"This is an outstanding contribution to literature from a world class academic. His contribution to the field of organizational studies is without parallel and this work is a monumental contribution to the global literature on organizational behavior."

Sir Cary Cooper, Lancaster University Management School

"John Child has done it again. This accessible and scholarly book brings the analysis of organizational forms where it belongs at the very centre of the fields of organization and strategy."

Andrew Pettigrew, Saïd Business School, Oxford University

"Conventional, sluggish bureaucracies are being introduced to a new structural vocabulary as they attempt to respond to the challenge of globalization. John Child provides a lucid and engaging guide to this changing world of organizations."

W. Richard Scott, Department of Sociology, Stanford University

"Written by one of the foremost scholars, John Child captures the leading edge of scientific and practical knowledge about organizations and organizing."

Andrew H. Van de Ven, Carlson School of Management, Minnesota University

"Professor John Child describes and analyzes clearly some of the important emerging forms of organization and management. The book offers valuable lessons and will appeal to MBA and students in general as well as executives of large and small organizations."

Marc Verstringhe, Past Chairman, Catering & Allied

"This is more than a reiteration of Child's best-selling textbook. The new work represents a powerful re-statement of the 'design' approach to management in the context of today's fluid and indeterminate circumstances."

Ray Loveridge, Saïd Business School, Oxford University

"A key text which draws together many of John Child's landmark contributions to the field of organization studies. The additional new material in this book reflects an impressive level of scholarly breadth and depth, revealing John Child as a master of understanding complex organizations and processes of organizing."

David C. Wilson, Open University Business School

"A lucid and comprehensive review of the theory and practice of organization written by one of the world's leading scholars in this field. John Child successfully combines a deep knowledge of organizational theory with acute appreciation of its relevance to modern organizations facing the challenges of the twenty-first century. It will be invaluable both as a text book for students and as a guide for those responsible for running organizations."

Mark Easterby-Smith, Lancaster University Management School

"Given his years of experience in China and in other international activities, Child has given the book a very intercontinental flavour . . . Its comprehensive review of effective management practices is accompanied by boxed cases that show the practices in action. The book will prove useful to graduate students in business schools, as well as managers in applied settings looking for a new perspective on the problems they face."

Howard Aldrich, Department of Sociology, University of North Carolina at Chapel Hill

"John Child excels once again at connecting the past, present and future of organizational thought and managerial practice. By deepening its theoretical foundations and expanding its discussion of 21st century topics, this second edition is an exciting and insightful journey for faculty and students alike."

Guido Möllering, Professor of Organization and Management, Jacobs University Bremen

ORGANIZATION

Contemporary Principles and Practice

2nd Edition

John Child

WILEY

This edition first published 2015
© 2015 John Wiley and Sons Ltd
First edition 2005 published by Blackwell Publishing Ltd

Registered office
John Wiley and Sons Ltd, The Atrium, Southern Gate, Chichester, West Sussex, PO19 8SQ, United Kingdom.

For details of our global editorial offices, for customer services and for information about how to apply for permission to reuse the copyright material in this book please see our website at www.wiley.com.

Wiley publishes in a variety of print and electronic formats and by print-on-demand. Some material included with standard print versions of this book may not be included in e-books or in print-on-demand. If this book refers to media such as a CD or DVD that is not included in the version you purchased, you may download this material at http://booksupport.wiley.com. For more information about Wiley products, visit www.wiley.com.

Designations used by companies to distinguish their products are often claimed as trademarks. All brand names and product names used in this book and on its cover are trade names, service marks, trademark or registered trademarks of their respective owners. The publisher and the book are not associated with any product or vendor mentioned in this book. None of the companies referenced within the book have endorsed the book.

Limit of Liability/Disclaimer of Warranty: While the publisher and author have used their best efforts in preparing this book, they make no representations or warranties with the respect to the accuracy or completeness of the contents of this book and specifically disclaim any implied warranties of merchantability or fitness for a particular purpose. It is sold on the understanding that the publisher is not engaged in rendering professional services and neither the publisher nor the author shall be liable for damages arising herefrom. If professional advice or other expert assistance is required, the services of a competent professional should be sought.

Library of Congress Cataloging-in-Publication Data

Child, John,
    Organization : contemporary principles and practices / John Child. – 2nd Edition.
        pages cm
    Includes bibliographical references and index.
    ISBN 978-1-119-95183-4 (pbk.)
    1. Organizational behavior.   I. Title.
    HD58.7.C4853 2015
    302.3'5–dc23   2014039494

A catalogue record for this book is available from the British Library.

ISBN 978-1-119-95183-4 (paperback)   ISBN 978-1-118-77987-3 (ebk)
ISBN 978-1-118-77990-3 (ebk)

Cover design: Wiley

Set in 10/12.5pt DanteMTStd-Regular by Thomson Digital, Noida, India
Printed in Great Britain by TJ International Ltd, Padstow, Cornwall, UK

CONTENTS

Preface to Second Edition

The first edition of *Organization* has been very well received, translated into several languages and used in many countries around the world. It was one of the few comprehensive treatments of its subject that drew on research and experience in order to advance guidelines for policy and practice. Nevertheless, after ten years, a new edition was called for.

My aim in writing this second edition remains the same as that set out in the preface to the original edition (which follows this one). Organization is a vitally important subject that affects our lives in all sorts of ways. Most times it shapes how we work with other people and how we interact with them. The environments in which we spend much of our time, whether work or leisure, are organized ones. This book describes the main features of contemporary organization, looks to their principles or rationales, and places them in a relevant context. My basic intention is to provide the insight that will enable us to appreciate the degree of choice that is available in how we go about organizing our collective activities. While it does not neglect well-established ways of organizing, the book focuses on newer forms of organization that are evolving to cope with the changing conditions of the 21st century. Some of these initiatives point to ways in which we may be able to cope better with the rising expectations we place on organizations. On the whole, there is nowadays much greater scrutiny of how private as well as public organizations perform in terms of both economic and social criteria.

This second edition has been thoroughly revised and updated. In addition, it includes two new chapters. One of them, Chapter 2, reviews the historical development of different perspectives on organization. I have added this chapter in response to suggestions that readers would benefit from having more historical background. It provides an insight into when, how and why conventional thinking on ways of organizing has come about. Despite its past-loading, such conventional thinking continues to exert great influence today.

The addition of the other new chapter, Chapter 18, reflects the fact that how we organize people and their work activities has huge consequences for people's well-being in society at large. Most attention given to organization sees it as a set of arrangements for ensuring that collective tasks are performed well in economic terms, so as to achieve efficiency, adaptation to changing demands and innovation – all in due measure. Chapter 18 examines the other face of organization, which distributes power, rewards, and personal fulfillment often very unequally. The strongly hierarchical basis on which we still tend to organize firms and institutions, particularly larger ones, contributes to a social problem that is growing to alarming proportions. The scale of the problem is borne out by the widespread breakdown of trust in leadership, the growing inequality of income and wealth, and the general sense of powerlessness that threatens the very principle of democracy itself. While there are no easy answers to this dilemma, Chapter 18 explores some of the successful organizational initiatives that can serve to reduce the problem.

A great many friends and colleagues helped and encouraged me to write this book in the first place and they are mentioned with gratitude in the preface to the first edition. Many have continued to play an important role in shaping the knowledge and awareness from which this new edition has benefitted. In particular, I owe a huge debt to my close collaborators Max Boisot (now sadly deceased), Suzana Rodrigues and Kenneth Tse. Homa Bahrami, Stuart Evans, Martin Ihrig, Ray Loveridge, Eugene McKenna, Guido Möllering, and Malcolm Warner have never ceased to encourage me and to feed me with new ideas and insights. I also owe a special debt to Joanna Kamowska who read every chapter in draft, and provided invaluable feedback which it is so difficult to obtain in these times when academics are experiencing ever increasing pressures of work. Jenny Ng, Emma Henshall, and others at Wiley steered the project through many technical difficulties. Rosemary Nixon, formerly at Wiley, kept me focused on the need to produce a second edition and she has constantly encouraged me to publish over the course of many years. I am deeply grateful to all of you and, by no means least, for the tolerance and support that my wife Elizabeth has shown to a project that too often shut me away from her company.

John Child
Birmingham
January 2015

Preface from the First Edition

Organizations in the contemporary world have to adapt and innovate in order to compete if they are firms, or to meet society's growing expectations if they are public service providers. It has become increasingly obvious that conventional forms of organization are not well suited to support these requirements, and a spectrum of alternative approaches is therefore being tried out. These alternatives are usually described as "new organizational forms."

The emergence of new organizational forms was heralded by Tom Burns and G. M. Stalker's path breaking 1961 book on *The Management of Innovation*, which identified an "organic" alternative to the machine-like approach of conventional organization. By the 1980s, the so-called "post-bureaucratic" organization was identified, in principle at least, as a clear alternative to the bureaucratic form that had for over a century reflected the philosophy of large-scale, hierarchical, and formalized business. It took until the early 1990s, however, for articles on new and alternative organizational forms to appear with any regularity and for case studies of companies that had applied such forms to become available. Even today, there are remarkably few books that address the subject.

The pace of experimentation and innovation in organizational practice, stimulated by major economic and technological changes, has therefore outstripped the ability of writers on organization to capture and explain what is taking place. The challenge here is not just to offer a systematic description of ongoing changes, important though that is. We also need to make sense of new organizational developments in an attempt to move toward a theory that explains them. Only sound theory can furnish practical guidelines on the consequences of adopting new organizational forms and their relevance to particular situations.

This book aims to describe the main features of contemporary organization, to discern the principles underlying them, and to relate them to their contexts. The intention in so doing is to understand and clarify the choices we have in deciding on particular ways of organizing activities. I believe that such choices should be of great concern to all of us. This is because organization is more than just a set of arrangements for achieving desired results through collective effort, vital though this is. The way we organize and govern our companies and other institutions also affects how benefits, opportunities, and privileges are distributed in society. There is increasing evidence that it has direct effects on our health and personal well-being. This book therefore draws upon research and experience in order to reach an informed view on contemporary organizational practices. Its scope and the contents of each chapter are summarized at the beginning of Chapter 1. Although the book concentrates on the organization of business firms, much of its analysis applies to other areas of organized activity.

Like its ancestor, *Organization: A Guide to Problems and Practice* (1977, 1984), this book has arisen mainly from my experience in research and consultancy. It has been refined through engagement with the members of MBA classes in the universities of Birmingham, Cambridge, and Hong Kong, who have contributed from their varied experiences of managing and organizing. In writing the book, I have had in mind both people who are practicing management and those who are studying it. For the benefit primarily of students, the chapters close with questions for discussion and endnotes on the main sources used. The endnotes also serve to indicate further reading. Each chapter also begins with a short overview and ends with a summary of key points.

Although organization tends to be regarded as a subject for managers and students of management, I do passionately believe it is a matter of direct and immediate concern to everyone in society. Organization affects all of us in so many ways that we should not be content to leave the decisions on it to "leaders" and "experts." Organization is not simply a technical matter of finding an optimum solution. It should become apparent from a reading of this book that there are normally alternative ways of organizing to meet a given functional requirement, and that the choice between them is as much a matter of social preference as of scientific rationality. It is important to appreciate that there is some choice in the ways that public, industrial, and other institutions are organized, because it is the expression of a preference between such choices that will take us closer to a fully democratic society.

I have been very fortunate to have enjoyed a great deal of help and encouragement in writing this book. Several friends, especially Homa Bahrami, Ray Loveridge, Eugene McKenna, and Stuart Evans, have for many years been urging me to apply to the contemporary scene the practice-oriented approach I had developed in the earlier book on *Organization*. It has taken a long time and I hope they feel the result is worth the wait. Suzana Rodrigues, my close collaborator in much recent work, has contributed many telling insights and has never allowed me to stray too far from my roots as a writer on organization despite the competing fascination of China. Periodic engagement with Max Boisot's outstanding analytical mind has been immensely stimulating, as has exposure to the wisdom that Marc Verstringhe has distilled from his career as a successful chief executive. I have also benefited from the exchange of ideas with many colleagues at the Universities of Birmingham, Cambridge, Hong Kong, and Oxford, including Andrew Brown, Peter Clark, David Faulkner, George Frynas, Sally Heavens, Sek Hong Ng, Yigang Pan, Christos Pitelis, Robert Pitkethly, Edmund Thompson, David Tse, and Malcolm Warner. The work of my former doctoral students in those universities has provided many new insights on organization and related topics. Here I should like particularly to mention Roberto Duarte, Said El Banna, Aldemir Drummond, Noreena Hertz, Yuan Lu, Livia Markóczy, Guido Möllering, Stephen Rudman, Terence Tsai, Eric Tsang, Niti Villinger, Roland Villinger, Christine Wong, Daniel Yan, and Yanni Yan.

The years of editing the journal *Organization Studies* from 1992 to 1996 significantly broadened my appreciation and understanding of the diverse perspectives on the subject of organization. This brings me to express a special appreciation to Sally Heavens, who assisted me in the *OS* editorial office and then collaborated in work on organizational learning and corporate evolution. Sally has contributed a great deal of editorial effort toward making this book more readable. I am also grateful for the countless ways in which my PA at the Birmingham Business School, Jane Whitmarsh, has helped to deal with many queries at short notice and generally made the preparation of this book run more smoothly. As always, my wife Elizabeth has both offered constructive criticism and suffered the deprivations of having to compete for my time with the word processor.

John Child
Birmingham
June 2004

PART I

The Broad Picture

◢ Introduction to Part I – The Broad Picture

Part I provides some necessary background about organization. It looks at the broad picture rather than specifics. Chapter 1 introduces the nature of organization and the contributions it can make. Chapter 2 then outlines the main developments in organizational design over approximately the past hundred years. Its purpose is to provide an appreciation of what have become "conventional" ways of organizing, which continue to be widely found in practice and are engrained in the thinking of many administrators and managers who make decisions about organization. By contrast, Chapter 3 considers "new" organizational forms in the contexts that have encouraged them to be adopted. The chapter examines the relevance for organization of major developments in the business environment – globalization, new information and communications technologies, the rise of information-intensive and knowledge-based competition, the growing numbers of knowledge workers, and the increasing social expectations being placed on business. The overall message is that new developments in organization can only be appreciated by reference to the changed context in which business now operates.

CHAPTER 1

Organization and Its Importance

WHAT THIS CHAPTER COVERS

This book focuses on new trends and options in how we organize collective activity. The present chapter defines the key terms *organizing, organization,* and *organizations*. It then introduces the components of organization. Some of these are structural in nature, some are concerned with key processes, while others define boundaries. The components of organization are the parameters along which policy choices have to be made. Although there are limits to what the design of organization can achieve, these policy choices are highly consequential because serious problems can arise from inappropriate organization. The chapter closes with examples of such problems and a checklist to help identify their symptoms.

◢ Purpose and Scope of This Book

In contemporary societies most work, and a good deal of leisure activity too, is carried out in cooperation with other people – it is collective. Often people are working with others in the same location, but increasingly it can involve collaboration across physical distances through Internet and satellite connections. The aim of this book is to provide you with useful insights into how good organization is a foundation for success in collective activity.

Although the book focuses on business companies, much of its content is also applicable to the many public and not-for-profit institutions that are also expected to organize themselves for delivering relevant services in an economic manner. The success of any company depends basically on two fundamental requirements: strategy and organization. The two are closely bound together. Strategy "establishes the criteria for choosing among alternative organizational forms."[1] Yet if its strategy is faulty a company's organization, however sound, cannot compensate for this deficiency. The failure of Kodak to recognize the strategic importance of digital photography is a case in point. On the other hand, an unsuitable organization will handicap a company from delivering sufficiently on its strategy, however well conceived this might be. For example, some business schools fail to capitalize on market opportunities because their faculty are organized in traditional supply-side departments rather than in customer-oriented program teams. Additionally, the formulation of a sound strategy in the contemporary business world relies on knowledge and insight being provided from all levels and units within a company. An inability to motivate and coordinate these inputs because of inadequate organization can prevent a good strategy from being formulated in the first place.

Superior organization offers one of the last sustainable sources of competitive advantage. The gains previously to be had from market entry barriers, proprietary technology, and scale economies have become steadily eroded by trade liberalization, technology transfer, and the development of flexible production technologies. Most resources and technologies can either be acquired from the market or imitated. Organization, on the other hand, is an asset that each company has to develop to suit its own needs and situation and it cannot be bought off-the-shelf. The globalization of markets and value chains, competitive pressures, and the ever-shortening cycles of innovation, place an increasing premium on the ability to organize a wide array of resources, especially human resources, so as to make speedy, intelligent, and coordinated moves in the competitive game.

We live in a challenging and dynamic time for organization. It is often said that the conventional ways in which companies and other collective endeavors have been organized in the past are inadequate for 21st century conditions. Also their two foundations – hierarchy and bureaucracy – today attract hostility because in the public mind they are associated respectively with exploitation and inefficiency. There has been a great deal of hype about an organizational revolution in which new forms are emerging that move away from the fundamental tenets of conventional organization. The gurus have had a field day and much of the discourse on the subject has left sober evaluation way behind.[2] Actually despite the availability of some surveys and case studies[3], it is difficult to gain an overall picture of the organizational innovations that are taking place. They appear to have progressed further in some parts of the world, such as the Nordic countries, than in others.[4] It is therefore timely to review new organizational ideas and practices, compare them with conventional wisdom, and on this basis offer guidelines for practice.

Organization aims to present state-of-the-art principles and practice in the organizing of collective activities, primarily with reference to business companies. While there is much to criticize about the wider social costs of the way most organizations are structured and governed today – these are discussed in Chapters 16 and 18 – the main focus of this book is on how people and their work can be organized so as to achieve the objectives of the unit in which they are employed or to which they are contracted. I appreciate that this begs some absolutely fundamental questions as to the appropriateness of such objectives and who has the power to determine them, issues which ultimately determine whether organization is a force for social good or evil. Others have discussed these issues and the way that the failure to resolve them threatens a major crisis in contemporary societies.[5] Without naively claiming that the design of organization can be treated as a purely technical matter, divorced from these wider issues, the main focus of this book will nevertheless be on the more practice-oriented question of the behavioral and performance consequences of organizational design. I return to the social evaluation of organization in the final chapter.

Organization consists of five main parts. Part I provides necessary background and looks at the broad picture rather than specifics. The present chapter introduces the nature of organization and the contributions it can make. Chapter 2 then outlines the main developments in organizational design over approximately the past hundred years. Its purpose is to provide an appreciation of what have become "conventional" ways of organizing, which continue to be widely found in practice and are engrained in the thinking of many administrators and managers who make decisions about organization. By contrast, Chapter 3 considers "new" organizational forms in the contexts that have encouraged them to be adopted. The chapter examines the relevance for organization of major developments in the business environment – globalization, new information and communications technologies, the rise of information-intensive and knowledge-based competition, the growing numbers of knowledge workers, and the increasing social expectations being placed on business. The overall message is that new developments in organization can only be appreciated by reference to the changed context in which business now operates.

Parts II and III turn to the specifics of organizational form. The chapters in Part II focus on the internal aspects of organization, while those in Part III examine various networked forms of organization spanning traditional boundaries. Chapter 4 is concerned chiefly with hierarchy, a fundamental structural feature of organization. It considers downsizing and delayering, which are moves toward smaller and slimmer management structures that have fewer hierarchical levels. The attempt to reduce hierarchy is often accompanied by the greater use of teams. Teams are an important means of improving the coordination and integration of activities, which is the subject of Chapter 5. That chapter discusses ways in which integration can be achieved, including the use of cross-functional teams and modern information and communication technologies. The management of projects is a particularly important capability today and the coordination of the specialized contributions required is usually achieved through teams. Control is the subject of Chapter 6, which is another fundamental aspect of organizing where new approaches have been developed to suit modern conditions. The next two chapters turn to reward policies and practices as further aspects of organizational design. Chapter 7 examines reward policies and the contribution they make within the employment relationship to reconciling managerial requirements with employee needs. Chapter 8 recognizes the importance of pay within the spectrum of rewards and it pays particular attention to the choice of alternative payment systems including the contentious issue of executive bonuses.

The four chapters in Part III turn outwards beyond the conventional boundaries of organizations. They discuss various arrangements that involve networking between firms and across national boundaries. Networking is a very general concept and it can take different forms in practice.[6] The chapters in Part III consider some of these variations. One of the main features of new organization lies in how it opens up and crosses boundaries through outsourcing, virtual value chains, alliances, and internationalization. These developments have led some commentators to speak of the "boundaryless organization." Chapter 9 examines the outsourcing of activities to external contractors. Chapter 10 looks at the special, but increasingly significant, case of "virtual" organization based on e-commerce and similar strategies. Chapter 11 is concerned with a particularly challenging case of networking across organizational boundaries, when two or more partners form a strategic alliance on a formal basis such as a joint venture in which they invest equity, management, and other resources. Chapter 12 turns to the crossing of another kind of boundary, that of nationality. It considers the organizational challenges of managing across borders.

The chapters in parts II and III are largely concerned with the structures and mechanisms that facilitate ongoing processes. These should permit, even encourage, a company to evolve successfully through adaptation and innovation. Successful evolution, however, requires further specific capabilities – those of managing change, learning and innovating, generating trust, and securing legitimacy for corporate governance. These abilities can be promoted in part by appropriate organizational policies, but they also rely significantly on the integrity and ethos of management. The chapters in part IV in turn examine each of these capabilities for evolving effective organizations.

Chapter 13 identifies the policies and practices that facilitate major change in companies when events and trends require this to take place. Chapter 14 focuses on the impact organization can have on learning and knowledge creation within companies, with particular reference to supporting innovation. Increasing attention is being given to the creation of trust in business and employment relationships, as part of a culture that encourages innovation. Chapter 15 identifies organizational policies that can promote trust. Poor corporate governance can seriously damage trust, and Chapter 16 recognizes the growing social demands for a wider and more transparent corporate accountability and the implications these have for organization.

Part V steps back from the detail of previous chapters to make sense of how organization can be designed to help meet the strategic business and social criteria of the present century. The twin chapters in this last part of the book reflect the two fundamental faces of organization. In one face we see organization as a set of arrangements for undertaking collective goal-directed activities in a cohesive and coherent manner. This is the side of organization that contributes to meeting strategic business needs. Chapter 17 illustrates how each strategic business need, and different combinations of them, has a corresponding appropriate form of organization. It has become increasingly necessary to use a mix of organizational forms within the one company or system while at the same time preserving consistency and integration between them. The capability of doing this has become known as "ambidexterity." Returning to the theme of Chapter 3, a consideration of how these needs are changing helps us to make better sense of how organizational forms are evolving and tending to become increasingly complex.

Chapter 18 turns to the other face of organization, in which we see a set of arrangements that distributes power, rewards, and personal well-being. If this aspect of organization is seen to be failing, it will have deleterious performance effects as well as calling the legitimacy of business into question. Deficiencies in this aspect of organization are not only undermining trust within companies and public institutions; they are also threatening the social contract that underpins society at large. Some firms have taken organizational initiatives that address this problem.

◢ Organizing, Organization, and Organizations

Before we go any further, some basic definitions are required. Virtually all the goods and services we consume come to us as a result of *organizing* collective activities that are carried out within business *organizations* – "firms" or "companies." The institutions that mold our lives through education, health care, the law, politics, and religion are also all highly organized through public organizations. The leaders of successful organizations generally attribute a significant part of that success to the quality of their *organization*. This use of similar terms to mean different things can be very confusing. It is important to distinguish between them at the outset.

Organizing is the process of arranging collective effort so that it achieves an outcome potentially superior to that of individuals acting or working alone. It almost always involves some division of labor, with different people or groups concentrating on different activities that then have to be integrated (coordinated) to achieve a successful result. Organizing also requires a degree of control, so as to monitor progress against original intentions and to make appropriate adjustments along the way. If more than a small group of people are involved, and if the organized activity is a continuing one, a form of hierarchy normally develops such that one or more people take the lead in formulating instructions, providing coordination and controlling results.

These manifestations of organizing, taken together, are commonly termed *organization*, as in "the organization of the XYZ Company." This term implies that the form of organizing used by a company persists in a recognizable form, at least for a while. It is important to bear in mind that not all organization is consciously designed and formal in nature. The ways that people organize themselves spontaneously can be extremely important both for the performance they achieve and for their personal satisfaction. It often does not correspond with the relationships that are laid down neatly in organization charts. This facet of organization has often been called "informal organization" and it often takes the form of social networks in the workplace.[7]

So essential is being organized to companies or institutions that it is quite usual to refer to such a bodies as "organizations" – shorthand for organized bodies or systems. This term refers to all the attributes of the collective body taken as a whole, which can lead to a great deal of confusion for two reasons. First, an entity such as a company has features that are not strictly organizational in nature but which can nevertheless influence its behavior and performance. These include its history, nationality, leadership, and reputation. The second reason follows from the first: *an organization* will have its own specific character and identity, whereas *the organizational attributes* with which this book is concerned apply across different companies or institutions.

This book is about organization and organizing, meaning the ways in which activities and the people performing them are organized in firms or other collective bodies. In the past, this focus was often called "organizational design." The term has fallen out of favor because it implies the conscious, rational pre-planning of formal organizational arrangements, whereas contemporary thinking places greater emphasis on a more adaptive emergent process of organizing to suit ever-changing circumstances. Unplanned and spontaneous organizing can turn out to be very constructive and even essential for the survival of an organization under stress. Also organizational scholars have come to appreciate that the sense that members of organizations make of their situations can have a strong influence on how they decide to act or react, whether or not these actions are prescribed by organizational arrangements. Organization is therefore a tool whereby management can endeavor to shape collective effort, but only up to a point.

◢ Components of Organization

Organization has structural, processual, and boundary-defining facets. These are listed in Box 1.1.

BOX 1.1 COMPONENTS OF ORGANIZATION

Structural:
   Basic structure
   Hierarchy: levels, layers, authority, reporting lines
   Specialization: roles, groups, and units
   Procedures
   Rules and standards
   Schedules
   Systems

Processual:
   Integration/coordination
   Control
   Reward

Boundary-crossing:
   Outsourcing
   Virtual organization
   Alliances
   Organizing across borders

Among the **structural** components of organization, there is a distinction between "basic structure" and "procedures." A basic structure distributes responsibilities among the members of a company. Its purpose is to contribute to the successful implementation of objectives by allocating people and resources to necessary tasks and designating responsibility and authority for their control and coordination. This division of labor has both vertical and horizontal aspects. Its vertical aspect provides for a specialization of discretionary decision-making responsibilities through specifying levels in a *hierarchy*. Hierarchies also usually depict reporting lines for instructions and feedback of results, though these can sometimes jump across levels. The horizontal aspect provides for a *specialization* of tasks according to functional specialty, business focus, or geography.

Basic structure takes the form of organization charts, job descriptions, and the constitution of boards, committees, working parties, task forces, and teams. A basic structure can only provide a general blueprint or constitution. Because it is a considerable upheaval to make structural changes, it may be wise to keep a basic structure rather general with scope for adjustments to suit local and/or emerging conditions. In fact, as we shall see, the more often circumstances change, the more such reliance on a given basic structure has to yield to a more flexible approach, often using task forces and teams. These bring people together from across the structure to focus effort towards specific problems and new projects as the need arises.

Procedures focus more closely on behavior. The intention of rules and standards is to clarify to people what is expected of them. For example, standing orders can set out the ways in which tasks are to be performed. In addition, or perhaps as an alternative when the manner of doing tasks cannot be closely defined, standards of performance can be established that incorporate criteria such as output level or quality of achievement. These would normally be accompanied by procedures for performance review. It is also usual to have other procedures for handling problems that are recurrent and whose parameters are reasonably well known. Many examples occur within the sphere of human resource management where the principle of equity requires consistency in the way people are treated. Standard procedures are commonly used for recruitment and selection, appraisal, the determination of rewards, and grievance handling.

Much work of a routine or recurrent nature can be ordered efficiently through the use of schedules. Reporting of information on performance, drawing up of accounts, plant maintenance, and personal appraisals are among the typical activities that can be planned and conducted according to set schedules. The use of schedules is intended to improve the efficiency of these activities by allocating time and other resources to be available when required.

Systems are more complex and comprehensive than either rules or schedules. In fact, they usually incorporate both. They are a set of procedures for the performance of connected activities that constitute a particular task, and they normally rely on the support of information technology. Systems for inventory control, knowledge management, and the communication of transactional requirements within organized networks of firms are examples that have become particularly significant in recent years. Systems generally rely on the collection, analysis, and distribution of information among different units within a company or business network. For them to work effectively, it is essential to have protocols (rules) that ensure the standardization of such information.

There are three key organizing **processes**: integration, control, and reward. The purpose of each is to help achieve a configuration of mental and physical effort that leads to good corporate performance.

Integration is concerned with ensuring that there is adequate coordination between the different but complementary activities that create collective value. Organizational mechanisms aimed at strengthening integration range from simple arrangements for the people concerned to meet periodically to complex, multi-dimensional structures in which the contributions of specialized units are coordinated through a matrix arrangement according to customer, process, regional, or other requirements.

Control involves setting goals, implementing them, and monitoring their attainment. Control "systems" in the narrow sense of information-processing support for disseminating what is required of people and providing feedback on results follow a standard principle. It will become apparent, however, that there is considerable choice and variation in the broader strategies of control open to management. Some of these strategies require elaborate organizational support, while others rely more on people's "self-control" through their understanding and acceptance of collective objectives.

Reward is a process fundamental to engaging the motivation among members of a company to contribute positively to the achievement of its goals. The design of reward systems is part of management's organizing toolkit. There are broadly two main requirements that reward systems are expected to meet. One is to attract people with the required abilities and skills to join a company. The other is to encourage people to offer a high degree of commitment to their employment, including a willingness to accept innovation and other change. Many issues arise with the design of reward systems, especially around the concept of performance-related pay.

The **boundary-crossing** aspects of organization have become more prominent with the growing flexibility and permeability of the boundaries to firms. In the past, much of the concern in organizing was directed at drawing lines of exclusion, both between units within companies and between companies themselves. Jobs were defined in ways that identified their exclusive areas of responsibility and authority. Similarly, overlaps between larger units such as departments and divisions were considered to be potentially confusing and wasteful. Outsourcing major activities and entering into alliances with other organizations was often regarded with suspicion on the grounds of jeopardizing control and independence.

In recent years, organizational practice is shifting in the other direction. Companies are moving away from locating staff inside strongly bounded roles and units, with the idea of controlling and focusing their efforts in an efficient manner. There is much more emphasis today on managing relationships between roles and units so as to achieve a creative and proactive synergy between them – hence the greater attention now being paid to integration. On the external side, companies are also moving away from valuing exclusivity and are instead prepared to cross, even break down, boundaries between themselves. They are entering into various arrangements that network them with other firms, often in value chains that have global reach ("global value chains"). More activities are being *outsourced* to sub-contractors in order to focus on core capabilities and benefit from the advantages in cost and expertise enjoyed by external specialist firms. Some value chains, bringing together various contractors into networks, are being organized along virtual lines. *Virtual organization* offers advantages that suggest it will come into progressively greater use. There are also a rising number of *alliances* between firms in order to secure global market coverage, to resource innovation, and to access sources of low cost production. Many alliances are formed between firms from different countries and this is part of the trend to internationalize the scope of business value chains.[8] In many sectors the multinational enterprise [MNE] has become the dominant, though not the most numerous corporate category. Together with the many small and medium-sized enterprises [SMEs] that are also internationalizing, MNEs face the challenge of *organizing across borders*. They may choose to accomplish this either within their own structures or through alliances with other firms.

The contribution organization can make to the performance of specified tasks and in a given environment comes alongside, and has to be consistent with, that of other factors. Among these, the people involved – their motivations and capabilities – and the technology that is applied – both "hardware" and "software" (know-how) – are particularly important.[9] Organization aims to provide a set of framework provisions within which the processes necessary for effective collective activity can proceed. It can, however, only make a partial contribution to the effectiveness of those processes. An assumption shared by those who advocate the adoption of new organizational forms is that in the future we have to rely less than before on "organization," as framework, and more on "organizing," as process.[10] Their argument is that frameworks focus on formalized roles and rules which articulate knowledge gleaned from the past, whereas we now need adaptive and innovative processes that respond to present needs and anticipate the future. These processes have to be based on intensive communication and knowledge-sharing between people. In modern conditions of high change and turbulence, structures may well be obsolete before they are even implemented, and can inhibit the flexibility on which the survival of companies increasingly depends. Self-generated spontaneous processes that allow for rapid and innovative adjustments to new circumstances are seen to be appropriate instead. In ways such as these, sharp distinctions are being made between conventional and new organizational forms. The evidence presented in later chapters will clarify whether such a wholesale dismissal of the conventional approach to organization is justified.

Organizational Choices

The contrasts that are drawn between conventional and new forms of organization serve to highlight the basic choices that are inherent in each component of organization. These are summarized in Table 1.1, and I shall discuss them in turn.

Table 1.1   Basic organizational choices

Component of organization	Choice
Hierarchy:	
Levels/layers	• Tall vs. flat
Authority	• Centralized vs. decentralized
Reporting lines	• Single vs. multiple
Specialization	• Which logic of specialization: function, process, product, region?
	• Specialized roles vs. general roles
	• Clear role definitions vs. fuzzy role definitions
Hierarchy and specialization	• Specialized hierarchies vs. use of mixed teams
	• High vs. low job autonomy and content
Rules and schedules	• Mandatory vs. discretionary
	• Rule-based orientation vs. relationship-based orientation
Systems	• Oriented towards reducing uncertainty vs. emphasis on signaling the need to adapt
Control	• Which strategy of control: personal, bureaucratic, target-based, cultural, or HRM-based?
Integration	• Vertical vs. horizontal
	• Degree of formalization: direct contact, liaison roles, task forces, coordinators, teams, matrix structures
Reward	• Criteria: hierarchical level, performance, market rate
	• Individual vs. group-based
	• Frequent vs. periodic
Boundary crossing and networking	• Intensity of network
	• Role of contract vs. trust
	• Short-term vs. long-term links
	• Dominated vs. equal partner networks
	• Virtual or non-virtual?
Outsourcing	• Outsourcing value-chain activities vs. peripheral support activities only
Alliances	• Equity vs. contractual
	• One-partner dominated vs. integrated management
Organizing across borders	• Global vs. local emphasis
	• Basis of integration: business, function, or region?

Hierarchy

Many writers on organization have shown a marked aversion towards hierarchy and its supposedly deleterious effects, which are discussed in Chapters 4 and 18. Despite this, hierarchy continues to provide the backbone of almost every company in every part of the world. Key choices in the design of hierarchies concern the number of layers they should contain, whether decision-making authority should be centralized at their apex or distributed down their levels, and whether people should have single or multiple upward reporting lines (the latter is known as "matrix organization.")

Specialization

There are two basic choices for specialization. The first assumes that, except in a very small unit, it will be efficient to have some degree of specialization in what people do. The question, then, is on what basis to specialize? There are several competing logics here. People can specialize according to the expertise they possess; when groups of people or departments are organized on this basis we commonly speak of a "functional organization." A related principle is that people concerned with the same process, perhaps employing the same plant or equipment, should be organized to work together. Another, contrasting, logic is to specialize people according to the product or service to which they are all contributing. In a company with several product lines or businesses, this logic can give rise to the so-called "multidivisional form" based on a range of product divisions. Another logic of specialization is by country or region, which may be particularly called for when the political, cultural, or other characteristics of geographical entities are distinctive.

The second choice is how far to take the principle of specialization itself. One approach is to define roles in a highly specialized way, so as to allow the people in them to develop the maximum of expertise and focused experience. The alternative is to define them in general terms, so as to encourage the capability and willingness among people to switch flexibly between different tasks as the situation requires. Linked to this choice is another one, namely whether to rely on clear role definition or to allow these to be fuzzy and open-ended. The same questions will also have to be raised for groups, units, and departments within a company. Should these be highly specialized and self-contained, or should they be more generalist, even with some overlap and rotation between their members?

Hierarchy and specialization

Combining the choices on hierarchy and specialization identifies some of the major organizational configurations used in practice. For example, the level of discretion (reflecting centralization vs. decentralization in hierarchies), taken together with the level of specialization, identifies different ways in which work can be organized, as illustrated in Figure 1.1 below.

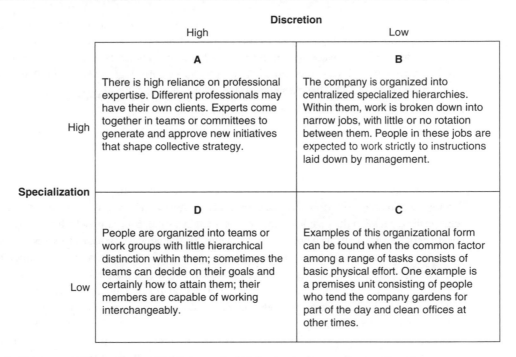

Figure 1.1 Different levels of discretion and specialization in the organization of work

Rules and schedules

One of the basic issues with rules and schedules is how far they should be made mandatory rather than discretionary. In some circumstances, when for instance legal regulations apply, rules have to be mandatory. In other cases, rules do not have this obligatory character, but instead derive from previous organizational experience and learning. Here it may be considered appropriate to adopt a more flexible approach to the use of rules by, say, encouraging people to replace them with new practices when they decide that existing rules are no longer functional.

This choice mirrors the contrast between a so-called "bureaucratic philosophy of organization" that favors the predictability of behavior stemming from an adherence to rules and the new philosophy that favors adaptation and innovation through relational dynamics. The latter perspective sees relationships leading to adaptation in a number of possible ways such as generating sensitivity to external changes through intensive networking, and the opening up of new opportunities through personal negotiation with parties outside the firm.[11] Similarly, most innovation is seen to arise today through the intensive, interpersonal process of qualified minds working together to find new solutions. In neither case can much reliance be placed upon existing rules, which may hinder rather than foster change.

Systems

A similar choice arises in the use of systems. One possibility is to orient systems towards reducing uncertainty by screening out as aberrant any non-conforming information or behavior. An example would be a production system rooted in the principle of economic batch size that did not permit the inclusion of special, one-off orders. The problem is that often the special order heralds a major new opportunity. The other choice is to design systems that strongly signal exceptions or new information at a sufficiently high level to impinge on the perceptions of people who have a say in strategy formulation. This approach emphasizes the potential of systems for signaling a need to adapt.

Integration

One of the key organizational choices to be made about integration is whether to secure it through a top-down, vertical approach or through direct, horizontal communication and relationships between the people or units concerned. In a small company, which has only a few constituent departments, it may be quite sufficient for the general manager to whom they all report to ensure that there is the necessary degree of common understanding and integration between their activities. In a large, complex company, however, this vertical approach is very likely to break down. Rather than passing information up and down hierarchies, it now becomes much more effective to rely on direct communications and relations between different parts of the company to ensure joint working and problem solving.

Other factors also make a horizontal approach to integration more effective. Modern information and communications technologies, especially email, have removed many of the barriers to direct, horizontal communications previously imposed by differences in geography and time. Another consideration arises from the needs of competition based on innovation today when relevant information and knowledge is dispersed among the people directly concerned and when quick results are called for. In this situation, it is more effective for them to exchange information directly and to ignite the sparks of creativity through direct interaction.

A further issue is whether to formalize the provisions for integrating activities and, if so, how elaborate these should be. The simplest way of organizing for integration is to facilitate direct contact between managers or employees who share a problem or need to exchange information. Progressively more elaborate (and costly) provisions are appointing people to act as liaisons with other groups or units, bringing people together in temporary task forces, appointing coordinators, and establishing cross-departmental teams or even more permanent matrix structures. Whichever use of formal arrangements is decided upon, there is usually merit in promoting integration through informal means as well, such as encouraging the wide circulation of information through email and the provision of shared social and eating facilities.

Control

Though the concept of control is essentially quite simple, its application is not. There are many different organizational possibilities for implementing control, which I have previously called "strategies of control."[12] Chapter 6 discusses six different strategies of control that may be adopted, either singly or in combination. Many factors are likely to bear on the choice between these strategies, including a company's culture and size, the tasks to be done, and the characteristics of the people working for it.

Reward systems

The key choices to be made about the organization of reward systems concern the basis of reward, whether rewards are to be individual or group based, and how frequently rewards are to be given. Rewards can be based principally or exclusively on hierarchical level. Salaries are normally determined according to this principle. Its justification lies in the claim that hierarchical level equates to the level of responsibility a person bears. Cynics would point out that it also relates closely to the level of power a person commands within a company and can therefore encourage self-serving behavior such as the award of unjustifiably high bonus payments. Another basis for reward is performance achieved, though serious difficulties can arise in apportioning an individual's responsibility for performance, in distinguishing short- from long-term criteria, and in ensuring a reasonable stability in earnings. Another principle is to pay the labor market rate for the work to be done. This principle can create so-called "anomalies" for bureaucratically organized companies, as when Giles – the famous cartoonist for Express Newspapers in the UK – was reputedly paid more than the chief executive of his employing newspaper company. It is, however, in tune with those new forms of business that are organized on the basis of a network of market contracts involving self-employed associates, consultants, sub-contractors, and other independent operators.

Rewards can be specific to individuals or they can be group based. The most collective reward would be an equal, annual share of company profits. While this may help promote a sense of corporate identity, one can see that it is far removed from the level of contribution that any individual has made. It is also a highly periodic reward, with long intervals between payments. This is also likely to weaken the reinforcement effects of such rewards on people's behavior. The frequency with which rewards are granted is therefore another choice that has to be considered in deciding on the organization of reward systems.

Boundary-crossing and networking

Networking in its broader sense is a form of organized transacting that offers an alternative to either markets or hierarchies. It refers to transactions across an organization's boundaries that are recurrent and involve continuing relationships with a set of partners. The transactions are coordinated and controlled on a mutually agreed basis that is likely to require common protocols and systems, but do not necessarily require direct supervision by the organization's own staff. Nowadays, encouraged by globalization, larger firms in many sectors have developed extensive networks of international partners who contribute at different points in those firms' value chains. This development has given rise to the concept of the "global value chain."[13]

Networking presents a number of organizational choices:

1 *The intensity of the network.* Possibilities range from outsourcing, where relations between a hub firm and its individual external contractors are confined to specific contracted activities, to a tightly-integrated alliance such as one between a set of technology developers in which most members work intensively with one another.

2 *Contract or trust?* Are the network relations to be based primarily on formal contract or do they involve long-term partnerships based on trust? This links to the third choice.

3 *Limited or long life?* Is the network intended to have a limited life, such as a consortium to build a particular infrastructure project, or greater permanency such as the system of suppliers that contribute to Apple and Dell Computers?

4 *Dominated or equal partner network?* Is the network to be dominated by a leading firm or to be one of more or less equal partners? In the former case, there will be a hub firm that decides which activities to carry out internally and which to outsource to network sub-contractors. Dell, Toyota, and Benetton provide examples of a dominated network solution. In an equal partner network, no single partner sets up and controls the network. The equal partner approach flourishes in environments like Silicon Valley where an entrepreneurial culture and ecology of intensive communications encourage the frequent reformation of new collaborative networks and limit the domination of major players.[14]

5 *How virtual?* To what extent is the network is to be managed on a virtual basis?

Outsourcing

The key decision on outsourcing concerns which activities to contract out as services to be provided by other firms or individuals. The criterion normally applied is to preserve within the firm those activities that are regarded as "core." One criterion for determining which are core activities is that the company should possess a relative advantage in performing them, such as to provide greater net added value than if they were consigned to other firms. Another is that they are activities having a particular competitive value as strategic assets; for example, proprietary brands, distribution systems, and research and development. It will be seen that companies vary considerably in the extent of their outsourcing – some only outsource peripheral support activities such as catering while others outsource significant parts of their central value chains.

Alliances

Outsourcing involves defining the activities to be undertaken within a company in relation to those performed externally and managing the connections between them. There is not usually any sharing of ownership or personnel, except perhaps people acting in a coordinative capacity. Alliances between companies can involve both a sharing of ownership and management, when they take the form of a new joint venture. Such alliances create truly hybrid forms of organization and there has been considerable debate on how they are best constituted. One key decision is whether to base an alliance on shared equity rather than confining it to a purely contractual arrangement. In addition to the fact that the venture may require new capital investment, an equity basis is more open-ended with regard to the timing and scale of returns to the partners; it also gives them long-term rights to determine the venture's policy and management.

The involvement of just a few, often only two, partners in equity joint ventures presents further fundamental choices for the way such ventures are to be organized and managed. Should, for example, one partner determine the venture's organization and supply its management? This could assist the venture's internal integration and also be justified if one partner is providing key inputs by way of brands, technologies, and/or expertise. Or, alternatively, should the partners jointly determine the venture's organization and staff its management? This could be in the interests of maximizing the learning and synergies between them and helping to build a sound, trust-based relationship that could be applied to other ventures in the future.

Organizing across borders

Cross-border operations make greater demands on a firm's organization than purely domestic ones. These demands inevitably grow as an MNE becomes more differentiated, both geographically and in the range of products and services it offers. A fundamental issue in an international firm's strategy is how to balance and combine advantages of global integration with the need for sensitivity and responsiveness to the conditions in the different localities where it operates and for which it produces goods and services. This strategic choice has implications for the way the firm organizes its main activities in terms of how much autonomy it grants local operations, the basis on which it secures integration and synergy between them, and whether to centralize via support functions rather than decentralize into product divisions and regions. Many MNEs are attempting to combine the benefits of global integration with those of localization in what has become known as a "transnational" approach. This approach is one of the most significant arenas for experimentation with new forms of organization because its complexity strains the limits to conventional forms based on hierarchy and bureaucracy. To secure the combination of flexibility, innovation, and integration that is required, the new approach to MNE organization depends significantly on the effective management of internal networks and the support of a well-developed corporate culture.

There are clear inter-dependencies between these organizational choices, especially in respect of structure and process. If the decision is taken to lean in a particular direction on one aspect of organization, this will impact on decisions in other areas. For instance, if centralization and hierarchy are preferred, this is likely to favor personal and/or bureaucratic control strategies, vertical integration, and rewards primarily based on hierarchical level. If, on the other hand, decentralized teamwork is preferred, this may well favor target-based and cultural strategies of control, horizontal integration, and performance-based reward. While there are a great many possible combinations of organizational elements, certain configurations have greater internal consistency than others and are therefore more likely to be used.

◢ **Consequences of Deficiencies in Organization**

The organizational choices just reviewed clearly have ramifications for all parts of a company's activities, but it is not easy to get them right. It is therefore very common for problems to arise as the result of organizational deficiencies. It is worth considering some of these because they can serve as warnings to a company of the need to attend to its organization.

Certain problems arise time and again in struggling organizations. Even at the best of times they can point to incipient dangers that have to be dealt with. High on the list are low motivation and morale, late and inappropriate decisions, conflict and lack of coordination, rising costs, and a generally poor response to new opportunities and external changes.

Deficiencies in organization can play a part in exacerbating each of these problems. The following lists identify some of these organizational deficiencies, though others could also be present.

Motivation and morale

Motivation and morale may be depressed because:

1 Decisions appear to be inconsistent and arbitrary in the absence of standardized rules.
2 People perceive that they have little responsibility, opportunity for achievement, or recognition of their worth because there is insufficient delegation of decision-making. This may result from too many layers of management and narrow spans of control. It can also signify an over-specialization of jobs.
3 Employees are not being recognized or rewarded for high performance, or recognition of achievement is not accompanied by a commensurate reward.
4 There is a lack of clarity as to what is expected of people and how their performance is assessed. This could be due to inadequate job definitions, a poorly worked-out reward system, and poor communication of corporate vision.
5 People are subject to competing pressures from different parts of the organization due to an absence of clearly defined priorities, decision rules, or work programs.
6 People are overloaded, either because they are not encouraged to delegate or their support systems are inadequate. For example, too much time is taken in searching for necessary information because the company's IT and knowledge-management systems are poorly organized.

Box 1.2 relates an example of how inconsistencies between the recognition of staff achievement and the reward offered to them can seriously damage motivation.

BOX 1.2 THE DEMORALIZING EFFECT OF AN INADEQUATE PERFORMANCE ASSESSMENT SYSTEM

Amy Wong* was a newly recruited MBA graduate of Chinese origin working in the training department of a large company. During her first year of employment, she designed and delivered three new programs on developing creativity and personal learning which participants found so useful that she was asked to repeat them several times. On her own initiative, she also arranged early morning "breakfast briefings" for divisional managers on doing business in China, which were also very well received.

Towards the end of her first year, Amy participated in a personal development meeting. The company required such meetings to be held annually. During the meeting, she discussed with her manager how she would like to build on her work and expertise during the coming year. Although this was not an appraisal meeting (the company did not have a formal appraisal system), her manager nevertheless talked about Amy's performance and expressed considerable satisfaction with it. Encouraged by what he said, and by the way her work had been received, Amy applied for an additional salary increment. Her case went to the company's pay review committee. Her manager was not a member of this committee, but submitted a strong recommendation in support of her case.

The committee turned down Amy's application for an additional increment. The reason it fed back to her was that she had been too short a time in her employment to be granted the increment. The committee was in fact under pressure to hold down salary increases because the company was experiencing a tight financial situation. Amy felt that the company was not recognizing her exceptional performance, and became more aggrieved when she found out that another graduate who acted as PA to the chief executive had been granted an additional increment for no obvious special merit. The experience prompted Amy to look for other employment and a competitor soon offered her a better-paid position.

Amy's resignation and signs of dissatisfaction among other professional staff prompted the company to look into its personnel procedures. It eventually realized that, by having a personal development system which inevitably dwelt on individual performance, but which was not linked to decisions on staff salaries, it was raising expectations that it often failed to meet in terms of rewards offered. Indeed, in cases like Amy's, it had allowed considerations other than staff performance to influence its decision.

*Name changed to protect identity

Decision making

Decision making may be delayed and lacking in quality because:

1 Necessary information is not transmitted on time to the appropriate people. This can result from an over-extended hierarchy.
2 Decision makers are too segmented into separate units and there is inadequate provision to integrate them.
3 Decision makers are overloaded due to insufficient delegation on their part.
4 There are no adequate procedures for evaluating and learning from the results of similar decisions made in the past.

Box 1.3 illustrates how inappropriate decisions can result from the failure to share information between different parts of the same company.

Conflict and lack of coordination

There may be conflict and a lack of coordination because:

1 There are conflicting goals that have not been structured into a single set of objectives and priorities. For example, people may be put under pressure to follow functional departmental priorities at the expense of product or project goals.

BOX 1.3 IMPACT OF INTERNAL BREAKDOWN ON A COMPANY'S DECISIONS

A diversified engineering company had several different operating divisions located in the same area of an industrial city. It was experiencing a long-term decline in the demand for machine tools, which could no longer match competition from Asia. On the other hand, it was expanding its production of electronic control systems. The two categories of production were organized into separate divisions, each with their own HRM departments. The company's central HRM department saw its role as one of professional development and therefore focused on the development and updating of HRM staff rather than on their everyday activities.

It was several weeks before the company discovered – as a result of a story in the local press – that its machine tool division had been making employees redundant, while the control systems division had been recruiting people with similar skills from the market. This breakdown in its internal information sharing had led the company into a set of inconsistent actions that were not only costly in themselves, but also damaged its reputation and image.

2   People are working out of step with each other because they are organized into separate units despite a high degree of interdependence between their activities.
3   The people carrying out tasks modify what they do in the light of changing circumstances, but there are no systems for ensuring that these changes are communicated to other parts of the organization.

Box 1.4 describes a case of serious conflict and breakdown in coordination.

BOX 1.4 A PROBLEM OF CONFLICT AND LACK OF COORDINATION[15]

A company had six sales groups and eighteen different plants. There was constant conflict between the production side, which wanted to limit the range of products in order to achieve a more economic level of output for each one, and the sales departments, which attempted to force production to comply with the customer's exact specifications regardless of the case for standardization. Conflict also arose between the different groups on the sales side, because each group tried to secure the earliest possible delivery date for its customers regardless of the system of priorities that the company had laid down. These priorities were intended to give preference to certain types of order, such as export, and to certain large and important customers. Some of the sales clerks had been recruited from production and they were able to organize preferential treatment for their "own" customers through informal deals with their former colleagues. These problems gave rise to major internal inefficiencies as well as creating uncertainty for customers.

Changing circumstances

An organization may not respond innovatively to changing circumstances because:

1   It has not established specialized jobs concerned with forecasting and scanning the environment.
2   There is a failure to ensure that learning and innovation are mainstream activities backed up by top management through appropriate procedures to provide them adequate priority, programming, and resources.
3   There is inadequate use of teamwork to bring together all the people who can bring relevant perspectives to bear upon new projects, in addition to purely technological solutions. These other perspectives include market potential, ease of manufacture, likely return on investment, and any relevant regulatory requirements.

Box 1.5 provides an example of a company that was failing to generate commercially successful innovative products.

BOX 1.5   A CASE OF UNCOMMERCIALIZED INNOVATION

A leading company in the field of computing and other office equipment made a major investment in a brand new research center sited close to a top research university. It recruited a highly qualified body of young, enthusiastic scientists and technical specialists to staff the facility. Over the center's first ten years, it generated a number of significant technological breakthroughs, none of which was, however, taken into commercial production by the company. Eventually, many of the research center's best brains left to join other companies. In some cases, their inventions and prototypes were then developed into new products that enjoyed a high level of success in the market.

Several factors contributed to this costly failure to commercialize the stream of inventions forthcoming from the company's research center. The center's self-contained organization and location over 2,000 miles from the company's headquarters and main production plants accentuated the sense of cultural distance and lack of a common identity between it and other units. It also meant that few projects enjoyed the understanding, let alone support, of senior corporate executives when the point came to decide on the investment required to bring them into production. Fearing to discourage creativity, the company did not involve non-scientists in new projects until they had reached quite an advanced stage. It did not therefore include commercial, production, and accounting specialists in project teams. As a result, the case for adopting new products on the grounds of scientific novelty was generally more convincing than that made for their market appeal, ease of manufacture, and value added.

Rising costs

Costs may be rising rapidly, particularly overheads, because:

1   The organization has a long hierarchy with a high ratio of "bosses" to "workers."
2   There is an excess of rules, procedures, and paperwork, distracting people's attention from productive work and requiring additional personnel to administer.
3   Some or all of the other organizational problems are present.

The list of symptoms can readily be converted into a simple but useful diagnostic tool to warn of possible design deficiencies in an organization. The form this can take is shown in Box 1.6.

BOX 1.6 CHECK LIST FOR IDENTIFYING SYMPTOMS OF ORGANIZATIONAL DEFICIENCIES

Read through the questionnaire and tick the questions (if any) for which you answer "yes" for (1) your organization as a whole and (2) your team or unit within it.

Symptoms	Your Organization	Your Team or Unit
Do morale and motivation seem noticeably low?		
Do decisions seem inconsistent and arbitrary, without reference to rules or criteria?	☐	☐
Are people unclear about what is expected of them and how their contribution might be assessed?	☐	☐
Do people perceive they have too little responsibility and opportunity for achievement?	☐	☐
Do people think they are not being rewarded for their achievements?	☐	☐
Are individuals subject to competing pressures from different parts of the organization?	☐	☐
Are people overloaded?	☐	☐
Is decision-making delayed and lacking in quality?		
Does vital information fail to reach decision-makers in time?	☐	☐
Are decision-makers segregated in separate units with insufficient coordination of their activities?	☐	☐
Are decision-makers overloaded because they have failed to delegate sufficiently?		☐
Are there inadequate procedures for evaluating the results of similar decisions made in the past?	☐	☐

Is there noticeable conflict and lack of coordination?

Do individuals or groups have conflicting goals that are
not in line with overall organizational objectives and
priorities? □ □

Have opportunities been missed for coordinating
people's activities by forming teams or other ways of
ensuring liaison between them? □ □

Are systems lacking for ensuring that information on
operational changes is communicated adequately to
other parts of the company? □ □

**Does the organization fail to respond innovatively
to changing circumstances?**

Is it no-one's special responsibility to monitor change
that is going on outside the organization? □ □

Do innovation and the planning of change get
inadequate support from the top? □ □

Is there inadequate coordination between the people
who can identify new opportunities and those who
might be able to develop ways of satisfying them (for
example, between sales and R&D or between R&D
and production)? □ □

**Are costs rising (over and above inflation),
especially in the administrative areas?**

Does the organization have too many managers and
too few people carrying out the work? □ □

Is there too much procedure and paperwork,
distracting people from productive work and requiring
additional administrative staff? □ □

SUMMARY

1 Organization is the product of "organizing," namely the process of arranging collective effort so that it achieves an outcome potentially superior to that of individuals acting or working alone. The term implies that the form of organizing used by a company persists in a recognizable form, at least for a while.

2 Superior organization offers one of the last sustainable sources of competitive advantage. It is an asset that each company has to develop to suit its needs and situation, and cannot be bought off-the-shelf.

3 The conventional ways in which companies and other collective enterprises have been organized in the past are widely regarded as inadequate, in most cases, for twenty-first-century conditions.

4   Organization has structural, processual, and boundary-defining facets.

5   Structure consists of a basic structure and procedures. A basic structure distributes responsibilities among the members of a company. Procedures focus more closely on behavior.

6   There are three key organizing processes: control, integration and reward. The purpose of each is to help achieve a configuration of mental and physical effort that leads to good corporate performance.

7   The boundary-defining aspects of organization have become more prominent with the growing flexibility and permeability of the boundaries to firms. They arise in the organization of network arrangements such as outsourcing and alliances with other companies.

8   Choices arise for each of these facets of organization and their constituent components. These choices are highlighted in the contrasts between conventional and new forms of organization.

9   Organizational choices have ramifications for all parts of a company's activities, and it is not easy to get them right. Many problems can arise as the result of organizational deficiencies. Low motivation and morale, late and inappropriate decisions, conflict and lack of coordination, rising costs, and a generally poor response to new opportunities and external changes may all signal the presence of organizational failures.

QUESTIONS FOR DISCUSSION

1.1   Why is organization important?

1.2   What is the difference between organizing, organization and organizations?

1.3   How in practice could you distinguish between formal and informal organization?

1.4   How do you see organizational structure affecting organizational processes?

1.5   Apply the checklist for identifying symptoms of organizational deficiencies (Box 1.6) to your own organization. [Or, if you are not currently working in an organization, apply it to the organization in which you are studying.] What results do you get?

NOTES

1   Jay R. Galbraith (1995), *Designing Organizations: An Executive Briefing on Strategy, Structure and Process*, San Francisco, Jossey-Bass, p. 13.

2   Some considered assessments of the extent to which there has actually been a revolution in organization away from the conventional forms described in Chapter 2 and 3 can be found in Thomas Diefenbach and Rune Todnem By (eds) (2012), Reinventing Hierarchy and Bureaucracy – from the Bureau to Network Organizations, *Research in the Sociology of Organizations*, 35, Bingley, UK: Emerald.

3   See for example John Child and Rita G. McGrath (eds) (2001), Special Research Forum on "New and Evolving Organizational Forms," *Academy of Management Journal*, 44(6); Andrew M. Pettigrew and others (eds) (2003), *Innovative Forms of Organizing*, London, Sage; Special issue on "Designing Organizations for the 21st-Century Global Economy," *Organizational Dynamics*, 39(2), (2010).

4   Perr Hull Kristensen and Kari Lilja (eds) (2011), *Nordic Capitalisms and Globalization: New Forms of Economic Organization and Welfare Institutions*, Oxford, Oxford University Press.

5   For example, Chris Grey (2013), *A Very Short, Fairly Interesting and Reasonably Cheap Book about Studying Organizations*, London, Sage, 3rd edition, especially Chapter 5.

6   For a discussion of the various meanings given to the term "network" and forms of network organization see Grahame F. Thompson (2003), *Between Hierarchies and Markets: The Logic and Limits of Network Forms of Organization*, Oxford, Oxford University Press.

7   David Krackhardt and Jeffrey R. Hanson (1993), Informal networks: The company behind the chart, *Harvard Business Review*, July-August, pp. 104–111.

8   OECD (2013), Interconnected Economies: Benefitting from Global Value Chains. Paris: OECD, DOI:10.1787/9789264189560-en; UNCTAD 2013. Global Value Chains and Development. New York: UNCTAD, http://unctad.org/en/publicationslibrary/diae2013d1_en.pdf, accessed April 6, 2014.

9   Jay R. Galbraith (1995), op. cit.; Harold J. Leavitt and Homa Bahrami (1988), *Managerial Psychology: Managing Behavior in Organizations*, Chicago University of Chicago Press, Chapter 22.

10 Karl E. Weick (1979), *The Social Psychology of Organizing*. Reading, MA: Addison-Wesley, 2nd edition.

11 The "network" concept is discussed in Chapter 3. A system that emphasizes managing through networks of relationships within an organization that cut across departmental boundaries is often called "the networked organization." A system of managed networked relationships between an organization and external organizations can be called "an organized network." The chapters in Part III focus on different aspects of organized networks.

12 John Child (1973), Strategies of control and organizational behavior, *Administrative Science Quarterly*, 18(1), 1–17.

13 Gary Gereffi (2014), Global Value Chains in a Post-Washington Consensus World, *Review of International Political Economy*, 21(1), 9–37.

14 Homa Bahrami and Stuart Evans (2010), *Super-Flexibility for Knowledge Enterprises*, Berlin, Springer, 2nd edition.

15 Adapted from A.J.M. Sykes and J. Bates (1962), Study of conflict between formal company policy and the interests of informal groups, *Sociological Review*, November, 313–327.

CHAPTER 2

Perspectives on Organizational Design until Recent Times

WHAT THIS CHAPTER COVERS

This chapter outlines the main developments in organizational design over approximately the past hundred years. Its purpose is to provide an appreciation of what have become "conventional" ways of organizing, which continue to be widely found in practice and are engrained in the thinking of many administrators and managers who make decisions about organization. It focuses on both the search for "one best ways" of organizing, of which so-called "classical organization theory" and scientific management are prime examples, and on the more recent "contingency approach." The contingency approach argues that in order to contribute to successful overall performance, how a work unit is organized must adjust to features of both its internal context and external environment. The internal context includes technology, size, diversification, people and purpose. The external environment includes the cultural environment in which the unit is located and its operational environment, especially the level of variability and uncertainty with which it has to cope.

"Conventional" ways of organizing continue to be widely found in practice and are ingrained in the thinking of many administrators and managers who make decisions on the subject. They developed initially through a search for "one best ways" of organizing, of which both so-called "classical organization theory" and scientific management are prime examples.[1] More recently, the conventional model has also been influenced by the so-called "contingency" perspective. The chapter offers an overview of these developments, rather than a detailed account. There are, in fact, several comprehensive sources that I recommend to any readers who are interested in the history of organization.[2]

A Brief Look Into History

Ancient civilizations such as those of China, Egypt, and India managed and organized people on a large scale for purposes of administering their empires, commanding their armies, and constructing monumental projects. The practical task of designing modes of organization to cope with these demands has a long history. Even several thousand years ago, there were examples of large-scale, formalized organization employing similar principles of hierarchy, functional sub-division and coordination.[3] The Han Dynasty in China (206 BC to AD 220) established a highly formalized central government bureaucracy that lasted until the beginning of the twentieth century. This incorporated the recruitment of officials by examination as well as systems for performance appraisal and promotion.[4] Through the Middle Ages in Europe, the monasteries continued to elaborate principles of organization such as the specialization of roles, carefully defined hierarchies, reliance on rules, and even the use of project teams to solve major new problems. Their highly formalized organization was functional for the accumulation of wealth, though it left little room for individual self-determination.[5]

However, it was only with the industrial revolution that systematic and widespread attention came to be given to the question of how best to organize. The advent of the factory system brought together large workforces which could be organized on a formal and systematic basis, while distance-spanning technologies such as the railroad and telephony facilitated the management of geographically dispersed workplaces. By modern times, organizational form had evolved into the ubiquitous presence of bureaucracy among large public and private corporations. Bureaucracy was founded on legal-rational principles of administration and management and was often complemented by principles of work organization enunciated by F.W. Taylor, the "father of scientific management." Bureaucracy appeared to be well suited to meeting organizational imperatives under conditions where there was reasonable continuity and stability.

During the second half of the twentieth century, the momentum developed towards a fundamental break from the long-established bureaucratic model. First, carefully conducted case studies showed that in practice bureaucracies were not necessary helpful to the achievement of organizational goals, especially ensuring good service to the customer. It was often necessary to deviate from its formal rules and structure for a firm to operate effectively.[6] "Working to rule" in fact became a form of industrial action in protest against an employer.

Next, students of organization came to the conclusion that, rather than adopting one model, different forms of organization were best suited to different contingent conditions ("contingencies") such as size, technology, and environment. Burns and Stalker, in a particularly seminal publication, identified a form of organization that was considerably more organic and less hierarchical than the typical bureaucracy.[7] They concluded that this organic form was more conducive to success in a turbulent, unpredictable environment than the more common "mechanistic" (bureaucratic) alternative. Alternatives to bureaucracy thus began to be recommended on the grounds that they were more functional for certain conditions.

In addition to the mounting evidence of bureaucratic dysfunctions, there was concern over the restrictive, even oppressive, impact that bureaucracy could have on individuals. Many people working in organizations, together with their clients and customers, were becoming increasingly dissatisfied with conventional organizational forms based on a combination of Taylorist work systems and hierarchical bureaucratic managerial structures. Social scientists articulated these discontents in the 1950s and 1960s through landmark studies such as Argyris's *Personality and Organization* (1957), subtitled *The Conflict between System and the Individual*, and Blauner's *Alienation and Freedom* (1964).[8] Intensive case studies exposed the use of organizations by particular groups such as managers to accomplish their own self-interests.[9] A radical critique of conventional organizational forms developed on the grounds that these embodied inequalities of power and thus encouraged exploitation. This critique was directed against both the failings of bureaucracy and the newer contingency perspective because it rejected any functionalist approach that justified organization in terms of its efficiency. It maintained that efficiency simply reflected a pursuit of elite interests and that this orientation did not seriously challenge existing structures of power and control.[10]

A look at history is valuable because it helps us to understand the importance both of continuity and context.[11] Continuity is evident in the fact that much pioneering thinking on organization offers insights that are still relevant. For example, the recommendation that the responsibilities allocated to a member of an organization should be accompanied by a level of authority appropriate to carrying them out. Or that there is a limit to the number of subordinates that a person can effectively manage as direct reports (the so-called "span of control"). These are simple guidelines, which strike many people as either too vague or self-evident, and which in any case may have to be adapted to suit a particular situation. However, when they are ignored, as is often the case, there can be serious negative consequences. Because some pioneering thinking and practice remains useful, one finds that organizational design has progressed incrementally over time. As Miles and his colleagues note, "each new organizational design builds on the most useful features of previous designs. Experiments with a new design are undertaken because of the problems and limitations of existing designs. The solutions that are developed help to preserve and extend the strengths of existing designs while bypassing their limitations."[12]

History also provides an appreciation of how certain organizational designs emerged and survived because they suited a particular context. The relevance to organizational forms of the context remains equally significant today. Among the features of historical context that helped to shape organization has been the undertaking of monumental projects, advances in technology, and changing social assumptions about the right to exercise authority. Reference to context helps us to appreciate that different organizational forms may each have a contribution to make depending on the situation. For instance, we shall see in Chapter 17 that older "bureaucratic" forms of organization continue to suit some purposes and operating contexts, especially those of many public institutions.

This chapter reviews two phases of thinking about organizational design. The first phase laid the foundations for what were in the first half of the twentieth century widely regarded as principles for optimal organization. It was founded on the belief that there are "best ways" of organizing which can be expressed as basic principles. The so-called "classical" theory of organization and the bureaucratic model made one of the major contributions to this first phase, while "scientific management" made the other. The second phase grew from a critique of one best way thinking which gathered pace from the 1960s on. By contrast, it argued that to secure optimum performance, it was necessary to vary the design of organization so that it suited the "contingencies" inherent in an operational situation. The organizational templates arising from these two phases mostly retained long-established principles such as hierarchy and specialization, and so they can be described as "conventional" ones. Although conventional organizational practices are still frequently followed, their limitations in contemporary conditions of high competition and rapid change, with a resulting premium on fostering innovation, have led to a search for new forms of organizing as will be described in Chapter 3.

◢ One Best Ways of Organizing

Classical organization theory and bureaucracy

Classical organization theory was primarily formulated by practitioners such as Henri Fayol and Lyndall Urwick. Fayol drew on his experience as a successful chief executive of a French mining and metallurgical company. Urwick's experience had been in the military and in the Rowntree confectionery company. Classical theory was prescriptive in that its advocates believed that it articulated the principles of sound organizational practice.[13] The theory, or more correctly the conceptual model, of bureaucracy was developed primarily by the German sociologist Max Weber.[14] Weber's intention was not prescriptive and in fact he was alarmed at what he saw as the threat to democracy that bureaucracy might pose.[15] Rather Weber's intention was to analyze the underlying principles of what had become the dominant organizational mode of modern societies.[16] Despite these different sources and their contrasting intentions, the key features of classical organizational principles and of bureaucracy were similar.

Fayol developed 14 principles of management and organization, from which he argued that good practice would follow. The principles specifically concerning organization are:

1 Division of labor – that jobs and units should specialize on different tasks.
2 The matching of authority with corresponding responsibility.
3 Unity of command – receiving orders from one superior (manager) only.
4 Centralization of decision-making, depending on the abilities of managers at each level.
5 The hierarchical ordering of positions, giving rise to a chain of command ("scalar chain").
6 Equitable remuneration.

Two of these principles – "unity of command" and "scalar chain" – require some clarification. Unity of command maintains that the hierarchical chain of authority should not be mudded by multiple reporting links. According to unity of command, people working in an organization should only report to one manager or "superordinate." The reasoning is that if people report to more than one manager, they are likely to be given conflicting instructions that will confuse their responsibilities and make it difficult for them to be held accountable for their performance. Scalar chain is synonymous with hierarchy. It maintains that authority should be apportioned up and down a linear scale in which the members of an organization report to persons at the next level up.

Fayol's principles were highly influential among early writers on organization, many of whom based their own statements on at least part of Fayol's list. Urwick was the main person responsible for bringing Fayol to the attention of the Anglo-Saxon world and he can be regarded as the most authoritative exponent of classical organization theory. He built on

Fayol's analysis to propose a set of 10 principles which he believed would offer a technically correct organization structure within which people could work purposefully towards a common objective.[17] These principles are:

1   The principle of the objective – the purpose of the undertaking must be clear.
2   The principle of specialization – people should perform specific functions.
3   The principle of coordination – to facilitate unity of effort.
4   The principle of authority – the need for a clear line of authority to every member of the organization (sometimes called the scalar principle).
5   The principle of responsibility – by the superior for the actions of his/her subordinates.
6   The principle of correspondence – the responsibility and authority in every position should correspond.
7   The span of control – no person should supervise more than five direct subordinates whose work interlocks.
8   The principle of balance – that the various units in an organization should be kept in balance.
9   The principle of continuity – that reorganization is a continuous process and provision should be made for it.
10 The principle of definition – all the above should be clearly defined in writing.

Urwick was greatly encouraged by the conclusion that Mooney and Reiley, both senior executives in General Motors, reached from their detailed comparative study of the organizational forms adopted by key historical institutions such as the state from Roman times, the Roman Catholic Church, and the military.[18] They concluded that the same principles of functional specialization, scalarity (hierarchy) and coordination had been applied in these diverse organizations throughout history, and that these were equally applicable to modern industry. Their analysis suggested to Urwick both the necessity for industrial management to organize on a systematic formalized basis and the likelihood that a study of organization structure would uncover principles that had a universal applicability.

The classical principles of organization are inflexible and mechanistic in nature and we shall note later how they have come to be dismissed, even ridiculed, for that reason. They are highly formal and some, such as the principle of continuity, are stated in very vague terms. Nevertheless, they do draw attention to pitfalls in management and organization that remain common today and can lead to failure. For example, Chapter 5 of this book illustrates the sometimes catastrophic failures that have resulted from ignoring principle #3 in Urwick's list – the need for coordination. Chapter 16 points to the problems of ensuring adequate corporate governance that can result from the absence of principle #6, leading to a failure to identify who takes responsibility for their actions. The principle of continuity (#9) draws attention to the need to view organizational change as a continuous process and to recognize the value of what Chapter 13 calls "emergent change."

Max Weber regarded bureaucracy as the purest type of exercise of legal authority in society, and as the system of organization best suited to the success of modern capitalist societies. I use the term "system" because Weber understood bureaucracy to be more than just an organizational form. It was founded on certain social criteria that defined the selection, rights, obligations and remuneration of appointed officials who worked in an entirely separate role to that of ownership. Weber believed that the bureaucratic type of organization was equally suited to a wide range of fields, including profit-making business, political and religious organizations as well as to government departments.

The strictly organizational characteristics of bureaucracy, according to Weber, are the following:[19]

1   Work is conducted in accordance with laid-down rules and procedures.
2   Impersonal criteria are laid down that define and delimit the duties of each employee. This definition of tasks provides the basis for specialization.
3   Each employee is given the authority necessary to carry out these assigned functions.
4   The responsibilities and authority of each employee (administrator, manager or other employee) form part of a hierarchy of offices.
5   Official business is conducted on the basis of written documents.
6   The holder of "offices" (formal positions) do not own those positions or the resources necessary for carrying out assigned duties, though they are accountable for the use of such resources.

The bureaucratic form of organization therefore depends on a high level of formalization, both of people's roles and how they are to carry them out. Essentially it lays down rules for the execution of tasks. Its underlying structure incorporates both horizontal specialization (division of labor) and vertical differentiation (hierarchy of authority).

Both Weber and the classical organization theorists were describing the form of organization that had by the beginning of the twentieth century come to typify large enterprises and public bodies. Although coming from different perspectives, they shared the belief that under the conditions of the time a definable form of organization made for both efficiency and propriety. The two organizational models shared many common features and these are summarized in Table 2.1 according to the basic dimensions of specialization, hierarchy, control and coordination. The main difference between the two models stemmed from their primary empirical points of reference. For classical organization theorists this was the large business

Table 2.1   Dimensions of classical organization theory and bureaucracy

Dimension	Classical organization theory	Bureaucracy
Specialization	Division of labor according to specific functions	Designated roles & "offices" Horizontal specialization (job positions & departments); Vertical specialization (hierarchical levels)
Hierarchy	Clear vertical lines of authority; authority to correspond to the responsibilities of each position	Clearly defined formal hierarchy based on officially assigned responsibilities and authority
Control	Control by hierarchical superiors through unity of command	Insistence on following codes and rules – "bureaucratic control" through "formalization"
Coordination	Achieved primarily by managers with limited spans of control	Through adherence to rules and procedures; also through formal committees

enterprise, whereas Weber took the Prussian civil service as an important reference for bureaucracy. This helps to explain the emphasis that classical organization theory placed on the role of the manager as the key to making the organization structure function well. By contrast, Weber focused on the contribution of clear rules and officials who were carefully selected and technically well-trained.

The principles of classical organization theory were evident in the so-called U-form (unitary) model which became common among large-scale single-business firms in the early part of the twentieth century.[20] The purpose of the U-form was to achieve economies of scale through functional specialization. The combination of functional specialization and hierarchy was an essential feature of this organizational form. Lower-level units were normally differentiated according to functional contributions. In the U-form organization, the coordination of different functions and units was performed by a manager at a higher level where he or she had authority over them, and similarly decisions were referred upwards on a management-by-exception basis. The exception principle was enabled by the regular reporting upwards of performance data in standardized formats. Vertically integrated U-forms had parallels in the public sector, to the benefit of the efficiency of government agencies as Weber described.

Scientific management

Frederick Winslow Taylor's grave bears the inscription "The Father of Scientific Management," but other pioneers such as Frank and Lillian Gilbreth, and Henry Gantt, also made important contributions.[21] The context in which scientific management developed was one of the growing size and complexity of business enterprises, the application of electric power and other technological advances, growing competition from an increasing number of newly industrialized countries, and the rising cost of skilled labor. This changing context made it increasingly necessary to bring in managerial personnel to supplement the personal direction of entrepreneurs and also to improve efficiency through a scientific study of work and increased control over how it was organized.

Taylor was concerned to develop what he called a "true science of work" which would replace the old rule-of-thumb approach and also bring the organization of work under the control of managers and out of the hands of work groups and their informal leaders. By science, Taylor meant systematic observation and measurement. The "science of work" entailed the application of job analysis, time study and a piece-rate payment system. Once a job had been analyzed into its essential component elements, these were to be timed. Adding together the times for individual elements gave a total time for the whole job. Identification of the components of a job also opened up possibilities for that job to be broken down into narrower tasks, each of which less skilled and lower-paid workers could perform – hence the association of Scientific Management with de-skilling. Certain allowances were added to the time allowed for the job, actually on a fairly arbitrary basis, to cover fatigue, variations in materials, accidental interruptions and so forth. Taylor proposed to motivate workers to maintain a high pace of work by means of an individual piece-rate system based on the standard work pace established through time study. This system of payment is discussed in Chapter 8.

While the attention of Taylor and the other industrial engineers who comprised the backbone of the scientific management movement was directed primarily at the planning, supervision and execution of shop floor work, they formulated certain organizational principles as well.

Fundamental to Taylor's thinking were the "triple S" of specialization, simplification, and standardization. These could be applied to managerial as well as shop floor work. For example, Taylor considered that the work of a typical factory foreman was composed of a number of different functions (such as cost clerk, time clerk, inspector, repair boss, and shop disciplinarian). He argued that these could be separated out and performed by different specialists who would each be responsible for controlling different aspects of the work and the workers. He called this system, "functional management," and he believed that it would provide increased efficiency by allowing for the development of specialist expertise applied to defined areas of work. These more limited, simplified tasks would be more amenable to scientific measurement and standardization, while they could be staffed by lower caliber, less scarce and cheaper employees than would otherwise be the case. Taylor also formulated the principle of "management by exception," which was informed by the same logic of specialization, simplification and standardization. This principle laid down that management reports should be condensed into comparative summaries giving in detail only the exceptions to past standards or averages – the especially good and bad exceptions. Through this standardized procedure, management information would be comprehensive, yet at the same time immediate in impact.

Scientific management was founded on the hierarchical premise that thinking should be separated from doing. Managers should carry out the thinking, in terms of setting objectives and systems of work based on the three Ss, while workers performed their tasks according to scientifically-determined methods. Thus the specification and verification of the methods, times, prices and quality standards of the jobs were to become management functions. Management was also to undertake the continuous supervision and control of the workers concerned, mainly through foremen (first-line supervisors) who would occupy an intermediate position in the hierarchy. Taylor claimed that the operation of managerial authority on scientific management lines was not arbitrary, because managers would be continually demonstrating that their decisions were subject to the same discipline as the workpeople – namely the scientific study of the work. Taylor believed that this supposedly objective standard would eliminate the main source of industrial conflict. At the same time, he maintained that scientific management would improve efficiency through both the scientific study of work and the motivating effects of payment by results.

The keyword for scientific management was measurement, which in turn provided a basis for formalization and managerial control. When categorized by the same dimensions that Table 2.1 applied to classical organization theory and bureaucracy, we can see that there are parallels between the principles articulated by all three approaches. Table 2.2 summarizes the

Table 2.2 Key organizational features of scientific management

Dimension	Scientific management
Specialization	Division of work into narrow carefully defined tasks – this provided the basis for de-skilling
Hierarchy	Clear differentiation between managers, foremen and workers based on the distinction between thinking and doing.
Control	Careful measurement of work done; control also supported by the motivation of payment by results
Coordination	By managers and supervisors

highlights of scientific management according to the dimensions of specialization, hierarchy, control, and coordination.

The Contingency Approach

Scientific management was criticized at an early stage, not so much for its emphasis on measurement and systems, but for the unsympathetic view that it was alleged to take of workers. There were critiques of the physical strain imposed by the "speeding up" of work, of the treatment of the worker as a "living tool" who was permitted minimal discretion and variety in his or her work, and for its attempt to win the allegiance of employees away from labor unions.[22] However, most of these critiques came from industrial psychologists who did not specifically challenge the search for a one best way of organizing work.

Classical organization theory came under attack somewhat later. Probably the earliest critique was that made by Herbert Simon in his classic book *Administrative Behavior* (1947).[23] Simon likened the classical principles to proverbs or slogans that were "essentially useless." Like proverbs, he said, the principles when taken together were mutually contradictory: specialization and unity of command; span of control and limited number of hierarchical levels; centralization and decentralization. Dichotomies like these, Simon argued, provided little practical guidance and could not legitimately be claimed as "one best ways." The main thrust of his criticism, however, was that the anatomical focus of the classical principles failed to consider some of the most significant features in the operation of organizations, such as how managers as actors made decisions, communicated these, and translated them into action.

The most enduring challenge to the "one best way of organizing" school came from the results of a growing body of empirical social science research from the late 1950s onward.[24] This produced mounting evidence that there was no necessary correlation between operational effectiveness and individual classical principles such as span of control, but rather that the most effective form of organization varied according to the nature and circumstances of the enterprise. The implication was that organization should be designed to fit the prevailing situation, a perspective that had been foreshadowed by Mary Parker Follett. Follett coined the term "law of the situation," by which she meant the course of action that became manifest when all the facts relating to a particular situation or issue are established.[25] Rather than determining a solution on *a priori* grounds, Follett argued that it had to follow from an analysis of circumstances. The requirements stemming from the situation in which the firm or institution concerned is operating represent identifiable contingencies, and ignoring them is seen to risk operating with a maladapted organization.

There are multiple contingencies and they come at different levels, ranging from those close to the task being undertaken to more environmental factors. Contingencies close to the task are primarily internal and have been categorized as the immediate "context" of organization.[26] They include the technology a plant or office uses, its size, the characteristics of its people (as employees or members), and its guiding purpose. External contingencies include the prevailing culture of where an organization is located, and the characteristics of the market a firm is serving (such as geographical dispersion, degree of competition, rate of change and innovation) or the nature of the domain in which a public organization is operating. The contingency perspective is distinguished both by the wide range of relevant factors it collectively identifies and by the fact that its conclusions are evidence-based. It resulted from a significant flowering of social science research into organization and its effects on performance under identifiable conditions.

Different writers focused on different categories of contingency. Among the more internal contingencies, considerable attention was given to *technology*. This ranged from the machinery applied to specific types of work to the configuration of whole plant-level production systems. The contributions of Joan Woodward and the Tavistock Group were prominent here. Another contingency was the *size* of the unit being organized, and here the Aston Group made one of the leading contributions. Organizations often grow through expanding the range of products or services they offer and also the geographical areas they serve. Growth through *diversification* was recognized as an important contingency for organizational design. A further internal feature identified as a contingency for organizational design was the type of *people* involved, in terms of their expectations, values, and skills. Mary Parker Follett was a pioneer of this human-centered view, which was taken forward by social and cultural psychologists and has been applied more recently to the increasingly important category of "knowledge worker."

Geert Hofstede is the best-known contributor on the ways that national or regional *culture* is a contingency for organizational design and behavior. Consideration of national *culture* as a factor shaping people's values and expectations takes us across an organization's boundaries into the realm of contingencies that have external sources. Apart from national cultures, two authorities have been particularly influential for their analysis of the organizational implications of external contingencies, usually referred to collectively as the *"organizational environment."* Tom Burns and G.M. Stalker identified the rate of external change, promoted both by competition and innovation as a key contingency. Paul Lawrence and Jay Lorsch developed the analysis further by identifying the need to secure and process new knowledge as a major contingency for appropriate organizational design. These contributions, and many others, add up to an impressive body of knowledge, which I now review with specific reference to its implications for organizational design.

Technology

Joan Woodward's research on 100 manufacturing firms in the UK drew attention to the relevance of their overall production technology as a contingency for organizational design.[27] She found that the more successful firms adopted an organizational structure that varied systematically with the integration of their technology. Among firms engaged in one-off or small batch production, the appropriate structure was one that had relatively few hierarchical levels and wide middle management spans of control. Moving up the scale of technological integration through large-batch, mass production, to process production, the structure of good performing firms tended to become taller and narrower, with longer hierarchies and smaller middle management spans of control.

Other studies also pointed to implications for organization arising from production technology or from features closely associated with it. For example, Khandwalla, in his research on American manufacturing companies found that those firms which had adjusted their structures according to the "mass output orientation" of their technologies were more profitable. Highly performing firms producing large quantities of standardized products (mass production and continuous process firms in particular) tended to employ sophisticated control systems and also to delegate more decision making. The key factor here appears to be that standardized work permits a form of organization that is more formalized (makes more use of standard rules and procedures) and incorporates more delegation than less standardized work.[28]

The relevance today of technology as a contingency has changed enormously with the advent of information and communication technologies (ICTs). As Chapter 3 will note, ICTs have opened up many new possibilities for both internal organization as well as for the management of transactions and integrated operations between firms. They have in this respect relaxed many of the constraints that made production technology a prominent contingency for organizational design.

The view that technology is a contingency for organizational design arose for some writers out of a belief in "technological determinism." This maintains that technical innovations and their embodiment in technology are the key movers in history and social change. Taken to an extreme, it implies that technological requirements eliminate any choice in how work is organized. Evidence from studies such as Woodward's, that the matching of organization to the technology in use had performance consequences, lent support to this view. Even when considered alongside other contingencies, technology was seen to have "implications" for organizational design.[29] This view subsequently came to be challenged by detailed studies of how work could be organized in relation to the technology used, even conventional technologies of mechanization and automation. Experiments in Swedish and other plants had shown by the 1980s that an organizational culture that was open to unconventional solutions could lead to innovations in work organization even in long-established production plants. Moreover, studies of new computer-controlled and ICT-based technologies demonstrated that their inherent flexibility allowed for considerable choice in organizational design both at workplace and managerial levels.[30]

Detailed investigations conducted by members of the Tavistock Institute in London into the organization of work also found that technology did not necessarily impose rigid constraints.[31] They saw the technology in use and the way that work units are organized as combining to form "socio-technical systems." The Tavistock researchers assumed that the aim was to optimize on both technical and social criteria. They concluded that within socio-technical systems, there was a degree of choice as to how work is organized in relation to the use of technology. This was conceptualized as "organizational choice." The decisions that managers made about organizing the work around a technology such as coal mining were found in studies by Eric Trist and his colleagues to have consequences for autonomy and social cohesion among workers, with knock-on effects for productivity and morale.[32]

Subsequent work by Tavistock researchers, notably Fred Emery, Eric Miller and Ken Rice, broadened out from the work group to consider organization as a whole and how adapted this was to the broader economic environment. Rice extended the focus from work design to the level of whole organizational systems, "identifying the 'primary task' of an organization as the overarching design principle."[33] Miller recognized that work was subject to boundary conditions established by technology, territory, and time, and that this posed a challenge of organizing so as to integrate the different subsystems that consequently arose. Emery and Trist developed insights into how the design of an organization as a whole could embody the degree of adaptive capacity necessary to respond to turbulent environments that created considerable uncertainty – for example through encouraging self-organization among teams. They later suggested that joint ventures and collaborations between groups of organizations could help to reduce this uncertainty.

Size

It has been widely noted that larger organizations tend to develop bureaucratic forms of organization. They generally have more extended hierarchies, and delegate non-strategic decisions down those hierarchies within the controls imposed by rules and other aspects of formalization. As we shall see in Chapter 6, large and complex organizations tend to adopt more formalized systems of control whereas smaller ones tend to rely on personal relationships to maintain control.[34] Past studies have found that better performing large companies (large in terms of employment) tended to use more bureaucratized structures in terms of greater specialization, more developed systems and procedures and more extensive delegation of decisions. It is instructive that this connection between size, formalized structure and performance was strongest for firms operating in relatively stable environments.[35] As Chapter 3 notes, high levels of innovation and of competition in open markets have resulted in very few stable environments nowadays, and much attention has therefore been given to how to reconcile large size with adaptation to change through new less bureaucratic forms of organization.

As the numbers employed in an organization grow, so does its complexity. Vertical complexity is manifested in the number of hierarchical levels and the link to size here lies in spans of control – the number of people reporting to a manager. Although the span of control principle of classical organization theory is now interpreted much less rigidly, there remains a limit to the number of subordinates that a manager can have as direct reports without problems arising such as overload and inadequate communication. It is a mathematical fact that, with a given average span of control, larger organizations will have more hierarchical levels. Size is therefore a relatively constraining contingency for the vertical aspect of organizational structure.

An increase in size makes it economically possible to utilize specialist support services, as well as to take advantage of specialization between individuals and groups which allows them to concentrate on given tasks and functions. However, specialization increases the horizontal complexity of an organization and the challenge of ensuring that an adequate degree of coordination and integration is maintained between the specialized roles and units. Additional organizational procedures are therefore required for coordination and communication, and these have also to be managed, thus further adding to the administrative burden imposed by larger size.

Growth remains a proclaimed corporate aim for many executives and there are various reasons for seeking larger size. In some industries, there are economies of large-scale production to be gained. There can also be benefits from spreading the overheads of R&D and specialist support services over a larger sales turnover. Diversification into other fields or industries in search of new profitable activities can also add to a company's size. Such diversification is often accomplished through mergers or acquisitions which clearly add to size, at least in the short run. Other less economically rational reasons include the prestige of belonging to the elite of the Fortune 500 or FTSE 100 list of leading corporations.

Nevertheless, company executives prefer growth in sales and assets rather than in numbers of people. This is because most of the implications that a larger employment establishment has for organizational design are negative. The fact that managing larger workforces tends to breed hierarchy, rigid boundaries between units, and formalization can inhibit the inter-disciplinary teamwork needed to support key competitive requirements today, namely innovation and the ability to adapt creatively to external changes (see Chapter 17). This is one reason why downsizing has become an attractive policy among employers in recent years (see Chapter 4) and likewise outsourcing (see Chapter 9). Both are policies that reduce size of employment, with an additional attraction of outsourcing being that it may be a way of simplifying and focusing organization onto core activities. Within the boundaries of a large firm, the multi-divisional (M-form) has often been adopted as a means to create smaller semi-autonomous units.

Diversification

After a certain stage of a firm's development, its path to profitable growth typically comes to require the diversification of products or services it offers and/or the range of geographical markets it serves. Scholars following up on Alfred Chandler's observation that "structure follows strategy" concluded that the diversification had organizational implications, notably a requirement to adopt a multi-divisional (M-form) structure and the procedures to make it work.[36] Pioneered by Alfred P. Sloan at General Motors in the 1920s, the M-form structure had become widely adopted among large American firms by the end of World War II and was copied by large European and Japanese firms during the 1950s and 1960s. The M-form required corporate managers to learn to discard the top-level control and coordination modes common in the U-form and instead to delegate decision making within a formalized framework of agreement on joint corporate division goals – a procedure for which Peter Drucker coined the term "management by objectives."[37] As Miles and his colleagues note, comparable approaches were adopted to manage the relations between federal and state levels of government.[38]

The fundamental rationale here is an attempt to combine an overall integration of policy with the benefits of responsiveness and innovation at the local level. It recognizes that the activities associated with different products or geographical markets generate their own specific knowledge and require their own specific skills. It therefore makes sense to group the people concerned into their own organizational units so as to concentrate and simplify communications and joint working among them. This helps to promote the benefits of diversity and innovation adapted to local circumstances. Even though an M-form organization can incur some additional costs due to a duplication of functions across divisions, the attempt to manage increasing diversification through a functional U-form type of structure will almost certainly give rise to serious problems such as slow adaptation and poor coordination.

Studies suggested that large American corporations which grouped their operations into divisions once those operations had become diversified tended to achieve higher levels of performance. For example, Rumelt found among 246 large industrial corporations that the match between diversification strategy and divisional structure affects performance. Firms that followed strategies of related diversification and adopted divisional structures attained the highest level of economic performance.[39] Stopford and Wells found that more successful firms had usually adopted the kind of divisionalization – an international division, global product divisions, global areas divisions, a mixed or grid structure – that their level of involvement in foreign business, level of product diversity or global regional spread logically dictated.[40] These and other studies led to the influential "strategy–structure–performance" (SSP) paradigm, which maintains that when an organization's strategy and its structure are congruent, the organization's performance is likely to be higher than if they do not match.

However, the association between diversification and structural design has not usually been found to have a strong connection with firm success. Rumelt's finding that firms pursuing unrelated diversification performed the worst suggests that diversification strategies themselves may have a more significant impact on a firm's financial performance than does the extent to which organizational structures have developed in line with these strategies. Many factors other than organization can also affect performance. These include external factors such as unfavorable competitive conditions as well as internal ones such as human resources limitations. It may be that the kind of people working in a company make it more viable to operate with a certain form of organization (as discussed in the following section), and that these two sets of capabilities, human and organizational, point to some strategies being feasible rather than others.[41] It also has to be borne in mind that the SSP paradigm is based on business models of the 1970s which continued to emphasize hierarchical relations and formal processes. In current less stable conditions, and with the emergence of many knowledge-based organizations, more flexible modular organizational forms based on loosely-coupled networked relations, often within multidimensional structures coordinated through matrix arrangements, have become more prevalent.[42]

People

It is a fundamental assumption of psychological theories that managements which adopt forms of organization consistent with the expectations and perceived needs of their employees or members will attract a greater contribution from them. The views of influential organizational psychologists such as Chris Argyris, Frederick Herzberg, Rensis Likert, Douglas McGregor and Richard Hackman have been consistent on this point, and have become the standard fare of many textbooks on management and organizational behavior. They have argued for structures and styles of management that secure a higher level of commitment from people to the goals of their organization through more adequately meeting their expectations and their needs as mature adults. The psychological perspective has clear implications for organizational design, favoring empowerment, teamwork and rewards related to what employees value.[43] The implications of this perspective for reward policies are discussed in Chapter 7. In terms of work organization, it argues in favor of granting employees greater autonomy and responsibility in their work, either as individuals or as members of teams, and improving the intrinsic quality of jobs through increasing the variety and significance of the tasks involved, recognizing achievement, and enhancing workplace social relations. Many organizational psychologists have also argued for non-hierarchical structures and open communications, in order to promote closer inter-personal relationships, to foster a shared organizational culture and through policies of transparency to facilitate a feeling of equity among employees and their acceptance of corporate goals.

This perspective assumes that all human beings share common needs and motivational structures. Insofar as motivation drives people's behavior in organizations, it is argued that the design of work organizations as well as organizational systems for control and reward must treat this as a major contingency. But although this perspective takes people to be a contingency for organizational design, it harks back to the universalism of pre-contingency thinking. It focuses on our common biological and physiological features, while ignoring the variations in cultural and social context that can shape people's values and expectations in important ways. As I have noted previously:[44]

It is precisely because many needs are socially-defined and reflect what is valued culturally, that the universal applicability of psychological theories has been heavily questioned. They have been criticized for their universalism – for assuming that the same theory can be applied to all people regardless of their social origins, upbringing, education and culture. They have also been criticized for their imperialism. Hofstede in particular has argued that these psychological theories actually reflect American cultural values, especially individualism, with their emphasis on achievement and self-actualization as the highest level needs.[45] Some psychologists have themselves urged the need to develop theories of behavior and motivation that are indigenous to different societies rather than universalistic in nature . . . If the general applicability of current psychological work-related theories can be questioned, then their prescriptions for organizational design have to be treated with caution.

People and their culture

While theories of human nature, and also of personality to a degree, emphasize the attributes that people everywhere share, the cultural perspective draws attention to ways in which people's thinking and behavior are importantly shaped by the cultural values and norms that they acquire – mainly through their upbringing but also open to some modification later in life. Cultural values are deep-seated and enduring, and they vary systematically between social collectivities. We tend to associate cultures primarily with nations or regions, but they can also vary according to other social identities such as those of religion, ethnicity, occupation and social class. Culture is a contingency for organizational design because it conditions what is acceptable organizational practice. With the global spread of many companies and supra-national public agencies, and with the increasing multi-cultural mix in many countries, cultural differences have become increasingly significant as organizational contingencies. On the other hand, globalization and more intensive international contact and communication may over time be reducing the *degree* of difference between cultures.

Although there is a vast body of research and discussion on cultural differences,[46] relatively few models of national culture have stimulated thinking about its organizational implications. The most influential (and controversial) has been Geert Hofstede's, but other widely used models of national culture relevant to organization are those proposed by Kluckhohn and Strodtbeck, Hall, Trompenaars, Schwartz, and House and his associates in the GLOBE project. Nardon and Steers note five relatively distinct common themes that emerge from a comparison of these models.[47] These concern values and beliefs on:

1 *Hierarchy versus equality* – "power distance": the distribution of power and authority;
2 *Individualism versus collectivism:* the centrality of individuals versus groups as a basic social building block;
3 *Mastery or acceptance of the environment* – controlling the environment or adapting to it;
4 Orientation towards and use of *time*;
5 *Universalism versus particularism* – especially reliance on uniformly applied rules and controls versus making modifications to suit particular circumstances or personal ties.

The argument that culture is a contingency for organizational design is based on the assumption that particular forms of organization will best suit given cultures, and that a good fit between the two is likely to enhance people's commitment to organizational goals and high performance. Thus values and beliefs concerning *the distribution of power and authority* are likely to shape preferences for organizing vertically or horizontally. A high "power distance" culture (in which there is an acceptance that power is distributed unequally and that authority differences are legitimate) is therefore consistent with a strong emphasis on hierarchy, tall organization structures, large differentials in rewards, and centralization of decision making. By contrast, a culture with low power distance is likely to generate a preference for minimal hierarchy, flat structure, participative management, and bottom-up initiatives. Arab, East and Southeast Asian and Sub-Saharan African countries tend to have strongly hierarchical cultures, while Nordic countries tend to have strongly egalitarian ones.[48]

Values of *individualism versus collectivism* are likely to have implications for whether individual or group working and decision-making is preferred, and whether authority and responsibility are granted to individuals or to groups. For example, an individualistic culture is likely to favor giving clear-cut responsibilities to individuals, while a collectivist culture encourages giving them to teams or committees. This cultural dimension is also likely to differentiate between whether organizational sanctions are designed to reinforce independence and personal responsibility rather than conformity to group norms; and whether payment should be individually or group-based. Anglo-Saxon countries tend to be highly individualistic while Arab, East Asian and Sub-Saharan African countries tend to be strongly collectivistic.

Mastery versus harmony with the environment is likely to be reflected in organizational cultures rather than structures, with mastery being associated with achievement, competitiveness and performance-based extrinsic rewards, while harmony is associated with quality of relationships, mutual adjustment, and a preference for intrinsic rewards. The main contrasts here tend to be between Anglo-Saxon countries which have strongly mastery-oriented cultures, while East Asian ones tend to be strongly oriented toward harmony.

Time. Some national cultures are "past oriented" valuing the preservation of past traditions, while other are "future oriented." This aspect of time orientation can overlap with the dimension of mastery versus harmony in that in future oriented cultures people are more likely to believe they can influence the turn of events and therefore to engage in planning for the future. Another aspect of time orientation is that some cultures are oriented toward the short-term while in others people tend to take a longer-term view. A further cultural aspect concerning time is whether people are more comfortable dealing with tasks sequentially or are happy dealing with multiple tasks at the same time. Also in some cultures, time discipline (punctuality and keeping to time schedules) is highly valued, in other somewhat less so. Various organizational implications follow from these cultural attitudes towards time. For instance, people belonging to cultures in which time discipline is valued are more likely to respond well to being organized according to formal schedules and deadlines. Cultures oriented to the longer-term future and in which people can readily pay attention to multiple tasks are more likely to be able to sustain newer organizational forms which (as Chapter 3 describes) emphasize the achievement of innovation and adaptation to change through a low definition and specialization of jobs, flexible ways of working, networking, and taking local initiative. Latin American cultures tend to display flexibility toward time and comfort in dealing with multiple tasks, while Anglo-Saxon countries tend to be the opposite.

Universalism versus particularism. In universalistic cultures like the United States, there is a heavy emphasis on controlling behavior and maintaining order through promulgating a wide range of laws, rules, regulations, bureaucratic procedures and strict social norms. People have a high respect for the law and expect it to be applied equally to every citizen without exception. In particularistic cultures, the opposite applies. People belonging to particularistic cultures regard it as legitimate to make exceptions according to circumstances or according to the people involved, especially if they are powerful. Things tend to be done much more on an informal basis with regard to personal connections and relationships. As a contingency for organizational design, universalistic cultures favor a high level of formalization, clearly spelt out policies, rules and responsibilities, an emphasis on legal contracts and meticulous record-keeping, and it is expected that these will be applied equally to all members whatever their hierarchical position or social standing. Anglo-Saxon, Germanic and Nordic cultures tend to emphasize universalism, while Arab, East and Southeast Asian, Latin American, and Sub-Saharan African cultures tend to be strongly particularistic.

Organizational purpose and values

This book focuses primarily on one type of organization – the business firm. Although prominent in economic terms, this is of course only one category of organization that is active in the modern world. Other types of organization can be distinguished from the business firm by a number of factors, all of which can be regarded as contingencies for organizational design. Professional service firms (PSFs), such as accounting, law, engineering and management consulting firms, advertising, and private medical firms, are characterized by a professionalized workforce, a reliance for their output on a substantial body of complex knowledge (knowledge intensity), and a norm of trusteeship towards their clients.[49] In highly professionalized occupations such as medicine and law, it is expected that key staff will have internalized a strong occupational culture which stresses values such as autonomy, informal relations with colleagues, and ethical codes. The organizational form appropriate to this occupational culture will place a low emphasis on hierarchy and a strong emphasis on coordination and knowledge-sharing through internal networking.[50]

Certain areas of public service work, such as social services, are expected to exhibit similar cultural and behavioral characteristics though the conduct of their work may be more subject to bureaucratic control in the form of externally imposed rules and regulations. Other public organizations, notably government departments, normally operate in ways that correspond closely to the bureaucratic model. Yet another significant form of organization is the membership organization. This category includes labor unions, professional associations, and political parties. These organizations combine a bottom-up representative system whereby officials are elected to represent their members' interests with a top-down administrative system often managed by those same officials. The dichotomy between representative and administrative rationales creates inherent organizational tensions.[51] Social enterprises which endeavor to combine business and commercial principles with the goal of serving communal and other social goals are also generally constituted so as to allow for the active participation in their governance of their stakeholder groups.[52]

The purposes and values of these other types of organization contrast with those of the conventional firm. The contrast is sometimes dramatic as in the case of membership organizations, but less so in the case of PSFs. PSFs operating in traditionally professionalized fields have to reconcile the profit motive with the historically primary value of placing the client's interest first, a reconciliation that can prove particularly difficult in for-profit medicine.

The growing complexity of PSFs over recent decades, in size, range of specialized services offered, and geographical spread, has had organizational consequences. It has encouraged greater specialization in depth complimented by client management systems to integrate specialized contributions, and the establishment of formal operating standards. However, the senior partners of PSFs continue to be the key liaison with important clients and provide the leadership of client teams.[53] Moreover, PSFs rely on the contributions of knowledge workers and cannot motivate them effectively though applying conventional forms of organization. The growth of knowledge work in organizations such as PSFs has been a factor in the emergence of new organizational forms and this is discussed further in Chapter 3.

Organizational environment

A groundbreaking and very influential research project conducted by Tom Burns and George Stalker in the electronics industry distinguished between "mechanistic" and "organismic" (organic) forms of organization.[54] Mechanistic forms are the descendents of classical organization theory and Weber's model of bureaucracy. They are highly structured, with considerable formalization and specialization, which encourages their members to work in watertight boxes and discourages informal horizontal communication. Organismic forms, by contrast, are less rigidly structured and have greater integration between parts of the organization. They accord more to a biological model of cellular systems rather than to the engineering analogy of separate mechanical parts.[55] The identification by Burns and Stalker of the organismic model led to one of the first descriptions of what in this book I am calling "new" organizational forms.

Burns and Stalker concluded that while mechanistic organizations are suited to stable conditions, they are very poor at promoting innovation, largely because their R&D departments are separated from the rest of the business, and also often unable to cope with change because of the poor communication between their constituent departments. On the other hand, organismic organizations "are adapted to unstable conditions, when new and unfamiliar problems and requirements continually arise which cannot be broken down amongst specialist roles within a hierarchy. Jobs lose much of their formal definition. The definitive and enduring demarcation of functions becomes impossible. Responsibilities and functions, and even methods and powers, have to be constantly redefined through interaction with others participating in common tasks or in the solution of common problems. Each individual has to do his job with knowledge of overall purpose and situation of the company as a whole. Interaction runs laterally as much as vertically, and communication between people of different rank tends to resemble 'lateral' consultation rather than 'vertical' command. Omniscience can no longer be imputed to the boss at the top."[56]

The mechanistic and organismic models are "ideal types" of organization, just as was Weber's characterization of bureaucracy. In other words, they captured the essence of two significantly contrasting approaches to organizing without necessarily being exactly or fully applied in practice to any specific situation. Since they capture many of the differences between the conventional organizational forms on which this chapter had focused and the new forms described in Chapter 3, it is instructive to reproduce Tom Burns's summary of their characteristic features in Table 2.3.

Table 2.3 Contrasting features of mechanistic and organismic organizational forms

Mechanistic	Organismic
Specialized differentiation of functional tasks	Contributive nature of special knowledge to the common task of the concern
Abstract nature of each individual task	Individual tasks set by the total situation of the concern
Reconciliation of individual task performances for each level of the hierarchy by the immediate superiors	Adjustment and continual redefinition of individual tasks through interaction with others
Precise definition of rights and obligations and technical methods attached to each functional role	Responsibility not seen as a limited field of obligations, rights and methods
Obligations, rights and methods defined as the responsibilities of a functional position	Spread of commitment to the whole concern beyond any given job
Hierarchical structure of authority, control, and communication	Network structure of authority, control, and communication
Reinforcement of the hierarchical structure by locating knowledge of existing conditions exclusively at the top of the hierarchy	Omniscience no longer imputed to the head of the concern; knowledge may be located anywhere in the network, this location becoming the center of authority
Tendency toward vertical interaction	Lateral rather than vertical direction of communication
Tendency for operations and working behavior to be governed by instructions and decisions of superiors	Communication consists of information and advice rather than instructions and decisions
Insistency on loyalty to the concern and obedience to superiors	Commitment to the concern's tasks more highly valued than loyalty
Greater importance attached to internal (local) than to external general knowledge, experience and skill	Importance and prestige attach to affiliations and expertise valid in the industrial, technical and commercial milieu external to the firm

(Adapted from Tom Burns, Industry in a new age, *New Society*, 31 January 1963, reprinted in Derek S. Pugh and David J. Hickson. *Writers on Organization*, London, Penguin 2007, pp. 70–71.)

Another influential study that explored the implications for organizational design of environmental conditions was that conducted by Paul Lawrence and Jay Lorsch of ten American companies.[57] Six of the companies were in plastics manufacturing, an industry characterized at the time by considerable market and technological change, and by much uncertainty about future developments. The other four companies, in container manufacturing and food processing, were operating in more stable environments. There was considerable differentiation in the time horizons of functional departments within companies in volatile environments. Their research departments had to work to long time horizons while also achieving adaptations to new developments. Marketing departments had to work to shorter time horizons than did research, but still faced more uncertainty than the production function. The challenge posed by the differentiation of time horizons in conditions of environmental uncertainty was one of achieving effective integration between the departments. When organizational arrangements were in place to achieve integration and to resolve conflicts between highly differentiated departments, the firm was more successful. In a volatile environment integration had to be achieved through direct horizontal contacts and open discourse between departments, whereas in more stable environments it could be achieved mainly though the managerial hierarchy. Lawrence and Lorsch's broad conclusion is similar to that reached by Burns and Stalker. In relatively stable industries where uncertainty is fairly low, more formal and hierarchical forms of organization may be appropriate, while in high-uncertainty environments more open and flexible approaches are suitable and likely to be more common.

Research by Lorsch and Morse followed up the Lawrence and Lorsch study by incorporating people as a contingency – or more specifically the personality predispositions of employees – alongside the organization-environment fit. Like Lawrence and Lorsch, the researchers selected companies to study which varied in performance and environmental uncertainty. They measured the internal variables included in the earlier study plus aspects of their members' personalities. They found that when there was congruence between the external environment, internal variables (including formality of organization structure), and members' personality dimensions, the units in both certain and uncertain environments were successful and individuals felt a high level of competence. Although their evidence is not conclusive on causality, they argue that a three-way fit between members' personality predispositions, internal and external environmental factors is conducive to higher per-formance. In other words,

> "Like other studies from the contingency perspective, the central message of our findings for managers is that there is no one best solution to the administrative and organizational issues they face. Rather, questions of managerial behavior and organizational design must be considered in light of the external environment which each organizational unit faces and the predispositions of its members."[58]

Conclusion

The contingency perspective covers a wide range of internal and external factors. Its common theme is that the design of organization should be "fit for purpose." This means that it should fit the contingencies that prevail both in the operating context and broader environment of a concern, be this a business firm or other kind of unit. By bringing organizational design into alignment with situational contingencies, the concern can evolve in response to changing circumstances in an adaptive manner that should ensure its survival.[59] Although the contingency perspective brings with it many practical difficulties – such as what to do when the implications of different contingencies are in conflict – and while evidence on its contribution to performance remains patchy, it does offer a practical portfolio of considera-tions to take into account when people are thinking about the organization of the unit they work in or belong to. In this respect, the contingency perspective represents a considerable advance over the older "one-best-way" type of thinking, although the demanding analysis it requires makes it less attractive to many managers. And by paying attention to the variable nature of contingencies, it also helps us to understand the forces that have stimulated the new forms of organization introduced in the next chapter and considered throughout the rest of this book.

SUMMARY

1 A historical overview is valuable because it helps us to understand the importance both of continuity and context.

2 Continuity is evident in the fact that much pioneering thinking on organization offers insights that are still relevant.

3 History also provides an appreciation of how certain organizational designs emerged and survived because they suited a particular context.

4 Thinking in the first half of the twentieth century was focusing on finding "one-best-ways" of organizing. These suited the growth of large-scale units operating under generally stable conditions.

5 Investigations in the second half of the twentieth century challenged these one-best-ways. Based on evidence that the most effective form of organization depended on the contingencies in a unit's situation, a "contingency approach" superseded previous thinking and became the dominant orthodoxy.

6 Nevertheless, certain earlier principles continue to have relevance such as maintaining a correspondence between authority and responsibility.

7 The contingency approach identifies both internal contingencies for organizational design (sometimes called "context") and external ones stemming from the characteristics of the unit's environment.

8 The historical review presented in this chapter covers the development of what has become conventional thinking on organizational design. The following chapter, Chapter 3, contrasts this with so-called "new" organizational forms.

QUESTIONS FOR DISCUSSION

2.1 How relevant do "classical organization theory" and "scientific management" remain today?

2.2 Are they more relevant for certain types of organization and/or certain cultures than others?

2.3 Do different contingencies carry different implications for the design of organization? If so, what can managers do if these implications conflict?

2.4 Is the fit of organization with some contingencies likely to have a greater impact on organizational performance than its fit to others?

2.5 Are any contingencies open to some degree of managerial control?

NOTES

1 Another influential perspective which argued for a "one best way" was the so-called "human relations school." This first emerged in the 1920s as a reaction to the mechanistic view of work and

workers in Scientific Management (discussed below) and a response to high levels of industrial conflict, some of which arose from aggressive applications of Scientific Management by employers. It drew attention to the emotional element in employees' makeup – the "logic of sentiment." It stressed the importance of "democratic leadership" styles and personal relations with employees – especially understanding their psychology, using persuasion rather than authority, communicating with them and paying attention to their morale. Since the human relations perspective was a compliment to, rather than an aspect of, organizational design I do not discuss it in this chapter.

2   For comprehensive accounts of the history of thinking on management, including organization, from ancient times to the modern, see Morgen Witzel (2012), *A History of Management Thought*, London, Routledge; and Daniel A. Wren and Arthur G. Bedeian (2009), *The Evolution of Management Thought*, New York, Wiley 6th edition. For detailed appreciations of the pioneering contributions by Frederick Winslow Taylor, Henri Fayol, Mary Parker Follett, Chester Barnard, and other more recent authorities see the relevant chapters in Morgen Witzel and Malcom Warner (eds.) (2013), *The Oxford Handbook of Management Theorists*, Oxford, Oxford University Press. Other sources are Derek S. Pugh and David J. Hickson (eds.) (2007), *Writers on Organization*, 6th edition, London, Penguin; John Child (2011), *British Management Thought: A Critical Analysis*, London, Routledge (first published 1969); William H. Starbuck (2003), The origins of organization theory, In Haridimos Tsoukas and Christian Knudsen (eds.), *The Oxford Handbook of Organization Theory*, Oxford, Oxford University Press, Chapter 5, pp. 143–182.

3   J.D. Mooney and C.A. Reiley (1931), *Onward Industry! The Principles of Organization and their Significance to Modern Industry*, New York: Harper.

4   F.Y. Wong (1997), Human Resource Management in Traditional China: An Examination of how Imperial Officials were Recruited and its Legacy, unpublished PhD Thesis, University of Hong Kong.

5   Alfred Kieser (1997), Rhetoric and myth in management fashion, *Organization*, pp. 49–74.

6   Peter M. Blau (1955), *The Dynamics of Bureaucracy*, Chicago: University of Chicago Press; Alvin W. Gouldner (1954), *Patterns of Industrial Bureaucracy*, Glencoe, Il: Free Press.

7   Tom Burns and G.M. Stalker (1961), *The Management of Innovation*, London, Tavistock.

8   Chris Argyris (1957), *Personality and Organization: The Conflict between System and the Individual*, New York, Harper & Row; Robert Blauner (1964), *Alienation and Freedom*, Chicago, University of Chicago Press.

9   Melville Dalton (1959), *Men Who Manage*, New York, Wiley.

10   J. Kenneth Benson (1977), Innovation and crisis in organizational analysis, *Sociological Quarterly*, 18(1), 3–16; Charles Perrow (1972), *Complex Organizations: A Critical Essay*, Glenview, Scott, Foresman.

11   Witzel (2012), op. cit., Chapter 1 makes a convincing case for the justification of taking a historical view.

12   Raymond E. Miles, Charles C. Snow, Øystein D. Fjeldstad, Grant Miles and Christopher Lettl (2010), Designing organizations to meet 21st-century opportunities and challenges, *Organizational Dynamics*, 39(2), 93–103. The quotation is from p. 94.

13   Henri Fayol (1949), *Industrial and General Administration*, first published 1916, translated by Constance Storrs, London: Pitman; Lyndall F. Urwick (1928), Principles of direction and control. In John Lee (ed.), *Dictionary of Industrial Administration*, London, Pitman, pp. 161–179; Luther H. Gulick and Lyndall F. Urwick (eds.) (1937), *Papers on the Science of Administration*, New York, Institute of Public Administration.

14   Max Weber (1947), *The Theory of Social and Economic Organization*, translated by A.M. Henderson and Talcott Parsons, New York, Oxford University Press.

15   Weber was somewhat in two minds concerning bureaucracy. On the one hand he recognized that bureaucracies could protect citizens' rights by administering laws consistently and fairly. On the other hand, he was alarmed that the very efficiency of bureaucracy as a mode of administration might threaten democracy and freedom by placing officials at an advantage over elected

representatives. Robert Michel's "iron law of oligarchy" echoes the concern that officials in democratic political parties could accumulate excessive power through their central organizational positions – see Robert Michels (1915), *Political Parties: A Sociological Study of the Oligarchical Tendencies of Modern Democracy,* translated by Paul Eden and Paul Cedar, New York, Free Press. Weber also expressed concern at the dehumanizing effects of bureaucracy, which Franz Kafka amplified in his novels that depicted the powerlessness and alienation that bureaucracies could impose both on their employees and members of the public who had to deal with them – see Malcolm Warner (2007), Kafka, Weber and organization theory. *Human Relations,* 60(7), 1019–1038.

16 Weber's analysis of bureaucracy relied on an identification of its key characteristics rather than on what might be found exactly in any given empirical case. In this sense, they may be called "principles," in keeping with the term used by classical organization theorists.

17 Andrew Thompson and John Wilson (2013), Lyndall Urwick. In Morgen Witzel and Malcom Warner (eds.) *The Oxford Handbook of Management Theorists,* Oxford, Oxford University Press, Chapter 7, pp. 113–133. The statement of Urwick's 10 principles is taken from pp. 123–124.

18 James D. Mooney and Alan C. Reiley (1931), op. cit.

19 From Max Weber, *The Theory of Social and Economic Organization* as analyzed by Reinhard Bendix (1960), *Max Weber: An Intellectual Portrait,* London, Heinemann, 418–425.

20 Miles et al. (2010), pp. 94–95.

21 For accounts and analyses of scientific management, see Witzel (2012), op. cit., Chapter 5, pp. 82–103; Wren and Bedeian (2009), op. cit., Part II, pp. 119–280; and the chapters by Robert F. Conti on Taylor and by Bernard Mees on the Gilbreths in Morgen Witzel and Malcom Warner (eds.) (2013), *The Oxford Handbook of Management Theorists,* Oxford, Oxford University Press.

22 An early critique by a prominent executive was Edward Cadbury (1914), Some principles of industrial organization: the case for and against scientific management, *Sociological Review,* VII(2), 99–117. Cadbury saw value in, and applied, the systematic approach of scientific management in the Cadbury Brothers chocolate company, while rejecting its mechanistic view of workers.

23 Herbert A. Simon (1947), *Administrative Behavior: A Study of Decision-Making Processes in Administrative Organization,* New York, Macmillan.

24 John Child (2011), *British Management Thought: A Critical Analysis,* London, Routledge (first published in 1969), Chapter 6, pp. 168–214.

25 John Child (2013), Mary Parker Follett. In Morgen Witzel and Malcolm Warner (eds.), *The Oxford Handbook of Management Theorists,* Oxford, Oxford University Press, Chapter 5, 74–93.

26 Derek S. Pugh and David J. Hickson (eds.) (1976), *Organizational Structure in its Context: The Aston Programme I,* Farnborough, UK, Saxon House.

27 Joan Woodward (1965), *Industrial Organization: Theory and Practice,* Oxford, Oxford University Press.

28 Pradip N. Khandwalla (1974), Mass output orientation of operations technology and organizational structure, *Administrative Science Quarterly,* 19(1), 74–97.

29 For a review of the range of perspectives on the relation between technology and organization, ranging from technological determinism to organizational choice, see John Child and Ray Loveridge (1990), *Information Technology in European Services,* Oxford, Blackwell, Chapter 2, 17–34.

30 John Child and Ray Loveridge (1990), op. cit. See also P. Grootings (ed.) (1986), *Technology and Work: East-West Comparison,* London, Taylor & Francis; John Child and Penny David (1987), *Technology and the Organization of Work,* London, National Economic Development Office.

31 On the work of the Tavistock Institute see Frances Abraham (2013), The Tavistock Group in Morgen Witzel and Malcom Warner (eds.) *The Oxford Handbook of Management Theorists,* Oxford, Oxford University Press, Chapter 9, especially pp. 165–171.

32 E.L. Trist, G.W. Higgin, H. Murray, and A.B. Pollock (1963), *Organizational Choice: Capabilities of Groups at the Coal Face under Changing Technologies: The Loss, Re-Discovery and Transformation of a Work Tradition,* London, Tavistock Publications.

33   Frances Abraham (2013), op. cit., p. 167.

34   Joan Woodward (1970), *Industrial Organization: Behaviour and Control*, Oxford, Oxford University Press.

35   John Child (1975), Managerial and organizational factors associated with company performance – Part II A contingency analysis, *Journal of Management Studies*, 12(1), 12–27.

36   Alfred D. Chandler, Jr. (1962), *Strategy and Structure: Chapters in the History of the American Industrial Enterprise*, Cambridge, MIT Press.

37   Peter F. Drucker (1954), *The Practice of Management*, New York, Harper & Row, Chapter 11.

38   Miles et al. (2010), op. cit., p. 95.

39   Richard P. Rumelt (1974), *Strategy, Structure, and Economic Performance*, Cambridge, MA, Harvard University Press.

40   John M. Stopford and Louis T. Wells, Jr. (1972), *Managing the Multinational Enterprise: Organization of the Firm and Ownership of the Subsidiary*, New York, Basic Books.

41   See the discussion in W. Chan Kim and Renée Mauborgne (2009), How strategy shapes structure, *Harvard Business Review*, September, 73–80.

42   Noam Wasserman (2008), Revisiting the strategy, structure, and performance paradigm: The case of venture capital, *Organization Science*, 19(2), 241–259.

43   It should be noted that the term "empowerment" as used in the management literature does not mean "giving power to," but rather granting a degree of additional discretion, information and resources to employees so that they can take greater initiative to solve problems, improve productivity and enhance the quality of customer service. Giving employees the capacity to make choices may at the same time assist their personal development and as such be welcomed by them.

44   John Child (2000), Theorizing about organization cross-nationally, *Advances in International Comparative Management*, 13, 27–75. The quotation is from pp. 36–37. Emerald Group Publishing Limited.

45   Geert Hofstede (1980), Motivation, leadership and organization: Do American theories apply abroad? *Organization Dynamics*, 8, 42–63.

46   For comprehensive collections of papers on culture and its relevance to management and organizations see Gordon Redding and Bruce W. Stening (eds.) (2003), *Cross-Cultural Management*, Cheltenham, Edward Elgar, 2 volumes; Rabi S. Bhagat and Richard M. Steers (eds.) (2009), *The Cambridge Handbook of Culture, Organizations, and Work*, Cambridge, Cambridge University Press.

47   Luciara Nardon and Richard M. Steers (2009), The culture theory jungle: divergence and convergence in models of national culture. In Rabi S. Bhagat and Richard M. Steers (eds.) (2009), *The Cambridge Handbook of Culture, Organizations, and Work*, Cambridge, Cambridge University Press, Chapter 1, 3–22.

48   The tendencies on core cultural dimensions for different regions summarized here are taken from Nardon and Steers (2009), op. cit.

49   Andrew von Nordenflycht (2010), What is a professional service firm? Towards a theory and taxonomy of knowledge-intensive firms, *Academy of Management Review*, 35(1), 155–174.

50   Royston Greenwood, Tim Morris, Samantha Fairclough, and Mehdi Boussebaa (2010), The organizational design of transnational professional service firms, *Organizational Dynamics*, 39(2), 173–183.

51   John Child, Ray Loveridge, and Malcolm Warner (1973), Towards an organizational study of trade unions, *Sociology*, 7(1), 71–91.

52   Mirjam Schöning, Abigail Noble, Andreas Heinecke, Ann-Kristin Achleitner, and Judith Mayer (2012), *The Governance of Social Enterprises: Managing Your Organization for Success*, Geneva, World Economic Forum.

53   Royston Greenwood et al. (2010), op. cit.; See also David M. Brock, Michael J. Powell, and C.R. Hinings (eds.) (1999), *Restructuring the Professional Organization*, London; Routledge.

54 Tom Burns and G.M. Stalker (1961), *The Management of Innovation*, London, Tavistock. The "organismic" form is more commonly called "organic." Also Tom Burns (1963), Industry in a new age, *New Society*, 31 January, 17–20, reprinted in Derek S. Pugh and David J. Hickson (2007), op. cit. pp. 66–75.

55 Witzel (2012), op. cit., p. 191.

56 Tom Burns (1963), op. cit.

57 Paul R. Lawrence and Jay W. Lorsch (1967), *Organization and Environment*, Boston, Harvard Business School Press.

58 Jay W. Lorsch and John J. Morse (1974), *Organizations and their Members: A Contingency Approach*, New York, Harper & Row. The quotation is from pp. 117–118.

59 Lex Donaldson (2001), *The Contingency Theory of Organizations*, Thousand Oaks, CA, Sage.

CHAPTER 3

New Conditions, New Organization

WHAT THIS CHAPTER COVERS

There has been a retreat from the "conventional" organizational forms described in the previous chapter. New forms of organization have emerged, largely as a result of changed conditions in the external environment. The intention of this chapter is to provide an overall picture as a background to the specific aspects of new organizational forms and processes that will be examined in Parts II and III of this book. The chapter starts with a review of the growing dissatisfaction with the conventional form of organization that has been modeled around the paradigms of bureaucracy and hierarchical command. It goes on to discuss ways in which the present conditions under which business operates have created a momentum towards new organizational forms. These new conditions are connected with globalization, new technologies, the knowledge-based economy, hypercompetition, and demands for social accountability. The chapter closes with a comparison of conventional and new organizational forms based on the organizational choices examined in Chapter 1.

◢ The Retreat from Conventional Forms of Organization

Military, political, and religious activities have been organized, often on a large scale, throughout recorded history. As the previous chapter described, the forms of organization that evolved shared many common features, despite differences of location and purpose. These included statements of collective aims (charters), the specialization of functions and roles (duties and rights) both vertically and horizontally, rules of conduct, and other arrangements to control and coordinate behavior. By the 1950s, however, this conventional model came under increasing criticism both because it was found often not to work as claimed and because it was deemed to be oppressive of those who worked under it.

During the 1970s, organizational theorists developed multiple models and paradigms.[1] Some of this diversification derived from a growing attention to the politics of organization informed by in-depth case studies and critical theory.[2] This implied that the rational assumptions of bureaucratic theory and its focus on structure were untenable. There was also a growing realization that it was impossible to predict, let alone understand, the effects of organizational design upon behavior and performance without discovering how the people working in organizations interpreted and made sense of organization and its context.[3] At a more pragmatic level, the slowing down of productivity growth and deepening of the competitive challenge from Japan were leading to the conclusion that the pursuit of rationalization through bureaucratic and Taylorist methods had reached its limit and was now in crisis. This encouraged the search for new forms of organization that were conducive to higher productivity, quality, and innovation. The conventional bureaucratic form of organization therefore came under increasing fire from several directions. The perspective that informed it was seen to be faulty. As an organizational form, it was regarded as increasingly ill-suited to emerging environments and the changing expectations about the way people should work.

As a result of these developments, the so-called "post-bureaucratic" organization was by the 1980s identified, in principle at least, as a clear alternative to the bureaucratic form that had for over a century reflected the philosophy of large scale, hierarchical and rationalized business. Its enthusiasts argued for a move away from hierarchy, a return to smaller less differentiated, more organic units, an emphasis on personal interpretation and creativity rather than on conformity to rules, and other arrangements to encourage empowerment, flexibility, learning, innovation, and teamwork. For example, Peter Drucker wrote in 1988 that:

> "The typical large business 20 years hence will have fewer than half the levels of management of its counterpart today, and no more than a third the managers. In its structure, and in its management problems and concerns, it will bear little resemblance to the typical manufacturing company, circa 1950, which our textbooks still consider the norm. Instead it is far more likely to resemble organizations that neither the practicing manager nor the management scholar pays much attention to today: the hospital, the university, the symphony orchestra . . . it will be what I call an information-based organization."[4]

During the 1990s, the transition from an economy based on the processing of materials to one based on flows of information became ever more apparent, especially in the developed economies. This transition unfettered many aspects of organization from their former physical constraints, permitting, for example, activities in dispersed locations to be as effectively integrated as those gathered on the same site. Increasing information intensity is today the fundamental development to which new organizational designs must respond, because it challenges the very premises upon which bureaucratic organization's claim to economic performance rests: namely, the harnessing of efficient combinations of resources in an economy.[5]

Bureaucratically organized firms look to codify new knowledge as rapidly as possible. In an economy based on physical objects, the organization can then reap returns from deploying that codified knowledge to offer new and better products or more efficiently manufacture existing products. The firm that creates new knowledge and keeps it to itself, enjoying a pseudo-monopoly, can in this way gain economic rents, where the term implies supranormal profitability for an industry.

The problem for bureaucracies is that such a "hoarding" strategy for knowledge is impractical in the case of knowledge-based goods and services. For one thing, the knowledge must often be given away as part of an economic transaction. For another, the very act of codifying knowledge to make it useful also makes it easier to diffuse. It can very quickly become a public commodity.[6] One can as a result observe in many industries that existing regimes of safeguarding proprietary knowledge are largely ineffective at providing genuine control over knowledge flows.

One implication is that the only way to sustain superior performance is to promote faster learning. The problem is that the control and reliance on conformity to rules implied in the bureaucratic form has been shown to inhibit the accidental, highly fortuitous and creative processes that facilitate exploratory learning.[7] When coupled with the stability, routinization, and robustness of process at which bureaucracies excel, one has a recipe for rigidity in a company's core activities and consequently poor performance.[8]

There has been considerable interest in new forms of organization that can evolve with changing circumstances through providing opportunities for people to express themselves, achieve personal fulfillment, and, as a result, enthusiastically contribute to organizational learning. The empowered team provides one organizational mode that appears to meet many of the new criteria. It can be a favorable context for engendering the creativity and innovation that are assuming increasing competitive importance. It is also consistent with a renewed emphasis on the benefits of smaller units and of focusing on core tasks through "sticking to the knitting" as Peters and Waterman memorably put it.[9] Companies have therefore been urged to divest themselves of non-core activities. Rather than internalizing complete value chains and their supporting activities into large hierarchies, networks of smaller, focused units appear in many cases to offer superior economic and human returns.[10] A hybrid form of organization – the strategic alliance – has also come into prominence as a means to achieve benefits such as international expansion, economies of scale, and learning synergies (see Chapter 11). The most common arrangement is the joint venture. While this is not strictly speaking a new organizational form, its spread and significance has increased greatly in recent years. Alliances and networks have their own special dynamics that engender new managerial challenges.[11]

Today, the leading edge of organizational practice has progressed a stage further. The metamorphosis of unitary, formal organizations into "virtual" networked alternatives based on a combination of contracting and ICT (information and communication technologies) has become a serious proposition. It has been adopted as a model for coordinating value chains which have become increasingly complex and international motivated by a search for economic advantages to be gained via offshore outsourcing (see Chapter 9). Dell Computers and other companies successfully competing on the basis of speedy response to bespoke customer requirements under highly competitive conditions have progressed a long way down the road to virtuality. At the turn of the twenty-first century, the explosion of new "dot.com" companies using the Internet to provide information that links consumers and producers also epitomized the introduction of a virtual form of organization that approximates to the efficient marketplace. Even for "old economy" firms, organization was now taking on a more transitory nature. In order to meet changing demands and retain their share of more competitive markets, firms were coming under increasing pressure to reorganize frequently, in order to recombine or recycle their assets and key competencies as well as to take advantage of the possibilities offered by e-commerce.

Having introduced some aspects of so-called "new organizational forms," it is necessary to sound a word of caution before I examine them in more detail later in this chapter. There has been a lot of discussion, and no little evangelizing, of new organization. Some academics have argued that the novelty of "new" forms of organizing lies not so much in their individual elements but in how these are bundled together.[12] Also the evidence indicates that discussion and debate about new organizational forms has outstripped their actual adoption and spread. New forms have been adopted, at least in part, by a relatively few pioneering firms and almost not at all in the public sector. The firms that have shown most interest in new forms tend to be concentrated in certain countries – especially the Scandinavian ones – and in certain sectors – especially those in which companies are started by and employ creative and knowledge workers. Also many of the high emancipatory hopes attached to new organizational forms have turned out to be illusory, particularly as economic pressures following the 2008 financial crisis have often given rise to renewed top-down control and demands for higher performance combined with threats to job security.

New Conditions, New Organization

Experimentation with new forms of organization has been stimulated by a number of developments in the business environment that are placing novel requirements on organization. It is widely believed that conventional forms of organization can no longer adequately meet the challenge. The key message being expressed by most business executives is that "the corporate structure that has provided the basis for business formation and growth throughout the twentieth century is in a state of long-term decline."[13] Globalization, new technologies, the knowledge-based society, hypercompetition, and the social expectations placed on business are each creating new demands upon organization and, in the case of new technology, also offering new design opportunities. A 2013 report for executives on Emerging Approaches to Organisation Design began by stating that "Globalisation, technology advances and the changing competitive landscape are increasing the need for connection between businesses, countries and markets. Organisations need to develop to manage the complexity involved in global operations, and to adapt quickly to changing circumstances."[14] These developments and their implications for organization are now reviewed in turn.

Globalization

THE PHENOMENON

The term "globalization" is employed in so many different ways that it is in danger of losing any useful purpose. It has become such a large and diffused concept that it is difficult to capture its meaning, though at least one "Globalization Index" has been constructed that breaks it down into its more important component parts.[15] Globalization refers essentially to increasing levels of interdependence across the world. In business, it is evident in the erosion of boundaries between commercial and financial markets. These boundaries have previously been founded on regulatory restrictions, barriers to communication, and differences in nationality and culture. International agreements to liberalize trade and the emergence of modern information and communication technologies have been particularly important facilitators of globalization.

Globalization is a complex phenomenon. The term actually encompasses a range of developments that have come to prominence since the mid-1980s. They include an accelerated growth of world trade and direct investment, the global integration of currency and capital markets, and the spread across the world of value-added chains made possible through decreasing transport costs, the widespread application of new information technologies, and the dissemination of "best practice" management concepts.

Globalization is driven by powerful economic forces, including market, cost, competitive, and governmental factors.[16] There are several important market drivers. One is the growth of common customer preferences stimulated by successful global branding as for designer jeans, sports footwear, and hamburgers. Another is the development of global distribution and servicing channels as for cameras and personal computers. As a result, it has proved possible for some product categories to develop a marketing approach that is transferable across cultural and geographical boundaries, although certain specifics of the product offer have to be adjusted to suit local cultures as the Disney Corporation found in Hong Kong.[17]

On the cost side, globalization can offer the advantages of economies of scale and standardization, not just in production but also in items such as advertising costs when a standard advertisement is used. A global scale of production also offers cost advantages in sourcing. Competitive drivers come into play when companies can compete on a worldwide rather than national or regional basis and so gain from the economies just mentioned. The liberalization of trade has clearly added to the strength of this driver for globalization, but its relevance also depends on how homogeneous or segmented markets are. Governments have come to recognize the economic benefits of freer trade and capital movements, and many have opened up their economies in the past twenty years. Freer trade has also led to the development of compatible technical standards across countries, which in turn facilitates global production and marketing.

With these powerful drivers, it has been widely assumed that the globalization of business is advancing relentlessly. The reality is not so straightforward. Globalization has paused since the financial crisis of 2008 in terms of intensity of world trade and has actually taken a step back as assessed by global capital flows and cross-border direct investment.[18] Conflicts of interest between developed and developing economies have jeopardized further moves towards liberalization. The rise of international terrorism has led some to question whether there will have to be limits to the liberalization of international transactions, financial transfers, and freedom of movement.[19] Also many unsubstantiated and sweeping claims have been made about globalization, and we need to treat these with some care. In the first place, globalization is a trend rather than a condition that necessarily already exists. Globalization is not spreading evenly across the world, and it is more evident in some sectors than in others. It characterizes telecommunications and civil aviation, but far less so construction, personal services, and hospitality.[20] Most cross-border integration in trade and investment is actually located in regional trade blocks rather than on a truly global scale.[21] The trend towards globalization is undoubtedly a strong one, but it remains to be seen how far and how fast it will spread. It has powerful opponents.

At the same time as globalization pushes forward, people are becoming increasingly aware of their cultural and ethnic identity, and insistent that this should be recognized. The same increasingly intensive international communication through the Internet that promotes a convergence of market-economy ideology and business practice appears to be strengthening cultural and sub-cultural identities. The new technology enhances communication between the members of cultural and other social communities and provides opportunities for their self-expression. This self-expression is manifested at different levels. It shows itself widely, though perhaps more superficially, through the preferences people express as consumers and employees. Many companies have come to recognize that they will achieve new business opportunities through catering for local tastes, and run their operations more effectively through adjusting their policies to suit local employment practices. This has given rise to the criterion of "localization" with which they see that globalization has to be balanced and reconciled. This paradox is of profound significance for how companies organize. Localization speaks for decentralized initiative and organization, whereas globalization speaks for and facilitates the centralized standardization of organizational practices.[22]

Implications for organization

Globalization can improve the possibilities that firms have to secure greater economies of scale and standardization. With the barriers to market entry falling, firms can spread their product development and production costs over larger volumes, especially if standard platforms or modules are used. The liberalization of world trade also opens up new opportunities to diversify into different regions or countries, so as to benefit from low-cost sourcing or the opening up of new customer markets.

Standardization and diversification create new demands on a firm's organization, which are not always easy to reconcile. In order to take full advantage of the potential benefits of globalization, a firm has to have the flexibility to reconfigure its resources as the relative attractions of countries and regions shift. While there may be considerable advantage in coordinating activities on a worldwide scale and maintaining strict quality and other standards to support the firm's brand or reputation, it also has to organize with sufficient flexibility to recognize new developments at a local level and learn from them. Globalization therefore increases the requirement for firms to maintain *both* standardization and flexibility within the same organizational framework.

One of the motives for firms to expand internationally lies in the opportunity to apply their specific know-how to new locations. They can often compete and/or produce successfully in other countries through the advantages they secure by introducing their best practices. This is a further reason why many firms prefer to standardize their approach to management and organization as they expand globally. It can, however, be hindered by local circumstances, including cultural differences, as some major retailers such as Wal-Mart have found (Box 3.1). The international transfer of practices, including assessing how far to adapt them to local circumstances, can be a major challenge.[23]

Globalization also exposes a firm to a greater level of *external complexity* than was previously the case. It expands the number of other organizations – customers, competitors, governments, non-governmental organizations (NGOs) – whose actions are relevant. Many more

BOX 3.1 RESISTANCE TO THE INTRODUCTION OF GLOBAL BEST PRACTICE

Walmart has worked with Grupo Cifra, a Mexican retailer, since 1991 and has had a controlling stake since 1997. However, it only introduced a modern till-information system years after local rivals had installed one. The improvement in profit margins expected to arise from this standard practice was slow to materialize. Local managers were reluctant to announce the layoffs that the new technology allows. This was because local labor is so inexpensive and also because local communities would suffer in a society where a culture of collective mutual support is more pronounced than in the United States.

Adapted from The Economist, *Globalization: Making Sense of an Integrating World.* London: Economists Books 2001, p. 205.

events in the environment now have to be taken account of, and most firms are entering into more intensive dialogue with external parties than before. This applies across the board, including the greater emphasis on relationship management and the need to engage regularly with the concerns of NGOs over environmental policy.[24]

Greater external complexity stems both from a widening range of relevant relationships and events. It generates a higher variety of stimuli with which an organization needs to engage. Rising external complexity necessarily maps onto a firm's internal organization. Not only does top management have to devote more time and attention to external developments of strategic importance, but in so doing it also has to be supported by a larger number of appropriate specialists. External complexity therefore creates the need for a corresponding internal complexity in a firm's organization and information processing. Even though some firms may be able to reduce external complexity through the influence they have over markets and governments, there are definite limits to this. It is difficult, if not impossible, to cope with high levels of external complexity through conventional hierarchies, which is one of the factors encouraging use of an alternative network mode of organizing.

Complexity theory suggests that a more complex environment with a greater number of relevant players, which are themselves interconnected through networks, will also exhibit a greater rate of change.[25] The high level of interdependence between relevant players means that the actions of any one of them tend to impact on the system as a whole, especially if the relations between that unit and others are unstable, due perhaps to changing market, political, or technological circumstances. As a result, it is generally far more difficult to predict the outcome of events within a complex system.

As a firm globalizes its strategy and operations, this very extension of scope tends to increase the external complexity it encounters. The result can be a tension between securing the benefits of worldwide standardization and adjusting to the uncertainties generated by complexity. It thus presents a corresponding dilemma for organizational design. Is it best to attempt to "reduce" complexity to a form that can be handled efficiently by an organization's tried and tested standard paradigms and routines? While economical, this runs the risk of discarding external information that does not fit the existing paradigm, but which nevertheless may have fundamental implications for how the organization should change. The result could be an efficient pursuit of an option that proves to have no future viability. Is it therefore better to "absorb" complexity by organizing to take account of non-routine information and dissonance, developing multiple options and keeping them open as far as possible, albeit that this can be more costly and time-consuming?[26]

The first option calls for an organization that buffers and screens external factors as far as possible, in order to permit the core of the firm to continue with its familiar and efficient routines for managing activities. This might be achieved by trying to reduce external variability through increasing the dependence on the firm of external parties such as suppliers and even governments, or at least by increasing the firm's negotiating power with such parties. Clearly, this policy is more available to financially powerful and technologically advanced multinationals than it is to small and medium-sized enterprises (SMEs).[27] An alternative is for the firm to protect its core through outsourcing, not so much in this instance to achieve a focus on core competencies, but rather to introduce greater flexibility in its peripheral activities.

The second option calls for an entirely different form of organization, which decentralizes initiative to units that are in touch with external developments, quite possibly working closely with partners. In this way, internal complexity is increased to match that of the environment[28] and (as Chapter 5 discusses) this then needs to be complemented by arrangements to ensure adequate exchange of information and coordination between the different units concerned. Rather than aiming to buffer the core from external disturbance, this alternative is intended to enhance its sensitivity to external changes. It aims to allow routine thinking and behavior to be challenged by new information rather than to force such information into existing frameworks. A firm adopting this solution will place a premium upon its ability to organize itself in a way that permits its rapid adaptation to new circumstances.

New technologies

THE PHENOMENON

The use of information and communication technology (ICT) in general and the Internet in particular continues to expand rapidly. E-business is exploding across a wide range of areas such as electronic commerce, procurement, knowledge management, and customer relationships. Social media have become significant avenues for marketing as well as for the mobilization of public opinion on corporate conduct. 3-D printing technology promises to revolutionize the economics of large scale, enabling small-scale customized production to become increasingly cost-competitive.[29] Despite eye-catching instances, many in the public sector, where huge sums of money have been wasted on failed ICT projects, overall it appears that investment in new technology pays. Firms investing in ICT and carrying out complementary organizational changes, have been found to achieve improvements in performance.[30] An analysis of over 400 global firms also suggested that investment in information technology, especially when directed at boosting revenues rather than reducing costs, has a positive effect on firm profitability.[31]

Two conclusions can be drawn from experience so far with the Internet and ICT in general. First, the impact of ICT is not even. It is greater and potentially more revolutionary in some sectors than in others. As a communications technology, it has the ability to effect most change in communications-based fields such as financial services, education, entertainment, direct sales retailing, health care transactions, and public information. It can play a significant, but more focused, role in manufacturing supply chains, travel, and the energy sector. The Internet dramatically lowers the cost of communication. This means it can have a fundamental impact on any activity that relies heavily on communication and information flow, both in the marketplace and within a company's own system for producing and delivering goods or services to the customer.

ICT and the Internet are facilitating the development of interdependence between organizations. In response to these new possibilities and starting in the 1990s, large corporations learned to "unbundle" their various activities, some of which were considered to lie at the core of their business, while others were sold off. In order to maintain the ability of the system to deliver a complete product or service to customers, firms have had to develop sufficiently disciplined networks with suppliers and contractors. The most advanced examples of such networks are generally to be found among the producers of ICT related equipment, (e.g., Cisco Systems, Dell Computers, and Palm) and service sectors that are heavily information-based, such as financial trading (e.g., E*Trade and Charles Schwab) and retailing (e.g., eBay).

In information-intensive business systems like these, leading firms have divested themselves of many component activities and no longer own all of the assets that are employed. They do not have legally to own an asset in order to utilize it. By contrast, traditional business organization presumed tight linkages between the outputs of assets, ownership of assets, and control of assets. Performance had to do with how efficiently the assets were deployed, relative to those of other firms. The option of being able to coordinate a range of complementary activities among network members through the use of ICT has opened up a whole new area of choice about how to organize provision to customers and what to retain within the direct purview of a particular management team.

The second conclusion is more cautionary and resonates with the history of technological change ever since the early days of the Industrial Revolution. The pace at which ICT can be introduced will be limited by regulatory barriers in fields like financial services and government, and by institutional resistance in highly professionalized areas such as education and health care. These barriers will slow down the rate at which ICT is used to change working practices and organization.[32]

ICT, however, is part of a wider trend in which technological innovation has come to play an increasingly important role in competitive strategy. The economic rents that can be earned from innovation, especially if increasing returns apply – as they often do – when the first mover can establish new technical standards, encourage technological development as a competitive strategy. The obsolescence of established competencies and techniques as a result of new technologies is not a new phenomenon. It was a fundamentally disruptive feature of the first industrial revolution which encouraged a shift from domestic production in favor of a then revolutionary new organizational form, the "factory system." The swift and dramatic impact that electronic technology had on the clockwork-based Swiss watch industry is a well recognized example from more recent times. The introduction of a new technology can generate the gust of creative destruction that Schumpeter identified as a characteristic of business cycles, but which today can in extreme cases herald the demise of an entire industry.[33]

The process of technological displacement has become frequent and widespread both in the nature of products and how they are produced. This is apparent in areas of manufacturing where new technologies such as biotechnology, genetic engineering, and electronic publishing have had fundamental impacts. It is even more evident in service industries that deal in information flows, such as banking, education, publishing, share dealing, and telecommunications. Here, ICT is not only being used to transform the type of services offered and how their production is organized, but is also greatly facilitating the entry of new competitors and the formation of alliances across traditional sector boundaries.

Implications for organization

Information and communication technologies have opened up new possibilities for both internal organization and the organization of transactions between firms. Internally, the moves in many large firms towards the reduction of levels of management ("delayering") and more horizontal structures can only be accomplished through improved communications between remaining personnel, which ICT facilitates. Intranet technology has hugely improved internal communications and encouraged the spread of formal and informal networks within companies. ICT assists the formation of networks across different functions and geographical locations, which has in turn greatly facilitated the now widespread use of team and project work. The Danish company Oticon A/S provides an illuminating example of how ICT was used to support a new way of organizing (Box 3.2).

BOX 3.2   THE USE OF NEW TECHNOLOGIES FOR NEW ORGANIZATION

Oticon, an affiliate of William Demant Holding, is a world leader in the production of hearing aids, with its headquarters near Copenhagen. By the later 1980s Oticon was suffering from increasingly strong competition from larger companies such as Philips, Siemens and Sony. It desperately needed innovative breakthroughs. Incoming chief executive, Lars Kolind decided that the way to achieve this turnaround was to break away entirely from a conventional mode of organization. In his view, the staff needed to "become more creative, action-oriented, and efficient" and he regarded formal hierarchical organization as standing in the way of this requirement. He introduced a new organizational form, which was called the "spaghetti organization" in order to emphasize the point that it should combine flexibility with coherence.

The company's hierarchy was reduced to just two levels with Kolind and ten managers forming the management team and other parts of the organization being organized into projects. Departments gave way to "Competence Centres" in areas such as audiology and mechanical engineering in order to break down the boundaries they had imposed. Projects rather than functions or departments became the defining units of work. Teams formed, disbanded and reformed again as the work required. Projects had to be approved by a Projects and Products Committee, consisting of Kolind and three other managers, which subsequently monitored their progress every three months. Otherwise the teams worked with a high level of autonomy. The company had a hundred or so projects at any one time and most people worked on several projects at once. Employees were allowed to join as many projects as they wished and were encouraged to develop new skills outside their existing portfolio. Vestiges of hierarchy, such as personal desks and offices, were abolished. Instead employees located with their colleagues working on the same project, taking with them portable caddies to hold necessary files.

Oticon has used a number of new technologies to support this mode of organization. Every morning incoming mail is electronically scanned, with paper usually shredded and recycled at the end of the day. Scanning permits access from terminals throughout the building and makes traditional filing redundant. Email and mobile phones are used for communication, especially for contact with customers and suppliers. Teams can use a large computer-filled conference room equipped with groupware systems and videoconferencing equipment for brainstorming and problem solving. Kolind claimed that these tools accelerated the company's intellectual processes by a factor of five.

After installing the new technology and breaking with conventional organization, Oticon experienced a complete turnaround. The new approach promoted knowledge sharing dramatically, resulting in a stream of product innovations and a reduction in product development time by 50 percent. During the 1990s, the company achieved significant improvements in sales revenue, profit margins and return on equity. Nonetheless, after 1996 Oticon reduced its radical bottom-up approach so as to avoid a number of unanticipated costs that it incurred, including problems of coordination and employee time allocation, and the need for management to intervene once projects had been approved which caused a serious loss of motivation. Management also sought to align initiatives to start new projects more closely to its strategic objectives. Chapter 17 discusses the wider organizational design implications of this case.

Sources: Polly LaBarre. This organization is dis-organization. *The Fast Manager*, June-July 1996. www.fastcompany.com/magazine/03/oticon.html; www.oticon.com; Nicolai J. Foss. Selective intervention and internal hybrids: Interpreting and learning from the rise and decline of the Oticon spaghetti organization. *Organization Science*, 14(3), 2003, pp. 331–349.

New communications technologies are also helping firms to internationalize their operations and manage them comfortably from a distance. This is apparent from work I conducted with internationalizing Hong Kong companies, whose top managers attach great importance to receiving frequent information on their operations and maintaining close control over them. Before the availability of modern ICT, the establishment of branches or subsidiaries abroad placed a severe strain upon their ability to retain this intensity of information. Now, the technology permits frequent access to operating information as well as less formal, quasi-personal contact through videoconferencing and email. In other words, ICT facilitates "arm's-length control" within geographically diversified organizations.

Externally, the extent to which an organization could previously operate interdependently with other organizations was constrained by limits on information processing capacity and the exigencies of physical distance. As ICT has advanced, interdependent operations are a much more cost-effective possibility. Combined with the changes in regulatory regimes and capital flows that are part of globalization, this has made interdependent operations desirable. Although any social system exhibits interdependence, it is widely agreed that the level of interdependence prevalent today is unprecedented and growing.[34] Companies now routinely exchange bulk information with suppliers, customers, alliance partners, regular consultants, distributors, and agents. They often use ICT to facilitate joint development work with suppliers and for the scheduling of activities within tightly-coupled value chains. Working in this ICT-assisted manner enables lead firms to leverage the use of assets within wider networks, without necessarily owning them.[35] The virtual organization is a highly developed organizing form for doing this, made very familiar through the approach adopted by Dell Computers and discussed in detail in Chapter 10.

Companies therefore have to learn how to organize themselves in ways that support the relationships and flows of information across their boundaries, which ICT has now made feasible. They must also be prepared to manage their boundary relationships actively, outsourcing activities and working through external networks when a combination of economics and technological possibility makes this attractive. Whereas ICT makes greater interdependence feasible in terms of information processing, to operate effectively it also requires new organizational supports in the form of practices designed to foster coordination and trust between network members.

Interdependence between firms presents several new demands on their capacity to organize. How is a sufficient level of coordination to be built into a network so that all the constituent members contribute adequately to a collective activity that is effective in delivering to the customer? How can the different units be linked appropriately? To what extent is their willingness to coordinate and cooperate weakened by the loss of a shared corporate identity when major components of a business are externalized? Can new organizational processes retain some of this common identity? To what extent does cooperation of a virtual nature require organizational support, such as standard data protocols and assistance with coordination across time zones, in order to compensate for the lack of a physical contiguity?

The need to integrate interdependent activities is also present within a large, diversified corporation, though the ways it is achieved may be more conventional in nature. In this sense, we can usefully distinguish between *external* and *internal* interdependence. External inter-dependence arises when a firm operates with an external network. Internal interdependence arises when a firm is diversified and/or requires a high degree of vertical integration along its value chain. Recent thinking has assumed that the externally networked solution, combining an internalized core competence with the externalization of other activities, is generally superior to internal diversification and interdependence.

The combination of globalization and the enabling effects of new communication tech-nologies creates a further challenge that organization design must address. This is *velocity*. Greater velocity has come to characterize virtually all aspects of organizational functioning, from internal communications, through product development, to competitive interchange. Changes in strategic conditions are also accelerated, as informal barriers to market entry are lowered by the growing ease of long-distance communication.

With greater velocity in the environment comes an increase in the unpredictability or volatility of events to which organizations have to respond. This is evident when capital investment can be moved swiftly and inexpensively across borders and change the configuration of supply chains and market competition. Similarly, the ease by which corporate stock can today be bought and sold internationally through purely electronic transactions, has rendered corporate managements much more vulnerable to acquisitive raids. A third consequence of velocity is to decrease the necessary stimulus-response times of even prosaic organizational activities. Thus, companies are experimenting with how they use time, for example through passing software programming work from a group based in India to one based in North America and back again.[36]

In order to cope with high velocity and make strategic decisions with corresponding speed, firms need to be organized so as to provide decision-makers with more information and the capacity to develop more alternatives, as well as to promote integration and conflict resolution among decision-makers. These are emerging as significant requirements for success in high velocity conditions.[37]

The Knowledge-based economy

THE PHENOMENON

As a result of new technologies and patterns of demand, a fundamental shift is underway in the basis of value creation. Value is increasingly being created through the processing of flows of information and knowledge rather than of flows of materials. The value created by manufacturing and production represents ever-smaller portions of the value added by an organization, thereby changing the nature of the critical contingencies within them.[38] Consequently, organizing to maximize the efficiency of production is becoming less crucial to economic performance. This is particularly true of societies like the USA in whose key industries knowledge rather than low-cost material processing provides the competitive edge. Increasingly, the work being done is not so much production work, in which raw materials are transformed into physical outputs, but knowledge work, in which activity relates to the creation and distribution of information.

This does not, of course, mean the demise of low-cost, mass production manufacturing, but rather the fact that it has been concentrated in developing and newly-industrialized countries. In the 1990s and 2000s, a great deal of production was progressively outsourced by developed nation firms to these countries (see Chapter 9), and local manufacturing firms in countries like China became increasingly competitive on the basis of cost and price leadership. A significant factor has been the reduction in the time it takes for such firms to learn higher value-adding technologies and know-how. Chinese firms in industries such as computers and telecoms equipment are already world-class, and new competitors in automobiles and aviation are emerging. Together with their lower factor costs, rapid learning and catching-up among emerging economy firms is one of the main forces heightening global competition. It means that established market players must learn how to acquire differentiation advantages based on innovation and adaptation to specific customer requirements and to combine these with offering value for money.

The shift to knowledge work is naturally accompanied by an increase in the numbers of knowledge workers. Taking a broad definition to include managerial, professional, technical, sales and administrative support workers, knowledge workers accounted for approximately two-thirds of the total US workforce in May 2012, up from just over half in the later 1980s.[39] Doubts have been raised as to how many workers classified as knowledge workers are really highly skilled rather than merely processors of information.[40] Highly trained people are, however, certainly to be found within the R&D, engineering, legal and other specialist units of firms, in the increasing number of professional service organizations such as consulting, accountancy, legal and market research practices, and in the public service specialties.[41]

The possession of superior knowledge, and the organizational ability to use it, has become one of the last inimitable competitive advantages a company can enjoy. As a result, there has been a steady acceleration in the pace at which companies need to learn. The race to gain advantage through learning has promoted an intensification of relationships between and within companies, especially in sectors like biotechnology where new discoveries and advanced science are often spread around large numbers of new venture firms. Many companies have for some time used alliances with other firms and research institutes to accelerate the process of learning. Toyota learned twenty years ago how to manage American labor and market to the American consumer through forming NUMMI (New United Motor Manufacturing, Inc), a joint venture with General Motors. More recently, the use of ICT to support international communications between the members of virtual teams has speeded up knowledge transfer and learning. The ability to acquire and digest relevant new knowledge rapidly and efficiently lowers an important intangible barrier to market entry, with the result that it is less and less the case that an established position in product and geographical markets provides any guarantee for the future. In some cases, as with Amazon.com, the Internet has enabled new "born global" companies to achieve access to worldwide markets and inputs in ways that were previously not possible.[42]

IMPLICATIONS FOR ORGANIZATION

The growth of the knowledge-based economy has major implications for organization that arise from twin needs. The first is to motivate individuals to contribute enthusiastically to the process of organizational knowledge generation. The second is to devise organizational arrangements that support various types of organizational learning.

In terms of motivation, many professionals and other specialists appear to respond well to organizational arrangements that draw from the traditional model of professional practice but are also akin in certain respects to the "organic" form discussed in Chapter 2. These are characterized by a high degree of self-management in everyday work applying trained judgment, participation in setting practice norms and performance criteria, close interaction with other specialists (often in groups or teams), and attractive career opportunities based on competitive performance. Whereas a conventional hierarchical form of management by non-specialists may serve to alienate many knowledge workers, these alternative forms, deriving at least in part from professional tradition, may better mobilize professional social identities in ways that serve corporate goals.[43]

As so often with organization, the requirements for supporting learning processes present a design dilemma, for the ability to compete on the basis of intellectual rather than physical assets can entail both the effective exploitation of existing knowledge as well as the creative exploration of new possibilities.[44] The managerial and organizational supports for these two processes are not the same, and the recognition of this divergence has given rise to the view that "ambidexterity" is a necessary capability for coping with it (to be discussed in Chapter 17). Exploitation requires a *capacity to adapt existing knowledge* and routines in the sense of improving them, whereas exploration requires *a capacity to innovate*.

The exploitation of known possibilities is intended to make more efficient use of existing knowledge or to apply that knowledge to new purposes. The exploitation of existing knowledge does not necessarily involve the contribution only of knowledge workers. It may also harness the operational experience of less skilled employees. Organizationally, this approach calls for procedures that define good performance in terms of incremental improvements within the existing scheme of doing things – what Argyris and Schön called "single-loop learning."[45] These procedures include discussion groups and suggestion schemes to elicit the tacit knowledge held by employees, and the setting of targets for the achievement of improvements. They have been used by some companies for many years, though not always effectively, and can readily be slotted into a conventional organizational design. However, because the process of exploitation can to a large extent be routinized, it runs the risk of encouraging conformity and so eventually weakening the culture of divergence that provides a fertile climate for creativity.

As well as exploiting the knowledge already held within an organization, external sources of knowledge are usually very important. Careful consideration should therefore also be given to arrangements that facilitate the identification of relevant new knowledge from external sources, its transfer into the organization, and any modification or development that is necessary. These arrangements include channels through which suitable trained staff can interact with external sources of knowledge, and incentives to encourage members of the organization not to resist such knowledge on the grounds of "not invented here."

By contrast, innovation – the exploration of new possibilities – calls for more significant modifications to conventional modes of organization, particularly the intensive use of teams in order to encourage synergy between people who can contribute their different specialist knowledge and perspectives to the creative process. Because new possibilities have first to be recognized before they can be exploited, successful innovation also calls for arrangements that encourage this early recognition. One such approach is the flexible definition of roles and working practices to facilitate fortuitous networking with external contacts by people at all levels of an organization. Another is the encouragement of open communication between different parts of the organization, even to the point of creating some redundancy of information.

In other words, the maintenance of both a sufficient range of specialists (differentiation) and their intensive integration are critical organizational policies for the exploration of new possibilities.[46] Interdisciplinary teamwork is a favored way of meeting these requirements. The teams concerned must also be permitted a considerable degree of initiative in what they do and propose, so that their creativity is not stifled. This type of learning approximates to "double-loop learning," in Argyris and Schön's terminology, and it cannot readily be accomplished within the scope of a conventional organizational form that is hierarchical and heavily reliant on established rules and procedures.

Hypercompetition

THE PHENOMENON

New technologies and the knowledge explosion have given rise to a huge wave of innovation that is redefining markets by creating new consumer wants. The formerly identifiable and relatively fixed boundaries of industries have become eroded. Because they can no longer reckon on sheltering behind entry barriers and relying on old assumptions, the pressures on companies to be flexible in responding to events and proactive in identifying options for the future has dramatically increased. The conditions under which many companies now operate amount to what has been called "hypercompetition."[47] This term has been coined to capture the essence of the intense competition and resulting uncertainty now being experienced by many companies. Hypercompetition is characterized by "markets fraught with uncertainty, diverse global players, rapid technological change, widespread price wars, and seemingly endless re-organization."[48] It is both a consequence and driver of other changes in the business environment, namely globalization, trade liberalization, and rapid technological change. It is exacerbated by additional forces of change, such as the shifting age structures of populations, rapid industrialization, and urbanization. Together, these factors are reshaping the competitive landscape across the world.

Although there is much that we do not understand about this new competitive environment, the ways in which it differs from the past and the implications for a firm's strategy and organization have become evident. A company's survival is no longer assured simply by selecting a high margin industry and defending it against the entry of new competitors. The speed at which competitive conditions are changing, including new entry, is so rapid that it may not even make much sense to define an attractive market. Rather, the onus has fallen on the ability of companies themselves to develop and exploit new capabilities that will generate their attractiveness to the market. This calls essentially for a more aggressive and proactive strategy to attack competitors' existing strengths and then move forward before they can catch up. It also calls for a continuous search for opportunities that can lever the company's competencies to advantage in new areas of business.

The implications for the ways that firms organize are that these must permit, indeed encourage, spontaneous reconfiguration, rather than tolerating the forces that resist change and promote rigidity. This places a premium on self-organization, which is the capacity for spontaneity and adaptability, the facility to absorb random events, and the self-guided discovery of creative alternatives. As we shall see in Chapter 17, organization is being required to cope with the paradoxes that a policy of creative adaptation has to resolve without the luxury of time and other slack resources. This is asking a lot. It means, among other things, that ways have to be found of simultaneously differentiating and integrating activities, continuously fragmenting and recombining teams and work units, and encouraging experimentation while maintaining control.

Silicon Valley is often regarded as a forerunner of the hypercompetitive, high velocity business environments that are becoming the norm today. In the words of Homa Bahrami and Stuart Evans:

> "High-technology firms in Silicon Valley prosper in a constantly changing environment of incessant novelty and innovation, which fuels their volatile and occasionally spectacular growth trajectories. This unique domain is characterized by fleeting opportunities, shifting customer preferences, cascades of technological innovations, brutally short product life cycles, and furious global competition. These forces collectively precipitate a never-ending stream of kaleidoscopic changes that can stimulate the rapid growth of an enterprise and also instigate its sudden demise."[49]

Competitive conditions in the computer industry were changing dramatically as early as the 1970s. The pace of new product introductions accelerated at the same time as the cost of developing new products increased. This forced firms to concentrate on what they did best and to acquire the rest of their inputs from an increasingly dense network of suppliers, both within the region and outside. The focus on key expertise and an ability to rely on equally focused suppliers enabled companies like Sun Microsystems to stay ahead of clone makers through the sheer pace of its new product introduction. This strategy required changes in the way companies managed their boundaries, so as to develop closer, longer-term relations with suppliers extending to considerable joint development.[50] At the same time, the availability of venture capital, mobile engineering and managerial talent, and a highly developed network of contacts maintained the flexibility and intense competition that characterized Silicon Valley's broader eco-system as a whole.

Rita McGrath has argued that the combination of hypercompetition, high velocity environments and relentless innovation has reached the point where many firms find it impossible to maintain their existing competitive advantage.[51]

IMPLICATIONS FOR ORGANIZATION

Hypercompetition places new demands on how firms must organize in order to survive. The keyword here is *flexibility*, so that strategies, deployment of competencies, and activities can be reformulated in anticipation of new competitive opportunities and threats. The idea of the "flexible firm" has grown out of these needs.[52] A mode of organizing is required that encourages initiative and innovation aimed at retaining a strategic advantage over competitors. Simply adapting in response to events may not be enough for a firm to survive under conditions of hypercompetition.

The complexity and velocity that accompany globalization and hypercompetition mean that companies have to learn how to organize their work in ways that permit frequent and rapid adjustment, informed by a knowledge of external market, technical and regulatory conditions that is not just up to date but anticipatory of new developments. Innovation and change could come from almost anywhere, and certainly across a much wider horizon. In open global markets, this applies equally to the next commission and the next competitor. Globalization and new technology are increasingly removing the protection from competition that used to be afforded by traditional market niches and barriers to new firms entering established industries.

The old stability associated with impregnable bureaucracies, underwritten by a dominant market position and the accumulated capital of ages past, has gone for most companies. Even the apparent exceptions, in fields such as electricity supply, face the unsettling effects of new entry into their markets and vocal criticisms of their price and profit levels. Virtually all companies now require the ability to reconstruct their processes and outputs with increasing frequency in the light of rapid change. One of greatest contrasts between conventional thinking about organizations and the newer models is that the latter take change for granted. Rather than stable structures designed to absorb uncertainty, as organizations used to be conceived, today many thinkers suggest that building in flexibility and the capacity to handle constant change are required of the new organization.

Innovative flexibility requires that activities and the resources to support them have to be reconfigured spontaneously. Reconfigurations cannot wait for approval from the top. It may not, however, be a simple matter to reconcile such a high degree of decentralized autonomy and "self-organization" with the conventional disciplines of resource allocation and coordinated control. The rigidity that tends to accompany traditional practices, such as budgeting, can be entirely non-functional for developing a capacity to handle new uncertainties in an adaptive and innovative manner. One way of handling this potential tension is for a company to bifurcate its organizational forms, operating its established core business through a conventional mode of organization while applying a much freer form to those activities where it seeks to be flexible in its response to hypercompetitive conditions. This was the approach adopted by two regional Bell Telephone companies (see Box 3.3).

BOX 3.3   ADJUSTMENT TO HYPERCOMPETITION

In January 1984, seven new corporations were spun off from AT&T. They were the new regional telecommunications companies, known as the "Baby Bells." Much of their business was initially in local telephone services where their monopoly was closely regulated. By the early 1990s, however, these local services were facing dramatic change and the companies could see clear signs of impending hypercompetitive conditions. Powerful potential new entrants were emerging in the form of long-distance, wireless and cable companies, which were securing new licenses, collaborating across traditional sector borders and developing new networks.

Two of the Baby Bells responded to this challenge by creating strategic flexibility in one of the unregulated areas, namely the international sphere. In order to do this, they developed a pocket of capabilities in international activities that was separate from their local service activities. Subsequently, the growing threat of hypercompetitive conditions in the traditional local telephone service provision led them to integrate the new capabilities acquired from international initiatives into their organization as a whole.

The new capabilities were generated through a flexible form of organization. Management proceeded to experiment on a largely trial-and-error basis through a wide variety of new international projects, in areas such as digital and satellite systems, voice mail, intelligent buildings and paging. The managers heading them were ambitious and unconventional – referred to as "mavericks" and "renegades" – and they were allowed considerable discretion. They often made deals with local partners who had relevant expertise or connections. Each project, however, was small-scale and thus posed little overall risk to the companies.

Learning was essential to success in this unregulated and highly entrepreneurial area of operations. The managers of these international initiatives had to learn quickly how to secure new contracts, how to manage international partnerships, and how to operate new telecoms systems and networks. They also had to learn how to work without the large bureaucratic support staff typical of the companies' US operations, and how to share knowledge across different projects. All of this required a non-conventional mode of organizing and working.

Source: Anne D. Smith and Carl Zeithaml. Garbage cans and advancing hypercompetition: The creation and exploitation of new capabilities and strategic flexibility in two regional Bell operating companies. *Organization Science*, 7, 1996, pp. 388–399.

Coping with hypercompetition places a huge premium on a company's ability to learn. In many sectors, where specific capabilities can be acquired from the market, it is the ability to learn how to combine these capabilities innovatively and uniquely to match new opportunities and threats that remains the only sustainable competitive advantage available to firms.[53] The secret of a firm's success under hypercompetition is to keep ahead of the game and mobilize available resources in a way that is smarter than its rivals. Experience has made it abundantly clear that the way its people and their activities are organized and managed can have a major impact on the effectiveness with which it learns as a unit.[54]

Demands for social accountability

THE PHENOMENON

While few companies, even the strongest, can avoid the impact of turbulent hypercompetitive environments, it is at the same time evident that significant asymmetries of economic power are emerging between winners and losers in the game. Competitive pressures are encouraging companies to join together through mergers, acquisitions, and alliances, with the result that the assets and revenues of large corporations are increasing. Again we are dealing here with a paradox. Amid the search for the "beauty" of smallness in organization, the trend towards consolidation continues apace among the Fortune 500. The growth of mega global firms was a key phenomenon of the late twentieth century and seems likely to continue over the long term despite the considerable amount of divestment after the onset of the financial crisis in 2008.[55] Ironically, one of the forces pushing corporate managers towards a consolidation of assets and market shares is the intensity of competition and the fear of failure. At the same time as firms are growing larger, they generally compete more fiercely and over a broader global terrain. The pressure on smaller firms to ally with their larger brothers or face extinction is intense in many parts of the "old economy," even as start-ups inject new blood into the new economy. Also many entrepreneurs starting up new firms hope to capitalize on their success through selling them later on to larger firms.

The trend towards the mega global firm creates a growing asymmetry of power between the managerial agents in charge of giant corporations and most other groups in society, including consumers, employees, and members of the local communities where the firms' plants are located, as well as shareholders.

Multinational enterprises (MNEs) are accused with some justification of unduly shaping public policy, and in some instances getting away with criminal behavior, through their influence over both national politics and supranational institutions such as the WTO.[56] Non-governmental organizations (NGOs), as well as informally organized protest groups, have become a significant force for dissent against what they see as the threat to basic human rights and values posed by globalization through the actions of MNEs and their sub-contractors. The development of social media and mobile telephony, as means of mass communication, has helped dissident groups to mobilize and coordinate worldwide. It is ironic that in this way the critics of globalization have harnessed new technology, one of its main facilitators, to oppose it.

Another stakeholder group has been ramping up the pressure on corporate managements. Activist investors are launching more campaigns to pressure corporate managements to improve their performance. In the USA, they launched an average of 240 campaigns in each of the years 2011 to 2013, more than double the number a decade previously, and this shareholder activism has been mirrored in other countries as well. Shareholder pressure of this kind can bring positive benefits such as strengthening the board of directors, improving strategy and operations, or moderating pressures to prioritize short-term performance.[57]

Advances in ICT have also assisted the management of operations at a distance and so enabled a shift away from organizations' previous linkages to specific geographic and cultural roots. This creates strains on conventional notions of the relationships between business organizations and wider society. Corporations operating through extended supply chains and diffused networks are being taken to task for all manner of negative social phenomena, from child labor to lost social cohesion.[58] One of the emerging challenges for organization is that of governance in the broadest sense: how to combine the benefits of scale and global reach with effective accountability to the local interests of the societies in which companies operate.

The governance issue has been heightened by a serious loss of trust in companies and their managers. Several developments related to globalization, new technology and hypercompetition have contributed to this problem. Chapter 15 cites evidence of a growing breach of trust as, starting in the 1990s, increasing numbers of employees became marginalized through downsizing, the contracting out of non-core activities, and moves away from long-term employment contracts and benefits. These trends are explicable in terms of a response to competitive pressures. They have been facilitated by the introduction of ICT, through which communication could become direct rather than passing through office intermediaries and middle managers. They are part and parcel of the shift towards slimmer organizational forms that increase flexibility through outsourcing activities into networks and through reducing the economic burden of direct employees. This is financially rational from the perspective of the employer, but it is changing the distributive balance to the disadvantage of employees and former employees. The growing imbalance is evident on both sides of the cost-benefit equation. On the benefit side, over the period from the mid-1980s to the late 2000s, income inequality increased in 17 out of the 22 OECD countries for which data were available.[59] On the cost side, even though many laid-off employees eventually find new opportunities as contract and self-employed business people, the social costs of this adjustment in terms of lost benefits, stress, and domestic disruption are very evident.

The trust of the general public in corporate managers has been further undermined by the corporate scandals that surfaced in 2001, and the combination of managerial incompetence and fraud exposed by the financial crisis of 2008. New cases continue to be exposed, and not only in the private sector. As employees, people lost their jobs and pension rights as a result; as consumers they have been mis-sold products, and as investors, they have seen the value of their savings and pensions cut. These misdemeanors have raised serious questions concerning the need for further legislated controls over the accountability and conduct of top executives, which are discussed further in Chapter 16, and more fundamentally they undermine the legitimacy of organizations and the system under which they operate.

IMPLICATIONS FOR ORGANIZATION

The social costs being attributed to the actions of corporate managers have a bearing on organization because the way it is structured can contribute to perceived injustices. Organization has two faces. One is a system for allocating and managing work. Here, organizational form amounts to a necessary technology of potentially positive social value. The other face, however, is that organization is a means for differentiating and allocating power and reward. In this respect, organization is a distributive mechanism that is far from socially neutral. Organization cannot therefore just be a technical issue. It is also used for determining the economic and other returns (such as personal fulfillment at work) that people receive. An immediate consequence of designing vertical distance into corporations, or of making organizational distinctions between core and periphery categories of employment, is the production of significant differentials in compensation, opportunities for advancement, and other benefits. It also makes it more difficult for lower-level organizational members to hold top management to account.

One of the intrinsic features of new organizational forms is the reduction of hierarchical distance through slimmer structures and devolving decision-making and initiative down the organization. Although reducing hierarchical levels may incur costs to displaced employees, movement in this direction offers an opportunity to reduce the distance and inequality that employees experience in relation to top management. If this is accompanied by an increased circulation and transparency of information, it should also improve the ability that employees have to exercise their voice within companies and thus expose and correct misdemeanors by senior management.

The social problems attributed to the actions of firms, of course, raise questions about their social accountability, or more precisely that of their leading executives. This is the central concern of corporate governance and it is coming to be realized that organization is related to the effectiveness of such governance. The conventional, narrow definition of corporate governance focuses on the role and rights of the board of directors or other bodies exercising supervision on behalf of owners. Concerns over the social accountability of business have strengthened demands for a wider definition of corporate responsibility to stakeholders in their roles as employees, consumers, and members of the communities concerned to protect their environments. If accepted, the broader view of social accountability will mean that the process of governance has to be extended into a firm's organization and value chain networks, so as to permit mutual accountability between top executives, employees and network partners. This imposes a further demand upon our organizational capabilities. For instance, it intensifies the need for control that is centered far more on shared values and the unobtrusive monitoring of results through ICT, so as to maintain ethical and socially responsible conduct without interfering directly with local initiatives and creativity. It also puts the onus on lead firms within business networks to take responsibility for the conduct of all members of their value chain and hence to go far beyond the obligations contained in commercial contracts.

It has traditionally been assumed that good corporate governance can be implemented within the firm through strict hierarchical accountability and control. Moves away from hierarchy therefore require new forms of accountability and control in order for effective governance to be preserved. The Enron scandal points to the challenge we face here. It remains an open question as to how far the problems that arose at Enron have to be attributed to the loosening of accountability through the company's use of non-conventional organizational forms involving the decentralization of initiative and diffused systems of control.

◢ New Conditions, New Forms Summarized

In the light of dramatic changes in the business environment, the potential offered by new organizational forms has become a major concern both for managers and business school

Table 3.1   Summary of new conditions and new organizational forms

New Conditions	New organizational forms
Globalization	• Adjustment to (1) the need for global integration through standardization combined with (2) the need for local sensitivity through flexibility • Handling of complexity via (1) reduction strategy to preserve existing routines *or* (2) absorption strategy through decentralization and partnership
New technologies	• Lean management structures (fewer layers and more horizontal communication) • Greater interdependence between units within and between organizations • Fuzzy boundaries and networks • Ownership of assets separated from their use • Use of "remote" control procedures • Information systems for decisions in high-velocity situations • Knowledge management support for organizational learning & innovation
Knowledge-based society	• Procedures to encourage effective application and exploitation of existing knowledge, within the framework of a conventional organizational design ("adaptation") • Decentralized initiative to teams and networks to promote creative synergy for exploring new possibilities ("innovation")
Hypercompetition	• The "flexible firm" • Organizing to maximize organizational learning, with a strong emphasis on innovation
Social accountability	• Normative controls backed by monitoring of conduct • Management of network conduct by lead firms over and above the legal limits of contracts

academics. Table 3.1 summarizes the new forms that appear to fit the new conditions just discussed. It should be noted that much of Table 3.1 remains speculative as we await further evidence, especially on how the proposed matching of new forms to new conditions impacts on performance.

◢ New and Conventional Organizational Forms Compared

The network paradigm

Underlying the shift from conventional to new organizational forms has been the emergence of a different paradigm – a new way of thinking. This is the idea of the network. A network is a group or system of interconnected people or units. It draws attention to how people relate with one another – raising questions such as who relates with whom, how they relate, what they relate about, and what sustains their relationship. This focus on relationships tends naturally towards horizontal links between organizational members that cut across formal divisions, and to the fact that such relationships may arise informally, even spontaneously. Interest in the network concept has also come from the realization that formal organizational arrangements do not of themselves necessarily result in the behaviors they are intended to promote. For example, we shall see in Chapter 5 that this can be the case with matrix organization, which is designed to improve integration between different units through making people jointly responsible to those units.

Relying on this structural arrangement alone does not however guarantee that staff from the different units will actually cooperate better. Further effort, in the form of training and socializing activities, will normally be required in order to encourage them to form an effective network based on shared understanding and mutual trust.

The network paradigm is one that informs a shift from conventional thinking about organization and also emphasizes non-structural complements to formal organization. It is applied both to internal organization (intra-organizational networks), discussed in Part II of this book, and to relationships between organizations (inter-organizational networks), discussed in Part III.

As an internal approach to organization, the network concept is part of a shift from the centralized vertical emphasis found in conventional organization toward a decentralized horizontal emphasis. The conventional approach assumed that control and coordination could be achieved through hierarchies without the need for staff lower down to relate directly among themselves. The newer approach places much more store on control and coordination being achieved through direct contact between people who will often, though not necessarily, be located at a similar organizational level. Direct relationships are seen to provide the means for rapid information exchange and coordination of effort, in circumstances where rapid informed adjustments to new events is required. They are also seen to be a necessary condition for innovation to be achieved.

The ideal for some advocates of the network principle is that networking becomes an inherent way of working that to a large extent substitutes for the need to rely on a formal structure. In other words, with networking in place, it should not be necessary to create a new horizontal structure that replaces or supplements the traditional vertical one. For example, the Global Integration consulting company states the following on its website:

> "Networked organization . . . is a reflection of the need for organizations to work across the traditional 'vertical' silos of function and geography, but without creating a horizontal structure to replace it."[60]

Other authorities would not go as far as recommending networking as a complete replacement for hierarchy, let alone for any form of formal organization. Although hierarchy and network are often presented as opposite modes of organizing, the question has to be asked whether in practice network is a complement to hierarchy rather than a substitute for it. Many regard it as a complement in which hierarchy and network in different ways both contribute to strategic objectives and can be combined in a hybrid manner.[61] We shall see in Chapter 5 that the matrix structure is a mix of the two principles. Also Chapter 17 will suggest that the appropriate balance between, or combination of, the two has to be resolved through a careful assessment of the strategic priorities of the organization.

Chapter 1 identified the structural, processual and boundary-defining components of organization and the basic organizational choices that occur among these components. We can now compare conventional and newer organizational forms in terms of the same components. The comparison is put into context by grouping these components into the three sets of activity for which organization is essential. The first activity is identifying, disseminating, and implementing the collective goals of the unit, be this a business company or a not-for-profit institution. Here, organization is concerned with arrangements for providing inputs to decision making, communicating its outcomes, and controlling the results. The second activity is to identify, and make provision for governing, the rights and functions (roles) of members within the unit or working in association with it. Organization in this respect contributes through a pattern of horizontal and vertical specialization. The third activity is maintaining the unit's value-adding system, principally by regulating the flow of resources across organizational boundaries. This is where the boundary-defining aspects of organization come into play.[62]

Using this framework, the contrasts between conventional and new organizational forms are set out in Table 3.2. In reality, as we shall see later, particular companies need not be

Table 3.2   Contrasts between Conventional and New Organizational Forms

Activity and Organizational Components	Conventional Organization	New Organization
Goal setting & dissemination		
Hierarchy	Centralized initiative and authority	Distributed initiative and authority
	Leadership through formal authority	Leadership through guidance
	Use of hierarchical channels	Use of teams, with fewer hierarchical levels
Rules & schedules	Mandatory; rule-based orientation	Discretionary; relationship-based orientation
Control	Centralized: personal or rule-based	Decentralized: target, culture and/or HRM-based
Reward	Based on individual's hierarchical level	Based on group performance
Identifying duties & roles		
Specialization	Specialized clearly-defined roles	General fuzzy roles
	Preference for confined roles	Preference for larger expanded roles
Degree of integration	Emphasis on differentiation rather than integration	Strong emphasis on integration
Maintaining a value-adding system		
Systems	Oriented to reducing uncertainty	Oriented to signaling need for change
Mode of integration	Through formal procedures and roles	Through direct contact and ICT
Networking	Only with major stakeholders	Integral to value-chain
Outsourcing	Vertical integration into large units; little outsourcing	Horizontal integration between smaller units; non-core activities outsourced
Alliances	Avoided due to fears of control loss and conflict	Extensively used
Organizing across borders	Either a loose financially-coordinated conglomerate or coordinated via an international division. Integration primarily vertical	Complex multidimensional organization that attempts simultaneously to gain benefits of global coordination and local initiative. Integration both vertical and lateral

located at either extreme, and the organizational profiles they adopt may vary for different work locations or specialties. It will also become apparent that opting for a position on one particular dimension is often consistent with a specific position on another dimension. For example, reliance on hierarchy for the maintenance of organizational goals will often be supported by the formulation of rules.

Setting and disseminating the goals of the organization

The contrasting ways in which organization can be designed to support the setting of goals and their dissemination fall between centralized top-down hierarchy, on the one hand, and decentralized, bottom-up teamwork, on the other. In the conventional model, a company's vision is prescribed from the top and disseminated downwards. This approach relies a great deal upon hierarchy as the basis for authority, control, and coordination. Rewards are based primarily on the individual's position in that hierarchy. In the new organizational model, there are arrangements to encourage wide participation in the formulation of an organization's vision. This approach is a collective one that depends on a common acceptance of a shared organizational culture, which is guided rather than imposed from the top. Teams bringing people together horizontally play a much more important role in coordination and decision-making within this second approach, and they are encouraged to contribute actively to the leadership process through local initiatives. It is seen to be appropriate to base rewards to a significant extent on group or team performance.

The approach inherent in the conventional model accords with the classic model of bureaucracy. This assumes that the higher managers are in an organization, the more information they possess, including information relevant to setting goals and making decisions. In a textbook bureaucracy, goals are set by the senior team and acted upon by line managers. Decisions that require coordinated action across units are referred to higher levels in the organization for resolution. The senior team acts as policy-maker for the rest of the company.

The advantage of the bureaucratic approach lies in its potential economy, both of personnel and time. A vision formulated centrally, and disseminated through a clear hierarchy, should not require the efforts of a large number of people and can be implemented rapidly. By contrast, the secondment of people to teams can take them away from their normal activities, and teams themselves eat up time and money in settling down before they even start to function. Bureaucracy also promises to produce consistency in the implementation and maintenance of organization goals, which might otherwise be threatened by a high degree of decentralization to local initiative. It is possible that some of the rigidities associated with goal-setting in bureaucracies can be offset by deliberate efforts on the part of top managers to break down the communication and interpersonal barriers that stand in the way of a wider participation in the process. In so doing, they can make a determined effort to steer the organization's culture away from using conformity to precedent as a performance criterion and replace this with criteria that support more forward-looking goals.[63]

In new forms, hierarchical organization is seen to give way to operating "horizontally" – a network approach in which initiative and decision making is decentralized among teams of people organized around specific tasks and processes. This organizing mode has similarities to the business process reengineering (BPR) paradigm that advocated cross-functional processes, delayering, and empowerment.[64] The objective is to push decisions to where relevant knowledge and information reside, then to use information technology (ICT) for support. This approach offers the potential benefit of being able to adjust rapidly to new or changed circumstances because the people "on the spot" are allowed to make the relevant decisions. It also allows the members of an organization to have a sense of owning its objectives rather than feeling that these are imposed on them. This is likely to increase their commitment to the success of these objectives. If, additionally, those members possess valuable knowledge, or access to sources of such knowledge, their active involvement in decisions and in proposals for innovation should again be to the company's advantage.

The conventional approach to setting and disseminating organizational goals is therefore oriented to satisfying the needs of efficiency. The new approach is oriented to meeting the needs of organizational adaptation and innovation.

Identifying duties and roles

New and conventional approaches to identifying duties and roles within organizations also contrast in terms of specialization and integration. The prime choice is between organizing with a clear specification of differentiated roles and departments, on the basis that this will prove to be a relatively permanent structure, or favoring a more fluid approach. This latter leans heavily towards flexible roles that are fuzzy in the sense of overlapping with others, so that integration is emphasized rather than clarity. The assumption behind this alternative is that circumstances will not permit a given set of roles to take on any permanency. It therefore aims at keeping roles flexible so as to encourage cooperation and mutual adjustment between the people in them, and also to avoid formal definitions of the role inhibiting initiative and innovation.

Conventional bureaucracies are organized to reflect the principle of specialization. The various functions of the firm – finance, marketing, production, and so forth – each specialized on the efficient production of their own outputs, are coordinated by general managers who exercise command and control influence over the functions, at least in theory. The advocates of new organizational forms propose to alter this basic system. Instead of employees being expected to respond to hierarchical authority and perform well-defined tasks, the new paradigm emphasizes the value of engendering their commitment and contribution as trusted organizational "members." This means organizing to "treat people more as assets to be developed than as costs to be controlled, and as renewable strategic resources rather than as replaceable operating parts."[65] Organization members in the new forms are increasingly responsible for larger, but less well-defined roles.

Whereas previously, possession of assets and the know-how to make them productive was key, in today's organizations organizing for knowledge creation is increasingly seen to be central, suggesting dramatic shifts in roles and tasks as well as in ways to integrate their activities. Nonaka and Takeuchi propose a specific form of organization, the "hypertext," to facilitate the knowledge-creating process. This combines the steady state advantages of the functional form with the strategic flexibility of a flat, cross-functional task force as an independent, parallel structure. The functional form offers specialization of expertise, whereas the horizontal task force overlay helps to bring together and synergize the specialist contributions. It aims to create a productive internal network. Based on the practice of innovative Japanese firms such as Sharp, it is one of a number of hybrid organizational forms that have been suggested as ways of ensuring ambidexterity, so as to combine a capacity to innovate with the ability to operate efficiently; to explore new possibilities as well as to exploit already existing knowledge.[66]

Maintaining a value-adding system

The conventional approach to organizing a value-adding system is to use vertically integrated, often large, units whose integration depends significantly on standardized procedures and rules. The new approach advocates outsourcing non-core activities and basing the value chain on inter-organizational networks of units linked through relationships that can re-form flexibly as circumstances change. Vertically integrated units are likely to have clear and relatively fixed boundaries, which embrace all or most of the value-chain. They are also likely to have a single legal ownership and be correspondingly larger. Bigger is better in a typical bureaucracy. By contrast, horizontally integrated networks will tend to have less defined or fixed boundaries between their constituent units. These units can be quite small, unless economies of scale are significant. Within a network, there will be a number of separately owned companies, as well as some strategic alliances each having several owners. The scope of ownership therefore no longer coincides with the scope of the value chain as it does with the vertically integrated model.

The new thinking around networks expects their constituent units to be relatively small and to concentrate on core activities for which they have developed a distinctive competence. Smaller focused units are thought to be more responsive to market requirements and better able to adapt to external changes more rapidly. Small units can more readily organize themselves than can larger ones. Their ability to do this and to arrive at constructive solutions in the face of high uncertainty has led this new form to be labeled the "chaordic organization," able to generate order out of chaos.[67]

The conventional approach, based on vertical integration and standardization through rules, has some advantages. Its systems are oriented to reducing uncertainty, by ensuring that both the strategy and operations of a value-adding system are consistent and unified. While the more open network approach is likely to be effective in providing early warning of the need for change, one of the underlying problems of networks is that it can be difficult to maintain agreement between different partners over the goals and modes of operation for their partnerships. Secondly, the conventional approach should also help to eliminate wasteful overlaps and foster an economic utilization of resources. Third, it ought to be more economical in terms of managerial effort, being a single entity as opposed to a wide scatter of different units all contributing to the value chain.

There are, inevitably, potential disadvantages to the conventional organization of value-adding systems, and these provide the arguments in favor of the new organizational approach. A reliance on standard rules and vertical, top-down coordination will present a handicap to adjusting to changing circumstances, *unless* these can be foreseen and incorporated into the organization's standard procedures. The incorporation of all or most value-adding activities within the same organizational unit forgoes opportunities to specialize on those activities that represent core competencies and to outsource others. Thirdly, the focusing of capital provision onto one source of equity may create difficulties in funding innovation from sources internal to the value chain. Innovation can also be inhibited in the vertically integrated organizational model because it involves few, if any, partners who can provide access to new knowledge and insights.

The new approach therefore aims at an optimization of the contributions to the value-adding system by encouraging flexible combinations and re-combinations of both intra- and inter-organizational relationships. These relationships are often formed between small units, each offering a contribution that can draw upon their own distinctive competency. Overall, the arguments for new organizational forms accord priority to adaptation and innovation as requirements for organizational survival rather than economy and efficiency.

The tension in maintaining organizational boundaries – how to respond to the twin pressures of being consistent and efficient, on the one hand, and being adaptive and innovative (flexible) on the other – is a fundamental one. Bartlett and Ghoshal have wrestled with this issue in the context of the large, diversified MNE. Their "transnational solution" envisages the use of an integrated network format in which the corporate center guides the process of coordination and cooperation between subsidiary units in a climate of shared decision making. The transnational solution attempts to blend hierarchy with network, but to retain value creation largely within the corporation.[68]

Later chapters will go further into the contributions that conventional organizational forms can continue to make, sometimes in combination with new forms even within the same firm. Senior management has to find organizational solutions that suit various areas of activity within the same firm that may be differentiated from each other by function, national (and hence cultural) location, and so forth. Also, as already noted, organizational design has to be sufficiently "ambidextrous" to support both knowledge exploitation and knowledge creation within the same firm.[69] The continuing contribution that conventional organizational forms may be able to make, in appropriate circumstances, is a reminder that we should not get so carried away by the excitement and hype about new organizational forms as to assume that the old is no longer relevant.

SUMMARY

1   Many business executives and organization analysts believe that conventional forms of organization can no longer meet present requirements.

2   Bureaucracy has been the most prominent conventional form of organization, with a long history of over 2,000 years. It embodies a considerable amount of accumulated experience.

3   The critique of bureaucracy strengthened from the 1950s onward. It was at first prompted by evidence of malfunctioning and, more recently, on the grounds that even well run bureaucracies are insufficiently flexible to suit modern competitive conditions.

4   Each of the major developments in the business environment places new requirements on organization.

5   Globalization requires firms to maintain both standardization and flexibility within the same organizational framework, as well as increasing the need for companies to organize to cope with increased complexity in the environment. In handling complexity, one option is to organize in an attempt to reduce it; the other is to organize to absorb complexity, seeing it as presenting new opportunities and therefore keeping choices open.

6 New technologies open up new organizational possibilities. Internally, they enable a simplification of management structures. Externally, they make it easier to manage information flows and relationships across their "boundaries," so facilitating international operations, outsourcing, and networks.

7 Greater interdependence between firms, encouraged by globalization and new technology, generates new demands on the organizational capacity of those firms. These demands result partly from the additional complexity of multiple transactions and partly from the greater speed of change and new events associated with more open and intensive information-processing across the world.

8 The increased significance of innovation as a competitive strategy within the knowledge-based economy also calls for modifications to organization, particularly the intensive use of interdisciplinary teams.

9 Hypercompetition places a premium on the ability of firms to organize flexibly so as to adjust in anticipation of new competitive opportunities and threats.

10 Pressures for social accountability place a further demand on organizational capabilities, especially to maintain socially responsible conduct within devolved business networks.

11 Contrasts between conventional and new organizational forms can be drawn for each of the components of organization identified in Chapter 1.

QUESTIONS FOR DISCUSSION

3.1 What have been the main problems with so-called conventional forms of organization?

3.2 What are the strengths of conventional forms of organization?

3.3 What are the salient contrasts between conventional and new forms of organization?

3.4 How "new" are new forms of organization? To what extent do they borrow from the creative and information-based sectors?

3.5 What circumstances are new forms of organization best suited to?

3.6 Is it possible to combine the strengths of conventional and new organizational forms?

3.7 To what extent do the new conditions said to require new organizational forms apply to your organization or to your country?

NOTES

1 Reviewed in Gibson Burrell and Gareth Morgan (1979), *Sociological Paradigms and Organizational Analysis*, London, Heinemann.

2 John Child (1972), Organization, environment and performance: the role of strategic choice, *Sociology*, 6(1), 1–22; J. Kenneth Benson (1977), Innovation and crisis in organizational analysis, *Sociological Quarterly*, 18(1), 3–16.

3 Karl E. Weick (1969), *The Social Psychology of Organizing*, Reading, MA, Addison-Wesley.

4   Peter F. Drucker (1988), The Coming of the New Organization, *Harvard Business Review*, 66(1), 45–53. The quotation is from p. 45.

5   The discussion in this section draws upon John Child and Rita G. McGrath (2001), Organizations unfettered: organizational form in an information-intensive economy, *Academy of Management Journal*, 44, 1135–1148.

6   Max Boisot (2002), The creation and sharing of knowledge. In C.W. Choo and N. Bontis (eds.), *The Strategic Management of Intellectual Capital and Organizational Knowledge*, New York, Oxford University Press, pp. 65–78.

7   Rita G. McGrath (2001), Exploratory learning, adaptive capacity and the role of managerial oversight, *Academy of Management Journal*, 44, 118–131.

8   Dorothy Leonard-Barton (1992), Core capabilities and core rigidities: a paradox in managing new product development, *Strategic Management Journal*, 13, Special Issue, 111–125.

9   Thomas J. Peters and Robert H. Waterman Jr. (1982), *In Search of Excellence*, New York, Harper & Row.

10   Nitin Nohria and Robert G. Eccles (eds.) (1992), *Networks and Organizations*, Boston, MA, Harvard Business School Press; Remo Häcki and Julian Lighton (2001), The future of the networked company, *McKinsey Quarterly*, (3), 26–39.

11   John Child, David Faulkner, and Stephen Tallman (2005), *Cooperative Strategy*, Oxford, Oxford University Press.

12   Phanish Puranam, Oliver Alexy, and Markus Reitzig (2014), What's "new" about new forms of organizing? *Academy of Management Review*, 39(2), 162–180.

13   Economist Intelligence Unit (EIU) in cooperation with Andersen Consulting (1997), *Vision 2010. Designing Tomorrow's Organization*. New York, EIU.

14   Susan Mohrman and Gillian Pillans (2013), *Emerging Approaches to Organisation Design*, London, Corporate Research Forum.

15   A.T. Kearney (2001), Measuring globalization, *Foreign Policy*, Jan/Feb, 56–65.

16   George S. Yip and G. Tomas Hult (2011), *Total Global Strategy: Managing for Worldwide Competitive Advantage*, 3rd edition, Englewood Cliffs, NJ, Prentice-Hall.

17   Jonathan Matusitz (2011), Disney's successful adaptation in Hong Kong: A glocalization perspective, *Asia Pacific Journal of Management*, 28(4), 667–681.

18   *The Economist* (2013), The gated globe: Special report on the world economy, 12 October.

19   *Business Week* (2001), What's at stake. How terrorism threatens the global economy, 22 October, pp. 22–25.

20   To be more precise, sectors such as construction, personal services and hospitality serve local markets but often source their labor internationally.

21   Alan Rugman (2000), *The End of Globalization*, London, Random House.

22   Ulrich Steger (ed.) (1998), *Discovering the New Pattern of Globalization*, Ladenburg, Gottlieb Daimler-und-Karl Benz Stiftung.

23   Francesco Ciabuschi, Oscar M. Martín and Benjamin Ståhl (2010), Headquarters' influence on knowledge transfer performance, *Management International Review*, 50(4), 471–491.

24   On managing external relations, see John Child, Kenneth K-T. Tse, and Suzana B. Rodrigues (2013), *The Dynamics of Corporate Co-evolution*, Cheltenham, Edward Elgar, Chapter 7. On engagement with NGOs, see John Child and Terence Tsai (2005), The Dynamic between firms' environmental strategies and institutional constraints in emerging economies: evidence from China and Taiwan, *Journal of Management Studies*, 42(1), 95–125.

25   Eve Mitleton-Kelly (ed.) (2003), *Complex Systems and Evolutionary Perspectives on Organisations: The Application of Complexity Theory to Organisations*, Bingley, Emerald.

26   On the choice between reducing or absorbing complexity, see Max Boisot and John Child (1999), Organizations as adaptive systems in complex environments: the case of China, *Organization Science*, 10, 237–252.

27   John Child and Suzana B. Rodrigues (2011), How organizations engage with external complexity: A political action perspective, *Organization Studies*, 32(6), 803–824.

28 Max Boisot and Bill McKelvey (2011), "Ashby's law of requisite variety: A complexity perspective," in P. Allen, S. Maguire, and B. McKelvey (eds.), *Handbook of Complexity and Management*, London, Sage, pp. 279–98.

29 Richard D'Aveni (2013), 3-D printing will change the world, *Harvard Business Review*, March, http://hbr.org/2013/03/3-d-printing-will-change-the-world/ar/1, accessed April 5, 2014.

30 Surenda Gera and Wulong Gu (2004), The effect of organizational innovation and information technology on firm performance, *International Productivity Monitor*, 9, pp. 37–51.

31 Sunil Mithas, Ali Tafti, Indranil Bardhan, and Jie Mein Goh (2012), Information technology and firm profitability: Mechanisms and empirical evidence, *MIS Quarterly*, 36(1), 205–224.

32 John Child and Ray Loveridge (1990), *New Technology in European Services*. Oxford, Blackwell.

33 Joseph Schumpeter (1939), *Business Cycles*, New York, McGraw-Hill.

34 Marina N. Whitman (1999), *New World, New Rules: The Changing Role of the American Corporation*, Boston, MA, Harvard Business School Press. Manuel Castells (2000), *The Rise of the Network Society, The Information Age: Economy, Society and Culture*, 2nd edition, Oxford, UK, Blackwell.

35 For how this is taking place in global multinational media companies see Amelia H. Arsenault and Manuel Castells (2008), The structure and dynamics of global multi-media business networks, *International Journal of Communication*, 2, 707–748.

36 John Child and Rita G McGrath (2001), op. cit.

37 Kathleen M. Eisenhardt (1989), Making fast strategic decisions in high-velocity environments, *Academy of Management Journal*, 32, 543–576; Ian P. McCarthy, Thomas B. Lawrence, Brian Wixted, and Brian R. Gordon (2010), A multidimensional conceptualization of environmental velocity, *Academy of Management Review*, 35(4), 604–626.

38 James B. Quinn (1992), *Intelligent Enterprise: A Knowledge and Service Based Paradigm for Industry*, New York, The Free Press.

39 US Bureau of Labor statistics.

40 Paul Thompson and David McHugh (2002), *Work Organisations: A Critical Introduction*, 3rd edition, Basingstoke, Palgrave, pp. 171–172.

41 *Organization Studies* (2003), special issue on "Knowledge and Professional Organizations," 24(6).

42 Noemi Pezderka, Rudolf R. Sinkovics, and Ruey-Jer (Bryan) Jean (2012), Do born global SMEs reap more benefits from ICT use than other internationalizing small firms? In Mika Gabrielsson and V. H. Manek Kirpalani (eds.) *Handbook of Research on Born Globals*, Cheltenham, Edward Elgar, Chapter 11.

43 See notes 49 and 50 in Chapter 2.

44 James G. March (1991), Exploration and exploitation in organizational learning, *Organization Science*, 2, 71–87.

45 Chris Argyris and Donald Schön (1978), *Organizational Learning*, Reading, MA, Addison-Wesley.

46 Paul P. Lawrence and Jay W. Lorsch (1967), *Organization and Environment: Managing Differentiation and Integration,* Boston, MA, Harvard Business School Press.

47 Richard A. D'Aveni (1994), *Hypercompetition*, New York, Free Press.

48 Anne Y. Illinitch, Richard A. D'Aveni, and Arie Y. Lewin (1996), New organizational forms and strategies for managing in hypercompetitive environments, *Organization Science*, 7, 211–20. The quotation is from p. 211.

49 Homa Bahrami and Stuart Evans (1995), Flexible recycling and high-technology entrepreneurship, *California Management Review*, 37, 62–89. Quotation is from p. 62.

50 Annalee Saxenian (2000), The origins and dynamics of production networks in Silicon Valley. In Martin Kenney (ed.), *Understanding Silicon Valley*. Stanford, CA: Stanford University Press, pp. 141–162.

51 Rita Gunther McGrath (2013), *The End of Competitive Advantage*, Boston, Harvard Business School Publishing.

52 Henk W. Volberda (1996), Toward the flexible form: How to remain vital in hypercompetitive environments, *Organization* Science, 7, 359–374. Also Henk W. Volberda (1998), *Building the Flexible Firm*, Oxford, Oxford University Press; Homa Bahrami and Stuart Evans (2010), *Super-Flexibility for Knowledge Enterprise: A Toolkit for Dynamic Adaptation*, 2nd edition, Berlin, Springer.

53   Robert M. Grant (1996), Prospering in dynamically-competitive environments: Organizational capability as knowledge integration, *Organization Science*, 7, 375–387.

54   John Child and Sally J. Heavens (2001), The social constitution of organizations and its implications for organizational learning. In Meinolf Dierkes, Ariane B. Antal, John Child, and Ikujiro Nonaka (eds.) *Handbook of Organizational Learning and Knowledge*, Oxford, Oxford University Press, pp. 308–326.

55   Deloittes (2013), *Divestments: Creating Shareholder Value.* http://www.deloitte.com/assets/Dcom-UnitedKingdom/LocalAssets/Documents/Marketinsights/uk-ma-upfront-in-brief-divestments.pdf. Accessed November 7, 2013.

56   Hadjikhani, Amjad (2000), The political behavior of business actors: The case of Swedish MNCs and the EU, *International Studies of Management and Organization*, 30(1), 93–117; Russell Mokhiber and Robert Weissman (2005), *On The Rampage: Corporate Predators and the Destruction of Democracy*, Monroe, Maine, Common Courage Press.

57   Joseph Cyriac, Ruth De Backer, and Justin Sanders (2014), Preparing for bigger, bolder shareholder activists. *McKinsey Insights*, March, http://www.mckinsey.com/Insights/Corporate_Finance/Preparing_for_bigger_bolder_shareholder_activists?cid=other-eml-alt-mip-mck-oth-1403, accessed April 8, 2014.

58   E.g., Humanity United (2013), *Exploitative Labor Practices in the Global Palm Oil Industry.* Report prepared by Accenture. http://humanityunited.org/pdfs/Modern_Slavery_in_the_Palm_Oil_Industry.pdf, accessed November 7, 2013. See also Carnoy, M. (1999), The family, flexible work and social cohesion at risk, *International Labour Review*, 138, 411–429.

59   Organization for Economic Cooperation and Development (OECD) (2011), *Divided We Stand: Why Inequality Keeps Rising*, Paris, OECD Publishing, December.

60   Global Integration (2013), *Networked Organizations: A flexible organization based on skills and networks, not structure.* www.global-integration.com/matrix-management-training/networked-organization, accessed December 10, 2013.

61   E.g., John P. Kotter (2012), Accelerate! *Harvard Business Review*, November, 45–58.

62   John Child and Rita G McGrath (2001), op. cit.

63   For an example of how a large conventionally organized multinational corporation was able to adopt an effective process for evolving organizational goals, see D. Charles Galunic and Kathleen M. Eisenhardt (2001), Architectural innovation and modular organizational forms, *Academy of Management Journal*, 44, 1229–1249.

64   Michael Hammer and James Champy (1993), *Reengineering the Corporation: A Manifesto for Business Revolution*, New York, Harper Business.

65   Christopher A. Bartlett and Sumantra Ghoshal (1994), Beyond strategy, structure, systems to purpose, process, people, Reflections on a voyage of discovery. In Paula B. Duffy (ed.), *The Relevance of a Decade: Essay to Mark the First Ten Years of the Harvard Business School Press*, Boston, MA, Harvard Business School Press, pp. 323–345. The quotation is from p. 345.

66   Ikujiro Nonaka and Hirotaka Takeuchi (1995), *The Knowledge Creating Company*, New York, Oxford University Press; Michael L. Tushman and Charles A. O'Reilly III (1996), The ambidextrous organization, *California Management Review*, 38, 8–30; James G. March (1991), Exploration and exploitation in organizational learning, *Organization Science*, 2, 71–87.

67   Peter Senge (1997), Through the eye of the needle. In Rowan Gibson (ed.), *Rethinking the Future*, London, Nicholas Brealey, pp. 123–145.

68   Sumantra Ghoshal and Christopher A. Bartlett (1998), *Managing Across Borders: The Transnational Solution*, 2nd edition, Boston, MA, Harvard Business School Press.

69   Michael L. Tushman and Charles A. O'Reilly (1996), op. cit.

PART II

New Internal Forms

◢ Introduction to Part II – New Internal Forms

The chapters in Part II focus on the specifics of organization as it occurs largely within the boundaries of firms and institutions. Chapter 4 is concerned chiefly with hierarchy, a fundamental structural feature of organization. It considers downsizing and delayering, which are moves toward smaller and slimmer management structures that have fewer hierarchical levels. The attempt to reduce hierarchy is often accompanied by the greater use of teams.

Teams are an important means of improving the coordination and integration of activities, which is the subject of Chapter 5. That chapter discusses ways in which integration can be achieved, including the use of cross-functional teams and modern information and communication technologies. The management of projects is a particularly important capability today and the coordination of the specialized contributions required is usually achieved through teams.

Control is the subject of Chapter 6, which is another fundamental aspect of organizing where new approaches have been developed to suit modern conditions. The next two chapters turn to reward policies and practices as further aspects of organizational design.

Chapter 7 examines reward policies and the contribution they make within the employment relationship to reconciling managerial requirements with employee needs. Chapter 8 recognizes the importance of pay within the spectrum of rewards and it pays particular attention to the choice of alternative payment systems including the contentious issue of executive bonuses.

CHAPTER 4

Simpler Structures – Reducing Hierarchy

WHAT THIS CHAPTER COVERS

The chapter is concerned with hierarchy and the possibilities for minimizing it. It begins by noting how hierarchy has attracted considerable criticism because of its negative effects, yet it remains a widespread feature of organization. Hierarchy has provided the backbone for conventional forms of organization and it continues to perform a number of seemingly indispensable functions. At the same time, we note that hierarchy has some clearly negative features. The newer approach to organization therefore endeavors to reduce hierarchy and in so doing to simplify organizational structures. The chapter goes on to examine ways in which simpler structures can be achieved through downsizing, delayering, and the use of teams. Delayering is usually a concomitant of downsizing, reflecting the close association between the number of personnel in a company and the extent of its hierarchy. The introduction of teams can help to collapse the number of hierarchical levels by replacing vertical coordination through middle managers with direct coordination and decision making within the team itself.

◢ Hierarchy

Unloved but ubiquitous

Hierarchy has become almost universally derided. As Elliott Jaques has said, "At first glance, hierarchy may seem difficult to praise. Bureaucracy is a dirty word even among bureaucrats, and in business there is a widespread view that managerial hierarchy kills initiative, crushes creativity,

BOX 4.1   THE PERSISTENCE OF HIERARCHY

Early in 2002, the Industrial Society surveyed "The State of the Office: The Politics and Geography of Working Space." The most remarkable feature of its report is how it reveals the persistence of hierarchy and the continued use of symbolism in the office to convey status. It also pointed to the negative performance consequences that this can have.

The Industrial Society study found that a great deal of the time and energy people should have devoted to doing their jobs was instead taken up in vying with each other for prime window space or a larger desk. One woman interviewed for the report said that she had arrived at her new office to find the names of people in it listed in alphabetical order outside. Since she was the manager, she rearranged the list to put her name at the top. The consequences of this for staff morale can be imagined.

The research found that a traditional hierarchical order was generally reflected in how ostentatiously office space was used. Managers at the top of the hierarchy generally occupied a top floor office with the best view and most light. Service employees were liable to work in the basement, with middle-ranking employees sandwiched in between.

Source: Max Nathan, *The State of the Office: The Politics and Geography of Working Space*. London: The Industrial Society 2002. Reported by Richard Donkin, *Financial Times*, 17 January 2002, FT CareerPoint section: XII.

and has therefore seen its day."[1] It has been blamed for failings in prominent UK public organizations including the BBC and the Bank of England.[2] Nevertheless, despite attempts to move away from hierarchy, most companies that have grown beyond the small start-up stage find it very difficult to do without it. Ricardo Semler claims that his company in Brazil has done away with hierarchy, and even inverted it for decisions on pay increases.[3] James Dyson's appliances company has a policy of minimizing hierarchy and marks of status. Though chairman and owner, Dyson says he likes nothing more than working with his engineers.[4]

These attempts to reduce hierarchy or its effects are, however, still exceptions rather than the rule. The evidence presented in Box 4.1 illustrates just how persistent hierarchy is and suggests that it arises from deep-seated human instincts.

In fact, hierarchy is ubiquitous both in the natural world and throughout human society. It appears everywhere in society and has done so throughout recorded history.[5] Some claim that it is intrinsic to all collective life, animal as well as human.[6] Historically, hierarchy has been the organizing principle of the ancient empires of China and Rome, the Catholic Church in Europe, and the modern multinational corporation. It characterized the management of major projects such as building the ancient pyramids of Egypt and the Great Wall of China, as well as the medieval monasteries.[7] Hierarchy has been taken for granted from the very beginning of writings on organization. As we saw in Chapter 2, one of Fayol's (1916) fundamental "principles" of organization was the "scalar chain" of hierarchical command, while Weber also recognized how hierarchy is central to legal-rational authority in bureaucracies.

Although some of the reasons for the widespread presence of hierarchy may not meet with overt approval in contemporary society, they continue to apply. One such reason is the drive among people to feel more important than others. In this respect hierarchy offers a pecking order that meets people's needs for status and power. Through the "ladder to the sky" that it offers, hierarchy can motivate people to strive upwards through promotion and career progression.

Other reasons for hierarchy are more attuned to the effective functioning of an organization. As the number of people working in an organization grows, it becomes increasingly difficult to maintain adequate control and coordination purely on the basis of face-to-face interactions between them. People will inevitably become divided into separate groups doing different work, possibly located in different premises, and personal contact will no longer arise naturally during the course of work. If reliance on direct personal contact continues, it will entail an increasing loss of time in the carrying out of jobs. As a result, managers have to be appointed to facilitate communication, control and coordination.

Hierarchy also emerges because it is appropriate to distinguish between different levels of authority and responsibility. It amounts to a vertical form of specialization. The tasks carried out in an organization vary in complexity, from the routine to the strategic. Likewise, the responsibilities people have to undertake vary from those of limited short-term consequence, usually of a routine nature, to those of major long-term consequence where failure could bring a company to ruin. It is logical to differentiate between roles on the basis of responsibility, which in itself is conducive to hierarchy. In this respect, hierarchy is a natural consequence of the widely accepted notion of leadership.

With these considerations in mind, it is not surprising that hierarchy has a very long history in human organization. Of course, this long historical legacy could simply mean hierarchy is an arrangement that has over time become a mere convention, embedded in our expectations. It is more plausible, however, to suggest that hierarchy embodies a wisdom born of experience in organizing complex activities that involve large numbers of people. If so, then the challenge we face is not so much how to get rid of hierarchy as how to reform it so as to enhance its contributions and minimize its drawbacks. This is what much of the thinking on new organizational forms has addressed.

The next section examines the nature of hierarchy in conventional forms of organization. We then consider the contributions that hierarchy makes to the organizing process, before turning to its negative features. These negative aspects explain why newer organizational practice is endeavoring to move away from traditional hierarchical forms.

Hierarchy in conventional organization

Hierarchy provides the backbone for conventional forms of organization. In conventional organization, hierarchy normally has the following characteristics:

- Positions are segmented into clearly differentiated levels according to the degree of authority and responsibility accorded to them.
- Higher levels have greater authority and responsibility.
- People at higher levels in the hierarchy take decisions that are more complex in the sense of the risk and uncertainty attaching to them, the implications for policy, and the financial commitment involved.
- People within the same designated areas report for instructions and guidance to managers with responsibility over them.

- These features give rise to a "chain of command" in which managers or officers in positions higher up a hierarchy have the authority to issue instructions or requests to those lower down. At the same time managers take responsibility for the work of the people reporting to them.
- Leadership is exercised from the top of an organization through a "command and control" system down its various hierarchies.
- Hierarchy provides the main channel for control and coordination.
- Information is passed down the hierarchy and is made available to people of a higher rank before those lower down.
- Although it is not a necessary feature of hierarchy in conventional organizations, there is in practice a tendency for the number of levels (layers) to increase over the course of time and as the total number of employees rises. As a result, conventional organizations are liable to have "tall" management structures with large numbers of hierarchical levels.

Conventional hierarchical structures are based on three principles derived from classical organization theory. These were discussed in Chapter 2. The first is the "scalar chain of authority" which is virtually a statement of hierarchy itself. The second principle, "unity of command," maintains that this chain of authority should not be muddied by multiple reporting links. The third principle is "span of control." This addresses the extent of a given manager's responsibility for subordinates in the sense of how many people should report to him or her. Cautions are raised regarding the breakdown in communication, control and coordination that may arise if a manager's span of control becomes too large. The significance of span of control for the slimming down of hierarchies through delayering (removing one or more levels) will become apparent later in this chapter.

The intimate connections that are made in conventional organizational thinking between hierarchy, authority and responsibility bear closer examination.[8] Authority is an essential feature of hierarchy. To be effective, according to Elliott Jaques, a manager's authority must include four elements:

1   The right to veto the appointment of any applicant to a job within the manager's area of responsibility who falls below the minimum standards of ability.
2   The power to assign work to members of her or his team.
3   The power to carry out performance appraisals and to make decisions about pay raises and merit awards.
4   The authority to initiate removal from the job, at least from the manager's own team.

Authority should also equate to the responsibility placed upon a manager. Although it has been criticized as unnecessarily rigid, this is a longstanding principle of management that is intended to avoid serious problems. For if a manger is allocated a level of responsibility exceeding his or her authority to obtain the resources and cooperation necessary to fulfill that responsibility, the result is liable to be ineffectual for the organization and stressful for the individual. On the other hand, if there is authority (power) in excess of accountability and responsibility for one's action, it becomes tempting to engage in arbitrary behavior and even downright corruption. In a literal sense, this imbalance breeds irresponsibility.

The contribution of hierarchy

I have already alluded to the ways in which hierarchy can meet some fundamental requirements in organizing large-scale activities. The most important of these lies in the way it identifies and nails down accountability. All organizations require a process through which work is allocated and its execution judged against performance criteria. This is necessary for aligning what people do, in a coordinated manner, with collective objectives. Although people can form their own judgments about how well they are performing, and make adjustments accordingly, the fact that they are not working in isolation requires a manager with responsibility for a group of people or units to assess their performance bearing in mind how each person or unit contributes in relation to the others. Even if people are organized into teams that have a group responsibility for what they achieve, they will still need to be accountable to a leader or manager. In some cases when a team's work is consequential for several different departments or even for the company as a whole, it may have to account to a group of managers sitting as a board or committee. The principle of accountability to a higher level in the organization, however, remains the same.

The hierarchical ordering of positions according to level of responsibility matches and supports this process of upward accountability. The clear identification of the positions in a company's hierarchies, so as to accord with different areas and levels of responsibility, makes it correspondingly easier to allocate unambiguous accountability for the exercise of those responsibilities. The contribution that hierarchy can make to nailing down accountability is, in principle, quite compatible with the mutual accountability of managers and their subordinates to each other, as occurs in the so-called "180 degree" assessment of individual performance. The reporting relationship between the two remains the same. Equally, there will still be a distinction in their responsibilities and therefore in the criteria for assessing whether or not they are carried out satisfactorily.

Decisions that a company has to make range between the routine and non-routine in a way that is also consistent with the logic of hierarchy. Routine decisions have relatively short-term consequences, relate to known parameters, and are amenable to procedures based on previous experience and precedents. It is often possible to apply decision rules that can be incorporated into IT based systems, for example in the re-ordering of standard stock items such as stationery. Although they are significant for the company, most routine decisions do not require high levels of judgment and discretion. In this sense, the taking of routine decisions does not represent a high level of responsibility and does not require a high level of authority. It may even become automated.

By contrast, non-routine decisions are normally more strategic in nature. They have longer-term consequences, involve larger commitments of expenditure, and require the exercise of judgment under conditions that are often highly uncertain. Even though some routine operational decisions do carry significant risk, especially if they have potential consequences for personal safety or the environment, the risks attending bad decisions at the strategic level are usually much greater. This means that much more responsibility attaches to strategic decisions. The relationship between routine and non-routine decisions is also hierarchical in nature. Routine decisions collectively comprise the parameters of a company's capabilities and as such have to feed upwards into higher-level strategic decisions. Procedures such as SWOT analysis (strength, weaknesses, opportunities, threats) underscore how a company's operational strengths and weaknesses should be taken into account when formulating strategies.

In these ways hierarchy mirrors a natural order in decision-making and can provide structural support for it. The hierarchical ordering of levels of decision responsibility has corresponding requirements in the abilities and skills that are required of people working at these different levels. The ordering of jobs into a hierarchy makes it easier to place people with the necessary competence at each organizational level.

The clear distinctions between different levels of decision-making that hierarchies reinforce become less tenable under conditions of rapid change and high innovation. It then becomes likely that developments at the operational level lose their previously routine nature, as when technological advance becomes increasingly rapid and innovations are introduced more frequently. Innovations can have major strategic implications, even to the point of rendering existing competitive strategies redundant. In such circumstances, it is no longer sensible to keep the people closely involved with routine decisions at arm's length from strategic decision-making and the rationale for hierarchy begins to break down accordingly.

A further contribution claimed for hierarchy also turns out to be a mixed blessing under conditions of rapid change and severe competition. Many people welcome a hierarchical structure that offers them the apparent security of "knowing their place" and being able to limit their liability for blame by kicking responsibility upstairs to their boss. A tall hierarchy also offers the prospect of promotion by relatively easy small steps. These characteristics help to account for the widespread acceptability of hierarchy as the natural structure for management. On the other hand, the coziness of hierarchy can readily breed a comfortable complacency and unwillingness to change that are not compatible with the turbulent conditions many businesses are experiencing today.

Negative features of hierarchy

Conventional hierarchy has therefore become increasingly dysfunctional for many companies. The barriers it imposes against adaptability and innovation offset the contributions it makes to efficient and orderly management. With its concern for the delineation of authority, responsibility and accountability, hierarchy tends to underwrite the status quo rather than an emergent adaptive mode of organizing. It breeds inflexibility. Not only that, but over time hierarchy tends to grow on itself adding appreciably to overheads.

It is a matter of simple mathematics to see that the more extended a hierarchy becomes, the more it increases the overhead cost of management. For example, if a company has 3,600 non-managerial employees, and a fixed number of 200 first-line managers, the number of managers it requires above the first-line level would amount to 102 with five levels in the hierarchy and only 41 with three levels.[9] The intervening factor here is span of control – the number of people reporting to each manager – as we shall see shortly when discussing downsizing and delayering. For each manager's salary that is saved, one can add further substantial savings in office and support costs. An approximate rule of thumb is that a manager's salary only accounts for about one-third of his or her total cost. There are also savings to be gained in less tangible costs, such as the additional time in meetings and other activities required to coordinate and control the activities of a large managerial group, the more complex communication process that is entailed, and so forth. The more that hierarchy can be reduced, the lower should be the level of managerial overheads a company has to bear.

One of the factors that can easily lead to a costly proliferation of managerial layers is confusion between the task-related justification for hierarchy, in terms of the authority and responsibility levels required, and non-task considerations to do with status. Jaques' field-based studies led him to the conclusion that there is never any justification for an organization to have more than six levels of management however large it is. Yet in practice, companies often have more levels than that, and public organizations even more still. One of the reasons for this is that titles become attached to pay grades, and responsibilities at a particular level get divided up in order to demonstrate status differences. Both these factors can result in a proliferation of titles such as deputy manager, assistant manager, and the like. Before long they easily become converted into distinct reporting levels where none is actually justified in terms of the work to be done or the decisions to be taken. This can easily lead to the kind of confusion and demoralization illustrated in Box 4.2 below. There is a strong argument for aligning salary structures to responsibility levels and, if appropriate, applying wide salary bands to each level to reflect experience and performance at that level.

BOX 4.2   A DEMORALIZING OVERLAP OF RESPONSIBILITIES

Elizabeth Mitchiner worked for the public corporation responsible for developing a new town in the UK. Her immediate manager was an older man, with general responsibility for the development social facilities in the new town. Elizabeth was responsible for designing and subsequently operating children's play and youth leisure facilities. These were located in a series of local district community centers, which opened one by one as the new town was built. As a university graduate, Elizabeth felt that she was capable of shouldering this level of responsibility. Indeed, she normally exceeded agreed targets. Her work was well received by users of the facilities, and she established good relations with medical staff, teachers, pastors and other professionals working in or near the community centers.

In the course of her work, Elizabeth needed to correspond frequently, especially with other units in the development corporation and members of the general public. She wrote these letters herself. Her immediate superior, however, despite having far less detailed knowledge of each case insisted not only on checking each letter, but also signing it under his name. This usually delayed the mailing of these letters, sometimes by several days. Return correspondence also came to his office, which he passed on to Elizabeth without any comment but often with further delay. The whole process impeded her ability to respond promptly to concerns or other requirements expressed in the letters.

The effect of this intrusion by a manager into her activities was extremely demoralizing. It was a factor behind Elizabeth's decision eventually to quit her job. It is possible that her manager had a high psychological need for control and had less confidence in Elizabeth because she was a woman and much younger than him. Laying aside such subjective issues, however, the level of his managerial responsibility was not sufficiently differentiated from Elizabeth's. Yet his superior position in a hierarchy gave him opportunity to interfere with damaging consequences.

Another factor that can encourage the extension of hierarchies is that promotion within tall structures, often accompanied by some symbols of status, is cheap and easy for a company. It is a popular non-financial reward that contributes to the status and most importantly to CV and future career prospects of an employee. Nevertheless, it can easily lead to a divorce between the formal levels in an organizational chart and real differences in responsibility.

In addition to the extra financial cost that results, unnecessary levels in a hierarchy can generate confusion even though paradoxically a fundamental justification for hierarchy itself is precisely the opposite, namely that it creates order. Having too many levels leads to overlapping responsibilities. In turn this gives rise to an unnecessary passing of problems up and down the system rather than their being resolved straightaway at the appropriate level. Managers will be liable to supervise work closely, and even contradict actions taken by those reporting to them, when in fact this should be unnecessary. When subordinates seek to have actions approved or decisions made, they will be tempted to bypass their immediate superior if in fact the latter are not located at a truly higher level of authority and cannot therefore give the necessary approval.

It is highly likely that negative motivational consequences will flow from this situation. People will feel that they are too closely monitored and that they are given too little scope for initiative. Box 4.2 provides an instance of the kind of problem that can arise. It was related to me personally.

The example in Box 4.2 provides an instance of how hierarchy can alienate a competent and motivated member of staff. It also brings to light another major problem associated with conventional hierarchy, namely its inflexibility in responding quickly to events. As in the example, action can be delayed by unnecessary interference across organizational levels, which compromises the ability of staff to react quickly to clients or other external parties.

One response that employees sometimes make to this problem has further negative consequence for the management process. They may try to carve out the autonomy they think they need by restricting communication upwards and reinterpreting the instructions coming down to them. In this way, staff can perhaps retrieve the ability to respond more rapidly and flexibly to changing events within their area of work. But further problems can result because it is not a way of doing things that higher management either recognizes or sanctions. It can lead to a serious restriction of upward communication that undermines the ability of senior managers to understand relevant events. It can also result in the hoarding of information within different sub-hierarchies rather than its dissemination to people in other parts of the organization who need it.

A large number of levels in the management hierarchy generally gives rise to communication problems and a feeling of distance between the top and bottom of a company. While electronic communications, especially email, can in principle go a long way to facilitating the sharing of information and opinions across organizational levels, these do not substitute for the exchange of views on an informal basis that can be extremely important for building a sense of identification between managers and different staff groups. Also I say "in principle" because in practice emails are often used for a top-down dissemination of information rather than for bottom-up communication and sharing of ideas.

Box 4.3 describes how communication problems arose in a medium-size company with many levels in its main hierarchy.

BOX 4.3   COMMUNICATION PROBLEMS IN A TALL HIERARCHY

A company producing drinks had approximately 1,200 employees and managers. There were eight levels in its main production hierarchy above the factory floor. The chief executive who valued his staff was keenly aware of what he called "communication problems" between himself and the company's operatives. He attempted to overcome these by somewhat unorthodox methods such as paying spot visits to the shop floor almost every day, working some days at operative jobs, and accompanying drivers unannounced on their runs to the company's distribution depots.

In themselves, these actions generated a high regard for their CEO among employees. This was at a cost, however, and did not solve the real problem. Production managers and supervisors greatly disliked this approach. They were apprehensive about what from their perspective was persistent "bypassing" of their authority. It was galling for them to be challenged by the factory staff on the basis that "the boss" had said something that went against their judgment. It was in any case questionable whether so much time and effort by the CEO aimed at improving communications was being judiciously balanced against the time required to perform other duties unique to his role such as developing long-term strategies for the company.

When asked to advise on the situation, I concluded that the effect of the CEO's methods was to generate a diffuse feeling that status barriers were being broken down, rather than to create the conditions for precise information to be communicated effectively on an everyday operational basis up and down the hierarchy. I recommended a reduction in the number of managerial levels through widening many of the spans of control within the managerial hierarchy. This turned out to make a significant contribution to resolving the problem and restoring greater balance to the CEO's use of time.

Source: Author's consultancy.

Hierarchy in new organization

These negative features of hierarchy can severely handicap companies subject to the forces of modern competitive conditions, which place a premium on adaptability and innovation. The evolution of new organization is therefore characterized by an attempt to minimize the aspects of hierarchy that are least suited to such conditions. The new approach to hierarchy is characterized by the following:

- Vertical relations are defined by the authority vested in a team or work unit rather than in an individual according to hierarchical rank.
- An imbalance between authority and responsibility may be tolerated rather than spending time and effort in trying to define them precisely in a fast-moving situation. Managers are expected to use their initiative and leadership qualities to overcome any ensuing problems.

- Decentralization is favored, along with distributed authority and initiative.
- Leadership is exercised through guidance based on collective vision rather than a system of command-and-control.
- Communication is open, with relevant information being widely and simultaneously distributed to all concerned.
- Control is no longer maintained primarily through personal supervision and adherence to rules and procedures. Instead, targets are agreed as performance markers; HRM policies for selection, training and appraisal are used to reconcile individual abilities and goals with collective requirements; and efforts are made to develop a common corporate culture and identity.
- There is a conscious attempt to minimize the number of hierarchical levels.

The revolution in communications technology has profound implications for the attempt to reduce traditional hierarchy and to shift from vertical relations towards more horizontal collaborative ones.[10] Intranets and the Internet facilitate the efficient working of flatter corporate structures and web-like teams that integrate different functions. With the aid of the new technologies, companies can more readily strip out layers of management and shift the pattern of communications from a downward flow along prescribed, hierarchical routes to a more multidirectional and networked process.

One of the factors that has traditionally led to the elaboration of hierarchical levels is organizational growth. For this reason, many companies have seized the opportunity to reduce the levels in their management structures (to "delayer") as they downsize. The movement to downsize has therefore been a major driver for the achievement of simpler structures.

◢ Downsizing and Delayering

Size and hierarchy

One of the most universal features of conventional organization has been the close relation between size and number of hierarchical levels. Size pushes up the layers of management, although at a decreasing rate. In studies conducted before the movement to downsize got under way in the mid-1980s, the typical figures for the configuration of size and levels are shown in Table 4.1.[11]

Table 4.1 Relationship between size and number of hierarchical levels

Total employment	Number of management layers above non-managerial employees*
100	2
500	3
1,000	5
3,000	6
10,000	7

*i.e., not including non-managerial employees as a level

The link between size and hierarchy lies in the average span of control, namely the number of people reporting directly to one manager. For an organization of a given size, the higher the average span of control, the fewer will be the number of levels in its management structure. There is, however, a limit to the span of control that a manager can accommodate. Once that limit is reached any further increase in size will push up the number of managers and eventually the number of levels in the managerial hierarchy.

The case of a university summarized in Box 4.4 illustrates how a chief executive's concern at having a large span of control led to a reorganization that added a hierarchical level within the structure. This had some significant negative consequences. An alternative solution, avoiding adding an extra level, would have been to reduce his span of control by delegating more decisions to subordinate levels in the organization, letting them handle them without reporting back to him. However, this solution appears not to have been considered.

BOX 4.4 NEGATIVE CONSEQUENCES OF ADDING A HIERARCHICAL LEVEL

The chief executive (president) of a university was experiencing overload. He had 24 different people reporting directly to him and decided that this was an untenable arrangement. This decision triggered a reorganization of the university's structure, which added an additional hierarchical level. At the new level, five colleges were created to which the existing schools covering broad subject areas such as Business, Law and Mathematics would now report. Each college recruited its own specialized staff for functional activities such as Alumni Relations, Human Resources, Marketing & Communications, Operations, Research, Teaching & Learning. These staff normally duplicated ones already in post in each school.

In addition to the considerable extra staff and overhead costs incurred by this additional hierarchical level, it led to several other negative consequences. These can be illustrated by the experience of the college concerned with social sciences. Micro-management by college officers of school matters gave rise to duplication of effort, with both upward flows (such as for approvals) and downward ones (such as communication of information) now passing over extra desks. Meetings in the schools were duplicated at the college level. Whereas previously the schools had discussed and formulated their own strategies, this initiative was now taken out of their hands. For some schools, such as the business school, this was a serious threat since one of the criteria for their external accreditation was that they could demonstrate a clear strategy. The introduction of the college level accentuated the already existing tendency to treat schools that were attractive to students, and hence large income earners, as cash cows to subsidize less successful schools. In the attractive schools, the ratios of students to staff increased with consequently growing pressure on academic staff time, including that to undertake research and writing. Their research performance suffered as a result and with it their esteem among peers within the college. The business school's ranking in annual international quality tables began to fall steadily. Annual surveys among academic and professional staff indicated a sharp deterioration in morale and trust in college leadership. Turnover among staff accelerated.

The early pioneers of management science maintained that six was an absolute limit to the span of control that a manager can effectively cope with when the work of subordinates interlocks and therefore requires coordination.[12] More recently, we have come to understand that the limits to spans of control are variable depending on a number of considerations. A very important one is the willingness of a manager to delegate decision-making to his or her subordinates. However, the following factors tend to limit a manager's span of control:

1   The manager has to devote a portion of time to non-managerial duties, as might be the case with a chief engineer.
2   Subordinates (the people reporting to the manager) need to interact intensively and they are not able to do this of their own volition.
3   Subordinates are working on dissimilar tasks.
4   New problems regularly surface in their work.
5   Subordinates are physically dispersed.
6   The competence and level of training of subordinates is low.
7   It is necessary to control the work of subordinates through an extensive amount of direct personal supervision.
8   A high proportion of the communication between managers and those reporting to them requires face-to-face interaction and cannot be conducted through other means such as email.

Clearly the way that work is organized and the extent to which it can be supported by information and communications technologies will have a bearing on the spans of control that can be sustained without either a breakdown of the managerial process or of the overloaded manager. Although the qualifying factors listed allow for a considerable variation in spans of control, there is always an upper limit beyond which serious dysfunctions start to occur. This upper limit means that as employment in an organization grows, so do pressures to add to the number and levels of management. The reversal of employment growth through downsizing therefore offers an opportunity to delayer management.

Downsizing

Downsizing is the planned elimination of positions or jobs. Jobs are categories of positions that are similar in their main duties, such as cost accountants or computer programmers. Downsizing can occur as a result of falling demand, the automation of work, or the decision to reduce the amount or range of work taken on through, for example, outsourcing some of it (see Chapter 9). Downsizing achieved through the elimination of functions and units can reflect a reduction in the diversification of a company's outputs, and/or the outsourcing of certain activities. It can also be achieved through reducing hierarchical levels and the number of managers. Downsizing and delayering are complementary insofar as reducing hierarchical levels is a means to achieve downsizing, while delayering is facilitated by the reduction in a company's overall employment.[13]

There is an important distinction to be made between "reactive" downsizing and "strategic" downsizing. Reactive downsizing refers to situations in which reductions in employment are made, often across the board, in response to external events and short-term needs. This form of downsizing was prevalent among American companies in the 1970s and early 1980s, when many adopted it as a response to increasing international competition, especially from Japanese firms in the manufacturing sector. At that time, it was common to require each department to cut a given percentage of its employees without regard to that department's strategic value. This indiscriminate form of downsizing fails to consider whether different departments can bear cuts without disproportionate losses in efficiency, or indeed whether certain parts of the company embody unique competencies or areas of special knowledge that must be protected.[14]

Strategic downsizing is sometimes called "rightsizing." It refers to a process that is carefully thought-out and designed to support long-term organizational strategy. In other words, this approach to downsizing recognizes that it provides an opportunity to achieve an organizational transformation towards lean production, re-engineering, a focus on core competencies or other aspects of organizational reform. By the mid-1980s, the combination of worldwide competition and recession forced large numbers of American firms to compete more effectively and to adopt a more strategic view of downsizing. Downsizing began to be combined with attempts to reorganize onto a more effective basis through re-engineering, and in the 1990s through drawing a clearer distinction between core and peripheral activities.

A purely reactive approach became evident again in the economic downturns post-2000 and post-2007, when the temptation was to cut costs in any way possible across the board in the attempt to restore profit margins.[15] Nonetheless, some companies in recent years have gone beyond regarding downsizing as simply a reaction to economic downturn. They now take a strategic view and accept the benefits of smaller size, including the opportunities for organizational reform that it offers. Others, however, still take the view that if they ask everybody to cut a little, it will not hurt in any one area too much and they can keep all their activities intact.

The adoption of downsizing in America and other developed economies was rapid and widespread. For example, between 1987 and 1991, over 85 percent of the *Fortune 500* corporations downsized their white-collar personnel. Huge numbers of people were involved. IBM cut its size down by 400,000 workers in 1992 and by mid-1993 the US Postal Service eliminated 30,000 of its 130,000 management jobs.[16] The economic downturn of 2000–2002 led to a fresh wave of downsizing. In 2000, American companies cut 614,000 jobs and announced almost 2 million job cuts in 2001.[17] It was estimated that 8.6 million jobs were lost from the start of the recession in 2007 to the beginning of 2010.[18] One of the largest downsizing programs was that of the UK Post Office, which at the beginning of 2002 announced plans to shed up to 30,000 jobs, 10,000 of these being in middle management. The company's board clearly associated downsizing with delayering. It was reported to believe that "huge savings can be achieved by stripping away layers of 'inefficient' middle management."[19] Subsequently, downsizing programs were announced in both Canadian and US postal organizations.

Context and reasons for downsizing

Many of the reasons for downsizing arise from economic and technological changes in the business environment. The competitive pressures arising from deregulation and the lowering of market entry barriers have forced firms to deflate their previously oversized bureaucracies and slim down their management structures in order to reduce overhead costs and speed up decision-making. Rationalization is one of the most important benefits claimed for mergers and acquisitions, and the periodic waves of M&A have been one of the drivers of downsizing.

Another factor has been investment in more efficient, labor-saving technology, which has reduced the numbers of direct employees required. ICT has also reduced the numbers of middle managers required for the preparation and processing of information.

In addition to the economic arguments for downsizing, there are other less evidently rational reasons. The motivation to enhance "shareholder value" through downsizing has not always been beneficial to the companies concerned. It has resulted from hostile takeovers by other companies calculating that their targets could be made to deliver better returns, at least in the short term, through being forcibly slimmed down. Leveraged buy-outs financed by aggressive finance houses have had similar effects. These developments produce financial gain for the raiders, and they have made corporate managers more alert to the need to use shareholders' investments productively. The generally short-term orientation adopted by corporate raiders, however, renders them asset strippers rather than asset enhancers, and it is by no means proven that their activities are rational in terms of the long-term viability of the firms concerned.

Leveraged buy-outs in particular, as the term indicates, are financed through large amounts of borrowed money. This involves indebting a company and then slimming down its structure, if not stripping its assets such as R&D, in order to help pay off the debts. This hollowing out can be at the expense of the competitiveness and productivity of the company. The route to downsizing through acquisitions and buy-outs therefore tends to lead to a distribution of corporate assets to stockholders. It contrasts with the earlier period up the 1970s when most companies adopted a policy of retaining and reinvesting profits in the company.[20]

An even clearer instance of non-rationality is seen in the way that downsizing became a management fad. Many corporate managers felt that their company should adopt a downsizing program because others were doing so. As Newsweek commented in 1996, "Firing people has gotten to be trendy in corporate America, in the same way that building new plants and being considered a good corporate citizen gave you bragging rights 25 years ago."[21] In swimming with the collective tide, managers frequently failed to attend sufficiently to the organizational logic of downsizing, to the experience and skills that were being lost, or to the effects on the commitment and morale of the staff who remained.

Performance consequences of downsizing

Downsizing is expected to provide various performance benefits. Among the economic benefits are lower costs, the adoption of a "lean and mean" managerial psychology, and a number of organizational benefits. Lower costs are seen to offer a more predictable contribution to a company's bottom line in periods of economic downturn than increased revenues, which may be difficult to achieve at a time of falling or stagnant demand. A lean and mean managerial psychology is seen to focus on the reduction of waste and to concentrate effort on activities that contribute most added value.

Downsizing is also expected to convey a number of organizational benefits, especially when it is used as an opportunity to reduce the number of levels in a company's management hierarchy. It can then be a means to cut administrative overhead costs. A slimmed-down management structure should provide a basis for reducing bureaucracy, especially the reliance on formal meetings and elaborate procedures. Other benefits expected to flow from a simpler and less bureaucratic management structure are improved communications, speedier decision-making, and the spreading of initiative through the organization.

Although it may be achieved in part by outsourcing certain activities, downsizing is anticipated to result in greater productivity for the activities that are retained. For downsizing to result in higher productivity, however, certain conditions must apply. These can be tough, and are often ignored in practice:

- Work has to be reorganized so that tasks previously carried out by others, including managers, are now added to the jobs of people remaining in the company. This job "enrichment" will not necessarily be unwelcome to the people concerned if it means a genuine enhancement of their responsibility and authority, matched by increased compensation. If these criteria are not met, disaffection and demotivation are likely to result.
- A downsizing program should not have a psychologically negative impact on the staff who remain. One of the problems with downsizing is that it often gives rise to a "survivor syndrome" in which the remaining managers and staff experience negative effects in terms of anxiety, guilt, apathy, disengagement and other mental and emotional states that result in poor morale, productivity loss, decline in quality, and more workplace injuries.[22] Both employees who lose their jobs and those that remain can see this as an employer breaching the trust that they may previously have had in the organization as a "good" employer. Downsizing achieved through layoffs appears to have a more negative effect on survivors that does downsizing achieved through offshoring and outsourcing, or where efforts are made to help departing employees achieve a transition to new jobs through "outplacement."[23]
- The people who leave the company should not be essential staff with special knowledge and capabilities and who subsequently have to be re-hired, often at inflated consultancy rates. Box 4.5 provides an example of the disaster that can follow the loss of essential specialists and the critical knowledge they possess.
- The tasks retained by the downsizing company should add greater value than those it has chosen to terminate or outsource.

BOX 4.5 DOWNSIZING AND LOSS OF CORPORATE MEMORY

In 1999, there was a serious rail crash at Ladbroke Grove, London in which 31 people died. The public inquiry that followed revealed evidence to show how the loss of critical knowledge and expertise by the train companies was an underlying cause of this disaster. Specialists had lost their jobs after British Rail was privatized in 1996 and the middle managers who remained did not understand the everyday activities of their staff. A loss of "corporate memory" gave rise to inconsistency and confusion over procedures for train drivers. Also many of the new recruits to jobs where train safety was an issue were inexperienced or inadequately trained.

Source: Alison Maitland. "If downsizing, protect the corporate memory." *Financial Times*. October 16, 2001, p. 18.

Although the direct costs of laying off employees can be significant, the often long-term indirect costs may be even greater. If it is not managed strategically, downsizing can undermine the success of a business in several ways. Productivity can drop when high performers leave as morale decreases. Business can be lost as a result of fewer salespeople. The company may be able to introduce fewer new products because it now has fewer R&D staff members.[24]

Survey results indicate that downsizing of employment has not, on the whole, had a positive effect on financial performance, either in terms of return on assets or stock price. By contrast, the downsizing of assets, through selling off businesses and outsourcing, has been found to improve ROA.[25] Negative effects of employment downsizing on company profitability were found to be particularly marked in industries that are R&D intensive, labor intensive and fast growing.[26] One of the reasons for these poor performance outcomes undoubtedly lies with the elements of non-rationality and unconcern for a company's long-term benefits noted above. There are, in addition, problems in ascribing changes in company performance to downsizing. For instance, while companies that are doing badly have the most incentive to downsize, the root of their poor performance may lie elsewhere. If there are more fundamental causes, such as a poor record in new product development, downsizing will not necessarily lead to improved corporate performance.

The way that downsizing is planned and implemented can also have a major impact on its success. The incidence of survivor syndrome is likely to be greater when downsizing is carried out in a manner that appears arbitrary and threatening. In other words, the most negative reaction to downsizing and associated layoffs is liable to occur when:

- Job insecurity increases, perhaps because redundancies are compulsory rather than voluntary.
- The process is perceived as unfair, both in the procedure followed and in the way that people are selected for disengagement.
- The company fails to adopt a socially responsible approach in assisting the people affected by downsizing to transfer to new jobs.
- The intrinsic attraction of the job is reduced, perhaps because of the additional pressure of work now bearing on the employees who remain.[27]

When downsizing is planned in advance so that it can be accomplished through voluntary redundancy rather than being imposed, it is less likely to lead to survivor syndrome. Similarly, downsizing has more chance of achieving positive financial results when a company makes an effort to assist redundant people, and to retrain those who remain to shoulder greater responsibility. If a company handles downsizing badly and creates considerable insecurity, it runs the risk of losing its core group of employees to competitors as well as discouraging talented people from applying to join it in the future.

Box 4.6 gives examples of the socially responsible stance towards implementing downsizing that is likely to produce better results both for a company and its employees.

As Chapter 13 will show, the members of an organization are much less likely to accept changes that they perceive as arbitrary and threatening. This means that the opportunity downsizing creates for more extensive changes in organizational form is very likely to be jeopardized if employment is scaled down in an unacceptable manner. This may result in a wide mistrust of the organization not just among its members but in the wider community as

---

BOX 4.6   A SOCIALLY RESPONSIBLE APPROACH TO DOWNSIZING

Some companies like Hewlett-Packard and Volkswagen have minimized the layoff of employees through a flexible and socially responsible approach. The measures they have taken include reducing standard hours and wages, redeployment and retraining, laying people off (or granting sabbaticals) for limited periods without pay but without losing pension rights, voluntary severance, and confining recruitment as far as possible to sources inside the company.

In the UK, Pilkington Glass undertook major restructuring over a long period of time in the face of competition and technological change. This resulted in substantial job losses. In a socially responsible initiative, the company established a trust that sponsored job-creating schemes. These schemes helped with advice on financing new businesses and securing facilities for them. They assisted nearly 1900 start-ups and created 15,800 jobs.

Source: L. Bilmes and K. Wetzker. "Wise tending in the jobs garden." *Financial Times*, 3 June 1996, p. 12.

---

well, which could have negative impacts on the attitude of government agencies and consumers in the marketplace. The implications of how downsizing is introduced are therefore of wider consequence than simply the reduction of employment or assets per se.

Delayering

A flatter structure is central to new forms of organization and is achieved by a reduction in the number of layers in the management hierarchy. Delayering has been advocated as a means of simplifying management structures, reducing bureaucracy, cutting communication paths, speeding up decision-making and pushing responsibility down to lower organizational levels ("empowerment"). While downsizing should facilitate delayering according to the span of control criterion, the two are not necessarily connected. Companies might seek to secure the benefits of delayering for their own sake without downsizing as well. For instance, Craig Littler found from surveys of Australian firms conducted in 1995 and 1998 that almost 11 percent had delayered without downsizing.[28]

Littler and his colleagues found from surveys of 2,964 firms in Australia, New Zealand and South Africa conducted in the mid-1990s that delayering had become a widespread managerial strategy. The incidence of firms that had delayered in the previous two years ranged from 37.5 percent for New Zealand to 44 percent for Australia and 45.5 percent for South Africa.[29] A survey of 3,500 large and medium size European companies found that during the period 1992 to 1996, 30 percent of them took out organizational layers.[30] Rather surprisingly, 20 percent of the firms actually increased their management layers during the same period, presumably as a consequence of increased size or complexity. Among the firms in Littler's three-country surveys that had delayered, some 10–11 percent subsequently relayered. The overall trend, however, appears to be a largely one-way street, towards reducing layers of management.

Delayering impacts primarily on managers, especially middle managers. The flattening of the management hierarchy reduces opportunities for promotion and hence appears to restrict career paths. I say "appears" because its real impact on managerial advancement need not be negative. Delayering offers managers an opportunity to assume greater responsibility at an early point in their careers and also to receive more favorable compensation for so doing. The process of delayering, however, can generate survivor syndrome effects similar to those of downsizing. The greatest negative impact on managers and employees is therefore to be expected when delayering and downsizing are introduced together, especially when there are repeated bouts of downsizing.

Downsizing and delayering are liable to incur considerable psychological and social costs. A forward-looking and enlightened approach to both, intended to minimize negative effects and to offer the maximum assistance to people who are displaced from their jobs can mitigate these effects. As already noted, a knee-jerk approach to downsizing and delayering in response to crisis is likely to create anxiety, hostility and stress, with these symptoms typically being manifested by increases in the length of sickness absence.[31]

From Hierarchies to Teams

Delayering is conducive to the decentralization of authority and initiative. By simplifying management structures, delayering also makes it easier to introduce better communications and teamworking between different departments and units. Teams can be formed to bring together people from different units. They can also comprise people who were previously located at different hierarchical levels. Delayering and teamworking are complementary. The collapsing of hierarchical levels into teams is one of the ways in which organizational structures can be simplified and the activities within them made more focused. The move from hierarchies to teams means that instead of authority being vested in individual managers, it becomes vested in a team or work unit. This may have the benefit of reducing inter-departmental rivalry if the reorganization of staff into teams means that department heads can be removed. Teams have to include people who have the necessary expertise, skills and information to reach decisions. Similarly, they must have the authority and ability to ensure that decisions reached by the team are efficiently and effectively executed. The faster that operating cycles become, and the more integrated that the processes supporting them are required to be, the more appropriate is a team-based approach than a traditional hierarchical one. As Lynda Applegate observed:

> "Once operating processes have been integrated and streamlined, the rigid boundaries that enabled segregation of authority to a single boss in a single functional unit are destroyed. So are the time and inventory buffers that allowed managers to sift through information carefully and pass it up the hierarchy for decision. Now marketing, sales, manufacturing, and purchasing must meet together to decide whether to change a price or offer a special promotion and the decision must be implemented within weeks rather than months."[32]

Applegate identifies common examples of teams. Operating teams are comprised of middle managers from a range of relevant specialties who are given authority to define, execute, and manage operating strategy. In the flatter delayered structures that characterize new organizational forms, these teams are usually located between the two levels of front-line employees and senior management. A major petroleum products firm provides an example of restructuring from a traditional hierarchy to area operating teams. In the mid-1980s, the firm had nine levels in its managerial hierarchy above its operators. With restructuring, the levels above operators were reduced to four. Area operating teams reporting to operations managers were now located immediately below them. The teams replaced what had previously been four levels of middle management. Other kinds of team include those that manage their work autonomously, process management teams created to coordinate, control and improve operating processes, and knowledge-creating teams established to generate new ideas and solutions in line with corporate objectives.

Teams and teambuilding are discussed further in the following chapter, regarding their contribution to organizational integration.

SUMMARY

1   Despite the widespread disparagement of hierarchy, most companies find it very difficult to avoid it once they have grown beyond a very small size.

2   In conventional organization, hierarchy is characterized by a clear ladder of authority and responsibility that forms a "chain of command." Hierarchy amounts to a vertical form of specialization, based on the three historic management principles of a scalar chain of authority, unity of command and span of control.

3   One reason for the persistence of hierarchy is that it meets people's needs for a "pecking order" of status and power. Other reasons, however, relate to the efficient functioning of an organization, such as:
    • the appropriateness of differentiating levels of authority and responsibility in order to distinguish different levels of decision-making and accountability;
    • the belief that hierarchy follows naturally from leadership;
    • the need to appoint layers of managers to control and coordinate a large, complex organization.

4   Conventional hierarchy, however, has become increasingly ill-suited to modern business conditions in which a firm's capabilities to adapt and innovate are essential to its competitiveness. Its negative features include:
    • maintaining the status quo;
    • creating vertical communication barriers;
    • making poor use of the talents that people lower down the organization can offer;
    • increasing managerial overheads;
    • generating poor morale among employees and a sense of distance from senior management;
    • corrupting genuine levels of responsibility into mere differences of status.

5   The evolution of new organization forms is characterized by an attempt to reduce the aspects of hierarchy that are least suited to current conditions. The aim is to minimize hierarchy and introduce simpler structures in which there are opportunities for

bottom-up initiatives, more open and wide-ranging communication, and the greater involvement of all staff. Authority is increasingly vested in teams, rather than being confined to specified hierarchical positions. Communication is more open, with information being widely distributed. Control is maintained less through direct managerial supervision than through targets and internalized norms.

6   There is also a conscious attempt today to minimize the number of hierarchical levels. Delayering is closely associated with downsizing because size has a major impact on the number of hierarchical levels. In many cases, downsizing is simply a reaction to a short-term deterioration in company performance. A more strategic view of downsizing, however, recognizes the opportunity it provides to introduce organizational reforms.

7   The performance consequences of delayering and downsizing are affected by the way they are introduced. Without careful planning, safeguards for employees and incentives to retain vital staff, downsizing can have major negative effects on the remaining managers and staff, and also lead to a serious loss of corporate memory.

8   One of the ways in which delayering can be achieved is to collapse hierarchical levels into teams. Teams offer other potential organizational advantages, especially for integrating cross-departmental or specialist contributions.

QUESTIONS FOR DISCUSSION

4.1   What are the chief features of hierarchy in conventional organizations? What are the principles on which these features are based?

4.2   Describe and evaluate the negative aspects of hierarchy.

4.3   How is hierarchy modified in new forms of organization? What are the principles on which these modifications are based?

4.4   If we wished to, could we eliminate hierarchy in the way we organize collective activity?

4.5   What are the main reasons for the persistence of hierarchy in organizations?

4.6   Distinguish between downsizing and delayering, and discuss how they are potentially related.

4.7   How might delayering be achieved in a constructive manner – in other words, to avoid potentially negative consequences?

4.8   Do you think we are making sufficient use of teams in contemporary organizations as a means of reducing hierarchy?

NOTES

1   Elliott Jaques (1990), In praise of hierarchy, *Harvard Business Review*, Jan/Feb, pp. 127–133.

2   On the BBC see Robert Budden and Robert Cookson (2012), Corporation in crisis: "Bloated" ranks of managers under fire, *Financial Times*, 13 November, p. 2. On the Bank of England see Chris Giles,

Brooke Masters and Claire Jones (2012), Bank of England's culture attacked: Reviews criticise deference and hierarchy, *Financial Times*, 2 November, p. 1.

3   Ricardo Semler (1993), *Maverick!* London, Random House.

4   Jane Simms (2002), Keeping up appliances, *The Director*, February, 46-49.

5   J.D. Mooney and C.A. Reiley (1931), *Onward Industry! The Principles of Organization and their Significance to Modern Industry*, New York, Harper. Joe C. Magee and Adam D. Galinsky (2008), Social hierarchy: The self-reinforcing nature of power and status, *Academy of Management Annals*, 2, 351–398.

6   Kipfer, B.A. (2001), *The Order of Things: How Everything in the World is Organized into Hierarchies, Structures and Pecking Orders*, New York, Random House.

7   Kieser, Alfred (1987), From asceticism to administration of wealth. Medieval monasteries and the pitfalls of rationalization, *Organization Studies*, 8, 103–124.

8   This discussion draws on the work of Elliott Jaques (1956), See in particular his books: *Measurement of Responsibility*, London, Tavistock Publications and *A General Theory of Bureaucracy*, London, Heinemann (1976).

9   C.W. Barkdull (1963), Span of control: a method of evaluation, *Michigan Business Review*, 15, 25–32.

10 Frances Cairncross (2002), *The Company of the Future: How the Communications Revolution is Changing Management*, Boston, Harvard Business School Press.

11 For a summary of evidence see John Child (1984), *Organization: A Guide to Problems and Practice*, London, Sage, Chapter 3.

12 Lyndall Urwick (1956), The manager's span of control, *Harvard Business Review*, May–June, 39–47.

13 Garry D. Bruton, J. Kay Keels, and Christopher L. Shook (1996), Downsizing the firm: answering the strategic questions, *Academy of Management Executive*, 10, 38–45.

14 Wayne F. Cascio (2002), *Responsible Restructuring*, San Francisco, Berrett-Koehler.

15 Michael Skapinker (2001), How to manage in a downturn, *Financial Times*, 9 April, p. 21; Douglas McIntyre (2010), The Layoff Kings: The 25 Companies Responsible for 700,000 Lost Jobs, *Daily Finance*, August 18, http://www.dailyfinance.com/2010/08/18/the-layoff-kings-the-25-companies-responsible-for-700-000-lost/, accessed April 8, 2014.

16 Wayne F. Cascio (1993), Downsizing: What do we know? What have we learned? *Academy of Management Executive*, 7, pp. 95–104.

17 Rewarding employees, *The Economist*, 2 February 2002: 65.

18 Zuckerman, M. (2010), The great recession continues, *The Wall Street Journal*, 22 January: A19.

19 John Waples and Rory Godson (2002), Consignia to cut 30,000 jobs in drive for mail efficiency, *The Sunday Times*, 13 January, p. 2.

20 William Lazonick and Mary O'Sullivan (2000), Maximizing shareholder value: a new ideology for corporate governance, *Economy and Society*, 29, 13–35.

21 *Newsweek*, 26 February 1996: 44. Quoted in James R. Morris, Wayne F. Cascio, and Clifford E. Young (1999), Downsizing after all these years: questions and answers about who did it, how many did it, and who benefited from it, *Organizational Dynamics*, Winter, pp. 78–86.

22 Craig R. Littler (2000), Comparing the downsizing experiences of three countries: a restructuring cycle? In Ronald J. Burke and Cary L. Cooper (eds.), *The Organization in Crisis*, Oxford: Blackwell, Chapter 4.

23 Carl P. Maertz Jr., Jack W. Wiley, Cynthia LeRouge, and Michael A. Campion (2010), Downsizing effects on survivors: Layoffs, offshoring, and outsourcing, *Industrial Relations*, 49(2), 275–285.

24 Wayne F. Cascio (2010), *Employment Downsizing and Its Alternatives*, Alexandria, VA, Society for Human Resource Management Foundation.

25 James R. Morris, Wayne F. Cascio, and Clifford E. Young (1999), op. cit. These authors report results from a survey of 3,628 American companies over a period of 15 years.

26 James P. Guthrie and Deepak K. Datta (2008), Dumb and dumber: The impact of downsizing on firm performance as moderated by industry conditions, *Organization Science*, 19, 108–123.

27   Kenneth P. De Meuse, Mitchell L. Marks, and Guangrong Dai (2010), Organizational downsizing, mergers and acquisitions, and strategic alliances: Using theory and research to enhance practice. In Sheldon Zedeck (ed.), *APA Handbook of Industrial and Organizational Psychology*, Washington, DC: American Psychological Association, 3, Chapter 21.

28   Craig R. Littler (2000), op. cit.

29   Craig R. Littler, Retha Wiesner, Richard Dunford (2003), The dynamics of delayering: Changing management structures in three countries, *Journal of Management Studies*, 40, 225–256.

30   Andrew M. Pettigrew and Evelyn M. Fenton (eds.) (2000), *The Innovating Organization*, London, Sage 2000, 37.

31   Mika Kivimäki, Jussi Vahtera, Amanda Griffiths, Tom Cox and Louise Thomson (2000), Sickness absence and organizational downsizing. In Ronald J. Burke, and Cary L. Cooper (eds.), *The Organization in Crisis*, Oxford, Blackwell, Chapter 5.

32   Lynda M. Applegate (1995), Designing and managing the information age organization, Harvard Business School Note # 9-196-003, pp. 14–15.

CHAPTER 5

Achieving Integration

WHAT THIS CHAPTER COVERS

This chapter focuses on the contribution that organization can make to the achievement of integration. Integration is a condition of cohesion and synergy between the different, but complementary, activities that collectively create value. It is a vital product of good organization, though often under-emphasized.

The first section looks at the need for integration, which has become harder to achieve as organizations become more complex and differentiated. Various areas in which integration problems can arise are then identified. The chapter goes on to illustrate how poor integration can lead to disaster while good integration can create a valuable dynamic capability. A further section points out warning signs that integration needs are not being met, and a helpful diagnostic tool is presented. There is a choice of organizational mechanisms intended to promote integration, each suited to different levels and types of integration need. The closing section discusses teamwork as an important and frequently used way of improving integration.

The Concept

Integration signifies cohesion and synergy between different roles or units in an organization whose activities are different but interdependent in the process of creating value. Its meaning comes very close to that of coordination. I shall use coordination to refer to the process of aligning the activities of people or their units so as to achieve a state of integration. In their review of coordination in organizations, Okhuysen and Bechky define coordination as "the process of interaction that integrates a collective set of interdependent tasks" and they view it as "a central purpose of organizations."[1]

One can look for integration in vertical relations, where it would refer to the result of a process of cohesive control, in which plans are implemented as intended and adequate feedback is provided on results. This is the subject of Chapter 6. The term integration is, however, more usually applied to horizontal or lateral relations across an organization, or between a number of organizations that form a network to accomplish a given task. This chapter focuses on coordination and integration within organizations, while Part III, chapters 9 to 12, considers aspects of integration between organizations.

The Need for Adequate Integration

Integration needs are more pressing than ever as companies adopt increasingly complex operational configurations in response to globalization and intensive competition. To take advantage of the opportunities offered by globalization, companies are widening the scope of their international markets and sources of supply. Multinationals are also distributing their production globally, to locations that offer favorable cost and resource benefits, while international service providers are opening a wider range of locations so as to be close to major new clients. As a company develops its international activities in these ways, it is no longer sufficient to manage them through the mechanism of a single, dedicated division. Their multi-functional and multi-regional nature becomes too complex for that solution. Such companies now require integration through a system that pulls together multi-dimensional activities – typically some form of matrix organization.

The growing intensity of competition is another key factor that presents new integration needs. The effects are evident within all major functional areas, but especially marketing, R&D, and quality assurance. Markets can be expanded and margins increased through a greater sensitivity to different market segments. This gives rise to a wider variety of products and services, which in some industries have to be complemented by local after-sales support. In order to maintain some consistency within this more complex marketing portfolio and to ensure it is aligned with the capability to supply, more intensive coordination is required.

Within R&D, there are three salient factors that are increasing integration requirements. One is the need to achieve shorter times-to-market in order to compete in terms of new product availability. Getting new products or services to the marketplace in less time than before obliges companies to engage in concurrent rather than sequential development activities. Concurrent development imposes new integration requirements between upstream and downstream activities, particularly in preventing information lacunae. A second factor is the trend toward locating its R&D activities close to a company's major markets, both to align projects better with market needs and also to tap into new sources of scarce, highly-qualified, scientific personnel. Companies are also entering into an increasing number of R&D and technology partnerships with each other. The more that R&D and related activities are dispersed around the world and/ or between different companies, the greater the challenge of integrating them around the goals of particular projects and programs. Third, while the huge expense of R&D in some industries is encouraging technology partnerships, it makes the duplication of research effort within a company extremely expensive. This can support the case for a company to concentrate at least its core R&D strengths. If this policy is adopted, the company's R&D facilities may have to serve a number of its businesses simultaneously, which creates another kind of integration need. The rationalization of R&D within pharmaceutical companies provides an example of this third trend.

The shift in developed economies from manufacturing to service work has also seen the expansion of new forms of creative work such as software design, media services and medical treatments. This shift presents new coordination demands as the range of specialisms has grown, as multiple solutions are often possible and as creative work involves networking between the staff of an organization and external collaborators. As a result, formal mechanisms cannot be relied upon to produce adequate integration and informal modes of collaboration and coordination have become more salient.

Quality assurance is a further area in which coordination has become increasingly vital. Companies are generally expanding both their product range and geographical focus. In order to maintain the integrity of a company's brands and reputation, it has to ensure consistent levels of quality across a broader range of production and distribution locations. This generates both a control and an integration requirement. The coordination requirement is primarily one of ensuring that information on product manufacturing and delivery, or on service delivery, is adequately transmitted to a central quality assurance unit, and that the company prepares its dispersed staff adequately to ensure consistent quality policy and standards.

Achieving Integration is a Challenge

Lack of integration is one of the charges most frequently leveled against organizations. "The right hand doesn't know what the left hand is doing" is an often-heard complaint of clients and customers.

It is relatively easy to state the need for adequate integration, but it is not so straightforward to achieve it. Curiously, it was for some time given less attention than other subjects in the literature available to managers. Achieving integration generally presents a greater challenge in countries that have strongly individualistic cultures, such as Britain and the USA, than in countries such as Japan whose cultures are more oriented toward group and other collective activities. Integration problems are common in many walks of organizational life. The following examples illustrate how wide-ranging these problems can be.

Integration between functions

One of the most common problems of integration appears in the relationship between different functions or specialties within a company. It presents most noticeably in the relations between functions that have continuously to adapt to the external environment, such as sales, customer relations, and purchasing, and those that are responsible for maintaining standards of production and design. This is the problem of integrating the "peripheries" of an organization with its "core." Without this integration, an organization cannot remain viable.

A problem concerning integration between sales, production and engineering functions in a manufacturing company is described in Box 5.1. The company in question tackled the problem by introducing greater product modularity and a method to facilitate the exchange of information between the three functions. The result was a performance improvement in terms of better delivery punctuality, reduced loss of time due to reworking, and a reduction in obsolete stock.[2]

An example of a significant failure due to inadequate integration between the different sections of an organization concerns the failure of General Motors to withdraw faulty ignition switches

BOX 5.1   IMPROVING INTER-FUNCTIONAL COORDINATION

A project was carried out in the Italian subsidiary (employing around 300 people) of a large multinational group – Finn-Power Italia – manufacturing automated bending machines. Its products are characterized by high variety and frequent product changes. The aim of the project was to devise ways to better align sales, production planning and engineering goals and to coordinate their activities. A team of researchers worked in close contact with managers, participating in the project's design and implementation.

The problem being faced was that the simultaneous presence of both high product variety and frequent product changes led to "coordination problems mainly due to the difficulty of carefully exchanging information on product changes, proposed both by designers and salespeople, and aligning forecasting/purchasing activities with sales-people's estimates and product change plans."

Two main changes were introduced following the study. The first was great product modularity which reducing internal variety i.e. the proliferation of components and subassemblies. This helped to align sales and production goals. Also by simplifying design activities, greater product modularity helped to reconcile the need of sales for frequently changing products and the engineering goal of reducing the number of components subject to redesign. The second change was the introduction of a "product configurator" which was seen by the project members as "an additional tool to facilitate inter-functional coordination by supporting the exchange of information or forecasting/ purchasing activities, aimed at overcoming inter-functional barriers caused by different functional area perspectives."

Source: Pamela Danese and Pietro Romano (2004), Improving inter-functional coordination to face high product variety and frequent modifications. *International Journal of Operations & Production Management*, 24(9), pp. 863–885.

from several of its models. The faulty switches may have caused airbags not to deploy in frontal-impact crashes contributing to over a dozen fatalities. Even though some staff had known about the problem for over eleven years, the company did not take appropriate action. A report by Anton Valukas, a former US attorney, released in June 2014 pointed to the "information silos" created by GM's fragmented structure as one of the factors contributing to this lack of action. Information was not shared among the relevant sections of the company, including information on fatalities, which should have engendered a sense of urgency. The report recommended a number of steps be taken to prevent such communication breakdowns in the future. These included a formalization of coordination between functional groups concerned with safety issues through, for example, establishing an appropriate cross-functional committee; the introduction of systems for disseminating information and sharing expertise; and the specific allocation of responsibility for overseeing the company's scheme for employees to voice safety concerns and to ensure that these were followed up.[3]

Operational integration

A major challenge in operations is making available to production a range of necessary support services on a continuous and reliable basis. These services concern technological support (such as industrial engineering, production engineering, and quality control); finance (budgetary control, costing, and management control information); personnel (such as recruitment, training and performance management); and planning (production control). In a large and complex multi-product, multi-line facility, the integration of these services to production management is a formidable task.

One attempt to achieve more adequate integration in this area was made in the large confectionery plant of a multinational food corporation. The concept employed was that of the "factory director's team." This was first applied to functional heads and then progressively cascaded down in the form of integrated teams at lower levels. Previously, production, quality control, industrial engineering, maintenance, management accounting, labor relations, employment, and other activities were organized in a strictly functional manner. This was not, however, conducive to an effective working relationship between production and the service-providing functions. For example, departmental production managers found that the information on costs and variances being presented by management accountants was not in a format suited to their needs, but one that was dictated by conventions originating in the financial director's office.

By contrast, the factory director's team is highly integrated across functions, comprising the factory director and his immediate production subordinates, the senior management accountant, the manager in charge of production services (primarily factory and employment services), the labor relations managers, and quality control managers. At the next level down in the production hierarchy, senior production managers are in turn supported by their own teams, comprising management accountants, production services, and quality control specialists. The management accounting function has been broadened into a "financial performance" role oriented to assist in performance improvement as well as financial control.

This method of integrating production and ancillary services has greatly improved both the quality of information available to production and the standards of production performance. Over a period of years, it has also facilitated the planning and introduction of new plant in which, through the use of IT, production scheduling, quality, cost, and maintenance aspects are combined into an integrated information and control system. In addition, the development has permitted a considerable reduction in staff numbers, the process of which has been handled by personnel in close conjunction with forward production planning.

There is always room for debate as to which functions should be integrated with production in the formal reporting sense. In the case described, quality control and HRM were not directly accountable to production. The reasons for this were to preserve an independent view on the quality standards that are particularly critical in a food company and, with HRM, to preserve what are seen to be economies of scale and functional rationalization given that it also services all the office areas on the site (including several divisional and head office departments). Another feature worth noting in this case is that, in addition to lateral integration via the creation of production management teams, vertical integration has been fostered by the overlapping hierarchical membership of those teams. Following the principle of "linking-pins" first advocated by Rensis Likert, production managers are members of their hierarchical superior's team.[4]

Other integration problem areas

Other areas in which problems of integration commonly occur are in: (1) the coordination between head office and divisions in a multidivisional company; (2) innovation; (3) concurrent development; and (4) the coordination of complementary services offered by members of different professions.

INTEGRATION BETWEEN CORPORATE AND DIVISIONAL LEVELS

The case of a large, diversified company illustrates how the separation between corporate and divisional levels within a multidivisional structure can create a serious problem. In this instance, business development was the uncoordinated activity. The company had a head-quarters corporate planning function, which saw its role as gathering information to assist in finding completely new areas of business into which the company could diversify. Each of its divisions also had its own planning department, securing and evaluating outside information that might indicate desirable modifications to existing products. These two levels of scanning and planning activity were totally uncoordinated, so that no effort was being put into possibly the most fruitful area for expansion, namely the development of new products within the company's existing area of business. Planners at each level, both corporate and divisional, assumed that the other was covering this particular aspect of R&D.

INNOVATION

A great deal of attention has been devoted to scientists and other creative specialists and how their work can be organized to promote more effective innovation of products and processes.

This challenge breaks down into two potentially conflicting integration requirements, relating to the invention and implementation stages of the innovation process. In broad terms, these two stages focus respectively on what James March called the "exploration" of new knowledge and the "exploitation" of existing knowledge.[5] For effective invention, a key requirement is to integrate the contributions of the different creative specialists themselves. From this point of view, informal team working is usually desirable, provided the necessary autonomy is granted to develop creative solutions. This helps to provide the group with an identity and freedom from interference, which should motivate the creative processes and encourage cohesive working practices. The second requirement, however, is for creative and inventive developments to be integrated with a company's strategy and main-line activities. This means that the creative group must be given clear goals and not be isolated from other departments or units on whose work the successful implementation and commercialization (in the case of a new product) of the innovation depends. The creative group has to maintain a bridge to the rest of the organization for its work to be guided appropriately and for new developments to be accepted. This reflects the basic requirement that, for profit-seeking companies at least, invention has to be informed by considerations of commercial implementation and adoption.

The organizational mode commonly employed to satisfy these requirements is the project team, which is discussed later in this chapter. This is set up for the life of the project to see it through to completion. Although their mode of working is normally informal, project teams are typically provided with some structure in terms of objectives, progress milestones and budgets. The team draws together all the people who can make relevant contributions, though its composition may change as the project passes through different stages. In order to meet both the invention and implementation requirements of innovation, it is important to include as members of the project team, not only appropriate scientific and technical staff, but also representatives of the other main-line areas that are concerned with a new project's economic viability. In the case of a new product, this concerns its potential attractiveness to the marketplace and whether it can be produced efficiently and reliably. The other relevant areas here include the marketing or customer contact functions, costing, and production engineering or its equivalent function. Studies of innovation indicate that one of the most frequent reasons for commercial failure in new products is a lack of understanding of customer needs, pointing to a serious absence of integration between research and marketing personnel.

CONCURRENT DEVELOPMENT

This refers to the practice of executing linked development activities in parallel rather than in sequence. It has become the common mode of organizing product development in industries such as automotive manufacturing in which, since the 1980s, time-to-market has gained in importance as a competitive factor. The following observation by Christian Terwiesch and colleagues succinctly describes the nature of the integration challenge in such a situation:

> "Given tight project schedules, many engineers cannot afford to wait until all required information is available, and have to start 'in the dark,' requiring close coordination with other independent activities. Coordination among tightly coupled (interdependent) and parallel tasks forces parallel teams to share preliminary information about work in progress. Production tool orders have to be based on rough sketches of product designs, product concepts must be developed while uncertainty remains about the customer's needs, and components must be specified while interacting systems are still under development."[6]

These considerations give rise to two fundamental coordination problems. The first concerns how people working upstream in the project can inform people downstream that the information they pass on is only preliminary in nature. The second is how the downstream people should use the preliminary information, and ascertain its level of accuracy and whether it will change. These problems represent the challenge involved in integrating interdependent upstream and downstream activities to achieve the most efficient outcome.

COORDINATION OF PROFESSIONAL SERVICES

The integration of different professional specialties is always difficult because of differing cultures and strong persuasions of occupational identity. Many MBA students will have experienced this problem among their instructors, which has led most business schools to make special efforts to integrate subject specialists within effective program teams. Social services constitutes another area of professional work, and here poor integration has had tragic consequences. In Britain, several recent cases of child death might have been avoided had there been closer working relations between the specialist groups involved. The Seebohm Report on the development of the social services in England and Wales, published in 1968, specifically called for the improved integration of specialist contributions through a move away from existing divisions between health, children, welfare, psychiatric, and other fields toward the creation of a "generic" approach. Too often it had been the case that, for example, a problem of family breakdown had been treated separately by different professional specialists, at the expense of coordination between them and to the bewilderment of the clients. Following the Seebohm Report, social services departments have tackled this problem in several ways – normally either by creating generic social work teams in which specialists work together, or by giving individual social workers sole responsibility for cases. The problem, however, has not been resolved. An official report of October 2002 on *Safeguarding Children* noted inconsistent interpretations of their responsibilities by the eight separate services that work closely with children.[7] More recently, the failure of the authorities in London to prevent the battering to death of a 17-month-old boy ("Baby P") was partly ascribed to failures of communication and coordination between the different specialists involved in his case – health, police and social services. Box 5.2 contains an extract on this point taken from an official report presented to the UK parliament in 2009 on arrangements to safeguard vulnerable children that was prompted by the case.

Healthcare is another field in which the integration of different professional contributions remains a continuing challenge. Healthcare is provided by a range of professions and disciplines, which in most countries are organized in discrete, specialist hierarchies along functional lines. In the British National Health Service, laterally related teams and working groups have been used for many years in an attempt to coordinate across these specialist boundaries. For example, the use of teams has been considered necessary to integrate contributions from the different areas of expertise and perspectives of medicine, nursing, administration, and finance at the local district level of health service administration. There are also numerous teams of healthcare and related service providers, such as doctors, nurses, social

---

BOX 5.2 CONTINUED INTEGRATION PROBLEMS BETWEEN PUBLIC PROFESSIONAL SERVICES

"It is evident that the challenges of working across organisational boundaries continue to pose barriers in practice, and that cooperative efforts are often the first to suffer when services and individuals are under pressure. Examples of poor practice highlighted to this report include child protection conferences where not all the services involved in a child's life are present or able to give a view; or where one professional disagrees with a decision and their view is not explored in more detail; and repeated examples of professionals not receiving feedback on referrals. As a result of each of these failures, children or young people at risk of neglect or abuse will be exposed to greater danger . . . This needs to be addressed if all local services are to be effective in keeping children and young people safe."

Source: Lord Laming 2009. *The Protection of Children in England: A Progress Report*. London: HMSO, paragraph 4.3. Department for Education, protected by Crown copyright.

workers, and psychologists. One constraint on the working of such grass-roots teams lies in the individual responsibility that doctors carry for the patients under their care. This militates against the principle of team responsibility and accountability.

Poor Integration Can Lead to Disaster

The example of professional personal care highlights the fact that a failure of integration can literally be disastrous. Avoidance of potential disaster is one on the prime reasons why organizations need to ensure the adequate integration of their interdependent activities. There are indeed cases where the system virtually breaks down when this is neglected. The result is at best delay, frustration, and waste. At worst, the consequence may be loss of life. Let us consider three examples, one some time back and the others more recent.

A special report of the Carnegie Endowment brought to light the misadministration by two of the world's largest famine relief organizations of aid, for 22 million people affected by the West African drought after 1968. The American Agency for International Development (AID) and the United Nations Food and Agriculture Organization (FAO) were the two agencies in question. The aid that countries donated was generous in itself – up to October 1973 over 20 countries had provided over $150 million. Yet sickness and malnutrition continued at an alarming level, considerably worse than that recorded at the time in Bangladesh. The report identifies inadequate bureaucratic organization as the culprit, with several instances of poor integration. For instance, warning telegrams from the drought-stricken area were not sufficiently collated or acted upon – instead they were tucked away in filing cabinets scattered around the world. Even when the rescue operation got under way, plans proved to be uncoordinated. Grain piled up in Dakar, Senegal, because there was insufficient transport to move it inland. An observer said that the only plump animals he saw in the area were the rats of Dakar port. The report alleges that these failures were due in part to a lack of cooperation between different groups; it states that, in spite of the dedication of many officials at all levels, the entire program was overlaid by the shadow of bureaucratic factors in the USA or UN that bore hardly any relation to the human suffering in Africa – programs continued or initiatives neglected out of institutional inertia, rivalries between offices and agencies, and an unwillingness to acknowledge failures to the public.

Is this an extreme case? In terms of its human impact, yes, but as an example of inadequate organizational integration, no. Here is a somewhat more recent example.

The case relates to a company called Railtrack, which as part of the privatization of Britain's railways in the mid-1990s, was set up to maintain and develop the network, so providing the infrastructure services for the privatized train operating companies. In October 2001, the company was taken into administration by the UK government, a move that forced trading in its stock to be suspended and which was a precursor to its restructuring into a not-for-profit organization called Network Rail. Public and political frustration with Railtrack stemmed from several problems, including massive cost overruns on modernization projects, heavy losses, and the daunting imposition on public funds all this threatened.

Another, more dramatic, source of public loss of confidence in Railtrack, however, was the fatal derailment that occurred at Hatfield, north of London, on October 17, 2000. This disaster, which followed a previous fatal crash outside London's Paddington terminus in 1999, exposed a significant failure of integration in the company's arrangements for track maintenance. The *Financial Times* outline of events leading up to the Hatfield crash is reproduced in Box 5.3 below. Interestingly, the

BOX 5.3 "COUNTDOWN TO DISASTER"

Winter 1999: tell-tale pieces of flaking rail are first spotted on the track near Hatfield during a weekly routine inspection by Balfour Beatty. The company reports the problem to Railtrack's zone headquarters at York and recommends "grinding" the rail to get rid of the cracks. Six hundred trains a day pass over the tracks.

December 1999: Balfour Beatty decides the problem is serious enough that the rail needs to be replaced – which would be done by another contractor, Jarvis Fastline.

January 2000: Balfour Beatty tells Railtrack that the rail needs to be replaced.

February 2000: Railtrack engineer inspects the problem rail.

March 2000: Railtrack decides that the rail is in such a bad state that it needs to be replaced as a "priority #1," the highest category of urgency. This means that the rail should be changed within one month. No speed restriction is put into place. A "possession" – when no trains would run so that work could be done – is timetabled for Sunday, March 19, and a special train is booked to deliver the rails to the site three days before. But the train – owned and run by Railtrack and managed by Jarvis – is late. The rails cannot be dropped, and the re-railing possession is lost.

April 2000: Two weeks later another rail drop is booked but fails because the overhead electricity lines – run by Balfour Beatty – have not been depowered. The following week a third drop is frustrated because the train is late again and can only set down some of the rails before having to move on. At the end of the month, a fourth attempt is made six weeks after the first try. The rails are delivered.

May–August 2000: Railtrack takes four months to agree a time to complete the re-railing with Jarvis – even though it has a regular four-hour gap between trains every night and eight hours every weekend.

August 2000: Managers from Railtrack and Jarvis finally agree to a possession, and a date for re-railing is set for the last week in November.

September 2000: Railtrack becomes increasingly alarmed about the deteriorating rail and orders it to be "ground" by another contractor, Serco. Balfour Beatty's track inspector walks the line after grinding and it looks much better. But engineers now fear that grinding the rail in such a bad condition might have done more harm than good.

12.23 pm, Tuesday, October 17: The rail breaks under the wheels of the 12.10 GNER London to Leeds express – just hours before the Balfour Beatty inspector starts out on his weekly check. Four people in the buffet car die, 70 more are injured, and the UK railway crisis begins.

Source: Financial Times, February 22, 2001: 4.

integration problem arose from the company's adherence to one of the orthodoxies of new organization, namely focusing on its core competence – managing and developing the railway network – and outsourcing routine, low value-added tasks such as maintenance.

Track maintenance may have been considered a routine, low-value-added activity, but it is of course vital to train safety. To carry it out, Railtrack had seven prime contractors, which in turn farmed out the work to over two thousand subcontractors. Evidence submitted after these crashes brought to light alarming consequences of these organizational arrangements. It pointed to a breakdown in the old comradeship between track workers that used to mean problems were easily spotted, repairs made, and people could talk to each other. It also pointed to a growing lack of control over the staff and the standard of their work.[8]

There was a fundamental lack of integration within the system that followed the break-up and privatization of the former state railway organization. The failure was evident both in the organization of maintenance work and in relations between the constituent companies that now comprised the system. The constituent companies constantly battled among themselves. The contractors fought with Railtrack to get access to the tracks, and Railtrack fought with the train operating companies who did not want their schedules disrupted. Even within Railtrack, there were constant disputes between departments, such as production and signaling. Three years after the disaster, in a move to improve integration, Network Rail (the successor to Railtrack) decided to bring all maintenance in-house across the rail network and to transfer maintenance functions from private contractors to itself.

The third example of a major disaster in which poor integration was a contributory factor is the Columbia Space Shuttle accident of February 1, 2003. The physical cause of the disaster was a breach in the Thermal Protection System on the leading edge of the shuttle's left wing, caused by a piece of insulating foam which separated and struck the wing shortly after launch. The official Columbia Accident Investigation Board identified a number of organizational shortfalls that led up to this accident, and these are summarized in Box 5.4. Poor integration was one of these failings, including barriers to communication between mission managers and working engineers over the problem of the foam strike. The report concluded that: "deficiencies in communication . . . were a foundation for the *Columbia* accident. These deficiencies are byproducts of a cumbersome, bureaucratic, and highly complex Shuttle Program structure and the absence of authority in two key program areas that are responsible for integrating information across all programs and elements in the Shuttle program."[9] More specifically, "within the Shuttle Program, the Orbiter Office handles many key integration tasks, even though the Integration Office appears to be the

---

BOX 5.4 ORGANIZATIONAL CAUSES OF THE COLUMBIA SPACE SHUTTLE ACCIDENT

"Cultural traits and organizational practices detrimental to safety were allowed to develop, including: reliance on past success as a substitute for sound engineering practices (such as testing to understand why systems were not performing in accordance with requirements); organizational barriers that prevented effective communication of critical safety information and stifled professional differences of opinion; lack of integrated management across program elements; and the evolution of an informal chain of command and decision-making processes that operated outside the organization's rules."

Source: Columbia Accident Investigation Board, Report. Washington, DC: Government Printing Office, August 2003, p. 9. Sourced from NASA at http://www.nasa.gov/columbia/home/CAIB_Vol1.html

more logical office to conduct them; the Orbiter Office does not actively participate in the Integration Control Board; and Orbiter Office managers are actually ranked above their Integration Office counterparts. These uncoordinated roles result in conflicting and erroneous information . . ."[10]

The Columbia Shuttle and Hatfield rail accidents may be extreme and thankfully rare examples of how a failure in integration can lead to disaster, but shades of the same problem affect many organizations quite frequently. A more typical example, which was mentioned in Chapter 1, concerned the company that had one division laying people off while another division was recruiting similar staff in the same locality. This instance of poor integration did not threaten human life but was nonetheless quite damaging to the reputation of the company involved.

◢ Good Integration Can Create a Dynamic Capability

While inadequate integration can have serious negative consequences, the other side of the coin is that possessing a superior integrating capability can offer a clear advantage to companies facing strong competition.

The crucial difference between a company's simply possessing a set of good resources and having a distinctive competitive competence lies primarily in its ability to integrate those resources and apply them flexibly to take advantage of new opportunities. This ability is captured by the concept of "dynamic capabilities." David Teece defines these as "the capacity to sense and then to seize new opportunities, and to reconfigure and protect knowledge assets, competencies, and complementary assets and technologies so as to achieve sustainable competitive advantage."[11] The creation of a dynamic capability requires effective integration between the people who are sensing new business opportunities and those who decide on the configuration of assets and competencies to take advantage of these opportunities.

The conventional organizational approach relies on securing the integration between opportunity and response through top management coordination and decision making. The new organizational thinking favors the decentralization of such initiatives so that the people directly concerned can come together and decide on how to reconfigure capabilities without having to rely on, and wait for, the decision of senior managers distanced from the scene.

The use of direct integration in this decentralized manner has been termed "the lateral organization," in contrast to the traditional "vertical" or hierarchical organization.[12] The decentralization is accomplished by recreating an organization in microcosm for the issue at hand. Each unit, holding or representing a relevant asset – knowledge, technology, human resources, connections to external resource providers, and so forth – contributes a representative to the collective resolution of the issue. This forms a decision group by drawing together relevant people laterally across the organization. The group is the equivalent of a general manager for the matter being addressed. It clearly has the potential to act quickly and flexibly because it integrates the people with the relevant knowledge directly, without relying on any intermediaries or external coordinators. If an organization uses a lateral approach, it can increase its capacity to make decisions more frequently and/or more rapidly. There is also likely to be an enhancement of decision quality because this approach gets people with the requisite knowledge and resources directly involved. Lateral integration therefore aims to bring together the capabilities needed to seize an opportunity or deal with a problem in a dynamic and creative way.

Jay Galbraith notes that there are three general types of lateral organization. One coordinates across functions. The second type coordinates across business units. The third type coordinates across countries.[13] We have already observed several examples of the need to integrate across functions, and briefly looked at some of the solutions adopted. The case of the SMH company, established to rescue the Swiss watch industry, provides an example of how integration across business units *and* countries was used to revitalize an organization threatened with extinction.

As Box 5.5 relates, Nicholas Hayek rescued a situation in which the two giants of the Swiss watch industry, SSIH and ASUAG, both faced bankruptcy in the face of low-cost competitors from Japan, Hong Kong, and the USA who had adopted new electronic technologies in watch

BOX 5.5   INTEGRATION AT SMH TO CREATE A DYNAMIC CAPABILITY

On becoming CEO of SMH, Hayek had to decide how to restructure the company so as to achieve his strategic objective of winning back the mass market for watches and restoring profitability. In the event, he was able to move from a situation in which SMH suffered a loss of $124 million on sales of $1.1 billion in 1983 to a profit of $2.1 million on sales of $2.1 billion in 1993.

His strategy was to combine the Swiss reputation for excellence with technologically innovative production techniques and exciting, sharply delineated product lines to compete across the entire spectrum of the global watch business. The task was to devise an organization that could support this strategy. He integrated product development and manufacturing across business units by combining more than 100 small, inefficient manufacturing and assembly operations into one. This provided major economies of scale and justified the subsequent introduction of new, state-of-the-art technology. The combination of mass production and new technology massively reduced production costs.

Hayek also decentralized marketing, sales, and distribution in order to integrate these functions across countries around the company's major product lines. These functions were placed under global product managers. At the same time, SMH appointed a country manager wherever it sold watches, in order to maintain and strengthen its localized customer connections.

The dynamism of SMH's capabilities was tremendously invigorated by these new groupings, which provided for integration around key competencies and focal points. The company was fashioned into a decentralized global operation totally dependent on the dynamics between its managers, namely their willingness and ability to negotiate and cooperate across the boundaries of function, product, and geography. In order to have managers in place who could operate in this flexible manner, Hayek eventually replaced every member of the original executive team.

Source: David A. Nadler and Michael L. Tushman. *Competing by Design: The Power of Organizational Architecture*. New York: Oxford University Press 1997: 71–72, 85–86.

design. When Swiss bankers took over the two companies, they combined them into a new company called SMH. They asked Hayek, the founder of one of Switzerland's leading consultancy companies, to advise them on how to save the combined operation. They then persuaded him to purchase a controlling stake in SMH and become its CEO.

The operation that Hayek took over was extremely fragmented. It had a collection of over 100 different brands, each with its own research and development, manufacturing, and marketing functions. The brands were mostly aimed at customers in countries around the world. So when it was formed, SMH was a hodgepodge of competing fiefdoms. In order to restore a competitive edge and profitability to SMH, Hayek had to find a way of integrating across functions, business units, and countries.

Signs that Integration Needs Are Not Being Met

Conventionally organized companies are increasingly unlikely to cope with the integration needs imposed by the requirement to make and implement decisions under conditions of uncertainty and time pressure. There are some common warning signs that integration needs are not being met and that action has to be taken to improve the company's integrative capacity.[14]

1. *Persistent conflict between departments.* The important point here is to recognize when the same matters of dispute keep recurring. When this happens, conflict has become inherent and amounts to much more than the occasional disagreement which is to be expected on new issues as they arise and which can produce a healthy variety of suggested solutions. Persistent conflict indicates a basic failure in integration. It becomes particularly insidious when the people or units involved start to accept it as normal. This is the point of danger at which a threat to performance arising from an underlying integration problem has come to be taken for granted.

2. *Fudging integration issues through a proliferation of formal meetings.* Formal meetings, such as committees, are themselves important integrative mechanisms that have the advantage of representing various interests and hence of preserving a balance of view and power between departments. Committees and working parties can, however, end up by fudging inter-departmental disputes and may delay their resolution. They are easy to set up and can readily proliferate into a hierarchy. They only meet periodically and their very balance of interests coupled with established committee procedure can give rise to procrastination and inadequate compromises. A spreading of committees is therefore paradoxically a sign that adequate integration is probably not being achieved through more appropriate means. Committees can be effective mechanisms for achieving consensus over matters that involve the application of given rules and procedures. They are extremely poor mechanisms for achieving an integration of effort around a task to be done or for encouraging the informal exchange of views and tacit knowledge.

3. *Overloading of top management.* One mode of integration is to refer matters requiring coordination between departments further up the hierarchy, ultimately to the chief executive. This clearly places an additional burden on that role, which will conflict with the time demanded by other matters that also have to be attended to, and can only be dealt with adequately at that level – in particular major policy issues and relationships with important parties outside the organization. Top management overload can therefore be another sign of inadequate integration. In its extreme form, chief executives and senior managers may protect themselves by deliberately avoiding contact with departmental heads seeking to see them with

coordination problems. If this happens, the hierarchical relationship will have broken down and clearly it would be a better solution to encourage middle managers to work together on issues at their own level rather than pushing them upwards for a decision.

4. *The ritual of "red tape"*. The use of procedures and rules set out on paper, and perhaps monitored by reports on paper, is another conventional way in which management may seek to ensure that integration takes place. The procedures can, for example, specify that consultation should take place between two departments on certain matters. A warning sign is when managers and other members of an organization cease to follow the procedures or to take paper reporting seriously, and these simply become rituals. This does not mean that the red tape should then be enforced; probably the contrary since it may well signal that the procedures are inappropriate and that this is perhaps an unsuitable way to secure integration in the situation concerned.

5. *Empire-building by coordinators*. Later on in this chapter, we mention the need that often arises to support the coordinator's position so the person in that role can exercise sufficient influence over the departments he or she is supposed to coordinate. This may mean providing the coordinator with support staff. It is important, however, to ensure that coordinator roles are not built up too much. A sign that they have outlived their usefulness comes when coordinators start to oppose attempts at simpler forms of direct integration that appear to bypass them. If coordinators attempt to monopolize coordination and block more innovative solutions to achieving integration, then the writing is clearly on the wall.

6. *Complaints by clients, customers, and other external parties*. A sure sign of inadequate integration is when persons who have dealings with the organization from outside complain, for example, that they are told one thing by one department and then given conflicting information by another department; when they have to contact a succession of people from different departments over a single issue; or when staff in one department profess ignorance and even indifference as to who elsewhere in the organization may be of assistance. These are actually very common failings that clearly detract from the quality of service an organization is providing and which may, in a commercial context, lead to the loss of valuable business.

◄ A Diagnostic Tool

These warning signs point to the distinct possibility that an organization has a significant integration problem. One can then apply a simple and economical diagnostic tool, which I designed, and which in my experience is useful for the initial task of identifying the areas of difficulty. It asks the managers and/or members of the units involved in a system in which problems are indicated to provide their own perceptions of where the issue is focused and what is going wrong. They are asked to complete a form of the kind shown in Figure 5.1, either privately or in a short interview.

The example shown in Figure 5.1 comes from an international airline, for which the form was originally designed. It shows how a particular respondent has scored the relationships between different units of the airline. In this case, integration between Flight Operations and In-flight Services is seen as very poor. Since these two specialties must coordinate closely in providing the airline's direct service to the public, their failure to do so would give rise to serious delays, and this was in fact happening. It was also indirectly creating poor morale among aircraft crews, which had a deleterious effect on the atmosphere around the passengers.

We would like to know about relationships between different parts of the organization.
Listed below are 8 statements; each of these might be thought of as describing the general state of the relationship between various units.

Would you please select the statement which you feel is most descriptive of relationships between each of the units, even if you are not directly involved in them.

Scoring of relationships
Relations between these two units are:

1. Sound – full unity of effort is achieved
2. Almost full unity
3. Somewhat better than average relations
4. Average – sound enough to get by even though there are many problems of achieving joint efforts
5. Somewhat of a breakdown in relations
6. Almost complete breakdown in relations
7. Couldn't be worse – bad relations – serious problems exist which are not being solved
8. Relations are not required.

* In-flight Services Scheduling is part of Marketing while pilot scheduling is part of Flight Operations thus creating frequent conflicts between two groups.

Matrix of relations between operation units

	SALES	AIRPORT SERVICES	IN-FLIGHT SERVICES	SCHEDULING ADJUSTMENTS	OPERATIONAL CONTROL	FLIGHT OPERATIONS	MAINTENANCE	RELATIONS BETWEEN REGIONAL DIVISIONS
SALES								
AIRPORT SERVICES	3							
IN-FLIGHT SERVICES	4	3						
SCHEDULING ADJUSTMENTS	3	4	2					
OPERATIONAL CONTROL	3	2	2	1				
FLIGHT OPERATIONS	3	3	6*	1	1			
MAINTENANCE	8	2	4	2	1	2		
REGIONAL DIVISIONS/ OFFICES	2	2	3	2	1	3	2	1

Figure 5.1 Example of a method to assess perceptions of integration within an organization

The form itself can be adapted to suit any type of organization. The matrix it contains can be used to build up a collective assessment of the adequacy of inter-unit relations. When inadequacies are indicated, by a score of 4 or more, the form can be followed up by inquiring (1) what the respondent thinks are the reasons for the inadequacies and (2) the problems that arise from them. Having responses from people in each unit helps to indicate whether perceptions of the problem are shared and whether there is a large measure of agreement across the organization on what is going wrong. As with other systematic ways of seeking opinion from within an organization, this method provides a basis for identifying and then discussing possible improvements.

◢ The Choice of Integrating Mechanism[15]

We have just discussed ways of identifying integration problems. Integration is, however, a fundamental need in any organization and will not simply happen by default once a unit larger than a primary group with face-to-face relations is involved. It is therefore always necessary to decide on what the appropriate integrating mechanisms are for a given situation. This is especially important because an inadequate approach to integration runs the risk of inviting the kind of failures discussed earlier in this chapter. On the other hand, an over-elaborate approach will add unnecessary costs and may have the demoralizing effect of being seen as irrelevant and time-wasting by the staff involved. So, how can one make the right choice?

Fundamental questions to ask

The warning signs of integration failure are often the start of a diagnosis leading to the identification of improvements to be made. The kind of diagnostic tool just described can also help to pinpoint the location of the problem. A good management, however, will try to assess the effectiveness of its organizational integration without waiting for a crisis to develop. It can do this by asking some relatively simple questions.

The first step is to reflect on whether the following circumstances apply:

1   Are the activities performed by different people or units within the organization highly *interdependent*? Would the quality of the product or service benefit from a better organizational adjustment to that interdependence? For example, would the quality of an advertising campaign benefit from copy and graphics specialists working in the same client team?

2   Are *unanticipated changes* arising in the activities to which different people or units contribute and which the normal processes are not dealing with satisfactorily? For instance, do people have to deal with these changes in an ad hoc manner on the run, as it were?

3   Would a company's competitiveness, or a public institution's ability to meet public need, benefit from a *compression of the time* it takes to respond to requests or offer its products and services?

4   Is *management time* being taken up unnecessarily with organizing meetings and ensuring that information is communicated between different staff and units, at the expense of dealing with other matters?

Affirmative answers to these questions strongly suggest that the organization needs to improve its levels of integration. The next set of questions that have to be asked then become more specific:

1 What kind of integration is required?
   1.1 What information needs to be exchanged and/or decisions made?
   1.2 What form does the information take? For example, is it formalized and explicit, or is it informal, judgmental, and tacit? Are the decisions routine in nature or do they concern new developments?
   1.3 Who needs to exchange or share the information or participate in the decision process?
   1.4 How frequently does the information need to be exchanged and decisions taken?
   1.5 Is it possible to predict when these requirements will occur?
2 What are the difficulties of achieving the required kind of integration?
   2.1 What difficulties arise from differences of specialty and perspective?
   2.2 What problems arise from the physical location of participants?
   2.3 What problems arise from the inherent difficulty and uncertainty of the issues to be resolved?
3 What are the pros and cons of alternative integrating mechanisms?
   3.1 Effectiveness in meeting requirements.
   3.2 Costs, including the opportunity costs of people's time and concentration, and possible costs of personal travel.

Diagnosis along the lines suggested prepares management for the choice it has to make between alternative integration mechanisms, including possibilities of using different mechanisms to suit different requirements. We now review the approaches to integration commonly used in conventional organization, and follow on with the emphasis on lateral coordination that characterizes new organizational thinking.

There are basically two traditional approaches to ensuring integration. One relies on passing all issues requiring coordination up to the manager that has overall responsibility for the activities concerned; the other on anticipating all or most integration requirements by relying on formal procedures, plans, and/or schedules drawn up in advance.

Integration by a higher manager

Relying on a higher manager to provide integration is an effective and economical approach only under certain conditions. First, the need to coordinate should not arise too frequently, otherwise the manager will become distracted from other tasks and probably overloaded. Second, the manager must be in a position to communicate closely with the people whose work requires coordination. Third, the situation should be one in which the manager is actually the person best able to exercise judgment as to what needs to be done. Fourth, the staff reporting to the manager must respect his or her judgment and be happy with referring matters upward rather than dealing directly with them.

These conditions favoring integration through personal managerial involvement often no longer apply. If a company is operating with a flat structure, managers' spans of control will be too large for them to become involved in day-to-day coordination. If the members of their teams or reporting departments are scattered around the world, then time differences will also require a different solution. If the work around which different people's contributions have to be integrated is of a creative or problem-solving nature, then they are likely to possess more relevant expertise than a higher manager. This also speaks in favor of coordination through direct contact. In these circumstances, people working interdependently will still require guidelines and regular approval from a higher manager, but that manager cannot effectively integrate the work itself.

Integration through formal procedures and planning

The traditional bureaucratic approach to integration relies on three primary mechanisms. The first is integration via standardization. This involves the establishment of rules, procedures or specified duties that are intended to channel the actions of each jobholder or department into a direction consistent with the actions of others. Job descriptions and rules for the membership and conduct of committees are examples. Procedures can be devised to cope with emergencies, so long as their nature can be anticipated even though the timing of their occurrence cannot, and this is essentially what public emergency services do. The second bureaucratic mechanism is to establish plans and schedules so as to coordinate the actions of separate units. Integration via planning is somewhat more flexible than standardization in that plans can usually be modified fairly quickly. The third mechanism is the formal standing meeting, typically the committee.

Rules and procedures are modified and extended over time. They formalize what experience has shown to be best practice in handling a set of recurrent problems. By formulating a body of procedures and operating plans, the contributions of separate departments can be clearly specified and so integrated into the task of the organization as a whole. If exceptions occur, and these are really seen to be aberrations from a routine, then they can be referred up the hierarchy to a point where the various departments concerned share a common boss. Integration, in other words, is also maintained by hierarchical referral when something out of the ordinary crops up. This is the principle of "management by exception." If matters of procedure and operating policy require some discussion or modification from time to time, the third bureaucratic mechanism for integration can be actuated, namely the committee meeting. Committee meetings allow for members of the organization to come together and agree on adjustments to procedures and policies.[16] If the matter falls outside their defined decision powers, committees can refer a recommendation up the hierarchy for approval. Under stable conditions, a program of such meetings is often arranged for twelve months ahead.

There are some merits to this bureaucratic system of integration, which can operate quite adequately when conditions are stable and predictable. Many people like to know where they stand, and bureaucratic integration is based on a system of clearly defined roles and procedures that are there for all to see. It is also a relatively cheap approach to integration, once its procedures and systems have been well tried and tested. It does not require any overhead of special coordinating staff, nor does it necessarily call for a great deal of manpower to be locked up in "endless meetings." Nevertheless, once an organization moves into less stable conditions and the requirement for information processing increases, the traditional bureaucratic approach to integration begins to creak in its joints.

This has been the experience of many companies. They have found it necessary to increase the intensity of direct contact between groups and departments at approximately the same level. In the absence of any formal provision for such lateral integration, informal contact will often arise. One often hears people say, "If we had to go through the official channels, we would never get anything done on time." The problem is that one cannot necessarily rely on effective informal arrangements emerging and those that do may not reflect the policy priorities set down for the organization as a whole. There is also the danger that informal coordination will not yield an adequate record for others to use in the future. So there can be great benefit from adopting a considered policy of developing lateral coordination as a normal rather than exceptional process.

Lateral coordination

Lateral coordination is an approach to integrating the contributions of different people or units in an organization all performing parts of a common task. It does this through fostering direct contact and mutual adjustment between the contributors so that they, rather than higher management, can make the decisions necessary to achieve their task. Lateral coordination is in this way "a mechanism for decentralizing general management decisions."[17]

As information processing requirements in an organization rise under conditions of greater change and complexity, so the bureaucratic approach becomes increasingly unable to cope. There are then four alternatives. First, the organization can increase the manpower resources it commits to maintaining integration, or accept lower standards of decision-making efficiency. This is clearly a path to the lowering of performance. Second, the organization can be divided up so as to group people in clusters according to the most intensive communication needs. This is the divisionalization approach and will tend to incur additional costs of resource duplication. Third, the organization can improve its vertical information systems so as to relieve the load on the hierarchy. Improvement of vertical information systems in the past normally required additional investment in clerical staff and computer time. The advent of ICT-based systems, however, has considerably enhanced the cost effectiveness of this option through the combination of speed, accuracy, ease of operation, and falling hardware costs. (The use of ICT to enable integration is further addressed in Chapter 10). The fourth alternative is also powerfully assisted by modern ICTs such as email and video conferencing. This is to increase the capacity to process information via the development of lateral relationships at appropriate points down the hierarchy, along with a complementary delegation of discretion to the people concerned. While, as we will shortly see, the use of lateral relationships can entail additional overhead costs, it also offers the greatest potential for improving integration.

The following passage, taken from an internal corporate consultative document, illustrates how managements have come to appreciate the value in moving beyond traditional structures by incorporating lateral integration:

> "In organization terms we appear to have learned a healthy disrespect for formal structures and relationships, and functional boundaries. In a number of areas, task-oriented arrangements have been developed which transcend the traditional structures in the interests of overall effectiveness.

In an organization of our size and complexity we need a formal structure and clear definition of accountability, but it is a promising sign that we appear to be capable of adapting and evolving appropriate structures to meet changing requirements. Examples of developments in this area include the increasing use of the project team approach (notably in the new product development and engineering areas) and the evolution of our whole long-range planning process. Elsewhere there has been an acceptance of the viability of matrix structure (working for more than one boss), and the need for more emphasis on team building, with an acceptance of team objectives."

The various forms of integration through lateral relationships are listed in Box 5.6. They form a "ladder" of increasing sophistication, difficulty in design, and overhead cost. By and large, the heavier the information processing load, deriving from pressures and complexity in the tasks to be done, the further up the ladder a management will have to go in order to secure an adequate level of integration. In practice, as managements move up the ladder, they generally adopt the more sophisticated integration mechanisms as additions to, rather than simply substitutes for, those lower down.

Research has confirmed that, to remain effective, organizations operating in more dynamic environments, with greater differentiation in the pace of innovation and change between their major functions, need to invest in more comprehensive arrangements for lateral coordination. It has also emerged that, the more difficult and variable the work to be done, and hence the

BOX 5.6 THE LADDER OF LATERAL COORDINATION

1   Bring about direct contact between managers or employees who share a problem.
2   If departments are required to have a substantial amount of contact, one or more of their staff can be given special responsibility to act as a liaison officer with counterparts in other departments.
3   If a development or problem arises that calls for the contribution of several departments until its completion or solution, then it will probably be appropriate to set up a temporary task force to deal with it, with members drawn from those departments.
4   If such inter-departmental problems constantly recur, then permanently established groups or teams can provide an appropriate method of integration.
5   If the management of lateral relationships becomes a problem, perhaps because of their complexity, then a special integrating role can be set up – that of a "coordinator" or similar title. It may be necessary to endow the coordinator with support staff.
6   A further development of the separate integrating role is to decide that it should have a definite claim upon the resources of functional departments. Indeed, these may even disappear as separate departments. In industry, such integrator-managers are often defined as product managers who have charge of the total operations required to market, develop, produce, and service a product.
7   The most elaborate and sophisticated method of ensuring lateral integration is to establish a matrix system. Here, an attempt is made to combine the integration of personnel within each of their functionally specialized departments with an integration of specialists from different departments to focus on their common contribution to specific products or programs.

greater the uncertainty, the more intensively the different contributors have to interact. These circumstances will encourage an organization to go further up the ladder of lateral coordination measures.[18]

Combinations of integrating mechanisms are often used by organizations facing high levels of uncertainty in which the tension between inter-departmental differentiation and inter-dependency is high. The managements of such organizations, particularly the more successful ones, appear to secure integration through a portfolio of mechanisms rather than by simply adopting one approach rather than another. Although they go high up the ladder of lateral coordination for some activities, they also use the lower rungs for other requirements. This recognizes the fact that, even in an organization experiencing a high rate of change and operating with complex interdependencies between departments or workgroups, some communications and decision processes can still be handled adequately by means of simpler arrangements that are less costly in time and administrative overhead.

A detailed case study of literally millions of electronic mail messages, calendar meetings and teleconferences within a large US IT and electronics company provides some clues as to which individuals may be expected to engage most actively in communications that help to coordinate across organizational, spatial and social categories within an organization. These turned out to be women, junior-to-mid level executives, and members of the sales and marketing functions. Since formal organizational positions and the spatial locations of offices sharply delimited interaction patterns, these "boundary spanners" appeared to be performing a valuable coordinative role.[19]

A note on matrix organization

The matrix structure or system is the most elaborate and sophisticated method of ensuring lateral integration. It is widely used in organizations like advertising agencies where a difficult balance has to be struck between two equally important but potentially conflicting criteria – encouraging creativity and responding rapidly to the demands of (often large) client organizations. As described in Chapter 12, the matrix is also widely applied in multinational corporations that need to organize their activities according to several dimensions – typically function, product and geographical location.

Matrix organization is designed to improve understanding and integration of effort between different units through making people jointly responsible to those units. The challenge is that relying on the matrix as a structural arrangement alone does not guarantee that staff from the different units will actually cooperate better. A matrix structure might show workers from different departments belonging to a team in which they share responsibilities for, say, the same product line or for teaching the same programme in a business school, but this does not mean they will necessarily have an effective relationship based on a sense of common purpose, a desire to communicate, and fulfillment from working together. The question is what will effectively align the people who are formally integrated according to a matrix.

An insightful article by Katzenbach and Michaels argues that matrix organization has a dual nature.[20] One side is the structural, which requires collaboration across traditional silos and boundaries. The other side is a culture that "fosters and energizes correspondingly collaborative behaviours." As an example of how a company achieved this cultural alignment, the authors cite the example of PepsiCo's large and high-performing food subsidiary in Mexico. It took responsibility for a merger between two of PepsiCo's Mexican subsidiaries, and introduced a matrix structure to integrate their activities. The matrix consisted of four business units and eight functions. Most departments in the new organization reported both to a function and to a business unit. While the structural and formal parts of the merger and matrix design were put in place quite rapidly, collaboration at the level of actual behavior was not satisfactory. With the backing of his corporate headquarters, the Mexico CEO therefore embarked on a deliberate process of cultural alignment, through measures such as insisting on the customer as a shared top priority, creating a common vocabulary of terms, and introducing training to share the methods and strengths of the formerly separate sales forces. At the time of writing the article, the indications were that these measures were proving to be successful.

Costs of managing integration

The costs of integration are an important consideration. They tend to increase in parallel with the sophistication of the integration mechanism. As just illustrated, getting a matrix solution to work as intended can require additional training and re-socialization costs. Such costs have to be weighed against the value and necessity of the benefits attained when assessing whether a particular set of arrangements is inadequate, overelaborate, or about right. In deciding when and what to invest in integration, it is therefore wise not to assume that it is the Holy Grail, otherwise it can accumulate costs, waste energy, and eventually generate cynicism.[21]

The costs of managing integration can include:

1   The costs of time and human resources involved in more intensive and extensive communication. Time that is spent communicating with people in other units is time not spent on developing new staff or on relations with customers and suppliers.

2   The time and effort required to resolve conflicts. Although conflicts are inevitable in organizations and have to be resolved one way or another, the intensity of lateral coordination can sometimes appear to exacerbate the level of conflict, partly because of the additional stress it imposes on people.

3   Additional overhead costs. These include the costs of coordinators, if appointed; also the costs of required training in matters such as how to handle conflict and teambuilding.

4   Possible side effects. For instance, arrangements to improve communications between departments, including perhaps the relocation of offices, can be at the expense of communications within these departments. The members of one unit working in a team with staff from another unit can become extremely dissatisfied if they then find that their terms of employment are inferior.

5   Last but not least, it may be that the quality of decentralized decision making through lateral coordination proves to be no better than that carried out by higher management. This is a possible cost, but one that becomes less likely when decisions have to be made quickly in response to local changes and when they need to be informed by expert opinion.

Another worry that senior managers often have about the lateral approach to integration can also have cost implications. This is their concern not to weaken the element of control. For this reason, they often prefer to rely upon conventional integration methods, even when these are not effective for information processing or decision making and incur greater costs of time and delay. So they insist on the referral of matters requiring coordination up the hierarchy, or on dealing with coordination as far as possible through formal procedures, or relying on coordination by committees on which senior managers sit and can exercise considerable influence. This may be partly a matter of culture and style in which managers seek to preserve the approach with which they are familiar. It serves to illustrate further the point that a portfolio of integrative mechanisms is likely to be used even where integration needs are greatest. It also reminds us that some ways of dealing with the need for integration suit a given culture of management better than others.

Requirements for coordination

The more elaborate arrangements for direct lateral integration require the designation of coordinators. This is a particularly difficult role to play because coordinators are likely to have more responsibility than authority. They are expected to achieve results, but are not granted full managerial authority over either the people or resources they are coordinating. Another source of frustration for coordinators can arise if they stay in the role for long, because their future career line may then become unclear.

The ability of coordinators to exercise any real influence over the staff from different units whom they are integrating depends importantly on backup from higher management. They require the ability to appeal to a general manager's authority when necessary. The understanding and determination of top management can in this way play an important part in the success of integration even when emphasis is placed on achieving this via direct, lateral relationships. If conflicts arise between the people or units that are being coordinated laterally, it may be beyond the capacity of a coordinator to resolve them.

There are other ways of enhancing the influence and potential for success of coordinators. These include:

1   Filling such positions with persons who are already influential in the organization and are known to have earned the respect of the departments or groups they are called upon to coordinate.
2   Making sure that coordinators have sufficient understanding of the work of the departments to be coordinated.
3   Selecting as coordinators people who can cope with the ambiguity inherent in their position.
4   Clarifying the rights that formally attach to the position, such as the right to call meetings and set schedules for project work, and if necessary providing the coordinator with backup resources and staff.

The "product champion" or "business innovator" is somewhat of a mixture between a coordinator and a manager. These are people who are given a leading or intrapreneurial role in driving innovation within a company. They are committed to the success of an innovation. They may be the original creative force behind an innovation or business idea, and also lead the commercialization of that innovation. The product champion role is the most common way of capturing and directing the enthusiasm of people who have to contribute to the success of innovation. The product champion takes the initiative to integrate the contributions necessary for the success of an innovation, typically developing a network of communications at the creative stage and leading cross-functional teams at the development stage. It is a necessary role, given the tendency to resist change and maintain functional separation within organizations. While many product champions are self-selecting, they may need to benefit from the managerial supports we have identified for coordinators.

Teamworking: An Aid to Integration

The trends in organizational practice towards breaking down functional boundaries, and the increasing amount of work based on projects that require input from people with different expertise and experience, have led to an increasing use of teams, or "teamworking." Teams integrate individuals around tasks and are intended to create tight networks of those people. It is expected that teams will normally perform better than individuals working on their own when the tasks to be done require multiple skills, judgment, and experience.[22] There is in fact evidence that productivity and other gains can be achieved as a result of adopting teamworking. For instance, as a result of reorganizing employees at its Trenton, Ohio facility into 31 self-directed teams of between 9 and 16 members each, the Miller Brewing Company achieved a 30 percent reduction in labor costs compared to its plants organized along traditional, non-team lines. K Shoes in the UK reported that a move to teamwork resulted in a 19 percent increase in productivity, a reduction in rejects produced from 5,000 per million to 250, and an on-time delivery improvement from 80 percent to 97 percent.[23] Such benefits have led to a noticeable increase in the reliance on teams in organizations. Having studied the use of teams in 20 "world-class organizations" located in both the USA and other countries, Wellins and his colleagues concluded that "teams can work in just about any type of organization."[24]

Types of team

In simple terms, a team is a group comprising people with complementary skills who are working to a common purpose for which they are collectively accountable. The concept is a very broad one, and there are many types of team. An important distinction is between teams that are "permanent" and those that are established to meet a specific, one-off purpose. *Permanent teams* continue over time and their membership is usually quite stable. They are organized around the operations leading to a product or service. *Temporary teams* are often called "task forces" or "working parties" and are set up to achieve a given project or tackle a particular issue. Temporary teams are often given a deadline and progress "mileposts" to work to.

Many types of team can be distinguished by their membership and/or purpose.[25] They are all intended to promote better integration and include:

TOP MANAGEMENT TEAMS

These are formed to coordinate policy formulation and implementation across the different units of an organization – business, functional, or regional – through bringing their managers together. These teams do not always achieve the integration desired because of the high level of individualism that characterizes many senior managers, as well as the difficulty of bringing them together in person. Modern information and communication technologies, especially videoconferencing, can assist in overcoming the latter problem.

CROSS FUNCTIONAL TEAMS

These teams consist of middle managers and staff representing various departments or functions. They can be permanent, such as a standing, plant-wide, safety team. Other cross-functional teams are temporary, such as those established to develop a new product or improve a major organizational process.

Cross-functional teams have become a commonly used integrating mechanism. They are responsible for a product, service, or process and enable work to be designed around processes rather than functions. They are typically multi-skilled, with their members trained into competencies that cut across traditional occupational boundaries. Support staff and their skills are often incorporated into cross-functional teams. Once established, it is quite common for cross-functional teams to expand the scope of their responsibilities, especially if they are permanent in nature. They may take over some managerial roles and also wider organizational responsibilities such as advising on human resources policy or customer service requirements. The development of cross-functional teams at the Hannaford Brothers Company provides an instructive example (Box 5.7).

Cross-functional teams have also been used successfully to accomplish major overhauls of organizational practice. An example is provided by the remarkable turnaround of Nissan following its strategic alliance with Renault. Carlos Ghosn, the new chief operating officer (and later CEO) who came from Renault, had successfully used cross-functional teams both there and in Michelin. Shortly after taking office in June 1999, Ghosn established nine cross-functional teams to focus on business development, purchasing, manufacturing, sales and marketing, research and development, financial costs, management costs, organization and decision-making systems, and rationalization of model range. These teams comprised middle managers from different sections of the company and were led by corporate vice presidents. The teams achieved five main results: (1) breaking down departmental sectionalism; (2) gathering information and ideas across the company; (3) providing opportunities for younger staff to be rewarded and/or promoted; (4) fostering collaboration within the company; and (5) disseminating the philosophy behind the Nissan Revival Plan which Ghosn had announced in October 1999. Cross-functional teams were central to the turnaround process. They highlighted essential factors that could be incorporated into the revival plan. At the same time, the teams helped to transform the company's formerly rigid organizational structure and conservative culture.[26]

PROJECT TEAMS

A project team is normally established for the duration of the project for which it is given responsibility. Once the project is completed, team members return to their different units or are re-assigned to a new project team. While some members continue to serve throughout the life of a project and thereby provide integration through their continuity, other members may

BOX 5.7   CROSS-FUNCTIONAL TEAMS AT THE HANNAFORD BROTHERS COMPANY

The transformation of Hannaford Brothers from a food wholesaler to a regional supermarket powerhouse in North East USA was an impressive success story. The company's rapid growth, however, led to problems behind the scenes. In particular, it severely strained the company's distribution system and there were signs of considerable employee dissatisfaction at its main distribution center at South Portland, Maine.

The company planned a new distribution center in New York State and senior executives were determined not to re-create the problems of South Portland. A design team conducted an exhaustive study of operational requirements and consulted extensively both within the company and with retail store personnel (the distribution center's customers). The result was an approach toward organization that was new for the company and based on cross-functional teams.

The main functional tasks required within a distribution center are inventory control, selecting products from inventory and loading them onto pallets, forklift operation, scheduling assignments, and general supervision. In the new organization, teams of between five and twenty-five people became responsible for all these previously specialized duties. Each team focused on specified customers – up to three supermarkets that it supplied directly. Six teams served Hannaford supermarkets and were specialized only in that different teams handle different categories of food, such as frozen foods or perishables. The seventh team, with ten members, provided specialized resources to the other teams. Team leadership was elected and rotated, with a maximum tenure of one year, and within teams most decisions were reached by consensus.

Considerable time was invested in training and development. As much as 20 percent of time was spent on this during the first year, and thereafter typically 15 percent was devoted to meetings and training. As the teams matured, they took on additional responsibilities, including scheduling work assignments, inventory control, developing and delivering training, setting team goals, team budgeting, hiring new team members, safety, quality assurance, peer performance reviews, and dealing with disciplinary and performance problems.

The payoff to the company from adopting cross-functional teamwork was spectacular. The new distribution center's operating costs were much lower than those of similarly sized distribution centers, mainly because of its lean staffing, negligible absenteeism, and low staff turnover. Fewer on-the-job accidents reduced workers' compensation costs by over $500,000 a year compared with similar centers. Team-led operational improvements also provided additional cost savings.

Source: Richard S. Wellins, William C. Byham, and George R. Dixon, *Inside Teams: How 20 World-Class Organizations are Winning Through Teamwork*. San Francisco: Jossey-Bass 1994, Chapter 12.

join and then leave the team depending on the stage at which their contributions are necessary. A project team will not normally be self-managing. It will usually have a coordinator who plays the roles both of leading the team towards fulfillment of the project's goals and integrating the members' contributions. The challenge of integrating contributions by members from diverse specialist areas can be a difficult one.

Other commonly used types of team include *quality circles, self-managed teams,* and *affinity groups*. Quality circles are teams concerned with improving quality, the effectiveness of working methods, use of equipment, and cost and safety matters. A key attribute of the quality circle is the involvement of employees at all levels. Quality circles became an integral part of the management system in Japan. Difficulties often arose with transplanting the concept to other countries and today many companies have subsumed the quality circle concept into the broader concept of team-based structures.

The teams introduced at Hannaford Brothers (see Box 5.7) illustrate the principles of self-management. They are often considered to be the ideal way to counteract the worst features of organizational life, such as a lack of meaning in work, stress, and social isolation. Certain key issues have to be resolved when embarking on self-managed teamwork, such as what happens to managers, how they can be helped to adjust from managing people directly to coaching and facilitating teams, and what limits may need to be placed on the freedom enjoyed by teams.

Affinity groups are teams composed of professional or knowledge workers. They meet regularly to share information, capitalize on opportunities, and solve problems. While powerful information technology systems are available to codify and distribute knowledge within organizations, there is no guarantee that their potential will be used effectively. Affinity groups, and indeed other types of team, can help to create a culture that encourages the sharing of knowledge and the breaking down of barriers within organizations. Whenever they regard knowledge as power, people become reluctant to share information and knowledge. Many of the integration problems experienced by companies and other organizations stem from this basic human tendency, and the most fundamental contribution offered by teams and other integrative mechanisms lies in the ways they counteract it.

Further advantages offered by teams

There are other advantages of teamwork, in addition to the contribution it can make to organizational integration. Teams substitute a peer-based control of work for traditional hierarchical control. In so doing, they typically increase the commitment and involvement that people have in their work. Teams have therefore been found to reduce absenteeism and increase employees' sense of accountability and responsibility. At the same time, the devolution of managerial responsibilities to teams enables hierarchical levels to be reduced and administrative overheads to be cut. Because teams can now make more of their own decisions, without having to wait for managerial approval, and because colleagues within the team can now communicate with one another on the spot, the introduction of teamwork normally speeds response times and increases the organization's ability to adjust flexibly to new circumstances.

The integration offered by teams should also facilitate learning and innovation. It is necessary here to distinguish between "invention," the creative phase of innovation and "implementation," the applied phase.[27] Teams are not necessarily superior to individuals in achieving creativity. There is always the danger of "group think" leading to conservative conformist solutions.[28] Teams can, however, assist in refining ideas through discussion and mutual feedback. Teams are likely to prove their worth in the implementation of new ideas and proposals. Here it is essential to integrate different functions such as hardware and software engineering, operations, costing, and marketing. The use of teams at this stage can also help to align implementation to overall organizational objectives and the broader, organization-wide picture. Earlier in this chapter, we noted how important this integration of implementation tasks has become in supporting a policy of concurrent engineering.

Teamwork best practice – a summary

Wellins and his colleagues have distilled a set of "best practices" for teamwork from their detailed study of twenty companies.[29] These can be summarized as follows:

1 Moving to teams must be informed by business needs. In the 20 cases studied by Wellins and colleagues, the overwhelming reason was increasing competitive pressure. The implications of these business needs must be clearly understood, especially the integration requirements they establish, so that teams are not adopted simply because it is fashionable to do so.
2 Senior management has to drive and support the change effort. This is a general requirement for achieving successful organizational change, which Chapter 13 discusses in detail.
3 The approach to introducing teams among the twenty companies usually involved a steering group with top management participation, complemented by a design team that did the detailed work. Design teams were normally composed of a cross-section of organization members from different levels. Visits by steering groups and design teams to other organizations in which teams had already been implemented provided valuable information that speeded up the learning process and avoided typical pitfalls.
4 New team roles and responsibilities have to be defined. Teams cannot function effectively, let alone attain their full potential, if they are constituted on the basis of previous definitions. Wellins et al. found six recurring principles guided the redesign of processes and responsibilities. These contrast with traditional design principles (Table 5.1):[30]

Table 5.1 Traditional versus team design principles

Traditional structure	Team Design
Work designed around functions	Work designed around processes
No sense of ownership	Team owns a product, service, or process
Single-skilled jobs	Multi-skilled / cross-trained jobs
Leaders govern teams	Teams govern teams
Support staff / skills outside team	Support staff / skills incorporated into team
Managers make all organizational decisions	Teams involved in organizational decisions

5   A basic principle of the team concept is to create a sense of ownership. This usually involves giving teams responsibility for whole products, services, or groups of customers.

6   For the flexibility offered by teamwork to be fully realized, a premium has to be placed on developing multi-skill capabilities.

7   In addition to extensive cross-training of this kind, employees in successful teamwork situations can be required to assume a broad range of other responsibilities, many of which may previously have been reserved for supervisors and managers.

8   Support services have to be integrated into teams. Among the 20 companies studied by Wellins et al., this was done in one of two ways. The first approach was to keep the support specialists together as a team, with their contributions now being directed toward each operational team or set of teams. A second, more far-reaching approach was to incorporate support specialists within the teams themselves. In this situation, the specialists may even transfer their skills to team members. Though this is a bolder approach, it is likely to provide greater job satisfaction to team members as well as greater efficiencies to the organization.

9   Because of the significant changes to managers' roles that teamwork implies, it is important to take time to restructure management, and to build the commitment of managers to the team process. Teamwork implies larger spans of control, fewer management positions, and fewer hierarchical layers.

10 Attention must also be given to leadership within the teams. Here practice varies widely. Some organizations have designated team leaders, and this can be on a rotating basis. Others have no person formally responsible for team leadership; instead, various governance responsibilities are shared among team members. This latter solution does not necessarily mean less control over the teams, because they can still be held accountable for their performance.

11 As with any change in organizational form, other contingent organizational systems will have to be realigned. For example, team members are likely to wish to be involved in selecting new members. This may raise problems in respect of ethnic discrimination and other ethical issues. Considerable training will have to be offered in the early stages of teamworking to develop appropriate team skills as well as to enhance multi-skilling. Traditional reward and compensation systems will need to be redesigned to match the new team responsibilities and to support new priorities such as the enhancement of skills. It is likely that a significant part of each team member's remuneration will be tied to the attainment of team goals. Over time, as teams assume new responsibilities and are given new performance criteria, so the ways in which their members are recognized and rewarded must also be adapted.

Coordination has to be managed

It has become clear that integration does not occur naturally in organizations, even in very small ones that consist of just a group of people. The process of coordination to achieve integration has to be managed on a continuing basis.[31] For there are ways in which everyday dynamics in organization can erode coordination. One is turnover of staff because new entrants will generally not be familiar with existing staff or have a good understanding of the organization's task. These are both conditions that may stand in the way of coordinating them with existing staff. Second, integration is also threatened if one of the parties that need to work or exchange information closely with others regularly makes mistakes or underperforms. Managers therefore need to be aware of the task performance as well as of the relationship quality involved in collaboration. Third, even if formal barriers are bridged through integrative mechanisms, status differences between groups can stand in the way of effective cooperation and information exchange, and become barriers to mutual recognition and trust.

SUMMARY

1 Integration is a condition in which there is adequate coordination between the different, but complementary, activities that collectively create value. It is a vital product of good organization, though often neglected.

2 From a cautionary perspective, integration is essential to avoid failure, or even disaster, in the delivery of an adequate service to customers and the public.

3 From a more positive standpoint, sound integration is one of the factors that can turn the people and knowledge at a company's disposal into a distinctive and dynamic capability, lending it a competitive edge and enabling it to adjust successfully to changing demands.

4 Integration is unlikely to occur spontaneously within an organization, beyond the scope of face-to-face relations within a working group. It is therefore extremely important to recognize signs that the integration being achieved may be inadequate.

5 Integration problems are likely to be more challenging as an organization becomes larger and more complex.

6 The coordination of people and units so as to achieve integration between them therefore has to be managed.

7 There are various mechanisms aimed at strengthening integration. These range from simple arrangements for the people concerned to meet periodically to complex, multi-dimensional structures in which the contributions of specialized units are coordinated through a matrix arrangement according to customer, process, regional, or other requirements.

8 Teams play a very important role within this range of possibilities, and they are today one of the most commonly used means for achieving integration.

9 Teamworking reflects the strong emphasis in new organizational practice on achieving integration alongside the devolution of initiative to people who possess the requisite information to adapt or innovate an organization's activities. IT based methods of integration are discussed further in Chapter 10.

QUESTIONS FOR DISCUSSION

5.1 Briefly describe the concept of integration and how it may be applied within organizations.

5.2   What are the main problems that management can encounter in achieving integration?

5.3   Describe traditional approaches to achieving integration within organizations.

5.4   What additional challenges are likely to arise in securing adequate collaboration between organizations such as partners within a supply chain or professional agencies dealing with community problems?

5.5   What are the main approaches to securing integration in new organizational forms?

5.6   How should teamwork facilitate the integration process?

5.7   What might be the problems of introducing teamwork into a conventional organization structure?

NOTES

1   Gerardo A. Okhuysen and Beth A. Bechky (2009), Coordination in organizations: An integrative perspective, *The Academy of Management Annals*, 3(1), 463–502.

2   Pamela Danese and Pietro Romano (2004), Improving inter-functional coordination to face high product variety and frequent modifications, *International Journal of Operations & Production Management*, 24(9), 863–885.

3   Valukas, Anton R. (2014), *Report to Board of Directors of General Motors Company Regarding Ignition Switch Recalls*, May 29.

4   Rensis Likert (1961), *New Patterns of Management*, New York, McGraw-Hill.

5   March, James. G. (1991), Exploration and exploitation in organizational learning, *Organization Science*, 2(1), 71–87.

6   Christian Terwiesch, Christoph H. Loch, and Arnoud De Meyer (2002), Exchanging preliminary information in concurrent engineering: Alternative coordination strategies, *Organization Science*, 13(4), 402–419. Reprinted by permission, copyright 2002, the Institute for Operations Research and the Management Sciences (INFORMS), 5521 Research Park Drive, Suite 200, Catonsville, MD 21228 USA.

7   Richard Ford and Alexandra Frean (2002), National offenders register will protect children, *The Times*, 14 October, p. 13.

8   Juliette Jowit (2001), Why an accident like Hatfield was waiting to happen, *Financial Times*, 22 February, p. 4. Peter Martin (2001), Lessons from Railtrack, *Financial Times*, 9 October, p. 21.

9   Columbia Accident Investigation Board (2003), *Report*, Washington, DC, Government Printing Office, August, p. 187.

10   Ibid., pp. 187–188.

11   David J. Teece (2000), *Managing Intellectual Capital*, Oxford, Oxford University Press. Quotation is from p. 26. See also David J. Teece, Gary Pisano, and Amy Shuen (1997), Dynamic capabilities and strategic management, *Strategic Management Journal*, 18(7), 509–533.

12   Jay R. Galbraith (1993), *Competing with Flexible Lateral Organizations*, 2nd edition, Reading, MA, Addison-Wesley.

13   Galbraith (1993), op. cit., Chapter 2.

14   These warning signs were first identified in Derek Pugh (1979), Effective coordination in organizations, *SAM Advanced Management Journal*, 44(1), 28–35.

15   A more detailed review of "mechanisms for coordination" can be found in Okhuysen and Bechky (2009), op. cit., pp. 472–481.

16   It is, however, important that committees clearly allocate responsibilities to their members for the actions on which they decide. Otherwise committees can be ineffective because of dispersed and ill-defined responsibility.

17   Galbraith (1993), op. cit., p. 6.

18   See Paul R. Lawrence and Jay W. Lorsch (1967), *Organization and Environment*, Boston, Harvard Business School Press; Andrew H. Van de Ven, Andre L. Delbecq, and Richard Koenig, Jr. (1976), Determinants of coordination modes within organizations, *American Sociological Review*, 41(2), 322–338; Galbraith (1993), op. cit.

19   Adam M. Kleinbaum, Toby E. Stuart, and Michael L. Tushman (2008), Communication (and coordination?) in a modern, complex organization, Harvard Business School Working Paper 09-004, 31 July.

20   Jon R. Katzenbach and Adam Michaels (2013), Life in the matrix, *Strategy +Business*, issue 72, Autumn, New York, Booz & Co.

21   Michael Goold and Andrew Campbell (1998), Desperately seeking synergy, *Harvard Business Review*, Sept–Oct, 131–143.

22   S.A. Mohrman, S.G. Cohen, and A.M. Mohrman, Jr. (1995), *Designing Team-Based Organizations*, San Francisco, Jossey-Bass.

23   Richard S. Wellins, William C. Byham, and George R. Dixon (1994), *Inside Teams: How 20 World-Class Organizations are Winning Through Teamwork*, San Francisco, Jossey-Bass.

24   Wellins et al., (1994), op. cit., p. 299.

25   A good discussion of different types of team and their effectiveness is provided by Eugene F. McKenna (2012), *Business Psychology and Organizational Behaviour*, 5th edition, Hove, UK, Psychology Press, Chapter 11. See also Michael A. West (2012), *Effective Teamwork: Practical Lessons from Organizational Research*, 3rd edition, Malden, MA, British Psychological Society and Blackwell.

26   Piero Morosini (2006), Nurturing Successful Alliances across Boundaries. In Oded Shenkar and Jeffrey J. Reuer (eds.), *Handbook of Strategic Alliances*, Thousand Oaks, CA, Sage, Chapter 15: 273–296.

27   See Michael A. West (2002), Sparkling fountains or stagnant ponds: An integrative model of creativity and innovation implementation in work groups, *Applied Psychology*, 51(3), 355–387. See also the commentaries and response following this article in the same issue.

28   I.L. Janis (1972), *Victims of Groupthink: A Psychological Study of Foreign Policy Decisions and Fiascos*, Boston, Houghton Mifflin.

29   Wellins et al., (1994), op. cit., Chapter 21.

30   Wellins et al., op. cit., (1994), p. 308.

31   This section is based on Okhuysen and Bechky (2009), op. cit., pp. 493–494.

CHAPTER 6

Control

WHAT THIS CHAPTER COVERS

Control is an elusive concept, even though it refers to a central process in management. The chapter therefore begins by clarifying the nature of control. It identifies a number of foundations upon which control within an organization can be built. The chapter goes on to make several key distinctions relevant to the exercise of control. One is the difference between strategic and operational levels of control. A second concerns the three principal features of control on which a policy decision has to be made: its extent, focus, and the mechanisms through which it is to be exercised. Yet another distinction relevant to mechanisms is between control based on authority and control achieved through the management of relationships and/or of identity. These distinctions help us to understand the options for control. These options are classified into six basic strategies of control and discussed in detail.

Certain of these control strategies are associated with conventional organizational forms, while others are more in keeping with newer approaches. The choice between them, and the configuration of control strategies adopted, reflects the circumstances of a particular organization, and the contingencies it faces. The chapter closes by considering these contingencies.

◢ An Elusive Concept

Control is an essential and central process of management. Chapter 2 indicated that early writers on organization, especially from the "classical" school, gave considerable thought to control and emphasized formal control mechanisms such as rules and the definition of responsibilities. Then for a long time, the subject was neglected by most writers on organization and is still not given the attention it deserves.[1] There are several possible reasons for this period of neglect. Some may take it for granted that managing is about control and that for this reason there is no need to treat the subject separately. However, it is hardly conducive to a discussion of control to treat it implicitly in this way. Another possibility is that control has a sinister ring to it, associated in people's minds with associations of power and manipulation. As a result, there may be some reluctance among many business school writers to discuss control, in order to avoid embarrassment for their sponsors in positions of corporate power. The claim, sometimes made, that control is a purely technical process concerned with accounting and operational feedback, also amounts to a de-sensitizing of the subject.

The standard English definition of control is "to order, limit, instruct, or rule someone's behavior."[2] Within the context of organization, control may be defined as *a process whereby management or other groups are able to initiate and regulate the conduct of activities such that their results accord with the goals and expectations held by those groups.* Control amounts to more than just formulating goals and/or rules of appropriate conduct; it also extends to ways of encouraging the members of an organization to attach significance and give attention to what management deems to be important.[3] Seen in this light, control is a fundamental process of organization and much more than just the system that supports it. A "control system" is a mechanism that is designed to convey information to assist the initiation and regulation of activities, but this does not guarantee that the activities are carried out satisfactorily. The process of control, taken as a whole, aims at ensuring that a predictable level and type of outcome (performance) is attained and maintained.

Though control is rightly regarded as an essential aspect of management, we should bear in mind that managers are not the only group who will attempt to exercise control. Workers, technical staff, professional employees, and other organizational groups will also do so. This accounts for the paradox that control in an organization is not simply a process in which everyone shares with the same goals in mind; there can also be resistance and counter-control in pursuit of objectives that do not fully accord with those of management.

There is considerable ambiguity surrounding the term "control" despite the fact that it is in common, everyday use. In part this is because the term has both the narrow and broad meanings just mentioned – namely, control as a system and control as a process. Another source of ambiguity lies in the close relation that control bears to an equally fuzzy phenomenon: power. On the one hand, there is a purely functional aspect to control. In one form or another control is essential for an organization of people to achieve their objectives and to inform the future direction of their efforts. On the other hand, control depends upon power and it can therefore easily become perverted towards supporting exploitation.

Managers appointed by the owners of a company or their representatives, or by state agencies in the case of the public sector, enjoy legal authority over the conduct of the organization subject to periodic review. This legal position does not in itself guarantee that employees will accept managerial power. However, in organizations that they join voluntarily and are free to leave, employees are likely to accept a great deal of this power as being legitimate. They may be assured by an ability collectively to oppose a misuse of power by managers, and by the possibility of quitting the organization if the situation becomes intolerable.[4] Under these circumstances, power becomes legitimated as "authority" which employees are normally prepared to accept, at least in the conduct of everyday activities. Authority can be greatly enhanced when employees are offered rewards that they value for accomplishing what management wishes them to do.

Power and authority do not only reside with managers. For example, those members of an organization who possess relevant special knowledge enjoy the authority that stems from their expertise. Power can also be shared as a matter of policy. This is the principle of "empower-ment." which can extend as far as self-managed organizational control, whereby decisions both on the determination of objectives and the means to attain them are shared. Whatever the distribution of power, however, organized activities will require a degree of control. This intimate relation between control and power gives rise to an alternative definition of control, namely *the use of power to secure the achievement of specified goals through organized effort*.

To summarize, control in an organization can be achieved through a number of attributes including:[5]

- *power*, such as the command of resources;
- *authority*, such as the rights delegated by legal owners;
- *expertise*, such as the possession of specialized expertise relevant to the organization's operations;
- *rewards*, such as the offering of payment at levels acceptable to employees, especially when elements in that payment are linked to performance goals. As discussed in the next chapter, non-financial rewards may also support control.

The following section looks beyond definitions and makes some key distinctions. The first is between strategic and operational control. The concept of control is also unpacked so as to identify different aspects concerning its extent and focus, and the characteristics of control mechanisms. An important distinction within the spectrum of control mechanisms is that between control based on authority and control achieved through the management of relationships and/or of identity. These basic distinctions help us in the next section to address the question of the options (strategies) for control and to link these to conventional and new organizational forms. The third main section then identifies the contingent factors relevant to choosing between different strategies of control. The issue of control is also discussed in later chapters that deal with two of its specific contemporary applications. Chapter 12 includes a section on control within multinational corporations, while Chapter 16 considers control in relation to the question of accountability in corporate governance.

◢ Control in Organizations: Key Distinctions

Levels of control

There are two broad levels of control in organizations: *strategic control* and *operational control*. *Strategic control* is control over the means and methods on which the whole conduct and future direction of an organization depends. These include its capital, the form of assets in which the capital is embodied, and its strategic dispositions such as the markets or areas of need to be served, the communities and labor markets in which the organization is located, its external relations with suppliers, competing organizations, and government agencies. This is the level of control that those concerned about effective corporate governance normally have in mind.

The ability that management has to exercise power within organizations derives primarily from control at this strategic level. For this level of control allows it to re-deploy capital, which may entail closing sites and entertaining bids from communities to open new ones. Control over the provision of investment capital has, for instance, provided a basis for securing cooperation from local government authorities in development areas to secure "captured" local labor markets in which the one company becomes a dominant employer, and also for securing guarantees of assistance from workers' leaders in removing restrictive working practices, reducing manning levels, and promoting "industrial discipline." If management has the ability to recruit selectively from an ample supply of job applicants, this enables it to take on employees who appear more likely to accept managerial authority and to replace them should they not perform as management expects. The provision of company housing, of mortgages tied to employment in the company, and of non-transferable benefits such as pensions, are further examples of how control over strategic resources can be used to encourage, even coerce, employees into accepting management control within the organization – control which the mere provisions of an employment contract itself do not guarantee. A similar analysis could be made with respect to control in other strategic areas, such as dominance in a product market or monopoly over the provision of a public utility service. The general point is that the ability to exercise control within an organization at the operational level is largely dependent on, and certainly facilitated by, control at the strategic level.

The second level of control, *operational control*, comes closer to the main focus of this chapter. This is control over the work done within an organization, in the sense of determining how employees perform their jobs. The possibility of exercising operational control depends on the possession of power, especially if the people concerned are unlikely to cooperate spontaneously. Power may be used in an overtly coercive way, as when employees are threatened with the threat of dismissal, particularly in conditions of high unemployment when this would impact significantly on their livelihood. Power can also be used to offer material persuasion, such as incentives for attaining certain targets. A third use of power is through the command of the means of ideological persuasion. Examples are the ability to establish symbolic events such as periodic ceremonies or to finance a company magazine, both of which are intended to promote a sense of community and a cultural identification with the organization and its management.

Operational control, then, is a realization of the potential offered by the possession of power within organizations. While top management is likely to hold the largest share of such power because of its control over strategic resources, other groups will also possess some power to affect operations. Workers who have special skills required to carry out certain tasks, and who cannot readily be replaced, provide an example of a potentially powerful group. For example, when there is an IT failure, the services of the IT support staff are usually required urgently. Management, however, cannot easily predict when these services will be required and therefore make arrangements to bring in alternative assistance in the event of non-cooperation from their in-house specialists.

It is at the strategic level of management that objectives are established and translated, first into policies and then into specific plans of action. Whoever controls strategic resources and the means to secure them, such as raising finance, also determines objectives and policies for the organization. Despite the existence of extensive employee shareholding in some companies, such as retailers Publix Super Markets in the USA and the John Lewis Partnership in UK, it is not very common for ordinary members of a company to participate in the formulation of its objectives. As a result, these members may not fully share or understand top management's objectives, so giving rise to potential resistance to management control.

This possibility is heightened by the potential conflict of interests inherent in the employment contract due to the fact that wages and salaries are deficits on bottom line profitability. If this conflict of interests remains at the forefront of employees' minds, it will tend to sustain an active, and probably collectively organized resistance to managerial control. Such resistance will appear to those engaged in it to offer the best hope of protecting their interests in terms of, for example, the balance between effort required and payment offered, or the preservation of labor market power through restrictions on management's ability to erode employees' skills. Competitive pressures in the world economy are obliging managers to exercise more stringent control in an attempt to reduce costs, increase productivity, and respond more swiftly to market changes. Chapter 4 noted how cost reductions are often achieved through downsizing in a manner that threatens employees' immediate interests. In these circumstances, the short term quite reasonably tends to take precedence in people's minds, with some employees finding themselves no longer invited to share in the long-term rewards being promised. The result may be to generate demoralization among employees to the point where it more than offsets any cost savings that were originally contemplated.

Aspects of control

There are three principal aspects of control. These are the *extent* of control, the *focus* of that control, and the *mechanisms* through which it is exercised.[6]

EXTENT OF CONTROL

The extent of control concerns the degree to which control is exercised over a particular activity. It can be assessed in a direct way by reference to the range of decisions or areas of activity that a manager controls, either solely or jointly with others. The range of activities on which a manager receives information that could lead to his or her intervention, if deemed necessary, provides a less direct, but broader, assessment of the extent of control. The same distinction applies to the case of control within an alliance between companies, referring to the range of activities controlled by a partner company.

It is important to view control as a continuous variable rather than an all-or-nothing phenomenon. In other words, managers can exercise different degrees of control over their organization, and also distribute it to various levels and positions, rather than the issue being one of having either total control or no control. This allows for the possibility of devolving decision-making and other initiatives among different levels and sections of an organization without necessarily losing overall control in so doing. A basic tenet of new organizational thinking lies in the recognition that centralized control may no longer produce the best performance results. Chapter 4 noted how it can lead to costly administrative overheads, demotivate staff, and inhibit innovation and flexibility. The locus and distribution of authority is therefore an important policy choice, and specific mechanisms of control can be adapted to suit. As Chapter 11 will discuss, similar considerations apply to the organization of activities through alliances between partner companies, such as joint ventures. While gaining sufficient control over the alliance to safeguard its interests is an important consideration for any partner company, there is also a danger of over-control. The attempt to exercise more control than is necessary will not only incur additional direct costs – it could have negative consequences. If a company tries to exert too much control within an alliance, this may threaten the quality of its relations with its partners. Moreover, if partners either singly or together try to control their alliances too much, this may inhibit the flexibility that the latter need in order to develop within their own competitive environments. So, as Ohmae has argued, "managers must overcome the popular conception that total control increases chances of success."[7]

FOCUS OF CONTROL

The realization that control in organizations does not have to be an all-or-nothing phenomenon raises questions concerning the activities and issues to which a control system should be primarily directed and at what level in an organization should control be exercised. These questions have to do with the appropriate focus of control. Given that exercising control entails management costs and has potential demotivating effects on the people subject to it, it is wise to give serious consideration to how control should be focused.

In practice, companies typically focus a more intensive level of control onto specific activities, decisions, or processes. For example, many multinational corporations (MNCs) consider it essential to control product quality centrally from the corporate level, through enforcing rigid standards. The intention is to protect the integrity and reputation of their global brands, which could be severely damaged by a local failure in quality. The potential threat to their corporate reputation of an environmental failure in a given locality is similarly a consideration leading many MNCs to control their environmental standards centrally. By contrast, an MNC may consider it appropriate to exercise a looser form of indirect control over the HRM and marketing practices of its foreign affiliates because it is functional to adjust these to local cultural and market conditions. Even within a given unit of a company, control may be focused more on some activities than on others.[8]

The implication of the focus dimension for managerial control policy is that it is normally optimal to exercise control selectively. This means, first of all, making a clear distinction among activities and decisions for which it might be appropriate to adopt a different level or type of control. Studies that provide checklists of common activities and decisions can be useful here.[9] Secondly, a view has to be taken about the intensity and method of control appropriate to each of them, which raises questions such as what operational information to require, and what discretion to permit the persons carrying out the work to evaluate their own performance and decide on any corrective action. Looked at internationally, the criticality of some activities in foreign markets is likely to be greater than that of others. For example, the resource deficiency of many developing countries in technology and marketing systems may lead an international company to consider these among the key items for it to supply and control in order to achieve their viability and to protect corporate reputation. In view of the problem of corruption in many developing countries, MNC also usually deem it necessary to control the financial management of their affiliates there.

MECHANISMS OF CONTROL

A large range of control mechanisms is available and it is usual to employ several of them in combination. The main configurations of control mechanism become distinct strategies of control, and these are described in the following section. The characteristics that distinguish different control mechanisms concern:

- their negative or positive nature;
- their formality or informality;
- how they work;
- their emphasis on the feedback of past information as opposed to the "feed forward" of predictive information.

The first distinction is between *negative* and *positive control mechanisms*. Managers use negative mechanisms to prevent other members of an organization from taking unapproved actions. A typical example is the laying down of a requirement that specified decisions have to be ratified by higher levels of management or even the board of directors. This is likely to apply to matters such as capital expenditure plans and budgets, and senior appointments. Negative control depends principally on rules and other formal provisions. Employment contracts, for example, can lay down restrictions on the disclosure of information to parties outside the organization, a notorious example being the restrictions imposed on UK government officials by the Official Secrets Act. Many companies insist on similar contractual restrictions with regard to proprietary technology.

Other mechanisms are positive in nature because they are used to encourage and promote desired behaviors. Positive control lies at the core of many contemporary HRM practices. The provision of HRM programs and systems for selection, training and development, appraisal, career advancement, and compensation, can both help to control the quality of an organization's staff and generate understanding of, and commitment to, the norms of a strong corporate culture.[10] MNCs, in particular, are interested in promoting their corporate cultures to improve the control, as well as the integration, of their foreign affiliates. Even processes like consultation and participation, which may be desirable for other reasons such as improving the quality of decision-making, can serve as positive control mechanisms if they result in a greater commitment among employees to the implementation of decisions.

Secondly, control mechanisms can be *formal* or *informal*. Procedures for making staff appointments and the specified criteria for awarding rises in salary are among the more significant formal controls. The formalization of upward reporting relationships and planning and approval processes for capital budgeting plus resource allocation are other prominent examples. As with any formalization, the problem of rapid obsolescence arises in the fast-changing conditions of today.

Consequently, there has been a growing interest in the potential of more flexible, informal control mechanisms. One approach is to foster regular contact between managers and lower-level staff in the organization, in the expectation that such contact will lead to several benefits: (1) greater personal commitment to management's objectives for the organization; (2) a more flexible readjustment to changing circumstances, and (3) a larger number of innovative suggestions. It may be possible to do this on a personal, face-to-face basis through meetings and social events or, failing that, through regular, personalized video and other communication. Technical, advisory, and managerial inputs given by corporate staff to affiliates on a continuing basis, accompanied by the maintenance of close relations between staff at the two levels, can have considerable potential for enhancing the corporate center's operational control. This more informal and personal approach to control is recommended by advocates of new organization as being compatible with devolved initiative among employees and teams. It does not necessarily involve much reliance on personal supervision in the sense of the traditional, personal, centralized control strategy to be discussed shortly. Rather, it can serve as reinforcement of a strategy that fosters control through normative and "cultural" means (see "cultural control" below).

The third distinction concerns *how control mechanisms work*. They can influence the nature of what is done, the context in which it is done, and/or the processes by which activities are carried out.

Content-oriented control mechanisms rely on the specification of items of substance, such as the prohibition of theft from factory workshops. *Context-oriented* controls, by contrast, are those that aim to create an attitude of mind among the members of an organization that supports the attainment of managerial goals. The fostering of a strong corporate culture would be one approach toward generating an understanding and acceptance of such goals. A norm expressed by a corporate culture may, for instance, be the desirability of working flexibly as the situation requires. This illustrates a potential advantage of this approach, namely that it can in principle apply to any situation, including unforeseen circumstances. *Process-oriented* controls rely on the control effect of shaping the process whereby things are done in or by the organization. A prime example, already noted, is to encourage staff to participate in making decisions with a view to securing their commitment to getting the decisions implemented successfully. This approach is characteristic of the approach to decision-making in larger Japanese firms through the so-called *ringi* system in which proposals are widely circulated for comment by organizational members.[11]

The fourth distinct aspect of control mechanisms concerns whether they are based on *feedback*, or whether they incorporate *"feedforward,"* or both. Traditional systems of management control operate on the basis of providing information on past events. The problem in a rapidly changing environment is that much of that feedback soon becomes irrelevant. The contrasting principle is to promote feedforward. This takes place when predictive information is used as a basis for assessing whether and how it is necessary to adapt. It can enter the management control process through various channels, such as upward reporting by employees who are in direct contact with external events, or information secured by managers through their networking and subscription to information sources on trends and new developments. Feedforward thus tends to rely on a wide range of information sources, which brings it into line with the new organizational thinking that control can no longer be placed exclusively in the hands of top managers.

Strategies of Control

It has become apparent that control is a complex process that organizational design can shape only to a certain degree. The paradoxes and contradictions inherent in organizational relationships mean that there is likely to be resistance to management control by other groups seeking to enforce their own measures of control. This in turn means that it may be misleading to account for resistance to control and attempts to subvert it, purely in terms of the control strategy being inappropriate. Much has been written about how certain control strategies, such as close supervision and a heavy reliance on rules, are incongruent with the personal psychological needs of mature adults.[12] There is also a growing interest in finding approaches to organizational control that can at the same time be experienced by employees as fair and not destructive of their trust in management.[13]

There are two areas of interpretation at play here. The first concerns the way that control is applied and whether this is positive with regard to the sense of personal dignity, norms of fairness and conditions for trusting others that individuals carry with them. This first area is primarily to do with the means of control and how these suit psychological needs. The second area is primarily to do with the content of control, including the criteria that management is applying in the control process to specify objectives and performance levels. This second area constitutes a wider context for the application of organizational control. If applied without regard to this wider context, an emphasis on control mechanisms and how far they suit psychological needs could give rise to the expectation that resistance to control would disappear once an appropriate strategy of control were adopted. While the psychology of control is certainly relevant, it does not tell the whole story, except perhaps for those members of an organization who are entirely committed to management's goals and policies. In their case, the problem would simply be one of finding a style of management control that was acceptable – there would be no conflict with its content and rationale. But when employees do see themselves to be in conflict with management, no control strategy, however sensitive to psychological considerations, is likely to be received entirely without resistance.

One of the paradoxes about control in organizations is that it is directed at some issues on which there may be consensus between management and employees, but also at others over which there can be conflict. When there is a matter in dispute, an increase in control achieved by employees over that issue would be at the expense of the amount of control available to management, and vice versa. Control then takes on a "win–lose," zero-sum character. An example might be control over the level of manning in a department. Where there are issues on which the different parties may be able to agree readily, such as safety, control avoids this win–lose character. It is possible to share control and for an increase in the devolution of control to employees not to mean a loss in control by management. In practical terms, this conjunction of conflict and consensus indicates the appropriateness of adopting a portfolio of control strategies rather than just one. Each strategy would be directed toward different issues according to the degree of conflict or consensus involved and, similarly, different approaches might be followed toward different groups within the organization.

For example, where conflict is liable over the rate at which employees work, one might expect to find management primarily relying on control through direct supervision of the work being done or, where performance can be measured, through tying payment directly to work rate. Where there is a high degree of consensus, such as over safety, one might expect management to maintain control on the basis of an appeal to the identity of aims, such as campaigns urging workers not to take personal risks. On matters of consensus, discretion is more likely to be delegated to the employee. Moreover, categories of employees whose acceptance of managerial aims can generally be taken for granted and who are usually highly trained as well – development engineers are one such example – will tend to be subject to a far less direct mode of control than will groups of employees who are likely to resist managerial objectives and/or who may require more technical guidance.

Another reason for management finding it appropriate to pursue a portfolio of control strategies is that control is not likely to be aligned to a single objective. Management has to have regard to efficiency, which tends to be a short-term, "here and now" objective. At the same time, it also has to ensure that the organization can adapt to new circumstances, which requires preserving some flexibility in working arrangements. Management may, in addition, be concerned to encourage the creative capabilities of employees and the whole organization's capacity to innovate and learn. This will require some space to permit creative thinking and experimentation. A mix of objectives speaks for a corresponding balance between control strategies. For instance, an all-out emphasis on controlling for efficiency may jeopardize attainment of other objectives if it destroys the goodwill among those employees required to adapt working arrangements, eliminates creative space, or removes investment in staff development. The need to design a mix of organizational arrangements to suit a combination of strategic priorities is elaborated further in Chapter 17.

The appropriate position for an organization to adopt on each control dimension will therefore vary according to its circumstances. These dimensions are not, however, independent of each other, but in fact serve complementary functions for management. For example, the use of formalization as a means to "structure" the activities of people within an organization can facilitate both an increase in delegation and a reduction in close supervision. Research on the structural development of Canadian post-secondary colleges illustrates this complementarity between dimensions of control. It is also one of the few investigations to have examined how the use of control mechanism changes over time as organizations grow, as described in Box 6.1 below.

BOX 6.1 CHANGES IN CONTROL MECHANISMS AS ORGANIZATIONS GROW

A study of 23 post-secondary colleges in Alberta and British Columbia provides interesting insights into how methods of control tend to change as an organization grows. Changes in control are also to be expected if organizations diversify their activities and locations.

As the colleges grew larger and older, the following changes occurred. They steadily increased their reliance on formal controls. At the same time, they increased their delegation of decisions over the earlier years. The amount of delegation then fell back before increasing again in later years. Reliance on personal supervision by middle managers and supervisors rose at first in step with delegation by top management, but later on tended to decline.

These relationships point to a number of tentative conclusions. First, the difference between smaller, younger versus larger, older organizations was marked. The small, young organization tended to have little formalization, was highly centralized, and had a moderate amount of personal supervision by middle managers. As growth proceeded, delegation increased, but this was accompanied by a rise in both personal supervision and, after a while, formalization. Then a crisis of control appears to have been reached in which formalization was increased quite markedly, delegation decreased, and the use of personal supervision declined. At this point, it appears that formalization was rapidly being instituted as a control strategy in place of reliance on direct supervision and that, while formal procedures and job definitions were being implemented, some degree of re-centralized decision-taking had to compensate for the reduction in direct supervision. In later stages of development, formalization tended to increase fairly steadily, and delegation was re-instituted and extended.

Source: D. Friesen, R.P. Heron, E.A. Holdaway, J.G.T. Kelsey, and L.E. Sackney. *Organizational Structures: The Educational Sector*. Edmonton: The University of Alberta, February 1978.

These interpretations of Friesen and his colleagues' findings make the point that managers are presented with some choice in their approach to control, in that different configurations of control dimensions are possible. This choice will probably be constrained by the prevailing situation, but should nonetheless allow for some expression of what is felt to be desirable managerial philosophy. Today, in view of the need to secure sufficient flexibility to cope with present rates of change and the need to motivate employees and make best use of their capabilities, there is a growing interest in finding ways of promoting committed self-control and relaxing the more structured control mechanisms.

There are six particularly significant strategies of control in organizations. Their features are summarized in Box 6.2. Each control strategy is based on a different configuration of control mechanism dimensions. Although more than one strategy can be adopted within a single organization, these will tend to be applied to different types of unit undertaking different types of work, or located within different cultural milieus. The attempt to apply more than one strategy to a particular group of people engaged on similar work could be counter-productive. It runs the risk of exposing employees to inconsistencies and destroying initiative, if not actually provoking active resistance due to resentment at what is perceived as control overkill.

This may even be the case with what is termed "cultural control" in Box 6.2. Cultural control can be used to reinforce the other five types, especially "HRM control." Nevertheless, employees who accept cultural control in its fully developed form may well resist a heavy application of other strategies. In Anglo-Saxon cultures at least, with their emphasis on individualism and personal independence, a cultural approach to control will normally be allied to a philosophy of empowerment and self-control. There is some evidence to suggest that the heavy imposition of control through the simultaneous use of more than one strategy may be more common in situations where passive acceptance of authority is the norm, combined with low trust and low skills, e.g., the employment of migrant workers from developing economies. This is not, however, normally the recommended basis for a healthy organization.

Personal centralized control

This control strategy is often found in the small, owner-managed firm. It is also a form of control historically associated with the subcontractor in building and civil engineering, the "butty" in coalmining, and comparable arrangements in general engineering and iron and steel making. Centralization of decision-making and initiative around a leadership figure is fundamental to this approach. Decisions are passed to the person at the top of the organization or whoever is in charge of the unit concerned. The control process consists largely of ensuring, through personal inspection and reporting, that such decisions are carried out. The leader may in fact spend a significant proportion of his or her time personally supervising the work being done. When an organization becomes large enough to employ someone to supervise the details of everyday operations, a separation occurs between centralized decision-making and close supervision. Both continue to be done in person, with the supervisors of work now reporting personally at frequent intervals to the leader. The leader's authority generally rests on rights of ownership, very special personal qualities (charisma), or technical expertise. A major criterion in allocating rewards and punishments is likely to be obedience to the leader's authority. Under these circumstances it is, of course, easy for favoritism to develop and distort the feedback of information to the leader.

BOX 6.2 SIX STRATEGIES OF CONTROL IN ORGANIZATIONS

1 *Personal centralized control*
   1.1 direct supervision of people's activities
   1.2 centralized decision taking
   1.3 personal leadership: founded upon ownership rights, charisma, and/or technical expertise
   1.4 rewards and punishments reinforcing conformity to personal authority
2 *Bureaucratic control*
   2.1 breaking down of task into easily definable elements
   2.2 formally specified methods, procedures, and rules applied to the conduct of tasks
   2.3 budgetary and standard cost-variance accounting controls
   2.4 technology designed to limit variation in the conduct of tasks, with respect to pace, sequence, and possibly physical methods[14]
   2.5 routine decision-taking delegated within prescribed limits
   2.6 reward and punishment systems reinforcing conformity to procedures and rules
3 *Output control*
   3.1 jobs and units designed with responsibility for complete outputs
   3.2 specification of output standards and targets
   3.3 use of "responsibility accounting" systems
   3.4 delegation of decisions on operational matters: semi-autonomy
   3.5 reward and punishment linked to attainment of output targets
4 *Control through electronic surveillance*
   4.1 speed and quality of work recorded and assessed remotely via information and communication technology (ICT)
   4.2 employee's performance assessed against that of other employees and trends
   4.3 such monitoring of performance used to reward and discipline employees
5 *HRM control*
   5.1 use of selection methods to ensure that new recruits "fit" the profile of attitude, behavior, and capabilities desired by management
   5.2 training and development designed to reinforce this desired profile
   5.3 assessment procedures and reward systems used to encourage conformity
6 *Cultural control*
   6.1 development of employees' personal identification with management goals
   6.2 strong emphasis on the collective and mutually-supportive character of the organization – e.g., analogy with the "family"
   6.3 employment characterized by security of tenure and progression within the organization
   6.4 semi-autonomous working: few formal controls

BOX 6.3   A PERSONAL CENTRALIZED CONTROL STRATEGY

A five-star hotel was purchased and redeveloped in a world famous resort by a property company belonging to a family of Mediterranean origin. The hotel offered a range of services. In addition to guest accommodation and food and beverages, it also provided conference facilities, shopping, apartments for rent, and public parking. Each morning, all the heads of department would assemble in the owner's office. The owner's two sons, who were being groomed to assume senior positions, were normally present as well. During the meeting, the owner would question the managers in turn about events the previous day, as well as the intentions for that day and the near future. He then issued instructions to each manager. Sometimes, the owner would also mention future developments concerning the hotel as a whole or one of its associated properties. The tone of the meetings, which I witnessed personally, was very deferential and there was an implicit process underway whereby the loyalty of each manager to the owner was reaffirmed. As a control and motivational procedure, these meetings appeared to work well. Given the relatively small size of the organization and high profile of its operations, it seemed unlikely that the significant power distance between the owner and his managers would permit the latter to distort the feedback information they provided. Their loyalty was further reinforced by the fact that they were all long-service staff who were treated generously. They and their families were, in effect, "retainers" of the owning family.

Source: Author's personal observations.

Box 6.3 provides an illustration of the personal centralized control strategy in use.

Bureaucratic control

The bureaucratic control strategy is a familiar one, not only in the public services where it may be said to have originated, but also in larger organizations of all types. Its rationale is the attempt to ensure predictability through the specification of how people in the organization should behave and discharge their duties. The most characteristic feature of the bureaucratic control strategy is formalization in the sense of written and standardized definitions of responsibilities and procedures. Scientific management was a classic example of this control strategy as applied to manufacturing industry. It advocated the "three Ss:" *Specialization* that, through the *Simplification* involved, permitted the specification of *Standard* methods for how each element of the job should be carried out. This approach to control remains in wide use throughout the world, even in recently emerged types of work unit such as call centers.[15]

Reward and punishment systems can be designed with the intention of reinforcing this control strategy. Compliance and "keeping your nose clean" can be rewarded by upgrading, admission to staff status, the award of more favorable employment benefits, and (not least) job security. These prospects of admission to the privileged sector of employment – which labor economists call the "primary" segment of the internal organizational labor market – have close affinities with the offer of job security and progression of benefits available to the compliant official in a public service bureaucracy. Non-compliance will, by contrast, normally involve an increasing order of sanctions ending with dismissal.

The accounting control systems that are most compatible with the bureaucratic strategy of control are budgets and control of variance from standard costs. Budgetary control involves a regularly repeated process of formulating a budget, often on an annual basis, followed by a set of budgetary reports usually submitted on a more frequent basis (often monthly). Since budgets are typically broken down into expenditure norms for specific tasks or operations, they are in effect structured controls over the behavior of units, groups, or individuals. Similarly, a standard cost-variance control system involves a process of determining what the level of costs should be under specified operating systems, using these costs as standards of performance, measuring actual cost performance, and then evaluating this against the standard costs. The determination of standard costs in effect establishes a major parameter for the ways in which subordinates can set about their work. The whole bureaucratic strategy is aimed at the control of how things are done and how people in organizations should behave. It is in this sense a "behavior control" approach that contrasts to the "output control" approach discussed below.[16]

The bureaucratic strategy of control clearly allows for only limited flexibility. If budgets and standards have to be revised frequently, this becomes a very costly exercise that diverts effort from value-adding work. A more flexible approach would not attempt to specify behavior so closely, if at all, but would rather focus on overall objectives and how people were progressing toward their achievement. For example, a close monitoring of cash flow would replace the use of detailed budgets. If a unit were a cost center, its total expenditure would be monitored against targets rather than specific elements that it would be functional to change as tasks were accomplished. These developments are more compatible with the devolution of overall performance responsibility to units and teams and represent a shift toward output control.

Another problem lies in the way that bureaucratic control attempts to impose norms and procedures uniformly on all employees, regardless of their personal strengths or weaknesses. As the example in Box 6.4 illustrates, a bureaucratic control system designed to suit most employees can for this reason end up alienating one of the company's best performers. You might like to consider how this dilemma could be resolved.

Output control

This control strategy depends on having the ability to identify tasks that are complete in themselves, in the sense of having a measurable output or criterion of overall achievement. An output in this sense does not have to be an end product – it could be a piece-part manufactured to agreed specifications, a batch of microchips, or a sub-assembly. Common criteria of achievement are quantities of items processed, value added, and profitability. These criteria can be applied to individuals, groups, product lines, and whole units, as is appropriate according to how work is organized. In the case of many services, the measurable output would be the whole service based on satisfaction expressed by the customer, though some services like transportation can have their performance broken down into separate elements like punctuality, comfort, and staff courtesy.

BOX 6.4 "DEAR HOME OFFICE: DO YOU READ ME?"

Charles (Hap) Clonninger is an outstanding life insurance salesman – he knows it and the company knows it. His monthly total of policies written in dollar value consistently places him in the top ten percent of all company agents. And, the more he sells, the easier it becomes. As Hap (for Happy) himself put it some time ago, "sales build confidence in a man and confidence in himself is what motivates a man to do still more. It just builds and builds."

Clearly, Hap Clonninger is a highly motivated and productive insurance agent. The company has recognized Hap's contribution over and above the usual generous sales commissions. For example, in the past three years, Clonninger has received:

1   a two week, all expenses paid trip for himself and his wife to Nassau in the Bahamas as one of the top ten producers for the year;
2   a weekend in Mexico City (paid, of course) for top dollar sales in the month of January;
3   free tickets to numerous theatrical and sporting activities;
4   a weekend in Pasadena, California, for the annual Tournament of Roses Parade and two tickets to the Rosebowl Game;
5   numerous sales citations and plaques that are prominently displayed in his downtown Atlanta office.

Hap Clonninger has also been recognized by industry professionals outside his company and was recently elected to the position of Vice-President, Georgia Chapter, of the Insurance Executives Association.

Cloninnger thoroughly enjoys his work and claims he wouldn't trade places with anyone. "I don't really think of myself as a salesman," he often says; "I prefer to think of myself as someone who helps people build their estates . . . a sort of financial planner and advisor. It is very satisfying work and I can immediately see the rewards for my efforts."

It seems, though, that no job is perfect in every respect and there is one part of his work that does irritate Hap Clonninger: a required company report in narrative on sales prospects.

"That damned report kills a whole day each month!" says Clonninger. "Imagine, *an entire day* a month filling in six pages of questions in straight narration on how I propose to close sales for the next month.

"I mean, I can see the company's point of view, particularly with new and inexperienced salesmen. A detailed form such as this one forces a new man to work out a sales plan for the coming period. It helps the man because it transforms fuzzy or vague ideas in his head into a workable plan on paper. The form also helps the company because it shows that the agent really does have a well-defined sales plan. It can also serve as a basis for monitoring his progress . . . how well he actually does compared with what he said he would do.

"But that monthly Sales Plan doesn't really have any value to the company or to me so far as my efforts are concerned. It probably has little or no value to any other top agent either. We have so many deals cooking all the time that we don't bother to work from a plan.

"One month, about a year ago, I didn't send in the report for the first time since I've been an agent for the company. I thought if nothing was said I'd skip it from then on. Wow! You'd think I'd committed grand larceny! I received formal notices from two vice-presidents and several, more lower-level bureaucrats about the omission and so I figured it wasn't worth fighting the system . . . I'd continue submitting sales plans as in the past.

"Some time later though it occurred to me that the *only time* I had heard any feedback about my monthly report was in the month that I failed to turn it in! *At no other time in recent years could I recall anyone commenting on or questioning my sales plan.*

"Four months ago, on the day of the report, I was feeling pretty good. I had just sold a big policy to a supermarket executive and was in no mood to write the report. But, conditioned by years of compliance, I started plugging away at it.

"About halfway through, on page 3 or 4, I suddenly wrote, 'If anyone has bothered to read this far, I, Hap Clonninger, will personally buy him a martini.' You know, I didn't have to buy a single martini . . . and that report crosses at least four desks!

"The next month I wrote in the middle of the text, 'This report has been prepared by the world's greatest insurance salesman.' Again, no response from home office.

"Still there was the possibility that the report was being read, but that my remarks were being ignored as whimsy. So, I decided last month to really test the system. On page 2 under the heading of new prospects, I wrote:

'Edgar Millikan (company president) is a dirty old man and a poor insurance risk.'

Would you believe that I got no response? Nobody reads the monthly report . . . but if I don't turn one in . . . Wow!"

Reproduced from Robert D. Joyce, *Encounters in Organizational Behavior*. New York: Pergamon 1972: 17–19.

Once outputs or criteria for overall performance have been identified, it is possible for management to specify output standards and targets. Rewards and sanctions can be linked to the attainment of performance expressed in output terms. In this way, a direct incentive is created for employees to meet and surpass output standards. The effectiveness of this incentive will depend greatly on the degree of trust in management's intentions to honor the equation between rewards and performance. If this trust is lacking, both the incentive value of the system and the accuracy of information released to management are likely to suffer. Assessments of performance are liable to create tension and resentment if any suspicion of inequity is present.

"Responsibility accounting" is the kind of financial accounting system most suited to an output control strategy.[17] This assigns financial responsibility to specified organizational sub-units, measures the performance of those units, and provides feedback on performance both to the people assigned responsibility and to their manager. The assignment of responsibility for a rounded activity may be in terms of *investment centers* in which the people concerned have authority over revenues, costs, and capital investment; *profit centers* where authority is delegated over revenues and costs, but not investment; or *cost centers* where authority is delegated over costs, but not over revenue-generating decisions or capital investment.

An output control strategy is aimed at facilitating the devolution of operational decision-making without incurring the costly and potentially demotivating paraphernalia of bureaucratic controls or of relying on close personal supervision, which can also be demotivating and adds to managerial overheads. Once output standards have been agreed with staff, it is often possible to leave them free from detailed control over how they do things, in a semi-autonomous relationship to management. This strategy also has the merit of directing the process of control toward the issue that really counts for the long-term survival of an organization – its performance. It is, however, important to minimize the conflicts that can arise between the criteria assigned to different sub-units competing for resources or (sometimes) for custom in the same market.

Output control is therefore in principle an attractive strategy and one that is generally consistent with the adoption of new organizational forms. What then are possible obstacles to its adoption? One problem is that the autonomy given to working groups or teams, which output control encourages, can stand in the way of introducing technological advances that require a more integrated process combining tasks previously performed separately by each group. An example would be the introduction of automated transfer equipment. In this case, it may be feasible to shift the focus of output control up a level to plant rather than group output. Another problem can arise if workgroups resist management's suggestions for improvement because they suspect that these are the prelude to renegotiating downwards their rate of payment per unit of output. The question of trust is clearly an issue here. A technical problem with output control may lie in the difficulty of establishing suitable and agreed measures of output. For instance, while it may be possible to measure the output of advisory and staff groups in terms of, say, the number of reports they produce, it may be more difficult to judge the quality of those reports. On the other hand, if the processes whereby results are achieved are not well understood, and therefore not codifiable by management, a form of output assessment may be called for because it is not feasible to apply a bureaucratic approach. Some professional and industrial research activities fall into this category.

Control through electronic surveillance

Surveillance itself is not a new form of control. It is central to control through direct personal supervision. The new aspect of surveillance lies in the application of electronic means for performance monitoring.

The essence of control through electronic surveillance is that the speed and quality of work is recorded and assessed remotely through the use of information and communication technology, including video. This avoids costly reliance on personal supervision, and also has the advantage that the control data captured is precise rather than impressionistic and subject to managerial bias. An employee's performance can through these means be assessed against that of other employees and with reference to trends over time. This precise monitoring of performance can in turn readily be used as the basis for rewarding and disciplining employees.

Electronic surveillance is being applied to many types and levels of activity. As early as 1990, some 10 million workers in the USA, including many managerial and professional employees, were subject to it.[18] By 2001, nearly 80 percent of the large to medium-sized companies surveyed by the American Management Association were checking employee's email, Internet, or telephone connections, or videoing them at work. This percentage had jumped from 35 percent in 1997. A subsequent American Management Association survey in 2007 of 304 US companies concluded that:

> From e-mail monitoring and website blocking to phone tapping and GPS tracking, employers increasingly combine technology with policy to manage productivity and minimize litigation, security, and other risks. To motivate compliance with rules and policies, more than one fourth of employers have fired workers for misusing e-mail and nearly one third have fired employees for misusing the Internet . . . Computer monitoring takes many forms, with 45% of employers tracking content, keystrokes, and time spent at the keyboard. Another 43% store and review computer files.[19]

One of the earlier applications of control through electronic surveillance was the recording of the keystrokes achieved by operators at workstations or PCs. Pressure for university teachers to place their materials on organizational websites and communicate with students via email and computerized "chat rooms" provides an example of the potential electronic surveillance of professional work.

Call centers provide an increasingly common example of tight control relying partly on electronic monitoring. By 2002 call centers accounted for 3 percent of the working population in the USA, and it was estimated that in 2011 they accounted for 3.5 percent of UK employment, or over one million people.[20] Automated call distribution systems (ACDs) enable management to direct the allocation, character, and speed of the tasks to be done. The performance of individual call center staff ("customer service representatives") can be monitored and evaluated, and compared within or across sites.

In a case study reported by Callaghan and Thompson, the call center had specified 19 core standards of behavior and 7-point scales to measure the skills of operators during appraisal. The surveillance of calls from customers was undertaken by a "research department," which conducted random checks and responds to customer complaints, as well as by team leaders who listened to at least five calls per week. Statistics on how many calls are taken, how they are handled, where they are directed, and their average time, are collected and graded as the basis for feedback, discipline, and appraisal. The target is that no more than three calls out of every ten thousand should generate complaints.[21] Needless to say, the front-line call center staff dislike the pressure that this form of control places on them, and there is evidence that it leads to emotional exhaustion.[22] Many challenge the objectivity and appropriateness of relying on electronically produced statistics to encourage a uniformity of response and pressure for speed that does not take account of the individual needs of each customer. Although call centers may well attract recruits who do not expect to stay many years in the job, the nature of the control to which they are subjected contributes to high labor turnover and low morale.[23]

HRM control

The primary activities of human resource management (HRM) are identified in Figure 6.1, which also indicates how they are seen to relate in the form of an HRM cycle.

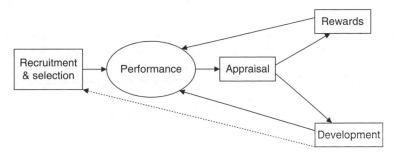

Figure 6.1 The Human Resource Management Cycle

The recruitment and selection of new employees is intended to improve an organization's performance through matching individuals to the work or activities that need to be carried out, as well as through attracting people with good developmental potential. The performance of managers and staff is appraised at regular intervals. Appraisal should provide feedback to the people involved, assessing their needs for further development and training, and allocating recognition and rewards. If the reward system is appropriate, it should help to motivate the kind of achievement and behavior that contribute to better performance. Similarly, if the training and development programs offered to employees are attuned to their needs in relation to the requirements of their job, these again should contribute to better performance. If it turns out that a significant amount of investment in development is necessary for people to perform adequately, this information provides feedback relevant to the selection process because it indicates that the people being selected for employment do not possess the right kind of capabilities at that time.

HRM procedures can be used both to develop people at work ("human resources") and control their behavior and performance. They are part of management's control armory in that they enhance the contribution that people at work make to the achievement of organizational goals and objectives. Systematic selection techniques are designed to ensure that new recruits fit the profile of attitude, social skills, and technical competencies that management is seeking. Performance evaluation and appraisal provide feedback both to management and to employees themselves. In many organizations today, these processes are highly formalized. Feedback on performance is increasingly expected to be constructive, in the sense of identifying possibilities for achieving more ambitious goals and the improvement in capabilities and job conditions needed to accomplish this. As Chapter 7 discusses in detail, a further contribution that HRM can make to the process of control is through designing rewards that provide incentives for people to achieve such goals.

Cultural control

Cultural control has been strongly associated with moves away from conventional organizational forms. Its rationale is one of maintaining control by means of internalized compliance rather than external constraint. It aims to ensure that the members of an organization willingly comply with managerial requirements on the basis both of accepting the legitimacy of management's authority and identifying with its goals. This is an approach to control that relies on shaping employees' understandings of how they stand in relation to their work and their employer. This kind of organizational control is accomplished through employees willingly accepting a managerial interpretation of their work and their organization, and with which they come to identify.[24] Trust in management is a condition for such identification.

Perhaps the most striking example of cultural control is to be seen in the larger Japanese corporations where extremely high levels of productivity and employee loyalty have been the norm. An important foundation for this commitment has been a common socialization into the corporate culture and the ready acceptance of its values and beliefs. In Japanese companies, and many larger corporations elsewhere too, programs have been devised to break down sectional identities and instead to generate an awareness of, and commitment to, a common corporate identity. The methods employed for this purpose include "awareness training" at education centers, corporate videos and other communications, and social gatherings organized by managers and team leaders.

Critics have called such activities a form of "compulsory sociability."[25] The cultural control strategy places a heavy emphasis on the collective and mutually supportive character of the organization and often invokes an analogy with the family. For this to remain credible, employers must also be willing to accept the obligations of family heads to protect their members, especially with a guarantee of job security and opportunities for employees to progress within the organization. It remains to be seen, however, when faced with severe pressures to rationalize and restructure, how many of the major Japanese companies will continue to offer this baseline support. Certainly, many American corporations, when faced with a squeeze on earnings, have shown little compunction in laying off employees, thereby pulling the rug from under the credibility of corporate culture programs and destroying the trust that is essential to them.[26]

It is actually quite difficult for employers and senior managers to avoid entanglement in contradictions when they espouse cultural control, as many have sought to do. One contradiction concerns the way that a strong corporate culture is supposed to provide an alternative to control. Despite the claim that the development of a strong and widely accepted corporate culture permits the granting of high levels of autonomy, in practice strenuous efforts are usually made to ensure that employees conform to the norms and rituals of that culture. Corporate culture building is in fact usually undertaken or advocated with control in mind. It is regarded as an exercise to develop an appropriate social order that provides the basis for desired behavior. Working as it does through the shaping of people's attitudes, cultural control is often combined with an emphasis on HRM control. The thinking is that, in order to let people loose to be "autonomous," they have to be mentally programmed first, with a key role here for selecting suitable candidates and then socializing them though appropriate training. As Thompson and McHugh have commented, "through team practices and family rhetoric, the company produces 'designer employees' who buy into the secure identity offered by the simulated community."[27]

Similar to output control, managers have to accept that subordinates who are subject to an effective regime of cultural control can be given considerable discretion on how to go about their work, assuming that they possess the necessary skills and abilities. For they will have an understanding of the goals set for the organization and an enthusiasm to work towards them. Management can contemplate semi-autonomous modes of working if there is a high degree of consensus within the organization. Acceptance of a common corporate culture can assist in maintaining cohesion between the activities of teams and other component units of the organization, and this acceptance is more likely if the staff concerned have participated in a process of defining organizational goals.

These features of cultural control offer clear advantages over other forms of control in companies seeking to encourage informed and flexible behavior on the part of well-educated members. For a company that is seeking to achieve a differentiated market appeal based on superior products and services, most other forms of control have significant drawbacks. Centralized personal supervision is liable to create top management overload and be unduly restrictive of initiative and innovation. Bureaucratic control relies on the prior prescription of actions and behaviors that in present conditions can become obsolete even before they are introduced. Both personal and bureaucratic control can also be highly demotivating, especially for knowledge workers. Output control does permit devolved autonomy, but it also relies on the ability to specify standards and targets. At the very least, these may have to be revised at frequent intervals under conditions of hypercompetition and rapidly changing environments. Electronic surveillance also depends on the ability to specify performance standards, which may be feasible with relatively routine work, but less so with non-routine, creative activities.

Despite the psychological and social manipulation, even sheer hypocrisy, that has often accompanied the use of cultural control, it is actually in tune with two long-term trends noted in Chapter 3. One is the increasing numbers of professional and other knowledge workers in the working population; the other is the growing use of organizational clusters, alliances and networks in supply and value chains. Cultural control has long been applied within the professions, where it has combined with personal autonomy to follow strongly internalized norms of competence and correct conduct. Professional people, more than most, resent having external managerial control imposed on them when they become employees of, or contracted to, large institutions. The rising proportion of knowledge workers is therefore establishing the need for a new approach to control that relies more heavily on internalized self-control.

The second trend is that increasingly organizations are working cooperatively, whether this be cooperation between companies or public agencies. Part III of this book focuses on this phenomenon. In such collaborative and partnership relationships, control has to rest primarily on a definition and acceptance of mutual obligations, supported by trust between the parties who are involved. This means substituting relational control for the more traditional hierarchical approach. As John Hagel and his co-authors have written, this is "a trust- and relationship-oriented concept of organizational 'control' that acknowledges mutual obligations and responsibilities among partners across firm boundaries and the network . . ."[28] The development of a common culture to give meaning and purpose to the cooperation can therefore provide an important support for guiding and sustaining the cooperative effort.

In principle, cultural control is also compatible with industrial democracy and the equalization of power within organizations. Indeed, this is probably the only way to guarantee that cultural control rests upon a true consensus rather than one imposed by senior management. Given that any organized activity requires control, participation can become a means of organizational control based on legitimacy. In the vision of new organization, a widely accepted organizational culture would establish the values to guide more specific goals and targets by which the progress of the collective activity could be monitored. This approach is consistent with self-managing units or teams that accept responsibility for meeting agreed targets and completing collectively endorsed projects. If underwritten in this way by genuine legitimacy, the combination of cultural and output control strategies can reconcile the underlying need for managing with employees' desires to have more participation and self-fulfillment.

Conventional and newer approaches to control

The strategies of control differ in their compatibility with conventional and newer approaches to organization. Three strategies of control broadly speaking correspond to conventional modes of organization, while the others are more consistent with new organizational forms. As Chapter 3 described, control in conventional and traditional organization tends to be heavily reliant either on personal supervision and centralized decision making, or on the application of rules and norms of conduct. Electronic surveillance is also consistent with these conventional approaches to control, even though it employs a highly contemporary technology.

The other three control strategies are, by contrast, emphasized more heavily in newer approaches to organization that endeavor to foster devolved initiative in order to encourage innovation and a flexible response to change. Devolved initiative is much better managed through the monitoring of how well people achieve agreed goals than either direct supervision or the laying down of rules. The newer organizational philosophy also stresses the value of human capital and the appropriateness of managing knowledgeable employees through the fostering of their potential and commitment. This is consistent with an HRM approach to control. The development of identification with a corporate culture and the management goals it articulates is highly compatible with the new organizational philosophy, so long as it does not become over-manipulative.

◢ Control Strategies and Relevant Contingencies

The choice between organizational forms has to be made with contingencies in mind; such as how affected a company is by competition and change, and the kind of people it employs. This applies equally to the question of control. For example, should several strategies be applied in combination? Should different strategies be applied to different areas of activity or types of personnel?

The case of Hap Clonninger described in Box 6.4 illustrates the dilemma of whether to vary control according to the type of employee. The monitoring function of the monthly report was clearly not appropriate for a high-performing salesman like Clonninger – it took time away from doing his job and the discovery that nobody was reading his reports became seriously demotivating. In any case, the company could readily assess salesman performance by the new business each one signed up. As Clonninger himself admits, however, the monthly monitoring could be helpful in the case of new and inexperienced salespeople. It could be allied to HRM procedures that offered mentoring and training for less experienced staff. Should the company therefore only require reports from certain categories of salespeople? It could do this, so long as it made the criteria for determining who had to complete the report very clear – for example, lack of experience, newness of tenure, or even level of performance. Otherwise, a differential application of the control could easily be interpreted as arbitrary behavior on management's part.

Table 6.1 summarizes the implications for choice of control strategy presented by different contingencies. The first is the *competitive strategy* that a firm is pursuing.[29] If it is aiming to secure an advantage over competitors based on lower cost, it necessarily has to rely heavily on tight cost control and incentives for achieving quantitative targets. Tight cost control can be

Table 6.1 Strategies of control and related contingencies

Contingent factors	When	Control strategies likely to be appropriate ($/$ = and/or)
1. Competitive strategy	Cost leadership	Bureaucratic/electronic surveillance (ES)/output
	Differentiation	HRM/cultural/output (qualitative)
2. Extent of diversification	High	Output/HRM/cultural
	Low	Personal centralized (PC)/bureaucratic
3. Environmental variability: unpredictability of activities and need for flexibility	High	PC (small organizations)/HRM/cultural
	Low	Bureaucratic
4. Task characteristics: outputs	Measurable	Bureaucratic/output/ES
	Not measurable	PC/HRM/output
5. Task characteristics: knowledge of transformation processes	Good	PC/bureaucratic
	Limited	Output/HRM/cultural
6. Importance of achieving innovation	High	Output/HRM/cultural
	Low	PC/bureaucratic/ES
7. Employee expertise and skill	High	Output/HRM/cultural
	Low	PC/bureaucratic/ES
8. Position of employees in labor market	Strong	Output/cultural
	Weak	PC/bureaucratic/ES
9. Size of the organization	Small	PC
	Large	Other types

assisted by various bureaucratic control procedures. These include the requirement of prior managerial approval for items of expenditure, the specification of economical working methods aimed at waste reduction, and the formalization of conditions for other expenditure such as the class of air and rail travel permitted. Electronic surveillance can also help to reduce the cost of services provided by recording in detail items such as the time taken to complete a transaction and the added value achieved. Output control, where it is feasible, can also keep down the cost of each activity or transaction by specifying appropriate targets that are then monitored at regular intervals.

A contrasting strategy is for a firm to achieve an advantage over competitors based on securing a price premium for a superior, or even unique, product. Michael Porter has called this a "differentiation" strategy.[30] Differentiation requires an ability to adapt to different customer requirements, if not the ability to innovate products and services. This in turns needs strong, cross-functional coordination, creativity, and an emphasis on qualitative targets. If quality can be measured, then suitable output controls can be used to monitor it. A differentiation strategy can be supported across the organization as a whole through the use of HRM processes to recruit, develop, and motivate high quality and creative people, and by a corporate culture that stresses the importance of creativity, customer orientation, quality, and other desired features.

The *extent of diversification* is a second contingency that carries implications for the choice of control strategy. If geographical diversification is extensive, it becomes more difficult to rely on personal centralized control, even with the use of communication technologies such as videoconferencing. If a firm's product or service lines are highly diversified, the use of personal control from the top of the organization is constrained by limitations of knowledge about the details of the different operations and their markets. It may also be problematic to adapt bureaucratic controls to the variety of regional, technological, and/or market circumstances that characterize a diversified firm. Diversification therefore obliges a firm to consider the use of output controls, supported by HRM and cultural controls, to encourage whatever level of consistency is desired across diversified units.

Environmental variability means that the conditions under which a firm operates, and the activities it has to carry out, are characterized by significant uncertainty. High variability puts a premium on organizational flexibility. Bureaucratic controls tend to be too rigid to permit such flexibility. Great reliance has to be placed on personal centralized control, if the firm is small, or otherwise a combination of HRM and cultural controls. If performance measures can be devised that allow for a flexible response to unanticipated demands and other external developments, it may be possible to use electronic surveillance and output controls. It is, however, unlikely that these approaches will be sufficiently adaptable to meet all cases of environmental variability. Low environmental variability makes it more feasible to employ bureaucratic control, assuming that other circumstances are favorable to that approach.

Two aspects of *the tasks to be done* in an organization are particularly relevant to the choice of control strategy. These are, first, whether the tasks are *measurable* and whether there is good *knowledge of the transformation processes* involved – i.e., how to carry them out. The performance of tasks that have readily measurable parameters can be monitored by bureaucratic controls, when methods can be measured, and output or electronic controls when outputs can be measured. Tasks that are difficult or impossible to measure require personal supervision or the arm's length support of HRM and cultural strategies. Tasks normally involve the transformation of physical materials or information. If the processes used in such transformations are well known, so that best practice can be specified, personal or bureaucratic control can be used. The choice between them depends on factors such as the size of the firm and its constituent work units, and the attitude of employees towards personal rather than impersonal monitoring. On the other hand, when transformation processes are poorly known, so that they have to be worked out by the employees directly involved, management cannot specify the methods to be used and other control strategies therefore become more appropriate: output, HRM, and cultural.

Two further contingencies are likely to be associated with a limited knowledge of transformation processes. These are *innovation* and high levels of *employee expertise and skill*. It is becoming more important across virtually every sector to compete on the basis of innovation in products and services. Innovation by definition involves working on new tasks with new parameters and conditions, so that the transformation processes involved have to be discovered or worked out as the innovation proceeds. The employees working on innovation and new developments require high levels of relevant expertise and skill. By contrast, purely routine work involves little or no innovation and lower level skills. The tasks comprising the work and the jobs of the people concerned have well-understood transformation processes. Therefore, control strategies suited to both innovation and highly skilled employees are output, HRM, and cultural, whereas personal centralized control and bureaucratic and electronic surveillance are more suited to routine work and lower skilled employees. While electronic surveillance is not well suited to the control of innovative activities, it is sufficiently flexible to be applied to assessing skilled as well as routine operators, including some aspects of their behavior. For example, some call center work requires high levels of skill in handling interpersonal communications, which can be monitored electronically through listening remotely to a sample of calls.

The *position of employees in the labor market* can impact upon the effectiveness of different control strategies. Some categories of personnel, and indeed some individuals, hold a strong labor market position – they can readily quit their job for another one if they do not like the way they are being controlled. Such people are normally the outstanding performers who possess certified skills and/or have an exemplary track record. Hap Clonninger precisely fits this category; Box 6.4 above illustrates his frustration with a formalized bureaucratic control procedure that wastes his time and, worse still, is not being followed through in his case because it is actually unnecessary to do so. Employees enjoying a strong labor market position are therefore likely to respond better to output and cultural controls, especially if they are tied to a reward policy of good performance through incentives and public recognition within the firm through awards and other symbols. By contrast, the use of personal centralized or bureaucratic controls and electronic surveillance are likely to be tolerated by employees with a weaker labor market position, even though they may not necessarily like them.

Last, but not least, there is the factor of *organizational size*. In many instances, Table 6.1 lists personal centralized control against the same contingencies as bureaucratic control. Both control strategies are attuned to cost control, low levels of diversification, low environmental variability, limited need for innovation, low employee skills, and a weak position of employees in the labor market. It is primarily the size of the organization that will dictate which of these two forms of control to adopt, though other factors such as the personal charisma and drive of the chief executive are also significant. The example given in Box 6.1 illustrated how as an organization grows, it becomes increasingly difficult to rely on personal centralized control even with the assistance of modern communication technologies, and the balance of advantage therefore tips toward the bureaucratic approach. Other, less direct control strategies – output, electronic surveillance, HRM, and cultural – are not so constrained by the size factor, though it becomes increasingly difficult to sustain a common corporate culture the larger and more diversified a firm is.

To summarize: the choice of control strategy has to be made with reference to the type of activities undertaken by the organization, the qualities of the people it employs (including their scarcity), and a range of factors in its context. This is a highly complex area for managers to decide on, and one that is still poorly informed by research. While Table 6.1 draws attention to the main contingencies bearing upon the choice of control strategies, it does not address the full complexity of the decisions to be made. These decisions are made more complicated by the presence of multiple contingencies and different conditions within the same firm. As Chapter 12 will indicate, many large MNCs, diversified by function, product, and region, face this high level of internal complexity, and as a result they find it appropriate to employ a range of control strategies within the same company.

SUMMARY

1 Control is a core process within organizations, yet it has been accorded relatively little attention.

2 It is often linked to the exercise of managerial power, though other groups may also attempt to control what goes on within an organization and how it is done.

3 Further ambiguity surrounds the concept of control, because it is used to denote processes that range from the exercise of power and influence in a broad sense to very specific and focused control systems.

4 It is therefore helpful to unpack the notion of control and bring to light its different aspects. One distinction is between strategic and operational levels of control. Other aspects concern the extent and focus of control, and the characteristics of control mechanisms.

5 Basic distinctions such as these help us to identify the options for control. These options can be classified into six strategies of control, some of which are consistent with conventional forms of organization while others fit more readily with newer forms.

6 Contingent factors are relevant for the choice between different control strategies. They include a firm's competitive strategy, the extent to which it is diversified, the nature of its environment, the tasks it is carrying out, the quality of its employees, and its overall size.

7 Control is considered further in two later chapters that deal with specific, contemporary applications. Chapter 12 includes a discussion of control within multinational corporations and how the maintenance of control can present a problem for small and medium-sized enterprises that are expanding abroad. Chapter 16 relates control to the question of accountability in corporate governance.

QUESTIONS FOR DISCUSSION

6.1 Discuss the different meanings attached to the concept of control and their relevance for organizing.

6.2 What are the key features of control in organizations?

6.3 What is the significance of distinguishing between strategic and operational control?

6.4 Describe the main strategies of control in organization. What are the main advantages and disadvantages of each?

6.5 What considerations would be relevant to choosing between different strategies of control or combining several of them?

6.6 How does each control strategy fit with (1) conventional and (2) new forms of organization?

6.7 Would you expect different strategies of control to be prevalent in different parts of the world? Explain the reasons for your answer.

NOTES

1 The principal exception was the work of some behavioral accountants who continued to focus on control. See for example, Anthony J. Berry, Jane Broadbent, and David Otley (2005), *Management Control: Theories, Issues and Performance*, 2nd edition, Basingstoke, UK, Palgrave Macmillan. Another notable exception to the neglect of control was Paul Thompson and David McHugh (2002), *Work Organizations*, 3rd edition, Basingstoke, UK, Palgrave, who aimed to write "a critical alternative to the standard, often American, texts." The neglect of organizational control has recently begun to be rectified, especially with the publication of Sim B. Sitkin, Laura B. Cardinal, and Katinka M. Bijlsma (eds.) (2010), *Organizational Control*, Cambridge, Cambridge University Press.

2 Cambridge University Press. *Cambridge Dictionaries Online.* http://dictionary.cambridge.org

3 William Ocasio and Franz Wohlgezogen (2010), Attention and control. In Sim B. Sitkin, Laura B. Cardinal, and Katinka M. Bijlsma (eds.), *Organizational Control*, Cambridge, Cambridge University Press, pp. 191–221.

4 These possibilities are discussed by Albert O. Hirschman (1972), *Exit, Voice and Loyalty: Responses to Decline in Firms, Organizations and States*, Cambridge, MA, Harvard University Press.

5 J.R.P. French, Jr. and B. Raven (1960) offer a classic analysis of the foundations for power and control in organizations in their essay, The bases of social power, In D. Cartwright and A. Zander (eds.), *Group Dynamics: Research and Theory*, 2nd edition, New York, Harper & Row, pp. 607–623.

6 These dimensions are derived from J. Michael Geringer and Louis Hébert (1989), Control and performance of international joint ventures, *Journal of International Business Studies*, 20, 235–254.

7 The quotation is from Ken Ohmae (1993), The global logic of strategic alliances. In Joel Bleeke and David Ernst (eds.), *Collaborating to Compete*, New York, Wiley, p. 42.

8 For examples of varying focuses of control within MNCs, see John Child and Sally Heavens (1999), Managing corporate networks from America to China, *Asia Pacific Business Review*, 5, 147–180.

9 For example, John Child and Yanni Yan (2003), Predicting the performance of international joint ventures, *Journal of Management Studies*, 40, 283–320; Arran Caza (2012), Typology of the eight domains of discretion in organizations, *Journal of Management Studies*, 49, 144–177.

10 A corporate culture is the pattern of shared beliefs and values that shapes the meaning of an organization for its members and provides them with norms of behavior and performance. When management articulates a corporate culture, it is attempting to shape a way of thinking that pervades an organization with the intention of increasing the identification of employees with, and their commitment to, its goals.

11 Charles L. McMillan (1996), *The Japanese Industrial System*, 3rd edition, New York, De Gruyter.

12 A short review is provided by Jay A. Conger (2000), Motivate performance through empowerment, in Edwin A. Locke (ed.), *Handbook of Principles of Organizational Behavior*, Oxford, Blackwell, pp. 137–149.

13 Chris P. Long (2010), Control to cooperation: Examining the role of managerial authority in portfolios of managerial actions. In Sim B. Sitkin, Laura B. Cardinal, and Katinka M. Bijlsma (eds.), *Organizational Control*, Cambridge, Cambridge University Press, pp. 365–395.

14 Some authorities distinguish this as a separate control strategy. For example, Richard Edwards (1979), *Contested Terrain: The Transformation of the Workplace in the Twentieth Century*, New York, Basis Books.

15 For an example see George Callaghan and Paul Thompson (2002), 'We recruit attitude': The selection and shaping of routine call centre labour, *Journal of Management Studies*, 39, 233–254.

16 The distinction between behavior and output control was first made by William G. Ouchi (1977), The relationship between organizational structure and organizational control, *Administrative Science Quarterly*, 22, 95–113.

17 Paul D. Kimmel, Jerry J. Weygandt and Donald E. Kieso (2009), *Accounting: Tools For Business Decision Making*, 3rd edition, Hoboken, NJ, Wiley, Chapter 21.

18   Jeffrey Pfeffer (1997), *New Directions for Organizational Theory: Problems and Practices*, New York, Oxford University Press, p. 114.

19   Extract from "2007 Electronic Monitoring & Surveillance Survey" press release (http://press .amanet.org/press-releases/177/2007-electronic-monitoring-surveillance-survey/). Reproduced with permission of American Management Association International.

20   Alex Hudson (2011), Are call centres the factories of the 21st century? March 11, London: BBC. http://www.bbc.co.uk/news/magazine-12691704. Accessed 03-12-2013.

21   George Callaghan and Paul Thompson (2002), op. cit.

22   Stephen Deery, Roderick Iverson, and Janet Walsh (2002), Work relationships in telephone call centers: understanding emotional exhaustion and employee withdrawal, *Journal of Management Studies*, 39, 471–496.

23   George Callaghan and Paul Thompson (2002), op. cit.

24   Mats Alvesson and Hugh Willmott (2002). Identity regulation as organizational control: Producing the appropriate individual, *Journal of Management Studies*, 39, 619–644. Elizabeth George and Cuili Qian (2010), Organizational identity and control: can the two go together? In Sim B. Sitkin, Laura B. Cardinal, and Katinka M. Bijlsma (eds.) (2010), *Organizational Control*, Cambridge, Cambridge University Press, 167–190.

25   Paul Thompson and David McHugh (2002), op. cit., p. 203.

26   Wayne F. Cascio (2002), *Responsible Restructuring*, San Francisco, Berrett-Koehler.

27   Paul Thompson and David McHugh (2002), op. cit., p. 204.

28   John Hagel III, John Selly Brown, and Mariann Jelinek (2010), Relational networks, strategic advantage: collaborative control is fundamental. In Sim B. Sitkin, Laura B. Cardinal, and Katinka M. Bijlsma (eds.), *Organizational Control*, Cambridge, Cambridge University Press, 251–300.

29   Michael E. Porter (1985), *Competitive Advantage*, New York, Free Press.

30   Idem.

CHAPTER 7

Questions of Reward

WHAT THIS CHAPTER COVERS

The subject of reward policies and systems in organizations is so far reaching that two chapters are given over to it. Chapters 7 and 8 together present the main issues and choices concerned. They consider how reward and payment systems can be adapted to suit contemporary conditions and the adoption of new organizational forms. For rewards to contribute effectively to the process of organization, they need to reconcile the purposes of both management and employees. Chapter 7 reviews theories and concepts that have been developed to aid our understanding of rewards. Chapter 8 focuses on the specific issue of pay.

This chapter begins by discussing the role of reward policies and their systemic nature. It then distinguishes between extrinsic and intrinsic rewards, and continues by examining the criteria that management and employees respectively apply to rewards. Managerial criteria reflect the contingencies that a reward policy is intended to meet, such as attracting the desired kind of employees and motivating them to achieve the required performance of tasks. The criteria that employees apply to rewards are a guide to their motivational potential. We consider the psychological and sociological research that has informed such criteria. The chapter then discusses two perspectives that suggest how contingent factors and motivational aims can be linked together in an effective reward policy. These perspectives are expectancy theory and conditioning theory.

◢ The Role of Reward Policies

A wide range of rewards is applied daily within organizations, and they are central to the process of employment. An employment contract specifies the remuneration, and possibly other benefits, offered to an individual in return for making available to the employer his or her capacity for work. That capacity, however, still has to be converted into an active contribution toward the attainment of organizational objectives. A reward policy is intended to elicit this contribution through a number of inducements. It is therefore an essential complement to the process of control discussed in the previous chapter.

The term reward (or reward management) "system" is commonly used and this refers to linkages both between the integral components of a reward policy and the need for that policy to be attuned to the strategic objectives of an organization as well as to relevant external factors such as labor market conditions and cultural setting.[1] Internal components are pay (normally termed "compensation" in North America), intrinsic work experience, benefits such as health and pension plans, flexible working time, and symbols of status such as having one's own office. A reward system can therefore comprise a portfolio of rewards and ways in which they are offered, with the intention of attracting and retaining high quality employees and motivating them to contribute effectively to organizational objectives. The fact that a wide range of rewards is available, which can be applied in different forms, and that there are multiple objectives to be achieved, together make this an extremely complex subject on which many contrasting opinions and theories are voiced.

While rewards and punishments might be used together, their nature and objectives are different. Rewards are in principle intended to encourage the type of behavior that precedes them, while punishments are intended to discourage the behavior that precedes them. For management, the criterion of success for reward policies is that they motivate employees to commit high levels of physical and/or mental effort toward performing required tasks well. A further condition for their success is that the employees concerned regard the rewards offered to them as attractive and fair, and any punishments as legitimate and merited.

The design of reward systems complements that of organization and it is appropriate to regard it as an aspect of organizational policy. Previous chapters have drawn attention to several examples of the interdependence between organization and reward systems. Chapter 4 discussed the problem of aligning a salary structure with the design of hierarchical levels of authority. Chapter 5 noted how modifications to work organization aimed at improving integration could require the abandoning of individually based incentives in order to support a group or team mode of working. Chapter 6 indicated that suitably designed rewards should contribute toward the operation of an organization's control system by encouraging employees to achieve given standards or targets. What is rewarded must be compatible with the tasks and structures laid down for the organization, and these can therefore be regarded as contingencies for the design of reward systems.

◢ Extrinsic and Intrinsic Rewards

The most tangible rewards are *extrinsic* ones. These are attached to positions within an organization, rather than deriving directly from the actual content of those jobs. The principal extrinsic rewards are pay, fringe benefits, security of tenure, promotion, special awards, and status symbols. Pay is a highly visible reward that attracts the lion's share of attention from both employers and employees. For the employer, pay is usually a major element in an organization's costs. For the employee, pay not only provides the means to a livelihood and the satisfaction of material wants; it can also have symbolic value as a mark of achievement and social status.[2]

BOX 7.1 INTRINSIC REWARDS ARE IMPORTANT SOURCES OF SATISFACTION AT WORK

A report by the Confederation of British Industry in 2000 found that only 45 percent of those surveyed rated material rewards among the main factors in building and sustaining employee satisfaction. By contrast, 68 percent rated "good working relationships," and 57 percent "interesting work," as important sources of satisfaction.

Data from the 1998 and 2004 Workplace Employment Relations Surveys in the UK paint a picture compatible with the CBI Survey's findings. They indicate a higher mean score on a 1–5 scale given to satisfaction with a sense of achievement (3.59 in 1998 and 3.75 in 2004) and with influence at work (3.52 in 1998 and 3.53 in 2004) than was given to satisfaction with pay (2.86 in both years).

Sources: *Employment Trends Survey 2000: Measuring Flexibility in the Labour Market*. London: CBI & William Mercer. Andrew Brown, Chris Forde, and David Spencer 2008. Changes in HRM and job satisfaction 1998–2004: evidence from the Workplace Employment Relations Survey. *Human Resource Management Journal*, 18(3), pp. 237–256.

By contrast, *intrinsic* rewards arise from the nature of jobs themselves and the working relationships created in carrying out those jobs. These are less tangible than extrinsic rewards and more difficult to adjust, but this is not to say that their effects are less important. For instance, a report published in 2000 found that intrinsic rewards were more satisfying than extrinsic ones (see Box 7.1). The features that can generate intrinsic rewards for employees include variety in job content, responsibility, recognition, autonomy, social interaction, participation in setting targets, and determining methods of work and feedback of information. For the employer, intrinsic rewards are advantageous in that they do not necessarily add to costs and may even improve productivity. Changes to intrinsic rewards can often be accomplished without new investment or modifications to technology. In fact, modern automation and information technologies generally permit considerable choice in how work is organized.[3]

The movement toward devolved initiative, more responsible jobs, and teamwork to be found in new organizational forms therefore represents a policy shift toward higher-level intrinsic rewards for organizational members. Nevertheless, the extent to which intrinsic non-financial rewards motivate performance, as opposed to financial rewards, is likely to depend both on an employee's personal circumstances and on contextual factors such as cultural norms and the local income tax regime.[4]

Punishment is involved whenever an otherwise expected reward is withheld, or any other sanction is applied, with the aim of discouraging a specific behavior. For instance, management may refuse to make a bonus payment under certain circumstances, as in a plant where an agreed monthly bonus is withheld from any individual or group refusing to be redeployed between jobs according to the terms of a flexibility agreement. To quote from one such agreement, "refusal to carry out the work required without good reason will be treated as a disciplinary offence."

Delaying a person's promotion would be another example of withholding a reward. A more severe sanction, that of dismissal, actually terminates the employment contract and is normally linked to specific offences, such as theft at work. When considering the points this chapter makes about reward policies, the punishment aspect should also be kept in mind. Indeed, at times of high unemployment, the threat of punishment in terms of losing their jobs assumes major proportions for many people. Punishment nevertheless has a negative implication that is more readily associated with authoritarianism than the treatment of organizational members as potentially responsible people who have a valuable contribution to make. We shall therefore concentrate on rewards, though it remains the case that withholding a reward is in effect a punishment.

◢ Criteria Applied to Rewards

Managerial criteria

There are six criteria that management may apply to a system of rewards, in terms of the behaviors that it is aiming to encourage. These behaviors are necessary to achieve the goals established for the organization, though their relative saliency will depend on the type of work the organization undertakes and the conditions in which it is currently operating. The six criteria are:

1. Attraction and retention of valued staff
2. Predictability of behavior
3. The extra percentage
4. Flexibility
5. Innovation
6. Alignment of the reward system with an organization's structure

1 Attraction and retention of valued staff. People have to be attracted to fill job vacancies in an organization and feel sufficiently satisfied with the rewards these jobs offer not to leave for another employment. Labor-market conditions are clearly relevant to the level of reward that will satisfy this criterion, particularly in respect of alternative employment opportunities offering superior rewards (and/or fewer disadvantages), better career prospects, and physical accessibility from where the employee is prepared to live. The cost of labor turnover to the organization is, however, itself contingent. It depends on the investment in skill, experience and beneficial informal practices that is lost when an employee leaves in relation to the cost of obtaining a replacement. This cost includes any time and expenditure required to bring the new recruit up to the necessary standard, the loss of valuable tacit knowledge held by departing staff, the disruption of informal organization that improves efficiency, and the potential negative impact on other employees. In some circumstances labor turnover may incur less net cost. For example, when a firm seeks to downsize, labor turnover provides an opportunity to adjust employment levels downward without incurring severance payments or creating a climate of fear about job insecurity. There are also occasions when people decide to leave their jobs because they are not suited to them, and this in effect rectifies an error in their original selection.

Another aspect of the "join and remain" criterion of reward policy is the avoidance of absenteeism. Often absenteeism reflects disappointment on the part of employees with the rewards they are being offered, and a negative attitude toward their employer while they bide their time and look for another job. The costs incurred by organizations as a result of absenteeism usually far outweigh those due to industrial disputes.

2 Predictability of behavior. This is the criterion that reward policies should encourage employees to be dependable in the sense of carrying out the duties requested of them consistently and to reasonable standards. For instance, opportunities for upgrading or even promotion will tend to increase the likelihood of desired behavior among ambitious employees if it is apparent that such behavior enhances their prospects of career advancement. Some critics have suggested that reward policies of this kind can generate behavior that is over-dependable in the sense of conforming unduly and uncritically to the expectations of higher management. This could run counter to the criterion of innovative behavior discussed below.

3 The extra percentage. A good management should look to its reward policy to encourage above-average performance. This "extra percentage" is a level of commitment and effort from employees that goes beyond mere predictability and dependability. The extent to which the extra percentage is forthcoming may make a significant difference to the competitiveness of a business company or, in the case of a public agency, to the quality and cost of services provided.

These three criteria primarily address the goal of organizational efficiency – the attainment of high employee productivity and the minimization of costs. Nowadays, with the high rates of change, fierce competition, and pressures to innovate being experienced by many organizations, two further criteria that were mentioned in Chapter 6 in connection with control have become increasingly important. These are flexibility and innovation.

4 Flexibility. We have seen how the conditions faced by business today oblige managers to seek flexibility in the way people work and the activities they undertake. Flexible deployment economizes on manning and facilitates the running of more complex and varied configurations of work through, for example, computer programmed production facilities. Competitive strategies that attempt to combine cost-leadership with differentiation of products and services depend on such flexibility. It is appropriate that reward policies should encourage employees to accept a steady broadening of their jobs, through (1) extending the skills they acquire and apply, and (2) working together with members of other specialties or departments when required. Examples of the application of this flexibility criterion to reward policy are the offering of upgrading in return for employees acquiring relevant new and tested competencies, and the payment of a bonus for accepting flexible deployment provisions.

5 Innovation. For an organization to renew itself and its products, its members must be encouraged to suggest, and indeed argue for, change and innovation. Certain people occupy jobs in which it is particularly important that they recognize and deal with new problems and challenges in an innovative way. Some specialized groups are particularly charged with the task of innovating products and processes on a systematic basis, with research and development personnel being the most obvious example. While this specialist contribution is a vital one, it is increasingly recognized that valuable ideas and initiatives can come from all organizational members. A reward policy should encourage these contributions, despite the difficulties that can arise in rewarding suggestions for change and innovation from any member of the labor force. For example, employees lacking the necessary training or experience with problems may offer impractical suggestions that cannot in themselves justify a reward despite the positive intentions and work that are behind the proposal. Problems like this usually pale into insignificance, however, when compared to the ability of a suitable reward policy to encourage organizational members to release the tacit knowledge they possess.

The above five criteria that management may apply to rewards are clearly contingent on the type of personnel required, the nature of the work being undertaken, and the particular pressures for change and innovation being experienced by the organization. In some situations, some of the criteria will be more salient than others. Some criteria may apply to given sections of the workforce rather than to others, and particular criteria will be more readily satisfied through one kind of reward than another. For example, incentives intended to encourage a high level of individual effort may inhibit the willingness of workers to accept flexible deployment between tasks if they believe that some of the tasks do not allow for equally high levels of measured output. The evolution of a policy on rewards will therefore require a decision on the balance of emphasis that management considers appropriate to its priorities and its assessment of contingencies, and the choice of reward systems should in principle follow from this decision.

6 Alignment with an organization's structure. The five criteria just mentioned are each concerned with the kind of behavior management seeks to encourage among employees. The intention of a sixth criterion is, by contrast, structural. It is the requirement that differential levels of reward, particularly pay, should accord with the structure of the organization, at least in terms of the relative hierarchical position of job categories. The traditional means of meeting this structural requirement has been through *job evaluation.* Job evaluation is the process of analyzing and assessing different jobs on a systematic basis in order to establish their relative worth for purposes of payment. Job evaluation begins with an analysis of the function in order to obtain a job description. The job description is then related to the organization's pay structure in order to determine the relative value of that job or group of jobs. Skills, knowledge, and accountability are typical of the factors taken into account by job evaluation schemes. Monetary values are then fixed by establishing rates for each group of jobs based on their relative contribution. Job evaluation can be allied to the use of rewards to promote desired behavior (performance), if it is used to establish a base level of reward that specifies a differential between one job category and others, on top of which additional rewards linked to behavior and performance are offered.[5]

The argument behind this sixth managerial criterion is that it is necessary to align the basic structure of rewards to the general structure of the organization, not only to preserve orderliness but also to reflect the logic of that structure in terms of features such as the hierarchical differences in the work it incorporates. This structural criterion is also compatible, in principle, with the importance that employees attach to differential payments and their concern that these should "fairly" reflect differences in the intrinsic nature of jobs and the qualifications required to fill them. There can, however, be a number of problems with job evaluation:

1   It assumes a reasonable degree of stability in an organization's structure, with the danger that it can encourage too much rigidity in employee behavior under conditions requiring considerable flexibility and even frequent change. As an organization changes, job evaluation schemes deteriorate.
2   It can be costly to install and maintain.
3   It is dependent on subjective evaluations; no scheme has proved to be wholly valid and reliable.
4   Schemes applied to an organization as a whole tend to oversimplify, whereas more specific schemes can introduce apparent inconsistencies and inequities.

Another consideration is that, if the number of hierarchical levels is reduced as part and parcel of moving to a simpler structure (see Chapter 4), the number of basic wage and salary grades will have to be reduced correspondingly. This means that the payment bands attached to any one grade will need to be broadened, for two reasons. First, broadening will reflect the greater range of skills and competences now expected at a given hierarchical level. Second, with fewer payment bands, the broadening of each one will retain the incentive that progression between bands previously offered for employees to acquire new competences and improve their performance over time.

Employees' criteria

The criteria that employees apply to rewards are a guide to their motivational potential. Psychologists have tended to regard these criteria as deriving from the individual needs of people at work. They have debated whether individuals differ considerably in their perceived needs, preferences, and values, or whether instead there is a single model that can be applied more generally, across the employee spectrum. By contrast, those adopting a sociological or industrial relations perspective emphasize that the most influential criteria applied by employees to rewards are social in nature. This means that the criteria are collectively defined by social groups, such as the members of a given occupation, and are informed by comparisons with other social groups. This fundamental contrast in approach therefore boils down to whether the value that people at work place on rewards, and the basis on which they assess their adequacy and reasonableness, derives primarily from employees' human needs or from the norms shared within their social group.

THE PSYCHOLOGICAL VIEW

Although some psychologists maintain that human beings seek to satisfy a wide range of needs, others have tried to reduce this complexity by means of grouping, classifying, and developing a typology of needs. Clearly, if any such ordered typology could validly be established, it would suit the purposes of managers who are concerned with the practicality of motivating people to act in certain ways, and who cannot apply too complex a model without incurring undue cost and possible confusion.

This helps to account for the popularity of Maslow's grouping of human needs into just five categories. He suggested that these categories formed a hierarchy such that, only when the needs in one category were satisfied did those at the next level up become salient for the individual concerned. This *"need hierarchy"* envisages an upward progression from fundamental "physiological" or material needs, through "safety" or security, "social and affiliation," "esteem" and "self-actualization" needs, at the highest level.[6]

Although Maslow's formulation of this need hierarchy lacked an empirical foundation, it achieved wide acceptance and has influenced many managerial and academic views about employees' likely motivational responses to particular rewards. The need hierarchy suggests that, as people become more affluent, they attach a diminishing value to further increments of pay (in real terms at least) and an increasing value to other, intrinsic, rewards. Herzberg, in what was in effect a further simplification, distinguished two categories of rewards relating to Maslow's need hierarchy. First, rewards that satisfied lower order needs such as pay and working conditions were considered as components of a *"hygiene"* factor. Any inadequacy in meeting hygiene needs would create dissatisfaction, but satisfying them would not generate the motivation to perform the work itself any better. Second, rewards such as achievement, responsibility, recognition, and interesting work that are addressed to Maslow's higher needs were considered to form part of a *"motivating"* factor. Such rewards, Herzberg argued, will encourage commitment to high performance in the conduct of work as well as generate satisfaction.[7]

Herzberg's ideas gave a considerable impetus to the principle of job enrichment. The methodology of the studies from which he derived his theory has been criticized, however, and many subsequent investigations have failed to support the admittedly elegant simplicity of his formulation. This returns us to the problem of oversimplifying people's needs and the criteria they apply to rewards. It is doubtful whether in reality people think of their needs or goals in terms of just a few categories, whether any two people share exactly the same hierarchy of preferences, or whether such hierarchies remain consistent over time as circumstances and stimuli change. The static universal model implied by the Maslow and Herzberg formulations fails to address the much more realistic discussion of employees' reward criteria advanced by sociologists.

THE SOCIOLOGICAL VIEW

At first sight, needs like subsistence and personal safety might appear to be absolute and universal in nature. Yet further consideration indicates that even these are subject to a social definition that varies from society to society as well as between classes within a society. This is clearly apparent with definitions of what constitutes a "poverty" level, and also in the varied definitions of what constitutes a "safe" environment. In other words, norms of what is acceptable and expected are socially defined. They do not arise directly from individual needs without social mediation. The sociological view cautions that, in practice, it is very difficult to generalize about the criteria by which employees assess rewards.

The role played by social norms is particularly important in the case of pay. These norms may vary across different national cultures as well as between different social groups within a culture. Norms of fairness are extremely significant for employees when they evaluate the rewards they are offered. Research suggests that people make two comparisons when assessing fairness. The first is a comparison of their balance of reward to inputs (such as time and effort), relative to their expectations. The second is how this balance compares with the rewards others are receiving for their inputs.

SOCIAL COMPARISON

The comparison to which people attach greatest significance here is with others who are in the same socially defined group, such as people doing the same job. This gives rise to the so-called "comparability principle," that people doing the same work should be given the same pay regardless of whether they are employed in the public or the private sector, in flourishing or in ailing organizations. In theory, a perfect labor market would ensure comparability. The evidence as to what people will do when they perceive themselves to be over-rewarded is rather mixed. The effects of perceived under-rewarding are much clearer. Under-rewarded people will typically protest. If that does not improve their situation they will reduce the level of their inputs, making less effort or personal sacrifices, or will leave their employment at the first opportunity.

Norms of fairness in the context of comparison with others also help account for the fact that differentials in rewards between people occupying job levels that are adjacent in terms of skill, qualification required, or authority, generate more frustration and conflict than do absolute levels of reward. If, for example, a fifty-year-old manager has a much younger assistant appointed at almost the same salary level, he or she is likely to feel aggrieved, if not actually threatened, by the absence of a significant difference between the two salaries. If employees only applied criteria relating to their levels of personal need, one would expect absolute levels of reward to be the main issue, but in practice they do not. Elliott Jaques therefore argued that an acceptable policy for the allocation of incomes will not be found until the problem of equity in differential payments is understood and resolved. He concluded from his studies that members of the population share deeply-felt norms about fair differentials, based upon differences in intrinsic levels of responsibility.[8] The comparisons that enter into a person's notion of fair reward are also informed by long-established traditions which have become institutionalized within particular sectors of work. For example, workers with certified skills expect to secure a higher level of pay than non-skilled workers, even if the two groups are able to perform the same tasks equally well. Comparability is therefore a basic principle that employees apply to rewards.

Several points of reference may enter into the comparisons that people make. For example, a study of Cadbury-Schweppes' cocoa bean processing factory at Chirk in Wales found that three bases of comparison entered into employees' evaluations of their levels of pay.[9] The first comparison was with rates of pay offered by other jobs in the local community. The comparison here was favorable. This favorable local point of reference had a more marked effect on employees' motivations and willingness to accept managerial requirements in the early days of the plant, which provided jobs for unemployed local coal miners when it first opened. A second dimension of comparability was that of skill, which meant that qualified workers expected to enjoy a differentially higher level of payment, even if doing the same work as unskilled employees. A third dimension involved reference to the balance between rewards and inputs that prevailed in other plants within the same division of the company but located elsewhere. This comparison became easier to make as the new workforce at Chirk developed its system of union representation and those representatives came into contact with their equivalents in the other plants, a contact encouraged by the initiation of company-wide participation and communication structures. The comparison with other plants in the company gave rise to a less favorable evaluation of the rewards that management offered at Chirk.

EQUITY THEORY

Equity theory derives from psychology in that it focuses on the cognitive processes leading an individual to decide whether or not to put effort into an activity.[10] Nevertheless, social comparison provides its rationale. Equity theory maintains that people are motivated to secure what they perceive to be a fair reward for their efforts. A sense of fairness, or equity, is seen to derive from a comparison between people of each other's inputs and outputs. Inputs may include effort, skill, education and experience. Outputs are rewards such as salary, promotion and other forms of recognition, and fringe benefits like medical insurance and subsidized meals.

People are likely to compare themselves with others who are doing similar work or occupying similar positions. Someone perceiving that another person is receiving better rewards for the same or less input will feel a sense of inequity. Feelings of inequity could well be demotivating, leading individuals to do less work or offer a reduced contribution. On the other hand, someone perceiving that another is receiving inferior rewards for the same or greater input may experience a sense of guilt or embarrassment and attempt to raise the level of his or her effort. However, for some people the comparison could give rise to smug complacency. The key point of present interest lies in equity theory's prediction that people will reduce their effort or commitment if they consider themselves to be unfairly and detrimentally rewarded.

LABOR MARKET

The criteria that employees give to rewards will also tend to vary according to their position in the labor market. This will impact on the level of reward they find acceptable for the job they are asked to do and on the employment conditions under which they are expected to perform it. The relative importance attached to different rewards may also be subject to labor market considerations. There is evidence that, at a time of widespread unemployment, employees give less prominence to job enrichment or participation – which according to Maslow and Herzberg meet higher order needs – than they give to retaining a job itself and the income it provides. (It has to be said, however, that evidence on the effects of unemployment demonstrates how most jobs also provide people with significant social and status rewards that are then sorely missed.) In other words, the criteria that employees apply to the rewards offered them are not only based on norms of comparability and fairness, but also refer to their standing in the labor market.

The factors identified so far imply that a reward policy should ideally be sensitive to the following considerations:

1   the contributions that management wants from the members of its organization, expressed as performance criteria;

2   norms of fairness, so that all members of an organization perceive they are treated according to the same rules of the game;

3   the criteria and priorities attached to particular rewards by different categories of organizational member.

In practice, these three considerations can come into conflict. Thus, a highly differentiated reward system aimed at suiting different groups of employees can easily start to appear unfair. This problem arose in a small family firm known to the author. The owner ran the firm on very paternalistic lines. He knew all his employees firsthand, and he tried to recognize their individual needs by making special provisions for each one. For example, he allowed one person with an ailing mother to work reduced hours but for the same pay, and he made special ex gratia payments to help another employee who was in financial need. Although the owner's intention was to keep these variations in reward confidential, the word got out and they led to a general feeling of favoritism, which caused resentment and undermined morale.

It may even be difficult to meet any one of the three considerations. For instance, the dilemma that managements normally face in attempting to apply trade-offs between potentially contradictory performance criteria, such as efficiency and innovation, means that it will be very difficult to strike the right balance between the components of a performance-related reward policy. Nonetheless, it is better to have some consistency between employees' expectations, managerial performance criteria, and rewards than none at all. Managers have to find ways of designing reward policies that link these elements together. Some useful guidance as to how this may be accomplished can be drawn from two lines of social science research. The first is associated with what has come to be known as "expectancy theory." This draws attention to the conditions that are necessary if rewards are to direct people's behavior at work towards high performance. The second line of research is associated with what is known as "conditioning" and draws attention to the behavioral consequences of the scheduling of rewards.

◢ Expectancy Theory

Expectancy theory in essence states that people will decide how much effort they are going to put into their work according to: (1) what they perceive they are going to receive as a reward for that effort, and (2) how much they value the reward (or dislike it in the case of sanctions or punishments). As with many ideas in social science, this sounds like common sense. Yet it draws attention to a number of requirements for directing motivation that are frequently neglected in practice. Expectancy theory arose from a realization that it is vital to ensure a clear relationship between performance and rewards and that, as far as possible, rewards match employees' expectations.

There are several links in the chain that expectancy theory regards as vital for an effective reward system. Lyman Porter and Edward Lawler have integrated these into the model set out in Figure 7.1. The expectancy theory model suggests that four key linkages and feedback loops need to be in place for employees to be motivated toward achieving the performance requirements set out by (or with) management:[11]

1   the extent to which employees see their effort leading to better performance;

2   whether performance is seen to be rewarded;

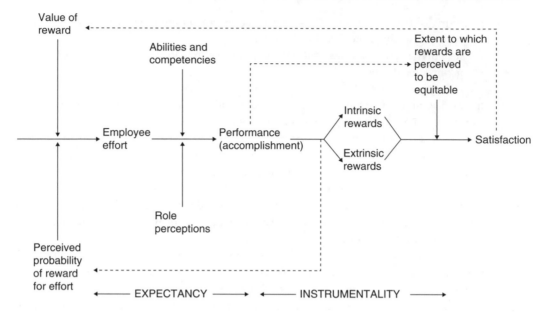

Figure 7.1 Relationships between reward, effort and individual performance
Adapted from: Lyman W. Porter and Edward E. Lawler III, *Managerial Attitudes and Performance* (Homewood, Ill: R.D. Irwin 1968, p. 165).

3   the legitimacy attached to the way rewards are administered;
4   the value attached to the rewards that are offered.

Link 1: Expectancy

The first link gives its name to the theory – "expectancy." This concerns the relationship that employees perceive to exist between the amount of effort they put into their work and the level of performance they are recognized as having achieved. In other words, do the members of an organization expect greater effort or application on their part to lead to better performance? Employees must believe that they can control the quality of their job performance; if they do not, they will see no point in trying harder. Note that it is what management recognizes as performance that is important here, because this will provide the basis for any feedback and rewards that employees receive. The model also suggests that the relationship between employees' efforts and their performance will be mediated by (1) their abilities and competencies, and (2) by their perceptions as to what their job entails and the best way to carry it out ("role perceptions"). These mediating factors point to the potential contribution of training and the setting of understood and accepted goals toward the translation of effort and goodwill into effective performance.

Link 2: Instrumentality

The next main link in the chain has been called "instrumentality." This refers to the relationship that employees perceive between their performance and the outcomes of that performance in terms of rewards and punishments. At issue here is the extent to which "good" performance, as evaluated by management, is actually rewarded and whether the rewards offered adequately offset the costs and risks borne by the employee. The probability of increased effort leading to increased reward is very likely to affect the amount of effort people will think it worthwhile to expend in the first place. It therefore constitutes an important feedback loop of information to them. Even if people do conclude that greater effort on their part leads to better performance, this effort is hardly going to be encouraged if it is not seen as leading to any additional reward. As noted earlier in the chapter, rewards may be of an extrinsic or intrinsic kind.

Link 3: Legitimacy

The third main link in the expectancy theory model concerns the legitimacy that employees attach to the rewards they are offered for their performance. Fairness and equity come into the picture here. The notion of fairness will enter employees' minds to the extent that they have a view as to the level and kind of rewards that "ought" to be available to the type of person performing the work required in a particular job. The issue of equity also enters into the way people see rewards being distributed between different individuals in relation to their perform-ance and also to any deprivations suffered, such as working on a night shift. The important point here is that employees are unlikely to be satisfied with the rewards they receive if these are not perceived to be equitable. Dissatisfaction will weaken the motivating power of these rewards.

Link 4: Valence

Finally, the motivational potential of rewards will depend not only on their legitimacy, but also on the value employees attach to them. In other words, if rewards are seen to be fair and equitable, but are not the kind of rewards to which employees attach much value, then their motivational potential is likely to be low. To quote one example:

> "Yes, I can see that if I apply myself more my performance goes up. Yes, management recognizes the improvement in my performance and, when my performance goes up, it rewards me more. Yes, it also seems to be fairly administered as between my colleagues and me. But, I don't want any more ****** luncheon vouchers, so why should I bother?"

The concept of "valence" has been coined to draw attention to the positive or negative value that people ascribe to the reward outcomes of how they behave in their jobs.

From a practical point of view, the utility of the expectancy model lies in the way that it draws attention to basic conditions that have to be met in order for rewards to assist in linking motivation to performance requirements. To repeat, these requirements are that (1) employees must expect that additional effort leads to higher performance; (2) they must perceive that higher performance leads to greater reward; (3) they must regard the administration and distribution of rewards as legitimate; and (4) they must attach value to the particular rewards offered to them. Box 7.2 provides an instructive example of how these principles of expectancy theory proved to be of practical use in the case of a factory in the South of England where management faced a problem.

BOX 7.2   A PRACTICAL APPLICATION OF EXPECTANCY THEORY

Managers in a southern English factory could not understand why operatives drove site vehicles so badly, generating additional maintenance and downtime costs, and sometimes damaging plant and materials as well. It was reasonable to conclude that the drivers' motivation to meet contingent requirements was pretty low. Application of the expectancy theory model pointed to certain weaknesses in key linkages that contributed to this low motivation and effort. There was no training scheme at all for site drivers. The link between a driver's level of effort and his performance could have been improved if he was given some training, and if a number of dangerous corners and other accident hazards on site were removed. Secondly, management's definition of performance was deficient; it had never decided upon acceptable driving standards. Thirdly, there was no link between driving performance and level of reward for the driver. There were returns to management from more careful driving in terms of reduced costs in respect of damage and maintenance. Yet, if anything, drivers secured rewards they valued from poor driving: speeding, for example, was exciting, and also gave them slightly more free time in the recreation room. It was necessary for the company to find a means of rewarding drivers for good driving. Finally, there was no general feedback to drivers about the standard of their driving and its consequences. However good or bad the driver, no one said. A policy linking rewards to quality of driving would also have to bring this informational feedback loop into being.

None of the points in this analysis are revolutionary. In fact, half of them were mentioned at various meetings called to deal with the problem. Nevertheless, setting out the problem systematically in terms of the expectancy theory model greatly assisted managers in obtaining new insight, on which they acted with good results.

Source: Jeremy Baker, *Accounting Age*, February 24, 1978.

Expectancy theory clearly places the onus on management to reward what it wants to happen, not something else. If a reward system is to support organizational control, then it has to encourage employees' to focus on what is significant.[12] As Steven Kerr points out, writing on "the folly of rewarding A, while hoping for B," it is surprising just how often this misdirection of reward can be found in practice.[13] The problem often arises when the quantification of some objectives is more difficult than that of others. For instance, in most cases of performance-related pay, objectives or targets go unspecified in areas such as creativity or teamwork where it is difficult to measure them. This leads to management formally rewarding the attainment of certain objectives only, at the expense of not motivating employees to achieve the others however important they are to the long-run success of the organization. A comparable problem arises in non-business organizations where it poses an equal challenge to the designers of reward systems. For example, in universities it is hoped that teachers will not neglect their teaching responsibilities, but they are rewarded primarily for their research and publications. Doctors are liable to a great deal more punishment, increasingly through litigation, if they err in declaring a sick person well than if they prescribe treatment that is not necessary. Both are errors that can have serious consequences for the patient, yet, the balance of punishment and reward is far from symmetrical between the two.

Expectancy theory also brings out the importance of knowing what employees value for rewards. Do they place a higher value on an increment of certain intrinsic rewards or of particular extrinsic rewards? How are employees' evaluations likely to shift over time and can this be predicted in relation to changing conditions in the economy as well as by reference to the changing domestic and personal circumstances of individual employees? A precise application of expectancy theory would lead one to consider the individual employee. While this is not usually a practical proposition from the point of view of administering a reward system, it does nonetheless suggest the usefulness of distinguishing different categories of employee for whom different reward policies would be appropriate according to their particular values.

Expectancy theory is a cognitive theory. It assumes that employees will adopt a stance toward work and its reward that is thoughtful and rational in terms of their objectives and preferences. It almost certainly overstates the extent and frequency to which people really go through a process of deliberate and precise calculation when deciding how to respond to the rewards they are offered. Nevertheless, this cognitive emphasis is a valuable corrective to earlier psychological theories that tended to look upon people at work as responding to relatively inarticulate needs in a manner not too far removed from the behavior of animals. While expectancy theory does not explicitly take account of social influences such as custom and practice or cultural norms, it is consistent with the need to locate the issue of how people respond to rewards within the context of perceptions of equity and trust that are so important in organizational relations. If employees do not regard the rewards they are offered as fair, and if they do not trust management's intentions, then according to expectancy theory they will not be motivated to work towards management's contingent requirements. Skepticism over management's long-term intentions to continue to honor the scale of rewards attached to performance helps to explain why, on many occasions, workers fail to respond to such incentives. It would be rational for them to do so if they could trust management's intentions to honor the scheme or not withdraw other benefits such as job security once productivity rises. Failing this trust, it may be more rational for workers to continue to restrict their level of contribution.

◢ Conditioning Theory

Conditioning theory contrasts with expectancy theory in that it is behavioral rather than cognitive. Rather than being concerned with what people think about rewards, it regards them as organisms that respond to rewards as positive or negative stimuli. In fact, the classical conditioning research was performed on animals, the most famous being Pavlov's dog, which was conditioned to salivate at the sound of a bell. Conditioning is concerned with methods that induce behavioral change in people.[14]

There is more than one kind of conditioning, though all involve stimuli that are either positive or negative for the individual concerned. "Instrumental conditioning" is the kind most relevant to a discussion of reward policies. Here a person is placed in a situation such that he or she learns that certain behaviors trigger a reward or a punishment. A reward is commonly called a "positive reinforcer" and a punishment a "negative reinforcer." A basic law of

BOX 7.3   A CASE OF INADEQUATE BEHAVIOR REINFORCEMENT

Alex Smith* was hired by a catering agency as project coordinator in their commercial department. Over time, it became apparent that he was not doing his job properly: failing to answer the telephone, failing to enter new jobs on the company database, and failing to make systematic records of sales orders and invoices. He was also resistant to instruction, giving the impression that he "knew it all." He had a postgraduate degree (though not in a relevant subject) and this might, in part, explain why management failed immediately to address the situation beyond an occasional comment, which was never strong or detailed enough to modify his behavior. Also he was paid a straight salary so that his poor performance did not register in the level of his earnings. In effect, this situation meant that he was given enough rope to hang himself: having messed up a job with an important client, he was summarily dismissed. This came as a huge shock to him, as well as to his colleagues, since management had given no prior indication of there being a major problem. It was, of course, by then too late to have any effect on Alex's work performance.

*Name changed to protect identity. *Source*: Author's research.

instrumental conditioning is that behavior that is rewarded is likely to be repeated, while behavior that attracts punishment is less likely to be repeated. Rewards and punishments are not always reinforcers, however; for example, when they are not substantial enough to modify a person's behavior or are administered too late to have an effect. The example in Box 7.3 clearly illustrates a management failure in this regard due to an absence of continuous performance management.

Studies of conditioning also point to some more subtle considerations. First, there seems to be a wide measure of agreement that reinforcement should be positive rather than negative, constructive rather than destructive. This is partly because negative reinforcement can generate a great deal of emotional upset, and also because it is directed at training people in what not to do, rather than in the desired behavior. Negative reinforcement is therefore unlikely to encourage the innovative activity that is so critical for organizations today. The ratio between positive and negative reinforcement also has to be considered. A high incidence of negative feedback is more likely to demotivate: "All you get around this place is kicks." On the other hand, the frequent use of positive reinforcement combined with the occasional deserved reprimand or punishment is likely to be regarded as fair, and more likely, therefore, to be effective: "The boss doesn't usually complain about my work; it must have been really bad for him to have done so on this occasion."

Another consideration is that reinforcement has more effect if it is immediately contingent on the behavior. Reinforcement serves two functions – to sustain motivation and provide feedback – and the value of the feedback function in particular is lost if delay occurs. On the other hand, it can be costly to administer rewards or punishments immediately. If this is to be done by an employee's manager, it implies that the manager must continually be diverted from other matters in order to review the employee's performance. A balance has obviously to be struck, but the point about immediacy and contingency of feedback helps, for example, to account for the very limited conditioning value of rewards such as annual profit-sharing bonuses. They are welcome, of course, but employees cannot readily link variations in bonuses to any particular actions for which they personally were responsible. This is partly because of the long time delay and partly because any one individual lower down in the organization is not likely to perceive that his or her behavior has had much effect on a company's profitability.

There are a number of alternative possibilities in the way that reinforcement can be linked to behavior. The basis on which reinforcement is designed to track behavior is known as a "schedule of reinforcement." Reinforcement can be "continuous:" each time a behavior occurs there is positive or negative feedback. This may take an intrinsic form such as a manager's comment, or an extrinsic form, i.e. reward or punishment. In contrast to continuous reinforcement, there is the possibility of intermittent reinforcement by which the reward or punishment is given after some, but not each, occurrence of the behavior. Intermittent reinforcers can be given at set time intervals, such as a weekly bonus. This is an "interval" schedule. Ratio schedules entail the delivery of reinforcement after a certain number of actions have been performed, such as a scheme that allows employees to go home early once a given quota of work has been completed.

A further distinction lies between fixed intermittent schedules where the frequency of reinforcement does not change, and variable intermittent schedules where it does. A monthly paycheck is an example of the former, while a personal tour of the factory by the managing director at varying intervals illustrates the latter (assuming that employees appreciate this personal attention). Based on the results of laboratory experiments, it appears that, while continuous reinforcement may be the fastest way either to establish or to stop a particular behavior, ratio schedules are conducive to the highest incidence of a desired behavior. Up to a point, it may be possible to "stretch" a ratio schedule so that reinforcement is given at progressively less frequent intervals yet still have the same effect. From a managerial perspective this has the advantage of economizing on the expenditure of resources. There is, however, the obvious risk that stretching may destroy the credibility of a reward policy, and one also has to question its morality. If stretching means delaying an agreed incremental payment, then rather than employees still eagerly anticipating being rewarded, they are more likely to regard it as a breach of trust. This was how British firefighters were treated in 2004 and it greatly harmed the quality of labor relations encouraging much more militancy in subsequent years. Any short-term gain to local authority employers was cancelled out by the long-term downside. It reminds us that people do apply norms and values to the rewards they are offered in a thoughtful way. The fact that they can think for themselves and apply their own subjective standards sets severe limits to the validity of the conditioning approach.

The whole subject of conditioning also raises ethical problems, because it amounts to a refined form of manipulation. It can be argued, of course, that this is what sophisticated management is all about. There is a fine line to be drawn between "getting the best out of people" and "getting the most out of" or exploiting them. It can also be argued that it is better to discuss the matter openly rather than ignore it in the hope that it will go away. Conditioning does not take a cognitive view of mankind; its originators thought in terms of stimulus–response rather than in terms of a calculated reaction to rewards and punishments. Most of the research into conditioning has been conducted in laboratories rather than in the real world of work. The approach therefore has its limitations, yet is nevertheless addressed, like expectancy theory, to the very practical question of how to design reward systems that will encourage the performance that management judges to be required. The fact that this latter can change frequently and radically, especially in current conditions of hypercompetition, is just another factor to be thrown into the melting pot. Reciprocal flexibility – on the part of the employee in adapting to changing managerial and market requirements, and of management in offering appropriate reward for such flexibility and performance – is key.

Whereas expectancy theory focuses on the *linkages* necessary for a reward policy to be effective, conditioning theory draws attention to the *scheduling* of such rewards in relation to people's behavior. The considerations raised by conditioning research are primarily concerned with the balance between rewards and punishments, and with their timing. They complement the considerations raised by expectancy theory concerning the fundamental linkages required to render a reward system operational in the first place.

SUMMARY

1   There is no "one best way" for the design of reward policies.

2   Rewards play a crucial role in directing people's efforts toward the implementation of an organization's strategy. They must therefore be sensitive, as far as possible, to employee and managerial criteria; in other words both to considerations of personal motivation and task requirements. Each of these considerations varies between different people and organizations, and also changes over time.

3   This suggests that reward systems require frequent fine-tuning, to suit individual and organizational contingencies. In practice, this is very difficult to achieve. Employees can be very unsettled by constantly changing formulae and rules of the game, further eroding their trust in management. It can also be prohibitively expensive for employers constantly to modify their reward schemes.

4   Some progress toward the flexibility that is today required of reward policies can, nevertheless, be made, with respect to both intrinsic and extrinsic rewards.

5   In the case of intrinsic rewards, people's work has to be arranged to suit their needs, including variety, personal growth, or social interaction, as far as is possible given the kind of contributions required by the organization's strategy.

6   This can be achieved through granting workgroups or teams autonomy to organize their own work, in consultation with managers who are sensitive to circumstances in which the need arises to change intrinsic rewards. Such changes can often be accomplished without new investment or modifications to technology. Indeed, modern information technologies generally permit considerable choice in how work is organized.

7   In the case of extrinsic rewards, as the following chapter indicates, the requirement is for schemes that enable performance criteria to be adjusted as circumstances change. Such adjustment is ideally carried out through mutual discussion between managers and employees.

QUESTIONS FOR DISCUSSION

7.1   What is the difference between extrinsic and intrinsic rewards?
7.2   What are the implications of this difference for reward policies?
7.3   It has been said that working people today are placing an increasing value on intrinsic rewards. Do you agree or not? Please explain your answer.
7.4   What are the key managerial criteria for an effective reward policy?
7.5   What are the key criteria that employees might apply to rewards?
7.6   What is "expectancy theory"? How can it inform the design of reward systems?
7.7   What is "conditioning theory"? How can it inform the design of reward systems?

NOTES

1   Stephen J. Perkins and Geoff White (2011), *Reward Management: Alternatives, Consequences and Contexts*, 2nd edition, London, Chartered Institute of Personnel and Development (CIPD).
2   Amy E. Mickel and Lisa A. Barron (2008), Getting "more bang for the buck": Symbolic value of monetary rewards in organizations, *Journal of Management Inquiry*, 17(4): 329–338.
3   Paul Thompson and David McHugh (2009), *Work Organisations*, 4th edition, New York, Macmillan.
4   Flora F.T. Chiang and Thomas A. Birtch (2012), The performance implications of financial and non-financial rewards: An Asian Nordic comparison, *Journal of Management Studies*, 49(3), 538–570.
5   For further detail on job evaluation see Michael Armstrong, Ann Cummins, Sue Hastings, and Willie Wood (2003), *Job Evaluation Handbook: A Guide to Achieving Equal Pay*, London, Kogan Page.
6   Abraham H. Maslow (1954), *Motivation and Personality*, New York, Harper.
7   Frederick Herzberg (1966), *Work and the Nature of Man*, Cleveland, OH, World Publishing Company.
8   Elliott Jaques (1961), *Equitable Payment*, London, Heinemann.
9   Alan Whitaker (1982), *People, Tasks and Technology: A Study in Consensus*. University of Lancaster, UK, Department of Behaviour in Organizations.
10 J.S. Adams (1963), Towards an understanding of inequity, *Journal of Abnormal and Social Psychology*, 67, 422–436.
11 Lyman W. Porter and Edward E. Lawler III (1968), *Managerial Attitudes and Performance*, Homewood, Il, R.D. Irwin.
12 William Ocasio and Franz Wohlgezogen (2010), Attention and control. In Sim B. Sitkin, Laura B. Cardinal, and Katinka M. Bijlsma (eds.), *Organizational Control*, Cambridge, Cambridge University Press, pp. 191–221.
13 Steve Kerr (1975), On the folly of rewarding A, while hoping for B, *Academy of Management Journal*, 18, 769–783.
14 I.P. Pavlov (1927), *Conditioned Reflexes*, New York, Oxford University Press; B.F. Skinner (1961), *Analysis of Behavior*, New York, McGraw-Hill.

CHAPTER 8

Payment Systems

WHAT THIS CHAPTER COVERS

This chapter concentrates on the major source of extrinsic reward – pay – and in particular on the choice of payment systems. This focus is justified by the undoubted importance of pay and also because some coverage has already been given to the organizational aspects of intrinsic rewards in connection with teamwork (Chapter 5), new approaches to control (Chapter 6), and employees' criteria in evaluating such rewards (Chapter 7).

Pay matters a great deal to most people, and reasons for this are discussed in the first section. We then classify different methods of payment in terms of four underlying dimensions: the features to which pay is tied, whether an incentive element is built into the method of payment, the frequency and scheduling of payment, and the organizational unit to which payment relates. Flat time rates, output incentives, merit rating, performance-related pay, gain sharing, and profit sharing and stock ownership are discussed. The chapter then highlights considerations in the choice of a payment system, and trends in payment policies that are consistent with new organizational forms.

The Importance of Pay

Although it is rightly said that happiness cannot be bought, money as the universal medium of exchange is obviously the key to a great many things that matter to people. As it says in the Bible: "Wine gladdens life, and money meets every need" (Ecclesiastes, 10: 19, NRSV). Even Frederick Herzberg, a major exponent of the theory that money does not motivate, is reported as admitting: "It sure as Hell helps me sort out my priorities!" In an age when consumers around the world are constantly urged by the media to "Spend, spend, spend!" and are taking on ever-increasing levels of personal debt, the amount they receive in pay is of obvious importance to them.

In fact, observation of the way people behave suggests that, for most, making money is a prime objective. This seems to apply no less to those who are fortunate enough to have jobs that offer considerable intrinsic rewards than it does to those for whom pay is one of the few rewarding features of their jobs. Many hospital consultants, for example, are keen to add lucrative private work to their salaried public duties, just as many senior executives attach considerable importance to their salaries, bonuses, stock options, and company cars.

Money is valued for a number of reasons. It is instrumental in fulfilling material desires. So, to some extent, the value of money to individuals is determined by the intrinsic worth of what it can buy; for example, one individual might take expensive holidays, while another might invest every spare penny in home improvements. The possession and spending of money is also a symbol of personal success and status. Money has an important symbolic meaning in most societies. Achievement and recognition are often associated with high pay, and with pay raises. Monetary rewards also convey status and respect, not just because they are associated with achievement but also because higher pay tends to go with a higher position in an organizational hierarchy and/or in society at large. The symbolic meaning of pay has its roots in an individual's psychology, in organizational culture, and in social norms.

The fact that monetary rewards have symbolic meaning carries practical implications for how such rewards, especially those for special achievement or merit, are distributed to the members of an organization. Who distributes the monetary reward, why it is given, how it is awarded and who receives it are all likely to make a difference. A reward is likely to have greater symbolic meaning the higher the hierarchical position of the person giving it, the more it is given for exceptional achievement, the more public and ceremonial its presentation, and more select the recipients of the reward (i.e. few recipients and including at least some at a high organizational level).[1]

Pay provides a basis – usually the most obvious basis – on which one person's standing and worth may be compared with another's. This helps to account for the importance that employees attach to the differential between their level of pay and that of others. People may acquire a drive to make money because its lack is associated in their minds with an inability to meet basic needs, a challenge that for many has been heightened by layoffs and falling real wages at times of economic depression. This condition naturally provokes extreme anxiety particularly where there are family dependents to support. Additionally, because money is associated with other desirable attributes, it can take on the incentive power of those features. This may result in people being conditioned to seek money apparently for its own sake, a phenomenon identified by some psychologists.

It is not surprising, therefore, that payment is a reward that evokes considerable interest among virtually all employees at all levels within organizations. This interest is not confined to the needy or to those for whom money may be in part a compensation for a low quality of working life, although the underlying reasons for an interest in pay may vary between different employees. It is instructive to note two points in the light of the fact that many advocates of job enrichment and an improved quality of working life have downgraded the motivational significance of pay. First, in Herzberg's original and highly influential study of accountants and engineers (employees who already enjoyed good pay and intrinsic rewards), pay was the one reward that was quite frequently reported as generating *both* satisfaction and dissatisfaction.[2] If pay can provide satisfaction, it is not necessarily just "compensation," as it is often termed, for giving up time, effort, and some personal freedom. Second, many schemes ostensibly aimed at enhancing intrinsic rewards via job enrichment or work restructuring have offered higher pay at the same time. There is reason to believe that this has been an important inducement for employees to accept the changes, particularly when staffing levels were also reduced. Pay and material fringe benefits remain central features in contracts of employment and are prominent issues in both collective and individual bargaining.

The value that people place on pay compared with other potential rewards from employment might vary according to external contingencies over which management has little control. Domestic circumstances can dictate the leeway an employee has to trade pay against other benefits. An international perspective identifies some societies in which materialism is less of a central cultural factor than it is in others. Also some countries have higher and more progressive systems of income tax, which can deflate the motivation to earn more. Such factors help to explain why the link between financial rewards and performance can vary in strength between countries.[3] Nevertheless, these are matters of degree and, even in traditionally less materialistic societies like China, evidence points to a strong attachment to materialistic values among the younger, urban population. There is very little evidence to challenge the conclusion that pay is a reward that has both a high positive and negative motivating potential. Also, pay is expressed in terms of a perfect scale of measurement that makes it easy to compute and adjust when linked to measures of performance.

Bearing in mind the message of expectancy theory described in the previous chapter, this means that, in principle, pay lends itself particularly well to two necessary conditions for linking motivation and the fulfillment of operational contingencies. First, it is a valued reward and, second, it can be linked to performance in a highly visible manner. Pay is also wholly compatible with the accounting basis of modern organizations operating within a money-based economy. It can be readily computed as a charge upon the organization, whereas the cost of some intrinsic rewards such as the time spent in "satisfying" social relationships at work cannot easily be quantified.

There are a number of methods through which pay can be offered as a reward, and certain pros and cons are claimed for each. As the role of pay is of such significance, it is important to consider these alternatives and their appropriateness to a particular organization's policies and circumstances.

◢ Methods of Payment

Methods of payment can be classified in terms of several underlying dimensions, of which the following are particularly significant:

- *The features to which payment is tied*. These may be intrinsic to the job (as with an assessment of job requirements and conditions in job evaluation schemes) or relate to performance in a job or collection of jobs. The features to which pay can be tied include:
  (a) *time*: the number of hours an employee gives to the job;
  (b) *effort*: the amount of work achieved or other measures of energy expended;
  (c) *skill* or *competence*: possession of, or requirement for, for the job;
  (d) *responsibility*: the significance of the job and of how it is performed;[4]
  (e) *status*: this may be an attribute of the individual, such as age or length of tenure, or the job itself, such as hierarchical position.

- *Whether or not an incentive element is built into the method of payment.* This dimension concerns the extent to which management matches variations in performance to variations in level of payment.
- *Frequency and scheduling of payment.* This relates in particular to whether payment follows immediately upon satisfaction of the criteria to which it is attached, or is deferred until later.
- *The unit to which the basis for payment relates.* While it is the individual who is paid, the level of payment may also be determined on a workgroup, department, plant, or whole organization basis.

Table 8.1 sets out six commonly used methods of payment, summarizing their broad characteristics in terms of the above four dimensions. Job evaluation has been omitted from this table on the grounds that it is intended to provide the foundation for a payment structure rather than constituting a method of payment per se. A summary such as Table 8.1 cannot include the detailed variations that are to be found in the practical application of each payment method. Its purpose, rather, is to facilitate the process of comparing different methods of payment and considering the requirements and conditions that impact on the appropriateness of each of these.

1 Flat-time rates

A flat-time rate system involves payment of a wage or salary at intervals specified in a contract of employment or similar agreement. The payment of a flat-rate wage or salary is dependent upon provision by the employee of an agreed number of hours of availability for work. It is "fixed" in the sense that adjustments are made infrequently, normally on the basis of periodic increments or through individual or collective bargaining. Payment may be made at an hourly "rate," a weekly "wage," or a monthly "salary." Salaries often have annual increments built into them, especially in the public sector. Part-time workers are either paid according to an hourly rate or salaried on a pro rata basis. If employees work above their normal hours of work by agreement with management, then overtime may be paid for the extra, often at an enhanced rate. Alternatively, time off may be given "in lieu" of the additional hours worked.

The criteria for assessing payment relate to an individual, though the rate of payment is likely to be fixed for a particular job or job category. Different grades of pay are typically determined on the basis of job evaluation, which takes into account the duties and requirements of the job and/or the skills and competencies needed to perform it. This means that the structure of pay grades can readily be designed to fit an organization's hierarchical structure. Flat time rates do not, however, reward work performance. They do not vary pay level according to quantity or quality of output or even according to flexibility and cooperativeness in the way a job is performed. In principle, it rewards dependability of attendance or availability, though this incentive is in practice often weakened by the ease with which employees can take time off for short-term "sickness." Also, many employers are reluctant to monitor closely the time-keeping of their staff, especially salaried staff, over matters such as lunch breaks, and adjust their payment levels according to time-keeping performance. As we saw in Chapter 6, such close monitoring can be expensive; it can also be demotivating, as it implies a lack of trust on the part of management.

Table 8.1 Classification of methods of payment and their key characteristics

Underlying Dimension	1 Flat time rates	2 Output incentives	3 Merit rating	4 Gain sharing	5 Profit-sharing and stock ownership	6 Performance-related pay
The feature to which payment is tied	Fulfillment of agreed hours of work. Basis of rate is often job evaluation. May also be status or going rate in labor market	A set formula relating to: level of output achieved (production incentive), or level of sales achieved (commission), and similar	Performance assessed subjectively by supervisor and his immediate superior according to agreed criteria	(1) Increase in productivity/saving in costs due to negotiated changes in work rules and methods; (2) Negotiated improvement in flexibility of manning	Profit sharing: increase in organization's profit; Stock ownership: Dividend payment and appreciation of stock values	Performance assessed according to agreed criteria which may contain objective and subjective elements
Presence or not of incentive element	No	Yes, payment may be entirely or primarily dependent on work achieved (e.g. piecework) or may consist of bonus additional to base rate	Yes, usually consisting of lump-sum bonuses. Incentive may be weak if criteria for merit are not stated clearly, or not seen to be attainable	Yes, may be one-off payment, or payment of agreed % of savings, or bonus guaranteed while improvement is maintained, or payment for additional skills used in flexible working	Yes, but weak and indirect	Yes, usually consisting of lump-sum bonuses
Usual frequency of payment	Weekly (wage) or Monthly (salary). Reward for additional hours may be deferred (e.g. time off given in lieu at later date)	Weekly	Usually a deferred bonus or increase in wage rate/salary level	Once-and-for-all; or deferred periodic bonus/payment of % of saving	Long deferred; profit distribution usually yearly; dividend distribution usually half-yearly	Varies, but usually six-monthly or annually
Unit to which basis for payment is normally related	Individual (once allocated to a specified job or job category)	Individual, workgroup or department	Individual	Often plant-wide; may be limited to specific groups with which agreement is negotiated (e.g. maintenance workers)	Whole company or could be profit-centre such as division, subsidiary.	Individual or group

A number of variants of time payment have become more commonly used. One is the two-tier system whereby one group of employees receives lower wages and/or benefits than another. The lower tier often consists of new recruits or less experienced workers. Informally, female employees have often been treated as a lower tier despite the presence of equal pay legislation. A two-tier policy may reduce an employer's overall wage bill and also be thought appropriate in industries where there is a high turnover of newly-hired workers, as in retailing. In times of high unemployment, it may also be welcomed by workers in the higher tier as a way of protecting their wage levels and even their employment. However, if the level and quality of work performed is not appreciably different between the two tiers, this system can lead to demoralization and high turnover among the lower-paid workers.

There has been a sharp increase in another variant of time-based pay, the so-called "zero-hours" payment contract by which workers are effectively "on call." Use of this system has been encouraged by pressures on employers to cut their labor bills and to find more cost-effective ways of meeting flexible staffing requirements, especially in sectors such as agriculture, education, healthcare, hospitality and tourism, and retailing. Under zero-hours contracts, staff agree to be available for work as and when required. On their part they have no obligation to accept a specific item of work that is offered, though usually their disadvantaged economic circumstances leave them with little option but to comply with an employer's requirements. They may also fear that if they turn down the work once, they will not be offered it again. In effect, this system provides employers with a pool of people who are on call and can be used when the need arises.[5] It is a system that might suit some groups such as students and retirees, but for many it created a serious level of unpredictability in their income stream and has attracted charges of exploitation.

There are several reasons for the widespread use of fixed-time rate, wage, and salary payments:

1   In the case of many jobs, performance cannot be accurately measured;
2   With the use of automated technologies in production and some fields of transportation, the previous requirement for effort is being replaced by the need for reliable monitoring in control rooms or aircraft cockpits, using cognitive and judgmental skills;
3   Fixed-time payment confines disputes over pay to relatively infrequent intervals, and so provides a more favorable basis for managements seeking to develop a "cultural" philosophy of control based on high normative commitment among employees.

Also, the fixed, flat-time rate system has a number of advantages:

1   It is relatively easy to administer;
2   It is "above board," i.e., open to inspection, and fair in the sense that people doing the same job will be on the same pay grade, though there may be incremental points built into each grade;
3   The transparency and relatively fixed nature of the system reduces the incidence of conflict over pay;
4   A flat-time rate system helps an organization to retain staff because it can be linked to a hierarchy of job grades and so offer the prospect of progression across grades as well as incremental increases within each grade;

5   A flat-time rate system does not emphasize quantity of work and output at the expense of quality. This can be particularly important for organizations competing on the basis of high quality and where the individual worker or team can have a direct impact on this, e.g., in personal services and customer relations.

The biggest drawback with the fixed, flat-time rate system lies in its lack of incentive to perform well. If some people on a particular grade are performing less well than others, why should they receive the same pay? Or, put another way, what incentive is there for a person to improve his or her performance if he or she receives no additional reward for so doing? For this reason, a basically fixed wage or salary system may be supplemented by negotiated productivity and flexibility agreements or profit sharing (both discussed below). While these modifications or extensions do link in with performance, this may just be on a once-for-all basis or, in the case of profit sharing, involve a long-deferred payment.

Another problem is that the attraction offered by time rate systems, of potential career progression up a hierarchy of grades, is not very compatible with moves toward delayering and flatter organizational structures. Also if time payment requires close, top-down monitoring of how jobs are being performed, it may negatively impact on any policies to encourage initiative among knowledge workers and to devolve initiative within organizations.

For reasons such as these, payment by time, and progression according to seniority or length of service, is declining. Many employers have moved towards payment systems that incorporate incentives linked to individual or group performance.

2 Output incentives

Output incentive schemes, by contrast, tie payment (normally a portion of total remuneration) to the output achieved either by an individual or a group. When the topic of "incentives" for non-managerial employees is discussed, it is usually with reference to these schemes, although they are not the only methods of payment to contain an incentive element. Examples of output incentives schemes are:

- *Piecework*: payment per unit produced;
- *Premium schemes*: part of take-home pay is fixed, but a percentage – usually between 10 and 30 percent – is a bonus linked to output achieved;
- *Commission schemes*: such as paying an additional amount of money to salesmen for each extra sale (or incremental sales value) secured.

The main attraction for employers of output incentive schemes lies in their motivational power. This can be substantial if the conditions highlighted by expectancy theory (see Chapter 7) are fulfilled. First, an opportunity to earn extra payment has to appeal to employees. This appeal may be weakened if, for instance, they face a high marginal rate of taxation. Second, the extra reward must be worth the additional costs in effort or personal inconvenience that are involved. Third, employees must trust management's good faith in offering incentives in at least two respects: (1) they must perceive that they can realistically achieve the bonus that management is offering; (2) they must have reason to believe that, on attaining higher levels of output, management will not attempt to renegotiate a lower rate of incentive payment simply because employees have benefited. This last requirement points to the necessity on management's part to avoid gross errors in fixing rates because of poor quality of work measurement, subsequently attempting to rectify such errors by renegotiating the agreed rate.

If output incentive schemes are based on a clear and unambiguous measurement of output, they can be regarded as fair by employees in the sense that level of reward is directly linked to level of production. Their motivational potential should also mean that employees require less supervision. The main downside with such payment schemes lies in two problems to which they often give rise: (1) an emphasis on quantity at the expense of quality; (2) increased conflict with management over determining a fair rate of pay per unit of output.

FLAT-TIME RATES VERSUS OUTPUT INCENTIVES: PROS AND CONS

The advantages and disadvantages associated with time rate and output incentive payment systems are pretty much diametrically opposed. The strengths of one approach tend to be the weaknesses of the other. The respective merits of fixed pay and output incentive schemes have usually been considered from a managerial standpoint only, despite the fact that the choice between the two systems has major implications for workers and their representatives. To a surprising extent, the debate has also been conducted in black-and-white terms without reference to the circumstances of particular organizations and their workforces, including the custom and practice that has become established among them over the course of time. The following is a review of the main arguments.

Arguments for output incentives and against fixed-time rate or similar schemes

1 *Higher output per person hour*. Studies, mainly in the USA, have indicated that output incentives can impact significantly to increase employee performance, especially when the work tasks are relatively simple and conducted by individuals.[6] Research by the former Swedish Employers Confederation found consistent evidence that output incentive payment schemes tended to enhance labor productivity. Among 36 Swedish plants that changed from piecework to fixed wages, there was an average fall in productivity of between 10 and 20 percent. This fall-off usually occurred within three to four months after the changeover to fixed payment. Thirty-seven other companies had changed to a premium scheme: 21 of these started with a piecework system and on average increased their productivity between 5 and 10 percent; 16 started with fixed wages and increased their productivity by between 25 and 35 percent. Conventional wisdom among those with experience in manufacturing industry is that a productivity loss of around 20 percent can be expected when changing from output incentives to time-related payment.

2 *Less supervision and greater freedom for employees*. An important criticism of piecework schemes is that they lead to a loss of managerial control over the production process. Employees, however, can see this as a virtue. Incentive schemes incorporate an output control philosophy that delegates control over methods and, by implication, output levels to the workers concerned. They can legitimately ask management to leave them alone to get on with their work as they see fit, on the grounds that they will be the first to suffer if a high level of output is not attained. The attractiveness of such arrangements to any workers who value

autonomy is clear. For management, there may be a considerable saving in supervision if workers are motivated by incentive payments to undertake some normal supervisory duties themselves, such as ensuring an adequate supply of materials, requesting maintenance of equipment when required, and generally preserving the conditions for efficient production. Under a fixed-time related payment system, the burden falls upon the supervisor to motivate workers to lift their performance, since the level of their pay is not at stake.

3 *Opportunities to achieve high earnings.* An output incentive scheme that successfully links performance to pay is not only likely to provide a high level of production for management, but also to afford employees the opportunity to increase their pay. In principle, this type of scheme allows them to decide their own trade-off between effort and earnings, though clearly the more this choice is actually exercised on a fragmented, individual basis within an integrated workflow the more likely are work imbalances and unacceptably high levels of buffer stock and work-in-progress to arise.

Arguments against output incentives and in favor of fixed-time rate or similar schemes

1 *Loss of management control.* There are several ways in which management control may be weakened by the use of output incentives. The first arises because it only makes sense to offer output incentives when it is within the power of workers to modify their levels of output through their own dedication and effort. If management can totally control the level of output, as in an automated process, there is little point in offering an output payment incentive. When employees can control the level of output, the notion of what is a reasonable target becomes a matter of formal negotiation or informal practice. Work measurement is far from being an exact science and workers have opportunities to take advantage of this to attempt to secure a more advantageous balance between their effort and their pay, or to protect the present balance. They may therefore attempt to control their output to reduce the risk of management seeking to cut incentive rates, raise production quotas, or even lay off surplus workers. "Don't work your colleague out of a job" is a long-established saying that illustrates this thinking, which itself indicates a breakdown of trust in management's intentions. Also, if the flow of production is variable, perhaps due to problems with materials supply or the condition of the plant, it becomes rational for workers to smooth the flow in order to provide more stable weekly earnings and thereby assist their personal budgeting. Informal action of this kind taken by employees can result in management being provided with misleading production information that creates scheduling and other problems.

Another control problem with output incentives is that they can easily lead to upward wage drift. Wage drift can disturb the parities and differentials in an organization's payment structure – between employees who are on incentives and those who are not, between direct and indirect workers, and between employees on incentives and their junior managers. If established parities and differentials are to be maintained, the earnings of people who are not on output incentives have to be raised, which will clearly add to overall employment costs. The process of making such adjustments can involve major disputes and upset. Output incentives applied to only one section of the workforce thus impact negatively on integration and harmony within the organization.

Management control also tends to be weakened in other respects by the use of output incentives. Workers are far more reluctant to be redeployed from jobs with which they have become familiar and in which they can earn higher bonuses, so it is difficult to achieve flexibility. Quality of work may decline because workers cut corners in search of higher output, unless a stringent and costly system of inspection is introduced. Disputes over piece rates or bonuses are liable to lose production time through industrial action and, more seriously still, lead to such disruption that customers are let down and orders lost.

2 *Encouragement of competition and conflict.* As just mentioned, the parallel use of output incentives and other payment systems within the same organization can lead to disruption and conflict between the different groups concerned. Any system of reward that is liable to give rise to frequently changing differences in payment between different groups of employees is likely to generate envy and conflict, leading to a breakdown in morale. The same applies at the level of individuals. Individual incentives have the potential to provoke envy, inter-personal conflict, and other dysfunctional behavior. They encourage people to concentrate on their own interests, which can be disastrous when, as is increasingly the case, jobs are interdependent and call for flexibility and cooperation between colleagues.

3 *Higher accident rates and mental illness.* The pressure for output can threaten safety at work. In plants where individual incentive schemes operate, there are often higher accident rates, especially when the output standard is set too high. The desire to increase earnings can lead employees to ignore safety regulations, such as the use of machine guards, generally cut corners, and lay themselves open to higher levels of personal risk. The pressure generated by such a situation also leads to greater levels of stress, which eventually take their toll on both general efficiency and individual well-being. In non-factory environments, pressures for output can result in mental health problems which, though often not reported, can be equally destructive to human well-being.

4 *Discouragement of innovation.* Output incentive schemes can discourage innovation, unless there is some arrangement for sharing the gains from improvements suggested by employees for raising productivity. Otherwise, the consequence of declaring improvements to management may be a downward revision of the output incentive rate. If the innovation eases the task for some workers, it is far more rational for those workers to keep the improvement to themselves, at least in the short term, as a means of easing the pressures they face. When management seeks to introduce a new product or service in a situation where output incentives are used, there is likely to be a period of heightened conflict, grievance, and negotiation because of the changes in job content, work measurement, and setting of new incentive rates that are required. Together with the problem of low flexibility already mentioned, one can see that output incentive schemes may well inhibit innovation and change.

5 *Cost of administration.* While output incentive schemes may save on the amount of direct supervision required, they are inherently costly to administer. Specialists in work measurement are normally required, though these specialists may be expected to provide benefits of a more general industrial engineering nature as well. Staff have to be allocated to the calculation of incentive payments, while additional supervisory time may well be taken up handling the larger number of workers' queries that generally arise under these complex payment methods.

3 Merit rating

Merit rating is another performance-based pay system. In contrast to output incentives, the idea behind merit rating is to include the ability to reward performance of a kind that is not particularly tangible, or measurable by "objective" or direct indicators. Criteria such as "willingness to bear responsibility" or "cooperativeness" are applied. Merit rating can focus on those aspects of work that management deems particularly important, which can include quantifiable elements such as eliminating returns of faulty products or reducing customer complaints. In this way, merit rating can provide a way of communicating management's objectives to its workforce. For example, several schemes have been introduced in the United States whereby schoolteachers receive merit payments for improvements in pupil performance or according to other criteria.

The rewarding of merit can take the form of a wage or salary increase, or a one-off bonus. A salary increase has traditionally come to symbolize consistently good performance. The problem is that, because it is very unusual for organizations to reduce a salary if performance drops back, the merit increase tends to become locked into the salary even when the employee no longer displays any special merit. This weakens the employee's perception of a link between pay and performance. The one-off bonus approach is a better alternative because this does enable the employee to see a pay–performance link. Under this system, a bonus would not be paid in a subsequent period if it were not deemed merit worthy.

The chief problem with merit rating lies in how merit is to be assessed. The basis for determining merit payment is normally a subjective assessment, usually made by a person's manager and the manager's immediate superior (and sometimes with inputs from colleagues). The information required for rating merit is provided by regular performance appraisals. A performance appraisal system plays an essential role in merit rating and it is vital to construct one that is seen to be fair. Merit rating schemes can generate considerable aggravation because their subjective basis lends itself to charges of favoritism and inequity. They can also degenerate from being a method of allocating rewards for individual merit into becoming annual, across-the-board awards so as to spare the embarrassment and rancor of rewarding some with merits increases, but not others.

Research into subjective ratings of performance has pointed to a generally weak level of agreement between those given by the superior and those perceived to be appropriate by the person being rated. Studies I conducted with Bruce Partridge into the ratings of first-line supervisors' performance came to the same conclusion and indicated how characteristics of the rater substantially influenced the rating given.[7] Although merit rating has the virtue of applying the incentive principle to jobs for which precise quantitative measures of performance are not available, it is often disliked by managers and held in suspicion by employees because of its subjective foundation.

Getting a merit rating system right is therefore quite a challenging matter. Four key steps need to be taken.[8]

1   First, there must be clarity about the definition of a person's job and its objectives ("goals"). One way of doing this is to work with employees to identify who receives or benefits from the outputs of a job; in other words, who is the "customer" of that job. The customer approach helps employees to become aware of the significance of their job and how it fits into the attainment of the organization's goals.

2   The second step is to set both expectations about what needs to be done in the job and standards of job performance. Research into goal setting is helpful here. It indicates that employee performance is greatly enhanced when the goals assigned to people are challenging but attainable.[9] They also need to be defined in specific terms and relevant to the objectives of the organization.

3   Step three is to monitor the employee's performance during the period between appraisals. This should be a normal part of the managing process. Done constructively, it can help employees to understand their level of performance and enable discussion of possibilities for improvement. It also allows for priorities and working methods to be modified in a changing situation that requires flexibility.

4   The final step is the formal appraisal. More time is likely to be required for the performance consequences of a senior manager's actions to become apparent than is the case with more junior staff.[10] Thought therefore needs to be given to the appropriate performance period for appraisal and merit rating. This may be up to two years for managers and as frequently as six months for non-managerial workers. As part of the appraisal process, the manager and employee each record their assessment of the latter's performance. This should provide all the information necessary for a fair review. If this is discussed in a constructive, forward-looking manner, it should appear non-threatening and generate a climate of trust. An approach that has gained favor is the 360-degree appraisal in which employees, including managers, are assessed by their peers and any people reporting to them in addition to their immediate superiors. In the case of some jobs, the opinions of clients and suppliers may be sought. This approach is aimed at maximizing relevant information and minimizing unfairness. It is particularly suited to new organizational forms that emphasize openness and bottom-up initiatives. Assessment by subordinates may, however, not be acceptable in some traditional cultures.

4 Gain Sharing

Gain sharing schemes are a broad category covering a range of arrangements to provide opportunities for employees to increase their earnings when they achieve or submit ideas for improvements in productivity, cost reduction, or other desired organizational objectives. In some cases, a collective bonus is paid for an agreement to introduce flexible manning, which is calculated to reduce overall labor costs. Gain sharing schemes are distinct from profit sharing in that they focus on improvements in the productivity of a group, unit, or plant over a period of time, rather than on overall profitability. In so doing, they recognize improvements that are brought about by employees' own contributions and are less influenced by external factors. Some of the benefits from such gains can legitimately be passed on to the employees who helped to make them.

Gain sharing schemes are group or unit-wide based, and intended for situations where the nature of the work process does not permit people to see a strong link between their individual efforts and output. Examples are steel, oil refining, chemicals, and other process plants. It is therefore no coincidence that early examples of these payment schemes emerged in the US steel industry, with the Scanlon Plan, and with so-called "Productivity Bargaining" in oil refineries during the 1960s. Gain sharing schemes have also been applied to services sectors including communication, financial services, transportation, and retailing. Because they often cover a whole establishment or plant, gain sharing agreements are usually negotiated collectively between employers and unions or other employee representatives.

Gain sharing is suited to situations in which individual performance is difficult or impossible to measure and where the operations involved are interdependent, requiring the cooperation of all employees. Gain sharing schemes encourage employee involvement both in their design and also in their implementation. They are founded on the belief that every employee can contribute to the overall success of the organization through participation. The emphasis on participation means that gain sharing plans also enable employees to experience non-financial rewards such as a sense of responsibility and social involvement. Kanungo and Mendonca in their detailed analysis of gain sharing schemes comment that:

> "The participative process is critical to the successful operation of the plan. The experience of Herman Miller, Donnelly Mirrors, Lincoln Electric, Nucor Corporation – to name just a few corporations that have successfully used gain sharing plans – suggests that gain sharing plans are more than a mere device to increase productivity; they represent a way of life. Some organizations have adopted a parallel structure, a steering committee that includes representatives of employees and management from all levels and functions as well as representatives of the union. Other organizations have used the suggestion system with special awards for suggestions that have proved to be effective."[11]

The benefits of gain sharing schemes can be significant so long as real and not pseudo improvements are rewarded. They direct the attention of both managers and employees toward beneficial change and productivity enhancements in a way that highlights the common interest and improves labor relations. When such schemes cover a whole plant or establishment, they can help break down demarcations between groups of workers and reduce the vertical barriers of hierarchy. Many companies have used forms of gain sharing in order to "buy out" established demarcations and achieve flexible deployment. Gain sharing is a way of ensuring that employees benefit financially from these developments. As noted in Chapter 4, they are likely to respond positively to this opportunity so long as the deal does not involve compulsory lay-offs.

5 Profit sharing and stock ownership

Profit sharing is a long-established feature of payment policies in some companies. It is a reward strategy that links employee pay to the financial performance of the firm. Under profit sharing, a certain annual percentage of annual profit is distributed among the staff and employees. The rationale for profit sharing lies in an attempt to eliminate fundamental conflicts of interest between the owners and employees of a capitalist firm. If both shareholders and employees have a share in a firm's profits, then they have a common interest in maintaining a steady improvement in those profits. This principle is similar to that underlying employee stock ownership plans (see below), including the allocation of stock options to managers, under which the members of a firm have an opportunity to share in its ownership and, in this way, to benefit from its prosperity through dividends and potential stock appreciation. For employees on fixed incomes, these schemes introduce an element of variability in pay based on the performance of the firm as a whole. They may well make a firm more attractive to high-quality employees who wish to share in the prosperity of the organizations in which they work.

Profit sharing, like gain sharing plans, aims to promote a sense of employee partnership. Unlike gain sharing, however, profit sharing does not encourage participative management by involving employees or their representatives in the design of the plan or in reaching productivity improvements. Profit sharing is often introduced in a top-down manner, solely at management's discretion.

As well as having the objective of increasing the general level of cooperation and commitment to the organization as a whole, some see in profit sharing an encouragement for employees to improve organizational performance specifically through increased effort and acceptance of change. The fact that the reward – a share in profit – can only be paid when profit is generated could be seen as another advantage, at least from the employer's point of view. Despite its critics, profit sharing may not do much harm to a firm unless it means that certain investments are foregone or that external financing through an issue of new equity becomes available only on less favorable terms. On the other hand, profit sharing is unlikely to have a dramatically favorable effect either. The long period of deferred payment (normally one year) makes the reward seem remote and uncertain in relation to any specific actions that an employee has taken. It is also difficult for individuals to relate profit to their own performance because it is a company-wide indicator. Profit is in any case determined by many factors unrelated to employees' efforts, including external factors.

Employee stock ownership plans (ESOPs) can be regarded as a component of reward policy, though they also have major implications for corporate governance as discussed in Chapter 16. Under a stock ownership scheme, employees are allocated company stock, or have the right to purchase it at a favorable price, usually after they have worked with the company for a certain period of time. Like profit sharing, the intention is to grant the members of an organization a share in the rewards from its prosperity, in the form of stock dividends and capital appreciation, and so enhance their commitment to its overall success. Often, an employee stock ownership scheme is coupled with a system of extensive participation in a company's policy formulation. As Chapter 18 indicates, this arrangement can help to offset some of the negative consequences of extended organizational hierarchies.

ESOPs are in tune with current organizational realities in two respects. First, many firms today are obliged to devolve initiative to individual employees or project teams so as to become more innovative and adaptive. One intention of co-opting employees into ownership is to reduce the risks of opportunism that arise with devolution by strengthening their commitment to the overall goals of the firm. Second, many workers are now providing firms with knowledge assets that constitute a scarce, key resource. As Peter Drucker has said, this in effect "means that knowledge workers collectively own the means of production."[12] Knowledge assets now assume as much, if not more, significance for corporate success as financial assets.[13] If this knowledge is of proprietary value to a firm, and some of it necessarily held in tacit form by employees, then the economic argument alone for increasing their commitment by granting them a formal stake in ownership becomes compelling.

In fact, the balance of historical evidence on the consequences of ESOPs is that they are economically beneficial for firms.[14] More recent reviews of studies conducted both in the UK and USA concluded that the introduction of ESOP schemes resulted in productivity, employment and sales gains, especially when combined with participation in decision making.[15] Such participation tends to go hand in hand with greater employee engagement in the organization and encourages their contribution to innovation.[16] Moreover, firms with ESOPs have been more resilient during the post-2008 period of recession.[17] Examples of the supposed failure of such schemes, such as United Airlines, on closer examination generally indicate the presence of other factors such as economic distress when the scheme was established or a lack of union cooperation.[18] Counter examples of successful firms, like the John Lewis Partnership, that have reaped many benefits from employee ownership and participation, have not received the attention they deserve.[19]

6 Performance-related pay

Performance-related pay (PRP) is a broad concept that may include output incentives, merit rating, gain sharing and profit sharing. The PRP approach started at the top of organizations with the introduction of more discriminating ways of determining base salaries and bonus schemes for executives. During the 1990s, PRP was extended to cover other groups of staff across many companies. It normally considers both results or output and the behavior of employees on the job. Kelly Global Services, which conducts an annual international survey of workforces, states that "performance-based pay includes any arrangement where an element of the total remuneration package is tied to meeting performance targets and may include profit sharing, performance bonuses and sales commissions." Its 2013 survey was based on approximately 122,000 respondents in 31 countries across the Americas, EMEA and APAC regions. It found that the adoption of performance-related remuneration has been gathering momentum. It was being applied on average to 44 percent of employees worldwide, and to 59 percent in the APAC region. China and Indonesia had the highest incidence – 75 percent – while the USA and UK had among the lowest (32 and 30 percent respectively). Significantly, 46 percent of the overall sample said that they would perform at a higher level on performance-related pay.[20] Other studies suggest that, when applied properly, PRP schemes typically lift productivity quite substantially.[21]

In principle, PRP is compatible with the adoption of new organizational forms. The idea behind PRP is to retarget the payment system so that it is more responsive to the needs of both the organization and the individual. It can be focused on either the individual or the group (team). PRP rewards people for the achievement of better-than-expected performance and is therefore intended to encourage individual or group initiative. As the removal of management layers makes it more difficult to reward people through promotion, PRP, together with a widening of pay bands, is seen to provide one solution to the problem. Some advocates of PRP in fact regard its principle of rewarding for actual contribution and achievement as being an important advance on older systems.

There are further reasons why PRP has been popular among employers. First, by creating differentials between people's pay, PRP not only rewards achievement, but also makes it less feasible for employees to get together to regulate their output in relation to their pay, as happened frequently with output incentive systems. PRP individualizes pay and weakens collective negotiation. Second, companies can achieve savings in salary costs when the introduction of PRP leads to an abolition of automatic increments on pay scales. Third, PRP enables people to be rewarded for achievement without having to do this by promoting them to a level that may be beyond their capabilities.[22]

As with merit rating, the setting of performance standards and the quality of the appraisal system are critical for the success of PRP schemes. In practice, experience indicates that it is very difficult to convince employees that PRP schemes are administered without the intrusion of subjective bias, or that they have sufficient influence in setting performance targets. PRP schemes have often demotivated employees. They can generate resentment and an unwillingness to cooperate when some people are rewarded more than others. Also, when performance criteria are not well thought-out, there can be a conflict in the balance between the achievement of quality versus quantity in people's work. Some of these problems can be mitigated when PRP schemes are group rather than individually based.

As in the case of merit rating, there is always a danger that PRP schemes become corrupted through managers and employees receiving bonuses because they have come to expect them, rather than as a true reflection of exceptional performance on their part. Some of the worst cases have been the payment of large bonuses to top executives in companies whose performance has been declining or, like some financial institutions, failed outright. In the USA, the payment of large bonuses to top executives for steering their companies through bankruptcy has been particularly controversial. An example is the Lear Corporation, a car parts supplier. As reported by the *Wall Street Journal*, when the Lear Corporation became bankrupt it closed 28 factories with the loss of over 20,000 jobs and left shareholders with no value. Despite this, Lear planned to pay $20.6 million in bonuses for its key executives including an eventual payout for its CEO. Although the US Justice Department objected to this package, a judge overruled this and approved the payouts. A statement from the company said that bonuses were "customary" and "fully market competitive."[23]

It is not just the level of so-called "fat-cat pay" that has caused widespread resentment, but primarily the cynicism and hypocrisy that has been evident in the abuse of the PRP principle. Not only has there been a manifest corruption of senior executive bonus schemes that have ceased to reflect performance; the charge is also made that such schemes can distort policy decisions in directions that harm shareholder interests. A study using data from all NYSE, AMEX, and NASDAQ firms listed on the Compustat Execucomp Database, the Compustat annual industrial files and the CRSP files from 1994 to 2011 supported this charge. It found that CEO pay was negatively related to future stock returns over the subsequent three year period and that this effect was stronger when CEOs received higher incentive pay relative to their peers. The authors also point out that, overall, there is surprisingly little direct evidence that incentive contracts actually lead to better future stock performance.[24]

A scheme for relating pay and even continued job tenure to performance that has also proved controversial, and some would say counterproductive, is the so-called "stack ranking" employee-review and compensation system. Sometimes the system is described in more euphemistic terms such as "talent management." General Electric under Jack Welch was a pioneer in introducing the system. With stack ranking, managers are required to grade employees against one another and rank them on a scale of one to five. These rankings can be used as a basis for deciding promotions and bonuses. They can also be used as the basis for removing the bottom 10 percent of employees. In practice, this approach can be highly subjective and disruptive of good relations and morale within an organization.[25]

While it is difficult to argue against the principle of performance-related pay, getting its implementation right is far from easy. Its acceptance requires clarity and transparency in the link between performance and reward and that all who contribute to an organization's success can share in its payback. The unequal system of status and access to information that normally accompanies organizational hierarchy can militate against these conditions and very often has.

◢ Considerations in the Choice of a Payment System

Different payment schemes suit different jobs and types of employee. There is, inevitably, a trade-off between fine-tuning pay policies to suit a wide range of circumstances, so that different categories and level of employee have their own scheme, and the costs of administering a complex approach of this kind. Also the willingness of employees to be flexible in the tasks they undertake, and to move between jobs when required, will be jeopardized if the different jobs have their own payment arrangements. These are important

BOX 8.1 INTEL EUROPE'S MIXED REWARD PACKAGE

Intel Corporation's operation in Europe extends from Ireland in the west to Kazakhstan in the east and Israel in the south, employing approximately 17,000 workers in sales and marketing, manufacturing and design. Intel's reward philosophy is based on matching or exceeding the market for fixed elements of the total reward package (base pay, benefits and employee share schemes) and rewarding exceptional performance with variable pay practices which allow repeat high-performers to earn at the very top of the market. An annual bonus is based on individual targets with a multiplier based on overall company performance, while a six-monthly bonus is awarded on size of revenue, operating margin and feedback from customers. What may be surprising in a large diverse employee population is that the bonuses are open to all, regardless of role, business group or location. The message to employees is unambiguous: performance drives earnings potential and performance is dependent on everyone – everyone will have a role to play, and a share, in company success.

Source: Chartered Institute of Personnel and Development [CIPD] 2013. *Reward Management, Annual Survey Report 2013*. London: CIPD, p. 24.

reasons why many employers have consolidated their payment systems across different categories of employee and why merit rating and PRP schemes focusing on individuals rather than jobs have found favor.

Nonetheless, it is possible and quite common to combine different payment methods. The most obvious is the combination of a time-based wage or salary with one or more incentive elements. A merit or PRP scheme offers bonuses for above-average performance on top of a person's basic payment. Profit sharing and ESOPs can be also be added to time-based schemes and/or merit and PRP schemes. Box 8.1 summarizes how this is done in the Intel Corporation.

Different incentive schemes can also be combined to reflect special circumstances such as seasonal variations in production. An example of this comes from a plant in Northern Ireland that bottled gas in cylinders. The plant's management negotiated a piece-rate agreement that gave workers more pay when the demand for output was high in the winter period, and allowed early finishing in the summer when the level of production required was lower, but when employees particularly appreciated additional leisure time in the afternoons. This combination of two incentive elements suited management's need for flexible production and the workers' lifestyle. The scheme led to greater cooperation from the workers, allowing supervision to be relaxed and workgroup autonomy to be increased. There were resultant increases in productivity and a decline in absenteeism.[26]

There are several trade-offs that have to be considered when designing a reward policy. One is the issue of simplicity versus complexity already mentioned. The main choices are between:

- A simple system *versus* one that addresses several relevant dimensions;
- A standardized system *versus* one that is sensitive to individual differences;
- A relatively fixed or rigid system *versus* a flexible and adaptive one;

Table 8.2   Broad choices in the design of payment systems

1 **Simplicity**	or **Complexity**
Example: flat time rates; traditional piecework without additional features	*Example:* job evaluation combined with various types of incentive or profit-sharing schemes
In a period of change and pressure, makes it easier for managers to exercise control and keep track of costs	Provides management with more options to respond to different requirements; but difficult to get the balance right or to predict cost implications
2 **Standardization**	or **Differentiation**
Example: all employees on flat time rates and grouped into few job categories	*Example:* merit rating; menu of additional benefits from which employees can choose
Ease and low cost of administration. Avoids risk of charges of favoritism	Recognizes individual differences and adapts payment system to these, thus enhancing motivational potential
3 **Relatively fixed or rigid**	or **Flexible and adaptable**
Example: times rates based on job evaluation	*Example:* performance-related pay
Attractive in terms of maintaining discipline and control in face of change and pressures	Attractive in terms of aligning people's efforts to a company's objectives and changing requirements
4 **Attempt to influence motivation or increase individual performance**	or **Emphasis on building harmonious collective relationships**
Example: output incentive schemes	*Example:* profit-sharing; employee stock ownership; gain-sharing
Maximizes motivational potential and helps to control direct costs in face of intensifying competition	Conducive to co-operative, harmonious industrial relations, and to achieving flexible manning

- Systems that attempt to influence motivation *versus* ones that are more conducive to the development of cooperative relationships.

Table 8.2 sets out these choices and summarizes the potential advantages of each. While the table provides illustrations of payment systems, the choices it lists also apply to the design of reward policies as a whole. For instance, standardization could mean the design of jobs according to specifications that apply to everyone within a given category, whereas differentiation would allow employees the freedom to decide on what they do and adjust the scope of their jobs, so long as they meet agreed performance criteria.

◢ Trends in Reward Policies Consistent with New Organizational Forms

Rigidities in pay structures have been one of the most significant obstacles to the introduction of new organizational forms. The search for ways to reduce such rigidities has in fact characterized recent approaches to reward policy, and it has brought some traditional approaches into disfavor. Job evaluation has proved to be too time-consuming a process to be adaptable to frequently changing new requirements. It has also discouraged employees from adopting a flexible approach to their work, an essential part of which is a willingness to work outside and beyond the tasks that are formally specified in their jobs. Output incentive schemes can also encourage resistance to flexibility because the employees concerned may well estimate that it will prove more difficult for them to achieve their bonuses if they are required to take on new and less familiar tasks.

Teamworking has increasingly become an integral part of contemporary organization, and one would have expected to see a corresponding take-up of team-based payment systems. Teamwork is in principle best supported by a group payment system that has an incentive element based on either objective performance measures (if these are feasible) or on a performance related formula. However, it appears that relatively few employers operate team pay systems. It is, for example, difficult to do so if teams are temporary. Nevertheless, the CIPD 2013 Reward Management survey of 444 UK organizations, across private, public and third sectors, found that of all PRP schemes, those offering group bonuses based on the group/team achievement of specific objectives ("goal sharing") were the most common form, especially in private sector companies.

PRP features prominently in the new approach to pay, which endeavors to improve performance in relation to the need for flexibility and innovation. Combined with regular appraisal and assessment of employees' development potential and training, reward policies today emphasize a connection between employee pay and employee performance through variable incentives that are linked to corporate objectives. This link is an important element in the so-called "strategic" approach to human resource management.

Pay structures are tending to incorporate broader bands, which are in line with fewer hierarchical levels and encourage flexible working and deployment. For example, the Norwich and Peterborough Building Society, starting in 1999, replaced its former 12-band grading structure with a simpler, 5-level job framework. The pay attached to each band was informed by the labor market rate. Pay progression now became linked to the attainment of skills and knowledge within a staff member's "career progression framework," which is a personal development plan. The change resulted in lower staff turnover, increased productivity, and greater satisfaction among both staff and customers.[27]

Some employers have also offered a wider range of options and benefits in the attempt to encourage people's commitment and motivation through suiting different individual needs, though others are wary of introducing too much complexity into their reward policies. In January 2003, a British bank, Lloyds TSB, launched a scheme of this kind through which its 72,000 staff can trade salary for extra benefits in a tax-efficient way. The menu of flexible benefits offered includes up to five days' holiday entitlement, private health insurance, pension contributions, computer purchase, subsidized learning, childcare vouchers, retail vouchers, and discounted insurance. Within certain limits, staff can choose to trade in these benefits for additional pay. The company's objective in introducing this scheme was to differentiate itself in attractiveness from other financial sector employers and, in particular, to retain younger and shorter-service staff whose turnover was disproportionately high.[28]

A further trend has been the decentralization of bargaining over pay within multi-establishment organizations. The purpose is to permit the development of pay policies that best suit the contingencies present in a particular establishment or unit within a company. This

BOX 8.2 INTRODUCTION OF AN INCENTIVE SCHEME AND ITS EFFECTS

A large retailer introduced an incentive scheme for its 40,000 store-based employees. The intention was to increase sales of four insurance plans covering products against accidental damage or breakdown. Financial services products such as these were important to the company, because they were a potential growth segment and already accounted for 6 percent of total profits.

The new incentive scheme offered rewards based on the achievement of store-specific, insurance-product sales targets. Cash payments were awarded to individual staff for different levels of target performance. An additional, competitive element was introduced to create some excitement, involving weekly prizes. Store managers also received "holiday points."

The incentive scheme was successful in increasing sales by 20 percent. It did, however, have several negative effects as well. It disrupted teamworking in the stores. Also the level of incentive payment offered was felt by most employees to be too low and this generated some discontent, while managers of smaller-volume stores felt discriminated against because they could not earn the level of reward of larger-volume ones. Most stores initiated local schemes to run alongside the official one. These included awarding time off for top sellers and organizing staff into teams that were then given rewards for achieving high sales. These local adaptations were perceived as more motivating and generating greater interest among employees.

Source: Malcolm Higgs and Hamish Renton. Recognition and Rewards. *IRS Employment Review*, No. 781, August 1, 2003: 20–23.

becomes a very significant consideration for companies that have internationalized across a number of countries and where both legal and cultural factors may require a variety of approaches to pay and other rewards.

The case described in Box 8.2 provides an example of the growing use of incentive schemes and also illustrates two of the issues we have discussed, namely: (1) incentives that are effective in raising individual performance can simultaneously disrupt teamworking; (2) schemes adapted to local situations can have more positive effects.

To summarize, emerging trends in pay policy include:[29]

1   *Market-driven pay*: a flexible approach to pay and benefits that reflects the worth of employees in the labor market.
2   *Performance-related pay*: a widespread application of individual PRP schemes and an increasing interest in team-based rewards as teamwork becomes increasingly used.
3   *Broadbanding (broader pay ranges)*: in order to attain increased flexibility in delayered organizations.
4   *Competence-based pay*: this reflects the growing use of competencies as criteria in managing performance in line with the recognition that the competitiveness of a firm can depend heavily on the quality of such competencies.

5   *Flexible benefits*: to reflect the needs of a diverse workforce, as well as target the costs of different benefits.
6   *Non-financial (intrinsic) rewards*: there is a growing recognition of the motivational power of intrinsic rewards and of their compatibility with new organizational forms that devolve initiative and responsibility to employees, either as individuals or in teams.
7   *Harmonization and consolidation*: to eliminate a source of division when management is attempting to promote integration and flexible deployment within organizations.

At the same time, certain reward policies are now less frequently applied:

1   *Incremental pay systems*: regular periodic increments are not regarded as responsive to an employee's market value, or to the linking of reward to performance and hence to the organization's strategic objectives.
2   *Inflation linked increases*: inflation linked increases in pay are falling out of favor in a climate of low inflation, which weakens employee expectations that such increases should be given. Inflation-linked pay was particularly common in the public sector and this link has been broken at a time of cutbacks in government expenditure.
3   *Traditional job evaluation*: there are concerns about the inflexibility of job evaluation when reward strategies are required that adapt to change and innovation.
4   *Annual pay reviews*: longer-term pay deals are becoming more common, especially when linked to productivity improvements.
5   *Allowances and add-ons*: these are becoming increasingly consolidated into simpler reward systems that are "clean" in the sense of being focused onto key organizational objectives.

SUMMARY

1   A payment system is intended to offer employees rewards that they value and that at the same time motivate them toward fulfilling an organization's performance criteria.
2   The ease with which money can be measured and linked as a reward to specific achievement criteria, lends payment an inherent flexibility that is attractive both to employers and many employees as well.
3   Each of the different payment systems discussed in this chapter has its strengths and limitations when assessed against the managerial and employee criteria discussed in the previous chapter. For this reason, it is quite common to combine two, sometimes more, of the systems.
4   At the same time, emerging trends can be observed in pay policy towards favoring systems that are more compatible with contemporary developments in employment and organizational form. Examples are performance-related pay and broader payment bands. Relatively inflexible systems such as job evaluation are losing favor in organizations that need to adapt and innovate.

QUESTIONS FOR DISCUSSION

8.1 Why does pay continue to play such a major role in relations between employers and employees?

8.2 Describe the most common methods of payment and compare their relative merits.

8.3 What are normally the key considerations that inform the choice between different methods of payment in organizations?

8.4 How can payment systems support other aspects of organizational design?

8.5 From a management point of view, evaluate the arguments against output incentive schemes.

8.6 Discuss the pros and cons of merit rating.

8.7 What appear to be the emerging trends in payment policy and how do they relate to developments in forms of organizing?

NOTES

1 Amy E. Mickel and Lisa A. Barron (2008), Getting "more bang for the buck": Symbolic value of monetary rewards in organizations, *Journal of Management Inquiry*, 17(4), 329–338.

2 Frederick Herzberg, Bernard Mausner, and Barbara B. Snyderman (1959), *The Motivation to Work*, New York, Wiley.

3 Flora F.T. Chiang and Thomas A. Birtch (2012), The performance implications of financial and non-financial rewards: An Asian Nordic comparison, *Journal of Management Studies*, 49(3), 538–570.

4 It is a challenge to measure responsibility. Elliott Jaques suggested the criterion of "time span of discretion" which is the longest length of time taken to complete discretionary work, or unsupervised tasks. In other words, it is the length of time before sub-standard decisions or work would become apparent. The longer the timespan of discretion, the higher the level of responsibility. See Elliott Jaques (1956), *Measurement of Responsibility: A Study of Work, Payment, and Individual Capacity*, London, Tavistock; and Elliott Jaques (1964), *Time-Span Handbook: the Use of Time-Span of Discretion to Measure the Level of Work in Employment Roles and to Arrange an Equitable Payment Structure*, London, Heinemann.

5 Advisory, Conciliation and Arbitration Service (ACAS) (2012), The rise of the 'zero-hours' contract, http://www.acas.org.uk/index.aspx?articleid=3886, accessed 21 November, 2013.

6 Stephen J. Perkins and Geoff White (2011), *Reward Management: Alternatives, Consequences and Contexts*, 2nd edition, London, Chartered Institute of Personnel and Development (CIPD), pp. 173–174.

7 John Child and Bruce Partridge (1982), *Lost Managers: Supervisors in Industry and Society*, Cambridge, Cambridge University Press.

8 Rabindra N. Kanungo and Manuel Mendonca (1997), *Compensation: Effective Reward Management*, 2nd edition, Toronto, Wiley, Chapter 9.

9 Edwin A. Locke and Gary P. Latham (2006), New directions in goal-setting theory, *Current Directions in Psychological Science*, 15(5), 265–268. See also Edwin A. Locke and Gary P. Latham (1984), *Goal Setting: A Motivational Technique That Works*, Englewood Cliffs, NJ, Prentice-Hall.

10 Elliott Jaques (1976), *A General Theory of Bureaucracy*, London, Heinemann/Halsted.

11 Kanungo and Mendonca (1997), op. cit., p. 224.

12 Peter Drucker (2001), The next society: a survey of the near future, *The Economist*, November 3, pp. 1–22. Quotation is from p. 8.

13 Max Boisot (1998), *Knowledge Assets: Securing Competitive Advantage in the Information Economy*, Oxford, Oxford University Press.

14 Frank Heller, Eugen Pusic, George Strauss, and Bernhard Wilpert (1998), *Organizational Participation: Myth and Reality*, Oxford, Oxford University Press.

15 Patrick Briône and Chris Nicholson (2012), *Employee Ownership: Unlocking Growth in the UK Economy*, London, Centre Forum; Graeme Nuttall (2012), *Sharing Success: The Nuttall Review of Employee Ownership*. https://www.gov.uk/government/uploads/system/uploads/attachment_data/file/31706/12-933-sharing-success-nuttall-review-employee-ownership.pdf, accessed 21 November, 2013.

16 J. Lampel, A. Bhalla, and P. Jha, (2010), *Model Growth: Do Employee-owned Businesses deliver Sustainable Performance*, Employee Ownership Association. Available via: http://www.employeeownership.co.uk/publications/model-growth-do-employee-owned-businesses-deliver-sustainable-performance/. D. MacLeod and N. Clarke (2009), *Engaging for Success: Enhancing Performance through Employee Engagement*, London: Department for Business Innovation and Skills. http://www.bis.gov.uk/files/file52215.pdf, accessed 21 November, 2013.

17 Lampel et al. (2010), op. cit.

18 *The Economist* (2003), Economic focus: a capital idea, March 29, p. 86.

19 Keith Bradley and Simon Taylor (1992), *Business Performance in the Retail Sector: The Experience of the John Lewis Partnership*, Oxford, Clarendon Press; Peter Cox (2010), *Spedan's Partnership: The Story of John Lewis and Waitrose*, Labatie Books.

20 Kelly Services Ins (2013), *Kelly Global Workforce Index 2013: Workplace Performance*, http://www.kellyservices.co.uk/uploadedFiles/United_Kingdom_-_Kelly_Services/4-Knowledge_Hub/Articles/KGWI_2013/KGWI%202013%20TOPIC%202%20REPORT.pdf, accessed November 29, 2013.

21 Tito Boeri, Claudio Lucifora, and Kevin J. Murphy (eds.) (2013), *Executive Remuneration and Employee Performance-Related Pay: A Transatlantic Perspective*, Oxford, Oxford University Press.

22 Eugene F. McKenna (2012), *Business Psychology and Organizational Behaviour*, 5th edition, Hove, UK: Psychology Press, Chapter 19.

23 Mike Spector and Tom McGinty (2012), Bonuses flourish for CEOs at firms, even in distress, *The Wall Street Journal*, January 30, 12–13.

24 Michael J. Cooper, Huseyin Gulen, and P. Raghavendra Rau (2013), Performance for Pay? The relation between CEO incentive compensation and future stock price performance, January 30. Working paper available at SSRN: http://ssrn.com/abstract=1572085 or http://dx.doi.org/10.2139/ssrn.1572085.

25 Shira Ovide and Rachel Feintzeig (2012), Microsoft ends dreaded 'stack', *The Wall Street Journal*, November 14, p. 20.

26 Lex Donaldson and Richard Lynn (1976), The conflict resolution process, *Personnel Review*, Spring, 21–28.

27 Building a new pay framework (2002), *IRS Employment Review*, no. 758, August 19, pp. 25–28.

28 Lloyds TSB develops a taste for flexibility (2003), *IRS Employment Review*, no. 768, January 24, 24–28.

29 For further discussion of emerging reward trends see Stephen Pilbeam and Marjorie Corbridge (2010), *People Resourcing and Talent Planning: HRM in Practice*, 4th edition, London: Financial Times Management; Stephen J. Perkins and Geoff White (2011), *Reward Management: Alternatives, Consequences and Contexts*, 2nd edition, London: CIPD.

PART III

New Network Forms

◢ Introduction to Part III – New Network Forms

The chapters in Part III turn outwards beyond the conventional boundaries of organizations. They discuss various arrangements that involve networking between firms and across national boundaries. Networking is a very general concept and it can take different forms in practice. The chapters in this part of the book consider some of these variations. One of the main features of new organization lies in how it opens up and crosses boundaries through outsourcing, virtual value chains, alliances, and internationalization. These developments have led some commentators to speak of the "boundaryless organization."

Chapter 9 examines the outsourcing of activities to external contractors. Chapter 10 looks at the special, but increasingly significant, case of "virtual" organization based on e-commerce and similar strategies. Chapter 11 is concerned with a particularly challenging case of networking across organizational boundaries, when two or more partners form a strategic alliance on a formal basis such as a joint venture in which they invest equity, management, and other resources. Chapter 12 turns to the crossing of another kind of boundary, that of nationality. It considers the organizational challenges of managing across borders.

CHAPTER 9

Outsourcing and Offshoring

WHAT THIS CHAPTER COVERS

Outsourcing has become a major feature of organizational restructuring. This chapter begins by defining outsourcing and describing its scale and scope. It identifies two categories of outsourcing, the first being of value chain activities and the second being the outsourcing of support activities. Examples are given of manufacturing outsourcing as well as of outsourcing by service companies. The chapter then discusses the attractions of outsourcing, followed by the problems and pitfalls that can arise. This leads naturally to the considerations that should inform a decision on outsourcing and the outlines of a methodology for creating successful outsourcing partnerships.

Outsourcing and Changing Organizational Boundaries

Outsourcing refers to the contracting out of activities that need to be undertaken on a regular basis, which otherwise would be conducted within an organization. Outsourcing has become a major area of restructuring, and one that is dramatically changing the traditional boundaries of organizations. James B. Quinn, best-selling author and business visionary, has called outsourcing "one of the greatest organizational and industry structure shifts of the century."[1]

The term "outsourcing" is not usually applied to the buying in of specialized services that are required only occasionally, such as legal advice, or that fall outside the scope of the organization's normal activities, such as arranging business travel. Outsourcing normally refers to the farming out of activities that were previously performed in-house. The strategic choice here is between conducting the activity inside the firm (in-house), conducting it cooperatively with a partner (through a partnership or alliance – see Chapter 11), or outsourcing it fully to an arms-length provider (a contractual market transaction). Outsourcing can be domestic, when activities are performed by an outside organization located in the same country; but it is often international with activities performed by an external organization located in a different country.

When activities are performed for a firm in another country this is normally referred to as "offshoring." (The term "nearshoring" is sometimes used to refer to activities transferred to neighboring countries, such as US business activities performed in Canada and Mexico.) Offshoring does not necessarily involve outsourcing, such as when activities are conducted by a foreign subsidiary of the firm. When offshoring also involves outsourcing, this is known as "offshore outsourcing."[2] Outsourcing together with offshoring are the foundations of business networks and global value chains. Estimates for the global market size of outsourcing vary considerably, partly because of inconsistencies in its definition. We know that the global market is large and that it has grown every year albeit recently at a slowing rate. One estimate put the total value of services outsourcing (business processes and IT) alone in 2013 to be worth over US $950 billion.[3]

Table 9.1 summarizes the four main configurations of outsourcing and offshoring.

From the late 1990s, a great deal of manufacturing was moved to countries like Mexico and China from previous bases within developed countries, largely because of cheaper labor costs. An increasing amount of service work, ranging from software design to call centers, was moved to India and more recently to the Philippines – with the knowledge of English in both countries being an advantage.[4]

Offshoring is a long-established phenomenon and is a fundamental characteristic of the multinational firm. There has been a trend toward the lowering of barriers to international trade and foreign direct investment, coupled with better communication technology and an increasingly sophisticated understanding of value-adding activities. This has encouraged multinationals to source intermediate goods and services from the most favorable locations. The organizational challenge that arises here is that of coordinating internationally dispersed, disaggregated value-adding activities while also having regard to the different criteria arising from product, regional, and functional considerations.

The rationale for outsourcing is also based on a disaggregation of a firm's activities and the advantage of sourcing these from the most efficient supplier – subject to the proviso that strategically key competencies and knowledge need to be protected in-house. An extensive use

Table 9.1 Configurations of outsourcing and offshoring

	Offshoring Activities performed in a foreign country	Onshore Activities performed in the home country
Outsourcing Activities performed by an external organization under separate ownership	*Offshore outsourcing*: Contracts to external organizations located in a foreign country	*Domestic Outsourcing* Contracts to external organizations located in the same country
No outsourcing	*Offshoring*: Activities performed by overseas affiliates or subsidiaries	Purely domestic divisions and subsidiaries

> ## BOX 9.1 METRO INTERNATIONAL: AN EXAMPLE OF EXTENSIVE OUTSOURCING
>
> Metro International, a Swedish-owned media company claims to produce the "world's largest global daily newspaper." It publishes its freesheet in 72 editions for over 150 cities in 24 countries across Europe, North and South America and Asia, reaching an audience of more than 18 million daily readers. It employs many fewer reporters per edition than traditionally organized newspapers, buying most of its content from news and picture agencies instead and presenting it under the Metro label. It also outsources its printing and most of its distribution. The company's non-traditional organizational model has been more successful in sustaining rapid growth than in helping to return a profit. Its advertising sales grew at a compound annual growth rate of 41% since launch of the first newspaper edition in 1995, but it has only occasionally returned a profit.
>
> *Source: Metro International,* http://www.metro.lu

of outsourcing leads to a "hollowing out" of the traditional organization. As companies shift an increasing number of activities to external contractors and partners, their boundaries contract. This leaves a smaller body of core staff within the company who possess its key competencies and can concentrate on the most strategic and value-adding activities. One of these key competencies is the ability to coordinate the web of transactions that have to be undertaken effectively within the network that the outsourcing company establishes with its contractors. The core company becomes a "network coordinator." Taken to a limit, and especially when supported by modern communications technologies, this network form approximates to the "virtual organization" discussed in the next chapter.

Metro International, a Swedish publishing company with its editorial office in London, provides an example of a company using a considerable level of outsourcing (see Box 9.1).

◢ The Scale and Scope of Outsourcing

The two decades of the 1990s and 2000s were characterized by a huge expansion of outsourcing. One important area of outsourcing is in the global supply chains of auto producers. Whereas there was a time when Ford's River Rouge plant made its own tires, electrics, glass, and steel, about two-thirds of North America's automobile industry is now accounted for by suppliers. Today, major auto corporations such as DaimlerChrysler, Ford, and GM mostly design and assemble vehicles, while their suppliers make most of their components. Toyota outsources about 70 percent of its production and, like many Japanese firms, has a long and successful history of doing so. The value of the global auto component outsourcing market is estimated to reach US $855 billion by 2016.

Another major area of manufacturing outsourcing is in the supply of electronic manufacturing systems (EMS). Flextronics, Foxconn, and Jabil Circuit are among the leading EMS companies. The EMS industry was born in the 1980s as large brand-holding producers sought to outsource component manufacturing. The main motives were to reduce their fixed costs, to take advantage of EMS firms' economies of scale, and to benefit from the higher operating efficiencies EMS providers achieve through specializing in manufacturing. The Dell Computer Corporation discussed in the next chapter provides an example of an electronics company that has used a particularly high level of outsourcing. Over time, EMS companies have also come to provide design and testing services in addition to component manufacturing.

A further significant category of outsourcing by value is services including IT and business process outsourcing (BPO). Estimates of the size of the worldwide outsourced services market vary greatly, with one estimate for global IT outsourcing alone in 2013 being US $288 billion. BPO divides into back-office services such as accounting, human resources and finance, and front-office services such as call center services. In 2010, the Philippines overtook India in having the largest business process outsourcing industry in the world.[5] "Knowledge process outsourcing" (KPO) is emerging from BPO as a new wave of services outsourcing. KPO has been hailed as the third generation of services outsourcing following the outsourcing of IT and then of relatively standardized business processes. It has been defined as "the outsourcing of firm activities that directly involve the production of knowledge and innovation, and that involve some degree of firm-specific capabilities . . . Included are potentially proprietary and core activities such as intellectual property research, market research, biotechnology and pharmaceutical research and testing, brand management, data mining, engineering and design, financial and insurance analytics, and legal services."[6] These activities are strategically important or form an integral part of a company's value chain. They require a high level of specialist expertise and skills.

The public sector has also been turning to outsourcing on an increasing scale. In the UK, for example, it is estimated that approximately £1 out of every £3 of government expenditure on public services goes to independent providers. These service areas include employment services, health care, education, and probation. As will be seen later in this chapter, there have been some major failures in the provision of these outsourced services, with a high cost both to clients and to taxpayers.[7]

Outsourcing is today conducted on a huge global scale. One of the controversial aspects of offshore outsourcing concerns job loss in the country from which activities are transferred abroad. Early predictions were alarming. For example, it was estimated that, by 2015, some 3.3 million US jobs would have moved offshore to low-wage countries such as India, China, Mexico, and the Philippines. Most of the jobs vulnerable to offshoring are white-collar: office support, computing, business operations, and management.[8] It was similarly predicted that 275,000 jobs would be moved offshore from the UK between 2004 and 2010.[9] However, a report to the US Congress in 2012 noted the lack of a database to provide an adequate answer to the question of how many workers have lost their jobs to offshoring. Reviewing available studies, the report noted that a number of them have concluded that about one in four US jobs are potentially offshorable.[10] This is far greater than the number of jobs that offshoring is likely to have caused to be lost. For instance, it is estimated that "the net number of business-services jobs in big American and European companies lost between 2002 and 2016 is likely to be around 3.7m, and only 2.1m of those will have been due to offshoring. That works out at a loss from that cause of just 150,000 jobs a year."[11] Moreover, the tide may have turned in that an increasing number of jobs are being brought back ("reshored") to the US for reasons discussed later in this chapter.

Globalization has been a significant driver behind the increasing use of outsourcing. The liberalization of international trade has exposed companies to increasing levels of international competition, and this puts ever more pressure on them to find ways of cutting their costs through outsourcing and offshoring. At the same time, outsourcing has been greatly facilitated by trade liberalization, which has provided easier access to suppliers across the world. Improved information and communications technologies, especially the Internet, are also leading to falling interaction costs and fewer imperfections in the marketplace. These powerful facilitators have given companies a hitherto unknown degree of choice in how they structure their businesses. Andrew Berger, a partner at Accenture, foresaw multinational corporations increasingly breaking up as between core areas of capability where they retain a capacity for operational excellence, and other areas within, or relating to, their value chains which are provided for by new service companies.[12] Contractor and his colleagues took up the same theme, but also cautioned that it imposes management and organizational costs:

> "The disaggregation of the value chain enables companies to make finer allocation choices, for each slice of their value chain. But disaggregation and dispersion of the firm – beyond an optimal degree – also entails more complexity and more costs in terms of added management and communication efforts."[13]

The examples from the auto and electronics companies are ones where manufacturing is being outsourced. They illustrate the first of two main categories of outsourcing, namely the outsourcing of core value chain operations. Outsourcing the supply chain, especially manufacturing, is the most common example, though other downstream operations such as distribution are also commonly outsourced. This category of outsourcing clearly has to be organized so as to preserve a high level of operational integration. This is particularly the case because, as we shall see, one of its main attractions has been the prospect of minimizing inventory.

The second main category is the outsourcing of support activities, such as research and development, IT, HRM, and facilities management. These activities are essential, but they support the value chain rather than being integral to it. This means that they do not create potential inventory costs or require such finely tuned integration with everyday value chain operations.

Much of the initial impetus toward outsourcing was to lower costs through transferring relatively routine work to low-wage countries. This has now changed, partly due to the rise of labor costs in countries like China that have provided much manufacturing outsourcing. Also, with the steady rise in skills and competencies in these emerging countries, companies have been increasingly looking to offshore high-end, higher value production and services. The considerations that informed Hewlett-Packard's location of the development and production of a new server provide an example (Box 9.2). Several emerging economies, including India and Taiwan, are producing large numbers of highly qualified scientific and technical graduates who are increasingly able to undertake the higher-level software and research work that has been hitherto concentrated in countries like the United States.[14]

Increasingly, manufacturing firms are offshoring and outsourcing higher value company functions including research and development. For example, in the pharmaceuticals sector,

BOX 9.2 OUTSOURCING WITHIN HEWLETT-PACKARD'S PATH TO MARKET

In 2003, Hewlett-Packard started to produce a new server, the ProLiant ML 150, for small businesses. The process of bringing this new product into being and eventually to market was carried out with little input from its American headquarters. The idea for the product was hatched in Singapore. Houston approved the project. Concept design was carried out in Singapore. Engineering design was done in Taiwan, where many computer components are made. Initial manufacture was also carried out in Taiwan. Final assembly of the server is located in Singapore, Australia, China, and India. The products made in Australia, China, and India are primarily for markets in those countries, while machines made in Singapore are destined for Southeast Asia.

The reasons for this distribution of activities concern local capabilities, logistics, tariffs, and costs. For instance, the location of design in Singapore and Taiwan reflects the technical capabilities now available in those locations. China would be too far from some markets for all manufacturing to be located there. Production in India is not only closer to that market but avoids the steep tariff levied on the import of finished products.

Source: Wall Street Journal Europe, 23 February 2004, p. A3.

contract research organizations (CROs) are being used more and more for outsourcing clinical trials. By 2010, CROs were accounting for over 40% of annual research spending by pharmaceutical firms, compared to 4% in the early 1990s.[15] GlaxoSmithKline provides a case in point, shown in Box 9.3.

BOX 9.3 GSK SPINS OUT STANDALONE PAIN RELIEF COMPANY

In 2010, GlaxoSmithKline spun out 14 of its scientists and several patents into a standalone company, Convergence Pharmaceuticals, specialising in pain relief. This arrangement allowed it to gain from any drugs developed and to cut overhead costs while minimizing job losses.

Andrew Jack of the Financial Times commented: "If contract services seem an obvious area for large companies to save costs in the long-term, more debatable are the implications of their divestment of research, highlighted by GSK's deal with Convergence. It increases their reliance on smaller, external – and potentially more poorly funded – biotech companies to do early stage drug development." However, at the time of writing Convergence was well-funded largely by a syndicate of America and European venture capitalists.

Source: Financial Times, 5 October 2010, p. 23.

◢ The Surge in Outsourcing During the 2000s

1. Manufacturing

According to information gathered by the Engineering Employers' Federation in 2003, 30% of British companies had moved part of their manufacturing abroad, and 49% of larger companies with more than 500 employees had some production abroad. One in three British manufacturing companies said that they planned to increase the proportion of foreign production over the following five years. Almost two-thirds of these companies (62 percent) said that lower cost was the main reason for moving their production abroad. Much of the manufacturing that has been moved abroad from the developed Triad region economies (North America, Western Europe, and Japan) went to China.[16] Some of this globally shifted production stays with directly managed overseas affiliates, and is therefore not outsourced in the full sense of being contracted out to other firms. Other production, however, is moved out of the original firm or is at least allocated to a foreign-partnered joint venture.[17]

The rapid and widespread use of outsourcing was inspired by the advice to focus on core competencies and to shed other activities.[18] Large corporations learned to "unbundle" themselves into their constituent parts, some of which they saw as lying at the core of their business, while others could be sold off. One of the prime exemplars for core-focused businesses was Cisco Systems, in terms of how to continue to deliver a complete product or service to the customer while integrating a network of other firms supplying vital parts of its value chain. Cisco was itself withdrawing from those parts of its value chain in which it did not enjoy a pre-eminent advantage. This did not mean, however, that it was disengaging from the other companies on which it depended for the smooth delivery of its products to customers – manufacturers, subcontractors, resource planners, and so forth. In fact, Cisco tightly coordinated its value chain network. For this, it used the Cisco Connection Online, a channel in the World Wide Web for coding and circulating information generated by its customers and network partners.[19] We shall see in Chapter 10 how Dell Computers managed its supply network in a similar way. Cisco provides an instructive case because, as discussed later in this chapter, the company's subsequent difficulties illustrate some of the problems that can arise if outsourcing is not adequately managed.

General Electric provides one of many examples where a major manufacturing corporation not only moved manufacturing operations to countries such as China, but also outsourced important support activities, especially to India. By 2003, more than 7,000 people in Indian software companies were working exclusively on projects for GE. GE's own call center and back-office business in India employs another 11,000 people. GE invested more than $80 million into creating in India its largest research center outside the United States, with more than 1,600 staff. A key factor behind moving from more straightforward outsourcing like call centers and software development to high-level research was the plentiful availability of world-class science and engineering graduates, whose annual salaries started at only around $5,500 in 2003. A more specific driver was the number of Indians already working on research for GE in the United States. Not only did they indicate the quality of English-speaking technical personnel from India, but they also encouraged GE's plastics division to create a research center in India, which opened up possibilities for some to return to their country of origin.[20]

2. Services

Financial services companies are among those that undertook the largest outsourcing of jobs, primarily to India. For instance, it was reported in June 2003 that Britain's largest banks and insurance companies were looking to move up to 200,000 administrative, processing, and clerical jobs to India over the coming five years. One recruitment firm was predicting the transfer of 100,000 jobs from Britain to India in call centers alone by 2008, but many union officials believed that the figure could be twice as large. A senior bank executive was reported as saying that he had met his counterparts in competing financial services groups and that all wanted to outsource jobs to cheaper locations. One of the largest global banks, HSBC, by end-2003 was estimated to have moved around 9,000 jobs to offices in China, India, and Malaysia.[21] Another dramatic example has been the UK National Savings organization, which offers a range of personal savings products. In the mid-1990s it used to employ 5,000 people. By 2002, it only employed 120 direct staff, having outsourced nearly all its functions. Three large UK services companies – BT (British Telecommunications), Powergen, and Thames Water – announced on the same day in March 2003 that they were transferring call center activities from Britain to India. BT opened two call centers in Delhi and Bangalore in 2004, creating 2,200 jobs for Indian workers. The Indian call centers carry out everyday BT business, including telephoning customers in the UK to remind them to pay their bills and handling directory enquiries.

At the time there were huge cost differences between average British and Indian call center workers, which motivated these instances of services outsourcing. The average British call center worker earned between £10,000 and £13,000 and worked 7 hours a day with a one-hour lunch break. By contrast, the average Indian call center earned £2,500 and worked 8 hours per day in three shifts.[22] However, the situation has since changed. A combination of rapidly rising Indian wages and a great many complaints from home country customers have led some UK and US companies to move call center operations back home or to other offshore locations. At the time of writing, India was facing strong competition for call center work from the Philippines, where many low-cost graduates speaking good English with a more neutral accent are available.[23]

One of the pioneers of outsourcing among UK service companies was the catering firm, Catering and Allied. Its experience is summarized in Box 9.4.

◢ Attractions of Outsourcing

The outsourcing undertaken by Catering & Allied and the other companies mentioned illustrates some of the attractions of this popular mode of organizational restructuring. Outsourcing has become a new corporate gospel because it can offer the following managerial benefits, at least in principle:

1 It enables companies to concentrate on what they do best.
2 At the same time, it allows them to select and utilize the best expertise available in the market to undertake other activities.
3 It offers significant, often immediate, cost savings. These may derive from access to cheaper labor abroad and/or from the saving on in-house managerial and facilities

BOX 9.4   CATERING & ALLIED: A HISTORY OF SUCCESSFUL OUTSOURCING

Catering & Allied (C&A) was founded in 1975 under the chairmanship of Marc Verstringhe. After its initial 18 months of operations, Catering & Allied moved into profit, and remained profitable for the rest of its history as an independent entity. The company became known for its introduction of new approaches to organization in pursuit of its aim to introduce high-quality restaurant standards to contract catering. Verstringhe attributes much of the company's sustained success in a highly competitive industry to these organizational innovations.

Outsourcing was seen by C&A's management to offer both intrinsic benefits and productivity gains. Important intrinsic benefits derived from the fact that working with outside specialists allowed the company access to a greater range of expertise on a flexible basis. The first step came in the area of financial and company secretarial work. In 1975 Verstringhe had been introduced by his solicitor to Keith Moore, a senior partner in an outside accounting firm. The reason for this introduction was that C&A's 10-year business and investment plan needed, in the opinion of the solicitor, to have its financial viability verified. From this initial meeting with Moore a working relationship developed. Moore was invited by the shareholders in November 1975 to carry out company secretarial activities in order to ensure that all the company's legal, administrative, and fiscal affairs were conducted in a professional and efficient manner from the outset. It soon became apparent that the highly experienced Moore was also invaluable in acting as company financial advisor in matters such as taxation, drawing up of accounts, and taking minutes of board meetings.

Another use of outsourcing was in the design of new client dining facilities. Access to external specialists in the design of a client facility provided additional flair, added to the company's authority in the client's eyes, and generally allowed for a more flexible approach to different projects. This was C&A's policy from an early stage, totally focused on gearing up to provide a superior service to clients. Verstringhe and his colleagues foreshadowed the idea of core competencies in that they recognized how the company's ability to offer a superior service to its clients could be strengthened by bringing in skills from outside to complement its own resources. Through such outsourcing, the company achieved the flexibility to work with appropriate specialists outside the company and to benefit from the innovative synergy this offered.

As time went on, the company realized that outsourcing could offer a range of intrinsic benefits, and by the end of the 1970s it had become an established approach for the company. One further benefit lay in meeting the challenge of how to retain the advantages of smallness while at the same time growing the business. Many of its clients were asking C&A to stay small, for fear that a larger company would lose its particular style, attention to detail, and above all, the close personal contact with them. Yet growth was the natural consequence of succeeding in the marketplace. The use of external specialists offered one way to achieve this aim of "growing small."

Productivity gains arose from the reduction of costs. Outsourcing reduced the costs of ongoing support services such as finance and company secretarial, PR and marketing, computing support, and HRM. The following figures from a lecture that Verstringhe gave in 1986 illustrate his calculation of this cost-saving benefit:[24]

Function	Outsourcing £	In-house provision £
Financial/secretarial	20,000	40,000
PR/Marketing	20,000	40,000
Computer Specialist	12,000	30,000
Personnel & Training Dept.	12,000	30,000
	64,000	140,000

Cost Benefits
Saving of £76,000 on income of £1,036,950
Also no office space, secretary, telephone, etc.

Source: Sally Heavens and John Child, with Marc Verstringhe. *Managing to Serve – Learning from Catering & Allied*. Cambridge: RH Business Books 2002.

overheads. Outsourcing also enables an existing fixed-cost structure to be turned into a variable one.

4   It rids companies of operational headaches and bottlenecks;
5   It avoids problematic labor relations situations and managerial deficiencies.
6   By hiving off activities previously undertaken in-house, outsourcing assists downsizing and de-layering.
7   Outsourcing, or more precisely the threat of outsourcing, can strengthen managerial control within an organization.

We consider each of these potential advantages in turn.

1 *Outsourcing enables organizations to concentrate on what they do best*. This is in line with one of the oldest principles of economies – the law of comparative advantage. Every organization has to draw a line around what it will undertake itself and what is beyond its capabilities. The rational approach is to decide this on the basis of assessing the activities it is best placed to perform. The outsourcing movement is simply redrawing that line so as to increase an organization's degree of concentration and focus on its core competencies. Telecommunications networks provide an example. Many large firms had literally constructed mini telephone companies within their facilities, even though that is not what they are in business for. Outsourcing a support activity like that allows these firms to devote their energies to other activities through which they create greater value. Outsourcing often means selling some of the existing assets of a company to an outside service provider and then working with experts from that provider to improve those assets and their use. Some companies have taken this principle to its furthest possible extent, running a multi-million dollar business as a network of outsourced operations with only a handful of core staff. One example is the fashion accessories company Topsy Tail, established by Tomima Edmark, who invented the best selling hair tool ever. She established an extensive network of outsourced vendors to deal with everything from manufacturing to servicing retail stores. She kept her own company very small (just 3 full

time employees) while creating an economy of scale. She focused on what she did best, which was managing the business and keeping an oversight of quality control.[25]

2 *Outsourcing allows organizations to select and utilize the best expertise available in the market.* This benefit also follows from the law of comparative advantage, adding to it the virtue of flexibility. Catering & Allied used outsourcing in this way when establishing new catering facilities for clients. It selected the designer for each project who could provide the best available expertise to suit the specific requirements of each client. By outsourcing the facilities design function rather than retaining it in-house, as do some companies in the sector, the company was able to switch between different external specialists in a flexible manner.

3 *Outsourcing offers significant, often immediate, cost savings.* This benefit has been very apparent in most instances of outsourcing. It is often the case that outside manufacturers or service providers can supply at lower cost than an internal department, even within the same country. The availability of modern ICT has made it easier to manage outsourcing on a global basis. In the case of some services such as call centers, software design and maintenance, and account management, ICT enables operations to be integrated across continents. This globalization of outsourcing can considerably enhance the cost savings it offers by enabling outsourced work to be located in low-cost regions such as India and China.

4 *Outsourcing rids companies of operational headaches and bottlenecks.* Companies sometimes face the problem of poorly performing operational areas or ones that create persistent bottlenecks in the value chain. Outsourcing offers a possible solution, either to add necessary capacity or bypass the problem area entirely. If a poorly performing unit is not essential to a company's primary activities, it can be closed down without securing an alternative. If the unit does play an essential role, closure would have to be offset through buying in its products or services through outsourcing.

5 *Outsourcing avoids problematic labor relations situations and managerial deficiencies.* The rationale here is similar to that of item 4. It can be very difficult and/or costly to turn around a unit that is plagued by a long history of poor labor relations and deficient management. A negative culture may simply have become too entrenched and a climate of mistrust too embedded. The challenge of effecting a transformation in such a unit through in-company managerial action is made harder by the fact that management itself is part of the problem equation in the eyes of employees. Outsourcing offers the alternative of selling off the unit and securing its product, either from another source or from the unit itself once it has been reconstituted under new ownership and management. A change of ownership and leadership has in fact often provided the key to the salvation of a failing unit.

6 *By hiving off activities previously undertaken in-house, outsourcing assists downsizing and delayering.* Chapter 4 noted the managerial and organizational advantages that come with smaller size. Outsourcing can dramatically reduce the scale of a company's employment and of its fixed-cost facilities. When Ford's River Rouge plant was opened in 1928, it employed around 100,000 workers. Today, largely as a result of extensive outsourcing, it employs around 6,000. A challenge that successful smaller companies face is how to retain the advantages of smallness while at the same time growing the business. As Marc Verstringhe, Chairman of Catering & Allied once put it, the problem is "how to grow and stay small." Outsourcing to what the company called its "strategic alliance" partners helped Catering & Allied to resolve this paradox and expand while remaining a small, compact organization. The retention of a small core organization can avoid the growth of hierarchy. Outsourcing offers the means to recapture smallness and to delayer. It is a condition for downsizing, just as downsizing is in

turn a concomitant of the drive to focus on core activities that powerfully informs outsourcing. Outsourcing is an integral part of the shift toward network forms of organization. As previous chapters have indicated, the new organizational model posits fundamental connections between (1) the reduction of hierarchy and delayering; (2) downsizing and focus; and (3) outsourcing that is integrated through networks.

7 *Outsourcing, or more precisely the threat of outsourcing, can strengthen managerial control within an organization.* As Chapter 16 discusses in detail, one of the concerns with new organizational forms is that they are more difficult to govern internally. The benefits for innovation and flexibility of devolving initiative to increasingly qualified and knowledgeable employees may be offset by a concomitant weakening of senior managerial direction. This is because high levels of innovation and change, together with the very initiative now offered to knowledge workers, renders it less feasible to rely on traditional bases for control such as hierarchical reporting and evaluation against pre-determined plans. Outsourcing, however, can offer a new governance discipline in that it now becomes a plausible potential sanction against inadequate performance. If a unit within an organization performs badly, there is the threat that it may be sold off or shut down, with its activities outsourced as an alternative.

◄ Problems with Outsourcing

Such was the enthusiasm for outsourcing in the 1990s and 2000s that it took the status of a new management gospel. This brings the danger that outsourcing is simply assumed to be the answer to a company's prayers. In the light of evidence that outsourcing can go seriously wrong, it would be wiser first to compare its potential disadvantages with its promised benefits in relation to each specific case. Although firms are reluctant to report outsourcing failures, substantial problems can arise. As *The Economist* commented in 2011, "Some of the worst business disasters of recent years have been caused or aggravated by outsourcing."[26] The problems that Boeing experienced with the development of its 787 Dreamliner provides a dramatic illustration – see Box 9.5.

In November 2012, The Zurich Insurance Group announced a survey revealing that:

> "Outsourcing failure is now a significant cause of supply chain disruption. Service issues attributed to outsourcing jumped to third place in the causes of supply chain disruption at 35%, up from 17% in 2011, highlighting the importance that outsourcing decisions have in supply chain resilience. It also showed that 73% of organisations recorded at least one supply chain disruption in 2012 with 39% of analysed disruption originating from below the immediate supplier. 532 organizations from across 68 countries and 14 industry sectors responded to the survey, which is supported by Zurich and conducted by the Business Continuity Institute (BCI)."[27]

The following organizational problems have frequently arisen with outsourcing:

1 outsourcing the wrong activities, leading to a loss of key skills and competencies;
2 unreliability of suppliers and poor quality service;
3 writing a poor contract;
4 loss of employee morale;
5 communication problems;

BOX 9.5   PROBLEMS OF OUTSOURCING AT BOEING

In developing its 787 Dreamliner aircraft, Boeing decided to rely heavily on outsourcing, both locally and internationally, as a way of lowering costs and accelerating development. Boeing outsourced more of the 787 than any other aircraft in its history – approximately 70 percent, with over 30 percent of its components sourced from overseas. According to a company executive, this approach aimed to "reduce the 787's development time from six to four years and development cost from $10 to $6 billion." It turned out to be a nightmare. The project was billions of dollars over budget and three years behind schedule.

"Some of the parts did not fit together. Some of the dozens of sub-contractors failed to deliver their components on time, despite having sub-contracted their work to sub-sub-contractors. Boeing had to take over some of the sub-contractors to prevent them from collapsing." [The Economist]

Sources: The Economist (2011). The trouble with outsourcing. 30 July 2011, p. 62; Steve Denning: What went wrong at Boeing? *Forbes*, 21 January 2013, http://www.forbes .com/fdc/welcome_mjx.shtml, accessed 29 August 2013.

6 losing control over the outsourced activity;
7 squeezing suppliers too hard;
8 suppliers exploiting client organizations' dependencies.

1 *Outsourcing the wrong activities.* The first problem is the loss of key skills and competencies, or at least the loss of control over them, through outsourcing the wrong activities. IBM decided to outsource the production of microprocessor chips to Intel and operating systems software to Microsoft when developing its PC, in the belief that this would speed up the introduction of the new product. In retrospect, it is apparent that the company gave away its potentially commanding position in two key competence areas. There have been cases where companies have ended up with higher costs and a dangerous dependency on external suppliers when they have outsourced IT applications that were too close to their core business – such as the reservation system for a car rental firm.[28] In the light of this problem, the recommendation is normally not to outsource those activities which represent areas of prime strategic importance and distinctive competence. Thus Toyota has chosen to retain in-house some processes such as stamping, welding, and injection molding that give it control over the fit and finish of its cars – for which it enjoys an outstanding reputation – even though some of these processes could be undertaken at lower cost elsewhere.

2 *Unreliability of suppliers and poor quality service.* Suppliers may turn out to be unreliable or unable to provide an adequate service. Quite often the quality of their work turns out to be disappointing and/or they are consistently late with delivery. It is, of course, possible in principle to retain multiple suppliers, but this may negate advantages such as achieving supplier economies of scale, working closely with a supplier on long-term technical developments, and persuading the supplier to commit its assets specifically to the company's special requirements.

The Deloitte 2012 survey of global outsourcing covered 111 companies located in 22 industries across 23 countries. Outsourcing was used as a standard practice by 60 percent of them, especially for IT, and most expected to make greater use of outsourcing in the future. However, almost half the companies (48%) had terminated an outsourcing contract early in the past, and poor quality of service was by far the most frequent reason (71%) for doing so.[29]

In 2003 Dell Computers moved its business support call center operation from India back to the USA following customer complaints about the quality of service. Problems included the failure of staff to adjust flexibly to customers' specific needs and difficulties of understanding Indian accents. "Language and cultural rifts between disgruntled US customers and Dell's bright but unseasoned Indian support staff fueled the flames. US customers say they got frustrated when Dell employees fielding calls seemed unwilling to depart from a script."[30] To take another example, research conducted by Lyda Bigelow and her colleagues at the University of Utah, indicates that outsourcing contributed to Toyota's need for major recalls. The company had increased its outsourcing to support a strategy of enhanced growth, including the manufacture of accelerators. Starting October 2009, the company recalled nearly 8.5 million vehicles due to problems with floor mat interference and a sticky accelerator pedal.[31]

Companies in some countries, like Germany, that favor long-term business relationships may for that reason be reluctant to risk a new relationship with a new supplier, despite the apparent cost advantages. One small IT business in Bombay reported, for example, that German companies "seem reluctant to try out a relationship and certainly not with a small Indian company."[32]

3 *Writing a poor contract.* Outsourcing contracts are sometimes insufficiently precise or complete. Incomplete contracts, as some economists call them, have been associated with a reliance on trust in customer–supplier partnership arrangements. They can, nevertheless, give rise to problems if, for example, fees are fixed too rigidly or there are no clauses specifying objective measures of supplier services. Contracts also need to have flexibility clauses that help both parties to adjust to changes in the business environment. A problem can arise when a company's contracts with suppliers are insufficiently flexible to handle sudden contingencies. Some contracts have, for example, proved to be inadequate to govern outsourcing in times of major fluctuations in demand. This caused Cisco Systems to have to write down $2.25 billion of its inventory in the second quarter of 2001. Cisco's vaunted supply chains were supposed to provide greater advance notice of impending slowdowns in demand than they actually did. Other companies, such as Sony, Apple Computer, Philips, Palm, and Compaq have suffered in the past from the inability of suppliers to meet upsurges in demand.

Three Booz Allen authors take the view that the problem here has been with the practice of outsourcing rather than with the principle. They conclude that the companies mentioned:

> ". . . had outsourced their manufacturing of essential components without a full understanding of the changes required in their business models. They didn't translate the old practices that had made them successful into their new business relationships. They hadn't adequately codified informal communications practices and channels within their supply chain. They didn't align incentives through contract terms and agreements, which rendered it almost impossible for the supply chain to scale up in relationship to a hit product, or scale down in response to declining demand."[33]

Persuading suppliers to agree to more flexible contracts, which earmark capacity without specifying exactly what is to be built, may help to reduce this problem, but only up to a point.

Outsourcing current assets (in the form of inventory) and fixed assets to suppliers does not remove the need to have such assets available to meet unforeseen changes in demand. If suppliers are expected to shoulder this additional cost burden, they will be obliged to raise their prices. If inventory is eliminated then, far from insulating a company from sudden swings in demand, it makes them more instantly damaging.[34]

4 *Loss of employee morale.* Outsourcing can provoke a serious loss of employee morale, both among people who are to be outsourced and among employees who remain. If outsourcing is not planned in consultation with employees and with regard to their interests, it can evoke fears similar to those of downsizing. Rumor can arise concerning security of employment, with the proposal to outsource being interpreted as an underestimation of employees' skills and value. The consequence can be a loss through job quitting of the very employees whose skills the company wishes to retain. These negative effects are often avoidable so long as management takes the relevant employees into its confidence. A company will need to retain employees with experienced, firm-specific knowledge in order to interface with the external vendor. This opens up new responsibilities and opportunities for them. For employees who are transferred to a specialist vendor, working for a successful external company is in many cases more attractive than working in an internal unit that is accorded low priority and even seen to be failing.[35]

5 *Communication problems.* Problems can arise when the outsourced activity involves or depends on personal communication. This is more likely when the communications are between different countries and encounter linguistic or cultural differences. Some call centers have been repatriated back from India because staff there were found to return an inferior level of productivity and service. The Dell Company has already been cited as an example. In January 2004, the Shop Direct Group, a mail order firm, announced that it planned to close its India call center and repatriate jobs to the UK. Problems have also arisen with the outsourcing of software development when this requires frequent communication between programmers. Valicert, for example, experienced difficulties when in 2001 it started to replace software engineers in Silicon Valley with much lower paid equivalents in India. As the Wall Street Journal reported, "The Indian engineers, who knew little about Valicert's software or how it was used, omitted features Americans considered intuitive. US programmers, accustomed to quick chats over cubicle walls, spend months writing detailed instructions for overseas assignments, delaying new products."[36] The company eventually ameliorated the problem by giving entire projects to its India team, thus reducing the intensity of communications required, and by having its US managers write more detailed specifications for each assignment.

6 *Losing control.* There is a danger of losing control over the outsourced activity. Relying on the provisions of a contract may not be enough to ensure that the outsourced activity is under sufficient control for it to be performed satisfactorily. For this reason, it has been recommended that, when an activity is outsourced, a small group of in-house managers is retained in order to handle the external vendor. Outsourcing an activity does not equate to abdicating managerial responsibility for it. This is particularly crucial when the activity is a core element in the value chain or an essential service, the failure of which would have a major negative impact and where a switch to an alternative source is costly or not feasible.[37] Grant Thornton's 2013 survey of 3,300 senior executives in mid-market businesses from 45 countries found that some 60 percent of them did not outsource or had no plans to do so. The impediment to outsourcing that they cited most often (44 percent of respondents) was an unwillingness to lose control of a key process.[38]

7 *Squeezing suppliers too hard.* This problem can arise if major companies strive for cost savings through outsourcing to the point of squeezing their suppliers too hard. To take a case

in point, in the automotive industry the manufacturers are substantially larger than their suppliers and hence enjoy greater bargaining power. In the United States, they have pressed suppliers to the point where their ability to invest in innovation and quality and, in some cases, their financial survival, has become compromised. Boeing's Chief Executive Jim McNerney, for example, in May 2013 announced that the company had plans to reduce costs by squeezing suppliers hard. Suppliers that do not agree to cut their prices will not find their contracts renewed or bid for work on new programs. Whether that is a wise move in the light of Boeing's supplier problems with the 787 remains to be seen.[39]

8 *Exploitation by suppliers.* This problem is effectively the reverse of squeezing suppliers too hard. It can arise when an outsourcing company commits assets that can only be used for a given long-term transaction with its supplier. If in this situation, the company is unable, or simply fails, to specify an agreed formula for handling unforeseen contingencies, such as the supplier claiming that its costs have risen beyond original estimates, it becomes vulnerable to renegotiation in the supplier's favor. What happens is that the supplier effectively locks its client organization into a relationship that is too expensive for the client to renegotiate, and is therefore in a position to exploit the client's dependency.

In the UK at the time of writing (2013), there is a storm of criticism against private outsourcing companies for supposedly exploiting public service providers both at central government level in areas such as health care, probation and welfare services and at local government level in areas such as building maintenance, IT, tax collection and customer contact.[40] Considerable doubt has been expressed regarding the ability of public officials to negotiate and manage outsourcing contracts. The pace of outsourcing has resulted in such officials being stretched to the limit and mistakes made on drawing up contracts that result in poor services and value for money.[41]

The Reaction to Outsourcing and Offshoring Problems

Business companies have reacted to these problems in a number of ways. Some, like Boeing, are bringing work back in-house, especially work that was previously outsourced offshore. The latter has come to be called "reshoring." As *The Economist* notes, "Well-known companies such as Google, General Electric, Caterpillar and Ford Motor Company are bringing some of their production back to America or adding new capacity there."[42] The principal reason has been the rising cost of offshore production, followed by concerns over quality and lead times.[43] The rapid rise of labor costs in emerging economies such as China, coupled with the costs of shipping, customs duties and other fees, and of inventory tied up in transit, have whittled away the advantages of manufacturing outsourcing. I have already mentioned instances in which business services such as customer contact have been returned to their home country. The reasons for bringing service activities back in-house can include the managerial and organizational problems I have highlighted, with changes in relative costs also playing a role.

Overall, however, outsourcing is still expanding and companies are approaching it more carefully rather than abandoning it. They are tending to favor smaller more flexible deals, signing shorter contracts and using a wider spread of outsourcers rather than relying on just a few. The process of "reshoring" or "onshoring" that has attracted attention in recent years in both the USA and UK appears to be largely one of switching back to domestic suppliers rather than a reversal of outsourcing per se. Nevertheless, in the light of sometimes negative experience, both companies and public authorities are having to address decisions on outsourcing more carefully and strategically.

Reaching a Decision on Outsourcing

In the light of the potential advantages of outsourcing as well as the problems that can arise, it is clearly vital that companies make a careful assessment before they decide to source any activity externally. It is not always the case that efficiency gains can only be achieved through handing processes over to suppliers, rather than making in-house improvements. Stephen Doig and his colleagues from McKinsey and Company suggest that, in making this assessment, the senior management of a company should consider three dimensions of performance:[44]

1   *Strategic:* is in-house ownership or preferential access to the asset or activity of strategic importance? A direct relationship with customers and ownership of design are normally key assets that a firm would not seek to outsource, because they provide it with the ability to keep in touch with market requirements and maintain a technological leadership that is sensitive to them. These, for example, are the two activities that Dell Computer chose to retain in an otherwise outsourced, virtual value chain.

  Over time, however, there has been an increase in the outsourcing of core activities such as finance, production or delivery of core products and services, sales & marketing, and R&D.[45] R&D outsourcing can tap additional sources of invention, as in new drug discovery, and also provide access to scientific knowledge. On the other hand, firms should carefully assess the strategic case for outsourcing R&D. Too much R&D outsourcing can lead to dysfunctional over-dependence on external providers. There also have to be adequate provisions for managing knowledge flows and protecting proprietary knowledge.[46]

2   *Operational:* here the key question concerns the optimal manufacturing and supply chain arrangements for meeting performance targets. This comes down to factors such as lead times, unit costs, and ease of integrating the different stages of a firm's operations. A supply chain has to be configured so as to support the organization's overall strategy.

3   *Organizational:* outsourcing implies an organizational change. Units or departments become redundant; control and coordination processes have to be changed. The question, therefore, is whether the company has the capability to make such changes, especially if it has been operating in a given mode for a long time. As Doig and his colleagues warn: "Established companies, whether they manage reconfigured networks or operate long-standing internal ones, seldom have the skills to transform their supply chains."[47] (See Chapter 13 for further discussion of organizational change management.)

  Table 9.2 sums up the factors that weigh in the balance between retaining an activity or process in-house and outsourcing it.

  The choice between retaining activities in-house, outsourcing them and going for offshoring can also be summarized by reference to three key questions: (1) Does the organization have a competitive or competence advantage in performing the activity (internalization advantage)? (2) Is the activity strategically key? (3) Does a foreign location offer an advantage in performing the activity? Tables 9.3 and 9.4 show the results of applying these three criteria.

Table 9.2   Retaining processes in-house or outsourcing?

There is a basis for retaining any process that:	There is a case for outsourcing a process when an external supplier offers:
• Can meet or exceed industry performance norms within three years • Confers a distinct competitive advantage that cannot be replicated • Is not available externally or likely to become available soon • Defines the distinctiveness of a company in its market	• Major cost savings from cheaper labor and procurement, lower capital intensity, or larger scale • A location, process technology, or set of skills that would be hard to acquire or reproduce • Greater productive capacity and a more diverse base for meeting end-user demand, which would help to reduce supply shortages and surpluses • The potential for sharing expertise that an external specialist organization has acquired in other markets or industries

Adapted from Stephen J. Doig, Ronald C. Ritter, Kurt Speckhals, and Daniel Woolson. Has outsourcing gone too far? *McKinsey Quarterly*, 2001 (4): 34–35.

Table 9.3   Outsourcing and offshoring choices with reference to the organization's competitive advantage and strategic importance

		Is the activity strategically key?	
		Yes	No
Does the organization have an advantage in performing the activity?	Yes	Retain in-house	Limited outsourcing allowing for downsizing and concentration on core activities
	No	Captive (managed) offshoring, but not outsourced	Outsourced, including offshore

Table 9.4   Outsourcing and offshoring choices with reference to the organization's competitive advantage and advantage of a foreign location[48]

		Does a foreign location offer an advantage?	
		Yes	No
Does the organization have an advantage in performing the activity?	Yes	Captive offshore	Retain in-house
	No	Offshore outsource	Domestic outsource

◢ Creating Successful Outsourcing Partnerships

PricewaterhouseCoopers interviewed 226 outsourcing customers and 66 outsourcing service providers. They found that as outsourcing moved beyond the "first wave" of commoditized services, such as IT, to include more bespoke services such as HR and R&D, so there was a preference for trust-based supplier management, joint teams, and collaboration through joint ventures. Successful outsourcers in their survey were more likely to have transparent dealings with service providers (including transparency on margins), joint decision-making on matters of mutual interest, and joint governance structures.[49] As outsourcing matures beyond merely a cost-reducing strategy toward one that takes advantage of the specialized competencies and knowledge of providers, so this partnership model becomes the appropriate one to develop.

A partnership relationship is likely to be more appropriate than an arms-length market one for the outsourcing of core activities, especially those involving knowledge processes. With knowledge production and innovation, synergy can arise from close cooperation between clients and providers especially in the sharing or co-production of tacit knowledge. A high level of trust is also required in order to protect knowledge resources. The more these factors apply, the more suitable an alliance to govern relationships between the parties is likely to be. Mudambi and Tallman argue that the more the outsourced activities involve tacit, complex, high value knowledge, and require considerable integration of tasks between client and vendor, the more appropriate it will be to govern the partnership through managerial controls and integrating mechanisms rather than relying primarily on contracts and other written agreements.[50]

The basis for successful outsourcing

Outsourcing arrangements appear to have approximately the same rate of failure as another type of partnership, namely joint ventures (see Chapter 11). About 50 percent of all outsourcing arrangements fail within five years. They are prone to concerns about equity and the apportionment of benefits to the two parties concerned. If a company has assessed the suitability of outsourcing according to the strategic criteria I have mentioned, it would then be well advised to consider the eight problem areas identified earlier and how best to cope with them if they should arise.

Many lists of do's and don'ts for outsourcing have appeared.[51] While recommendations need to be tailored to suit specific forms of outsourcing, the following are key points of general relevance:[52]

1 *Know what you want.* This requires establishing precise, measurable objectives for the outsourcing activity.
2 *Determine how it is going to help.* This concerns establishing which improvements for the company's core business are expected to result from an intensified focus on its core capabilities. It requires determining a measurable gain for the core business as a result of the benefits from outsourcing. For example, the objective might be to use the money saved to increase customer retention by 5 percent, through reducing the time taken to respond to customers' questions.
3 *Measure it.* This could involve creating a scorecard that quantifies each objective the outsourcing is supposed to accomplish.

4   *Share it.* This entails transparency of information between client and vendor. It is recommended to set up periodic reviews with relevant internal staff and the outsourcing partner to assess how things are going and whether objectives are being met.

5   *Actively manage the relationship.* This requires the appointment of a contract manager even with outsourced activities of a routine nature. In the case of more strategic knowledge-based activities, joint teams and governance are likely to be required.

SUMMARY

1   Outsourcing has become a significant feature of organizational restructuring and its use continues to expand, albeit less rapidly than before.

2   Globalization provides an incentive for offshore outsourcing because of the ensuing pressures of cost competition. At the same time, trade liberalization and the development of advanced information and communications technologies, have greatly facilitated outsourcing on a global scale.

3   Two main categories of outsourcing are evident within both manufacturing and services. These are (1) the outsourcing of operations within core value-chains and (2) the outsourcing of support activities.

4   Outsourcing offers a number of advantages, in principle at least. These include enabling companies to concentrate on what they do best, allowing them to access the best expertise available to undertake other activities, and ridding them of operational headaches. As well as offering cost savings, outsourcing can facilitate a policy of downsizing and delayering. The prospect of outsourcing may also strengthen managerial control.

5   At the same time, outsourcing often fails. Problems may arise through outsourcing the wrong activities, poor contracts, inadequate control over the outsourced activity, poor employee morale, communication failures, and difficulties with suppliers and vendors. Failures and problems have led to some reversal of outsourcing and to reshoring.

6   Decisions on outsourcing therefore have to be taken with due care and consideration. The case for outsourcing a process as against that for retaining the process in-house can be set out systematically in terms of a number of criteria. Similarly, there are a number of identifiable steps for establishing a successful outsourcing partnership.

QUESTIONS FOR DISCUSSION

9.1   Define the terms "outsourcing" and "offshoring," and discuss examples of each. How would you group these examples into useful sub-categories?

9.2   How has globalization encouraged outsourcing?

9.3   Describe and discuss the key advantages of outsourcing.

9.4   Describe and discuss the main problems that can arise with outsourcing.

9.5 What are the main organizational requirements to facilitate successful outsourcing?

9.6 What organizational benefits does outsourcing make possible?

9.7 What considerations might a company or public institution thinking of outsourcing be advised to take into account?

9.8 What lessons can be learned from cases of "reshoring"?

NOTES

1 Michael F. Corbett (2002), Outsourcing's next wave, www.fortune.com, p. S2.

2 Farok J. Contractor, Vikas Kumar, Sumit K. Kundu, and Torben Pedersen (2010), Reconceptualizing the firm in a world of outsourcing and offshoring: The organizational and geographical relocation of high-value company functions, *Journal of Management Studies*, 47(8), 1417–1433. See also Farok J. Contractor, Vikas Kumar, Sumit K. Kundu, and Torben Pedersen (2011), *Global Outsourcing and Offshoring: An Integrated Approach to Theory and Practice,* Cambridge, Cambridge University Press.

3 Horses for Sources (2013), http://www.horsesforsources.com/hfs-index-q12013_02221, accessed August 27, 2013.

4 Tech in Asia (2013), http://www.techinasia.com/companies-choosing-philippines-india-outsourcing-services, accessed August 27, 2013.

5 Gartner Inc., (2013), Press Release, Stamford, CN., July 17, 2013, http://www.gartner.com/newsroom/id/2550615, accessed 28 August 2013; IBM Global Business Services (2010), *Global Location Trends Annual Report 2010.* Somers: NY, IBM Global Services.

6 Susan M. Mudambi and Stephen Tallman (2010), Make, buy or ally? Theoretical perspectives on knowledge process outsourcing through alliances, *Journal of Management Studies*, 47(8), 1434–1456. Quotation is from p. 1436.

7 Institute for Government (2013), *Making Public Service Markets Work.* London, Institute for Government, July 18, 2013.

8 *Business Week* (2003), The new global job shift, February 3, 2003, pp. 36–48.

9 David Smith (2004), Job takeaway is good for you, *Sunday Times*, February 1, 2004, p. 3.4.

10 Linda Levine (2012), *Offshoring (or Offshore Outsourcing) and Job Loss Among U.S. Workers*, Washington, DC; Congressional Research Service (2013), December 17, 2013. www.fas.org/sgp/crs/misc/RL32292.pdfcrs/misc/RL32292.pdf?, accessed 28 August, 2013.

11 The Economist (2013), *Here, There and Everywhere. Special Report on Outsourcing and Offshoring*, January 19, 2013, p. 15.

12 *ECollaboration: How Supply Chains will Drive the New Economy* (2001), Introduction, produced by Accenture and *Management Today*, London.

13 Contractor, Kumar, Kundu, and Pedersen (2010), op. cit., p. 1421.

14 Special report: software. Will outsourcing hurt America's supremacy? (2004), *Business Week*, March 1, 2004, 52–60.

15 BIS (2010), *Life Sciences in the UK – Economic analysis and evidence for Life Sciences 2010: Delivering the Blueprint.* BIS Economics Paper No. 2. London: Department for Business, Innovation & Skills.

16 The exodus in manufacturing and services (2003), *Sunday Times*, June 8, 2003, p. 35.

17 UNCTAD (2001), Promoting Linkages, *World Investment Report.* New York, United Nations.

18 See Gary Hamel and C-K Prahalad (1994), *Competing for the Future*, Boston, MA, Harvard Business School Press.

19 Remo Häcki and Julian Lighton (2001), The future of the networked company, *McKinsey Quarterly*, (3), 26–39.

20   Joanna Slater (2003), GE reinvents itself in India, *Wall Street Journal Europe*, March 25, 2003, p. A6.

21   John Waples and Louise Armitstead (2003), Banks prepare to shift 200,000 jobs to India, *Sunday Times*, June 8, 2003, p. 3.1.

22   Laura Peek, Sam Coates, and Catherine Philp (2003), Unions accuse BT of exporting call center work, *The Times*, March 8, 2003, p. 5.

23   India losing 70% voice and call centre business to Philippines (2014), *Times of India*, April 7. http://timesofindia.indiatimes.com/business/india-business/india-losing-70-voice-and-call-centre-business-to-philippines-report/articleshow/33386127.cms, accessed 15 July, 2014.

24   Marc Verstringhe (1986), A different approach to management of a people's business, lecture sponsored by the HCIMA, November 17, 1986.

25   Joan Lefkowitz (2013), Topsy Tail, The $100 Million Hair Gadget That Could . . . and Did! http://www.accessorybrainstorms.com/articles/topsytail.php, accessed 29 August, 2013. Other examples are discussed in Bo Hedberg, Göran Dahgren, Jörgen Hansson, and Nils-Göran Olve (1997), *Virtual Organizations and Beyond*, Chichester: Wiley.

26   The trouble with outsourcing (2011), *The Economist*, July 30, 2011, p. 62.

27   Service failures by outsourcers reach top three causes of supply chain disruption (2012), Zurich Insurance, November 7. Extract is from p. 1. http://www.zurich.com/internet/main/en/media/newsreleases/2012/pdfs/2012-1107-01.pdf, accessed 30 August, 2013.

28   Jérôme Barthélemy (2003), The seven deadly sins of outsourcing, *Academy of Management Executive*, 17, 87–98.

29   *Global Outsourcing and Insourcing Survey Executive Summary* (2012), New York, Deloitte Consulting LLP, February.

30   Elizabeth Corcoran (2004), Dell moves outsourced jobs back to U.S. shores, *Forbes*, April 28, http://www.nbcnews.com/id/4853511/ns/business-forbes_com/t/dell-moves-outsourced-jobs-back-us-shores, accessed 30 August, 2013.

31   Outsourcing May Lead to Failure in Tough Times and in Good, Shows University of Utah Research (2013), PRNewswire 2013, http://www.prnewswire.com/news-releases/outsourcing-may-lead-to-failure-in-tough-times-and-in-good-shows-university-of-utah-research-99927534.html, accessed 30 August, 2013.

32   Khozem Merchant (2001), Software companies look beyond traditional borders, *Financial Times*, Survey of Indian Outsourcing, October 23, 2001, p. 22.

33   Excerpted with permission from "Why Cisco Fell: Outsourcing and Its Perils" by Bill Lakenan, Darren Boyd and Ed Frey from the Third Quarter 2001 issue of *strategy+business* magazine, published by PwC Strategy& Inc. © 2001 PwC. All rights reserved. PwC refers to the PwC network and/or one or more of its member firms, each of which is a separate legal entity. Please see www.pwc.com/structure for further details. www.strategy-business.com.

34   Peter Martin (2001), The limits of outsourcing, *Financial Times*, September 25, 2001, p. 14.

35   Jérôme Barthélemy (2003), op. cit., pp. 91–92.

36   Scott Thurm (2004), How US software firm fixed bugs in system of outsourcing to India, *The Wall Street Journal Europe*, March 3, 2004, pp. A1 & A6. Quotation is from p. A1.

37   Jérôme Barthélemy (2003), op. cit., p. 92.

38   *Outsourcing: Driving Efficiency and Growth* (2014), Grant Thornton International Business Report 2014, London. http://www.internationalbusinessreport.com/files/IBR2014_Outsourcing_report_FINAL.pdf, accessed May 10, 2014.

39   Dominic Gates (2013), McNerney: Boeing will squeeze suppliers and cut jobs, *Seattle Times*, May 22, 2013, http://seattletimes.com/html/businesstechnology/2021037931_boeingmcnerneyxml.html, accessed 30 August, 2013.

40   Tom Gash, Nehal Panchamia, Sam Sims, and Louisa Hotson (2013), *Making Public Service Markets Work*, London, Institute for Government; Alan White and Kate Belgrave (2013), Nine spectacular

council outsourcing failures, *New Statesman*, August 29, 2013. http://www.newstatesman.com/uk-politics/2013/08/nine-spectacular-council-outsourcing-failures, accessed 30 August, 2013.

41   Tom Gash et al. (2013), op. cit.

42   *Special Report on Outsourcing and Offshoring* (2013), *The Economist*, op. cit., pp. 3-4. See also: Majority of large manufacturers are now planning or reconsidering 'reshoring' from China to the US (2013), Boston Consulting Group, Press release of survey of over 200 corporate decision makers, http://www.bcg.com/media/pressreleasedetails.aspx?id=tcm:12-144944, accessed April 23, 2014; Brian Groom and Tanya Powley (2014), Reshoring driven by quality, not costs, say UK manufacturers, *Financial Times*, March 3, 2014, http://www.ft.com/cms/s/0/9757ffcc-9fc9-11e3-94f3-00144feab7de.html#axzz2ziop1WGp, accessed April 23, 2014.

43   Brian Groom (2013), 'Reshoring' gathers momentum, *Financial Times*, November 25, 2013, p. 4.

44   Stephen J. Doig, Ronald C. Ritter, Kurt Speckhals, and Daniel Woolson (2001), Has outsourcing gone too far? *McKinsey Quarterly*, (4), 25–37.

45   *Outsourcing Comes of Age: The Rise of Collaborative Partnering* (2008), PricewaterhouseCoopers, London.

46   Christoph Grimpe and Ulrich Kaiser (2010), Balancing internal and external knowledge acquisition: The gains and pains from R&D outsourcing, *Journal of Management Studies*, 47(8), 1483–1509; Nina Rilla and Mariagrazia Squicciarini (2011), R&D (re)location and offshore outsourcing: A management perspective, *International Journal of Management Reviews*, 13(4), 393–413.

47   Doig et al. (2001), op. cit., p. 32.

48   Adapted from Stephen Tallman (2011), Offshoring, outsourcing and strategy in the global firm, *Academy of International Business (AIB) Insights*, 11(1), Figure 1, p. 5.

49   PricewaterhouseCoopers (2008), op. cit.

50   Susan M. Mudambi and Stephen Tallman (2010), op. cit.

51   E.g., the guides to *Best Practice Outsourcing and Offshoring* regularly produced by WNS, a leading global outsource service provider.

52   Partly based on Dun & Bradstreet Barometer of Global Outsourcing (2000), http://www.dnb.com.

CHAPTER 10

Virtual Organization

WHAT THIS CHAPTER COVERS

Definitions and descriptions of virtual organization vary considerably and this chapter starts by identifying the features that are common to this new organizational form. It then examines the benefits that virtual organization promises to offer. Certain conditions are required for the benefits of virtual organization to be achieved and for it to be viable. The disadvantages and limitations of virtual organization are also considered. The chapter goes on to address three questions arising over the use of virtual organization: when to use it in preference to conventional forms of organization; whether virtual organization has to be managed in a different way; and how virtual organization can be managed when applied to teamwork. The chapter closes by examining the Dell computer company as a pioneer of virtual organization on a global scale.

What is a Virtual Organization?

A virtual organization exists within a space that is not bound by the legal and physical structures that define a conventional organization. As Malcolm Warner and Morgen Witzel put it in their path-breaking book on the subject, virtual organizations "use mental and technological constructs to represent certain aspects of organization that, in more conventional organizations, have a physical existence."[1]

Bo Hedberg and his colleagues describe virtual organizations in terms of the mental construct of the "imaginary system" which cuts across and transcends conventional boundaries defined by legal identities, accounting systems, organization charts and physical assets. This perspective reveals "new enterprises which can utilize imagination, information technology, alliances and other networks to organize and sustain a boundary-transcending activity."[2]

Warner and Witzel echo the view that virtuality involves a mental leap which allows for a highly fluid and boundary-transcending form of collective activity:

> "In virtual organizations the solid physical realities of bricks and mortar, offices and production plants, colleagues and customers met face-to-face, are to some extent – sometimes to a large extent – dissolved and replaced by virtual forms. Solid bricks become fine networks. Instead of managing within organizations that enclose us and envelope us, we are part of an organization that is fluid, flexible and to a large part invisible, and can be called into existence only by active mental effort on our part. In virtual space, we place less emphasis on our five physical senses, and much more on our inner knowledge and imagination."[3]

New forms of technology are seen as the most significant facilitators of virtual organization. In the words of one source, "Rapid technological advancements have led to a new paradigm of work – it can now be conducted anytime, anywhere, in real space or through technology."[4] Indeed, one definition of virtual organization is that it is a repertoire of variably connectable modules built on an electronic information network. It is, however, possible to have organized activity based on modules or groups that are flexibly connected without the assistance of modern communications and information technology (ICT). The clan mode of organizing come close to this description and has been functioning in societies like China (the Triads) and Southern Italy (the Mafia) for many centuries. Nonetheless, ICT has opened up a huge range of new possibilities and extended the potential scope of organizing in a virtual manner to the global level.

Certain phrases are commonly used to identify the virtual organization – lack of physical structure, reliance on ICT, fluidity and mobility, the transcending of conventional boundaries, networks, and flexibility. Definitions of the virtual organization tend to emphasise one or more of these characteristics and therefore vary considerably. Some stress the role of information and technology, regarding the virtual organization as one that organizes information and technology rather than people. Others stress the networking aspects, applying the idea of virtuality to webs of partnerships between individuals or firms that come together to achieve a task or make a product. Michael Dell, for example, takes the view that "virtual integration means you basically stitch together a business with partners that are treated as if they're inside the company."[5] A further variant is the idea of flexible workforces that are brought together to perform a given need and then disband. In all these respects, virtual organization is seen as an attempt to avoid the rigid hierarchies and boundaries that often characterize conventional organizations.

Virtual organization takes the notion of the network organization to a higher level. Cisco Systems coined the term "Networked Virtual Organization" (NVO) to refer to this as a new way of doing business.[6] The Dell Computer Corporation will serve to illustrate this later in the chapter. While companies within a network may still act as different entities towards the external environment, the virtual organization is seen as a single entity from the outside, within which the companies inside act much more in concert. A highly developed network for coordination, normally using ICT, is required to achieve this. A significant level of mutual trust focused on an acceptance of common business goals is also necessary.

Faced by this wide range of interpretations, Warner and Witzel suggest that it is useful to note the features that nearly all virtual organizations have in common. Box 10.1 summarizes the ones they identify.

BOX 10.1 COMMON FEATURES OF VIRTUAL ORGANIZATIONS

- Lack of physical structure: Virtual organizations have a lower physical presence than their conventional counterparts. They have fewer tangible assets such as office buildings and warehouses, and those they do have are often geographically dispersed. Some have suggested that in the future, firms may be structured in virtual reality formats with computer links taking the place of physical infrastructure and firms existing only in cyberspace.

- Reliance on communications technology: Modern ICT plays a vital role in enabling virtual organization, and many see it as being at the heart of the virtual organization. Whereas conventional organizations use physical structures to provide their framework, virtual organizations use networks of communication supported by the Internet and other systems. However, technology is an enabler of virtual organization rather than the organization itself.

- Mobile work: The use of communications networks rather than buildings and tangible assets means that it is now less important where work is physically located. As a result, departments and teams no longer have to work in close contact with each other. Project teams can be – and in sectors such as publishing, routinely are – assembled from persons in different countries or on different continents to work together without ever coming into physical contact.

- Hybrid forms: Because virtual organizations often involve collaboration between individuals or firms, they have been referred to as hybrids – networks, consortia or webs working together within a loose framework to achieve a mutual goal. Such hybrids can be short-term such as consortia with a limited life bringing players together to undertake risky research and development projects, or they can be longer-term such as virtual supply chains.

- Boundaryless and inclusive: This characteristic is associated with the way that virtual organizations are not confined to legal entities. They can encompass suppliers and distributors working in tight relationships with producers, and bring customers into the production process through the concept of relationship marketing. Online financial services are a highly developed example of this latter phenomenon.

- Flexible and responsive: Virtual organizations are, in principle, very responsive and flexible. They should be amenable to rapid assembly from a variety of disparate elements, used to achieve a certain business goal and then dismantled. Much in practice, however, will depend on the people involved: whether they can negotiate mutually satisfactory arrangements quickly, and whether managers and employees are willing to work flexibly.

Source: Malcolm Warner and Morgen Witzel 2004, *Managing in Virtual Organizations*. London: Thomson, Chapter 1.

◢ Forms of Virtual Organization

It is important to recognize that there can be different degrees and different forms of virtuality in organization. Every organization has some virtuality, because it cannot rely simply on its tangible assets and formal routines. It also has to depend on the knowledge and experience inherent in its people, and on their informal communication with one another. We have seen in previous chapters how these characteristics have become increasingly important with the premium attached to flexibility and innovation in current competitive conditions.

Some organizations may organize certain activities on a virtual basis while organizing others in a conventional manner. For example, the operations inside supermarkets are physical and tangible. By contrast, their links with many suppliers are often virtual through the use of automated reordering systems. In addition, specialist programmers working from their homes maintain the software for these and other systems. Very few companies, however, are suited to complete virtuality throughout all their activities. They may have to maintain a physical connection with their customers and they may also still be producing or processing tangible goods. For example, Amazon is in the eyes of the public the stereotype of a virtual online broker connecting the purchasers and suppliers of books and many other goods without a physical retail store presence, and contracting out delivery. Nevertheless, it also runs huge physical warehouses.

The exact mix of virtual and tangible aspects in an organization will depend on the nature of its product or service, and the way it adds value in relation to the needs of customers and suppliers. The most comprehensively virtual organization is found when both its assets and management system are highly virtual. Many financial service firms fall into this category. They are trading a largely virtual commodity – financial instruments and currencies – across dispersed networks of offices around the world, managing the transactions through various communication technologies. Other cases illustrate the management of virtual assets in a non-virtual way. These are often found in knowledge industries where intellectual property is created or processed through project teams, teaching program teams, or publishing houses. There is always the potential for the management and coordination of such virtual assets to be managed in a more virtual manner. There has been, for instance, a growing use of virtual global teams for research and development.

Another form in which both assets and management are highly virtual is found with companies that take outsourcing to its limits. When a company outsources all the activities in its value chain except for its strategic core, and coordinates these in a virtual manner, it can be large in trading terms but very small in terms of fixed assets and permanent staff. For instance, the fashion accessories company, Topsy Tail, has generated revenues of some $150 million with only three employees. It never even touches its products through the entire supply chain. It contracts with various injection-moulding companies to manufacture its goods; it uses design agencies to create its packaging; and it distributes and sells its products through a network of independent fulfillment houses, distributors, and sales representatives.[7] Cisco Systems' concept of the networked virtual organization (NVO) has as one of its key characteristics a reliance on multiple partners to perform necessary but non-core functions – the other two key characteristics being rapid response to customer needs and standardization of processes within the organization as well as with external partners.

The traditional way to manage tangible assets has been in a non-virtual way. This uses the conventional form of organization in which most people and assets are physically concentrated into factories and offices, and are managed through hierarchies. Examples are production lines and integrated process plants in industries such as glass, steel and papermaking. It is in fact difficult for technical reasons to envisage anything other than a non-virtual configuration and management of integrated process production, unless such processes can be completely automated.

Tangible assets can be managed in a partly virtual manner when the value chain – the sequence of production and assembly, or the steps involved in offering a service – can be separated into stages. Global virtual supply chains, which are common in the automobile and computer industries come into this category. In the case of computer manufacture, "micro-processors and other semiconductors may pass through as many as four or five different production facilities – often in as many different countries – as they move down the value chain through the various processes of etching, masking and so on to finished status. The physical production plants are controlled 'virtually' from the corporation or supply chain head-quarters."[8] Dell Computers provides a case in point and is often held up as an example of a highly successful virtual value chain network.

Potential Benefits of Virtual Organization

While the operation of virtual organization is greatly facilitated by the development of ICT, we have to look to other factors that encourage managements actually to adopt it. The benefits that virtual organization promises to offer become prime drivers for its adoption in the light of the trends in the business revolution that many companies are experiencing and the pressures to which they are subjected. However, we need to use terms like "promise" and "potential" in connection with these benefits because virtual organization is a complex development that needs to be implemented with considerable care – it is not an automatic remedy for success.

The potential benefits of virtual organization lie in its facilitating:

1   efficient coordination across boundaries of time and space;
2   a more flexible combination of activities and enhanced focus on the customer;
3   the reduction of costs by reducing overheads and eliminating mediated transactions;
4   the simplification of management.

The use of ICT-based systems opens the door to *efficient coordination across boundaries of time and space*. Email systems overcome the need to synchronize communication across time zones, and to ensure that the other party is immediately available, as is the case with telephone conversations. Moreover, they readily overcome limitations of geographical space by permitting the simultaneous distribution of information across a network of recipients in dispersed locations. Other systems, like videoconferencing, effectively eliminate spatial distance by creating the virtuality of a single space between people who are at a considerable distance. It is possible to hold meetings between people located thousands of miles from each other, and also to deliver services such as education simultaneously and interactively to different groups located far away from one another. Online financial services reduce the units costs borne by banks as well as being readily available at times outside the normal working day that suit many customers.

This aspect of virtuality clearly can provide considerable benefits for the organization of related activities across physical distances, such as with a global supply chain. The savings in time, cost, travel fatigue and so forth can be considerable. They offer the benefits both of reduced cost and faster speed of response. Organizing in a virtual mode therefore offers a constructive response to the coordinative and control requirements that follow from the trend toward the networking of business on a global scale.

A related set of potential benefits from virtual organization stems from the way that *it permits a more flexible combination of activities* that form a value chain. By providing an alternative means of managing linked activities to placing them under a unified hierarchical structure, virtual organization allows for their coordinated dis-aggregation, often spread between different firms. With virtual modes of management, it becomes easier to separate stages of production and other activities in the value chain, while retaining a basis for coordinating them effectively. The speedy communication of information through common protocols within a virtual system permits the disaggregated activities to be recombined in a variety of ways to meet the needs of the specific situation, especially to meet the needs of customers in a flexible manner. In addition to the competitive benefit of a flexible response to customer requirements, this approach promises considerable economic benefits:

1   It permits a firm to specialize in those activities for which it enjoys a relative advantage based on its core competencies and/or specific location. The firm can then concentrate on enhancing this core advantage so as to maintain the basis for its competitive position.

2   Similarly, the firm can select the most suitable partners, from a wider range of candidates, with which to join to form a complete value chain. The partners should also benefit from the ability to focus on their core competencies.

3   Partnerships within a network are bound together by contracts that can be subject to periodic review and renewal, and include provisions for contingencies. Such arrangements should permit greater flexibility in adjusting to changing market demand compared to a mode of organization in which all activities are integrated within a single company. If the adjustment is to a contraction in the market, a virtual network facilitates the discarding of activities no longer required. If it is to take advantage of opportunities for marketing new products, this can usually be achieved quite quickly by adding new partners to the network.

4   When a company focuses its staff down to a small central core and constructs a virtual organization to take care of other value chain activities, it can use flexible employment arrangements to permit the workforce to be expanded or contracted as needs change. This kind of arrangement is neither new nor confined to virtual organizations. Virtuality, however, can offer an extra degree of loose coupling which provides more flexibility in adjusting employment compared with a conventional organization. The extra loose coupling comes through the spatial dispersion of work units and flexible employment arrangements such as home-based contract work.

5   The use of communications networks rather than a physical concentration of people and equipment opens up much greater choice in the location of work. People and their activities can now be located in the least-cost places, which is one of the prime reasons why outsourcing has become so attractive to firms. Even staff working in the core organization do not need to be located in central offices; many can work at home or in their local community. This can dramatically reduce costs; for example, the overhead per capita cost of home working can be under one-third that of working in a city-center office. Removing the need for commuting should also reduce both costs and stress for staff.

Another benefit of a virtual organization lies in the way *it can reduce costs*. One way this is achieved has just been mentioned: organizing virtually can reduce overheads. It can reduce the expenses of in-house physical working spaces, such as rent, insurance, maintenance, and the cost of utilities. Having some staff working at home through telecommuting can also make more efficient use of office space.

Another way that virtual organization can reduce costs is by eliminating mediated transactions. In conventional modes of organization, the imperfections inherent in transacting in a mediated way through, for example, the intervention of staff placing orders for supplies, or requesting a technical specialist to visit a site in person to provide assistance, generate costs associated with waiting times because the physical and organizational distance between transacting parties creates delays. Components and parts have to wait in the form of inventory; people have to wait until personal assistance became available. By transacting in a virtual mode, it is often possible to reduce if not eliminate waiting costs such as these, as well as the costs of managerial intervention. Supplies can now be ordered automatically through electronic order placing guided by a stock check and re-order system. Technical advice can often be given speedily on the basis of an electronic representation of the problem parameters, either through applying an expert system or through electronic communication with technical staff working at their distant location – which may be their home. Managers do not need to spend time arranging these transactions because their previously mediated and arms-length nature has effectively been eliminated.

A number of the potential benefits offered by virtual organization are associated with a reduction in the need for managerial intervention. Partly by automating much information processing on the basis of shared protocols, and partly by facilitating direct communications between anyone in the network, it is natural to devolve initiative within a virtual organization, and this saves on management time and effort. As a result, *the use of virtuality should permit a simplification in management* and a corresponding reduction in administrative overheads.

In offering these potential benefits, virtual organization speaks to the needs that most companies face given the changes in their competitive environment. Companies face pressures to offer increased value along with lower costs. Virtual organization promises to reduce costs in several ways, not least by offering a viable way of managing outsourcing to lower cost sources of supply. Companies also need to respond more rapidly to changes in order to preserve their competitive advantage. The flexibility offered by virtual organization should assist this capacity for rapid response.

Virtual organization can also benefit small companies by combining their advantages with those of large companies. Independent but closely linked companies can cooperate within a virtual organization to achieve their common business goals in an efficient way. Their relatively small size helps them to be highly innovative and to react swiftly to changing market demands. On the other hand, their combination into a virtual organization allows them to act as a single large company and to benefit from their aggregated market power.

◢ Conditions for the Viability of a Virtual Organization

Certain conditions are necessary for a potentially beneficial set of links between people and units to be converted into a viable virtual organization. First and foremost, like any organization a virtual organization requires management. Warner and Witzel suggest that four managerial tasks will assume greater importance in a virtual organization: communication, assessment, learning and valuation.[9] Managing communication clearly presents a particular challenge in the planning, coordination and control of activities that are no longer located centrally under one roof. This means ensuring that the flows of information and knowledge are efficient, relevant and timely, so as to link all the elements of the organization to one another as well as to suppliers and customers. Second, because a virtual organization is composed of various quasi-independent units, it is necessary to make frequent assessments of how they are meeting the organization's goals and how they need to lock together. The form and structure of a virtual network is potentially flexible, which is why it requires regular assessment and, often, regular adjustment. Third, a virtual organization usually relies heavily on what Max Boisot has called knowledge assets rather than on tangible physical assets.[10] This stock of knowledge assets requires replenishing through activities such as training and education, research and development, and searching the environment for new relevant knowledge. Fourth, there needs to be a frequent reassessment of knowledge assets in terms of their value to the virtual organization. The more that virtuality is seen as a way of acquiring flexibility in the light of changing customer or client requirements, the more frequently the contribution to that end of different people and units in the virtual system, and the knowledge they provide, has to be reassessed.

The continuing significance of management in a virtual organization stems from the fact that such an organization requires both operational and strategic direction. At the operation level, it is necessary to put together a set of competent value chain performers that are able to deliver required output on time and to specification. This is the central nervous system of the virtual organization, as it were, providing communications and processes to assure necessary standards of quality, delivery and the like. While having such a system is an obviously necessary condition, it is not sufficient. For a virtual organization also requires strategic direction. It requires a brain as well as a central nervous system. The brain is a center that provides strategic direction and makes difficult choices according to a consistent vision, including whom to add, whom to discard from the collective network, and on which criteria.

In practice, a virtual organization is likely to be led, even dominated, by a company at its center possessing the brand name that is a mark of quality and market appeal. That lead company is also likely to serve as the central information systems "commander," taking responsibility for designing and maintaining a common information standard across the virtual network. This applies both to management systems such as accounting and to technical systems. Regarding the latter, it is especially vital that a common standard is adopted when the work performed at different stages in the value chain such as design, development, production engineering, component assembly, and software systems has to interface according to precise technical specifications. The organization that within a virtual network plays the dominant role in forming the network, establishes its standards and has the primary (if not sole) relationship with the customer is often called the "network orchestrator."

◢ Limitations of Virtual Organization

There are concerns about the limitations of virtual organization, especially with respect to maintaining communication and control, the stimulation of learning and innovation, the vulnerability that may arise from dependence on partners, and security risks.

The restricted face-to-face interaction in a virtual organization can limit communications. Communication breakdowns arising from cultural and organizational differences between geographically dispersed units or collaborating organizations are normally harder to resolve virtually. This in turn may make it difficult to develop trust among the people involved or to preserve it from breaking down. Trust is likely to be at risk if one or more parties to a virtual network withhold information or prove to be unreliable, and it is more difficult to manage such eventualities in the absence of face-to-face contact. The personal dimension of control is missing in a virtual organization, and reliance has to be placed on other approaches mentioned later in this chapter, such cultural control based on the articulation of a strong, shared vision.

Unlike strategic alliances between different firms, many of which are intended to transfer knowledge or bring about organizational learning, learning is not a fundamental objective of virtual organization. Rather, the main intention is to create a flexible organization of companies in order to allow each to specialize on its area of excellence so as to deliver a product competitively to the customer. One limitation of virtual organization therefore concerns its capacity to promote learning and innovation except within the confines of each firm in the network.

It may prove difficult to develop systemic innovation involving the commitment of large R&D funds to highly integrated projects within a virtual organization, because such investment requires there to be stability in the relations between partners over a period of years. The essentially flexible nature of virtual organization is likely to militate against this degree of stability, or at least present a high risk that it will not endure. The problem can be avoided if the lead firm in a virtual network can undertake the necessary R&D itself. If the product in question comprises relatively discrete units that can be assembled together in different configurations, as is the case with the microprocessor, disk drives, monitor, keyboard, and speakers in a computer, then the responsibility for innovation in such component units can largely be left to their producers. In this situation, a virtual relationship between them and the lead company designing and assembling the computer need not be problematic on these grounds.

A further limitation of the virtual organization lies in its restricted ability to communicate and share tacit knowledge. The virtual organization functions through arms-length relation-ships, despite the fact that its supporting technology can compress distances of time and space. This presents a barrier to the sharing of embryonic ideas and uncodified knowledge, especially when the willingness to share them depends on the people concerned knowing and trusting each other well. This implies that the processes required to achieve the initial creative stages of innovation may not be well served by organizing virtually. Later stages of innovation, when it is primarily a question of working out how to produce a well-specified new product or service, or a codified new technique, are more amenable to coordination and control on a virtual basis.

The risk of vulnerability when working within a virtual network is illustrated by a well-known example where an innovation partnership operating in a virtual fashion actually worked against the long-term interests of the lead company. When IBM, although far from being a virtual corporation itself, decided to develop and make its PC in a virtual manner, it coupled its hardware with Microsoft software and an Intel microprocessor. This gave Microsoft and Intel the impetus to grow from small beginnings to become larger than IBM itself. The company missed the opportunity to make the microprocessor and develop the software in-house, which it certainly had the resources to do. Instead, it effectively gave away some of its core competencies. It made a mistake in entering into a virtual partnership and not doing in-house the things that it was both good at and which had strategic importance.[11]

Another kind of vulnerability can arise from the heavy dependence of virtual organization on ICT networks. The danger of international cyber attack and espionage through sophisticated hacking has become newsworthy because of the potential threat it poses to national security.[12] A comparable kind of risk faces business companies. It was reported that the costs to US companies of intellectual property theft through the Internet amounted to at least $250 billion a year, which is far more than what businesses pay in federal corporate income taxes. The risk with Internet-dependent virtual organization is not just that intellectual property might be stolen but that highly integrated systems could be brought down.[13]

◢ Questions about the Use of Virtual Organization

Three questions often arise over the use of virtual modes of organizing. The first is when to use them in preference to conventional forms of organization. The second is whether virtual organization has to be managed in a different way. The third question is how virtual arrangements can permit people, who are located far apart, to work together as a team and to benefit from the coordination and synergy that team working is intended to provide.

When to use virtual organization

The point was made earlier that all firms comprise a mixture of virtual and physical components, using both tangible and intangible assets. The question is how to decide on an appropriate combination between the two.

This question can be addressed by reference to the combination of economic, technological and organizational requirements that a business faces:

ECONOMIC FACTORS

1 *Relations with customers.* How important is it to maintain personal face-to-face contact with customers? Do customers expect a high level of personal contact or not? If the product is standardized and an established brand, there will not normally be any need for customers to have personal contact with the producer, and the relationship can take a virtual form. This is because there is no requirement to choose the product through personal inspection; also the risk of a faulty product being supplied to customers is low and, should it arise, the problem can easily be identified and rectified. Moreover, many standard products do not require the provision of special installation or after-sales services. Internationally classified commodities, branded goods, and the delivery of power, light and water supplies are examples of products and services for which the relationship between producer and customer is therefore normally a virtual one.

In other cases, the transference of customer provision to a virtual mode is technically possible, but may hinder the provision of other linked services that customers prefer to receive through a more personal mode of delivery. For example, banks were concerned about losing touch with their customers once they introduced automated teller machines (ATMs). More recently British banks found that the quality of their relationship to customers declined after switching to call centres, so that one major bank is now making telephone access to local branch staff a feature in attracting new customers. Some personal services simply cannot be delivered on a virtual basis – such as hairdressing or personal therapy. Products like soft furnishings, where many customers want to make a personal firsthand choice between alternatives, might have only a limited appeal if offered solely through mail order or over the Internet.

2 *Relations with suppliers.* The extent to which the relationship between a firm and its suppliers can be put onto a virtual basis also depends on the nature of the goods or services being supplied. In manufacturing, components and parts require physical shipment and may be sourced very locally so as to facilitate just-in-time delivery. The physical shipment clearly cannot be done on a virtual basis, although the accompanying information processing – of components/parts specifications and their delivery schedule – can be. Normally, the organization of supplies, and indeed a whole supply chain, can be accomplished on a virtual basis, as we shall see in the case of Dell Computers described later in this chapter. Services that consist of information provision, or that can be transacted without any physical presence like booking airline flights, are increasingly being provided through the Internet. Other support services, such as consultancy and media promotion have to be tailored to the needs of a particular firm. They normally require personal interaction between the supplier and members of the organization, and cannot be conducted on a virtual basis. When the supply of goods or services can be provided and transacted on a virtual basis, considerable savings of cost and time are normally available through the elimination of "middlemen" such as wholesalers and travel agents.

TECHNOLOGICAL FACTORS

Many of the economic considerations just mentioned are tied up with the technological nature of the activities undertaken by a firm, and consequently the type of market it is supplying and the inputs it requires. A further technological factor is the kind of work that is carried out within the firm itself. If it undertakes advanced research and/or design work, the need to promote creativity and share tacit knowledge through group work may limit the extent to which this can successfully be carried out on a virtual basis. This is despite the keen interest now being shown in virtual teams which bring together geographically dispersed specialists to work on a common project. Managers may have to assess the trade-off between (1) optimising the *processes* conducive to creativity, and (2) optimising the availability and cost of creative *resources*, especially when these are spread across different regions and time zones. The first component of the trade-off speaks in favour of working in a non-virtual mode with teams of people who are in close physical proximity, whereas the second component speaks in favour of bringing together the most appropriate, but dispersed, people through a virtual system.

Other areas of work can operate, and be managed, quite well on a virtual basis. Sales teams are often physically dispersed and work through virtual links. They can be brought together periodically through sales conferences in order to share experiences and discuss possible improvements on a face-to-face basis.

ORGANIZATIONAL FACTORS

In addition to the work of different units within an organization, such as design and sales, consideration must also be given to relations between them, and those between management and employees. The conclusion that Lawrence and Lorsch reached in the 1960s continues to apply: organizations differ in the degree and form of internal integration they require, depending on the uncertainty and speed with which they have to deal with new requirements.[14] If they are frequently faced with fresh problems involving new parameters, especially problems they are also under pressure to solve quickly, then they have to organize in ways that facilitate intensive and creative interaction between the people who have to work on those problems. Virtual information processing systems may assist, but there will also be a need for inter-personal discussion and interaction. When the organization's work is relatively routine, or there is time to make adjustments, then a greater use of virtual methods may be possible. So the required relationship between the organizational units in a firm has to be examined very carefully before deciding on the appropriateness of virtual working.

In addition to these primarily "horizontal" relationships, consideration has also to be given to the vertical aspect – the relationship between management and employees. One of the problems that frequently arise when organizations adopt virtual modes is a loss of control and motivation. Control may not be too much of a problem if the quantity and quality of what people produce can readily be measured or assessed. Even so, people working at a distance from their organization can feel cut off and develop a demotivating sense of being neglected by management. Therefore, if virtual arrangements are to replace physical and social proximity between managers and employees, this will probably have to be compensated for with mechanisms that ensure the relationship remain sufficiently active.

To summarize, managers deciding on the balance between virtual and conventional organization could benefit from using a checklist along the lines of the following. This identifies the questions that have to be considered when deciding on the extent and form of virtual organization which can usefully be introduced.

1 Relations with customers:
   • How standardized is the product or service?
   • How well is the product supported by an established brand?
   • Are variations in style, or considerations of personal taste involved?
   • Is the product a personal service?
2 Relations with suppliers:
   • How tangible are the items being supplied?
   • Do suppliers need to be physically located close to their customers?
3 Technological factors:
   • To what extent does the work require creativity and innovation?
   • To what extent can employees carry out their work separately from their colleagues?
4 Organizational factors:
   • What form of integration is required between different people and units within the organization?
   • Can employees be adequately motivated working apart from each other and from their managers?
   • Is there a risk of serious loss of control if employees work apart from their managers?

Managing the virtual organization

Warner and Witzel ask how different the task of managing a virtual organization is, and suggest that it has affinities with the general management of conventional organizations. General managers necessarily have to take a broad view of their organizations, and in this respect the primary task is the same as that of managing the network of activities that comprise a virtual organization. General managers are not expected to get closely involved with operational control and coordination, though in practice some do,[15] and in a virtual organization ICT-based systems are expected to provide a considerable amount of the operational coordination that is required.

The traditional approach to identifying the specific activities of general management has derived from the following seven sets of tasks first identified by the French management theorist Henri Fayol, and generally known by the acronym POSDCORB:[16]

- Planning
- Organizing
- Staffing
- Directing
- Coordinating
- Reporting
- Budgeting

In the case of managing a virtual organization, some of these tasks are likely to assume greater significance than others. Planning in the sense of strategy formulation and implementation remains very important, as does "reporting" (i.e. control) and coordination across the whole range of value chain activities and functions. As we have noted, the people in a virtual organization may be almost its only asset, and HRM issues (the modern equivalent of "staffing") are therefore especially important. How HRM tasks are dealt with within a virtual organization will depend on how it is constituted. If it is a network between organized partners, such as distinct firms, then many HRM matters can be managed within those organizations. If, however, the virtual organization consists of many employees or contract staff working by themselves or in small, scattered units, HRM matters will have to become the responsibility of the virtual organization's central management. Other tasks such as organizing day-to-day work, directing (in the sense of personal direction), and budgeting are likely to be less salient in a virtual organization than in a conventional one where people work within a single physical, legal and financial entity.

The nature of a virtual organization means that its management process has to be characterized above all by:

1 guidance and motivation of the organization through a vision that is articulated through strategy and communicated effectively to its members;
2 a strong focus on information processing and knowledge management;
3 an emphasis on the coordination of others;
4 the constant reinforcement of skills and willingness to cooperate among staff.

The last requirement stems from the recognition that, while a virtual organization depends on advanced technology to facilitate its processes, its distinctive competitive edge depends primarily on its network of people and how this functions. A concomitant requirement is to give priority to the development of relevant skills, appreciating that these skills must include the ability to work together within a virtual format. It is therefore vital to manage the staff of a virtual organization in a manner that encourages their willingness to trust each other, and consequently to communicate openly in ways which enhance the potential competitive advantages of a virtual organization in respect of learning and flexible adaptation.

Managing a virtual organization involves some of the same issues that arise in managing outsourcing and strategic alliances, discussed in Chapters 9 and 11 respectively. When some, if not all, the members of a virtual value chain are independent partners – either firms or individuals – there is the overriding challenge of maintaining a strategic fit between them. The managers of the virtual network have to forge a unity between the members' objectives, or at the least create a compatibility between them. Much the same problem arises with reconciling compatibility between a firm and its contractors to which it has outsourced certain activities. It is also vital to the success of a strategic alliance that the partners continue to identify with its objectives and perceive that they are each gaining from their partnership in proportion to the resources they are giving to it. A further issue that arises with virtual networks, outsourcing and alliances is what to centralize into the lead firm and what to leave to the partners. With outsourcing, the question is what to outsource and how far to take the process. With an alliance the equivalent question concerns which tasks each partner should undertake and retain most influence over.

Drawing on research in telecommuting, globally coordinated product planning and supply chain integration, Fritz and Manheim identify what they term the "critical processes" that have to be managed in virtual organizations.[17] These are the management of people, relationships, work, knowledge, and technology. They argue that the effective management of these processes in a virtual organization can be a source of major business benefits such as shorter time to market, a superior response to competitors' moves, more effective management of integrated supply chains, and the better use of staff with flexible work schedules. The key difference between managing the processes in a conventional organization and a virtual organization lies in the very low incidence of face-to-face contacts in the latter. The following subsections summarize Fritz and Manheim's conclusions.

PEOPLE MANAGEMENT

In a virtual organization people work more autonomously and have to be prepared to make decisions independently while at the same time coordinating with others and often working collaboratively with distant colleagues. For such individuals, time management and self-management skills are particularly important operational competencies. They may also be concerned that their lack of organizational visibility could lead to reduced promotion and development opportunities. Their managers must be sensitive to concerns such as these, as well as to selecting appropriate people in the first place. This implies that managers in virtual organizations should be very sensitive to human resource management issues and develop sufficiently sophisticated systems.

RELATIONSHIP MANAGEMENT

Relationships between people are particularly important for the effective performance of virtual work. Many commentators have noted the significance of trust as a requirement for sustaining virtual relationships that are physically distant and not supported by frequent face-to-face contact or managerial support.[18] Trust is critical because virtual processes have to be open and transparent. Yet this quality is more difficult to create and sustain when people are working physically apart and less able to rely upon the informal shared understandings and inter-personal empathy that can help to build trust (see Chapter 15).

The managers of virtual organizations therefore need to make special provisions for nurturing and supporting the relationship between the people within the network and between those people and themselves. Essentially, these provisions are intended to offset the impersonality and sense of psychological distance that can otherwise reduce the quality of relationships and even lead to a sense of alienation among staff. For example, there can be arrangements to bring physically scattered staff together in periodic regional gatherings. These would combine the functions of discussing work-related issues with social events intended to help people who normally communicate only remotely to bond together personally. Managers themselves should be prepared to make personal visits to other partner organizations within a virtual network. There is evidence from studies of strategic alliances that such visits contribute importantly to building trust among the partners, and that this in turn assists them to optimize on their partnership through mutual learning, and a spirit of cooperation in adapting to changing requirements.[19] In between these interpersonal events and visits, news and other information can be distributed regularly throughout the virtual organization through its electronic channels.

WORK MANAGEMENT

In a virtual organization, the management of the work itself focuses on the two processes of coordination and control. The coordination of activities within a virtual organization becomes more complex because goals and priorities have to be communicated to people in a variety of different locations. Local needs and circumstances have also to be communicated back to managers. In a conventional work environment, managers can often achieve this coordination speedily and effectively through face-to-face interactions, either informally or through scheduled meetings. In a virtual organization, electronic protocols have to substitute and rules can be implemented to make this effective – for instance, an instruction that all staff must check their email boxes at least once a day and respond to them within a specified period. When the units of a virtual organization are distributed globally, special support is needed to assist their working together, as we shall see in the case of virtual global team working.

Chapter 6 discussed how as initiative is devolved within and between organizations, the approach to control has to shift from attention to how work is done and toward the outcomes of that work. In other words, there has to be a shift from control over the process towards facilitating the effective performance of the process. Initiative is generally highly devolved in virtual organizations, because to work effectively in geographically dispersed locations, workers must have the autonomy to make important decisions on how to perform their work – for example, how to respond immediately to specific client requests. This means that managers have to develop new approaches toward evaluating and monitoring the performance of remote workers.

KNOWLEDGE MANAGEMENT

Within a physically compact organization, a great deal of knowledge can be shared and created through direct interaction between people. In a virtual organization, the sharing even of explicit knowledge can become difficult. Data can be transmitted and distributed without undue problems, but the reasoning and understanding that distinguishes knowledge from mere data or information poses a greater problem for knowledge management in a virtual organization. Making sure that people get access to the information they need to perform their job is a critical and often more complex issue when they are not located in the same place. Experience with virtual team working (discussed below) suggests that the design of appropriate systems to coordinate the sharing of both structured knowledge and less structured opinions may play an important role in the effectiveness of working in a virtual mode.

TECHNOLOGY MANAGEMENT

Information and communications technology clearly plays a vital role in virtual organization. While it is by no means the be-and-end-all of such organization, the effective management of technology is crucial to its success.

The technology is required to support virtual working in a number of modalities:

1   structured, as in the use of systems for managing and reporting structured tasks such as sending purchase orders as EDI messages in a supply chain;
2   semi-structured, as in the use of Workflow Management (WF) systems, e.g. sending invoices for payment that may entail several levels of review in both the purchasing and selling units within a virtual network;
3   unstructured, which could use groupware and email to cope with distances and/or non-synchronized work schedules.

The need to service a number of interaction and transaction modalities, means that an ICT strategy for supporting the processes within a virtual organization has to take account of the entire range of interactions in an integrated manner. We also noted the importance of encouraging a social dimension to relationships within a virtual organization, so as to enhance identification and trust between its members. This means that managers need to give attention in their ICT policy to supporting the totality of virtual work, including personal interactions as well as purely business matters. It goes without saying, that relevant training forms an essential part of such support.

Virtual team working

Chapter 5 discussed how teams are being used increasingly to integrate the contributions of organizational members who possess complementary areas of expertise and types of experience, and to focus these capabilities onto a given project or task. Teamwork is a powerful organizational tool for coordinating interdependent activities. The activities may be either of a routine nature, as with many workgroup teams, or aimed at solving problems creatively such as when a project team is set up to design or plan a new development. The latter kind of team is likely to have a lifespan governed by that of the project.

Almost one-half (46 percent) of a sample of US organizations surveyed in 2012 were using virtual teams, particularly those with multinational operations.[20] There is evidence that virtual teams can outperform traditional ones.[21] The application of the virtual approach to team working can help to overcome some of the limitations of the traditional face-to-face method.[22] First, it is not possible to organize a team along traditional lines without personal meetings taking place in one location. This makes such teams very location specific. With the use of ICTs such as email, video conferencing, multi-media email and group support systems, a virtual team can communicate and proceed with its work without the necessity of gathering together in one physical place. Virtual teams can enrol the best expertise from any location, including from outside the organization when appropriate. Also they can reduce the time it takes to complete projects by using the "follow the sun" schedule. This means that members of the team located in, say, North Carolina, can leave a list of action items for their colleagues in Beijing to work on while their American colleagues are asleep.[23]

Second, the traditional team was restricted in numbers both to reduce the cost and time of meetings and to allow a manageable interpersonal process. With the use of virtual teams, it is possible to mobilize the contributions of a large number of people. This extended participation has the advantage of drawing on a wider range of contributions and spreading the sense of ownership and commitment toward a particular project. For example, the NCR Corporation created a virtual task force of over 1,000 people at 17 locations to develop a new-generation computer system. Applying high-speed telecommunication networks and information systems technologies, the virtual task force team completed the project on budget and ahead of schedule.[24]

A third set of problems that can arise in conventional non-virtual teams concerns the distinction between regular members (insiders) and outsiders. When the membership of teams is restricted to a small number of people, those left out can readily feel estranged and devalued. Friction can easily arise between the two sets of people. Even if they are motivated to contribute to the team's work or to respond to its ideas, the outsiders are handicapped by not knowing who is involved or what the team is doing. This was the problem at one time in the author's own business school when the school's "executive committee" failed to disseminate its terms of reference, let alone the outcome of its deliberations. This led to considerable resentment among other faculty members. When, later on, the committee's agendas and minutes were circulated electronically to everyone in the school, and the staff were also invited to contribute ideas and observations relevant to the items on the committee's agenda via email, their sense of estrangement reduced and the school benefited from much improved morale and commitment. In this case, applying some of the principles of virtuality to a team process yielded significant benefits by removing much of the barrier between insiders and outsiders. One of the arguments for restricting access to teamwork is that there may be a need for information security. Paradoxically, when the need for security arises, the electronic storage and circulation of information allows for control because it allows the flow of such information to be tracked.

There is increasing interest in the use of global virtual teams. Many technology-based firms are spreading out their research facilities to various parts of the world in the search for highly trained scientific and technical personnel. Large corporations like General Electric, IBM, and SAP have research labs and "centers of excellence" scattered around the world, whose staff often collaborate through virtual teams. Sometimes, the search for lower-cost graduate personnel is also a motivating factor.[25] A global virtual team is a group of geographically and temporally dispersed individuals who are assembled via the use of ICT to accomplish an organizational task. Activities of a global scope are both *dispersed* – carried out at different locations – and *asynchronous* – carried out at different times. Conventional teams normally operate in more or less the same space and time.

The technologies are now available to provide the possibilities for working on this global basis to take place. The real challenge is how to organize and manage global teamwork effectively; their superior performance depends on this. Virtual teams, established to overcome space and time barriers, cannot necessarily rely on traditional social cues and behavioural mechanisms. New ways have to be found to coordinate them and to resolve conflicts between their members.[26]

An experiment carried out with 35 five-person teams composed of graduate students located in the United States and Japan throws some interesting light on how to manage these requirements.[27] These teams were granted limited time to reach a solution to a given assignment. The team members communicated solely through custom-designed and access-controlled Lotus Notes (now IBM Notes) discussion forums, and the teams were therefore strictly virtual. The researchers assessed each team's performance in terms of (1) the range of issues covered in its decision rationale, (2) how well its decision rationale was organized, and (3) the depth to which each team explored issues. They found that:

1   Avoiding conflict had a negative effect on team performance. This negative impact was, however, reduced by the use of Lotus Notes to provide a temporal coordinating mechanism that revealed team members' initial positions, imposed progress-setting tasks such as required reviews, and set time limits for specific tasks.

2   Behavior that tried to accommodate conflict within the team – through, for instance, thoughtless agreement with what another member was saying – did not contribute anything to performance. Since this behavior focused more on maintaining harmony than on negotiating integrative optimal solutions, application of the temporal coordination mechanism to such behavior did not help.

3   When conflict within the teams was resolved through domination by one party or by collaborative behavior, team performance benefited. Handling conflict through compromise led to poorer team performance, though this negative effect was reduced through the use of the temporal coordination mechanisms. These mechanisms did not have any moderating effect on the domination and conflict and collaboration styles.

This pioneering experimental research suggests that an ICT-based mechanism to coordinate global virtual team members' contributions across space and time barriers can assist team performance under certain conditions. By providing a structure to the team process, and perhaps most importantly by encouraging transparency within the team, the ICT mechanism can reduce the otherwise negative effects of behavior that lead to sub-optimal performance by muting issues and opinions rather than expressing them openly and forcefully. It is likely that the clearly stated goal and time constraints also had a significant effect in focusing and motivating team efforts toward a successful outcome.

An intensive study of three global virtual teams within a US industrial technology company and two of its European strategic partners sheds further light on the conditions required for positive interaction within such teams.[28] Two of the teams proved to be successful, whereas the third was not. One requirement for success was to have a fit between (1) the form chosen for interaction (its medium and duration) and (2) the decision process and complexity of the communication required within the team. For example, building commitment requires team members to be highly involved in the decision process and necessitates the exchange of complex messages. Effective interaction in this situation requires a rich communication medium, such as videoconferencing. A less rich communication medium, such as email, would not be adequate, whereas it might be quite appropriate for arriving at simpler decisions and for less complex messages. Trying to discuss complex strategic issues via brief emails was an inappropriate fit and proved unsuccessful. Stepping away from virtuality through periodic, face-to-face meetings was found to inject fresh life into the teams' processes. This appeared to be particularly important in the early stages of a team's life and for teams with tasks that required a high level of interdependence. The successful virtual global teams also focused specifically on building relationships to increase trust and to develop shared views across the "borders" of country, culture, company, or occupation.

There is considerable agreement on the requirements for virtual teams to perform effectively.[29] A very important requirement is that their members have to trust each other. Trust is likely both to reinforce and be encouraged by other closely-linked relationship qualities such as low interpersonal conflict (but at the same time high respect for conflicting views), mutual liking, open communication, a willingness to contribute effort, and team learning.[30] Other important requirements are that virtual team leaders understand and fully use the diversity in their teams, plan team conference meetings and monitor progress, rotate virtual meeting times to accommodate members fairly, and give full recognition to team members' contributions. Careful consideration also has to be given to if and when the team should meet on a face-to-face personal basis – for example, to establish initial trust among the members and to iron out particularly challenging issues when these arise.

Ishaya and Macaulay examined the role of trust among the members of two experimental virtual teams.[31] They concluded that there were three main levels of trust in these teams. The first two concerned technology and media, namely the mechanism and software used for collaboration. If these failed, trust could not readily develop among team members. The third level of trust is more complex. It concerns the interactions between the team members and can therefore be called the "social" level. Interestingly, the researchers found that with virtual communication trust could be jeopardized because people could hide behind the relative anonymity of the technology. For example, people continued to criticize one another for a longer period, and to say things they would not normally have said in face-to-face communication.

Ishaya and Macaulay suggest that, in order to help build social trust in a virtual team, certain communication protocols or conventions need to be established by which each team member would have to abide. These relate to the five dimensions of integrity, ability, openness, benevolence, and expectations. Each dimension has certain defining characteristics, which the protocols states in specific terms, as Table 10.1 indicates.

Table 10.1   Dimensions and protocols of social trust in virtual teams[32]

Dimensions	Characteristics of Each Dimension	Protocols
Integrity	Honesty, truthfulness, loyalty, faithfulness, and commitment	Being honest Being straightforward Keeping promises Being faithful and truthful Responding in good time Being reliable
Ability	Interpersonal knowledge, skills, and experiences, competence	Demonstrating personal knowledge Demonstrating individual & group skills Sharing individual experiences Demonstrating personal competence
Openness	Willingness to share ideas and information freely	Informing team members Sharing ideas freely Sharing information freely Giving positive feedback Apologizing publicly
Benevolence	Wish to do good, goodwill, and generosity	Being helpful and supportive to others Being friendly to others Being kind and courteous Being considerate to others Empathizing with others Praising people for their good work Being humble
Expectations	Potential gains/losses, reliability, consistency, and judgment	Being open in one's expectations Being prepared to compromise on one's expectations Being fair in expectations Being consistent in personal expectations

◢ A Pioneer of Virtual Organization: Dell Inc.[33]

The Dell computer company was founded in 1984 by Michael Dell. It grew rapidly and joined the Fortune 500 list in 1992. In 1999 Dell became the world's largest PC manufacturer. As one commentator noted, "Through a career spanning almost two decades, Mr Dell has lined up the companies that dominate the markets for personal computers (PCs), notebook computers, servers, storage and network systems like bottles on a wall. From behind his desk in Austin, Texas, he has shot them down, one after the other."[34] Since 2005, however, the company has lost its pre-eminent position, though remaining number three in the world for PCs.[35] Nevertheless, it provide an instructive example of how virtual organization can offer significant business advantages.

A distinctive feature behind Dell's remarkable success was its "Direct from Dell" direct sales model, which entails an extensive use of virtual organization. By building its products to order and perfecting logistics and distribution, Dell streamlined its operations and cut costs to the point where it could undercut its competitors and gain market share. This approach kept inventory to a minimum and took advantage of the mass customization of computer system configurations, so permitting customers to define their preferred specifications and obtain them at a competitive price with the minimum of delay.

Michael Dell described the company's "strategies for success" as follows:

> Speed to market; superior customer service; and a fierce commitment to producing consistently high quality, custom-made computer systems that provide the highest performance and the latest relevant technology to our customers. And, as we as a company evolved, our strategies became more robust . . . once I bypassed the middleman and sold directly to customers, I set my sights on tightening the relationships we had with suppliers, reducing the number of steps involved in managing inventory, and improving the cost and time-to-market advantages we provided to our customers. Telephone sales worked just fine for a long time – and still do, for some customers – until we exploited the limitless potential of the Internet.[36]

Dell's build-to-order model meant that it could simplify its value chain by cutting out distributors and retailers or resellers. Whereas the indirect PC value chain is

The Dell Direct PC value chain is:

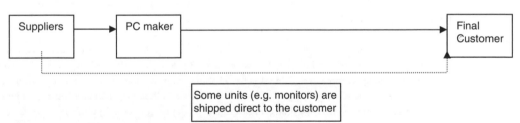

On the supply side, the Dell system was aimed at balancing the financial advantages of outsourcing with the operational benefits of vertical integration.[37] Dell Computer coordinates a global production network for assembly in its most important markets. While Dell does not manufacture its own components or subassemblies, unlike some other computer manufacturers it has avoided outsourcing the final assembly of its products, and it employs over 103,000 people worldwide. It increasingly ordered base units for notebooks from its suppliers and performed the final configuration in order to offer more options to customers. While in this way Dell prefers to keep direct control over product quality and configuration, it does permit some highly reliable units such as Sony monitors to be shipped to the customer without further inspection.

Most of Dell's sourcing is global: it sources the major components for all its assembly locations through a centralized information system. For major components, Dell looks for suppliers with global capabilities such as Intel, IBM, Samsung, Toshiba, Sony and Seagate. The sourcing of consumables such as cartons, shipping material and the printing of manuals, is done locally. As Dell receives an order for a computer, it shares the corresponding production requirement information electronically with its suppliers worldwide for immediate delivery to a Dell production facility, where the computer is assembled and shipped directly to the customer within a week.

The Dell model relies on demand-side pull rather than supply push. No computer is produced unless there is a corresponding customer requirement. This almost eliminates the massive queues of inventory usually sitting idle in retail stores, distributors and factories. Due to its made-to-order approach and highly sophisticated information technology, Dell is able to plan on a daily basis. The company can also discern whether movements in demand are specific to certain customer segments or are occurring across the market. Dell relays its assessment of this information to its suppliers, so allowing them to adjust their inventory to meet the demand. The advantages of this system are that Dell can operate with half the numbers of employees and one-tenth the inventory of its traditionally-organized computer competitors. It also enables the company to respond very flexibly to changing market trends and demands, and new technologies.

Dell manages its value chain in a virtual manner. It transacts all of its business via telephone and the Internet. The company is both the architect and cornerstone of this virtual organization. As the lead member and the single point of accountability for customers, Dell sets common goals for the entire virtual organization. In this role, Dell can select and evaluate its partners against a benchmark that it sets as the minimum requirement to belong to its virtual organization.

Dell Computer used technology and information to blur the traditional boundaries in the value chain between suppliers, manufacturers and end users. The company evolved in this way towards what Michael Dell calls "virtual integration." This mode of organizing has been described as follows:[38]

> The individual pieces of the strategy – customer focus, supplier partnerships, mass customization, just-in-time manufacturing – may all be familiar. But Michael Dell's insight into how to combine them is highly innovative: technology is enabling coordination across company boundaries to achieve new levels of efficiency and productivity, as well as extraordinary returns to investors. Virtual integration harnesses the economic benefits of two very different business models. It offers the advantages of a tightly coordinated supply chain that have traditionally come through vertical integration. At the same time, it benefits from the focus and specialization that drive virtual corporations. Virtual integration as Michael Dell envisions it, has the potential to achieve both coordination and focus. If it delivers on that promise, it may well become a new organizational model for the information age.

In a presentation to the US Institute for Supply Management's 2013 annual conference, the chief procurement and supply chain officer of Flextronics, Tom Linton, described how companies that were previously vertically integrated are now "virtually vertically integrated" (VVI). In similar terms to those of Michael Dell, Linton portrayed virtual integration as the "managed alignment of external supply chain capabilities that leverages multiple levels of those capabilities to improve profitability and cash flow." With virtual integration, suppliers are seen as an extension of the core enterprise behaving as though they were internal to that company.[39]

Through using ICT and information sharing with both suppliers and customers, the Dell system creates a strong link that is mutually beneficial to all the parties concerned. Not only can customers order the specification that suits their needs; they can also track the progress of their order electronically. In the case of large global customers, Dell has developed customized secure intranet sites that give them direct access to purchasing and technical information about the configurations they have bought. Dell also works closely with large corporate customers on a continuing basis. For instance, it routinely loads such customers' software onto machines in its factories. In the case of some customers, such as Boeing, it has staff working on site operating more like Boeing's PC department than as a supplier.

On the supply side, Dell works with a limited number of what it calls "partners." "Our rule is to keep it [the relationship with suppliers] simple and have as few partners as possible. Fewer than forty suppliers provide us with about 90 percent of our material needs. Closer partnerships with fewer suppliers is a great way to cut cost and further speed products to market."[40] Some of its partners are large corporations like Intel, Microsoft and Sony with which it enjoys a long-term relationship.

Dell uses online communications technology to communicate production needs to suppliers directly and in real time. Through an extranet, Supplier Web Pages offer real-time access to special business data and facilitate communication between the top twenty suppliers and Dell. The Supplier Web Pages are utilized in 85 to 90 percent of procurement transactions. This virtual link in turn provides Dell with information on suppliers' capacities, capabilities, inventories, and current cost structures. Dell in return relays gathered customer feedback to suppliers on their products and their performance so as to give the suppliers the opportunity to meet customer demands and improve the quality of their products. In this way, the concerns and needs of the customer are met directly.[41]

These virtual links reduce the time that a product is built according to customer specifications and then delivered directly to that customer. From the customer's own computer, the order is relayed to Dell's assembly facilities. With this information, the specified hardware and software is communicated to the suppliers and the necessary components delivered and assembled in one of Dell's plants. The individual product packages from Dell and the other fully built parts of the order, such as monitors, are then sorted out by Dell's delivery partner, such as UPS, and delivered directly to the customer who placed the order. The process gets the product to the consumer in the least possible time and with the least possible expense. Some of Dell's suppliers, such as Sony which produces its computer monitors, are so reliable that Dell does not even need to check the products they deliver. Thus the delivery partner just collects the products and on matching them with other parts of the order delivers directly to the customer.

The advantages of virtual integration for Dell are clear. By not having so many assets and people in-house, management of the value chain in simplified. As Michael Dell himself put it, "There are fewer things to manage, fewer things to go wrong."[42] Virtual integration also enables the company to be flexible in response to customer demand. As its products can be tailor-made, customers attach a high value to them. The flexibility of the system enables Dell's products to incorporate the latest technology, while the implementation of strict measures ensures their high quality. Being a virtual organization gives Dell access to a wide range of specialized resources. Dell can tap selected products from several sources, which gives the company further flexibility in choosing the best components for its computers. Individual members of the Dell value chain can retain their independence and continue to develop their niche skills, so adding further competencies to the overall virtual organization. Suppliers obviously have to accept some limitations in return for being part of a highly successful virtual network. They are very dependent on Dell for their production schedules. They are required to maintain inventory in Dell's plants or within 15 miles of them to support Dell's build-to-order production. They therefore have to bear additional costs for stocking some of the inventory that Dell avoids.

The Dell case raises two key questions about virtual organization. The first is what prevented its competitors from adopting vertical integration and reaping its benefits, especially at a time when it was clearly advantageous? The second question is why having created an advantageous supply chain system, has Dell in recent years lost ground in its industry?

Much of the answer to the first question seems to come down to a matter of corporate culture and philosophy. Founded only in 1984, Dell was a relative newcomer to the computer industry and was not encumbered by the established structures and norms of the industry's conventional value chain. Michael Dell's book and the Dell website strongly emphasized the company's distinctive philosophy. What they call the "Soul of Dell" stresses the following values:

1   teamwork;
2   meritocracy;
3   adherence to a common goal;
4   competitiveness and accountability for results;
5   directness in relations with customers, communications, confronting problems, and listening to subordinates' criticisms;
6   operating without inefficient hierarchy and bureaucracy;
7   good global citizenship.

While these are aspirations that many companies would publicly support, in Dell's case they played an important role in sustaining the approach to customers and suppliers that underlay the success of its virtual organization.

The fact that Dell has in recent years lost ground to its competitors can be partially attributed to the company's emphasis on selling established technology at low prices based on the supply-chain efficiencies offered by its virtual system. This emphasis diverted attention away from innovation; Dell has invested a low percentage of its revenue on R&D compared to its major competitors. The company remained heavily dependent on the declining commoditized PC market and it made little inroad into more lucrative and fast-growing segments such as mobile devices. Moreover, its direct selling model was also approaching its limits as the market increasingly came to include categories of customer, such as older citizens, who preferred to purchase in a retail environment with the personal advice and support this offered. Dell now sells through retail outlets as well as online. Nevertheless, the achievements and benefits of the virtual organization that Dell created continue to offer instructive lessons for other companies to consider.

SUMMARY

1   A virtual organization might be considered as the ultimate new organizational form because it is not bound by the legal and physical structures that define a conventional organization.

2 It is a highly developed form of networked organization, comprising different individuals, units or companies that act in concert through an advanced level of coordination.

3 Although virtual organizations vary considerably, they have a number of common features:
   • lack of physical structure
   • reliance on information and communication technologies
   • mobile work
   • hybrid form
   • inclusiveness across boundaries
   • flexibility and responsiveness

4 Different forms of virtual organization are characterized by varying mixes of virtual and tangible assets and systems. The most comprehensively virtual organization has both assets and management systems that are highly virtual, as is the case of firms trading financial instruments and currencies.

5 The use of virtual organization offers potential benefits, including efficient coordination across time/space boundaries, a significant reduction in costs, a more flexible combination of activities, and a simplification of management.

6 Certain conditions are required for a virtual organization to be successful and the form has a number of limitations. It may, for example, have a limited capacity to promote innovation and to allow tacit knowledge to be shared.

7 A number of key questions therefore have to be asked about virtual organization: when to use it in preference to conventional forms of organization; whether virtual organization has to be managed in a different way; and how the virtual approach can be applied to teamwork.

8 The possibility of virtual teamwork on a global basis is attracting considerable interest. Research has uncovered some of the requirements for global virtual teams to operate successfully.

9 The Dell company was a pioneer of virtual integration and it gained benefits from applying many features of virtual organization to its global operations; it illuminates many of the issues covered in this chapter.

QUESTIONS FOR DISCUSSION

10.1 What are the key characteristics of virtual organization? How does it differ from conventional organization?

10.2 What kind of networks can be supported by virtual organization?

10.3 What are the potential economic benefits of a virtual organization?

10.4 Discuss the key considerations for management when deciding on the balance between organizing in a conventional and in a virtual manner?

10.5 What are likely to be the key differences between managing a conventional organization and a virtual organization?

10.6   In which ways can ICT support virtual organization and team-working?

10.7   What advantages can virtuality offer to the composition and working of teams?

10.8   With reference to Chapter 9, compare and contrast a virtual organization to an outsourcing organization.

NOTES

1   Malcolm Warner and Morgen Witzel (2004), *Managing in Virtual Organizations*, London, Thomson Learning. The quotation is from p. 18.

2   Bo Hedberg, Göran Dahlgren, Jörgen Hansson, and Nils- Göran Olve (1997), *Virtual Organizations and Beyond: Discover Imaginary Systems,* Chichester, Wiley. The quotation is from pp. 13–14.

3   Warner and Witzel (2004), op. cit., p. 18.

4   Laura A. Hambley, Thomas A. O'Neill, and Theresa J.B. Kline (2007), Virtual team leadership: Perspectives from the field, *International Journal of e-Collaboration*, 3, 40–64.

5   Michael Dell (2000), *Direct from Dell,* New York, HarperBusiness, p. 185.

6   Cisco Systems (2003), An introduction to NVO, *The Bridge*, issue 1, p. 5.

7   Thomas W. Malone and Robert J. Laubacher (1998), The dawn of the e-lance economy, *Harvard Business Review*, Sept–Oct, p. 148. Scott Channell (2013), Tomima Edmark – New invention? Perspectives on reaping maximum profits and protecting your idea in a Topsy Tail world, November 29. http://www.scottchannell.com/tomima-edmark-new-invention-perspectives-on-reaping-maximum-profits-and-protecting-your-idea-topsy-tail-hair-world, accessed December 17, 2013.

8   Warner and Witzel (2004), op. cit., The quotation is from p. 6.

9   Ibid., Chapters 8 and 10.

10   Max Boisot (1998), *Knowledge Assets: Securing Competitive Advantage in the Information Economy*, Oxford, Oxford University Press.

11   John Child, David Faulkner, and Stephen Tallman (2005), *Cooperative Strategy: Managing Alliances, Networks and Joint Ventures,* Oxford, Oxford University Press, p. 178.

12   Conor Friedersdorf (2013), A Question For *60 Minutes*: Why would China want to destroy the global economy? The CBS program implies that Asia's biggest country has the intention and ability to damage every computer on Earth, *The Atlantic*, December 16. http://www.theatlantic.com/International/Archive/2013/12/A-Question-For-Em-60-Minutes-Em-Why-Would-China-Want-To-Destroy-The-Global-Economy/282376, Accessed December 17, 2013.

13   Spirent (2011), *Cyber Security for Virtual and Cloud Environments,* August, Sunnyvale, CA, Spirent. http://www.toyo.co.jp/file/pdf/spirent/Cyber_security_for_virtual_and_cloud_environments.pdf, accessed December 17, 2013.

14   Paul R. Lawrence and Jay W. Lorsch (1967), *Organization and Environment*, Boston, MA, Harvard Business School Press.

15   Henry Mintzberg (1972), *The Nature of Managerial Work,* New York, Harper & Row.

16   Henri Fayol (1949), *General and Industrial Management*, London: Pitman (originally published in French in 1916). For a critique of POSDCORB based on observations of the behavior of CEOs, see Henry Mintzberg (1972), op. cit.

17   Mary Beth Fritz and Marvin L. Manheim (1999), Managing virtual work: A framework for managerial action. In Pascal Sieber and Joachim Griese (eds.) *Organizational Virtualness and Electronic Commerce*, Bern, Simowa Verlag, pp. 123–135.

18   For example, Charles Handy (1995), Trust and the virtual organization: How do you manage people whom you do not see? *Harvard Business Review*, 73, May–June, 40–50; Sirkka L.

Jarvenpaa and Thomas R. Shaw (1999), Global virtual teams: Integrating models of trust, in Pascal Sieber and Joachim Griese (eds.), op. cit., 35–52; Christopher P. Holland (1999), The importance of trust and business relationships in the formation of virtual organisations, in Pascal Sieber and Joachim Griese (eds.), op. cit., 53–64; Tanko Ishaya and Linda Macaulay (1999), The role of trust in virtual teams, in Pascal Sieber and Joachim Griese (eds.), op. cit., 135–151; Debmalya Mukherjee, Robert W. Renn, Ben L. Kedia, and Deepraj Mukherjee (2012), Development of interorganizational trust in virtual organizations: An integrative framework, *European Business Review*, 24, 255–271.

19   John Child, David Faulkner, and Stephen Tallman (2005), op. cit.

20   Society for Human Resource Management (2012), Virtual teams used most by global organizations, survey says. http://www.shrm.org/hrdisciplines/orgempdev/articles/pages/virtualteamsusedmostbyglobal organizations,surveysays.aspx, accessed December 20, 2013. The sample for this survey was 379 randomly selected HRM specialists from the SHRM's membership, working in both public and private firms, plus some government agencies.

21   Frank Siebdrat, Martin Hoegl, and Ernst Holger (2009), How to manage virtual teams, *MIT Sloan Management* Review, 50, 63–68.

22   Sean B. Eom and Choong Kwon Lee (1999), Virtual teams: An information age opportunity for mobilizing hidden manpower, *SAM Advanced Management Journal*, 64, 12–15, 25.

23   Ernest Keith Ferrazzi (2012), Virtual teams can outperform traditional teams. *Harvard Business Review Blog Network*, March 20. http://blogs.hbr.org/2012/03/how-virtual-teams-can-outperfo-2/, accessed December 20, 2013.

24   J. Lipnack and J. Stamps (1997), *Virtual Teams: Reaching Across Space, Time and Organization with Technology*, New York: Wiley.

25   Pete Engardio, Aaron Bernstein, and Manjeet Kripalani (2003), The new global job shift, *Business Week*, February 3, 36–46.

26   Mitzi M. Montoya-Weiss, Anne Massey, and Michael Song (2001), Getting it together: Temporal coordination and conflict management in global virtual teams, *Academy of Management Journal*, 44, 1251–1262.

27   Montoya-Weiss, Massey, and Song (2001), op. cit.

28   Martha L. Maznevski and Katherine M. Chudoba (2000), Bridging space over time: Global team dynamics and effectiveness, *Organization Science*, 11(5), 473–492.

29   Arvind Malhotra, Ann Majchrzak, and Benson Rosen (2007), Leading virtual teams, *Academy of Management Perspectives*, 21, 60–70; Angelika Zimmermann (2011), Interpersonal relationships in transnational, virtual teams: Towards a configurational perspective, *International Journal of Management Reviews*, 13, 59–78.

30   Angelika Zimmermann (2011), op. cit.

31   Tanko Ishaya and Linda Macaulay (1999), op. cit., 135–151.

32   Adapted from Ishaya and Macaulay (1999) op. cit., Table 2, p. 146.

33   Sources: Michael Dell (2000), op. cit.; Joan Magretta (1998), The power of virtual integration: An interview with Dell Computer's Michael Dell, *Harvard Business Review*, March–April, 73–84; Nic Hopkins (2003), Computer pioneer aims for yet another bull's-eye, *The Times*, June 6, p. 32; Leo de Castro, Volker Ossendoth, and Maria E. Patino (2003), Dell – a virtual organization, Unpublished MBA term paper, Birmingham Business School, February 27, 2003. The company's website is www.dell.com.

34   Nic Hopkins (2003), op. cit.

35   For an up-to-date summary and sources, see the "Dell" entry on Wikipedia.

36   Michael Dell (2000), op. cit., p. 102.

37   Trevor Miles (2013), Virtual vertical integration: the best of all worlds, *The 21st century supply chain*, August 20. http://blog.kinaxis.com/2013/08/virtual-vertical-integration-the-best-of-all-worlds, accessed April 24, 2014.

38 Joan Magretta (1998), op. cit., p. 74.

39 Paul Snell (2013), Virtual vertical integration is the future of supply chain. *Supply Management*, May 9, http://www.supplymanagement.com/news/2013/virtual-vertical-integration-is-the-future-of-supply-chain, accessed April 24, 2014.

40 Michael Dell (2000), op. cit., p. 177.

41 This paragraph and the one following are adapted from Leo de Castro et al. (2003), op. cit.

42 Joan Magretta (1998), op. cit., p. 75.

CHAPTER 11

Strategic Alliances

WHAT THIS CHAPTER COVERS

This chapter begins by defining a strategic alliance and indicating the growing importance of alliances in contemporary business. It then details the different forms that alliances can take in terms of their level of integration, legal and ownership status, and the partners' strategic intention in forming them. Due to their hybrid nature, alliances present special managerial and organizational challenges. Five of these are discussed: the design of alliances, the challenge of generating trust within them, conflicts in the role of alliance management, clashes between partner cultures, and the issue of partner control. The last section identifies three configurations found among joint ventures, each of which suits different circumstances and requires different arrangements to achieve good performance. These configurations are the surrogate subsidiary, the balanced partnership, and the junior partnership.

◢ What is a Strategic Alliance?

An "alliance" is any medium to long-term cooperative relationship between organizations, normally between firms. It excludes one-off or short-term contracts and other agreements that do not involve some joint working between firms over time. Alliances are often termed "strategic" because they are normally formed to help the partner firms realize their strategic objectives on the basis that this can be done better through cooperation than alone. Strategic alliances are therefore the normal agents for what has come to be known as "cooperative strategy."[1] For the sake of simplicity, we shall normally just refer to this organizational form as an "alliance."

◢ The Significance of Alliances

Alliances and other forms of inter-firm cooperation have grown remarkably since the mid-1980s. They are one of the more important new organizational forms. Despite the managerial and organizational challenges they undoubtedly present, there is no sign that alliances are a transient phenomenon. Given the very wide range of forms that alliances can take, it is impossible to obtain accurate figures as to their total numbers. However, despite the historic growth in those numbers, there is evidence that the rate of new alliance formation declined during the first decade of the 2000s and is far below that for new mergers and acquisitions (M&A).[2]

Alliances are, along with outsourcing and virtual value chains, one of the defining forms of modern networking among firms. They represent a clear break away from the internalized, hierarchical model of the firm, of which General Electric and IBM were salient examples as recently as the 1980s. Today, leading corporations such as these have as many as 1,000 alliances. In the past, such corporations might have regarded alliances as a relatively peripheral activity, primarily for entering emerging country markets in which risks were high or government regulations required joint ventures (JVs) or licensing agreements. Today, alliances are regarded as a means to achieving fundamental strategic objectives such as a strong market position, significant knowledge acquisition, and major cost reductions.

◢ Alliance Forms

Alliances take a wide range of different forms. These differ along several key dimensions:

1   the degree of organizational integration between the partners;
2   their legal and ownership form;
3   their primary strategic intention.

Organizational integration

The highest level of integration between previously separate firms is a merger between them or an acquisition of one firm by another. A merger is not strictly an alliance because its aim is normally to subsume the firms into one overall structure in which they lose their previously separate identities. In the case of an acquisition, the acquiring firm either seeks to integrate the acquired company into its structure or to run it as a subsidiary. Again, the outcome is not an alliance in the sense of firms working together as partners. Moving to the other end of the scale, there are alliances that are purely informal, based simply upon a handshake without any contractual foundation. Other relatively informal alliances include arrangements to exchange information or share distribution channels. JVs fall into the middle range of integration, between wholly integrated mergers and informal partnerships. They are the most common form of alliance.

Legal and ownership form

The legal and ownership form of JVs themselves can vary quite considerably. Some are based purely on contract and do not involve any joint equity. An example of this type is the "build, operate, transfer" partnership often used for infrastructure projects such as constructing toll roads. Here one partner provides the finance and technology to construct the facility and then operates it for a period of time, collecting fees or royalties, before it is handed over to the other partner. Another type of contractual alliance is the technology partnership, in which firms agree to work together and share knowledge on a joint research project. Such projects may be one-off or long-term. An example of the latter is the Open Handset Alliance, which comprises 84 firms that have come together to develop open standards for mobile devices using the Android platform. The members include mobile operators, software companies, commercial-ization companies, semiconductor companies and handset manufacturers. Many arrangements between smaller firms and their overseas agents also take the form of a contractual partnership.

Other JVs involve an exchange of equity between partners, or the establishment of an equity JV in which the partners each take an equity stake. These equity stakes can either be equal or unequal, which means that equity JVs can themselves range from 50/50 or other equal partnerships where one partner dominates through having a large majority equity share.

Figure 11.1 combines the dimensions of degree of integration and legal status to identify the alliance forms normally found in practice. It locates these within the wider range of possible inter-firm links. Purely contractual agreements include traditional and non-traditional forms. Traditional contracts between firms, such as buying and selling, franchising, and licensing contracts, would normally not be considered as alliances unless the contracts were long term and formed the basis of a continuing, cooperative relationship. This takes us into the area of non-traditional contracts, in which there is a degree of joint organization between firms, such as joint project teams. Non-traditional forms of contract, such as joint R&D projects, joint manufacturing, and joint distribution, are becoming increasingly common, especially as the means of locating firms on a continuing basis within global value chains. Non-traditional contracts can offer benefits such as synergies from pooling technical knowledge and economies from establishing a joint distribution system in a new market territory.

Consortia formed by a number of partners are another alliance form that does not usually involve the sharing of equity capital. The airline industry is now dominated by three consortia – the Star, Sky Team and One World Alliances. These typically started with focused collaboration in code-sharing, joint marketing and timetable rationalization for given routes. They have subsequently expanded their range of cooperation to include activities such as common IT systems, seamless transiting, shared airport lounges, joint procurement, and shared maintenance facilities. Despite being the largest of these alliances with 26 members at the time of writing (2014), the Star Alliance runs with a modest central coordinating structure based in Frankfurt. The effectiveness of this economical organizational form is greatly assisted by a high level of trust between the alliance members based on their acceptance of clear basic principles and good personal relations between the principal airline executives.[3]

Other forms of alliance involve the commitment of some equity capital by the partner firms. The degree of equity ownership tends to correspond to the intensity of integration between the alliance and the partners, and between the partners themselves. When the alliance simply involves a minority equity investment or an exchange of equity, without any new joint entity being established, the level of integration between the partners may be quite low – perhaps confined to joint projects, shared distribution arrangements in selected markets, and the exchange of information. The partners' equity investments in this case symbolize mutual goodwill and commitment rather than providing the capital for establishing a new operational unit.

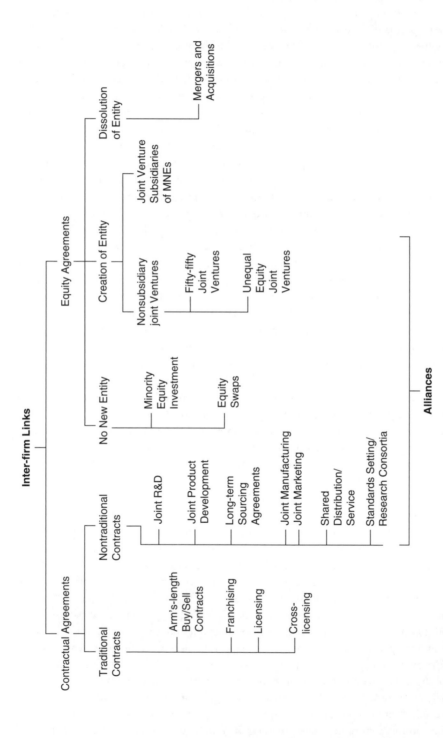

Figure 11.1 Alliance forms within the range of inter-firm links

Source: Michael Y. Yoshino and U. Srinivasa Rangan 1995. *Strategic Alliances: An Entrepreneurial Approach to Globalization.* Boston: Harvard Business School Press, p. 8.

Another form of equity arrangement involves the establishment of a JV. The JV could be quasi-independent of the parent companies or effectively a subsidiary of one of them, depending on the extent to which a single partner dominates the venture's ownership and management.[4] If the JV is run as a subsidiary of one firm, it is questionable whether this really amounts to a partnership between the equity owners. The third form of equity-based arrangement is the merger or acquisition. As already noted, this is not an alliance in the strict sense of the term.

Certain identifiable factors have emerged as predictors of the ownership form that will be adopted in strategic alliances. For example, a study of alliances formed by US companies found that they were more likely to take a substantial equity stake in those alliances when the objective of the collaboration was joint R&D, or in some cases joint marketing, when the partnership was with a non-US firm, and when the company's experience of managing alliances was limited.[5] Such research indicates a clear tendency to seek equity involvement in order to reduce perceived risks when entering an alliance.

Strategic intention

Another useful way of categorizing alliances is by reference to the strategic intention that partners have when forming them. Contractor and Lorange identify seven "more or less overlapping objectives" for alliance formation:[6]

1   *Reduction of risk:* Sharing the investment in a new venture can reduce the risk that a firm faces, especially if the partner has relevant local knowledge and connections.
2   *Achievement of economies of scale and/or rationalization:* Economies of scale may not be fully realizable through the production levels of a firm on its own.
3   *Technology exchange:* Given the high costs of R&D and the creative potential arising from synergy between the specialists from two or more collaborating firms, a technology alliance may offer cost and innovation benefits
4   *Pre-empting, countering or co-opting competition:* joining with other firms may enhance their market power.
5   *Overcoming government-mandated trade or investment barriers:* Governments in some emerging or transition economies require partnership with local firms as a condition for permitting trade or inward investment. This condition was reducing as more countries joined the World Trade Organization or signed bilateral investment treaties, but since the post-2008 financial crisis it has somewhat increased again in importance.
6   *Facilitate initial international expansion of inexperienced firms:* Alliances with a more internationally experienced firm can assist international expansion; many small and medium-sized firms internationalize as partners in the value chains of larger multinationals.
7   *Vertical quasi-integration advantages:* These can arise from linking the complementary contributions of partners in a value chain.

Dussauge and Garrette divide alliances into six distinct types based largely on the strategic purpose they are intended to fulfill. Three types are alliances between competing firms and the other three are between non-competing firms (Box 11.1).[7]

International expansion JVs are often established to overcome trade or investment barriers or facilitate initial international expansion to territories where risks are high, a firm has little

BOX 11.1 TYPES OF ALLIANCE

Partnerships between non-competing firms:
- International expansion JVs
- Vertical partnerships
- Cross-industry agreements

Alliances between competitors:
- Shared supply alliances
- Quasi-concentration alliances
- Complementary alliances

Source: Pierre Dussauge and Bernard Garrette. *Cooperative Strategy: Competing Successfully through Strategic Alliances.* Chichester: Wiley 1999, Chapter 4.

knowledge of local conditions, or where government regulations require partnerships with local companies. These reasons account for the fact that JVs predominated in the early period of foreign direct investment into China, whereas after 1997 wholly-owned subsidiaries became the most favored form.

Vertical partnerships are alliances between companies that operate at two successive stages within the same value chain. They are usually formed to achieve quasi-vertical integration advantages, to rationalize through specializing on core competencies, or to share new technology development costs. For example, Intel and Hewlett-Packard established a JV to design a new-generation microprocessor and the operating system to be built around it. In so doing, the two companies combined their complementary core competencies and also shared the considerable development costs.

Cross-industry agreements may combine complementary competencies, as well as assist diversification or pre-empt competition in a new field. For example, American Airlines (AA) and the French National Rail Company, SNCF, established a JV – ResaRail 2000 – to develop a new, computerized ticketing system for railway networks, applying technology that AA had pioneered for airline reservations. AA contributed its extensive experience and knowledge in computerized reservation systems, while SNCF contributed an in-depth understanding of railway services and users' needs. In another example, Philips and DuPont created a JV to combine the former's optical disk knowledge with the latter's chemical know-how to produce surface coatings for optical disks.

These three types of alliance are formed between non-competing firms, which generally makes it easier for the partners to develop a long-lasting cooperative relationship based on complementary interest and trust. The other three types of alliance identified by Dussauge and Garrette are between competing firms, the very fact of which might create serious tensions within the alliance relationship. The commercial benefits of such alliances must therefore clearly outweigh the risks involved.

Shared supply alliances are formed to achieve economies of scale and, often, to reduce risk by sharing R&D costs. An example is Butachimie, which was set up as a JV between two competing chemical companies – DuPont and Rhône-Poulenc – to supply both firms with a specialized intermediate chemical that they used for nylon production. Neither company was large enough in Europe to achieve the available production economies of scale on its own and this was especially significant given the high level of up-front capital investment required. Every one of the world's largest carmakers now has an alliance of some kind with another large auto producer.[8] Many of these alliances have been formed to develop and produce engines in order to share their high development costs, such as Peugeot with both Ford and BMW, and GM Europe with Fiat.

Quasi-concentration alliances may be established to co-opt or counter competition, as well as to reduce risk by sharing R&D costs. A highly successful and long-lasting alliance of this kind was Airbus Industrie, in which competing European airframe manufacturers came together to counter the competitive threat from US manufacturers, especially Boeing, and also to pool the enormously high R&D costs that characterize the industry. Airbus was reconstituted into a joint-stock company in 2001 following consolidations of European defense and aerospace companies.

Complementary alliances are usually formed to achieve potential synergies. Many of the alliances between biotechnology and pharmaceutical firms, as well as between pharmaceutical firms themselves, are of this kind. They are potential competitors who nevertheless seek to gain benefits from pooling complementary strengths such as the inventiveness of the small biotech firm and the financial, manufacturing, and marketing strengths of the large pharmaceutical firm. Paradoxically, the very complementarity between such different types of firm, with their contrasting approaches to organization and management, can result in serious problems that jeopardize their ability to work together.[9] Despite this, the number of alliances intended to promote knowledge sharing and joint technological development is today very substantial and they are often sponsored by governments.[10] An example is the UK's National Aerospace Technology Programme described in Box 11.2.

BOX 11.2 THE NATIONAL AEROSPACE TECHNOLOGY PROGRAMME

The Aerospace Growth Partnership (AGP) was formed in 2011. It is a collaboration between Government and industry working together to secure the future of UK Aerospace. The AGP has developed a National Aerospace Technology Programme (NATEP) aimed at aerospace supply chain companies including small and medium-sized suppliers to help them develop their own innovative technologies while enhancing their technology management capabilities, thus increasing their ability to win new business with higher tier companies anywhere in the world. NATEP is a £40m program over three years; its objective is to deliver 100 novel technologies through collaborative projects within the UK aerospace supply chain. By developing a supply chain with a high rate of innovation, rich in new technologies, it is expected that the UK will be better able to offer the right products and services, at the right time and ahead of competition. This should ensure that market opportunities are exploited with high value manufacturing work retained in the UK. NATEP is funded by the government's Advanced Manufacturing Supply Chain Initiative (AMSCI).

Source: https://www.adsgroup.org.uk/pages/40227907.asp, accessed 13 January 2014

◢ Organizational and Managerial Challenges Posed by Alliances

Alliances are a "hybrid" form of organization, in which staff seconded from, or appointed by, the different partners have to learn to work together.[11] If one partner dominates the alliance, it may be possible for that partner to manage it along the lines of a conventional unitary organization. If, however, the partnership is a relatively balanced one, to which the partners contribute equity and management in roughly equal measure, they have to find ways of reconciling their different structures, styles, and cultures of organizing.[12] This is not an easy task, especially if there is some conflict of interest or mistrust between the partners in which case each might be vying for control over the alliance or its critical functions.

So the potential benefits that alliances can offer might fail to materialize because of the organizational and management challenges generated by this hybrid form of organization. Many managers have stated to the author their view that, for this reason, alliances are their least-preferred organizational arrangement – to be avoided if at all possible. The majority of multinational enterprises (MNEs) seek to establish wholly-owned subsidiaries as an alternative to JVs or, if the latter are unavoidable, to aim for managerial control over them on the basis of a large majority equity share backed by clear contractual rights.[13]

In this section, I consider five particular challenges posed by alliances: their organizational design, the challenge of generating trust within an alliance, conflicts in the role of alliance management, clashes between partner cultures, and the issue of partner control.

The organizational design of alliances

Sascha Albers and his colleagues identify five key parameters in the organizational design of alliances.[14] These are familiar dimensions of organizational design and were discussed in Chapters 2 and 3. The first of these is the *interface* between alliance partners. Here the organizational design choice concerns the number and type of boundary spanners involved (people in the parent organizations who have some responsibility towards the alliance), the number of connections between them and the intensity of their interaction. On the whole a strong interface is likely to encourage better understanding, trust and learning between the partners and their respective staffs, although a very broad interface could complicate communications and even encourage conflicts for control. Examples of alliances that have benefitted from the design of strong interfaces are those between General Electric and SNECMA and between Renault and Nissan.[15]

The second design parameter is the *intraface* between the boundary spanners and non-boundary spanners in a partner's organization. This concerns the ties that link back into a partner's organization. They may take the form of a team whose work is oriented to the alliance but which has purely internal as well as boundary-spanner members. As Albers and his colleagues state, the intraface "is important for coordination between partners, since boundary spanners are often merely information conduits and relays who need other organizational members to plan, evaluate, and perform crucial activities for the alliance."[16]

The third parameter is *specialization*. This refers to the extent that alliance activities are differentiated from other activities within the partners' internal organizations. Specialization is high when there is a relatively high number of positions within a partner organization whose responsibilities are exclusively devoted to the alliance. The focus that specialization permits is likely to improve coordination with partners and the speedy recognition of problems arising in the alliance and it may foster the process of mutual learning though the alliance. While in the short run, greater specialization may increase alliance administrative costs, this may in the longer term be compensated by the benefits it offers.

Formalization is the fourth alliance organizational design parameter and refers to the specification and standardization of rules, plans, responsibilities and documentation related to alliance activity. In line with the conventional model of organization (see Chapter 2), formalization is often associated with specialization, the thinking being that the boundaries and duties of specialized roles need to be defined. For reasons discussed in Chapter 3, it is expected that formalization will assist alliance coordination and the ability of partners to cooperate, so long as conditions remain relatively stable but that it will probably inhibit fundamental "exploration" learning. Size also comes into the picture as a contingency. Formalization may become a necessity when coping with very large numbers of alliance partners such as licensees and independent software developers.

The fifth alliance organizational design parameter that Albers and colleagues identify is *centralization*. Centralization applied to an alliance can have two facets. One concerns the level in one or all partners at which decisions relevant to the alliance are taken. The second facet refers to the concentration versus dispersal of decision-making for the alliance. Concentration might take the form of a single alliance management board that makes most decisions or at least the key ones, whereas there would be dispersion when alliance-relevant decision-making is spread among a range of groups or functions. On the whole, centralization makes it easier to maintain consistency and coherence in decision-making. On the other hand, as in a unitary organization, a centralized regime can become overwhelmed by a large number of decision and coordination issues. It can also inhibit learning and experimentation partly by restricting employee initiative and partly because it limits the number and variety of contributions made to problem solving.

Achieving trust

As chapter 15 discusses in some detail, alliances have to rely on trust between the partners and their staff. Although they are mostly established on a contractual basis, they need to develop working arrangements and relationships that go far beyond the terms of contracts in order to perform successfully, let alone evolve progressively over time. The absence of trust will decrease the openness of communications and willingness to share resources between the partners and their staff in the alliance and waste management time in having to resolve misunderstandings and conflicts. It can lead to the eventual breakdown even of highly profitable alliances as happened with the TNK-BP alliance in Russia's oil sector (see Box 11.3).

The difficulty of resolving disputes between the partners in the TNK-BP alliance was increased by the fact that each held the same 50 percent share of its equity. This would seem to support the argument, discussed later in this chapter, that since ownership affords certain legal rights of control, possessing a majority equity share in a JV is essential to securing control over it. Others, however, have rightly pointed out that unduly emphasizing governance and control rights is likely to add to management costs and to demoralize partners and their staffs. For this reason, it is important not just to select an appropriate governance form for an alliance but also to manage it in such a way that the JV relationship gives rise to positive outcomes. It is here that trust makes a vital contribution.[17]

BOX 11.3   THE TNK-BP ALLIANCE—A BREAKDOWN OF TRUST

In 2003 BP formed a 50-50 joint venture (TNK-BP) with the Alpha Access Renova Company (AAR), run by four Russian billionaires. This alliance was Russia's third largest oil producer. Over the years to 2012, it was highly profitable and provided BP with over $19 billion in dividends. However, after a series of disputes leading to legal action by its partner, the governance of the joint venture had collapsed by 2012, with its board failing to meet and its CEO resigning. An earlier struggle in 2008 for control of the company had led to its then British CEO having to leave Russia after what BP called a campaign of harassment. There was a fundamental breakdown of trust between the partners.

Several factors contributed to the collapse of the TNK-BP alliance despite its inherent profitability. One was that the British and Russian partners had quite different conceptions of the role of managers and shareholders in the joint venture's corporate governance process. Also their strategic priorities did not coincide. The Russian partner was led by oligarchs who focused on short-term gains, whereas BP, as an experienced oil major, was more focused on long-term sustainable development. Cultural tensions arose in the process of governance because the Russian oligarchs were entrepreneurs whereas BP was a professionally managed bureaucracy. Another factor was the failure of the British partner fully to appreciate how the state and legal system in Russia tends to put national interest first. These strains compounded one another.

Matters were finally brought to a head by BP's attempt to strike an exploration deal with Rosneft, the Russian state oil giant, which broke one of the terms of the alliance agreement. This led to AAR taking legal action against BP. In October 2012, BP sold its stake in TNK-BP to Rosneft, receiving a combination of cash and 19 percent of Rosneft's shares. In March 2013, Rosneft completed its acquisition of the whole of TNK-BP.

Sources: various, including coverage by the Financial Times; BP and Rosneft: Unhappy families, The Economist, 20 October 2012, p. 63

Essential though it is to the success of an alliance, trust is nevertheless a fragile entity and can easily be threatened by a number of inherent sources of tension. If firms enter an alliance for only short-term gains and remain basically competitive, they can become as much concerned about not giving away benefits to their partner(s) than about working with them to mutual advantage. Chapter 14 describes how this has happened in situations where alliance partners are primarily concerned to use the alliance as an opportunity to secure technology or other knowledge from their partners rather than to share knowledge in order to innovate together or at least learn from each other. In an alliance relationship that remains fundamentally competitive, one partner cannot afford to allow another to gain too much of an advantage through the alliance. The conditions for this to happen, such as one partner establishing superior channels for information reporting from a JV, are likely to result in its gaining a dominant position within the alliance. One would therefore expect that the three types of alliance between competitors identified by Dussauge and Garrette to have more tensions and conflicts to resolve between the partners, who will therefore need to work harder at establishing mutual trust.

Managerial role conflict

The managers of JVs and other new units established by alliance partners can find themselves subject to conflicting pressures. This gives rise to a situation in which the manager is subject to conflicting priorities and pressures from different sources. Partner companies generally form alliances on the assumption that their objectives are sufficiently complementary to be achievable through a partnership. This does not, mean, however that their priorities for the alliance will be the same. For instance, one partner might seek short-term returns from the alliance whereas the other favors the reinvestment of surplus during the early years to strengthen the alliance's market position. This is commonly the case in JVs between partners from emerging and developed economies, with the former seeking more immediate returns because of their weaker financial position and less stable economic systems.

If each parent expects the general manager of a JV (JVGM) to pursue different priorities, this places that manager in a difficult position. Conflicts with the parent company can also arise through the JVGM seeking to develop the venture as a successful business in its own right. This will happen, for example, if the JV starts to compete with its parent companies in their existing markets.[18] As just noted, there can be disputes over whether to reinvest profits in a JV or distribute them to the parent companies. In addition, a JVGM has to deal with the pressures that normally face a chief executive coming from external stakeholders and various employee groups. If the JV's staff are seconded or appointed by its various parent companies, its GM may need to devote additional time to resolving conflicts within this mixed staff complement.

Incompatible expectations and pressures of this kind are likely to produce "role conflict" for a JVGM. Generally speaking, this conflict will tend to be more severe the greater the dissimilarity between the parent companies in their objectives, ownership forms, size, and cultures. The severity of role conflict may well be greatest when the alliance manager has to satisfy two equally strong parent companies that have different priorities. While experience, training, and level of education can all equip alliance managers to handle role conflict, it is nevertheless likely to result in negatives such as stress, dissatisfaction, inferior decision-making, and low productivity. Some role conflict is probably unavoidable due to the inherently hybrid nature of alliances, but it undoubtedly contributes to failure both in JVs and their GMs.

What can be done to mitigate this problem? If all that is done is to leave individual managers to cope, a number of non-functional behaviors might well result. They may be forced to buffer themselves against conflicting pressures by essentially saying different things to the different sources of pressure. They may keep on shifting their ground, "trimming their sails according to the wind," which can result in inconsistent decisions and policies that are very unsettling to the employees under them as well to the owning companies. They may prevaricate, so delaying the making of significant decisions. Or they may seek compromise, which often gives rise to a sub-optimum solution.

The constructive way out of the dilemma is likely to be a proactive approach. Research suggests that informal methods through which a JV's management can exert upward influence, such as persuasion and generating parental trust in alliance management, are the most effective.[19]

Other constructive proactive approaches include efforts by the JVGM to bring any role conflict out openly "onto the table" for discussion, requesting that parent companies clarify and reconcile the requirements they place on the alliance, and proposing constructive solutions that may serve to integrate those requirements. Pressures from parent companies may also reduce if the JV is sufficiently successful that it can stand on its own feet, no longer depending on them for resources and other assistance. As noted, the problem here is that some parent company managements fear that they may lose control over a JV that becomes too self-sufficient.

For their part, parent companies can take certain measures to minimize the role conflict that alliance GMs experience. These include:

1   Clarifying and backing the GM's authority;
2   Establishing special liaison positions to assist understanding and the development of a common policy approach toward the alliance, as well as to represent the alliance's own perspective. Such roles are sometimes known as "alliance guardians."[20]
3   Establishing clear mechanisms for resolving disputes between parent companies and/or other parties that are placing divergent pressures upon alliance management;
4   Creating processes for the wide dissemination of information and viewpoints within the alliance and its relevant network of parent companies, government agencies, suppliers, and so forth.

Clashes between partner cultures

Alliances require cooperation between partner firms that have their own different organizational cultures as well as their own interests. In the case of cross-border alliances, such as international JVs, differences in the partners' organizational cultures will be informed and, quite possibly, accentuated by differences in their national cultures. These cultural differences require careful management because otherwise they can generate misunderstanding leading to mistrust and a breakdown in the partnership. They were a contributory factor in the breakdown of the TNK–BP joint venture. For this reason, many consider it essential to assess the "cultural fit" between partners as part of the process of selecting an alliance partner.[21] The problem is that, for economic and strategic reasons, such as needing a local partner who can facilitate entry to a new market, it may not be possible to achieve a good cultural fit. If this is the case, then priority has to be given to ways of managing cultural differences. Although managers often regard cultural differences as barriers to effective cooperation, they have a potentially positive side as well. Culture is reflected in practices and an important part of a partner's contribution to an alliance lies in its unique "ways of doing," some of which other partners can adopt to advantage because they are more effective or better suited to the context in which the alliance is operating.

Culture has been defined in many different ways. Basically, it is a pattern of shared beliefs and values that provides people with norms of behavior and a common identity. Over time, cultures become embedded in various tangible forms. Norms become converted into social rules through the development of institutions such as legal systems and formal ceremonial. A society's culture is also expressed in its artifacts and technologies.

Similar dimensions can identify the culture of an organization such as a company. While there is always some variation in how people understand their national or regional cultures, there is likely to be even less agreement about what constitutes a company's culture.[22] This is because a firm is a pluralistic organization made up of groups or categories of people who differ by occupation, hierarchical level, and, quite possibly, nationality. In order to encourage some identification with the firm among these diverse groups, management often attempts to generate what is best called a "corporate culture" through, for example, mission statements, setting goals, training employees, encouraging certain norms and styles of behavior, and formalizing practices.

There are areas where cultural differences between alliance partners are likely to create particular difficulties for managing the alliance. These concern attitudes towards authority, relationships, uncertainty, and time. The following are some illustrations.

AUTHORITY

One of the problems most commonly voiced by western managers in alliances located in more traditional and emerging economies is that local staff are reluctant to take responsibility and exercise authority. This has been linked to a greater "power distance" between hierarchical levels in such societies – in other words, there is a greater deference to, and unwillingness to challenge, higher authority.[23] Alliances between large formalized and small informal companies can founder because their attitude and practices toward authority differ. For example, in the alliance between pharmaceutical giant Ciba-Geigy and small entrepreneurial AZ, managers from AZ would try to communicate directly with whomever in Ciba-Geigy's hierarchy seemed appropriate, regardless of formal authority level. This caused considerable resentment within Ciba-Geigy's management, adding to the mistrust that eventually aborted the alliance. In AZ's informal culture, people went directly to the appropriate person regardless of level; in Ciba-Geigy's formalized culture, people were expected to communicate with others at the same level.[24]

RELATIONSHIPS

Differences in cultural attitudes toward relationships often involve a tension between applying the same rules to everyone regardless of personal or friendship ties ("universalism") versus taking such ties into account ("particularism"). In an alliance between organizations that contrast greatly along the universalism/particularism dimension, it will be more difficult to establish the mutual trust on which a good relationship has to be based. This issue has impacted on the choice of recruitment and selection methods for JVs between MNEs and Chinese partners.[25] The former prefer standardized universal procedures, whereas the latter tend to see value in using family and similar connections.

UNCERTAINTY

Organizations and countries differ in the extent to which their cultures encourage people to avoid risk and uncertainty ("uncertainty avoidance.").[26] An organization with a risk-adverse culture is likely to emphasize control and certainty through establishing formal rules, not tolerating deviant ideas and behaviors, and rewarding its employees on the basis of career progression rather than performance-related pay. Although established companies frequently enter into alliances with entrepreneurial firms in an attempt to enhance their creativity and innovative capability, they may fail to achieve this objective if their culture scores highly on avoiding risk and uncertainty.

TIME

People's orientation toward time has long been noted as a fundamental dimension of cultural difference.[27] It can manifest itself at a surface level, when tension arises between alliance staff from different cultures because one group keeps strictly to time while the others do not. This can translate into a lack of trust if one party feels continually let down by the unreliability of the other, for example in meeting previously agreed deadlines. More fundamentally, corporate and national cultures can differ in the extent to which people adopt a long or short-term orientation. This can lead to basic disagreements within an alliance over policy decisions such as whether to pay out surpluses now or reinvest them for future development.

   If the potential damage that can result from cultural differences within alliances is recognized and measures are taken to address them, cultural diversity need not be a serious problem. The need is for those concerned to have an understanding and sensitivity toward cultural differences and respond flexibly and constructively. A case from my own research, summarized in Box 11.4 below, illustrates both the danger of cultural insensitivity and the possibility of avoiding it.

BOX 11.4 THE NEED FOR CULTURAL SENSITIVITY IN AN ALLIANCE

A joint venture between a Dutch multinational company and a Chinese partner almost collapsed because its first GM, a European with only limited international business experience, insisted on the introduction of practices from his parent company in an aggressive and culturally insensitive manner. Not only did he fail to consult his Chinese colleagues, he engaged in browbeating and shaming behavior in meetings with them, conduct that is particularly offensive to Chinese cultural norms. In this JV, the Chinese partners together held 60 percent of the equity and, through the majority this gave them on its board, were able to insist that the GM be replaced before relations broke down completely. His replacement, a Canadian with wide international business experience, was able to mend the relationship through adopting a much softer style that was culturally more acceptable to the Chinese. He consulted regularly with the Chinese deputy GM, especially before all senior management meetings. He also took care not to cause them public embarrassment (loss of face) in those meetings and brought Chinese managers much more into the process of communicating information to employees.

Source: Author's research

Control

Control is widely regarded as a critical issue for the successful management of alliances. There are, in fact, many firms that will not enter into an alliance unless they are assured of the right to manage them. This is true of alliances between multinational corporations and smaller, less experienced local firms, where the multinationals' managers with some justification claim superior technological know-how and managerial expertise. Control is regarded as a concern because the formation of an alliance requires each partner to share this, which introduces an element of uncertainty. Geringer and Hébert have expressed the issue quite graphically with reference to international JVs (IJV): "although each partner must, by definition, relinquish some control over an IJV's activities, such a move is often accompanied by great consternation."[28]

The way that an alliance is constituted and organized has clear implications for a partner's opportunities to exercise control over it. In the case of an equity JV, holding a majority equity share is normally reflected in a majority on its board of directors. This enables the partner to control the venture's policy and strategic decision-making, subject to a number of limitations. One limitation is that, under some countries' jurisdictions, a two-thirds majority on the board is required for certain key decisions and unanimity for vital decisions such as winding up the alliance. Another, more fundamental, limitation is that, if the rationale for forming the alliance is to secure the benefits of a cooperative partnership, these will be jeopardized if one partner tries to insist on forcing decisions through by right against the wishes of the other partner(s). A third limitation lies in the fact that strategic decisions need to be implemented. This means that a partner seeking overall control must also attend to the mechanisms and provisions that will provide it with operational control. Research has identified a number of these.[29]

The appointment of key alliance managers to take charge of critical functions can be an important means for a partner to secure operational control over an alliance. The partner may in fact decide to focus its control in the alliance onto certain areas, such as product technology, quality, and promotion in the interests of its international brand equity. Since senior appointments are often made by the board, possessing a majority equity share is the ultimate condition for securing this right to make them. Formal contractual agreements can be made that set out certain decision rights to a partner relating to issues of alliance management, including the management structure, key appointments, the management systems and practices to be used, and provision of training support. Moreover, contractual agreements can determine a partner's rights to the use of its technologies by the alliance.

Non-contractual methods can also improve a partner's control over an alliance's operations. For example, by providing HRM support for an alliance, a partner can shape selection procedures so as to ensure that people are hired who both have the required capabilities and will accept the alliance's culture and way of doing things. It can reinforce this acceptance through training and appraisal procedures. MNEs in particular are usually very interested in exporting their corporate cultures and practices to their alliances. This increases their control over them and enhances integration with the multinational's global network.[30] The offering of support in the form of practices and systems to an alliance increases a partner's influence over the operational areas concerned and is often done on a non-contractual basis.

There are a number of important informal methods that can enhance a partner's control over an alliance. One is the maintenance of regular, personal relations with the alliance's senior managers. I have often heard alliance managers complain that their influence with their parent company is undermined by the parent's apparent lack of interest in the alliance unit. Even if a partner only has a minority of seats on a JV board, the appointment of well-briefed, high quality, and experienced directors can considerably enhance their influence over important policy decisions. A great deal of additional influence can accrue to a partner if it shows an active interest in and support for its alliance, partly because of the impact of personal involvement and partly due to the goodwill and trust that this is likely to generate among the other partner(s). Another informal approach to control in joint ventures (and actually in all organizations) is social control, which inculcates norms and values through structured personal interaction, careful selection of staff and training.[31]

◢ Alliance Configurations

The variety of alliance forms suggests that there is no "one size fits all" solution to the way that alliances are organized. Different configurations of ownership, control, and management appear to be viable under different circumstances. Alternative alliance forms appear to suit prevailing contingencies.[32] My own detailed investigation of 20 equity JVs between Chinese and UK partner companies identified alternative configurations in the organization of equity JVs, each of which was capable of supporting satisfactory performance.[33] From the perspective of the UK (foreign) partners, these configurations could respectively be called the *surrogate subsidiary*, the *balanced partnership*, and the *junior partnership*.

The surrogate subsidiary

This configuration is based on one partner having a majority equity share. It is typically found in JVs where one partner (usually from a developed country) provides a large value of invested capital and/or an advanced proprietary technology to the venture. In such cases, the lack of capital and/or technology among the other partner enterprises limits them to a smaller equity share in projects. In contrast to the other two configurations, I found that partners having a majority equity share tend to be less insistent on contractual safeguards for other resources they provide such as brands and management systems, since they perceive they can determine the use of these inputs and secure a due return on them through their overall control of the JV. Their overall control is usually backed up with a heavy presence of expatriate managers and staff, especially as GMs and heads of the finance and technical functions.

Foreign partners having a majority equity share refer more decisions above the JV board to their corporate or regional levels than they do in the other two configurations. JV boards, which are the main channel for minority partner representation, assume a less substantial policy-making function in this configuration. Although the normal provisions for unanimity among JV directors on matters such as approval of JV business plans apply, most of the UK majority equity JVs I studied were in effect being run as subsidiaries.

The formative context of the surrogate subsidiary is distinctive. Most JVs in this category were established by MNEs with considerable international business experience. Western MNEs tend to favor having overall control, if not sole ownership, of affiliates. Japanese companies are somewhat less insistent on this point. The previous experience usually enjoyed by MNEs lends them additional confidence to manage new market entry without reliance on local partners. The granting of majority JV ownership became progressively easier in China as restrictions eased along with the dash for growth and foreign investment in the 1990s. At that time, MNEs were increasingly favored by the Chinese authorities as providers of foreign direct investment (FDI) because they were seen to have the most capital, advanced technology, and know-how to offer. In these respects, the surrogate subsidiary was representative of the growing numbers of MNEs entering China and other large emerging markets such as Brazil, with relatively large and capital-intensive projects.

A majority equity share is frequently recommended to alliance partners as a means of reducing the risk of control loss, securing unified management, and achieving consolidation among multiple partnerships. It does, however, run another risk: that of marginalizing and demotivating the local partner. It tends to limit the latter's contributions toward running the operation, providing relevant local knowledge, and facilitating network connections. The conventional advocacy of majority equity in effect looks to reduce complexity. It is prepared, if necessary, to sacrifice quality of partner relations for the perceived benefit of having policies carried out without argument or delay and according to the standardized procedures of the foreign parent organization. The downside is that if a local partner possesses valuable knowledge about the local market, about employment laws, or other aspects of the local context, then the risk of marginalizing that partner may destroy the JV management's ability to absorb and benefit from that knowledge.

There were two cases among the UK joint ventures I studied in China that were exceptions to this pattern. Importantly, they indicate that it is possible to combine having the final say in JV strategy-making that comes from majority equity with inclusion of the local partner in the decision-making process. Dominant equity share does not have to be used to run a surrogate subsidiary; it still allows for the option of running the JV as a partnership. Rather than trying to reduce complexity through unilateralism and standardization, this alternative policy allows for the local partner to contribute to a process of absorbing complexity and offering alternative options.[34] The quality of the partnership plays a more critical role in this variant of the majority equity configuration, a factor that was stressed by executives in both cases.

The balanced partnership

This configuration is based on an equal equity share among the partners, usually 50/50 between just two partners. This arrangement may be mandated by regulations applying to some sectors that prohibit non-domestic firms from acquiring majority joint venture owner-ship. It may also suit a situation in which both partners can make complementary contributions of similar value to the alliance. The joint ventures in which a balanced partnership is found generally have a low value of total capital invested in the JV, thus easing the possibilities for the local partner to match the foreign partner's contribution. Balanced partnerships are less likely than surrogate subsidiaries to have MNEs as their foreign parents.

To compensate for reduced income rights from equity and less control, the UK partners in this category tended to supply a wider range of non-capital resources on a fee-paying, contractual basis. Those offered without contract were generally confined to management services and training. Strategic and operational control of the joint venture was shared, though the foreign partner's influence normally prevailed in technical matters. There was a low incidence of expatriate managers. In this configuration, the quality of partner relations is particularly critical, and tensions between the partners will have more serious consequences than in the dominant share model. The balanced partnerships in which a strong trust-based relationship had developed between the partners and their staff benefited to the full from the partners' complementary strengths and they enjoyed a high level of success. Their success undoubtedly contributed to the further strengthening of the partnership. On the other hand, it was evident that when serious conflict arises within a balanced partnership, it is extremely difficult to resolve.

The junior partner

In this third configuration, the foreign partner holds a minority share of the joint venture's equity. This does not necessarily mean that the partner lacks significant influence. In each case studied, the UK company retained a degree of influence over strategic matters. Provision for unanimity in the JV board over decisions on its business plan and profit distribution undoubtedly worked toward enhancing the minority UK partner influence, but other factors were also significant. The fact that in each JV the UK partner provided the technological basis for both its products and processes was an important source of strategic influence, as well as providing for the dominant say in the technical aspects of operations.

Each of the JVs in which the international partner held a minority equity share either had a foreign GM or a manager designated by the international partner who regularly visited the JV. This provided an important means for the minority partner to exercise continuing influence in the JV. Another basis for such influence lay in the trust that it had developed with its local partner. This points to the important evolutionary aspect of inter-partner relationship building, which can generate a basis for sharing influence through mutual confidence in circumstances where contractual and other legal rights do not provide for formal control. With few expatriate managers allocated to minority-share JVs, however, the time and effort needed to build relations of this quality could impose a very heavy burden on the foreign managers concerned.

Most of the cases with foreign minority equity featured UK partners that did not have, or were unwilling to commit, the resources to assume a larger equity share. One of these investors had for many years preferred to benefit from international expansion through licensing its technology rather than through laying out capital. It had extended this philosophy to China. Others also preferred the lower-risk route of securing a significant part of their return from China through technology transfer rather than return on equity. Only in one case did Chinese regulations applying to a strategic industry determine its minority equity position, rather than the foreign investor's own preference.

Implications

The case studies throw light on the different requirements for achieving favorable JV performance in each configuration. Examination of the various configurations of ownership, resource, management, and control that were associated with satisfactory performance suggests that it is the *fit* between these factors that is particularly significant in this regard.[35]

For example, the best performers among the surrogate subsidiary joint ventures enjoyed considerable managerial and technical support from their UK parent companies and very active communications with those parents. At the same time, local managers were encouraged to play an active role in overseeing external activities to which they could contribute with their own particular knowledge, such as marketing and government relations. By contrast, the less well-performing surrogate subsidiaries were characterized by little local management contribution to these external activities. In two cases of relatively low-performing surrogate subsidiaries (one of which subsequently failed), the internationally branded products brought to China by the UK parent companies were too expensive to appeal to the local market. This was despite strong advice on this point from the local partner. The implication that arises from these contrasts is that, in surrogate subsidiaries, a combination of strong resource support with sensitivity to local conditions (both in terms of products and enlisting active local managerial contributions) will assist the achievement of good performance.

Another important implication of the case studies is that it is not possible to identify a single approach to the distribution of control in a joint venture that will be conducive to good performance.[36] It depends largely on the particular configuration. In a surrogate subsidiary where one partner has overall control, the trick appears to be to involve the other partner(s) in areas where it has special knowledge or connections. In a balanced partnership, a genuinely shared control and management approach based on a high level of personal communication and trust appears to be a necessary condition for good performance. The shared control may well involve a division of responsibilities between the partners according to their relative strengths.[37] In junior partnerships, where the international joint venture partner has minority ownership and control, good performance appears to be associated with continuing involvement by that partner in the alliance's overall management and the provision of necessary technical support. High mutual trust is an important condition for the minority partner to enjoy this level of involvement.

SUMMARY

1   Strategic alliances are an important form of boundary-crossing organization; they are part of the general move toward taking advantage of networking opportunities between firms.

2   Alliances take a wide variety of different forms, of which joint ventures (JVs) are the most common.

3   JVs present a number of organizational challenges and are not easy arrangements to manage.

4   If firms enter into a JV with short-term or exploitative aims, the venture may founder for lack of trust.

5   Even when partners have positive intentions toward their alliance, serious problems can arise around managerial priorities, the handling of cultural differences, and control.

6   JVs can be configured differently in terms of ownership, control, and management. Research suggests that the requirements for good performance vary according to which configuration is adopted.

QUESTIONS FOR DISCUSSION

11.1   What are the different forms that a strategic alliance can take?

11.2   What are the relative advantages and suitability of these different forms?

11.3   A strategic alliance has been called a "hybrid organization." In what ways is it a hybrid and what challenges stem from this?

11.4   How does a strategic alliance differ from an outsourcing arrangement?

11.5   What are the key motivations for forming alliances?

11.6   Discuss the relationship between alliance form and alliance performance.

NOTES

1   For further discussions of cooperative strategy and alliances see John Child, David Faulkner, and Stephen B. Tallman (2005), *Cooperative Strategy*, Oxford, Oxford University Press; Oded Shenkar and Jeffrey J. Reuer (eds.) (2006), *Handbook of Strategic Alliances*, Thousand Oaks, CA, Sage; Farok J. Contractor and Peter Lorange (2002) (eds.), *Cooperative Strategies and Alliances*. Oxford, Pergamon; J-L. Schaan and M.J. Kelly (2007), *Cases in Alliance Management*, London, Sage.

2   Ravi Madhavan (2011), A shift in the wind? Strategic alliances versus wholly owned units in global industries, in T.K. Das (ed.), *Strategic Alliances in a Globalizing World*, Charlotte, NC, Information Age Publishing, pp. 53–66.

3   Star Alliance (2014), *Facts and Figures*, March, http://www.staralliance.com/en/about/member_airlines/, accessed April 30, 2014; Interview with Jürgen Weber, Chairman of the Lufthansa supervisory board in *Lufthansa Magazin*, May 2007, pp. 32–43.

4   John Child (2002), A Configurational Analysis of International JVs Drawing upon Experience in China, *Organization Studies*, 23(5), 781–815.

5   Bing-Sheng Teng and T.K. Das (2011), Governance structure choice in strategic alliances, in T.K. Das (ed.), *Strategic Alliances in a Globalizing World*, Charlotte, NC, Information Age Publishing, pp. 93–115.

6   Farok J. Contractor and Peter Lorange (1998), Why should firms cooperate? The strategy and economics basis for cooperative ventures, in Farok J. Contractor and Peter Lorange (eds.), *Cooperative Strategies in International Business*, New York, Lexington Books, pp. 3–28.

7   Pierre Dussauge and Bernard Garrette (1999), *Cooperative Strategy: Competing Successfully through Strategic Alliances*, Chichester, Wiley.

8   Henry Foy (2013), Hybrid carmakers. *Financial Times*, December 11, p. 12.

9   See for example the alliance between Ciba-Geigy and AZ described in Yves L. Doz (1996), The evolution of cooperation in strategic alliances: Initial conditions or learning processes? *Strategic Management Journal*, 17, 55–83.

10   United Nations Conference on Trade and Development (UNCTAD) (2002), *Partnerships and Networking in Science and Technology for Development*, New York.

11   Bryan Boris and David B. Jemison (1989), Hybrid arrangements as strategic alliances: Theoretical issues in organizational combinations, *Academy of Management Review*, 14(2), 234–249.

12   J. Peter Killing (1983), *Strategies for Joint Venture Success*, New York, Praeger.

13   Stephen T. Rudman (2006), *The Multinational Corporation in China: Controlling Interests*, Chichester, Wiley-Blackwell.

14   Sascha Albers, Franz Wohlgezogen, and Edward J. Zajac (2013), Strategic alliance structures: An organization design perspective, *Journal of Management*, DOI: 10.1177/0149206313488209.

15   Yves L. Doz (1996), op. cit.; Piero Morosini (2006), Nurturing successful alliances across boundaries, in Oded Shenkar and Jeffrey J. Reuer (eds.), *Handbook of Strategic Alliances*, Thousand Oaks, Sage, Chapter 15, pp. 273–296.

16   Albers et al., op. cit., p. 14.

17   Anoop Madhok (2006), How much does ownership really matter? Equity and trust relations in joint venture relationships, *Journal of International Business Studies*, 37(1), 4–11.

18   For an example of this situation, see the case reported in Marjorie A. Lyles and Rhonda K. Reger (1993), Managing for Autonomy in JVs: A Longitudinal Study of Upward Influence, *Journal of Management Studies*, 30, 383–404.

19   Lyles and Reger (1993), op. cit.

20   See J.H. Dyer, P. Kale, and H. Singh (2001), How to make strategic alliances work, *MIT Sloan Management Review*, 42, 37–43.

21   John Child, David Faulkner, and Stephen Tallman (2005), op. cit., chapters 6 & 14.

22   Joanne Martin (1992), *Culture in Organizations*, New York, Oxford University Press.

23   For influential studies that have identified dimensions of culture, see Geert Hofstede (2001), *Culture's Consequences*, 2nd edition, Thousand Oaks, CA, Sage; Fons Trompenaars (1993), *Riding the Waves of Culture*, London, The Economist Books.

24   Yves Doz (1996), op. cit.

25   Yuan Lu and Ingmar Björkman (1997), HRM practices in China-western JVs: MNC standardization versus localization, *International Journal of Human Resource Management*, 8, 614–628.

26   Geert Hofstede (2001), op. cit.

27   F.R. Kluckhohn and F.L. Strodtbeck (1961), *Variations in Value Orientations*, New York, Row, Peterson.

28   J. Michael Geringer and Louis Hébert (1989), Control and performance of international JVs, *Journal of International Business Studies*, 20, 235–254. Quotation is from p. 236.

29   For further details see Jean-Louis Schaan (1988), How to control a JV even as a minority partner, *Journal of General Management*, 14, 4–16; John Child, and Yanni Yan (1999), Investment and control in international JVs: The case of China, *Journal of World Business*, 34, 3–15; Chang-Bum Choi and Paul W. Beamish (2004), Split Management Control and International Joint Venture Performance, *Journal of International Business Studies*, 35, 201–215.

30   Stephen T. Rudman (2006), *The Multinational Corporation in China: Controlling Interests*. Oxford, Blackwell. A good illustrative case study is *The Wuhan Erie Polymers Joint Venture (version A)*. London, Ontario: Richard Ivey School of Business, reference: 9B03C002.

31   Gerald E. Fryxell, Robert S. Dooley, and Maria Vryza (2002), After the Ink Dries: The Interaction of Trust and Control in US-based International Joint Ventures, *Journal of Management Studies*, 39, 865–886.

32   John Child, David Faulkner, and Stephen Tallman (2005), op. cit.; Anupama Phene and Stephen Tallman (2012), Complexity, context and governance in biotechnology alliances, *Journal of International Business Studies*, 43(1), 61–83.

33   John Child 2002 op. cit.

34   Max Boisot and John Child (1999), Organizations as adaptive systems in complex environments: the case of China, *Organization Science*, 10, 237–252.

35   For an overview of the many factors that can contribute to JV performance see Jeppe Christoffersen (2013), A Review of Antecedents of International Strategic Alliance Performance: Synthesized Evidence and New Directions for Core Constructs, *International Journal of Management Reviews*, 15(1), 66–85.

36   A point also made by Louis Hébert and Paul W. Beamish (1997), Characteristics of Canada-based international joint ventures, in Paul W. Beamish and J. Peter Killing (eds.), *Cooperative Strategies: North American Perspectives,* San Francisco, New Lexington Press, pp. 403–427.

37   The research reported by Chang-Bum Choi and Paul W. Beamish (2004) concluded that a division of areas of control between the partners according to their relative strengths was the approach most conducive to good JV performance. See note 29.

CHAPTER 12

Organizing Across Borders

WHAT THIS CHAPTER COVERS

This chapter focuses primarily on the organization of multinational enterprises (MNEs), which are firms comprising parent companies and foreign affiliates with operations in more than one country. They are both the product of globalization and one of its principal drivers. The chapter begins by examining globalization and the significance of MNEs. It then considers four main strategies that MNEs adopt for international expansion in the light of their requirements for global integration as against their need to be responsive to local situations. The four strategies are the multi-domestic, international, global, and transnational. Each of these strategies implies a different organizational configuration and approach to cross-border integration in terms of the balance between standardization and flexibility.

Despite these differences, their geographical spread and multi-level composition (headquarters and subsidiaries) mean that all MNEs to some degree face similar organizational challenges in regard to control, managing integrative processes, managing cultural diversity, and the cross-border transfer of knowledge and practices. Challenges such as these have encouraged both researchers and practicing MNE executives to propose new organizational forms. The last section of this chapter looks at the different case of internationalizing small and medium-sized enterprises (SMEs).

◢ Globalization and the Significance of MNEs

As noted in Chapter 3, there is considerable debate about both the meaning and extent of globalization. Some question whether globalization has been accorded too much emphasis. It is pointed out for instance that, in terms of trade, the world economy was actually more open and integrated in the 50 years prior to the First World War than it is today.[1] Further caution is urged by those who argue that the cross-border economic integration that is taking place is within regional blocs such as the European Union and NAFTA rather than on a truly global basis.[2]

There is, however, a crucial difference between the world economic integration of the mid-nineteenth century and that of today. The interconnections are now of a different kind. It is important to make a distinction here between two forms of integration, which may respectively be called "internationalization" and "globalization." Internationalization was as great before 1914 as today, but took the form of shallow integration: primarily arms-length trade between firms and movements of portfolio capital. Globalization processes, by contrast, bring in a new form of transnational economic activity. This is organized primarily within the value chain networks of MNEs and amounts to a deeper form of integration.

An increasing number of transactions are taking place between the internationally distributed units of MNEs. The growth of such units results from a considerable increase in the amount of direct investment undertaken by MNEs in foreign locations (foreign direct investment or FDI). This has brought the organization of cross-border interactions within MNEs into prominence. We shall see that difficult issues of both control and coordination arise. As a former CEO of Procter and Gamble told the author, "This is the biggest single challenge we face today."

There are conflicting definitions of what constitutes an MNE.[3] There is also some confusion of terminology in this area because, while most people speak of multinational enterprises, the term "transnational corporation" (TNC) is preferred by some authorities including the influential United Nations Conference on Trade and Development (UNCTAD).[4] Since the term "transnational" is also applied to a specific MNE strategy and mode of organization discussed later in this chapter, we shall refer to MNEs throughout in order to minimize confusion. Where some sources refer to TNCs, I have followed their terminology, but please translate to MNEs!

UNCTAD states that "a transnational corporation (TNC) is generally regarded as an enterprise comprising entities in more than one country which operate under a system of decision-making that permits coherent policies and a common strategy."[5] Normally, these are firms comprising parent companies and foreign affiliates, where affiliates may be subsidiaries, branches, or joint ventures. They have production or service-providing facilities in two or more countries, or at least have the power to control and coordinate operations in more than one country.[6] In addition, they may have worldwide sourcing and/or distribution networks. Another approach is not to apply an absolute criterion of whether a firm is an MNE or not, but instead to assess the degree of its "transnationality" in terms of indicators such as the proportion of its foreign assets to total assets, foreign sales to total sales, and foreign employment to total employment.

Dicken states with authority that MNEs have come to be regarded as "the primary movers and shapers of the global economy" more than any other single institution.[7] The facts bear out their massive economic importance. It is estimated that in 2009 there were 82,053 MNEs in the world with 807,363 affiliates.[8] By 2012 these affiliates accounted for 72 million jobs. In the same year, the foreign affiliates of MNEs generated sales worth $26 trillion, of which $7.5. trillion were for exports. These sales were 36 percent of world GDP.[9] However, the ways in which multinational business is organized have become more diverse. MNEs appear to be controlling a rising share of their foreign production through contracts rather than direct ownership which is consistent with a continuing rise in outsourcing and networked value chains. There are many more non-equity arrangements with independent firms, such as long-term customer-supplier relationships within international value chains, than there are equity-based arrangements. MNEs are also significant for the international standards that they set. The productivity of their foreign affiliates is generally higher than that of domestic firms in their host countries, with MNEs being regarded as sources of valuable advanced technology and management expertise by most emerging economies. They undertake the overwhelming amount of R&D effort in the world, with around 70 percent of international royalties on technology being accounted for by MNE parents and their foreign affiliates. Many MNEs today are of US origin, though there is also quite a large spread of countries of origin among the top 1,000. While many of the largest are headquartered in developed economies, such as Exxon Mobil in the USA and Volkswagen in Germany, there is also an increasing number of MNE from the emerging economies such as Brazil, China, and India. Moreover, it would be misleading to assume that all multinationals are large companies. For example, it was estimated that back in 1996 small- and medium-sized enterprises (SMEs), employing less than 500 people, comprised 80 percent of Swedish MNEs and 60 percent of Italian MNEs. SMEs are themselves internationalizing and playing an increasingly important role within networks of production across borders.[10]

Strategies for Global Expansion

Even within the same firm, potential economies of scale and standardization or other advantages of globalization often coexist with certain needs for localization. Whereas globalization refers to features such as the production of standard goods or services for a worldwide market and the global integration of a firm's activities, localization refers to features such as the provision of products tailored specifically for a regional or national market, or the adoption of local management practices. Local knowledge, not just of markets but also of cultures and institutions, is of strategic value and will speak for local adaptations. These two forces are often referred to respectively as pressures for global integration and pressures for local responsiveness.

Globalization can offer opportunities for a firm to benefit from economies of scale by opening up new markets. The more powerful its brands or reputation, the more readily they should appeal to new markets, unless those markets are subject to strong local specificities that reduce the attraction of internationally standardized products. In turn, having global product reach enhances the strength of brands. Firms providing inputs to globalizing customers, such as components or services like advertising, generally have to expand in parallel if they are to retain those accounts. Such accounts may be under threat anyway because, on the supply side, the global extension of a firm's value chain can allow it to access new, lower cost or superior quality inputs and hence optimize its sourcing of components, materials, support services, and innovation. Given the competitive importance of innovation today, a firm is also under pressure to exploit global sources of learning rather than rely purely on domestic capabilities. If factors like these apply and competitors are responding to them, a failure to globalize will soon lose a firm its competitive advantage.

It is not always possible for an MNE to create value by directly transferring its core competences to foreign countries. Some modification is usually required to suit local market preferences and adjust to the characteristics of local employees. Consumers in different countries may well demand different qualities from a given product, even highly standardized ones promoted through a global brand and worldwide advertising. The manufacturers of cola drinks, for example, add extra sugar to suit Chinese tastes, and McDonalds had a difficult time penetrating the South African market until it increased the size of its burgers to meet local expectations. These, however, are cases of relatively minor product modifications to strong global brands. In sectors where local tastes are heavily biased toward traditional indigenous products, the ability of firms to pursue a global product strategy will be limited. Similarly, some firms establishing production in developing countries have found it problematic to apply the work organization they use in their domestic plants, because of different skill levels and ingrained local working habits. In general, then, the greater the differences between countries in which an MNE is active, the greater will be the pressures for local responsiveness or differentiation.

There are a number of distinctive strategies that MNEs can pursue for global expansion in the light of the potential conflict between integration and differentiation. Table 12.1 indicates that four basic strategies for global expansion arise according to different combinations of pressure for globalization and localization respectively. In practice, MNEs may combine these strategies according to the circumstances of their different product or service divisions. They may also vary them according to the match between the internal competence of a subsidiary and the strategic importance of its local environment, which can give rise to a highly complex variant of the transnational approach discussed below.[11] It is useful to consider this strategic framework as significant organizational implications follow from it.

When the pressures for localization outweigh those for global integration or standardization, a *multi-domestic strategy* is likely to be pursued. This strategy is based on responsiveness to local markets. It aims to maximize the advantages of local differentiation in products, services, and production. Products, and the way they are marketed and distributed, are customized to suit the local market, and such customization is likely to be a strong selling point. Either there will be few significant economies of scale in producing such goods and services, or these can be realized within the scope of a local market. It is likely therefore that production will also take place in national or regional locations. Some of these localized products may be traditional in nature and require very little development over time, with the development that is required being carried out locally as well. A company pursuing this strategy transfers its core competences to its foreign divisions and decentralizes strategic control to them, treating them as relatively self-contained businesses that coordinate their own value-creating activities. It does not therefore look to benefit significantly from sharing facilities or knowledge between them. The multi-agency conglomerates in the advertising industry by and large pursue a multi-domestic strategy as does the international convenience store chain 7-Eleven mainly using a franchising model.

In cases where pressures for localization and global integration are both low, MNEs are likely to adopt an *international strategy*. This strategy is based on leadership from the home country. Firms in this situation face low pressures to customize their products or services to

Table 12.1 Four strategies for global expansion[12]

	Pressures for Global Integration	
	(Value creation activities are coordinated on a country-by-country basis)	*(Value creation activities are coordinated simultaneously on a global and a country basis)*
	Low	**High**
High *(Products and approaches are highly customized for each local market)*	(Goal of strategy is local differentiation advantage) **Multidomestic Strategy** (Organizational costs are lowest)	(Goal of strategy is both differentiation and low-cost advantage) **Transnational Strategy** (Organizational costs are highest)
Low *(The same standardized products are offered to customers in all countries)*	(Goal of strategy is global differentiation advantage) **International Strategy** (Organizational costs are low)	(Goal of strategy is low-cost advantage) **Global Strategy** (Organizational costs are high)

(Left vertical axis label: **Pressures for Local Responsiveness**)

local markets, so they can offer basically the same products to customers in all countries with only slight adaptations to suit local preferences. At the same time, they do not see any particular advantage in coordinating their activities simultaneously on a worldwide basis. They are not, for example, using global value chains to produce their standardized products and they do not benefit from significant economies through concentrating their production and coordinating it centrally. Firms like Coca-Cola, PepsiCo, McDonalds, and Toys "R" Us all pursue an international strategy. Pilkington Glass also adopted this strategy for many years in respect of its proprietary technology for producing float glass, which is used extensively in building construction. Pilkington pursued a policy of licensing this technology to local producers in foreign countries rather than investing in new plants that it would have to fund and manage itself. It obtained revenues through license fees normally related to value of sales, rather than from a return on direct foreign investment. Through this strategy, much the same standard product was offered to customers in different countries, but the company did not have to bear the costs of coordinating its production.

One of the limitations of an international strategy is that it does not strive to gain benefits from either local responsiveness or global coordination, although it offers some economies from having centralized R&D and standardized management systems. It has therefore become increasingly replaced by two other strategies that add to the value MNEs can create through their international scope.

In recent years, a growing number of MNEs have adopted a *global strategy* following the example of Japanese corporations such as Toyota, Sony, and Matsushita. This strategy is to manufacture standard products at a few low-cost locations, which are then marketed globally. There is at most only limited, local customization. Product standardization allows for significant global economies of scale, and the resulting lower unit costs can translate into highly competitive prices. When low price is accompanied by high and consistent quality, maintained uniformly across the globe, a firm has a very strong competitive advantage. A global strategy has been adopted in the production of automobiles, cameras, computers, and electrical goods. It sacrifices some potential advantages of differentiation in favor of high value-for-money products, where these are likely to appeal to most customers the world over. With a global strategy, a company locates value-creating activities in countries that can offer a cost advantage and uses a global network to source inputs – usually through long-term contracts – from whichever supplier can offer the lowest costs. The pressures on such suppliers continually to reduce costs can be intense.

Increasing international competitiveness is forcing many companies to aim simultaneously for the advantages of low cost *and* differentiation strategies. To rely solely on cost advantages is perilous in the face of new competitors from major emerging economies like China, who can combine lower costs with internationally acceptable product design and quality. The growing competitive challenge to the automobile and electronics industries in western countries is a case in point. The appeal of more sophisticated products is necessary. Equally, it is perilous to rely on differentiation advantages alone, when competitors are combining increasingly appealing products or services with the low cost benefits gained from a global strategy. Some European automobile producers have come under severe pressure for this reason.

A *transnational strategy* has therefore been recommended in order to obtain benefits from globalization and localization simultaneously: in other words, to achieve the advantages both of a global strategy and a multi-domestic strategy.[12] This strategy endeavors to balance scale with responsiveness and learning. On the one hand, a global scope and the coordination of capabilities and resources can offer significant cost benefits. On the other hand, the decentralization of relevant competences to local markets can help to provide differentiation advantages that suit those markets, as well as encouraging learning and innovation at the subsidiary level. The health care products multinational Johnson & Johnson provides an example of the transnational approach which is increasingly becoming the norm among large diversified MNEs. Gareth Jones describes the requirements to pursue a transnational strategy as follows:

> "First, the transnational organization must transfer core competences to the countries where they can be used most successfully to create value from both low costs and a differentiated appeal. Next, the organization creates a global network to provide the coordination that will allow domestic and foreign divisions to share skills and resources to improve their core competences. Each foreign division is expected to build on and develop the skills and resources it receives from the other divisions and to transfer enhanced products and processes to the other divisions. The goal of a transnational strategy is to develop a core competence in the global coordination of organizational resources between divisions throughout the world. In this way, the organization's products have a differentiated appeal, a low cost, and high quality. Unlike a company with a purely global strategy

Table 12.2 Factors affecting the balance between global and local organization in different activity areas

Activity area	Factors favoring global organization	Factors favoring local organization
Marketing	Homogeneity of taste, appeal of global brand, intrinsically standardized nature of product (e.g. chemicals)	Taste is culture specific (e.g. some foods), strong local brands, personalized service required
Operations (location)	Significant economies of scale; product has high value/transport costs, and/or low perishability (e.g. microprocessors)	Limited economies of scale, low value/ transport costs, and/or scale economies can be achieved locally (e.g. industrial gases)
Operations (methods)	Need for global standardization due to quality requirements (e.g. drugs)	Operational methods can be adjusted to local skill levels to take advantage of varying labor costs (e.g. garment manufacture)
R&D	Product development requires high level and intensely coordinated research activity (e.g. advanced ICT systems)	Lower level knowledge is used, relating to locally relevant extrinsic product characteristics (e.g. color) rather than intrinsic design
HRM (policies)	Standardization of product or service and production methods requires common HRM policies; benefits of inter-regional mobility of higher level staff require HRM standardization; firm's global reputation also requires HRM standardization, especially on personal rights and ethical aspects	Variations in culture and education/skill levels require local adaptation of HRM policies

that delivers a standardized product to customers in all countries, a company pursuing a transnational strategy has to act like a multi-domestic company and customize its products to meet the needs of global customers and, thus, increase demand for its products. Customizing requires a transnational company to locate value-creating activities such as manufacturing and marketing in almost every country or world region in which it operates . . ."[13]

The transnational strategy approach also takes account of the fact that the balance between global integration and local responsiveness can vary according to the requirements of different activity areas with a firm. Table 12.2 lists the factors that affect this balance. The need to allow for, and yet reconcile, internal organizational differentiation of this kind can pose a major challenge in terms of maintaining organizational balance and integration for a large MNE that is diversified both in terms of product businesses and geographical scope.

Ghoshal and Bartlett illustrate this challenge of reconciling simultaneous needs for global coordination and integration and for national differentiation and responsiveness with reference to Unilever.[14] Figure 12.1 reproduces their graphical representation of how these needs vary across Unilever's different businesses, functions, and tasks.

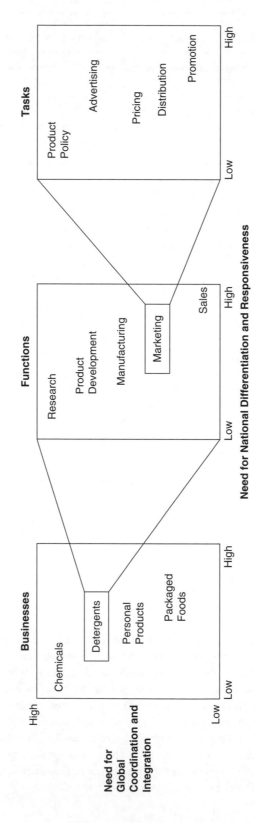

Figure 12.1 Integration and differentiation needs at Uniliver.[15]

Within Unilever's range of businesses, chemicals are highly standardized products that have considerable production economies of scale and little variation in local market requirements. A high level of global coordination and integration between economic production sites, suppliers, and markets therefore pays dividends, as does a centralized R&D activity. By contrast, packaged foods are subject to important differences in local tastes and cultures. Their processing does not offer very significant economies of scale and it is also appropriate to conduct most of their product development locally. Detergents occupy an intermediate position, because they can benefit from the innovations generated by a central R&D activity, whereas sales, distribution, and promotional tasks are better decentralized to suit different markets. Similarly, some functions can better be conducted globally, such as R&D, whereas others like sales need to be locally responsive. Even within the marketing function, there is some differentiation of needs, with product policy being best coordinated globally and product promotion best managed locally to suit national and cultural norms.

Given the mixture of global integration and local responsiveness needs across its various businesses, functions, and tasks, Unilever was obliged to move toward a transnational approach, primarily due to competitive pressure from Procter & Gamble, which by 1990 had reorganized its activities to pursue a transnational strategy. Unilever, however, continued to fall behind P&G's performance in terms of profitability, one of the reasons being the considerable difficulty it has faced in achieving the organizational and managerial requirements to support a transnational strategy. Although each of the four strategies mentioned has its own implications for organizational structure, it has become evident that the complexity of interactions and multidirectional communications required by a transnational strategy has to rely primarily on the management of organizational processes and cultures rather than on structures. This is, of course, in keeping with the general thrust of new approaches to organizing.

◢ Organizational Implications of Different Strategies

A *multi-domestic* strategy is organizationally the least demanding and least costly. The structure that suits this strategy is a global geographic one in which country or region-based divisions replicate and contain all the company's domestic value-creating activities, adapting these to suit their local situations (see Figure 12.2). The divisions may also market local brands, perhaps acquired through purchase of a local firm. Because the divisions operate in a relative self-contained manner, the need for integrating mechanisms between the corporate headquarters and divisions, and between the divisions themselves, is low. The divisions can operate satisfactorily with many strategic decisions delegated to them and the company can manage with a relatively flat hierarchy. The combination of a flat hierarchy and low integration requirements saves on managerial costs. The downside is that this structure does not facilitate the international exchange of information and learning between the divisions; the company may therefore choose to take specific measures to promote this, such as regular inter-divisional conferences.

An *international* strategy imposes greater need for coordination insofar as a company's core competences, such as R&D and quality assurance, are centralized, whereas other functions are decentralized. If the company is highly focused on a single product category, it may structure itself according to geographical divisions; otherwise, a global product structure can be adopted (see Figure 12.3). The foreign divisions tend to manufacture and market their products

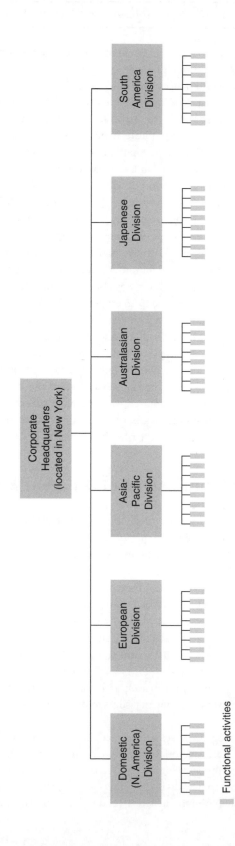

Figure 12.2 Global geographic structure

■ Functional activities

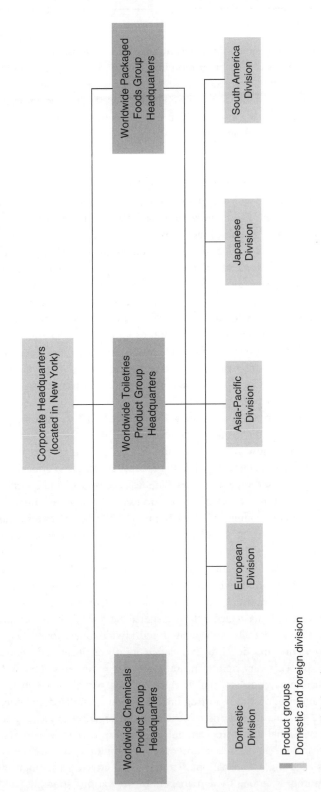

Figure 12.3 Global product group structure

according to technologies and policies developed by the parent company. Because of the mix of centralized core competences and decentralized operations, this strategy requires a taller hierarchy and imposes higher integration needs than in the case of a multi-domestic strategy. Its organizational costs are correspondingly greater.

A *global* strategy is intended to realize economies of scale and location, offering standard products of high quality at a low cost. There is relatively little local customization of products. A global product structure often suits this strategy, in which the resource requirements for standardized products, or groups of products, are decided centrally with a global focus. This arrangement can encourage the rationalization of production across the world and also concentrate resources for product innovation. It therefore requires a reasonably high level of centralized coordination, with a high level of supply chain integration based on IT systems and management networks. The manufacturers of consumer electronics and most automobile manufacturers pursue a global strategy, and the Dell model of virtual integration described in Chapter 10 is an example of a highly-integrated supply chain supporting that strategy.

Centralized coordination also tends to lengthen managerial hierarchies. This combination of relatively high integration needs and a tall hierarchy results in high organizational costs. Furthermore, if a company has several product divisions operating in the same territory, this structure provides for only limited local coordination between them. There can be negative consequences. In a country like China, for example, government agencies can intervene directly in business decisions through their power to withhold licenses and other measures. These agencies can resent having to deal separately with different divisions of the same company. Opportunities for global learning between divisions can also be inhibited by a global product divisional structure.

The *transnational* strategy is organizationally the most demanding and costly of all. It attempts to combine the benefits of learning from local units and encouraging local responsiveness with those of centralization in configuring global value chains, supplying key competences, and maintaining global corporate standards in critical areas such as product quality and socially responsible practices. The tasks of control and coordination become very challenging in a system of relatively autonomous yet interdependent subsidiaries which develop their own core competences and approaches to local markets. The transnational firm has to have the ability to be simultaneously "loose and tight" in combining a capacity for flexibility and learning with one to exploit the advantages of global scale and reach.

A transnational strategy requires a relatively flat hierarchy so as to enable managers in charge of centrally coordinated activities to respond quickly to new local needs and new information arising from decentralized national or regional units. It has a very high need to integrate the contributions made by these dispersed and specialized, but quasi-interdependent, units to the firm's centrally coordinated worldwide operations. The transnational firm endeavors to secure and develop knowledge jointly at local and central levels; this joint approach also presents very significant integration requirements. The preferred structure for meeting these requirements is usually a relatively flat, global matrix structure that establishes multiple communication and reporting lines between centralized and decentralized activities (see Figure 12.4). The intention is to structure the organization as a managed network.

A multidimensional structure can only go so far toward encouraging a transnational company's managers to take account of all its multiple requirements. For this reason, many MNEs adopting a transnational strategy also attach great importance to developing a personal awareness among their managers of the various strategic considerations that are

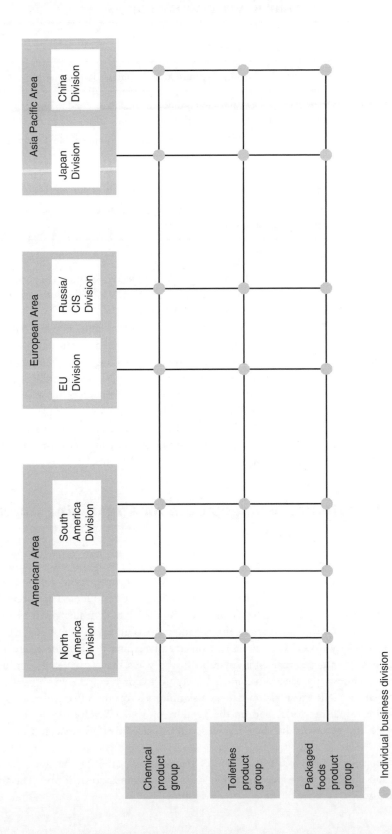

Figure 12.4 Global matrix structure

● Individual business division

Table 12.3   Organizational fit among more successful MNEs

Strategy	Organizational Configuration
Multi-domestic	*"Differentiated fit."* Organization is differentiated to respond to needs of local environments. Limited overall structural integration.
International	*"Ad hoc variation."* Little differentiation between locations. The limited integration required can be carried out centrally.
Global	*"Structural uniformity."* Little differentiation between locations. Common company-wide integrative structure and uniformity of practice.
Transnational	*"Integrated variety."* Structure of requisite local differentiation overlaid with strong company-wide integrative mechanism.

being taken into account. This means broadening their perspective over and beyond that of the unit or division in which they are located to take in one that is global as well as specialized, thereby creating what has been called "a matrix in the mind."[15]

There is some evidence to show that there are performance benefits when MNEs adjust their organization to their overall strategy in the ways just described. For instance, a study of 41 MNEs conducted by Sumantra Ghoshal and Nitin Nohria compared their organizational profiles with the environmental contingencies arising from the distinctive strategies they were following. The study provides suggestive evidence that those firms adopting an organizational profile predicted to "fit" their strategy on average achieved superior performance to firms not having an organization-strategy fit.[16] Table 12.3 summarizes the features of the organizational profile for each strategy that was associated with superior company performance. The terms used to label each organizational profile are Ghoshal's and Nohria's.

◢ New Organizational Arrangements for Organizing Across Borders

Cross-border operations present greater demands on a firm's organization than do purely domestic ones. These demands inevitably grow as an MNE becomes more differentiated, both geographically and in the range of the products and services it offers. The more it moves toward a transnational strategy, the greater the organizational challenge. It is no longer adequate to rely on conventional arrangements and new solutions have to be found. In order to develop a capacity to deal with new situations creatively and flexibly, these new solutions tend to involve greater internal differentiation in the ways that activities are grouped and coordinated, and new approaches to control. In relying less on hierarchy and bureaucracy, the new approach to MNE organization depends significantly on the effective management of internal and external networks, and on the support of a well-developed corporate culture. Corporate culture refers to the shared values and practices that are specific to a particular company.

The transnational MNE is therefore one of the most important arenas for new thinking about organization and for experimentation with new organizational forms. The following section discusses a number of these new developments.

◢ New Organizational Approaches within MNEs

This section considers organizational developments apparent within MNEs aimed at achieving the benefits of internal diversity and differentiation within a framework that preserves the requisite degree of overall integration. It discusses the following fundamental issues:

1   Hierarchy or network?
2   HQ-subsidiary relationships; control and autonomy
3   Managing integrative processes
4   Managing cultural diversity
5   Cross-border transfer of knowledge and practices

The emergence of new organizational forms in an MNE is then illustrated through the case of the leading pharmaceutical company, Eli Lilly.

1. Hierarchy or network?

Diversified MNEs that are attempting to maintain a competitive profile through being innovative and adaptive have learned that they cannot achieve this through a conventional hierarchically-oriented mode of organization. Instead they have to create effective networks both internally among their subsidiaries and externally with partners. Insofar as an MNE chooses to expand internationally through its own foreign direct investment, seeking to benefit from so-called "internalization" advantages,[17] it will build up a network of its own subsidiaries, which it then has to decide how best to manage. I have already suggested that logically this decision depends on the global strategy it is pursuing. However, the transnational strategy combining decentralization with integration has the considerable merit of recognizing the potential contribution that subsidiaries can make to a company's learning about new opportunities as well as to accessing new technical and other knowledge of strategic value. As discussed shortly, if subsidiaries are to be given this constructive responsibility, this implies a radically different, and somewhat diminished, role for the MNE corporate level.

Another, but not necessarily alternative, route to international expansion is for the MNE to build up external networks with key partners. These can include suppliers, key customers, selected key competitors and non-business institutions such as relevant government departments, research institutes and universities, all of which potentially perform value-adding activities for the MNE.[18] Some of these benefits became apparent in the previous chapters in this part of the book, and are achievable by organizing across company boundaries through outsourcing, strategic alliances and value chains. Similarly, the importance of networking with non-business agencies is highly significant today not just for business performance but for maintaining the very legitimacy of large companies in the light of the mistrust and public criticism they have attracted in recent years. While those at the top of corporate hierarchies retain a special role for the high-profile defense of their policies (such as before congressional or parliamentary committees) as well as for undertaking top-level lobbying, the myriad of other external network relationships necessarily have to be handled on a devolved basis, including those in host foreign countries. In other words, initiative has to be decentralized and localized within the corporation. The fact that MNEs cannot perform effectively on a traditional hierarchical basis has important implications for the management both of vertical and lateral relationships within their organizations.

The relative success of the Nordic countries in both innovation and general economic performance is relevant here. This success has been attributed, at least in part, to the approach to organization that characterizes the business and public sector organizations in those countries. While there are differences between each country, they all tend towards a decentralized networking mode of organization that allows for high level of individual autonomy and responsibility. This is coupled with a high work intensity. However, the pace of work is not set in a traditional way by demands coming from managers but rather by demands from other people (customers, suppliers, and colleagues) with whom staff interact directly. This networking channels in new information and encourages a shared evaluation of its significance. The Nordic approach suggests that learning and innovation derive from a combination of being confronted with new demands and being able to experiment with one's own ideas at work. This has implications for the organization of relationships not only within a single work unit but also those between the corporate level and subsidiaries within an MNE.[19]

2. Corporate–subsidiary relationships: control and autonomy[20]

In formal terms, subsidiaries or business units in MNEs are subordinate parts of the overall organization. They result from decisions to expand abroad through internalization rather than through forms of outsourcing or other arms-length relationship. At first sight, this arrangement appears to retain a traditional hierarchical relationship between subsidiary and corporate levels. However, the reality is normally not so straightforward because as subsidiaries evolve, they develop their own external relations in their host environment and they develop their own distinctive competences through learning how to prosper in that environment. They cease to be mere operational units and instead evolve their own unique charters. The MNE in this respect becomes a differentiated network rather than a traditional hierarchical organization, a political coalition rather than a military-like formation.[21] This evolutionary process enhances the value of subsidiaries to the parent company, but at the same time it gives them a voice of their own. The challenge is that as subsidiaries grow stronger they may become difficult to control, yet a tightening of corporate control may jeopardize their contribution through imposing inappropriate restrictions on their activities.

It has even been suggested that the corporate or headquarters level in MNEs is no longer necessarily adding any value because key market and technical knowledge is held by subsidiaries. This is seen to put in question the "parenting advantage" arising from the value-adding functions that headquarters are traditionally seen to perform. These include creating synergies between complementary activities, maintaining a balance between conflicting demands on resources (e.g. short-term versus long-term and between alternative investments), sharing knowledge and organizing common services. The question is whether in a complex network of subsidiaries distributed across many regions and lines of business, the headquarters still has the knowledge necessary to carry out these functions. If not, intervention by the headquarters might be detrimental to subsidiaries' innovation and performance because it would be based on ill-informed appraisals and expectations.[22] For a similar reason, direct interaction between subsidiaries rather than via headquarters may lead to more rapid and effective information exchange and knowledge transfer. To reduce the risk of such dysfunctions, it is necessary for headquarters personnel to invest in their relationships with subsidiaries, to understand the contexts in which the latter are embedded, and to grant them sufficient autonomy.[23] The implication is that rather than adopting a traditional command-and-control approach, the headquarters has to become more of a network coordinator, maintaining overall balance and integration through a "softer" and more inclusive approach to control.

The complexity of relationships within MNEs between their corporate units, regional units, and local affiliates is mirrored in the complexity surrounding the choice of control methods that such firms employ. Most MNEs today employ a variety of such methods of control and in particular combine formal controls with informal ones based on personal ties and the inculcation of a shared vision and values articulated by a corporate culture. MNEs have also learned to vary their methods of control to suit the needs of different functions and areas of activity.

Many MNEs have attempted to respond to the inadequacies of formal controls within their complex organization, where too much reliance on such controls might well inhibit local initiative and learning. They have done this by using corporate cultures and informal communication networks. Chapter 6 described the contribution that corporate cultures can make to the process of control. Acceptance of their values and practices should help direct the energies of personnel in an organization toward achieving its goals, which is precisely the purpose behind control. Expatriate managers can play a very significant role in spreading an MNE's corporate culture to its international affiliates. Once established, however, this culture-based approach to control has the considerable advantage that it does not require regular personal supervision and so reduces the overall need to employ expensive expatriates within foreign subsidiaries and affiliates. The informal nature of the norms and rules contained within a corporate culture also allows people to extrapolate them quickly to new situations and requirements, and therefore react efficiently to new situations.

In his study of US MNEs, Rudman found that they prefer to use the same control processes for all their overseas affiliates.[24] They also make no distinction in this respect between affiliates they wholly own and joint ventures in which they have part ownership, which appears to be a sustainable policy so long as MNEs have the majority share of joint venture ownership. In practice, however, the companies did distinguish between those affiliate activities that were purely internal and those that involved dealing with local markets and institutions. On the internal side, manufacturing and quality regimes, together with the nature and extent of financial reports, are subject to controls and practices that are standardized throughout the MNE. On the external side, control is more flexible, to permit an adjustment of certain marketing and HRM practices to suit the conditions in local product and labor markets. Some variation from normal company practices was also found to be necessary when relating to, and building trust among, local officials. My own studies of nine US MNEs with joint ventures in China found that they generally decentralized decisions on external matters such as the choice of markets and suppliers to their affiliates, whereas internal matters with implications for global product policy, such as modifications to the product, were controlled centrally.[25]

The considerable geographical and product diversity of many MNEs has obliged them to develop new configurations of control mechanisms so as to maintain central coordination and corporate standards in some areas of activity, while permitting local adaptation in others. As a result, these companies exhibit internal variations in their approach to control, and combinations of a variety of control methods, both formal and informal. Their use of informal methods such as corporate culture and intensive communication networks has become more significant over time.

3. Managing integrative processes

An MNE pursuing a transnational strategy cannot rely just on organizational configurations of a structural kind. It needs to develop its organizational processes to the point where they can transcend its structure. Processes refer to the actions that take place within an organization such as communication, decision-making, and workflows. Structures merely provide a framework for processes. Integration within an MNE depends on a number of corporation-wide processes. These include coordinating diversified activities and initiatives, building a shared vision and sustaining people's commitment to it, and opening channels for knowledge transfer and learning. In actively linking people and groups, these processes become the life-blood of "integrated networks."[26] While most attention has been paid to such networks within MNEs, the effective integration of external value chain networks is equally important (see Chapters 9 & 10).

The idea of networks draws attention to webs of organizational relationships, some of which may be formally prescribed, but others of which emerge informally. Informal networks may be based on friendship, advisory, or conversational relationships both within an organization and across its formal boundaries.[27] They are strengthened by their members' shared identification with each other and with a common purpose. Networks can help to realize the operational intentions of structures and, at the same time, contribute to structural evolution by, for example, developing new patterns of collaboration within a company.

Larger MNEs develop a number of levels at which activities are focused – typically corporate, divisional, and subsidiary or affiliate. These levels will to some extent frame the networks within the company. A key role is the "global network manager" who bridges and links these levels. Vertical integration is critical for MNEs that are trying to combine the corporate centralization of some activities and decisions with the decentralization of others to geographically dispersed affiliates. The manager who integrates vertical networks is akin to that of the lateral coordinator who links people and units to form a horizontal network (see Chapter 5). Some global network managers perform both roles.

Global network managers are the key participants and drivers of MNE networks and therefore have to manage the processes within them. They are the people between whom important communications flow; they consolidate information from various sources; they interpret and endeavor to reconcile corporate and local requirements; they act as a main point of transmission of information and policies to other parts and levels in the network. Global network managers may play this vital role by virtue of a hierarchical position that links key levels within the company. They may also be in a position to make significant contributions within the network because of their specialized competence and knowledge, and because of the respect and trust they command.

It cannot be assumed that the processes and networks required to organize an MNE across levels and borders will arise spontaneously. Global network managers of the right caliber and experience need to be placed at key points within networks. This is illustrated in Box 12.1 by the case of a US multinational that appointed a CEO of its China operations to improve both

BOX 12.1 AN MNE GLOBAL NETWORK MANAGER

Before being appointed as Chairman and CEO of a US multinational's newly formed China company, Jack Hislop had worked in various parts of the corporation, ending up as a corporate controller.* He was therefore quite well known in the corporation and trusted by managers at headquarters. This meant that he was able to deal directly with the corporate vice-president for international operations without having to go through any intermediary. On arriving in China, he immediately established direct links to the marketing and business development activities of the company's several product "businesses" (i.e. global divisions), whose managers were relocated to his office.

Hislop's main tasks were to formulate a coherent corporate strategy for China and get it implemented. In working toward an agreed China strategy, he had to ensure that the necessary communications and discussions took place between managers at different levels, so the corporate level would support the strategy and local managers would willingly act on it. He regularly informed his corporate boss on major developments taking place in China, while at the same time keeping managers within China informed on discussions and developments at the corporate level that could impact on their business areas. To further the operation of an open information network, Hislop's office arranged regular visits to China by corporate executives, including the heads of product businesses. Twice a year, Hislop himself attended a top-level discussion group involving the heads of the company's business divisions and the geographical entities. His staff regularly visited the USA and were making increasing use of video-conferencing as well as email.

His role as the manager of this vertical integration process was essential for the company to align its global product development strategy to the needs and opportunities of China's rapidly growing market. Business development staff in China had the task of identifying future local market opportunities in terms of how to capitalize on the company's products, what could be imported, what modifications were required, and the like. These market opportunities had to be conveyed upwards within the company and reconciled with what the corporate level could provide in terms of newly available products and others being developed for launch in two or three years' time. Hislop was central to these discussions and in particular made sure that they took account of the views of major customers in China with whom he kept close contact.

*Name has been disguised to protect identity.
Source: author's interviews

the vertical integration between corporate and country levels and horizontal links between product divisions in that country.

Managers who are serving as global network managers within MNE networks therefore have to perform a number of distinct and demanding roles. They have to be:

- boundary-spanners between different levels and units within their company, and often between the company and key external people;

- initiators of networks, by bringing together the geographically and organizationally dispersed people who have to collaborate to implement the MNE's international strategy;
- coordinators, synthesizers, and transferors of information within networks;
- conveyors of corporate vision downward and advocates of decentralized initiatives upward.

It is one thing to identify the role of global network manager. It is another matter to ensure that people with the appropriate qualities and preparation occupy this demanding role. This raises two questions. First, what qualities are required in global network managers who perform integrating roles within MNEs? Second, what practices can help to develop and prepare people to perform such roles?

Surveys and writings have identified key qualities that are required in global network managers.[28] It is widely agreed that a fundamental attribute is having the broad strategic awareness necessary for operating within an international network. In the example provided, the variety of Jack Hislop's previous assignments, finishing at corporate level, helped him to acquire this broader perspective. If the work of foreign affiliates is to be closely aligned with a firm's business strategy, the global network manager must be in a position not only to understand the firm's overall strategy, but also to reflect the opportunities and needs of the affiliates in its formulation and implementation.

At a personal level, the global network manager needs be able to understand the nature of conflicting priorities and to handle their resolution within the international corporate network. He or she has to cope with the exigencies of working with different groups within the company. This requires an ability to communicate effectively and flexibility in relating with others. Within the global scope of an MNE, an important skill in relating constructively to others can be the ability to manage cultural differences. These requirements point to relevant personal skills and sensitivities. They imply that, whatever training is offered, certain kinds of people are better suited to the demands of the job than others.

The relevant personal skills which have been identified for global network managers include adaptability, the ability to function in fluid conditions and cope with ambiguity and personal stress, the capacity to work with different groups of people whose views and cultures do not coincide, relationship and negotiating skills, and the capacity to communicate in more than one language. These skills are reinforced by a high level of sensitivity to others, especially sensitivity to and respect for different cultures, plus openness to learning from new situations and diverse points of view. Since these managers often have to initiate new networks, or expand existing ones, a high level of self-belief and self-reliance can be called for, so long as this does not degrade into personal arrogance.

Global network managers usually have to work with large numbers of people over whom they may have no direct authority. They may lack even downward authority when an MNE's foreign affiliates take the form of partnerships with other companies. In this situation, even more than in others, they have to possess the capacity to build trust among members of the network, some of whom may be on secondment from their own companies and will therefore tend to retain an identification with their own parent organizations rather than with the partnership.[29] This situation clearly places a premium on flexibility, finely tuned interpersonal skills, and personal integrity.

The pressures bearing on global network managers can be severe, especially when they are working with independent network partners in unfamiliar environments.[30] Quite a number are unable to stand the pressure and the cost is high both to the individual who has failed in a highly exposed position and to the network itself, which may be placed under severe strain as a result. Many global network managers are expatriates, like Jack Hislop, and the purely financial cost of extricating a failed expatriate can run to well over $1 million. It is therefore vital to select people who possess qualities suited to the demands of the role.

It is equally important to prepare people to undertake the position of a global network manager. The nature of the role and the capabilities it requires suggest that a policy for developing such managers should include a number of key elements:

- Select future candidates for this role for appropriate personal characteristics, including open-mindedness, emotional stability, and internal drive;
- Provide a career path that gives them exposure to both local and global tasks, and allow sufficient time for it to have positive developmental effects;
- Rotate the people in question between major functions, as well as some divisions, so as to develop a well-rounded view of the company and a widely-based credibility within the company;
- Encourage them to use these assignments to varied parts of the company as the means to develop a personal global network inside the company and with key external organizations as well;
- Provide appropriate training, such as the development of cultural sensitivity.

4. Managing cultural diversity in MNEs

An MNE, by definition, operates across a number of different national cultures. Even national cultures that are often grouped together, such as the so-called "Anglo-Saxon" category (primarily Australia, Canada, New Zealand, UK and USA), give rise to distinctive managerial practices that have to be reconciled in order to achieve adequate integration within the company. The approach to management within US companies tends to differ from that within UK companies. The policies that MNEs adopt toward managing cultural differences also reflect national orientations in management philosophy.[31] Differences in national culture are therefore a factor that MNE management has to take account of. If mergers and acquisitions are an important component in an MNE's growth policy, differences in corporate culture will also have to be addressed.[32] If newly acquired affiliates or partners are from a different country, their corporate cultures may reflect many aspects of the national culture, but one has to bear in mind that companies' cultures can themselves vary, even when they are of the same nationality.

Cultures are not simply obstacles to integration within MNEs. They also convey potentially valuable competences and practices, and understanding them can assist a company to orient itself to local markets and operating environments. Earlier in this chapter, we discussed the strategies for global expansion that MNEs can pursue and the balance of global and local needs that each strategy reflects. The recommendation follows that an MNE's policy toward managing its internal cultural diversity should correspond to the particular strategy for global expansion it is pursuing.

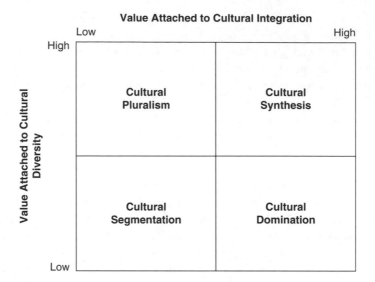

Figure 12.5 Policies for managing cultural diversity in MNEs

There are two basic choices that the managers of an MNE need to consider in defining the policy options for managing cultural diversity within their company:

1 whether or not to seek a basis for *integration* between the MNE's domestic culture and those of its foreign affiliates;
2 whether or not to retain *cultural diversity* within the company's practices, either on an integrated or non-integrated basis.

These two choices give rise to the four broad possibilities shown in Figure 12.5.

1 *Cultural pluralism.* When an MNE attaches relatively little importance to the integration of its various cultures and at the same time values their diversity, it is likely to seek a policy of cultural pluralism. This means that it will encourage rather than discourage its regional or national affiliates to operate according to their own cultural norms on the basis that these suit local conditions such as employment norms and consumer preferences. The preservation of cultural diversity should therefore provide greater flexibility. The active celebration of cultural diversity may become a prominent feature of a company's own corporate culture. For example, the company may seek to encourage comparisons between, and an active discourse about, its contrasting national and occupational sub-cultures, in order to exploit the potential to learn from their respective strengths and limitations.
2 *Cultural segmentation.* This is the case where an MNE attaches relatively low importance to cultural integration, yet at the same time does not value cultural diversity very highly. The consequence of this rather laissez-faire attitude to culture is likely to be a segmented situation in which the cultural norms that apply will reflect the origins of the activities or functions in question. Functions provided centrally will be accompanied by practices

reflecting the company's domestic cultural norms, while functions provided locally will reflect local norms. The difference between a pluralistic policy towards multiple cultures and a segmented one is that the former acknowledges cultural diversity as a resource, whereas the latter does not. The danger of a segmented policy based on cultural indifference is that it fails to capitalize on learning opportunities and may lead, by default, to harmful fragmentation within the company.

3   *Cultural domination.* When an MNE attaches low value to cultural diversity among its operational locations and affiliates, but is insistent on cultural integration within its organization, it is likely to favor the dominance of its domestic culture. Cultural domination is a policy aiming at integration on the basis of one national culture. The potential advantages of this policy are that, if successful, it creates a unified corporate identity, provides a common face to the customer, and makes it easier to implement standardized policies and practices. It may eventually encourage the development of informal, in-company networks. However, this and other potential benefits will be hard to achieve if a policy of cultural domination creates resentment among minority sub-cultures within the company. Such resentment could provoke opposition to company practices and reduce flexibility. A policy of integration through the dominance of one culture has to be "sold" to sub-culture members through a persuasive vision and the prospect of clear benefits to them.

4   *Cultural synthesis.* This policy arises when an MNE attaches value to the various national cultures within its organization, but also perceives a strong need to integrate them. Cultural synthesis is a policy aiming at cultural integration on the basis of a melding of all the cultures present within an MNE. In effect, it leads to the creation of a new culture within the company. This synthesis does not necessarily accord equal weight to each culture, but it does aim at achieving the fullest possible fit between them. Although this policy takes longer to implement than the others, it offers several potential benefits. It permits flexibility in the approach toward local markets and operational conditions, it retains the potential to learn from different subcultures and derive synergy from them, and it may be more successful than cultural domination in creating cultural integration throughout the company without the loss of goodwill. As discussed below, it is the policy for managing cultural diversity that best accords with a transnational strategy.

Table 12.4 summarizes the advantages and disadvantages associated with each of these four policy options for managing cultural diversity within an MNE.

These four broad policies for managing cultural diversity map quite closely onto the four strategies for global expansion discussed earlier. Figure 12.6 indicates which policy for managing cultural diversity is consistent with each of the four strategies.

A multi-domestic strategy can draw benefits from the preservation of cultural diversity, which helps affiliates to adapt to local markets and other conditions. Cultural integration within the MNE is not a priority because its need for global coordination is low.

An international strategy involves the transfer of some competences, usually in manufacturing and distribution, to foreign countries and retaining others centrally, like R&D, product development, and marketing. This mix of decentralized and centralized functions can coexist with a segmentation of cultures within the firm, although the low value placed on cultural integration may become sub-optimal. In fact as previously noted, one of the drawbacks of this

Table 12.4 Advantages and disadvantages of policy options for managing cultural diversity

Cultural Pluralism

Advantages	Disadvantages
• Addresses market or geographical differences • Allows stronger subcultures • Gives greater flexibility • Maintains productivity during merger • Comparisons encourage learning	• Reduces synergy gains • Inhibits solidarity of purpose • Slows movement of people, ideas • Reduces standardization of practices

Cultural Segmentation

Advantages As for cultural pluralism, plus:	Disadvantages As for cultural pluralism, plus:
• Avoids cultural conflicts	• Fails to capitalize on opportunities to learn from cultural diversity • Can lead to harmful fragmentation within the firm

Cultural Domination

Advantages	Disadvantages
• Creates unified identity • Provides one face to the customer • Allows for standardized policies and practices	• Minimizes subculture development • Fails to address market or geographical differences • Reduces flexibility • May cause resentment from minority cultures

Cultural Synthesis (new culture)

Advantages	Disadvantages
• Provides fresh face and identity to merged companies and to joint ventures • Creates more flexibility to adapt to market or geographical differences • Allows easier integration of companies or partners • Maximizes potential for mutual learning	• May cause high resistance to change • Could have negative impact on productivity during transition • Takes longer to implement

Adapted from Hewitt Associates, *Mergers and Acquisitions in Europe Survey Results 2003*. Amsterdam: Hewitt Associates, p. 30.

strategy is that it does not strive to gain benefits from either local responsiveness or global coordination.

A global strategy requires high levels of global coordination and favors a policy of cultural domination. In Japanese MNEs pursuing this strategy, their domestic national practices, and even cultural symbols and ceremonies, are usually applied with relatively little local modification throughout the companies' international operations.

Pressures for Global Integration

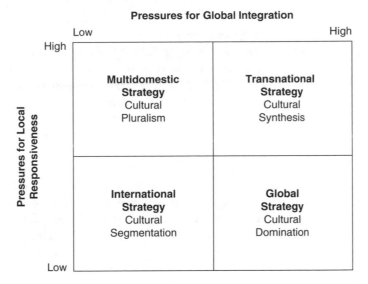

Figure 12.6 Policies for managing cultural diversity consistent with strategies for global expansion

The transnational strategy attempts to obtain benefits from globalization and localization simultaneously. An MNE pursuing this strategy endeavors to add value from the customization of its products and services, while at the same time capitalizing on its ability to locate operations in the most favorable locations and coordinate them on a global basis. A transnational strategy therefore relies on initiatives, proposals, and new knowledge flowing in from local affiliates and the ability to coordinate and disseminate these throughout the company. A policy of cultural synthesis is the one most likely to support this strategy and the methods for realizing it.

Cultural synthesis is also the policy best suited to encouraging the interpersonal bonding between the diversified groups that a transnational MNE seeks to form into a cohesive network. Cultural synthesis does not impose one culture on others, but rather treats each one with respect and recognizes the potential to learn from each. The intention with synthesis is to combine the better elements from each partner's culture to stimulate new ideas, deploy resources more effectively, and create more effective organizational processes. One might therefore equally call this a policy of cultural synergy. The concept of synergy is, of course, that the whole is greater than the sum of its parts. The key idea behind cultural synthesis is therefore that the "positive aspects of the various cultures are preserved, combined, and expanded upon to create a new whole."[33]

5. Cross-border transfer of knowledge and practices

Chapter 14 examines the transfer of knowledge and hence the potential to learn from other organizations through the formation of alliances between them, some of which may well cross borders. This section focuses on the cross-border transfer of knowledge and practices within MNEs themselves. The importance of effective cross-border transfer of the knowledge located at various points within MNEs is becoming increasingly important as competition among them intensifies. It is widely recognized that new knowledge provides a basis for firms to renew their capabilities and to secure a competitive advantage.[34] Cultural differences can impact on the success of this transfer, along with other factors.

Knowledge consists of information that has been collated and related to specific tasks and/or contexts. Thus a person might say: "I know how to achieve this task" or "I know what to do if that situation arises." Knowledge can be implicit (tacit knowledge) or well articulated and even codified (explicit knowledge). It can remain the possession of individuals, or contained within group or cultural norms, or embedded in organizational practices – systems, processes, rules, and routines. Knowledge can also vary from the simple to the complex, where complexity is associated with the need for more factual information in order to resolve causal uncertainty. Some knowledge is independent of given organizational situations and can be described by itself, while other knowledge can only be described in relation to specific situations.[35]

When taken into account alongside cultural differences, these distinctions between different types of knowledge help us to understand the likely level of difficulty in transferring knowledge between the diversified units of an MNE. The transfer of knowledge is likely to be most effective, in terms of the speed of transfer and richness of knowledge transferred, when the type of knowledge is simple, explicit, and independent. When a transfer across borders is involved, the transfer is expected to be most effective when it takes place between units that are culturally similar.[36] The greatest difficulty is likely to occur with the transfer of knowledge that is complex, tacit, and context-dependent, across units that are culturally very dissimilar.

From a strategic perspective, the most significant knowledge that MNEs need to transfer between corporate headquarters and affiliates, and between affiliates themselves, concerns new and long-term matters such as future market opportunities, creative ideas, potential business relationships, and incipient developments by competitors. It therefore tends to be complex, context-dependent, and not very explicit in nature. Much of this knowledge also has to be transferred across cultural boundaries. This combination of characteristics points to the difficulty that MNEs face in ensuring that the internal exchange of significant knowledge is both speedy and does not lose its richness and subtlety. Complex, tacit, and context-dependent knowledge requires a lot of explanation and interpretation when being transferred to others, and this is best handled in an interpersonal manner through discussions and personal presentations. If the knowledge is culturally sensitive, perhaps because it concerns idiosyncratic ideas coming from a foreign affiliate, personal advocacy and discussion among trusted colleagues may also be necessary to overcome resistance to its consideration by corporate management. These kinds of conditions do not permit an effective transfer of knowledge by purely formal means, such as documents. In fact, a company will probably wish to keep knowledge of a strategically important kind confidential, which also favors its transfer on an interpersonal basis.

The need to transfer non-routine knowledge within MNEs highlights another dimension of the contribution that global network managers can offer. Their management of MNE networks through personal contact and relations of trust is of a kind that is suited to overcome the difficulties facing such knowledge transfer. The more effective this transfer, the greater the capacity of the company to learn and hence achieve an edge over its competitors by being more innovative and smarter than they are.

For knowledge to provide its full potential benefit, it needs to be applied. Knowledge of a more routine kind can be converted into standard organizational practices. The cross-border transfer of superior practices by companies is also an increasingly important means through which knowledge is applied in a globalizing world. While practices are often explicit and codified, two important characteristics that should assist their transfer, differences in the contexts involved in the transfer may still present problems. For this reason, practices being transferred within an MNE will normally have to be "re-contextualized."[37] This means that, while the principles informing the practices can be transferred, their specific mode of application may have to be modified to suit the new organizational context.

For instance, the principles informing the Japanese practice of seeking continuous incremental improvements in production methods and quality are that a company should acquire the tacit knowledge accumulated through on-the-job experience and that continuous improvement should be integrated as an essential part of everyday work. However, the specific arrangements through which these principles are realized in Japan do not necessarily work in a different context like the United States, particularly in unionized plants with deeply embedded work practices. Indeed, early attempts to transfer the Japanese practice of quality circles to the USA generally ended in failure, being treated with hostility by workers and with indifference by many managers. Later attempts to apply the same principles through different means, such as incorporating them into the work of multifunctional teams, have generally been more successful. This organizational arrangement is consistent with the more frequent use of such teams as hierarchies are reduced.[38]

Research conducted by the author and his colleagues into the cross-border transfer of practices by 615 Hong Kong firms to affiliates located in mainland China, identified several other factors that assisted the process.[39] These include good quality local human resources, trust in affiliate staff, intensive controls, and international sourcing. The implications of these findings are that:

1   The successful transfer of parent company practices to a cross-border affiliate requires local personnel with sufficient competence to implement them. It is therefore important to recruit and/or train managers and employees of the right quality. If this is either not possible or too expensive, it is more appropriate not to apply the company's standard practices.

2   The trustworthiness of local affiliate personnel also helps the effective transfer of practices. For practices to function effectively in another situation, local staff have to show the goodwill to accept them as well as having the skills and competences to work with them. Trust in affiliate personnel is also likely to increase the motivation of headquarters managers to make the investment in transferring practices in the first place – to decide that it is worth the cost and effort.

3   The relatively intensive control of an affiliate, using a wide range of control mechanisms, helps the process of transfer to obtain the necessary momentum and then to be sustained. Once installed in affiliates, standardized practices should in turn assist the process of corporate control.

4   International, rather than local, sourcing by cross-border affiliates encourages the transfer of new practices to them. International suppliers of material and service inputs are originators and conveyors of new practices, as well as sources of advice for their application within a firm.

Larger MNEs are more likely than other firms to transfer practices effectively to their cross-border affiliates. There appear to be several reasons for this. First, their generally greater level of diversification creates the need to secure international integration in order to manage complex value chains, to maintain global quality standards, and to implement consistent HRM policies and ethical standards. The widespread implementation of standard corporate practices across affiliates can importantly support these control and coordination requirements.[40] Second, and partly for this reason, the larger firm will normally employ a formalized approach based on a highly developed set of standard practices. Third, the larger firm normally has superior resources to implement the transfer of those practices, such as staff to assist the process, funding for appropriate training, and the ability to sustain the costs associated with initial dysfunctional effects of introducing the required changes.

Eli Lilly: an example of emerging new organizational forms in an MNE [41]

Eli Lilly was founded in 1876 in the United States and is a pharmaceuticals industry leader with a long history of operating globally. At the end of 2013 it had 38,000 employees worldwide selling products in 125 countries. It manufactures in 13 different countries and its R&D facilities are located across eight countries. It conducts clinical studies in 55 countries. Like other major pharmaceutical companies, Lilly has experienced growing pressures "to innovate in developing a continual flow of new products, to speed the development and launch of new products, to improve the cost efficiency of all operations, and to be aggressive in selling products to major world markets."[42] These challenges have directly affected how pharmaceutical firms operate globally and the way they organize to do so.

Prior to 1990, Lilly's organization could be described as a functional silo structure in which research, manufacturing, and marketing/sales were located in separate divisions. The management of its national affiliates was centralized and they focused on local sales rather than on identifying new product needs and opportunities. This structure was demonstrating serious limitations, including communications inefficiencies, lengthy decision-making, a low rate of innovation and responsiveness to new market opportunities, information overload at the top management level, and a high cost of administration. Opportunities to learn and adapt were being lost.

During the 1990s, Lilly's organization evolved in several ways. It changed to a focused matrix structure, with product groups forming one dimension and national affiliates the other. Within the matrix, extensive use was now made of cross-functional teams and wider networking. Previously, the discovery of new compounds had been organized around scientific disciplines such as chemistry, biology, and pharmacology, with committees acting as coordinators for individual research initiatives. This structure had given scientists a great deal of freedom in conducting research, but it did not specifically orient their efforts to areas of market potential. In the new structure, executives responsible for global therapeutic areas now manage discovery operations and report to a cross-functional, senior management committee. The committee allocates resources, prioritizes and monitors the progress of each discovery team, and resolves conflicts. Similarly, by 1994 Lilly had introduced cross-functional teams dedicated to the development, regulatory approval, and launch of individual compounds. Figure 12.7 indicates the use of teams at different stages of the company's value chain.

Lilly also adapted its organization better to meet its requirements, including globalization, in another significant respect. It moved the organization of its core value chain processes (shown in Figure 12.7) toward globally oriented forms, though retaining a mix of structures between the different value chain stages. Thus, early phase development was structured around program teams, initial regulatory approval around cross-functional product teams, and bulk

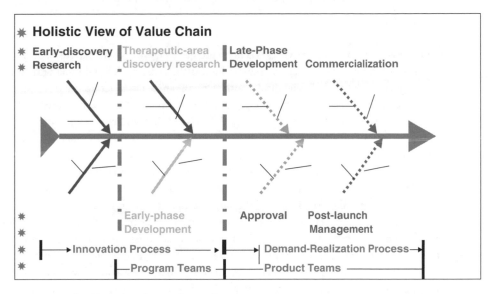

Figure 12.7 Eli Lilly: Value chain and use of teams

manufacturing around global functional structures. Support and delivery processes were also reorganized, with regional product structures for marketing support and regional functional structures for bulk formulation production and delivery. Through these organizational adaptations, Lilly was tuning its structures and processes to suit different activities and moving toward more common forms of organization for each activity. At the same time, this meant that it was increasing its overall organizational variation and complexity.

In recent years, Eli Lilly has been introducing an IT-based virtualized services system in which common processes are centralized at a regional level – or outsourced completely – to eliminate redundancies and cut costs. The company has been expanding the use of its existing SAP footprint to its global sales, manufacturing, and research facilities. While the intention is largely to reduce costs, it should also improve integration across its globally diverse businesses.[43]

Thomas Malnight's detailed investigation of emerging structural patterns found broadly similar trends during the 1990s within another major pharmaceutical MNE, Hoffman LaRoche. His comparisons with Lilly point to increasing divergence in internal company structures, but convergence between the firms in the specific structures they adopted for similar activities and processes. Both firms evolved multiple types of internal networks. Some of these focused on global knowledge sharing, some on global data sharing, and others on global facility sharing. Malnight suggests from his research that:

> "Rather than selecting a single structure, MNEs respond to increasingly complex pressures and opportunities from operating globally through increasing internal structural complexity, system-atically differentiating their structures to respond to the relevant sub-environments for individual processes. The organizational challenge facing managers at MNEs is . . . the development and integration of multiple types of internal networks sharing common and globally dispersed resources."[44]

Emerging issues

A major development in recent years has been the growing prominence in the world economy of emerging economies – especially the so-called BRICs (Brazil, Russia, India and China) and NITS (Nigeria, Indonesia, Turkey and South Africa). Their rapid economic development has attracted foreign direct investment (FDI) by MNEs from developed economies and has also given rise to a substantial increase in outward FDI by their own firms. The contrasts between these two sets of domestic (home) and foreign (host) environments, especially in terms of cultures, institutions and human competences, have raised questions about how MNEs may need to adjust their embedded managerial and organizational practices to suit their new host environments. The issue is made more complex by the fact that there can be considerable variation in the internal conditions of the larger emerging countries.

As noted earlier in this chapter, MNEs have some choice as to how they manage differences between their incumbent cultures and those of their host environments. Host-country institutions, however, are generally less amenable to MNE influence, although incoming firms with valuable financial and technological assets may have some leverage over them.[45] Emerging economies tend to be characterized by "institutional voids," meaning that they have absent or weak specialized intermediaries, regulatory systems and contract-enforcing mechanisms in their product, labor and capital markets.[46] Institutional voids in emerging markets are seen to offer both opportunities and challenges to firms seeking to do business in such markets. When institutional voids are present, governance tends to be relationship-based, as opposed to rule-based. This means that official approvals and other business arrangements are liable to be conditional on knowing or favoring the right people rather than governed by clear transparent rules. The practical implication is that whereas in a rule-based foreign environment MNEs can rely on formal procedures, based for instance on contracts, in a relationship-based environment they have to rely more heavily on informal processes such as hiring staff with useful connections and when necessary making exceptions to their internal rules.[47] Whether to sidestep formal rules by offering special personal monetary inducements, which may be the norm in such contexts, is a particularly contentious issue.

Despite the marked rise in the number of MNEs from emerging economies, much of our understanding of organizing across borders still comes from studies of large North American and Western European MNEs. Less is known about the forms of organization emerging economy MNEs are using to manage their international expansion, and whether these will differ from the organizational approaches of developed economy MNEs. One possibility is that they adopt the practices of western MNEs. Another is that their organizational forms and management styles will continue to reflect cultural and institutional features in their domestic environments even as they internationalize, which has been the case with many Japanese MNEs.

It has been argued that the management and organization of emerging economy MNEs has to be understood in the light of the competency and resource needs that arise from particular combinations of domestic (home) and foreign (host) environments.[48] The key question is whether the MNEs have acquired competences and ways of conducting business from their home environment that will suit their operations in a foreign country. This requires an understanding of the precise ways in which home and host countries compare. For example, in some emerging economies like China, the government is closely involved in many strategic MNEs. This can potentially reduce their need to adapt when operating in other countries if their home government has negotiated benign conditions for them with host country authorities. In addition, their executives may already have acquired appropriate skills in building relationships with government officials. The same factor of close identity with government has, however, proved to be counter-productive in other host countries such as the United States where politically connected incoming firms are regarded with suspicion.

When emerging economy MNEs expand into developed economies, they are likely to adapt their approach to organization and management to the practices prevalent in the host environment. These practices are well established and may well be regarded as "best practice" in terms of what is taught in business and other professional schools. In the highly rule-based universalistic systems of developed countries, the informal, particularistic and personalized practices familiar to emerging economy MNEs will be regarded as unacceptable. So there will be strong pressures for their modes of managing subsidiaries and their HRM systems to conform to those of the host country. By contrast, when MNEs from emerging economies enter other emerging or developing countries, they may opt to transfer their parent company systems and practices to their subsidiaries. This can be necessary to fill a void in local systems and to compensate for the limited availability of managerial and technical skills in such countries.[49]

Another issue concerns the rapid expansion of ICT capabilities, especially those based on the Internet, and how these can increase the variety of options for organizing across borders. When there is a standardization of interfaces between units, ICT opens up possibilities for the disaggregation of value chains both geographically and in terms of formal ownership. As noted in Chapter 10, it also facilitates the development of virtual MNEs.[50] These technology-enabled shifts from MNEs as traditionally organized, physically integrated entities to clusters of dispersed collaborating units are evident in the relatively new network forms of organization considered in the three previous chapters. As we shall see in the following section, ICT has also helped small- and medium-sized enterprises (SMEs) to internationalize and, in particular, has encouraged more small firms to be "born global" – to engage in international business immediately or soon after their inception. The combination of recent trends – the expansion of MNEs into qualitatively different markets, the growing pressures for innovation, and developments in ICT – is helping to bring about significant changes in the forms and the dynamics of MNE organization. Internally as well as externally, MNEs are taking on a network format, with multiple linkages between subsidiaries themselves and between subsidiaries and external parties. As part of making capabilities "dynamic" with the aim of enabling adaptation and promoting innovation, the roles of these units are becoming more flexible and, to a degree, interchangeable. As noted in Chapters 5 and 10, much work is now organized into projects that can involve people from across country as well as company boundaries. Ensuring the adequate integration of such diverse contributions has become a critical managerial competence.

Cross-border SMEs

Most discussions of organizing across borders focus on MNEs, and this chapter has so far been no exception. However, a number of the developments associated with globalization have made it possible, and often necessary, for many small- and medium-sized enterprises (SMEs) to expand beyond their domestic borders as well. The availability of efficient, worldwide communications technology and transportation has made it easier and less costly to extend their markets to foreign countries and keep in close touch with their staff or agents there. International expansion into new markets can be vital for SMEs because the liberalization of trade, and the consequent decrease in the number of geographically protected market niches, has heightened the threat to their domestic markets.[51] Extending their supply and operations to foreign countries is also sometimes a condition for SMEs to retain their existing business customers when the latter expand into new territories.

Compared to larger firms, especially those that are already established as MNEs, SMEs are relatively deficient in the resources required to support international diversification. Common areas of deficiency are:

1   information about the attributes of potential locations for international diversification;
2   investment and working capital;
3   experience of (a) international operations and (b) arrangements for achieving these, such as partnerships with foreign firms;
4   technology appropriate to foreign markets;
5   managerial and technical capacity (especially people to spare for investigating new foreign markets).

The risk for large MNEs in foreign expansion lies more in failing to secure a strategic position in product and/or supply markets early on, rather than in committing resources that could cripple the firm in the event of failure. The latter possibility is, however, likely to concern many SMEs. Deficiencies in information, experience, and capital increase the risk for an SME in going abroad, because they limit the firm's capacity to deal with the uncertainties of a new situation. Limited managerial resources and a generally centralized mode of control and decision-making may also present difficulties for managing activities at a distance. Although their involvement in internationalization is increasing, these limitations mean that SMEs are not yet as fully represented in the international economy as large firms.[52]

SMEs can basically choose between four main modes of internationalization. Each of these requires different arrangements.

1   *Exporting*, which for manufacturing SMEs normally requires the establishment of agreements with local agents. While a manufacturing SME will normally expect agents to promote its products in the foreign market, the other services required of agents depend on the nature of the product or service being offered. In the case of a one-off service, such as an overseas consultancy assignment, the role of the local agent may be no more than one of effecting initial introductions and arranging travel and associated logistics. In cases such as exporting sophisticated machinery, a company may have to rely heavily on local agents to provide services such as installation, after-sales service, and spare parts. SMEs offering services such as software which can be distributed and paid for via the Internet, or SMEs supplying to known customers within a well-established network, such as most biotechnology firms do, may not require overseas agents. For them, the problem posed by some export markets may lie less in organizing distribution and representation than in safeguarding propriety products and knowledge. On the whole, exporting can be considered a strategy that involves a low financial risk relative to other foreign market entry modes. Relying on exporting alone carries another kind of risk, however, namely that opportunities in new markets may not be fully exploited.

2 A *cooperative mode* based on alliances and other cooperative arrangements between firms. Although with this mode the internationalizing firm now enjoys some hands-on managerial control, it is still dependent on its partner(s) and faces a higher level of financial risk in terms of the resources it has to commit. The cooperative mode can take several forms, including a development project undertaken jointly with a local partner, contractual consortia, equity participation in an existing foreign firm, and equity participation in establishing a new joint venture (see Chapter 11). An SME may partner with one or more firms from the host country, with firms from its own country, or with firms from a third country.

Because of their limited financial resources, SMEs are more likely to enter into overseas alliances on the basis of an equity share of 50 percent or less. Chapter 11 noted how research suggests that the managerial requirements for success when partnering without a majority equity share are different to the case in which the firm is a majority partner. The creation of high trust between the partners appears to be particularly essential in this situation because the SME possesses neither the voting power nor sufficient managerial presence on the ground to be able to exercise control by direct means.

3 A *network mode* based on maintaining a position within the network value chains of larger firms and following them into new markets. Many Japanese SMEs have followed this strategy.[53] Industries where independent or affiliate SMEs have a significant presence acting as suppliers or sub-contractors within MNE value chains include automotive, scientific and precision instruments, software, tourism and film making.[54] The rapid internationalization of small software firms has at times been driven largely by their existing network relationships, with major partners often guiding foreign market selection and providing the mechanisms for market entry.[55] The quasi-subsidiary role that SMEs are liable to play within value chain networks involves a high level of dependence on larger firms, but it reduces the financial risks of internationalizing to a relatively low level – at least in the short term. This form may prove to be transitory in the medium to long term, however, because there is the risk that the major partner(s) might eventually choose to terminate its relationship with the SME.

A variant of the network mode of internationalization arises when foreign market entry is facilitated by the presence of compatriots who have migrated to the prospective host country. For example, in the case of Hong Kong SMEs expanding abroad, the availability in North America, the UK, and some South-East Asian countries of a Hong Kong Cantonese diaspora provided local staff who were seen to be trustworthy and who could help them cope with a new environment. Participation in business social networks with other firms, via membership of chambers of commerce and other business associations, also facilitated the internationalization of these firms through the sharing of experience and other relevant information.[56]

4 An *autonomous mode*, by which firms enter a new foreign environment in a way that is comprehensive and independent. They commit to foreign direct investment in the foreign locality, financing and managing the overseas diversification themselves. While this strategy is common for large firms, it is often beyond the reach of SMEs because of the resource constraints mentioned. It also presents a high financial risk mode due to the generally poor knowledge SMEs have of local conditions, their low bargaining power with local institutions, and the proportionately high commitment of their resources that

is entailed. If it can be achieved, however, the low dependence on other firms with this mode might permit SMEs more scope to deploy their advantage of small firm flexibility than do other, less independent, modes.

Even though MNEs have been externalizing some of their activities through outsourcing and partnering, typically many are retained within their internal hierarchies. These may include functions such as foreign business development and foreign governmental relations, which it is unlikely that an SME could afford to carry on its overhead. SMEs therefore generally rely on the support of agents, advisors and partners outside the firm to acquire information for recognizing new opportunities and to establish connections supportive of their international growth. This is likely to be particularly true of rapidly internationalizing new ventures.[57] The most common way for SMEs to cope with difficulties and uncertainties in exporting to foreign markets is through relying on the help of local partners.[58] Johanson and Vahlne have argued that "insidership" in relevant networks is, in general, a prerequisite for successful internationalization.[59] This is especially true for SMEs for which "internationalization is seen as an entrepreneurial process embedded in an institutional and social web which supports the firm in terms of access to information, human capital, finance, and so on."[60]

An SME's attachment to networks can include relations with other firms (e.g. large customers), institutional agencies, chambers of commerce, consultants, as well as other SMEs including those owned by extended family members. Such relations can vary in their quality. They may amount to "strong ties" which tend to be long-lasting and social in nature, such as those with family and friends, and have a markedly personal and trust-based quality. These contrast with "weak ties," typically business relations, which tend to be occasional and arms-length links, contractual and non-social in nature. Strong social ties enable access to and exchange of "fine-grained" and tacit information, whereas weak business ties can be focused more economically on providing non-redundant relevant information and brokering profitable connections.[61]

Because many SMEs seeking to engage in cross-border business are likely to depend heavily on external networking, the management of these relationships is a crucial issue for them. The distinction just made between strong and weak network ties indicates that SME entrepreneurs are presented with a degree of choice concerning the attachments to external network they should try to organize. This raises questions such as "Should strong or weak ties be cultivated? Is it better to have a dense or a diverse network?" When considering these options, they need to bear in mind the cost implications because time and effort has to be expended in maintaining network links, especially strong ones. Investigations into the internationalization of SMEs are beginning to throw some light on the factors that are relevant to these options.

One factor is the cultural and institutional character of an SME's home environment and that of foreign markets in which it does business. When the home environment has a well-developed range of institutions, following clear and predictable regulations and norms of conduct, SMEs can gain assistance from a similarly wide range of weak ties oriented to meeting specific needs. For example, they can pay for market intelligence and contact-making support from official export promotion agencies, and they can expect to secure working capital from financial institutions. The market is the prevailing social organization within a universalistic national culture in which all firms, small as well as large, are expected to be subject to the same rules. It should not be necessary to seek special treatment through cultivating strong ties. By contrast, when the home environment has institutional voids, as in many emerging countries, the culture is likely to be a particularistic one. This means that SME entrepreneurs have to rely on strong informal personal ties to effect connections with formal agencies in order to be heard in the first place and then hope to gain support as a particular favor rather than a universal right. They have to be selective in finding the right social ties. Their networks are likely to be relatively focused on such ties and restricted in scope but dense in nature. In effect, the entrepreneur to succeed has to belong to a relevant clan.[62] Such network links can take time and hard work to bring about, which represents a handicap for the development of SMEs in such an environment. A comparison of British and Egyptian internationalizing SMEs clearly illustrates how such contextual differences in their home countries shape the network ties that SMEs develop to support their international business.[63]

Turning to foreign (host market) environments, the earlier analysis of implications for MNEs can be extended to SMEs. If an SME from a developed country is seeking to expand into another developed country, especially one with a similar culture, it may be able to rely quite extensively on weak business-like ties to effect necessary local arrangements such as compliance with local regulations and securing necessary licenses and titles. Depending on the nature of its outputs, it may also need to sign contracts with local agents and distributors. If, on the other hand, the SME is seeking to expand into an emerging or developing country which has opaque institutions, a particularistic culture and perhaps high levels of corruption, it may need more substantial and continuing assistance requiring closer ties such as extended family connections, a partner in the host country, or assistance from its home government.

The burden of constructing and maintaining network ties can be a heavy one, which in the case of small firms falls heavily on the primary decision-maker. This is a significant potential deterrent to the expansion of SMEs into foreign markets that may be promising in terms of their size and growth but very challenging in terms of navigating their uncertain high-risk waters. Another challenge follows from the need for SMEs to be quick on their feet in response to new challenges and opportunities, and this in turn depends on the quality of their learning processes. Whereas MNEs can rely upon global network managers to integrate multi-level contributions to their learning processes, it is often the chief executive who performs the equivalent role in SMEs. In the Hong Kong SMEs I studied, their chief executives typically had to sustain heavy travel schedules, which they said were necessary to bring them into contact with new information and business opportunities, in addition to enabling them to keep in close touch with their foreign markets. This again illustrates how the heads of smaller firms tend personally to perform functions that in larger firms are fulfilled by specialists within the management structure.

SUMMARY

1   Multinational enterprises (MNEs) are firms with foreign affiliates in at least one country other than their domestic base. Through their foreign direct investment (FDI), they are key players in the process of globalization. An increasing number of transactions are taking place between their internationally diversified units.

2   There are four main strategies that MNEs adopt for international expansion in the light of their requirements for global integration as against their need to be

responsive to local situations. These are the multi-domestic, international, global, and transnational strategies.

3   Each of these strategies has its own implications for an MNE's organizational structure and the way it endeavors to manage organizational processes such as integration. The organization of their cross-border transactions is one of the biggest challenges that MNEs face today.

4   A multi-domestic strategy presents relatively low integration requirements and a global geographic structure is likely to be suitable.

5   An international strategy imposes greater integration needs and, depending on the degree of product diversity, may be implemented through either a global geographic or a global product structure.

6   A global strategy requires quite a high level of centralized coordination and, since there is little local customization of products, a global product structure often suits this strategy.

7   The transnational strategy is organizationally the most demanding because it attempts to combine the centralized control of certain activities with decentralized units that can adapt to local requirements. It presents very high integration needs with respect to communication and information processing.

8   While a multidimensional matrix is usually adopted to support a transnational strategy, its successful implementation also requires a broad level of awareness among managers and staff that transcends boundaries within the company.

9   MNEs are being urged to adopt a transnational strategy, which means that they have to recognize the benefits of internal diversity and differentiation within a network framework that preserves the necessary degree of overall integration.

10 Many of them have therefore been pioneering new ways of organizing to handle fundamental issues such as headquarters-subsidiary relations, control, integration, cultural diversity, and the cross-border transfer of knowledge and practices.

11 Eli Lilly provides an instructive example of how a large MNE has evolved its organization better to reconcile the benefits of globally coordinating some activities while decentralizing others such as marketing support and distribution. While differentiating its internal organization accordingly, it has come to rely on multiple internal networks to preserve the necessary level of integration between activities and the use of resources.

12 Less attention has been paid to the problems faced by small- and medium-sized enterprises (SMEs) as they strive to extend their activities across borders.

13 SMEs can choose between four main modes of internationalization: exporting, allying with a partner, following a larger company abroad as part of a supply chain network, and investing abroad on their own. They normally rely significantly on support from external network ties. The options open to them concerning the nature of such ties will depend on circumstances such as the cultural and institutional context of their home environment and foreign markets.

QUESTIONS FOR DISCUSSION

12.1 Referring also to Chapter 3, discuss the relationship between how the organization of multinational enterprises has evolved and the process of globalization.

12.2 What are the organizational implications of the different global expansion
strategies open to MNEs?

12.3 Describe and discuss the defining features of an MNE adopting the so-called
"transnational solution."

12.4 What are the key functions of a global network manager and the personal
attributes required?

12.5 In which ways are some MNEs pioneering new ways of organizing?

12.6 How are national cultures relevant to the operations of an MNE? What are the
main options for managing cultural differences within an international
organization?

12.7 Describe and discuss the key differences between how an MNE and an SME
might organize to achieve successful international expansion.

NOTES

1   Peter Dicken (2011), *Global Shift: Mapping the Changing Contours of the Global Economy,* London, Sage
    6th edition, p. 6.

2   Alan M. Rugman (2000), *The End of Globalization,* London, Random House.

3   UNCTAD [United Nations Conference on Trade and Development] (2003), *World Investment Report
    2003,* New York, United Nations, p. 231.

4   Also by Peter Dicken 2011, op. cit.

5   UNCTAD (2013), *Transational Corporations Statistics.* http://unctad.org/en/Pages/DIAE/Trans
    national-Corporations-Statistics.aspx, accessed 25 January, 2014.

6   Peter Dicken (2011), op. cit., Chapter 5.

7   Peter Dicken (2011), op. cit., p. 109.

8   UNCTAD (2009), *World Investment Report 2009,* New York, United Nations.

9   UNCTAD (2013), *World Investment Report 2013,* New York, United Nations.

10 This information comes from various issues of the *World Investment Report.*

11 Alan Rugman, Alain Verbeke, and Wenlong Yuan (2011), Re-conceptualizing Bartlett and Ghoshal's
    classification of national subsidiary roles in the multinational enterprise, *Journal of Management
    Studies,* 48(2), 253–277.

12 Notably by Christopher A. Bartlett and Sumantra Ghoshal (1998), *Managing Across Borders: The
    Transnational Solution,* London, Random House, 2nd edition.

13 Gareth R. Jones (2001), op. cit., Quotation is from pp. 244–245.

14 Christopher A. Bartlett and Sumantra Ghoshal (1998), op. cit., Chapter 6.

15 Christopher A. Bartlett and Sumantra Ghoshal (1998), op. cit., p. 227. The term was first coined by a
    senior MNE manager.

16 Sumantra Ghoshal and Nitin Nohria (1993), Horses for courses: Organizational forms for multi-
    national corporations, *Sloan Management Review,* Winter, 23–35.

17 Peter J. Buckley and Mark Casson (1976), *The Future of the Multinational Enterprise,* Basingstoke,
    Macmillan.

18 Quyen T.K. Nguyen (2011), The empirical literature on multinational enterprises, subsidiaries and performance, *The Multinational Business Review*, 19(1), 47–64.

19 Peer Hull Kristensen and Kari Lilja (eds.) (2011), *Nordic Capitalisms and Globalization: New Forms of Economic Organization and Welfare Institutions*, Oxford, Oxford University Press.

20 This section has been informed by Nora Ramadan (2014), *Vertical Inter-Unit Relationship Quality: The Concept and its Concomitants*. Unpublished PhD thesis, University of Birmingham.

21 Ram Mudambi and Pietro Navarra (2004), Is knowledge power? Knowledge flows, subsidiary power and rent-seeking within MNEs, *Journal of International Business* Studies, 35(5), 385–406; Alan Rugman, Alain Verbeke, and Wenlong Yuan 2011, op. cit.

22 Francesco Ciabuschi, Mats Forsgren, and Oscar M. Martin, (2011), Rationality vs ignorance: The role of MNE headquarters in subsidiaries' innovation processes, *Journal of International Business Studies*, 42(7), 958–970.

23 Phillip C. Nell and Björn Ambos (2013), Parenting advantage in the MNE: An embeddedness perspective on the value added by headquarters, *Strategic Management Journal*, 34(9), 1086–1103.

24 Stephen Todd Rudman (2006), *The Multinational Corporation In China: Controlling Interests,* Oxford, Blackwell.

25 John Child (2003), The management of joint ventures within international business networks: US companies in China. In Bruce McKern (ed.), *Managing the Global Network Corporation*, London, Routledge, Chapter 4.

26 Christopher A. Bartlett and Sumantra Ghoshal (1998), op. cit., Chapter 5.

27 Nitin Nohria (1992), Is a network perspective a useful way of studying organizations? In Nitin Nohria and Robert G. Eccles (eds.), *Networks and Organizations*, Boston, MA, Harvard Business School Press, pp. 1–22.

28 Henry W. Lane, Joseph L. Di Stefano, and Martha L. Maznevski (2000), *International Management Behavior,* Malden, MA: Blackwell, 4th edition.

29 John Child and Suzana B. Rodrigues (1996), The role of social identity in the international transfer of knowledge through joint ventures. In Stewart Clegg and Gill Palmer (eds.), *The Politics of Management Knowledge*, London, Sage, 46–68.

30 On managing partnerships, see John Child, David Faulkner, and Stephen Tallman (2005), *Cooperative Strategy*, Oxford, Oxford University Press, 2nd edition, Chapter 10.

31 On national cultural differences and their impact on managerial practices, see David J. Hickson and Derek S. Pugh (2001), *Management Worldwide: Distinctive Styles amid Globalization*, London, Penguin. Also R.S. Bhagat and R.M. Steers (eds.) (2009), *The Cambridge Handbook of Culture, Organizations, and Work,* Cambridge, Cambridge University Press.

32 For a useful discussion of cultural fit in mergers and acquisitions, see Hewitt Associates. *Mergers and Acquisitions in Europe: Survey Results 2003.* www.hewitt.com.

33 Rosalie L. Tung (1993), Managing cross-national and intra-national diversity, *Human Resource Management*, 32, 461–477. The quotation is from p. 465.

34 Bertrand Moingeon and Amy Edmondson (eds.) (1996), *Organizational Learning and Competitive Advantage,* London, Sage.

35 These distinctions are made by Rabi S. Bhagat, Ben L. Kedia, Paula D. Harveston, and Harry C. Triandis (2002), Cultural variations in the cross-border transfer of organizational knowledge: An integrative framework, *Academy of Management Review*, 27, 204–221.

36 Rabi S. Bhagat, Ben L. Kedia, Paula D. Harveston, and Harry C. Triandis (2002), op. cit., p. 208.

37 Mary Yoko Brannen (2004), When Mickey loses face: Recontextualization, semantic fit, and the semiotics of foreignness, *Academy of Management Review*, 29(4), 593–616.

38 Paul Lillrank (1995), The Transfer of Management Innovations from Japan, *Organization Studies*, 16, 971–989.

39   John Child, Leanne Chung, and Suzana B. Rodrigues (2004), Creating actionable knowledge through the cross-border transfer of practices, Paper presented to the Academy of Management Annual Meeting, New Orleans, August.

40   Stephen Todd Rudman (2006), op. cit.

41   Sources: Michael Y. Yoshino and Thomas W. Malnight (1999), *Eli Lilly – 1998 (b): Emerging Global Organization,* Harvard Business School Case. Reference No: 9-399-174. Thomas W. Malnight (2001), Emerging structural patterns within multinational corporations: Toward process-based structures, *Academy of Management Journal,* 44, 1187–1210.

42   Thomas W. Malnight (2001), op. cit., Quotation is from p. 1190.

43   Dave Hannon (2011), Lilly Brings Process Consistency to a Diversified, Global Organization, *SAP insider PROFILES,* April 1, http://sapinsider.wispubs.com/Assets/Case-Studies/2011/April/Lilly-Brings-Process-Consistency-To-A-Diversified-Global-Organization, accessed January 30, 2014.

44   Thomas W. Malnight (2001), op. cit., Quotation is from p. 1203.

45   John Child and Suzana B. Rodrigues (2011), How Organizations Engage with External Complexity: A Political Action Perspective, *Organization Studies,* 32(6), 803–824.

46   Tarun Khanna and Krishna G. Palepu (eds.) (2010), *Winning in Emerging Markets: A Road Map for Strategy and Execution,* Boston, MA, Harvard Business Press.

47   Deeksha Singh (2012), Emerging economies and multinational corporations: An institutional approach to subsidiary management, *International Journal of Emerging Markets,* 7(4), 397–410.

48   John Child and Svetla T. Marinova (2014), The role of contextual combinations in the globalization of Chinese firms, *Management and Organization Review,* 10(3), 405–409.

49   Mohan Thite, Adrian Wilkinson, and Dhara Shah (2012), Internationalization & HRM Strategies across Subsidiaries in Multinational Corporations from Emerging Economies – A Conceptual Framework, *Journal of World Business,* 47(2), 251–258.

50   D. Eleanor Westney and Srilata Zaheer (2009), The multinational enterprise as an organization. In Alan M. Rugman (ed.), *The Oxford Handbook of International Business,* Oxford, Oxford University Press, 2nd edition, Chapter 13, pp. 341–366.

51   Patricia Phillips McDougall and Benjamin M. Oviatt (2000), International entrepreneurship: The intersection of two research paths, *Academy of Management Journal,* 43, 902–906.

52   The Edinburgh Group (2013), *Growing the Global Economy though SMEs.* http://www.edinburgh-group.org/media/2776/edinburgh_group_research_-_growing_the_global_economy_through_smes.pdf, accessed February 1, 2014.

53   Jaideep Anand, R. Azimah Ainuddin, and Shige Makino (1997), An empirical analysis of multinational strategy and international joint venture characteristics in Japanese MNEs. In Paul W. Beamish and J. Peter Killing (eds.), *Cooperative Strategies: Asian Pacific Perspectives,* San Francisco, New Lexington Press, pp. 325–340.

54   OECD (2008), *Enhancing the Role of SMEs in Global Value Chains,* Paris, OECD Publishing. doi: 10.1787/9789264051034-en.

55   Nicole E. Coviello and Hugh J. Munro (1997), Network relationships and the internationalization process of small software firms, *International Business Review,* 6(4), 361–386.

56   John Child, Sek Hong Ng, and Christine Wong (2002), Psychic distance and internationalization: Evidence from Hong Kong firms, *International Studies of Management and Organization,* 32(1), 36–56.

57   Nicole E. Coviello (2006), The network dynamics of international new ventures, *Journal of International Business Studies,* 37(5), 713–731; John Child and Linda Hsieh (2014), Decision mode, information and network attachment in the internationalization of SMEs: A configurational and contingency analysis, *Journal of World Business,* 49(4), 598–610.

58   John Child, Suzana B. Rodrigues, and George Frynas (2009), Psychic distance, its impact and coping modes: Interpretations of SME decision makers, *Management International Review,* 49(2), 199–224; Pushyarag N. Puthusserry, John Child, and Suzana B. Rodrigues (2014), Psychic distance, its

business impact and modes of coping: A study of British and Indian partner SMEs, *Management International Review*, 54(1), 1–29.

59   Jan Johanson and Jan-Erik Vahlne (2009), The Uppsala internationalization process model revisited: From liability of foreignness to liability of outsidership, *Journal of International Business Studies*, 40(9), 1–21.

60   Jim Bell, Rod McNaughton, Stephen Young, and Dave Crick (2003), Towards an integrative model of small firm internationalization, *Journal of International Entrepreneurship*, 1(4), 339–362. The quotation is from p. 341.

61   Ronald S. Burt (1992), *Structural Holes*, Cambridge, MA, Harvard University Press.

62   For an analysis of markets and clans as forms of social organization, see Max Boisot and John Child (1996), From fiefs to clans and network capitalism: Explaining China's emerging economic order, *Administrative Science Quarterly*, 41(4), 600–628.

63   John Child and Rose Narooz (2014), Networking by internationalizing SMEs in the light of domestic institutional voids and cultures. Paper presented to the 2014 European Group for Organization Studies Annual Colloquium.

PART IV

Achieving Effective Organizations

◢ Introduction to Part IV – Achieving Effective Organizations

The chapters in Parts II and III were largely concerned with the structures and mechanisms that facilitate ongoing processes. These should permit, even encourage, a company to evolve successfully through adaptation and innovation. Successful evolution, however, requires further specific capabilities – those of managing change, learning and innovating, generating trust, and securing legitimacy for corporate governance. These abilities can be promoted in part by appropriate organizational policies, but they also rely significantly on the integrity and ethos of management. The chapters in Part IV in turn examine each of these capabilities for evolving effective organizations.

Chapter 13 identifies the policies and practices that facilitate major change in companies when events and trends require this to take place. Chapter 14 focuses on the impact organization can have on learning and knowledge creation within companies, with particular reference to supporting innovation. Increasing attention is being given to the creation of trust in business and employment relationships, as part of a culture that encourages innovation. Chapter 15 identifies organizational policies that can promote trust. Poor corporate governance can seriously damage trust, and Chapter 16 recognizes the growing social demands for a wider and more transparent corporate accountability and the implications these have for organization.

CHAPTER 13

Managing Organizational Change

WHAT THIS CHAPTER COVERS

This chapter examines the main approaches to achieving organizational change. Change has become a normal feature of organizational life, and it is widely appreciated today that organizations must evolve continually in order to survive. However, it is difficult to get change right. Many change initiatives fail and the types of change required vary according to different circumstances. After an introduction to the subject, the chapter discusses the various external and internal drivers of organizational change. It then identifies the different forms of change. These are compared and contrasted in terms of three main features: whether the change is radical or incremental, whether it is planned or emergent, and the focus of the change. Identifying these dimensions assists both in defining what organizational change is and in clarifying alternative approaches that suit different situations. The chapter concludes with a review of policies that support successful planned change and it summarizes key guidelines including those for addressing resistance to change.

The Challenge of Achieving Organizational Change

Organizational change refers to changes in how people's responsibilities, tasks and relationships are organized. Companies have had to adjust from a world in which they only needed to make organizational changes from time to time to one where they must be prepared to make them almost continuously. Change, paradoxically, has become an organizational constant.

In the past, it was sufficient for companies to reorganize periodically as their strategies and business scope developed beyond their organizational capabilities. In the relatively steady state period between reorganizations, it would normally be enough to revise the specifics of rules, procedures, and responsibilities in the light of experience, new external regulations, or to suit new business plans. Today, companies need to keep their organizational arrangements under continual review in the light of the disruptive change that now characterizes many industries.[1]

The nature of the change process itself has also changed in recent times. Organizing now relies less on what can be prescribed structurally, such as rules and formal job descriptions. It depends much more on people using their intelligence and initiative to adapt what they do and how they do it, when circumstances require. As a result, change is increasingly being stimulated by initiatives undertaken throughout an organization rather than through simply relying on schemes formulated by top management. In the past, organizational change programs would be planned by top managers or worked out in close liaison with them, whereas today companies are likely to use project teams to bring people together across levels and activities to work on proposals for improvement.

It is not easy to change entrenched organizational arrangements. There are many barriers to change and many attempts fail. Failure rates of between 60% and 90% have been quoted. Even though the evidence for these high rates has been questioned and it is not always clear what is meant by "failure," they point to the difficulty of implementing change in organizations, and imply that mistakes are often made.[2] As Bernard Burnes has observed, "Given the rapidly changing environment in which organizations operate, there is little doubt that the ability to manage change successfully needs to be a core competence . . . It is equally clear from the failure rate of change that the majority of organizations appear to lack this competence."[3] One of the more common mistakes is to underestimate the challenge of bringing about organizational change by assuming that there is a consensus over the need for change, that the change proposed is acceptable, and that therefore the process should not take too long.

Existing organizational arrangements are more than just ways of allocating responsibility and accountability for work. An organization involves structures that determine the distribution of power and reward among its members. The people who have vested interests in maintaining their organizational privileges as managers or professional specialists would be irrational not to defend them. The same is true for people who fear to lose income, or even their employment, through organizational change. An established organization is also a familiar working environment, to which people have adjusted and which they often wish to maintain. Change constitutes a disturbance that can have serious psychological ramifications. Economic, social and psychological considerations such as these can provoke a negative reaction to change and they help to explain why fundamental change initiatives so often fail.

There are people who are skeptical about the claim that the world is changing ever more rapidly and that organizations have to change in step with this. A quotation, often but wrongly attributed to the Roman Gaius Petronius Arbiter, captures this skepticism: "I was to learn later in life that we tend to meet any new situation by reorganizing, and a wonderful method it can be for creating the illusion of progress while producing confusion, inefficiency, and demoralization." In 1849, French journalist Jean-Baptiste Alphonse Karr wrote the famous epigram: "Plus ça change, plus c'est la même chose" ("The more things change, the more they stay the same") which expresses much the same cynicism about the outcome of attempts to introduce change. Chris Grey maintains that "the generalized claim of 'unprecedented' change is a significant rhetorical device to provoke fear and provide a justification for particular organizational changes."[4] While there is undoubtedly an element of truth in Grey's claim, pointing to a not uncommon combination of immorality and stupidity on the part of management, it does not invalidate the general premise that a failure to change can lead to a rapid organizational death.

There is no disagreement that change is extraordinarily difficult to accomplish in organizations, and is indeed a hazardous undertaking. Even when recommendations for organizational change follow the occurrence of extreme events involving loss of life, often these are not implemented.[5] While pioneering writers on the subject like Warren Bennis and John Kotter warn that we are not coping adequately with organizational change, they would not go along with the skeptics in saying that we should avoid making the attempt in the first place.[6] It is true that when organizational change is attempted but fails, the costs can be high in terms of time and money abortively expended, as well as in demoralization and lost managerial credibility. Nevertheless, avoiding the issue and trying to maintain the status quo is no longer an option. Everything that has been said so far in this book points to the absolute necessity for companies and other organizations to be prepared to handle change and to build this facility into their repertoire of core competences.

Internal and External Drivers of Organizational Change

There are both external and internal drivers of organizational change. Over the longer term, external developments shape fundamental ground rules that no company can afford to ignore. In this sense they are the ultimate drivers of organizational change. However, companies with the will and capacity to adopt innovative and aggressive strategies can proactively shape some of the conditions under which they operate. Being proactive implies a willingness and ability to adapt and change.

External drivers

The broadest category of external change drivers includes those factors that are active across a range of industries and countries. They offer inducements to introduce change in order to take advantage of new opportunities, but they can also trigger pressures to change, even among companies reluctant to do so. Many of the facets of globalization fall into this category. On the institutional side, these include new opportunities following from the liberalization of commercial and financial markets. It is now easier to expand into new markets and territories with the aid of local partners, service providers, and sources of finance. There are also new institutional constraints such as regulations on corporate governance and environmental standards. Equally broad developments of a non-institutional character include technological innovations, rising educational levels, demographic changes, the growth of critical social movements and the threat of cyber and physical terrorism. Another external "disturbance" has come from the ability of entrepreneurial firms such as Richard Branson's Virgin Group, Steve Jobs's Apple or Jeff Bezos's Amazon to shake up cozy arrangements among existing players in industries like passenger air traffic, consumer electronics and retailing. All these factors are drivers for the evolution of corporate strategies and configurations, which in turn generate requirements for organizational change.

A combination of more open markets, rapid technological change, and entrepreneurship has led hypercompetition to become a major driver for organizational change. Firms facing greater competition and a higher velocity of change in their industries are under pressure to speed up their rate of reorganization, and to redouble their attempts to acquire new capabilities through alliances or acquisitions. As we saw in Chapter 3, hypercompetition is brought about by the innovations of companies pursuing non-conventional strategies and prepared to adopt new organizational forms to provide them with a superior ability to adapt. The more that firms try to resist changes in strategy by sticking to the previously accepted rules of competition and maintaining their existing organizational arrangements, the greater the danger to their survival in the face of such competitors.

The way that the business environment is evolving at this broad, often global, level does not simply create pressures for change. It also offers opportunities for companies to reorganize themselves dramatically, especially in terms of actively managing their boundaries. As Chapters 9 and 10 described, the development of specialized competence nodes, such as that for software development in Bangalore, and the greater ease of managing extended value chain networks with the aid of modern ICT has encouraged companies to divest themselves of non-core activities in favor of sub-contracting work directly to the market. Similarly, it has become more feasible for many companies to distribute production to locations around the globe where it is economically more advantageous.

Internal drivers

Companies do not respond in the same way to external developments. Some pursue strategies aimed at creating new, first-mover advantages for themselves, as Toyota has done with its environmentally friendly and fuel-efficient hybrid automobiles. Others adopt a more defensive posture. The strategic choices senior managers make have direct implications for whether they are likely to opt for significant changes in their organization. Among these choices are whether to adopt a leader or follower role in the industry, whether to aim at above average or normal returns, whether to adapt through pursuing returns from innovation or from improved efficiency, and whether to diversify or focus. The more that top management opts for the first of these pairs of choices – a leader role, above average returns, and innovation – the more likely it is to encourage change and evolution in its organization. Toyota is again a good example in the automotive sector, having consistently pioneered both strategic and organizational innovations. Amazon also fits the profile, with innovations in its logistics and delivery systems.

Arie Lewin and his colleagues have produced a model of how environments, industries, and firms evolve in relation to each other over time.[7] By summarizing the external and internal drivers for change, and the connectedness between them, their model provides a useful guide to the context of organizational change. It is reproduced in Figure 13.1.

◢ Varieties of Organizational Change

There are many varieties of change underway among companies and labels to accompany them, including continuous improvement, organizational development, reengineering, refocusing, regeneration, restructuring, rebirthing, and transformation. The aims of change can range from the defensive, for example cost-cutting through downsizing and out-sourcing, to the proactive, for example releasing people's potentials and enhancing innovation. The scope

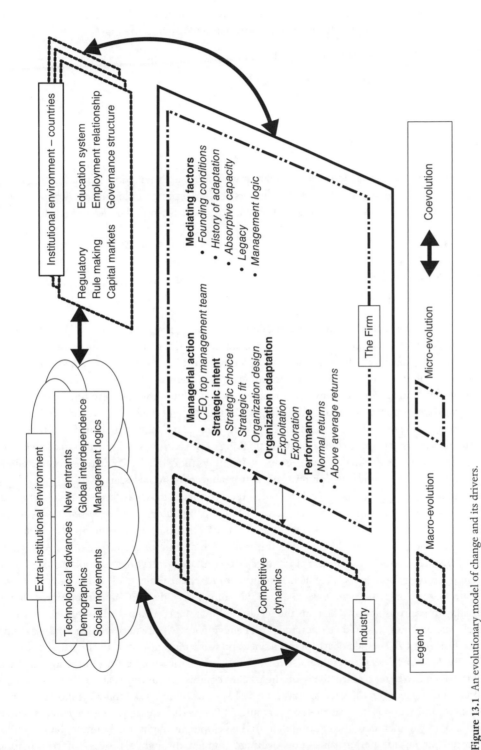

Figure 13.1 An evolutionary model of change and its drivers.

Reprinted by permission, Arie Lewin, Chris P. Long, and Timothy N. Carroll, 'The coevolution of new organizational forms', *Organization Science*, 10(5), 1999. Copyright 1999, the Institute for Operations Research and the Management Sciences (INFORMS), 5521 Research Park Drive, Suite 200, Catonsville, MD 21228 USA.

of the change can be primarily internal to an organization or extend to its external networking. The only way to make sense of this confused scene is to forget the labels for a while and look instead for key underlying features. Three are particularly important:

- How radical is the change?
- Is the change planned or emergent?
- What is the focus of the change?

How radical is the change?

Robert Marshak in a classic article argued that we tend to use metaphors when thinking about change.[8] He examined four change metaphors that incorporate different assumptions about how radical change should be and how it should be carried out. The four metaphors are:

1   fix and maintain;
2   build and develop;
3   move and relocate;
4   liberate and recreate.

The *fix and maintain* metaphor is basically about fixing things as they are. It looks upon the organization as a machine. If its performance starts to fail, the appropriate response is not to question the capability of the machine itself, but to adjust it, service it, or maybe refuel it. For instance, different units may not be communicating efficiently – therefore culling unnecessary emails and other clutter from the organization's communications network might be an appropriate response. In the face of falling sales, there might well be a recruitment drive for more salespeople. Although organizations do require fixing and maintenance, the metaphor militates against any more fundamental rethinking of the current set-up, which may no longer be adequate to cope with new circumstances. It betrays more of an attitude resistant to change, rather than a willingness to contemplate that change may be necessary.

Marshak relates the story of a large, high-tech company that was faced with a barrage of problems: erosion of its market base, entry of new competitors, inflated costs, low synergy, and insufficient responsiveness to customers. The corporation's top executives were aware of these problems, but their thinking was trapped in the fix and maintain metaphor. As a result they instigated a series of retreats, task forces, and employees' meetings, all looking for ways of fixing problems, but none of which produced more than minimal ideas for improvement. Matters got worse and morale declined, to the point where the CEO in desperation called in management consultants. The consultants advised that the company had to rethink its whole business and how it would be operated. Still believing it was only necessary to fix the existing machine, the CEO could not accept this advice and was later replaced by the board of directors.

The *build and develop* metaphor also assumes that the basic set-up is fine, but recognizes that it is possible to build constructively on the past. In contrast to the way that the fix and maintain metaphor screens out the need to learn, the build and develop way of thinking allows for what Argyris and Schon called "single-loop learning."[9] This is the search for improvements within the broad parameters of the existing system. Development might, for example, be driven by annual targets for performance improvement, agreed through a process of consultation between managers and individual staff, or conducted in groups. The delegation of more initiative to enrich the jobs of front-line employees, and the introduction of inter-departmental teams, are examples of the kind of organizational change that this metaphor encourages.

The *move and relocate* metaphor conceives of organizational change as a transition. This involves a move from one state to another – from A to B, with the parameters of the existing system therefore being changed. The end-state, however, is known and likely to be planned in advance. Top management and its advisors usually have a decisive role in steering this kind of change, although they may encourage the extensive participation of others in its detailed design and implementation. One common transition is that from carrying out some activities in-house or in the domestic country, to sourcing them externally or transferring them to another country (see Chapter 9). Another transition is the move from a centralized structure with only local sales and servicing units for different product groups to one in which decentralized divisions are sufficiently self-contained to be constituted as profit centers. A quite common case involves the integration of a company's structure and systems into that of a new parent following its acquisition. Some organizational transitions like the last two examples are quite major and entail considerable upheaval.

It is the fourth metaphor, *liberate and recreate*, that is most in tune with the change philosophy suited to organizing for the future. This metaphor conceives of transformation rather than transition, in the sense that is focuses on unleashing an organization's potential to create a new vision of the future, to reinvent itself, and so escape from its present hang-ups. Transformation is an open-ended process of evolutionary discovery, in which outcomes emerge from a process of active debate and experimentation, rather than the managing of a transition to a new state that is planned and specified in advance. It is not at all easy for the members of an organization to move beyond the anxiety and confusion that naturally come when they realize they have to let go of their previous organizational base and work out new solutions. Once they allow themselves to think of new possibilities that are not constrained by previous assumptions and norms, a wealth of ideas typically starts to flow. Argyris and Schon have called this more frame-breaking kind of learning "double-loop learning."[10] The biggest obstacle to achieving it usually arises from fear about how transformation will impact on jobs, especially in companies that are unwilling to provide guarantees about employment. Middle managers are often fearful that transformational change will make their functions redundant and lead to delayering. Claudio Ciborra and his colleagues relate how middle managers at Fiat for this reason blocked a potential transformation in the organization of production (see Box 13.1).

The different concepts of organizational change contained in the four metaphors are not mutually exclusive. It is a matter of judgment as to which metaphor is appropriate and when. It is however necessary to bear three points in mind. First, different people involved in bringing about change may find themselves adhering to a different metaphor and therefore working at cross-purposes. The case of the CEO who could not move beyond the fix and maintain metaphor, and so discourse constructively with the management consultants he hired, is an instance of this. It is vital to share and clarify assumptions about the kind of change required at a very early stage.

The second point is that the four change metaphors constitute a hierarchy in the sense that going up from metaphor 1 to metaphor 4 — from fix and maintain to liberate and recreate — broadens the horizon of possibilities whereas going down excludes possibilities. It is therefore wise always to aim for the top of this hierarchy, maintaining a company's capacity to apply the

BOX 13.1   THE BLOCKING OF TRANSFORMATIONAL CHANGE

In advising the company's management on how to achieve their aim of an integrated factory, Ciborra and his colleagues recommended that factory units comprising workers and supervisors be introduced to the concepts of systems dynamics. This would be a way for them to learn effective strategies to cope with complex breakdowns and bottlenecks. They concluded that acquiring new concepts and routines, such as distributed control over workflows, could support the development of important new capabilities.

In the end, Fiat management chose not to make this knowledge available to work units. Confronted with the challenge of sharing insights into systems dynamics and the mapping of a complex production flow, and so with sharing control with the workers in order to make the plant operate more effectively, managers took fright. They were ultimately unwilling to open the door to what they perceived as their privileged knowledge.

Sources: Claudio U. Ciborra, Gerardo Patriotta, and Luisella Erlicher (1996) Disassembling frames on the assembly line: The theory and practice of the new division of learning in advanced manufacturing, in Wanda J. Orlikowski, Geoff Walsham, Matthew R. Jones, and Janice I. DeGross (eds.) *Information Technology and Changes in Organizational Work*. London: Chapman & Hall, pp. 397–418. Also unpublished lecture by Ciborra, Judge Business School, University of Cambridge, 8 December 1995.

liberate and recreate metaphor and fostering a culture that supports it. Transformational solutions are becoming ever more necessary in contemporary business. The open-minded exploratory approach that goes along with the transformational metaphor still allows the members of an organization to revert to other metaphors when appropriate. This does, of course, require quite considerable mental flexibility but, as we have repeated many times, that is the name of the modern competitive game.

The third point also arises from the range across Marshak's four change metaphors from fixing the present to totally transforming it. It has become evident that a constructive process of change normally preserves an element of continuity in both people and practices.[11] The assurance that their security of employment, or that of their colleagues, will continue is likely to make a proposed change much more acceptable to the staff who have to implement it. It is a basis on which it may be possible to retain consensus and trust, which should motivate people to contribute to the specifics of making new arrangements work. This connects to another benefit of maintaining some continuity. Even if the impetus for change has come from a major crisis, an organization contains a fund of accumulated competences, knowledge and skills. It is almost certain that some of these accumulated invisible assets will be of considerable value in the post-change situation. In fact, they may represent the essence of the organization's distinctive competence and brand equity. It is therefore vital to preserve them.

Planned or emergent change?

In one sense, virtually all changes in organizations are planned in that either deliberate decisions are made to initiate a change or it is decided to encourage the emergence of changes through an active process of learning at all levels of an organization. It is, however, useful to make a distinction between "planned" and "emergent" change because they contrast in their sources of initiative and degrees of prescription.[12]

PLANNED CHANGE

Change is planned when a new set of arrangements and the process for moving toward them are articulated in advance. Planned change is usually driven from the top of an organization, and top management is influential in setting the agenda for change. The agenda involves a setting of goals or targets for improvement, and often includes a blueprint for specific changes in organization. By contrast, the emergent approach views change to an important extent as initiated and implemented from the bottom up.

The stages in planned change are considered in detail later in this chapter. The typical process may be described in simplified terms as follows. It starts when pressures or opportunities for change become evident. Top management then responds to external drivers for change or concludes from its own internal evaluation that new opportunities or new threats make change desirable. It then embarks on a problem-solving process that considers alternatives and ends with a decision on which to adopt. The change is implemented and subsequently assessed to provide feedback for an evaluation of the need for further change.

The planned approach to change usually involves the role of *change agent*, who is the person given the responsibility of managing the efforts directed at facilitating the change. The change agent may be an internal or external consultant, and we later discuss the merits of these alternatives. Whereas line management takes responsibility for deciding on a need for change and subsequently for its effective implementation, change agents normally focus on facilitating the process of gaining acceptance for the change, arranging for organizational members to work on the details, assisting implementation, and conducting post hoc evaluations.[13]

EMERGENT CHANGE

The emergent approach looks upon change as a continuous and decentralized process of learning and adapting as circumstances alter. This kind of change emerges not from the preconceptions of senior managers but rather from a process of learning and adaptation among people lower down the hierarchy who are closer to the scene of action. This contrasts with the tendency of planned change to take the form of periodic programs. The argument for an emergent approach rests on the observation that the complexity, pace, and uncertainty of the modern business environment make it impossible for a small group of top managers to decide on the most appropriate response. The sheer size of many corporations and business units also makes it difficult to judge from the top what will work best at the operating level. This is in line with the implications of complexity theory applied to organizations, namely that initiatives coming from their membership as a whole offer the best possibility of signaling the need to adapt to changing circumstances and of ensuring that such adaptation will actually take place.

In other words, the emergent approach to change is consistent with managing organizations as complex adaptive systems.[14]

Michael Beer and his colleagues concluded from a five-year study of American companies that pre-designed and planned change programs do not work. In many of the companies, top management, with the support of a corporate staff group, normally in HRM, had launched programs for education and training, performance related pay, quality circles, corporate culture, reengineering, and reorganization, none of which brought about any genuine change. Instead, the approach that did work was one in which top management encouraged innovations by the operating units themselves and then promoted their dissemination to other relevant locations throughout the rest of the company.[15]

There is growing evidence that the most effective senior managers are aware of their limited capacity to prescribe the nature of corporate renewal far from areas of operation. Their role, according to the emergent approach, is to specify the general direction in which change should go and to generate a supportive climate for it. Rather than trying to work out specific solutions at an early stage in the change process, they encourage new solutions to emerge at lower levels. Eventually, when this has happened, top management's role is to encourage their widespread adoption and to align the company's structure and systems with the change.

The emergent approach does not therefore diminish so much as modify the role of senior management in organizational change. Instead of senior managers actively directing change from a blueprint, in the emergent approach their role is to facilitate the process by providing vision, ensuring necessary resource and systems support, and reinforcing the will to implement newly emerged solutions in other parts of the organization to which they apply. The comprehensive changes introduced by the ASDA supermarket chain, which turned around its fortunes, illustrate the extensive use of an emergent approach heavily supported by top management (Box 13.2).

The focus of change

Change can be undertaken at different levels, ranging from the firm or institution as a whole, to the organization of a particular unit or area of activity, down to changes in individual jobs and the people who carry them out. Its focus can range from broad to narrow. It is, however, rather artificial and misleading to separate out areas and levels of change in this way, because each of them will certainly have wider impacts. The interdependence of the elements in organization means that it is not realistic to think about changing one part of the system without taking into account its knock-on effects.

This point is relatively easy to appreciate when the initial focus of change is the organization as a whole. When management initiates the reorganization of a company in order to support a major strategic shift such as diversification, the changes are likely to focus on the structuring of relations between its divisions and major functional units, and on the control, information, and other systems which link them together. To be implemented effectively, the overall reorganization will require more specific changes in how each unit is organized and staffed. The unit level changes are in turn likely to carry implications for individual members and their jobs.

It might appear that the reverse is not necessarily true. Why should changes in a specialized area or at a specifically operational level impact on a company as a whole? In practice, they

BOX 13.2 SUCCESSFUL CHANGE AT ASDA

ASDA is a UK grocery chain. In 1991 it was on the edge of bankruptcy. Its recovery to a highly competitive company illustrates the successful use of an emergent approach to organizational change. One of the key innovations introduced by Archie Norman, the CEO newly appointed in 1991 to turn the company around, was to identify three "renewable stores" in which managers would be given the freedom to innovate in their retail proposition, use of physical space, and how people were organized and managed. The staff in those stores were allowed to experiment without being penalized for any failures. Norman also made unannounced visits to many of the company's stores to discover what employees and store managers saw as barriers to better performance. Within nine months, the "renewable store" managers, working with a corporate cross-functional team, had created a wholly new approach. The innovation was then spread, through active top management insistence, to all the company's 200 stores. At the same time, Norman had also ensured that the company's culture and communications between corporate and store levels, and those of store managers with employees and customers, were reshaped so as to support the change. Among the measures taken to improve communication was the removal of top layers in the organization's hierarchy.

Sources: Michael Beer and James Weber (1997) *ASDA (A), (A1), (B), (C)*. Boston: Harvard Business School Case, Harvard Business School Press; Michael Beer and Nitin Nohria (2000) Cracking the code of change, *Harvard Business Review*, May–June, pp. 133–141.

often do not, but then the company will almost certainly suffer from failing to pursue an integrated organizational strategy. The argument is similar to that in favor of an emergent approach to change. Changes initiated at the operating level have the potential to strengthen the company's ability to make best use of its resources. They can also provide the source for product and service innovations. Successful grass roots changes have implications for the organizational arrangements within which operational groups are working. When an operating unit improves its productivity and quality performance by assuming greater decision power and responsibility, it takes over managerial work previously carried out at a higher level, which offers an opportunity to simplify and streamline the company's middle levels of organization. In turn, greater efficiency in resource use, improvements in innovation and quality, and economy of organization potentially provide the whole company with an improved competence advantage over competitors, which it can deploy strategically. Highly focused changes can have much wider implications, which it is normally in the best interests of a company to pursue. A similar point is made in Chapter 14 when we look at the links between different levels of organizational learning. In fact, learning and change are interdependent. Learning, when applied, normally speaks for some change, while the implementation of change provides feedback from which we can learn.

It is more useful to think about the focus or level of change in terms of where best to start it. Even if a company is facing difficulties, it is not necessarily best to launch into radical change across the organization as a whole. This approach has often been advocated and subsequently failed, as was often the case with Business Process Re-engineering (BPR) in the 1990s.[16] Total reorganizations like these are particularly drastic and risky, especially if all their components are set in motion at the same time. They almost certainly rely on a plan drawn up in advance. Such planning is liable insufficiently to comprehend the complex and fast changing conditions experienced today, and it will be difficult to control the process if many implementation problems arise at once. In this respect, Gaius Petronius Arbiter's warning is very apt for major reorganization.

The process of changing a company's work organization can start in a focused way within a particular operating section or system. Successful change in these limited areas should then provide the impetus for subsequent change in other parts of a company. For example, the ground was laid for a company-wide reorganization program in Air Canada by the successful implementation of pilot projects in the areas of aircraft maintenance and airport baggage handling. Their success provided a powerful reassurance to management and staff that change, well handled, could have positive outcomes for all concerned. The changes made in the organization of work had knock-on effects for the relevant supervisory, control, payment, support, and other systems. They served to open up the company's eyes to wider possibilities for constructive change.[17] Another instance of the way that focused changes can be drivers for more extensive developments is provided by moves to delegate responsibility for customer relations and feedback from managers, or specialist units, to operators who have direct contact with customers. This type of change has often proved highly successful and has broader implications for how a company organizes its marketing, complaints, and public relations activities.[18]

◢ Classifying Approaches to Change

Three dimensions of change have been identified. They are (1) how radical it is, (2) whether it is planned or emergent, and (3) the breadth of focus of the change. These dimensions describe key attributes of change on which practitioners are always obliged to take a view. Figure 13.2 shows how they also serve to contrast different approaches to organizational change.

Radical planned change – lessons from the example of BPR

One of the most highly publicized approaches to change has been Business Process Reengineering (BPR). BPR envisages planned change across a whole organization. Its proponents claimed that it was the most radical change in business thinking since the industrial revolution. It appealed to managers who felt that large investments in computerization and total quality management had not really provided the performance breakthroughs they had appeared to promise. This was partly because these were developmental rather than transformational changes. They involved organizing work in much the same way as before and with much the same workforce, but now using computers and taking more care over how things were done. Once most corporations had taken new technology and TQM on board, where were further competitive improvements to come from?

BPR offered a radical answer, summed up in Michael Hammer's phrase, "Don't automate, obliterate." In other words, processes that have become outdated should not be embedded in

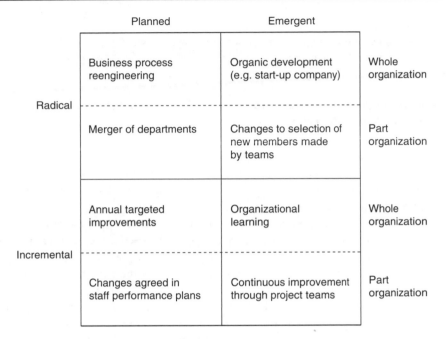

	Planned	Emergent	
Radical	Business process reengineering	Organic development (e.g. start-up company)	Whole organization
	Merger of departments	Changes to selection of new members made by teams	Part organization
Incremental	Annual targeted improvements	Organizational learning	Whole organization
	Changes agreed in staff performance plans	Continuous improvement through project teams	Part organization

Figure 13.2 Comparison of approaches to organizational change

new technologies that simply prop them up for a while. For this would amount to a misplacement of the investment in hardware and software. BPR called for fundamental rethinking and radical redesign to be incorporated into large-scale organizational change, away from a functional logic towards a focus on customer value-adding processes. It also insisted that this fundamental shift had to be complemented by a revolution in the role employees are permitted to play. It argued that dramatic improvements in process completion times, customized services, and so forth are unlikely to be achieved if key operational decisions cannot be made effectively by those who are closest to the action. The BPR approach therefore requires employees to be empowered to make relevant decisions and to have access to appropriate information. The people themselves need to have the appropriate skills and self-confidence, which implies a more active and positive policy of personal development.

By the end of the 1990s, BPR was seen as having failed to live up to its claims, although in some instances it did achieve dramatic short-term results in terms of downsizing and de-layering. There are several reasons for its failure. One is that it was too often applied with an eye to obtaining short-term cost reductions at employees' expense. In such cases, it became just another bottom line "fix" rather than the basis for long-term improvement based on the reorientation of work and employee responsibility toward the customer. Critics soon began counting the cost to people's morale and commitment through the way BPR was being implemented. Another problem arose because BPR was both too ambitious and too radical a model of organizational change. BPR potentially impacted every aspect of how a business is conducted. It entailed the overhaul of organizational structures, management systems, employee responsibilities and performance measurements, incentive systems, skills develop-ment, and a significant use of IT.[19] Massive fundamental change of this kind is extremely difficult to handle, especially if introduced in a climate in which staff fear for their jobs.[20]

As I note later, however, there have been some notable exceptions to this negative picture, which offer important lessons about the ways in which large-scale planned change is introduced and implemented.

A contrast between radical planned and emergent incremental change – BPR and Kaisen

The way that BPR was typically applied illustrated an American emphasis on getting quick results through a top-down initiative. The contrast has often been drawn between American and Japanese management practices, and it is not surprising that this applies to their favored approach to organizational change.

In Figure 13.2 the opposite corner to planned radical change is the emergent incremental approach. This is strongly present in the Japanese practices of continuous improvement (*kaisen*) and encouraging innovation through a widespread use of project teams. The preference here is for change to come about through the processes of learning and good example rather than for it to be imposed on people reluctant to accept it. Change is often focused on particular activities and oriented toward improvements in existing arrangements rather than transformation of the system. In Japanese companies, incremental change through emergent processes is assisted by the high value given to collective loyalty and skills development. Information both from external sources such as new patents and from internal experience such as engineers' visits to customers is carefully recorded. It is then effectively communicated and shared throughout the company, a process in which middle management is seen to play a vital role in connecting top management vision with a largely bottom-up flow of new proposals. Although many Japanese companies still require final approval for change to be given at a high level, their non-threatening culture, encouragement of rich and open information flows, and belief that initiative can be bottom-up, are all characteristics promoting the emergent approach.

Comparisons from research into how American and Japanese companies managed change in companies they acquired in the UK serve to highlight the contrast.[21] It was apparent that American companies tend to absorb firms they acquire into their parent corporate systems and practices. Many of them extinguish the previous identity of the acquired company through enforcing the adoption of the parent company's logo, brands, and corporate culture. They demand a rapid improvement in the new subsidiary's performance, with the threat of significant intervention if results are not forthcoming. A manager in one of the acquired companies described the approach as one where "there's a high degree of informality but on the other hand there's a very high degree of toughness and an insistence on conformity." This radical, even tough, approach to change can nevertheless get quick financial results, with most of the American companies achieving their objective of securing improved short-term profits from their acquired subsidiaries.

Japanese companies are generally quite different in the attitude they adopt toward acquisitions and in how they implement change following them. They bring about change much more through cooperative or indirect means. Most of the initiatives for change come from the new subsidiaries themselves rather than from the Japanese parent companies. Rather than exerting heavy pressure on a new subsidiary to undergo rapid and radical change, Japanese companies tend to rely on the personal "advisors" they appoint to the subsidiary both to encourage change and to provide feedback to the parent. As the British CEO of one Japanese subsidiary put it, "There is a feeling that we should know what we need to do and that we don't need to go to [our parent] for counsel. But they know what is going on and have been very supportive." It is instructive to note that this more emergent approach to post-acquisition change was generally successful in making previously unprofitable businesses profitable, and that it incurred less cost in terms of personal stress for the people experiencing the change.

The Japanese approach appears to lead to good value enhancement over the longer term. It is better geared to the mutual exploration of new possibilities than to offering a quick exploitation of existing assets.[22] It can require a significant initial adjustment on the part of people who are used to speedy decisions and clear directions from higher management. Some UK managers in Japanese subsidiaries complained about not being able to get a quick decision from their Japanese parents or having clear limits to their own discretion.

The context also has a bearing on these contrasting approaches to managing change. The American acquirers studied were generally more experienced in international operations, and operating in the UK did not in any case present major cultural and linguistic differences to them. They were also likely to purchase an already profitable company. It is understandable in these circumstances that they tended to introduce rapid change top-down, with an emphasis on exploiting that profitable base and integrating it with their corporate organization and product portfolio. By contrast, the Japanese companies generally had less international experience and often acquired a company for strategic reasons rather than for its current profitability. In addition to being prepared to adopt a longer-term view, Japanese managers were sensitive to the fact that they were not familiar with the Anglo-Saxon culture and other local differences. They therefore looked to an emergent and slower mode of change that reflected these factors.

◢ Contexts and Choices

The example of ASDA's turnaround showed that different approaches to managing change can be mutually supportive, especially to deal with a crisis. Strong top-down initiatives may be required to articulate the needs of the situation and to give the change process sustained momentum. Allowing scope for bottom-up initiatives may lead to solutions that are based on detailed local knowledge and are therefore realistic and acceptable to staff.[23]

Although forms of change vary in how radical they are, all can contribute to improvements in organizational performance. Earlier I noted Marshak's four categories: fixing, developing, managing transitions, and undertaking transformations. Things constantly go wrong in the day-to-day life of organizations and require fixing. For example, people can no longer cope with the demands of a particular job and have to be moved. Many ongoing productivity and quality improvements in companies come into the next category: developing the existing system. A company acquiring another will probably require the latter to change its financial controls and quite possibly its management structure to fit the arrangements in place within the acquiring company. This is a case of simple transition in that the end-point of the change is predetermined. Transformational change is the mode of change that is best suited to a process of continuous adaptation to turbulent business environments. It is based on a philosophy of organizational learning, but is at the same time limited by the resilience of the people and systems within a company in coping with continuous self-initiated change. So long as the members of a company are clear about which change metaphor they are adopting, there is every reason for an organization to include all four of them in its repertoire of practices.

Nevertheless, the contrasts drawn in Figure 13.2 suggest that different approaches to organizational change have their particular strengths and limitations. Each may therefore be better suited to certain situations and purposes than to others.[24]

Despite cautions about the limits to top management prescience, there are situations in which change has to be planned in advance by senior management. This arises when there is major new capital investment in assets that are indivisible and inflexible in the way they have to be used. It may also be vital to plan change when a company's capability to undertake emergent change has not been developed, perhaps because this was not in the past an accepted norm of that company's culture. In this situation, senior management has to initiate measures to develop relevant capabilities, such as cultural change programs, training, and a modification of the reward system, before more reliance can be placed on emergent processes. It was apparent that, even in a company like ASDA which had the capability to generate emergent change due to the decentralization of its operating units, top management has to play an active role when a major company-wide change is required.

Decisions on the focus of change will also have to be taken with regard to its context. The broader the focus given to change, the more demands it makes on management's capacity to handle it. Even incremental changes take considerable effort to consolidate across the organization. The portfolio of recommendations put forward by different project teams has at some stage to be brought together and work done on their implications for the organization as a whole. Although the encouragement of emergent change across an organization is generally to be recommended, there can be circumstances in which trying to cope with change on a broad front may lessen a company's ability to deal with an immediate crisis through more focused actions. A company finding itself in a downturn will need to focus on making changes that save costs through improving productivity. As mentioned in Chapter 4, the danger in such circumstances of an unfocused approach to change is that cost reduction can become an indiscriminating "slash-and-burn" operation in which strong, productive activities essential for the company's future are eliminated along with relatively unproductive ones.[25]

◢ Policies for Successful Planned Change

The point has been made that successful change cannot be planned precisely in advance and must rely heavily on emergent learning processes. Nonetheless, important aspects of a major organizational change can be anticipated, if not planned, and these are now discussed. The following chapter on organizational learning (Chapter 14) addresses the main foundations for successful emergent change.

What is "successful" change?

The notion of successful change begs a number of questions, such as what would have happened in the absence of the change, or if a different one had been introduced. The big question, however, is "successful for whom?" When organizational change is centered on downsizing, some people will lose from it. Even if the economic hurt is soon healed by generous severance terms and by a rapid return to work, psychological scars can remain. The fundamental ethical requirement for introducing change is therefore to make every effort to avoid its cost falling unilaterally on selected groups, and in situations of downturn and crisis always to seek solutions that are the least destructive in human terms. The practical implications of this ethical stance are that all members of an organization should be kept informed of its situation well in advance of any stage at which decisions to change have to be made, and that they should be granted the maximum opportunity to influence the changes introduced. It so happens that this approach is also usually the most effective way of managing change from the perspective of its impact on the bottom line. An ethical approach pays.

It is of critical importance for organizations to pay attention to how they manage change. There is evidence to show that, when the process is managed well, people are more likely to accept change even though it entails some sacrifice. Studies show that when trouble is taken to explain the reasons for change to the people affected and they perceive the process to be handled fairly, they are less likely to retaliate through measures such as theft from the company following pay cuts, or taking it to court for wrongful dismissal following termination.[26] Failure to manage change in an acceptable manner can be costly in other ways too. As Chapter 4 noted in connection with downsizing, highly valued staff will become disaffected if they perceive that their colleagues have been mistreated. This can be disastrous if it leads to the loss of skilled staff with a lot of embedded knowledge who are in short supply even during an economic downturn. The negativity provoked by the mishandling of change will also prevent management from accessing the pool of tacit knowledge among employees that can make all the difference to how effectively new arrangements will function. Eventually, a continued failure to manage change well can destroy all commitment to a company. Balanced against the price of mishandling organizational change, the additional costs of managing it well are relatively modest.

Stages of planned change

What is entailed in managing planned change "well"? Authorities such as John Kotter have set out the stages which experience indicates are necessary for major changes to be carried through successfully. This and many other models for conducting change owes quite a lot to the three-phase process model first described by Kurt Lewin of unfreezing, transition and re-freezing (see Figure 13.3).[27]

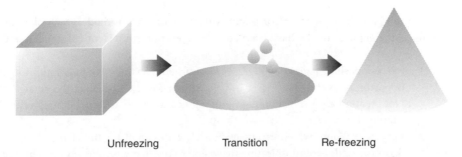

Unfreezing   Transition   Re-freezing

Figure 13.3 Unfreezing, transition and re-freezing

Unfreezing is the process by which people recognize and accept the need for change and become willing to discard existing practice. It is important for people to see that the current organizational activities to which they are attached are no longer sufficiently effective and that a change is required to rectify the situation. This means that a key consideration in the unfreezing process is to inform people about the importance of change and how it is likely to affect them.

Transition is the movement from the old situation to the new one. It may require considerable work to identify available options and is often facilitated by smaller-scale pilot projects through which lessons can be learned and people reassured.

Re-freezing amounts to bedding down the new practices and changed behavior of people so that they assume a routine aspect and are not easily eroded or reversed. This is sometimes referred to as the "institutionalizing" of a change. Care has to be taken at this stage to ensure that the organization's culture and systems support the new arrangements. This will usually require considerable retraining and changes in aspects such as the criteria for rewards, information, and control systems, and decision-making processes.

Lewin formulated his analysis just after World War II at a time when organizations could reckon on having to institute major change only periodically. Contemporary conditions seriously qualify the idea of re-freezing if this is taken to mean the re-implementation of stable and rigid organizational behavior and procedures. The institutionalization of a change today requires that it be implemented in ways that allow for flexibility and further adaptation. In other words, planned change has to be implemented so as to encourage constructive emergent change to become an organizational norm. Extensive participation is one of the key conditions favoring the seeding of future emergent change from a process of planned change.

Kotter formulated an eight-stage process model with the successful introduction of a major radical change in mind, or what he calls "transformation."[28] The eight stages are:

1 Establishing a sense that the need for change is urgent.
2 Creating a coalition to guide the change.
3 Developing a vision and strategy to guide the change.
4 Communicating the change vision and strategy.
5 Empowering broad-based action to remove obstacles to change.
6 Generating short-term wins.
7 Consolidating gains and producing more change.
8 Anchoring new approaches in the organization's culture.

Although their sequence is consistent with the basic Lewin model, each of Kotter's stages reflects the eight errors he has observed to be common sources of failure. These errors are:

1 Not establishing a great enough sense of urgency, based on an identification of crisis or opportunity as the case may be. This is necessary to kick start the change process.
2 Not creating a powerful enough guiding coalition, so as to generate a critical mass of support for change.
3 Lacking a vision, which can provide a clear direction for the change.
4 Seriously under-communicating the vision to the many people whose help is required to make the change happen.

5   Failing to remove obstacles that stand in the way of implementing the new vision. These obstacles can be managers trying to block change out of fear for their future, or organizational systems that fail to empower or reward people for carrying through the change, or information systems that are inadequate to sustain the desired new ways of operating.

6   Not systematically planning for and creating short-term wins. These wins can be projects selected because they look likely to provide quick returns and create satisfaction among the employees and/or customers involved. Short-term wins help to sustain people's motivation to a major change effort that can literally take years to complete.

7   Declaring victory too soon before the gains from change are consolidated. Because change can take so long, it is tempting to declare it completed prematurely before all the requirements for re-freezing have been completed. This can undermine the change and allow for the old ways to creep back in.

8   Not anchoring changes in the corporation's culture. Kotter identifies two factors that are particularly important in institutionalizing change in corporate culture. One is a deliberate effort to show people how new approaches, behaviors, and attitudes have helped to improve performance. The other is to take sufficient time to ensure that the next generation of top managers fully accept the change and are prepared to enhance it rather than allow it to erode. Anchoring the change, and indeed the need for continuing innovation and renewal, in its corporate culture is a necessary step for a company to be able to build upon it in the future.

Kotter's recommendations are directed towards radical planned change involving the whole organization. Nevertheless, much the same phased approach can be applied to a more focused area of change such as the redesign of operative work. Parker and Wall, bring together much of the available knowledge about job and work design, and they too recommend an eight-phase sequence for the restructuring of work.[29] This is reproduced in Figure 13.4, which illustrates the activities normally required at each phase. The figure is particularly instructive because it also shows how the approach was applied in an electronics company that had to change because it was under threat from competitors due to its poor performance. Deliveries to customer were only about 65 percent on time, costs were excessive, and quality defects frequent. All these problems were linked to its traditional form of work design, which the company therefore decided to change.

While understanding of, and commitment to, a change program on the part of senior management is vital to its chances of success, other actors located at different levels and in different segments of the organization will also have significant contributions to make at different stages of the process. For example, the process may be triggered initially by a specialized market intelligence group which warns of an impending change in a firm's competitive position. Developing and communicating a change vision will involve senior management, while the arrangement of detailed discussions to explain specifics of the proposed change and to receive staff views will probably fall to middle-level managers heading up departments and similar units. If generating "short-term wins" involves the setting up of pilot projects, people in the relevant segments of the organization will be the most closely involved. "Anchoring new approaches in the culture" is likely to require a combination of senior management presentations with focused training and development support from HRM

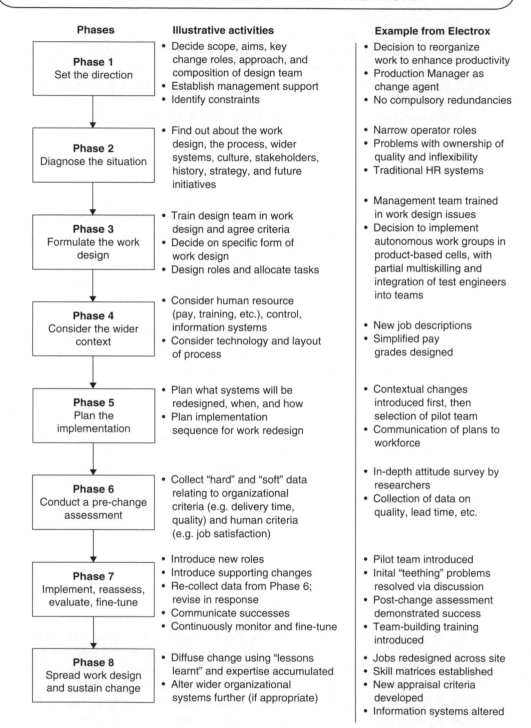

Figure 13.4 Key phases in the redesign of work structures.
Source: Sharon Parker and Toby Wall (1998), *Job and Work Design*, Thousand Oaks, CA, Sage, p.123.

specialists. In other words, the appropriate people to help drive a change forward will vary according to the stage in the process.[30]

Specific issues to consider

PARTICIPATION

The question of who is invited to participate in the change process presents a dilemma. From an ethical standpoint, it is always right that those affected by a proposed change should have the opportunity to share in its planning and implementation. From a position of expediency, however, the contribution that participation can make to the success of change depends on the situation. There are three main situations to consider:

1   In the first situation, there is underlying agreement about the objective of the change, but (1) people differ about the best way to achieve it and (2) no one party has a monopoly of relevant knowledge or power. In this case, extensive participation can make a constructive contribution to the process of organizational change. All the relevant people will be motivated to engage in discussions and there is a reasonable prospect of forging an eventual consensus.
2   In the second situation, management is sufficiently powerful to enforce its preferred solution. In this case, participation may well be dismissed as a waste of time. The danger, however, of pushing through change unilaterally lies in the way that the resentment created is likely to store up trouble for the future.
3   In a third type of situation, there is inflexible opposition to a proposed change based on a fundamental disagreement with the aims of its promoters. Here consultation and participation are likely to be used simply as opportunities for obstructing implementation. Whether the proposed change is pushed through, modified, or just postponed then depends largely on management's powers of action.

The long-term shift in the balance of power within labor markets toward the buyers of labor is significant because it strengthens the temptation to introduce change unilaterally. Many employers now perceive they have the opportunity to force through changes in manning and work organization more fundamental in nature and at a faster rate than would have been possible under a genuinely participative regime. Instead, employees are often presented with the stark choice of either accepting change or facing redundancy. It is also argued that, if people are working on a sub-contract basis, they may not be interested in any organizational issues beyond the specifics of their contracts. Nevertheless, a rejection of consultation, let alone more genuine participation, means excluding people with relevant experience and knowledge, who sometimes perform critical roles which gives them the power to defy the proposed change. Not only could this undermine the change; it could also forfeit the trust of the people concerned and their wider communities.

An example is how top management lost the trust of employees during its attempt to implement a significant change in the Norwegian airport and air traffic control administration, because of a withdrawal of participation during the process. This caused the change initiative to fail. This case, reported by Eric Lofquist, is summarized in Box 13.3.

BOX 13.3   A COLLAPSE OF CHANGE IMPLEMENTATION IN THE NORWEGIAN CIVIL AVIATION INDUSTRY

Due to the deteriorating economic conditions in the civil aviation industry following 9/11, the government-owned company administering Norwegian civil aviation – Avinor – faced a revenue crisis and needed to reduce its costs. Initially, there was broad acceptance that this required large-scale change aimed at reducing costs and stream-lining an overweight bureaucracy. Even the powerful air traffic controllers union, which had previously resisted major change, accepted the case for change in principle. At the planning stage, employees and union representatives were invited to offer contributions and recommendations. This led to many solutions being recommended by employees, who also expressed satisfaction with the genuine participation they perceived to be taking place. However, when the leadership presented its plan, the magnitude and speed of the changes – calling for a cut of over 25 percent of the workforce – was a shock for employees and did not match what they has been led to expect in the participation process. They realized that this process was not as genuinely participative as they had believed and that management's real intention was to achieve downsizing. This destroyed their trust in the leadership. The air traffic controllers union then challenged the basis for the published planned change and asked for a delay in implementation while the data supporting the decision were investigated. At this point the leadership attempted to move forward with implementation without offering any further discussion. The result was a prolonged industrial dispute, including a closure of airspace in southern Norway and the eventual collapse of the project. The leadership had failed to acknowledge the opposition of the air traffic controllers to several parts of the plan and it seriously underestimated their power to resist the change.

Source: Eric Arne Lofquist (2011), Doomed to fail: A case study of change implementation collapse in the Norwegian civil aviation industry, *Journal of Change Management*, 11(2), pp. 223–243.

Some other public sector organizations have provided examples of a totally inflexible opposition to reorganization. This is the other kind of situation in which a participative approach to implementing change is unlikely to suit. If a customary mode of operation is sufficiently embedded in a long established bureaucracy, the only way to change it is probably to attack both its structure and ideology unilaterally. In such situations, participation would tend to be used by the organization's incumbents simply to direct attention away from plans for action and to delay their implementation. For example, Donald Warwick in his book *A Theory of Public Bureaucracy* documents the resistance of the US State Department to attempts at structural reform.[31] This resistance was led by the Department's own senior career staff and was enhanced by their ability to mobilize external support in Congress. Warwick questions what he calls "the sometimes facile advocacy of employee participation in decisions about change" (p. 199) in cases like public bureaucracies where large size, rigid hierarchy, and the intrusion of different political power groups all make unworkable the notion of moving toward a consensus solution through participation.

If a proposed change is clearly contrary to the interests of those affected by it, it would be very appropriate, at least from an ethical standpoint, to initiate discussions in order to see whether an alternative way forward can be found. However, if this fails, further participation is likely to prove futile. People who stand to lose their jobs will be concerned with finding ways to block the change or, if that is not possible, with negotiating the best possible severance terms. This, of course, raises the possibility of offering guarantees of no job loss in connection with reorganization as a basis for eliciting the cooperation of employees and their willingness to participate in designing and implementing the change. A no-redundancy policy incurs obvious risks and is best suited to conditions where the level of activity is likely to remain buoyant; it could also give rise to an inappropriate labor force profile and block openings for recruiting people with new skills. On the other hand, it is a policy that some companies have successfully pursued in combination with careful manpower planning and agreements on flexible deployment between jobs. They claim that it provides significant benefits in terms of promoting a climate in which employees identify with management's objectives and of facilitating the process of adaptation to new requirements. This is the way that Corning Glass introduced BPR with constructive results and without meeting the opposition this kind of change typically encounters.[32]

Where zero-sum bargaining is not involved and an integration of interests is possible, the involvement of people concerned in the design and implementation of a change will normally offer the best chance for its success. One reason is that participation provides an opportunity for the rationale behind the proposed change to be explained and critically examined. This can help to lessen people's fears stemming from a lack of knowledge and a feeling of powerlessness. In fact, people cannot easily understand, let alone share, the vision guiding a major change if they are denied the chance to discuss it. If people contribute actively toward the premises for a proposed change, this helps to create among them a degree of commitment to the change and to making it work. It has been found in American companies, for example, that the probability of systems development projects being successfully implemented is much higher when user departments are fully involved in their design and feel some sense of ownership over them, than in situations where this degree of participation is absent.

A second consideration is that a great deal of the information required as a basis for planning a change – data on present problems, work activities, decision points, time cycles, files, costs, personnel, and so forth – will only be known in detail to the people who are affected. Their participation is therefore necessary if the reorganization is to be grounded in the realities of the situation. Thirdly, the process of employee participation should assist managers to learn about their employees' attitudes, values, and perceptions, and this learning experience should assist them to plan further changes in ways that provoke less conflict. Equally, the chance to influence and understand organizational change should create awareness on the part of employees of the need in modern business conditions for adaptation.

Participation, then, is in the majority of cases beneficial in the management of change. It offers the best prospects of developing an "adaptive learning capability" in organizations through harnessing the knowledge possessed by a wide range of organizational members and bringing forth alternative solutions. In addition, many people, the writer included, would also maintain that it is ethically the correct procedure for planning changes that affect other people. One can, however, expect too much from it, and we have indicated the kind of conditions under which it may not work. Participation is a way of confronting the political issues involved in change, not a means of avoiding or smoothing over them. If there is a deep-seated conflict of interest between the parties involved in a proposed change, participation will probably not turn up a mutually acceptable solution. Also, if hidden anxieties and hostilities are present, it may be necessary to introduce a skilled third party, a social consultant, to bring these into the open where they can be confronted and dissipated. So long as anxieties and conflicts are present, and not totally recognized, participation is likely to prove an unfruitful exercise.

A participative approach can be difficult for other reasons as well. It is usually very time consuming, the more so in a large-scale organization where participation has to cross so many hierarchical levels to link decisions on change initiated at a senior level to the people affected at a junior level. In some circumstances, that time may simply not be available, when a quick reaction to an unexpected event is required. The point is also made by managers that time spent in discussion is time lost to getting on with the job. These are genuine difficulties, though they are to some extent exaggerated by a failure to anticipate new developments in time to allow for their discussion, rather than having to react at the last minute.

A further problem that is often raised concerns the apparent lack of interest among employees in participation – an unwillingness to devote the effort and share in the responsibility. It is true that some experiments in adopting an American democratic management style have not evoked a positive response in European countries, such as Norway where one direct replication of an American experiment was made.[33] This, however, does not indicate employee resistance to participation so much as the fact that, in Europe, this has traditionally been undertaken by union officers and local elected departmental representatives rather than through direct personal relations with managers. We know of no evidence to suggest that members of organizations do not desire to enter discussions on matters of immediate relevance to their jobs and work, be this direct discussion or via representatives.

To summarize so far, the participative approach to handling change is not an easy one, and is not always functional for management. The consequences of managers refusing to participate can, however, be very costly where people are in a position to resist or even sabotage change, but where they would be willing to go along with it constructively if consulted.

The above discussion adopts a fairly narrow view of participation in organizational change, focusing on internal change and the people immediately affected by it. While this focus is important in itself, we have nowadays come to recognize that internal organizational practices and policies have wider social and environmental implications. Organizations and their managements therefore have to obtain the support and approval – legitimacy – from a broad set of stakeholders, as will be discussed in Chapters 16 and 18. Sustainability of the world's environment and resources is becoming ever more urgent for preserving the quality of people's lives, and indeed the future of the human race. This highlights the part played by organizational policies and practices regarding, say, energy saving and preserving the local environment. It draws attention to how supply chains can be managed so as to promote economic and social development and sustain the environment of poorer countries. So we appreciate better today that organizations are embedded in wider networks or systems. Organizational changes should therefore be informed by the realization that they can have wide consequences of real interest to a broad range of stakeholders who may be in a position either to contribute to change constructively or to resist it. For example, a report by Ashridge Business School on sustainability concluded that effective strategic change in this area has to be approached through the active participation of a network of stakeholders, overcoming conventional boundaries between internal and external participants in the change process.[34]

RESISTANCE TO CHANGE

Any organizational change is likely to meet with some resistance. Resistance to change is a universal phenomenon among groups who feel that their interests are threatened. It is found at all levels of organization from boardroom to shop floor and throughout history from the handloom weavers of the early 1800s to the protest groups of today. Research by the McKinsey consulting company and their clients' experience suggest that half of all efforts to transform organizational performance fail either because senior managers do not act as role models for change or because people in the organization defend the status quo.[35]

There is a high degree of consensus that the reactions to change of the people whom it affects and who are expected to work with it are key to determining whether that change is likely to succeed or not.[36] Resistance to change is often given as the reason why change initiatives meet difficulties and frequently fail.[37] It is therefore vital for managers to understand

---

BOX 13.4 WHY DO PEOPLE RESIST ORGANIZATIONAL CHANGE?

1   Most people will initially react to a proposed change with some suspicion because they see it as an unwelcome disturbance and interference to their established routine.
2   People will resist organizational changes that they perceive as negatively affecting their job security, payment and status differentials, working conditions, and value of their acquired skills. These are the "hygiene" factors singled out by Herzberg as sources of dissatisfaction when threatened.[41] This has become an acutely sensitive area due to the extreme levels of insecurity many people feel today as a result of downsizing and other moves away from the old, relatively stable structures of employment.
3   Line managers often resist changes proposed by specialists such as systems and HRM experts, who to some extent justify their presence by the projects they contribute for improvement and change. Managers often resist such proposals because they perceive a risk to the smooth running of their operations in accepting the potential disruption caused by something new. They may also resent what they regard as the implied criticism of having specialists tell them how to improve their management approach.
4   Specialists for their part are often uncomfortable with the emphasis that new forms of organizing place on their integration with other specialists in teams or other units that cut across traditional disciplinary or functional boundaries. They may therefore resist developments of this kind.

the reasons why people are resisting a particular change. Without this understanding, it is impossible to distinguish between fundamental and trivial factors, and to take appropriate action. So often, a change that appears rational and straightforward from a senior manager's perspective takes on quite a different aspect for people in other parts of the organization. It is therefore vital to understand the sense that people affected by prospective or actual change make of it – how they interpret the intentions behind it and what it will mean for their work, status and wellbeing.[38]

Resistance to change has been widely regarded as an adversarial phenomenon and a negative from management's perspective. This is a misleading view. Apart from the right of people to resist proposals that are detrimental to them, resistance can have positive consequences for the organization. It can, for example, encourage a collective identity among organizational members who feel that the proposed change will affect all of them. The resulting sense of common identity and purpose may encourage them to put forward constructive counter-proposals. Opposition to poorly thought-out plans can give rise to ones that are technically and socially superior, worked out by people who have relevant expertise and are closer to the tasks or operations that are affected.[39] Some would go further and argue that resistance has a positive effect in mobilizing a counter force to managerial power which leads to an effective reconciliation of opposing interests and organizational cultures rather than a one-sided enforced solution.[40]

People will resist reorganization if they believe that it is detrimental to aspects of their work life and roles that they value. Let us take some common examples that include negative reactions to change on the part of managers as well as workers:

1   Managers are alarmed at a proposal to streamline their company's organization structure, through reducing the number of hierarchical levels, because they see it as threatening their job security and the number of future openings for promotion.
2   Middle managers regard the enrichment of their subordinates' work as a threat to their authority and even the viability of their jobs.
3   Senior managers look upon the reallocation of responsibilities between the functions they head up as a threat to their claim on budgets and other resources rather than a sensible adjustment to new needs.
4   Workers react negatively to empowerment as imposing an additional burden on them.
5   A technical specialist sees the request that she work in a cross-functional product development team as a potential dilution of her standing and market value as a professional person.

The reasons why people resist organizational change are reasonably clear and therefore predictable (see Box 13.4). This means it is possible to follow a systematic approach to making such prediction and acting on its results.

In addressing resistance to change, it is helpful to recognize not only the reasons behind it, but also its different dimensions.[42] Researchers have distinguished between its behavioral dimension (how people behave in reaction to change), its cognitive dimension (what they think about change), and its affective dimension (how they feel about change). In terms of behavior, resistance to change may be active or passive (or both). It can be expressed overtly or covertly, and it can vary in strength. The cognitive dimension refers to how people understand the change and calculate its effects in terms of whether it will benefit or harm them or the unit they belong to. The affective dimension refers to emotions about the change such as anxiety and anger on the one hand or enthusiasm on the other. Management needs to appreciate these various dimensions of how people respond to change.

The challenge for management in coping with resistance to change has three aspects to it. First, how to minimize potential disturbances during the period of change. Second, how to turn resistance into a level of commitment to the change so people contribute their knowledge and experience to working out its details and ensuring its successful implementation. Third, how to move quickly to a new and stable situation that will produce a satisfactory level of performance. With these considerations in mind, it is recommended that care should be given to carrying out a rigorous diagnosis before embarking on the change process in addition to being receptive to feedback during the process.[43] The following suggests the steps in a diagnosis that is specifically oriented towards the possibility of resistance to change:[44]

1   List all the alternative ways of implementing a change, together with estimated time schedules.
2   Identify all the sections of the organization, occupational categories, or work groups affected by the change, however indirectly.
3   Estimate the likely reaction of these groups in general terms.
4   Calculate their likely reaction for specific issues such as wage rates, differentials, promotion prospects, retraining, working practices, and redeployment. Securing data of reasonable quality on these issues involves accessing the opinion of managers in close contact with all the groups and, even better, the direct reaction of the people concerned.
5   Conclude by estimating in a crude way the overall acceptability of the change and of each approach to implementing the change.
6   Decide on the extent to which people's likely objections to the change can be met through assurances and/or effective communication of the reasons for change.
7   Weigh up the importance of securing each group's contribution to the design and implementation of the change and the cost to the organization if some of its members should become alienated and decide to quit.
8   Tailor the process of how to involve different groups in the change according to the assessments made.

Information gathered on likely reactions to a proposed change, through applying an approach such as this, clearly remains highly subjective. It will, however, be systematically organized, which is much better than the alternative of sheer guesswork. A major requirement in gathering information is to ascertain whether spokesmen and sources accurately reflect the views of the people they speak for. This is one of the main considerations in favor of adopting a participative approach in the planning and implementation of change.

Drawing on their review of research and practice on resistance to change, Dennis Erwin and Andrew Garman set out a more detailed set of guidelines for change agents and managers under the following headings:[45]

*   Plan for resistance
*   Provide additional support
*   Address individuals' concerns
*   Provide support and training

- Communicate, communicate, communicate
- Ensure understanding of the change
- Examine policies and behaviors for their consistency
- Encourage and allow opportunities for participation in the change process
- Develop confidence and trust
- Emphasize effective management styles
- Develop quality manager–employee relationships

USE OF PILOT PROJECTS

If considerable resistance to a proposed change is anticipated, and if it is possible to introduce it first of all on a limited basis, then the use of a "pilot project" may be helpful. In a pilot project it is agreed that certain specific changes to the existing organization will be made on an experimental basis. After a given period of time, the change is evaluated on the understanding that it will be withdrawn if it is unsuccessful or unacceptable.

This approach can have a number of advantages. A favorable situation can be selected for the pilot scheme, perhaps enlisting volunteers. This contributes to the eventual success of the change by getting it over the early period of trial and error in circumstances likely to produce good results. Less committed and confident members of the organization may be more prepared to accept the change once the pilot is completed, and this category includes managers who may be wary of committing resources to any new development until they can assess its effect. Box 13.5 describes the successful use of pilot projects as a preliminary to implementing major change in Air Canada.

Pilot projects do, however, carry risks. They prolong the period of uncertainty that accompanies any change and, if this is a source of considerable anxiety, the result may be to increase rather than lessen hostility to the change. If the pilot scheme is located in too favorable an environment, it may not be possible to replicate any success it has across other parts of the organization. A pilot scheme that excludes people who are less receptive to change may also exclude those with power. Employee representatives are likely to be particularly cautious about proposed organizational changes because they have a responsibility to work out every possible ramification for their constituents' interests. For this reason it may not be easy to secure the open approval of employee representatives for a pilot scheme. There is also the danger that management could be understood to be making any further change totally conditional on the pilot project. In circumstances where change is unavoidable, it is important to explain this and to present the pilot scheme as an opportunity to learn and assess in a participative manner how best to move forward. A further problem is that, given the interconnectedness of functions and levels, it will in many situations be impossible to isolate a proposed change in organization and to pilot it on a limited experimental basis.

TIME REQUIRED

A planned organizational change almost always takes longer to accomplish than is first envisaged. The process has to run though a number of phases successfully, it is often punctuated by crises, and it requires a considerable investment of commitment and resource. It takes time to satisfy these requirements.

BOX 13.5 THE USE OF PILOT PROJECTS TO FACILITATE ORGANIZATIONAL CHANGE

As a prelude to introducing across-the-board organizational change, Air Canada initiated a number of specific projects during the period 1974 to 1976. The company's Vice-President for Personnel and Organizational Development, Phil Chartrand, saw in these projects an opportunity both to apply innovative principles of job design and to provide demonstrations of the benefits that could accrue to the company and its employees from a systematic program of organizational change within the company. They were in effect pilot projects that facilitated subsequent larger-scale organizational development by reducing anxieties about change and promoting recognition of its potential benefits.

Chartrand published a paper on two of these projects and the lessons to be drawn from them.[46] One involved the redesign of the system whereby ramp crews at Montreal's Dorval Airport accommodated incoming aircraft in terms of unloading passengers and their baggage, cleaning and servicing the aircraft, and ensuring that required provisions were on board. The team for the project was led by one of the company's organizational development specialists and consisted of the airport manager and three union stewards. It recommended a complete redesign of the basic method of organizing and managing the ramp operation. The result was better performance standards, reduced operating costs, and improved communications with passengers over delays and the like. Importantly, the previously skeptical union stewards were won over to accepting the value of this kind of change, and they subsequently applied to work as members of management.

The other project took place in the sheet metal shop of the maintenance base. Its objective was to achieve improvements in the servicing of honeycomb (a very light but very strong, expensive aluminum fiberglass material used on aircraft) to the point where the shop could gain official certification to service honeycomb for other airlines. A project team consisting of a lead hand, three licensed mechanics and an OD specialist met in company time for 10 sessions, and was able to call on the advice of foremen and an industrial engineer. The team achieved the goal of certification, which greatly expanded the company's markets for honeycomb servicing work. As a result of the project, return on investment, productivity, and working conditions also improved.

A major planned change has to pass through several major phases, which encompass the recommended actions that authorities such as John Kotter have identified. Although they tend to overlap in practice, four phases can be identified and defined separately. They are summarized in Box 13.6. The phases respectively involve (1) building a team to lead the change, (2) permitting resistance to surface, (3) securing identification with the objectives of the change, and (4) evaluating the change and building a learning capability for the future. When organizational change has failed, this has usually been the result of a management attempting to shorten or eliminate one or more of the phases.

These four phases are expressed primarily in terms of actions by management. They find a parallel in the reaction of organizational members. Dennis Jaffe and his colleagues identified

BOX 13.6   TIME REQUIRED TO ACCOMPLISH PHASES OF THE CHANGE PROCESS[49]

Phase 1 – Building the leading group and gaining acceptance. This phase follows an initial identification of the need for change. It involves the building of a leading group responsible for introducing an organizational change, which must then gain the acceptance of others. More than just personal acceptance by individual members of the group is involved here; it also includes acceptance of their role in the process (e.g. project team member, process facilitator) or of their legitimacy if they are consultants brought in from the outside. This phase could take six months.

Phase 2 – Surfacing of resistance to change. During this phase, which may last a further six months or so, underlying fears, hostilities, and suspicions regarding the proposed changes are brought into the open. Until such views and feelings are expressed openly, no matter how much information is given by management it will not be accepted at its face value.

Phase 3 – Identification with the objectives of the change. For this phase to begin, the underlying fears encountered in Phase 2 need to have been resolved. The people affected by the change can then begin to accept the objectives of the change program as their own and not something simply forced on them by higher management. Practical steps toward working on the details of the change and its implementation can now start to be taken. Depending on the scope and complexity of the change, this phase of active joint effort towards implementing the change may take as long as two years.

Phase 4 – Evaluating the change and building a learning capability for the future. At this stage the change in organization has been introduced and is evaluated. Some time may have to elapse before it is appropriate to conduct an evaluation. The monitoring of the change and subsequent adjustments should help the organization to move toward a mode of continuous learning. This in turn can provide a basis for it to undertake further change in a more emergent manner, rather than management waiting until it is forced to adapt to new circumstances.

"four reactions organizational members experience as they move through the change process: denial (refusal to believe the change will be implemented), resistance (not participating or attempting to avoid implementation), exploration (experimentation with new behaviors), and commitment (accepting or embracing the change)."[47] These reactions are emotional as well as cognitive. People's reaction to change can be intensely emotional, especially in the form of fear and hostility. Less often, the prevailing emotion is one of enthusiasm that at last something is being done about a clearly unsatisfactory situation or that overdue investment is being made. Those involved in planning or facilitating organization change need to give appropriate support, particularly when anxiety about it is objectively unfounded – when for example employees fear job loss although management has no intention for this to happen.[48] Sufficient time also has to be allowed for emotions to subside (see Phase 2 in Box 13.6 above).

The time scale envisaged in Box 13.6 is extremely lengthy, and it is becoming increasingly difficult to accept in contemporary conditions of turbulence and hypercompetition. In practice, most minor organizational changes, such as establishing new teams or units, will take nowhere near as long to plan and implement. However, a major change such as integrating a newly acquired company could take several years before it is bedded down satisfactorily.

The time required to accomplish change successfully therefore presents a real challenge. Forcing the issue heightens the risk of failure. However, developing a capability to achieve change on a more continuous and emergent basis will help to avoid large, disruptive, one-off projects and dramatically shorten time scales. The risk of not having the resilience to adapt to fast-changing circumstances is in fact one of the main reasons why companies should develop a capacity and culture for continual self-evaluation, learning, and making emergent changes.

USE OF THIRD PARTIES, INCLUDING ACTION RESEARCH

The term "third party" in the context of organizational change refers to any individual or group who assists in the process of diagnosing problems and implementing solutions, but who is not part of the organization system directly involved in change. Third parties could be outside commercial consultants, business school faculty, or members of an organization's development team. The benefits that they can bring include the contribution of analytical technique and experience developed elsewhere, an ability to assist in the resolution of conflicting views by standing outside the conflict, and the acceptability of their advice by virtue of their image as experts and (especially in the case of academics) on the basis of their relatively neutral position with respect to organizational politics. For reasons such as these, third parties have been frequently asked to assist in organizational changes.

The involvement of third parties can create certain problems. Commercial consultants are usually perceived by employees as being committed solely to top management interests, by virtue of their fee payment. There is also some temptation for consultants to apply a standard solution to organizational problems. This is partly because their experience lies largely in the application of standard techniques, and partly because the costs of consultancy can only be borne over a limited time so that a reasonably quick solution is called for. Standardized approaches, however, are not adapted to varied circumstances and they are unlikely to be in tune with the unique culture of a particular organization. If a management is going to engage commercial consultants in the field of organizational change, it would be well advised to ensure that solutions are not decided upon at the outset, or to the exclusion of other groups concerned in the change.

Business school faculty are potentially in a better position to enter into long-term collaborative relationships with organizations, and to extend this collaboration over the period of diagnosing and implementing change. It is easier for them to undertake the role of *action researcher*, which devotes some time to the formation of a consensus on the direction of change through research, feedback, and mutual discussion.

The typical sequence of events in an action research approach to organizational change would be: (1) research is carried out to provide data for problem diagnosis; (2) this is fed back to relevant management and employee groups; (3) the feedback is evaluated by all concerned; (4) there is then discussion with the researchers regarding options for action; (5) a decision is made on what action to take and a change is made. The researcher, possibly together with people from the organization, can then further investigate the effects of the change. There is further feedback and discussion, and the cycle continues. The research and feedback stages of the cycle are likely to identify problems and create an awareness of their existence in people's minds. This is roughly equivalent to the first two phases of the change process just mentioned. Discussion of options for action is likely to promote a sense of "ownership" of the change project and identification with the objectives of the change that are being clarified by the discussion itself (equivalent to phase three in Box 13.6).

If the organization is large enough to employ its own internal organizational planning and development teams, or internal consulting teams, then they may be able to play the part of action researcher instead. They have, of course, to gain credibility and to be seen as performing a relatively neutral service role. They may also have to rely on outside help for advice on techniques such as those of survey analysis. Internal consultants enjoy considerable familiarity with the organization's background and management will find them easier to program than outsiders.

Action research is a lengthy process, and careful control has to be retained over the programming of feedback reports and discussions if valuable time is not to be lost and expectations within the organization not disappointed. Business school faculty have other demands upon their time, and may not be able to provide the intensity of commitment that is desirable. Another point is that, while such staff with their professional academic standing are more likely to be seen as neutral to the political issues within an organization, the price of this independence may be that academics feel free to import values of their own into the organization.

Managers and employees alike should ascertain what they are taking on when the third party is an independent academic, because academics differ considerably in their values and approaches. Some go so far as to see action research as a means of subverting what they believe are oppressive and exploitative bureaucratic institutions. Others appear to confine themselves purely to a top management perspective, which is also a limitation of their potential contribution as third parties and facilitators of the organizational change process. Many business school staff are, on the other hand, sensitive to the difficulties of playing a role which inevitably brings them into organizational politics, but feel nevertheless that they have an obligation to offer their services as best they can and to apply their knowledge to practical use.

Bearing in mind that organizational change must gain the positive commitment and understanding of those who have to live with the new arrangements and make them work, it is appropriate that third parties adopt a role which facilitates this. In other words, they are not required to solve organizational problems. Rather, they are expected to collaborate with the parties immediately involved in reaching their own solutions through activities such as advising on surveys of attitudes, helping people to establish constructive working relationships, and facilitating the open confrontation of issues that are subject to conflict.

Those with experience in this field point out that there are situations in which progress can be made by the third party himself or herself taking on the role of expert problem solver, when for instance a technical matter is concerned. It has even been suggested that a dominant role, backed by top management, can speed up the progress of change. While it is true that to be effective a third party must have some influence, the adoption of a leading or dominant role is unlikely to prove an effective general strategy. Apart from the ethical considerations of power without responsibility, such roles can engender an undue dependence upon the third party. A successful implementation of organizational change in the long run requires that the people concerned participate actively in the process of working out the new arrangements both as a learning experience and as a basis for generating their personal commitment to the change. For they have to live with the change and assume responsibility for it.

The relationship between third parties and members of an organization is therefore not an easy one to manage. There can be differences in values and language, different ways of working, different time perspectives. These are compounded when the technical training of the people concerned also varies, as with a behavioral scientist working with engineers on a change in job design, or an organizational expert working with accountants on a change in control procedures. Integration into an effective team can be difficult, but this is the challenge of bringing together the people best suited to doing the detailed work on the many different facets that a change has to take into account.

SUSTAINING CHANGE

The final stage in both the Kotter and Parker/Wall frameworks of stages in the process of planned change is directed to the sustaining of change after it has been introduced. Sustainable change can refer both to a particular change that becomes the new norm in an organization and to regular organizational change itself becoming accepted as the norm. The challenge therefore is to how to make change "stick," as well as to build a capacity in the organization to undertake future changes in a smoother more emergent fashion as and when the need arises. As Brännmark and Benn comment, "Maintaining new ways of working and applying them to address the requirements of a rapidly evolving and increasingly complex business context is the real challenge of [change] sustainability."[50]

Buchanan and his colleagues identified from a review of the literature 11 sets of factors affecting the sustainability of organizational change. These range from the perceived centrality of the change for organizational performance, through factors that affect people's commitment to the change, to issues such as confidence in the organization's leadership and the question of whether sufficient time has been given to the change process. Buchanan et al. conclude that "the process of sustaining change is dependent on the interplay of multiple factors on different levels of analysis and timeframes."[51]

The primary condition for a change to be sustained is that it has to gain the understanding and support of key stakeholders, both within and outside the organization. Change is unlikely to be effective, let alone sustained, if one or more stakeholder groups oppose it. Regarding internal stakeholders, emergent bottom-up change promoted by employees and/ or internal specialists, is unlikely even to get implemented without the understanding and support of higher management. Equally, a change imposed from the top-down without participation and with undue haste is likely to encounter persistent resistance from employees, and this most likely will render it unsustainable. Regarding external stake-holders, changes that fly in the face of the values of customers, local communities or regulatory authorities are also likely to become unsustainable even if they get off the ground in the first place.

The report by Ashridge Business School mentioned earlier not only makes a strong case for stakeholder involvement as a requirement for effecting strategic change but also puts forward an insightful framework of the process required to embed and sustain change. This framework offers a more dynamic view of the change process than is portrayed by the sequence of steps depicted in Kotter's scheme. It views organizational change as being sustained through the continuing interaction between five processes: the *engaging* of stakeholders; the *enactment* of their preferences (often through experimental initiatives); the *encoding* (codification) of new behaviors and norms via appropriate structures, processes and systems; the *expressing* of change through the value network through appropriate communication and targets; and encouraging *sensemaking and reframing* so as to develop a shared understanding and sense of purpose around the change.[52]

SUMMARY

1 Companies today need to keep their organizational arrangements under continual review. They are undertaking organizational changes much more frequently than before in the light of developments in their environments and strategic initiatives of their own choosing.

2 Nevertheless, many (possibly most) attempts to bring about organizational change fail to reach a satisfactory outcome, which suggests that the subject remains rather poorly understood.

3 There are many varieties of organizational change and it helps to categorize these in terms of three key underlying features. These concern whether the change is:
   a. radical or incremental;
   b. planned or emergent;
   c. broadly or narrowly focused

4 In practice these features are often complementary. For example, the implementation of a radical new vision can proceed incrementally, step-by-step, if time permits.

5 In changing and uncertain conditions, it is hazardous to believe that senior management can plan the whole of an organizational change in advance, especially if it is of major proportions.

6 Many contributory elements have to be encouraged to emerge through the involvement of people who are close to the action. Emergent change can be a valuable learning process and is discussed further in the next chapter.

7 A change that is narrowly focused on, say, a particular work group or unit may soon come to have broader implications through its knock-on effects or though the precedent it sets for other parts of the organization. A narrowly focused change may also serve as a pilot scheme before undertaking a more extensive reorganization.

8 Planned change is a process that passes through a number of stages. Neglect of any one stage is likely to put the whole process at risk. This means that major complex changes are very demanding of effort and time. The time they take from initiation to successful implementation is typically much longer than originally anticipated. If an organization can develop a capability to change on an emergent basis through continuous learning, it is likely to adapt with more speed and less trauma to new circumstances.

9   There are certain specific issues to consider in connection with undertaking organizational change. One concerns the extent and role of participation in the change process. Another is the inevitability of resistance to change and how it may be addressed. The potentially beneficial consequences of resistance have generally been overlooked. A further issue concerns the conditions under which setting up pilot projects may be helpful to achieving change. The involvement of third parties, such as consultants, and the role they are to play also deserves consideration. And there is the question of the time likely to be involved.

QUESTIONS FOR DISCUSSION

13.1   What are the key external and internal drivers of organizational change? What kind of changes do they lead to?

13.2   Some argue that much of the emphasis on organizational change is pure hype and directed against the interests of ordinary organizational members. Elaborate your opinion on this matter.

13.3   Describe and discuss the key barriers to changes in organization.

13.4   Discuss the relationship between planned and emergent change.

13.5   What are the key requirements for successful change management?

13.6   What are the reasons for resistance to change and the options for addressing these?

13.7   Discuss the pros and cons of using pilot projects and third parties in carrying out planned organizational change.

NOTES

1   Brendan Buescher and Patrick Viguerie (2014), How US healthcare companies can thrive amid disruption, *McKinsey Insights and Publications*, June. http://www.mckinsey.com/Insights/Health_systems_and_services/How_US_healthcare_companies_can_thrive_amid_disruption?cid=other-eml-alt-mip-mck-oth-1406, accessed June 7, 2014.

2   Bernard Burnes (2011), Introduction: Why does change fail, and what can we do about it? *Journal of Change Management*, 11(4), 445–450; Mark Hughes (2011), Do 70 per cent of all organizational change initiatives really fail? *Journal of Change Management*, 11(4), 451–464.

3   Bernard Burnes (2005), Complexity theories and organizational change, *International Journal of Management Reviews*, 7(2), 73–90.

4   Chris Grey (2013), *A Very Short, Fairly Interesting and Reasonably Cheap Book about Studying Organizations*, London, Sage, p. 92.

5   David A. Buchanan (2011), Reflections: Good practice, not rocket science – Understanding failures to change after extreme events, *Journal of Change Management*, 11(3), 273–288.

6   Warren Bennis (1969), *Organizational Development*, Reading, MA, Addison-Wesley; John P. Kotter (2014), *Accelerate: Building Strategic Agility for a Faster-Moving World*, Boston, MA, Harvard Business School Press.

7   Arie Lewin, Chris P. Long, and Timothy N. Carroll (1999), The coevolution of new organizational forms, *Organization Science*, 10(5), 535–550. The Figure comes from Exhibit 1, p. 537.

8   Robert J. Marshak (1993), Managing the metaphors of change, *Organizational Dynamics*, 22, 44–56.

9   Chris Argyris and Donald Schon (1978), *Organizational Learning*, Reading, MA, Addison-Wesley.

10 Chris Argyris and Donald Schon (1978), op. cit.

11 John Child and Chris Smith (1987), The Context and Process of Organizational Transformation, *Journal of Management Studies*, November, 24(6), 565-593; Saboohi Nasim and Sushil (2011), Revisiting organizational change: Exploring the paradox of managing continuity and change, *Journal of Change Management*, 11(2), 185–206.

12 Piers Myers, Sally Hulks, and Liz Wiggins (2012), *Organizational Change: Perspectives on Theory and Practice*, Oxford, Oxford University Press.

13 Eugene F. McKenna (2012), *Business Psychology and Organizational Behavior*, 5th edition, New York, Psychology Press, Chapter 16.

14 Bernard Burnes (2005), op. cit.

15 Michael Beer, Russell A. Eisenstat, and Bert Spector (1990), *The Critical Path to Corporate Renewal*, Boston, Harvard Business School Press.

16 John Micklethwaite and Adrian Wooldridge (1997), *The Witch Doctors*, London, Heinemann, Chapter 1.

17 Phillip Chartrand (1981), *The Design, Implementation and Measurement of a Macrochange Programme*, Unpublished PhD thesis, University of Aston. See also Box 13.5.

18 See, for example, Hannaford Brothers Company in Richard S. Wellins, William C. Byham, and George R. Dixon (1994), *Inside Teams: How 20 World-Class Organizations are Winning Through Teamwork*, San Francisco, Jossey-Bass, pp. 179–191.

19 Business Process Reengineering. *Wikipedia*, http://en.wikipedia.org/wiki/Business_process_reengineering, accessed February 10, 2014.

20 For an insightful review of BPR and its story see John Micklethwaite and Adrian Wooldridge (1997), op. cit., Chapter 1.

21 John Child, David Faulkner, and Robert Pitkethly (2001), *The Management of International Acquisitions*, Oxford University Press.

22 James G. March (1991), Exploration and exploitation in organizational learning. *Organization Science*, 2(1), 71–87.

23 As well as the ASDA case, another example of how this dual approach led to another successful turnaround, that of the German retail company Adler Modemärkte, is described in Camilla Krebsbach-Gnath (2001), Applying theory to organizational transformation, in Meinolf Dierkes, Ariane Antal, John Child, and Ikujiro Nonaka (eds.) *Handbook of Organizational Learning*, Oxford, Oxford University Press, Chapter 40, pp. 886–901.

24 Andrew H. Van de Ven and Kangyong Sun (2011), Breakdowns in implementing models of organization change, *Academy of Management Perspectives*, 25(3), 58–74.

25 Armand V. Feigenbaum (2001), Managing cuts in a cold climate, *Financial Times*, 11 April, p. 17.

26 Joel Brockner (2000), Change: success is all in the detail, *Financial Times, Mastering Management*, Part 5, 30 October, pp. 8, 10.

27 John P. Kotter (2012), *Leading Change*, Boston, Harvard Business Review Press; Kurt Lewin (1951), *Field Theory in Social Science*, New York, Harper & Row.

28 John P. Kotter (1995), Why transformation efforts fail, *Harvard Business Review*, 73(2), 59–67.

29 Sharon Parker and Toby Wall (1998), *Job and Work Design*, Thousand Oaks, Sage.

30 Karen S. Whelan-Berry and Karen A. Somerville (2010), Linking change drivers and the organizational change process: A review and synthesis, *Journal of Change Management*, 10(2), 175–193.

31 Donald P. Warwick (1975), *A Theory of Public Bureaucracy*, Cambridge, MA, Harvard University Press.

32   John Micklethwaite and Adrian Wooldridge (1997), op. cit., Chapter 1.

33   Frank Heller, Eugen Pusić, George Strauss, and Bernhard Wilpert (1998), *Organizational Participation: Myth and Reality*, Oxford, Oxford University Press, p. 181.

34   Alexandra Stubbings and Nicolas Ceasar (2012), *Sustainability as Usual: A Change Leader's Guide to Embedding Sustainability*, Berkhamsted, UK, Ashridge Business School.

35   Geoff Cox (2014), *Cuttings 110*, April 1, 2014, geofcox@newdirections.uk.com, accessed April 1, 2014.

36   Jean M. Bartunek, Denise M. Rousseau, Jenny W. Rudolph, and Jenny A. DePalma (2006), On the receiving end: Sensemaking, emotion, and assessments of an organizational change initiated by others, *Journal of Applied Behavioral Science*, 42(2), 182–206.

37   Dennis G. Erwin and Andrew N. Garman (2010), Resistance to organizational change: Linking research and practice, *Leadership & Organization Development Journal*, 31(1), 39–56.

38   Piers Myers, Sally Hulks, and Liz Wiggins (2012), op. cit., Chapter 5.

39   Daniele Binci, Corrado Cerruti, and Stefano Antonio Donnarumma (2012), Resistance in HROs, setback or resource? *Journal of Organizational Change Management*, 25(6), 867–882.

40   David Courpasson, Françoise Dany, and Stewart Clegg (2012), Resisters at work: Generating productive resistance in the workplace, *Organization Science*, 23(3), 801–819.

41   Frederick Herzberg, Bernard Mausner, and Barbara B. Snyderman (1959), *The Motivation to Work*, New York, Wiley.

42   Dennis G. Erwin and Andrew N. Garman (2010), op. cit.

43   James M. McFillen, Deborah A. O'Neil, William K. Balzer, and Glenn H. Varney (2013), Organizational diagnosis: An evidence-based approach, *Journal of Change Management*, 13(2), 223–246.

44   These steps are based partly on Tom Lupton (1965), The practical analysis of change in organizations, *Journal of Management Studies*, 2, 218–227.

45   Dennis G. Erwin and Andrew N. Garman (2010), op. cit., Table 1, pp. 51–52.

46   Phillip J. Chartrand (1976), Job redesign: Progress or pipedream? *Business Quarterly*, 41(4), Winter, 65–77.

47   Quotation from Dennis G. Erwin and Andrew N. Garman (2010), op. cit., p. 40, referring to Dennis T. Jaffe, Cynthia D. Scott, and Glenn R. Tobe (1994), *Rekindling Commitment: How to Revitalize Yourself, Your Work, and Your Organization*, San Francisco, Jossey-Bass.

48   Piers Myers, Sally Hulks, and Liz Wiggins (2012), op. cit., Chapter 4.

49   This analysis is based on Hugh Marlow (1974), *Managing Change: A Strategy for Our Time*, London, Institute of Personnel Management.

50   Mikael Brännmark and Suzanne Benn (2012), A proposed model for evaluating the sustainability of continuous change programmes, *Journal of Change Management*, 12(2), 231–245.

51   David Buchanan, Louise Fitzgerald, Diane Ketley, Rose Gollop, Jane Louise Jones, Sharon Saint Lamont, Annette Neath, and Elaine Whitby (2005), No going back: A review of the literature on sustaining organizational change, *International Journal of Management Reviews*, 7(3), 189–205. Quotation is from p. 201.

52   Alexandra Stubbings and Nicolas Ceasar (2012), op. cit. See also Piers Myers, Sally Hulks, and Liz Wiggins (2012), op. cit., Chapter 13.

CHAPTER 14

Organizing for Learning[1]

WHAT THIS CHAPTER COVERS

This chapter is concerned with learning both within organizations and through cooperation between them. After identifying the strategic importance of learning, it moves on to discuss the nature of "organizational" learning and offers some important distinctions that help to unpack a complex phenomenon. Factors that can facilitate the process of learning within an organization are identified, notably managerial leadership, channels of communication, a balance between control and autonomy, the management of internal boundaries through methods such as cross-functional teams, and the ensuring of inward information flows across external boundaries. An organization's capacity to learn depends on a number of factors that are examined. The chapter then considers the increasingly important process of learning through the formation of strategic alliances. The closing section of this chapter indicates how organizational learning can be facilitated in practical terms.

◢ The Strategic Importance of Organizational Learning

The contemporary economy is increasingly knowledge-based and subject to rapid change. One of the main reasons why some organizations perform better than others is that they apply superior knowledge and can adapt more effectively to changing conditions. This means that they are better at what has come to be called "organizational learning." Organizational learning is the process whereby people belonging to, or working with, organizations develop their understanding and behaviors, which then become institutionalized into an outcome – organizational knowledge. In this way learning produces an organizational "knowledge asset."[2] It can take a cognitive form, as in new concepts, cultural norms and strategic thinking. It can also take a behavioral form, as in new or revised practices, routines, systems, and structures.[3] The terms "organizational learning" and "organizational knowledge creation" can for practical purposes be used synonymously.

Organizational learning therefore refers to both the process of acquiring or generating new knowledge and to its outcome. It encompasses both the acquisition of knowledge as an "intangible" asset and an ability to exploit that asset.[4] The outcome of learning is therefore the acquisition of a new competence. It can lead to an ability to apply new knowledge to enhance the performance of an existing activity or task. It can also help an organization prepare for new circumstances and in this way foster change on a continuing and emerging basis (the "emergent change" discussed in Chapter 13).[5] Increasingly, managers are seeking ways of promoting their organizations' capacities to generate new useful knowledge. The ability to learn therefore confers a competitive advantage on a firm and also makes a public organization a more efficient and effective deliverer of services. As with many of the subjects covered in this book, much more attention has been paid to learning in business organizations than in public service ones which provide a somewhat different context for organizational learning.[6]

For many years the dominant view among economists and strategy theorists was that superior performance could be explained in terms of the structural features of industries, such as barriers to competition. However, an alternative view has attracted much attention, which is that firm-specific resources and capabilities (learned processes and activities), play a critical role in enabling firms to achieve superior performance in the market.[7] Particularly key is having the ability to combine an organization's intangible assets synergistically and dynamically so as to enhance its competitive power – to create what have come to be called "dynamic capabilities."[8] This resource-based view of the firm highlights the contribution of organizational knowledge and its application as a foundation for competitive success. It has been argued that, in contemporary conditions, knowledge and the ability to learn faster than rivals is the only sure source of lasting competitive advantage. For instance, a consultant to the General Electric Company concluded that "Companies must learn better than their best competitor or their business is doomed to fall behind. Learning has become a key to organizational survival."[9]

Peter Senge, who popularized the concept of a "learning organization," went even further in stating that the pace of change in the modern world is so rapid that it is inadequate simply to learn how to adapt.[10] Adaptive learning needs to give way to a more pre-emptive type of learning which Senge calls "generative learning." In this way, firms can be proactive rather than reactive. They can surface latent customer needs to build new markets, explore the application of new technologies to meet those needs, and in these ways keep ahead of the competition and ensure long-term survival. In the terms coined by James March, firms have to organize so that they can "explore" new possibilities as well as "exploit" existing knowledge.[11]

It has been argued in somewhat similar vein that firms are better equipped to compete if they focus on their core competencies.[12] These core competencies are fundamental abilities, which it is difficult for competitors to imitate. They depend upon the firm possessing some specific knowledge and the ability to renew it. Various types of knowledge can contribute to a firm's core competence, including technical, organizational and strategic knowledge. Examples are, respectively, the special technical insight or design flair that lends a superior edge to products and services, the organizational ability to combine and recombine assets to meet new competitive opportunities, and the distinctive mindset that leads to innovative strategies.

While some of this knowledge is tangible and explicit, a great deal is intangible and tacit in nature.

The concepts of a learning organization and dynamic capabilities both draw attention to the fact that organizational learning may be facilitated, or alternatively hindered, by the context in which it takes place. Knowledge may be acquired from external sources or created within an organization. An important source of knowledge within an organization is information and reflection on previous task performance. These processes are both intrinsic features of organizational learning and both take place within a context.[13] Neither process is likely to take place very effectively, if at all, without certain supporting conditions being in place. One condition is the ability of the management team itself to be open-minded and to encourage learning throughout the organization. Is management, for example, receptive to market signals and does it have the ability to guide its organization's response accordingly? Another condition is management's ability to organize for learning by encouraging the free flow of information, and pooling of competencies, within and across the boundaries of a firm.

Context is also significant for learning in another respect. Much learning arises informally from interactions with co-workers performing shared collaborative tasks. For this reason, teamwork can be a powerful process for learning. Learning can be encouraged by people sharing an identity with others because then they are not only stimulated by the mutual interactions they have but are also more willing to open up their thoughts and ideas to those others. This insight has given rise to the notion of "situated learning" by which learning is viewed as a social process through which knowledge is constructed. That process is situated in a particular context and has to be understood by reference to the conditions of that context.[14]

This chapter describes the ways in which organizations can manage and organize themselves so as to achieve an effective capacity to learn. It focuses on firms, though its conclusions are normally applicable to all kinds of organization. The chapter first clarifies some key conceptual distinctions. It then considers learning within firms before turning to how partnerships through alliances between firms can promote learning. It concludes with implications for practice.

◢ The Nature of Organizational Learning: Key Distinctions

The concept

The term "organizational learning" has since the 1970s come to be used to emphasize that organizations, just as individuals, can acquire new knowledge and skills with the intention of improving their future performance. There has been a large amount of discussion and writing on the subject, much of it usefully reviewed in major reference sources.[15] Nevertheless, there is not a generally agreed model or even definition of organizational learning. Most writers agree that organizational learning consists of both cognitive and behavioral elements, equivalent respectively to understanding and the ability to apply that understanding. Villinger suggests that learning in organizations is "the process of developing a potential to improve actions (behavior) through better knowledge and understanding (cognition)."[16] While learning is clearly a process, some would go further and include its outcomes within the scope of the term as well. This extension is helpful, because it serves as a reminder that an organization does not necessarily benefit from the acquisition of knowledge and understanding unless these are applied, so that the "potential to improve actions" is actually realized.

Villinger prefers to use the term "learning in organizations" because of the uncertainty over whether organizations themselves can actually be said to learn. The idea of "organizational" learning does not resolve the paradox that "organizational learning is not merely individual learning, yet organizations learn only through the experience and actions of individuals."[17] In a strict sense, knowledge is created by individuals and an organization can only employ creative individuals and provide suitable contexts for them to create knowledge. The notion of "organizational knowledge creation" advanced by Nonaka and Takeuchi provides an indication of how this individual learning can become available, and retained, within the organization as a whole: "Organizational knowledge creation . . . should be understood as a process that 'organizationally' amplifies the knowledge created by individuals and crystallizes it as part of the knowledge network of the organization. This process takes place within an expanding 'community of interaction' which crosses intra- and inter-organizational boundaries."[18]

This touches on the very practical question of how learning by individuals, or groups of individuals, can become transformed into an organizational property. The challenge here is partly one of how to make explicit, codify, disseminate, and store the knowledge possessed by the members of an organization in ways that convert it into a collective resource. It is also partly a problem of how to reduce the barriers that organizational structures, cultures, and interests can place in the way of knowledge-sharing and learning.

The nature of the knowledge contributed by the members of an organization, or an alliance of organizations, is of considerable significance for the process of learning. An important requirement for converting knowledge into an organizational property is to make it sufficiently explicit to be readily disseminated. Here, Polanyi's distinction between tacit knowledge and explicit knowledge becomes very relevant.[19] The former is usually regarded as personal, intuitive, and context-specific. It is therefore difficult to verbalize, formalize, and communicate to others. Explicit knowledge, by contrast, is specified and codified. It can therefore be transmitted in formal systematic language. To make tacit knowledge available to an organization at large in a form that permits its retention for future use, it has to be converted into a codified or programmable form. It may not be possible to accomplish this, either for technical reasons or because the people with tacit knowledge do not wish to share and potentially lose their control over it. If this is the case, then the only way to put tacit knowledge to organizational use may be to delegate responsibility for action to the persons concerned and/or to persuade them to share their knowledge with other experts on an informal basis.

The degree to which knowledge is tacit or explicit is likely to parallel whether that knowledge is exploratory or exploitative in nature.[20] Exploration is commonly associated with the creation of new knowledge through fundamental or radical innovations. Until it has been codified, new knowledge will normally be in a highly tacit form and accessible only to the limited set of people who have generated it. Exploitation is associated with incremental innovations that build upon or apply what is already known. In order for exploratory knowledge to become available for exploitation, it needs to be structured in an explicit codified form. Codification enables it to be diffused through a range of applications to commercial or social purposes. Exploitation can also take the form of upgrading and efficiency improvements, in both cases applying existing knowledge.

The question of how to organize in ways that facilitate exploratory and exploitative learning or knowledge creation is discussed in Chapter 17. Organizing to encourage the development of tacit organizational learning can be particularly challenging in two respects. First, to ensure that tacit knowledge is mutually understood and shared. Second, to find ways of converting it into an explicit form. The tacit nature of much useful knowledge can present problems for cooperation in learning both between different specialized units within an organization and between different organizations. One problem between partner organizations arises when they regard each other as competitors or do not trust each other for whatever reason. If the partners are seeking to learn from one another in a competitive spirit, then they are likely to keep their knowledge in a tacit form as a defensive measure, because this means that only their trusted members have access to it. It is easier to protect tacit knowledge from leakage than it is to protect explicit knowledge.[21] However, if both or all partners adopt this tactic, then they will face major difficulties in converting the knowledge that each holds tacitly or covertly into a form usable for cooperative activities. This can, obviously, become counter-productive to the success of their cooperation, which almost certainly requires mutual learning in order to achieve other strategic objectives as well.

A second problem arises when the tacit knowledge held by the members of one partner organization is superseded by new knowledge and practices brought in by another partner. Their tacit knowledge may have considerable significance for individuals' own personal identities and sense of worth. The consequent threat to the personal and collective identity of the first partner's staff may generate considerable resistance to their accepting the new inputs. This situation often arises in alliances between companies from developing and developed countries respectively, where the latter are seeking to bring new ideas and practices into the alliance.[22]

Levels of organizational learning

Another distinction with important implications for practice is that between the different levels of organizational learning (see Table 14.1). Both theorists and those writing more from the standpoint of management practice have identified three main levels of organizational learning, in a broadly parallel way. The theoretical approach identifies routine improvements within the boundaries of existing organizational knowledge as the "lowest" level. The middle level involves changes to the boundaries or structures of existing knowledge bases, which imply a "reframing" of organizational systems and perspectives. The highest level is learning how to learn, in the sense of learning how to carry out lower and middle level learning, through reflexive cognitive processes; it is proactive and generative. These three learning levels correspond to the terms "single-loop learning," "double-loop learning," and "deutero-learning" coined by Argyris and Schön.[23] Single-loop learning is adaptive and similar to March's notion of exploitative learning that leads to new applications of existing knowledge. Double-loop learning is about discovery and similar to March's notion of explorative learning which leads to fundamentally new insights.[24]

The pragmatic practice-oriented approach distinguishes between technical, systemic, and strategic levels of organizational learning. The technical level refers to the acquisition of new, specific techniques, such as those for quality measurement or for undertaking systematic market research. This corresponds to routine learning. The systemic level refers to learning to introduce and work with new organizational systems and procedures. The focus here is on an integrative type of learning involving the restructuring of relationships and the creation of new roles. This parallels the notion of organizational reframing. The strategic level involves

Table 14.1 Levels of organizational learning

Level	Theoretical approach	Pragmatic approach
Higher	*Second-order learning – "deutero learning"*	*Strategic learning*
	Learning how to learn so as to improve the quality of the organizational learning process itself	Changes in managerial mindsets, especially in understanding the criteria and conditions for organizational success
Middle	*Reframing – "double-loop"*	*Systemic learning*
	Changes of existing organizational frameworks; involves questioning existing systems; oriented toward survival in changing environmental conditions	Changes in organizational systems, with an emphasis on learning how to achieve better integration of organizational activities
Lower	*Routine – "single-loop"*	*Technical learning*
	Improvements and adjustments to optimize performance *within the limits of existing* organizational frameworks and systems	The acquisition of new specific techniques such as advanced production scheduling or managerial techniques such as more advanced selection tests

Source: Child, John, David Faulkner, and Stephen Tallman 2005. *Cooperative Strategy*. Oxford: Oxford University Press

changes in the mindsets of senior managers, especially their criteria of organizational success and their mental maps of the factors significant for achieving that success. The emphasis on vision here is somewhat different from that on "learning how to learn," but there is a parallel in the reflexive cognitive processes involved with a view to generating new insights and being proactive.

Andreu and Ciborra point to the dynamic processes that link together these three levels of learning within an organization by means of three equivalent "loops."[25] Their scheme is reproduced in Fig. 14.1. At the lower level is the routinization-learning loop. This level of learning is aimed at mastering the use of standard resources and gives rise to efficient work practices. Most of the learning at this level will be technical in nature. Andreu and Ciborra cite as an example mastering the usage of a spreadsheet by an individual or a team in a specific department, to solve a concrete problem.

A company can internalize new work practices in the form of routines, and in this way they become part of its capabilities. This gives rise to a capability-learning loop, in which new work practices are combined with organizational routines. The learning process here is systemic in character because it involves generalizing work practices and techniques and placing them into a wider context. This defines not just what the practices do and how they work, but also the circumstances under which it becomes appropriate to use them and who has the authority or competence to apply them. The third and highest learning loop is the strategic loop. In this learning process, capabilities evolve into core capabilities that differentiate a firm strategically, and provide it with a competitive advantage. These capabilities are therefore critical to the firm's prosperity.

While the Andreu and Ciborra framework depicts a primarily internal process of upward learning cycles within a single firm, cooperation with partner organizations offers a potential

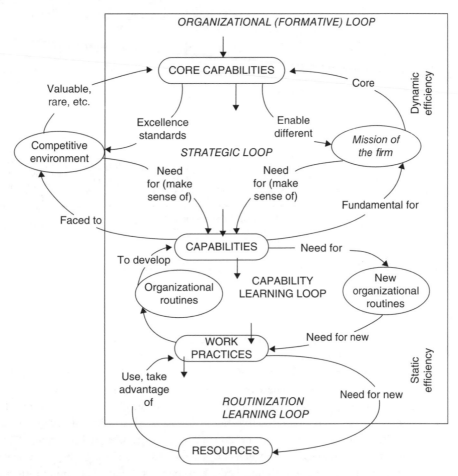

Figure 14.1 Organizational learning loops at three levels.[26]

for learning at all three levels. The level of learning which a collaborative venture aims to achieve will depend on its purpose and the needs of its partners. At the level of routine technical learning, collaboration may provide direct and fast access to improved techniques and specific technologies. At the level of system capability learning, collaboration can facilitate the transfer and internalization of new systems, such as lean production and project management. Cooperation can in these ways enhance a partner's capabilities, and these may assume greater significance if the cooperation also opens a door to new strategic possibilities through, for example, assisting market entry. However, the barriers to strategic learning through collaboration tend to be greater than at other levels of learning, a point to which I return later in this chapter.

◢ Requirements for Successful Organizational Learning

Figure 14.2 is a representation of the learning process in an organization and the requirements for it to be accomplished successfully. Much the same process is involved in learning through

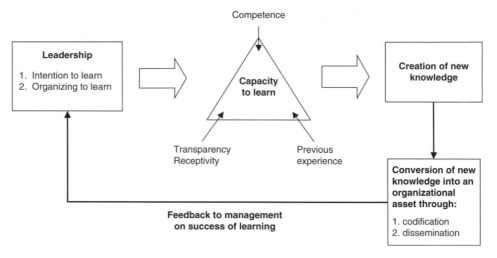

Figure 14.2 The organizational learning process and requirements for its success.

cooperation between organizations, though additional difficulties can arise if the partners have different learning objectives and modes of organization, or if they suffer from a lack of mutual trust. The first key requirement for successful organizational learning is that it has the support of adequate and appropriate *leadership*. Leadership has two particularly important components in regard to achieving organizational learning. The first concerns *intention to learn*. This means that management has the intention to promote learning and to take full advantage of learning opportunities, and fosters a culture conducive to organizational learning. The second component is that management *organizes to learn* – that it establishes organizational arrangements which will encourage learning. These arrangements concern communication channels, the balance between autonomy and control, the bridging of internal and external boundaries, and the use of teams.

The second key requirement is that the organization has the *capacity to learn*. Even if management is committed to learning and suitable organizational arrangements are in place, the organization also has to have a capacity to learn before new knowledge can actually be created (or imported) and absorbed. A capacity to learn depends on the receptivity of members to new knowledge, their ability to understand and apply it, and how much they have learned from previous experience. Although not an organizational capacity, the form that new incoming knowledge takes also impacts on capacity to learn.

If the requirements just mentioned are in place and learning has therefore taken place in an organization, one may assume that there has been a *creation of new knowledge*. However, this is not the end of the process. It is vital for the new knowledge resulting from the learning process to be *converted into an organizational asset*. For this to happen, knowledge that may be relatively uncodified has to be codified into guidelines, rules, routines or the like so that (1) the contributions of different specialists can be combined and (2) the knowledge is converted into a form that can be disseminated and stored within the organization. Moreover, it will be necessary to disseminate an understanding of the nature, importance and use of the new knowledge among those members of an organization who will be required to use it but who did not participate in its creation or development. This requires an investment in suitable training.

If these steps in the learning process are successfully achieved, this provides positive *feedback to management* that should help to convince it of the value of learning, so increasing its intention to foster organizational learning in the future. Although all of these requirements appear to be rather obvious, they are not easy to achieve in practice. There can be barriers to learning at each stage of the organizational learning process which may arise from a wide range of factors including failings in leadership; conservative mindsets, low motivation and limited skills among employees; an unsupportive organizational culture; inappropriate organizational structures; and politically-soured relationships. The nature of the information and knowledge being created, shared and applied in the learning process can also prove to be a barrier, especially if it is highly tacit and/or regarded as highly proprietary to a particular group within the organization or a particular external partner.[26]

The steps in the learning process just identified are now considered in greater detail.

Leadership

INTENTION TO LEARN

Leadership plays an important role in organizational learning. There are similarities to the role it plays in bringing about organizational change, and as noted in Chapter 13 change and learning are highly interdependent. The clear expression by senior managers of their strong intention to promote learning is often required to break the mold of established thinking and practice. "Unlearning" – the discarding of obsolete and misleading knowledge – is a perquisite for opening minds to new knowledge and practices.[27] Because unlearning can threaten people's identity and sense of value, it is an uncomfortable process which often requires a strong push from senior management to achieve. Indeed it sometimes requires a change of top management as a starting point. It is reported that in some major Japanese companies, CEOs have deliberately created a sense of crisis in order to create receptivity to unlearning.

Some leadership of the organizational learning process itself is necessary for it to be directed towards clear goals, coordinated, informed by open channels of communication and, not least, adequately supported with resources. Leadership at different levels can facilitate successful organizational learning. While the leadership of senior management is particularly vital to support and sustain organizational learning, the fact that such learning takes place at different levels means that the contribution of middle and lower levels of management is also important. Leadership has to be offered for what people actually do when learning and creating knowledge.[28] For this to happen, senior leaders have to prioritize the diffusion of a learning culture throughout their management structure.

The expression by top management of a clear and committed intention that its organization shall learn is an extremely significant requirement. One of the best-known examples of a company that has for many years displayed a strong intention to learn through the exploration of new possibilities is the 3M Corporation. 3M has a "thirty percent rule" which means that 30% of each division's revenues must come from products introduced in the last four years. Progress against this criterion is tracked rigorously, and employee bonuses are based on successful achievement of this goal.[29] 3M creates "garage projects" to foster new ideas, a concept that recalls the origins of Hewlett-Packard and Apple Computers. Employees at 3M can use 15 percent of their working time to develop new ideas, to challenge existing practices and to innovate.

Managers can also contribute importantly by fostering a culture conducive to organizational learning, if necessary by transforming the embedded legacy of the past from a barrier to an asset. Often, such barriers can be broken down through communication of a vision from the top. If the barrier to learning created by an embedded organizational culture proves insuperable, it may have to be demolished. Radical moves away from embedded organizational cultures, sometimes termed "frame-breaking" changes or "transformations," have to be led from the top (see Chapter 13). Jack Welch performed this role at the General Electric Company. The other side of the coin is that a conservative organizational leader, who clings to an established set of policies and practices, insulating himself or herself against changing realities, can have the power to prevent an organization from learning and adapting. It is therefore not surprising that radical changes and corporate turnarounds usually require the bringing in of new senior managers from outside, as well as the direct involvement of executives in all aspects of the process.

The introduction of radical change illustrates a rather dramatic connection between organizational leadership and learning. However, a culture supportive of learning also has to be sustained on a more everyday basis. Here tensions can arise between managerial controls and the freedom to explore alternative practices. Therefore, a further leadership role in promoting organizational learning is to establish a culture that permits the autonomy needed to encourage the creation of insight and new knowledge, within a sense of collective effort that is directed towards the development of the organization as a whole. This points to the need for management to ensure that appropriate organizational arrangements are in place to support learning, supported by leadership at all levels.

ORGANIZING TO LEARN

"Organizational structures and mechanisms that can influence the process of using, sharing, integrating and creating knowledge" have been categorized as "knowledge governance."[30] Although more research is required for us to fully understand knowledge governance, some guidelines can be suggested from what we already know.

1. COMMUNICATION

Three channels of communication and relationships across a firm's internal and external organizational boundaries are key to the learning process. These are shown in Figure 14.3, and it is vital that all three are kept open and effective.[31] The first channel is vertical and the other two are more horizontal.

- The first channel is between higher management and other, more specialized, groups within an organization. There is a division of function here in that higher management will normally be concerned with strategic knowledge, while other groups will work

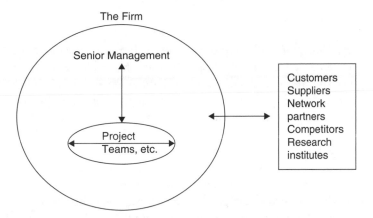

Figure 14.3 Three channels of communication and relationship necessary for effective organizational learning.[32]

more on organizational and technical knowledge. Each area of knowledge needs to be informed by the others. In particular, the degree of support that higher management gives to learning activities and systems at lower levels of an organization can have a major impact on their effectiveness.

• The second channel involves the integration of knowledge contributions between different specialties and units within an organization. It is a requirement for the operation of knowledge databases and for effective teamwork across departments and disciplines. It is often achieved through project teams.

• The third channel promotes flows of information and knowledge across the boundaries of an organization through communication with, and intelligence from, other organizations and groups including customers, suppliers, alliance and network partners, competitors, and research institutes. Cross-organizational knowledge flows can occur at any level of an organization, though flows relevant to strategic learning tend to be concentrated at the upper levels and those relevant to organizational and technical learning lower down. Information secured through external network links is particularly vital for the ability of smaller firms to acquire and learn from new technical and market knowledge which in larger firms is often provided by in-house specialists.[33]

Information is the lifeblood of learning. Some writers have for this reason advocated that firms provide for a "redundancy of information" in order to encourage learning, namely "information that goes beyond the immediate operational requirements of organization members."[34] Having effective channels to communicate and circulate information is therefore a vital requirement for organizational learning to take place. In this respect, modern information and communication technologies can greatly facilitate communication of information and knowledge over distances both in explicit and tacit forms. Media such as email can convey highly structured information, while video conferencing systems can convey relatively tacit information. Moreover, game-like technologies can also encourage brainstorming and experimentation in support of learning.[35]

2. CONTROL AND AUTONOMY

The second important aspect of organizing for learning concerns the difficult relationship between autonomy and control. Managerial leadership implies a degree of top-down direction and control which is not easily reconciled with the autonomy and open-mindedness commonly regarded as conditions for creative learning. Indeed, the pressures for change and reform that naturally result from organizational learning can readily be interpreted as a challenge to its senior leadership. The inherent tension between leadership and devolved autonomy can therefore be problematic for organizational learning.

This problem often arises in regard to the question of information and its availability. The question of *what* information is made available, and to *whom* within a firm, involves an element of choice. This choice is a prerogative of top management, insofar as it creates and resources the channels of information. At the same time, fast-changing organizational contexts, characterized by increasing discontinuity and turbulence, render it even less tenable than previously for top management to hold or even understand all of the information relevant to adapting their organization to these changing conditions. While it is the role of senior management to make sure that its organization has an appropriate sense of long-term direction, organizational learning also requires a degree of cognitive and behavioral initiative on the part of organizational members who are in closer touch with relevant events and developments. The challenge for leadership in facilitating organizational learning therefore lies in maintaining a judicious combination of *both* control, in the form of guidance and back up, *and* the autonomy required to motivate knowledge generators and encourage the free flow of information. It has to achieve *"controlled autonomy."*

Control can be directive and supportive rather than simply restrictive. Direction of a kind that supports learning can be implemented through the allocation of resources which are essential for knowledge creating projects: personnel, money, equipment and time. The latter resource is especially significant for learning, which requires a double time investment. The time that is taken up by personnel in standing back from a situation so as to assimilate and work on new information, or to learn new practices, is also time that is "lost" to the organization while learners step out of their usual roles and routines in order to accomplish the learning.

It is necessary to provide organizational learning with direction sufficient to ensure that it is regarded as significant, and thus adequately supported, while also allowing sufficient autonomy to the process so that it is capable of producing new insights. For example, a British contract catering company saved considerable costs in its purchasing by reducing the range of its suppliers without sacrificing food quality. This was achieved by its managing director setting such saving as a target but leaving it to teams of chefs, restaurant managers and other staff with operational knowledge to decide which suppliers the company should retain.[36] The turnaround of ASDA, described in Chapter 13, provides a similar example of how a sense of direction from top management was combined with bottom-up initiative to produce beneficial changes.

The concept of interactive control offers a constructive approach toward retaining control while opening up organizational dialogue so as to encourage learning.[37] A management adopting this approach attempts to reconcile the simultaneous need for control and creativity within a learning organization. It does this in tandem with active policies toward beliefs (by communicating core values and missions), boundaries (by specifying and enforcing the rules of the game), and diagnostics (by building and supporting clear targets). This approach endeavors

BOX 14.1 AUTONOMY AND LEARNING AT 3M

"Generations of top management at 3M have viewed their organization as growing from the bottom – the project team – up. Under a principle the company calls "grow and divide," successful project teams, consisting of an entrepreneur with an idea and a small team that believes in it, grow into departments . . . Top management has organized wide, collegial networks that scientists throughout the company can tap into for advice and assistance. . . . It routinely leverages new technologies across two or three divisions and applies them in multiple markets. It is the company's well-oiled competence-building process that has become 3M's real core competence."

In companies like 3M, "Top management entrusts the operating units with the challenge of creating the competencies needed to pursue local opportunities. It limits its own role to seeing that those competencies are shared through cross-unit flows of resources, knowledge, and people."

Source: Sumantra Ghoshal and Christopher A. Bartlett. Changing the Role of Top Management: Beyond Structure to Processes. *Harvard Business Review*, 73(1), 1995, pp. 86–96. Quotations are from pages 89–94.

---

to combine creative learning processes at the operational level with the maintenance by top management of an organization communications network through which these idiosyncratic learning experiences can be made accessible to other parts of the organization. Again, the 3M Corporation illustrates how management can actively foster learning and innovation through this kind of interactive control (see Box 14.1).

Since leadership also denotes status, power and privilege, those in authority are always liable to seek to defend their positions and, in so doing, may well suppress proposals from below which are at one and the same time opportunities for the organization to learn and challenges to the present establishment. In exercising the right to choose how much power it will delegate downwards, the leadership of an organization can determine how many learning opportunities it will make available to subordinates. When making this choice, some managers still accord with the precept of scientific management that in organizations thinking should be separated from doing. This tendency and the way it can militate against opportunities for learning is illustrated by the case of a major automobile manufacturer presented in the previous chapter (Box 13.1). This case points to the potential that external consultants have in promoting organizational learning, and also how their recommendations can be rejected due to considerations of maintaining managerial power. It highlights the relationship between learning, vertical differentiation and control. Control can readily be equated to the maintenance of vertical differentiation. This was certainly the perspective of the auto company's management. In reverse, it is also the perspective of employees who restrict management's access to operational and quality information.

An organic ("organismic") form of organization is more conducive to learning than is the more "mechanistic" conventional hierarchical organization (see Chapter 2, Table 2.3). The reason is that an organic form facilitates the crossing of organizational levels and boundaries, and the communication of information even to the point of redundancy.[38] A hierarchical form is not conducive to effective learning, especially in contemporary conditions. Relevant knowledge and expertise is today normally distributed widely among the member groups within organizations. Leaders therefore have to reconcile the need for control and autonomy in a manner acceptable to those groups and which elicits their positive contribution to the learning process.

Considerations of autonomy and control draw attention to how the *vertical* differentiation of firms can bear upon their ability to encourage learning. Chapter 4 discussed how organizational hierarchy can handicap adaptability and innovation, both of which depend on learning. There is in fact evidence that differences in power and status stifle learning within organizations by discouraging the commitment to collective goals of lower-level members and causing them to feel less safe in undertaking the experiments and initiatives on which learning can depend. To some extent these negative consequences of hierarchy can be offset if senior managers make an effort to encourage learning among all members and guarantee that they will not be penalized from any mistakes made in the process.[39]

Organizations are, of course, also differentiated *horizontally by* internal and external boundaries. A vertical emphasis on hierarchy encourages separate reporting lines among organizational units and so tends to make it more difficult to integrate those units horizontally. Yet organizational learning requires horizontal communication and cooperation across both internal and external boundaries, as Figure 14.3 indicated. In other words, these boundaries have to be managed.

3. INTEGRATION AND MANAGING INTERNAL BOUNDARIES

Unless they are extremely small, firms normally develop internal boundaries by delimiting different specialized groups, departments or sub-units. Each of these specialties will have its own set of competencies and knowledge. However, specialized groups attach their own values to their expertise, and articulate them through their own codes and terminology. As Lawrence and Lorsch noted, specialization within organizations tends to encourage a "difference in cognitive and emotional orientation among managers in different functional departments."[40] Specialized personnel may remain attached to their codes and language as reflections of their social identity and market value outside a particular organization. In the case of professionalized groups, membership of external occupational institutions reinforces this separate identity. It can therefore be difficult to bridge internal boundaries and integrate the contributions of different groups to organizational learning because of contrasts in the technologies they offer, and the goals they attach, to the process.

A firm, nevertheless, has to draw upon the specialist competencies and knowledge bases of different groups within its organization in order to provide the substantive contributions and insights required for learning. For this reason, effective organizational learning requires a certain level of differentiation and a complementary level of integration. The appropriate balance between them depends on contextual factors such as the complexity, rate of change and competitive pressures in the organization's environment. Lawrence and Lorsch concluded from their investigations that high performing organizations were those that achieved this optimum balance.

There is, however, no guarantee that integration across internal boundaries can always be realized as a wellspring of collective learning. For example, their embedded norms and practices can make individuals and groups unwilling to learn. The inter-group conflicts that are liable to arise with differentiation can also constitute an impediment to organizational learning. Studies of how private and public-sector organizations in European services responded to the availability of new information technology (IT) demonstrate that learning can involve contests as well as collaboration between the different organizational groups who are involved, such as technical specialists, higher management, personnel specialists, and employee representatives.[41] The introduction of powerful new integrated IT systems opens up the possibility of radical innovations in the organization of work as well as in the provision of services. It therefore exposes the conflicting interests and perspectives of different occupational groups that might otherwise remain relatively subdued.

Integration of the contributions to learning, which organizational sub-units have the potential to make, involves a willingness on their part to share with others the interpretation and use of their specialized knowledge. A condition for this to happen is a readiness to communicate openly based on a minimum level of mutual trust and respect, though open communication of itself is not sufficient to resolve underlying conflicts. Managers are the key personnel for mediating the differentiation/integration process and resolving inter-departmental conflicts. Managers have a responsibility to identify organizational members who possess the appropriate competencies, and then to bring them together and help them to align the different interpretations they apply to their knowledge.

In keeping with the organic model of organizing, investigations have generally found that when an organization takes on network characteristics, this encourages knowledge sharing and transfer both within that organization and with other organizations. The cognitive and relational aspects of networking seem to be particularly important in this regard. The cognitive aspect refers to having shared visions and systems, while the relational aspect refers to having strong trust-based relationships.[42] However, it can take considerable time and effort to foster and maintain active networks. It is therefore instructive that Kieser and Koch pointed out from their case studies of two German companies how rules can economize on the process of knowledge sharing and combination. They found that when the knowledge of different organizational specialists was codified into rules this could reduce the cognitive load on those specialists and also assist the combination of knowledge from different specialist sources. In this way, the codification of knowledge assists its diffusion, while also economizing on training needs and management time.[43]

A further type of integration also promotes learning – that of professional staff with management. Much of the expertise held by the more skilled professionals is based on tacit knowledge, and this is difficult to convert into organizational routines. Such professionals typically employ expert judgment that is not readily translated into rationalized, systematized procedures or delegated to others. If professional knowledge and judgment can be aligned with that of managers, their joint capacity to learn and make better-informed decisions should improve. As always, the challenge lies in how to achieve this. It requires reward and career development policies sufficient to motivate professional and specialist staff to contribute their expertise, and mechanisms such as task forces for bringing together and appropriating that expertise as an organizational competence.

Integration is therefore essential to organizational learning. An organization frequently knows less than the sum of its members. The first step consists of bringing together an organization's various bodies of specialist knowledge to maximize its knowledge resource. A further step is then to promote synergy between the holders of knowledge so that new insights are created and the organization, in terms of knowledge, can become more than the sum of its parts. The use of teams can play an essential part in achieving this synergy. They are commonly used to promote learning by bringing together people with relevant knowledge and skills within an organization, as well as to achieve learning synergies through collaboration between the members of different partner organizations.

4. TEAMS

Chapter 5 described the various types of team, their purposes, and the conditions for successful team working suggested by research and experience. Cross-functional or cross-specialty teams are probably the most frequently used type for purposes of achieving organizational learning. There are three dominant themes in discussions of how teams can promote learning and innovation:[44]

a. *The importance of the task that is given to the team.* Is the task sufficiently challenging enough to provide opportunities for creativity, yet also achievable in terms of the team's capabilities and the time and other resources provided for achieving the task?
b. *Diversity within the team.* Does the team have sufficient diversity of knowledge and skills among its members for them to have a good chance of generating new ideas and knowledge?
c. *Team integration.* How can the members of a team be encouraged to work together in integrated ways so that they can capitalize on their diverse knowledge and skills?

Two phases of organizational learning occur within the process of innovation: a creative phase and a phase of innovation implementation. The distinction is important for the way that teams engaged in learning are managed. While a team is at the stage of generating new creative ideas or proposals, external constraints are likely to inhibit its progress. This could happen through blocking off possible creative options or by reinforcing the different priorities that members bring into the team and so making it very difficult for them to achieve mutual consensus. When, however, it comes to the point of orienting new ideas to potential application, it is essential for external considerations to enter the discussion. For example, will a proposed new product meet a market demand; can it be manufactured at acceptable levels of cost and quality? The balance to be drawn between the exclusion and intrusion of external considerations during the life of a team engaged in innovative learning, raises crucial questions for its appropriate membership at different stages of its work, its reporting relationship to management, and the assumptions that guide the priorities and scope of its activities.

5. MANAGING EXTERNAL BOUNDARIES

The third channel of communication, shown in Figure 14.3, supporting organizational learning is that of securing relevant information and knowledge across the "external" boundaries of an organization. Tensions arise from the paradox that a firm's external boundaries have, at the same time, to be maintained and yet kept permeable. These boundaries are enclosures around the legal and contractual realities of ownership and employment. They define the limits to rights and obligations and can also demarcate a common corporate culture and identity. At the same time, these boundaries need to be kept open and information transferred across them so that organizational learning can be stimulated and informed by external developments.

It is vital to a firm's capacity to learn and innovate that it has access to relevant external information or knowledge. It can attempt to secure such information or knowledge through its own direct contacts or through forming alliances with other firms that possess it. In sectors such as biotechnology, which have a complex and expanding knowledge base and where sources of expertise are widely dispersed, alliances may be extremely important for this purpose.[45] Learning within and through inter-firm alliances is discussed further in a later section. External information is relevant to all levels of organizational activity: strategic, organizational and technical. Top management, through its external connections such as membership of other companies' boards, trade associations, and governmental working parties, can be an important conduit for the input of information relevant to strategic learning. At the technical level, which has been the focus for much of the research on innovation, relevant specialists and R&D project teams must maintain effective connections with external sources of technical information such as universities and research institutes. There are important parallels between the processes of bridging external and internal organizational boundaries, the use of teams with joint membership being one. Development or project teams with members from several collaborating organizations have become increasingly common.

The inputs to a firm's learning process flowing across its boundaries can vary from ill-structured and scattered items of news to highly codified sets of knowledge. The less codified and more tacit the knowledge, the more difficult it is likely to be for the receiving organization to make sense of it, even if it can gain access to it in the first place. One of the reasons why firms are encouraged to work closely in joint ventures or other forms of collaboration is that this enhances their opportunity to access and make use of the tacit, uncodified knowledge held by, and embedded within, their partners. The alternative is to recruit personnel from the other organization(s) who hold such knowledge, and then to graft them onto the "home" system.

It is not necessarily the case, however, that explicit knowledge can readily be imported across an organization's boundaries. Much depends on the receiving organization's capacity to absorb that knowledge, especially the experience required to interpret, store and use it. Problems can arise because different organizations codify knowledge to suit their own purposes. The imported knowledge may be codified in a form that is specific to a particular purpose or situation that does not apply in the receiving organization. In this case, it will be necessary to revert back to the more abstract principles that inform the knowledge and provide the bridge to its re-application and codification in the new organizational context.

"Boundary spanners," who work at the interface between their firm and its external environment, play a critical role in the process of transferring information and knowledge into an organization. Boundary-spanning involves accessing external knowledge, interpreting and refining it, and directing it to other members of the organization (such as other members of a project team, and appropriate senior managers). However, Figure 14.3 previously indicated that both external and internal boundaries have to be spanned for externally sourced information to contribute to internal knowledge enhancement.

This requirement translates into three necessary processes:

1   To gather outside information.
2   To communicate the information across internal horizontal boundaries, often through cross-functional teams.
3   To interpret the information for the benefit of higher management.

A commonly occurring problem is that persons who are effective as external boundary spanners, because they belong to the same speciality and share a common occupational identity with their informants, may face considerable difficulty in spanning the internal boundaries with colleagues who do not share these characteristics.

Capacity to learn

An organization's capacity to learn will be determined by a combination of factors: (1) the transferability of knowledge it receives from outside; (2) the receptivity of managers and staff to new knowledge; (3) their competence to understand and absorb the knowledge; and (4) their ability to apply the lessons from previous experience.

1. TRANSFERABILITY

Unlike the other three factors listed, transferability refers to a quality of the knowledge itself rather than to a feature of the would-be learning organization. Transferability concerns the ease with which a type of knowledge can be transferred from one party to another, whether this be from outside into an organization or between one of its units to another. Explicit knowledge is relatively easy to transfer and be absorbed and can normally be codified, such as in technical product specifications. Not so with tacit knowledge, which is implicit and often difficult to articulate.[46]

2. RECEPTIVITY

The more receptive people are to new knowledge, the more likely they are to learn. When the members of an organization adopt the attitude of students toward others who can provide new knowledge, they are being more receptive to fresh insights than if they assume that they already possess superior techniques, organizing abilities, and strategic judgment. For example, some managers make the mistake of assuming that they cannot learn useful motivational practices from their HRM staff because they are in closer everyday contact with their employees and "therefore" know better how to motivate them. Similarly, some multinational enterprises have unwisely ignored advice from their local partners on the best ways to relate to the governmental officials in the host country, who often wield an unusual degree of influence over the conditions for doing business.

Several factors can influence a partner organization's receptivity. Firms that are lagging behind often possess little enthusiasm for learning from other more successful firms, even if they enter into alliances with them, and they have little confidence that they can actually learn.

They tend to be trapped by deeply embedded cultures and behaviors, which make the task of opening up to new knowledge all the more difficult. In clinging to the past, they are not capable of unlearning, a necessary prerequisite to learning.

Receptivity also depends on the availability of time and resources for engaging in the processes of gathering knowledge and embedding it within the organization's own routines through staff training and investment in new facilities. The paradox of deteriorating competitiveness as both a pressure to learn and a constraint on being able to achieve learning becomes critical for poorly performing firms. If a firm has fallen a long way behind its competitors or partners in the skills and competencies necessary for it to absorb new knowledge, it may find it extremely difficult to close the gap.

3. COMPETENCE

A firm's "absorptive capacity" is a crucial competence for its learning and innovative capabilities.[47] Absorptive capacity is a firm's ability to recognize the value of new information (primarily arising from outside the firm), to understand it, to assimilate it, and to exploit it for commercial or usable ends through creating new outputs.[48] This capacity tends to benefit importantly from the firm's level of prior related knowledge and possession of the necessary skills to apply it. Hence, existing competence favors the acquisition of new competence. For this reason, if the skills necessary for handling new information are not available, the training of staff to acquire them should be an immediate priority.

Competence is required at all three levels of knowledge – strategic, organizational, and technical – if a firm is to take advantage of the opportunities for learning offered by access to new ideas and information. An important channel for such access is cooperation with other organizations, either through a formal alliance or through less formal networking. Cooperation that is perceived as peripheral to a partner's overall strategy will probably yield relatively few opportunities for the transfer of strategic knowledge from the collaboration back into the partner's main organization. This is because the lack of perceived strategic importance is likely to reduce the level of interaction between the organization and its partners. A related problem arises from a management's failure to appreciate that it can derive broad strategic lessons from the cooperation rather than ones restricted to comparatively narrow issues. General Motors, for example, approached its NUMMI joint venture with Toyota with the expectation that what it could learn from Toyota would be confined to production skills in the manufacturing of compact cars. As a consequence, although the lessons to be learned were actually of a systemic nature and of more general relevance, they were not immediately applied to General Motors as a whole.[49]

Competence at the organizational level is required in order to make the most innovative use of new knowledge or technology that is acquired. For example, the introduction of mill-wide computerization in the paper and pulp industry came about through close cooperation between paper manufacturers and system suppliers. It opened up radical, new possibilities for the constructive redesign of mill organization and to empower and enrich mill workers' jobs. By bringing all the information on paper mill operations into a single control room, the new technology made it possible for a small team of workers to run a whole mill and therefore to eliminate the previous middle management structure. However, the ability of paper manufacturers to take full advantage of this potential depended on their being able to envisage and accept radically changed roles and relationships. In practice, this organizational vision and competence was often lacking.

It is self-evident that the members of an organization also need to possess adequate skills to absorb and use new technical knowledge. With the complex nature of many modern technologies, and with the importance of deploying them in conjunction with the "human" skills and motivations of employees, multidisciplinary technical competence is required. In the case of international companies or alliances, inadequate competence in other relevant languages can impose significant limits on a company's ability to learn from its local affiliates or partners. In the case of some alliances between western and Japanese companies, the fact that almost all employees in the western firms lacked Japanese language skills and cultural experience in Japan limited their access to their Japanese partners' know-how. Their Japanese partners did not suffer from a lack of language competence to the same degree, and they benefited from the access that their linguistic skills gave them to their partners' knowledge.[50]

4. PREVIOUS EXPERIENCE

Two aspects of experience can facilitate learning. The first is the experience of having learned on previous occasions and understanding how this was achieved. The second is the experience of having learned through collaboration with long-term partners and the "relationship assets" this can build up.

Previous experience of learning can enhance an organization's capacity to learn in the future so long as the lessons of that experience are passed on to the persons involved in subsequent learning projects. Here regular reviews of how tasks and missions have been performed can provide valuable input into learning for future improvement.[51] The previous experience must also be relevant to the new requirements and situation.[52] If the circumstances of a subsequent learning project are very different, previous experience and its formalization into an organization's routines could even create a handicap to further learning. Many writers on learning recommend the creation of a "continuous learning capability" that provides the capacity to learn from experience and at the same time adapt it to new circumstances. The organizational procedures mentioned earlier that encourage and support learning within organization through reducing internal and external barriers are essential for a continuous learning capability to exist.

The experience of working together with other organizations in a long-term partnership should create relationship assets for the partners. They will acquire some understanding of each other's capabilities, and they are likely to have established a degree of mutual confidence and trust. The fact that they have already got through the initial period of working together will have generated a degree of commitment to one another. This should enhance the effectiveness of their collaboration to generate learning, whether through the exchange of knowledge between them or through working together synergistically to create new knowledge. From the standpoint of promoting learning, however, the partners should not in this process end up becoming too similar to one another. It is actually the fact that partners have very different competencies that enhances their mutual learning opportunity because of the different knowledge bases that they can offer each other.

Conversion of knowledge into an organizational property

Nonaka and Takeuchi, drawing largely upon cases of successful Japanese innovation, stress that the conversion of knowledge into a form that organizations can use is a "continuous and dynamic interaction between tacit and explicit knowledge." For this process to succeed, in their view, the conditions must be created for four different modes of knowledge conversion to take place:[53]

1 *Socialization* (tacit knowledge → tacit knowledge): "A process of sharing experiences and thereby creating tacit knowledge such as shared mental models and technical skills." Here organizational members, who have developed a personal understanding of their work and honed their skills at performing it, can pass these on to others through close personal contact involving observation and explanation. Industrial apprenticeships and the serving of articles in legal practices are traditional methods for tacit knowledge to be passed to new learners. They spread tacit knowledge more extensively within an organization.

2 *Externalization* (tacit knowledge → explicit knowledge): "A process of articulating tacit knowledge into explicit concepts." This form of knowledge conversion is typically seen in the creation of concepts that offer wider access to the knowledge and also link it to applications. Tacit knowledge is transformed into a more widely accessible organizational property through its codification. The construction of expert systems is an example of this process, but it is present whenever experience is converted into formal guidelines, rules and procedures.

3 *Combination* (explicit knowledge → explicit knowledge): "A process of systematizing concepts into a knowledge system. This mode of knowledge conversion involves combining different bodies of explicit knowledge . . . through media such as documents, meetings, telephone conversations, or computerized communication networks." The construction of integrated and systematically organized pools of knowledge is a central feature of modern "knowledge management."

4 *Internalization* (explicit knowledge → tacit knowledge): This process involves learning through the application and practice of explicit knowledge. Explicit knowledge is in this way incorporated into individuals' tacit knowledge bases. It becomes personal know-how. An important instance of internalization occurs when members of an organization attend training programs and bring back general concepts and/or techniques that then have to be adapted to the particular circumstances of the organization. Knowledge about the way the adaptation is achieved may, at least initially, be confined to the individuals concerned and is tacit in nature.

Nonaka and Takeuchi emphasize that organizational learning depends upon the tacit knowledge of individuals, and upon the ability first to combine tacit knowledge sources constructively and then to convert these into more explicit forms that are subsequently combined. Tacit knowledge itself can be enhanced by explicit knowledge obtained, for example, through training, reading the business press, or observing competitors' tactics. Nonaka and Takeuchi's framework provides a checklist of the processes that must be in place to maximize the opportunities for new knowledge to become an organizational property and hence constitute "organizational" learning. Nevertheless, as always in management, it is a case of "easier said than done" and we have already seen that significant barriers can stand in the way.

The most important requirements for knowledge to be converted into an organizational property or asset are that, so far as possible, it should be codified, combined and diffused. Codification converts knowledge into a form that can be readily stored within an organization's information system. Despite the need for familiarization with different classification and coding formats, the structuring of knowledge in this way also assists its combination – the "process of systematizing concepts into a knowledge system." For that knowledge system to be of general benefit within an organization, it will be necessary to disseminate an understanding of the nature, importance and use of the new knowledge among those members of an organization who will be required to use it but who did not necessarily participate in its creation or development. This requires an investment in suitable training.

Feedback

Feedback to senior management on the extent to which organizational learning has been accomplished, and with what results, will impact on its leadership of the process. If there has been successful learning, this should strengthen the leadership's intention to encourage further organizational learning. A review of the learning that has been should also lead to a refinement of the organizational mechanisms designed to facilitate learning. The question of implementation will arise if positive feedback from the learning process identifies opportunities to innovate in terms of new products, processes or organizational practices. In that case, the issues around introducing change discussed in the previous chapter become relevant.

◢ Learning through Alliances

As we saw in Chapter 11, companies often form alliances with the specific intention of acquiring new knowledge and know-how or of generating new knowledge through mutual learning. Even when alliances are formed for reasons other than learning and knowledge acquisition, such learning can be a desirable by-product of their collaboration. The prospect of acquiring relatively advanced technology and management expertise is a major reason firms from emerging countries favor alliances with those from developed countries. For their part, the partners from developed countries often view such alliances as an opportunity to learn about unfamiliar business environments. In sectors like biotechnology, which have a rapidly expanding but dispersed knowledge base, alliances form part of extensive networks of learning. To a considerable extent, what we can say about organizing to promote learning through alliances also applies to the increasingly network nature of relationships between the subsidiaries of multinational enterprises which have also become recognized as potential sources of valuable cross-national and cross-unit learning (see Chapter 12).

The nature of learning through strategic alliances

Strategic alliances are hybrid arrangements for they combine the strategic objectives and cultures of the partner organizations. When they are achieved through the establishment of a new joint venture, alliances may also have to combine elements of the partners' management structures and systems. The hybrid nature of alliances has a number of implications for the possibilities of learning through them. A positive feature is that the complementary expertise and knowledge brought to an alliance by partners can promote learning both through transfer and through the dynamic synergy that may be stimulated by the coming together of experts from different corporate, and perhaps national, backgrounds. Alliances between comparatively small, research-intensive biotechnology firms and rather large pharmaceutical companies with expertise in development, production, and marketing serve as one example. A problematic feature lies in the barriers to knowledge-sharing between alliance partners. Such barriers can arise for a number of reasons. For instance, the underlying relationship between the partners may remain fundamentally competitive. It may prove difficult to reconcile the different corporate or social identities of their staff. There can be incompatible features in the partners' systems and styles of management. The partners' staff may assume that they have nothing to learn from each other, or they may resist the changes that such learning implies. Companies may not have the experience or capacity to acquire and absorb the knowledge available from their alliance partners.

There are three different processes through which learning can take place in international joint ventures.[54] The first is the *transfer of knowledge* by the partners to the joint venture, much of it in the form of technology transfer. A similar transfer of knowledge may take place directly between partners who collaborate by means other than setting up a separate joint venture. This form of transfer involves the movement of existing technology, knowledge, or management practice into an organizational setting for which such transfer represents a new knowledge input.

The second learning process is different because it involves the creation of *new* knowledge, or at least a *substantial transformation* of existing knowledge, within the ambit of the cooperative venture. Here mutual learning occurs through a constructive integration of the different inputs offered by the partners and their members. This type of learning is qualitatively different from learning through knowledge transfer, and its realization presents a correspondingly greater challenge. It is, nevertheless, one of the potential prizes of cooperation between organizations that can offer one another valuable complementary knowledge.

The third learning process, *"harvesting,"* involves the retrieval of knowledge that has been generated in the joint venture or other collaborative unit and its internalization within the parent firms so that they can use it in other areas of operation.

These processes indicate that strategic alliances can provide a means to acquire or generate knowledge that might otherwise not be available. Alliances can also be an important vehicle for the incorporation of new knowledge into practice, particularly through the medium of joint ventures or cross-partner teams that work on the necessary adaptation and application of knowledge drawn from the partners.

Within strategic alliances, even the transfer of *existing knowledge* or practices presents difficulties. Abstract and codified knowledge reverts to the status of new data for people receiving it for the first time, if they are not in a position to validate it immediately. Members of alliances will be unable to validate such knowledge if it is not structured in a manner familiar to them. Technical knowledge should be easier to absorb if it is already classified and codified according to widely accepted and known standards, but this characteristic is less likely to be true of organizational and strategic knowledge.

The creation of *new knowledge* needs to draw upon and synthesize a number of different knowledge systems that the alliance has brought together, none of which may have been applied previously to the specific circumstances faced by the alliance. A number of attempts may be required to arrive at acceptable and effective schemes of classification and codification, and at least one pilot project may be necessary to demonstrate the appropriateness of the emerging approach for the new circumstances.

In addition to the problem of translation from the milieu of one alliance partner to that of another, the passage of information and knowledge between different actors or groups in the learning cycle implies that constructive relationships must exist between them for the process to be effective. Knowledge is socially constituted because it is created or compiled by social groups who have a sense of ownership over it. As noted earlier, this sense of ownership means that the groups will attribute value to the knowledge and will assume the right to arbitrate over this value. When knowledge is transferred between organizations, or when the members of different organizations pool their knowledge resources, how the people receiving the knowledge perceive its validity will impinge on the extent to which they are prepared to accept and work with it.

The issue of validity is likely to be more sensitive for organizational and strategic knowledge and practice than it is for knowledge of a primarily technical nature. Although technical knowledge is also socially constituted, several of its characteristics reduce its sensitivity to being transferred or shared between different organizations. One of these characteristics is that technical knowledge is often expressed in a widely accessible, standardized form, some of it in the form of international standards. Another is that trained specialists can accept the validity of technical knowledge because they share a conceptual language and occupational identity with the people who have generated the knowledge. This identity can bridge organizational boundaries. Problems can arise when knowledge generation requires the collaboration of people from different specialties, for then the presence of different validated technical standards can increase the problem of integration.

Competitive and collaborative learning between alliance partners

Strategic alliances face a trade-off between the opportunities they offer for generating and sharing knowledge and the possibility that a partner may act opportunistically. This question comes down to whether the partners' learning goals are complementary or competitive, either in terms of the cost–benefit calculus for forming and maintaining a specific alliance or, more fundamentally, in terms of their location within industry or market structures.

There are two qualitatively different kinds of benefit available to partners in alliances in which their primary objective is to learn from each other.[55] The first kind is private benefits, which a firm can unilaterally acquire through learning from its partner and apply to its operations in areas not related to the alliance's activities. In this case, the partners have divergent goals for learning through an alliance. The presence of private benefits is likely to encourage a race between the partners to exploit opportunities to learn from each other. Once they have done so, there is little incentive for the winner to continue the cooperation. Even out-and-out competitors may collaborate in order to benefit from learning opportunities, but they will be wary about sharing their knowledge. A fundamentally competitive relationship will render the balance between the contributions each partner makes to the alliance, and the benefits each is able to extract from it, a sensitive issue. Such a relationship encourages opportunism. In this kind of situation, the cooperation is often relatively short-lived, and the partners may well revert to competing with each other if and when their alliance breaks up.

The second kind is common benefits, which arise from mutual learning within the scope of the alliance and applies to the alliance's own operations. Common benefits foster continued cooperation and investment in the use of alliances as vehicles for mutual learning. Many strategic alliances are formed between organizational partners who perceive that they can benefit from their complementarities. This perception gives them a common interest in learning how to extract the potential synergies between their respective competencies. An absence of fundamental competition between the partners will also promote their sharing of knowledge and its accumulation as an alliance asset over time.

These distinctions identify two possible learning situations within a strategic alliance. One, *competitive learning*, is based on an underlying attitude of competition between the partners; the other, *collaborative learning*, is based on an underlying spirit of collaboration between them.

Competitive learning denotes a situation in which one alliance partner intends to learn as much as possible from the other rather than adopting mutual learning as the priority. Reporting on his investigations of international strategic alliances, Hamel described this as "competition for competence":

> "[M]anagers often voiced a concern that, when collaborating with a potential competitor, failure to 'outlearn' one's partner could render a firm first dependent and then redundant within the partnership, and competitively vulnerable outside it. The two premises from which this concern issued seemed to be that (1) few alliances were perfectly and perpetually collusive, and (2) the fact that a firm chose to collaborate with a present or potential competitor could not be taken as evidence that that firm no longer harbored a competitive intent vis-à-vis its partner."[56]

Hamel pointed to the possibility that asymmetric learning between alliance partners derives from the fact that they have failed, or are unwilling, to transform their partnership into a fully cohesive organization. The lack of perfect collusion is a failure by the partners to achieve total integration of their operations within the joint venture. A race develops between the partners to learn from the other, for their own advantage rather than for the benefit of the alliance as an organization in its own right. Performance in this race is associated with inter-partner bargaining power. The partner with the most bargaining power can, during the formation of the alliance, establish conditions favorable for it to achieve asymmetric learning by, for instance, insisting that the other partner's technology be made fully available.

Collaborative learning can occur when alliance partners do not regard themselves as fundamentally in competition or as having irreconcilable long-term interests. Alliances between organizations can enhance learning on this basis in two main ways. One involves learning *from* a partner; the other involves learning *with* a partner.

In the first case, collaboration provides access to the partner's knowledge and skills, which can include product and process technology, organizational skills, and knowledge about new environments (including how to manage relationships with significant people within those environments such as government officials). Transfer can be achieved in several ways, such as through the exchange of data sets and secondment of key personnel, with the intention of grafting new knowledge onto, or even having it transform existing activities. If the alliance takes the form of a new unit, such as a joint venture established for a specific purpose, the knowledge sought from partners may be relevant only to and embodied only in the outputs of that unit. Such learning may not have any general value outside the scope of the particular collaboration. There is, however, always a danger of underestimating the value that apparently specific knowledge can have for the receiving partner's organization as a whole, as noted earlier in the case of General Motors' collaboration with Toyota. There is also a risk that imported new knowledge, like any graft, will be rejected.

The second mode of collaborative learning in a strategic alliance involves learning with a partner. Many technology partnerships are formed with this objective. Another example is the accumulation of mutual knowledge about how to manage inter-organizational cooperation itself. This benefit is becoming increasingly significant in a world where more business activity is coming to be organized through strategic alliances, including those whose management has to cope with cultural differences and unfamiliar environments. Collaborative know-how might be used later in the design and management of other collaborations.

Box 14.2 is an illustration of both modes of collaborative learning: learning from and learning with a partner. The case refers to the alliance between Royal Bank of Scotland and Banco Santander which operated from 1988 to 2004 and which was dissolved to avoid a conflict of interest when Santander acquired Abbey National. Their cooperation therefore relates back to an earlier and relatively successful period in the Royal Bank of Scotland's history before its near collapse in 2008. In this particular case, a high quality of mutual learning was fostered by a high level of trust, reciprocity and personal friendship between the collaborating banks' "alliance directors." Other studies have also found that positive social exchanges and a willingness to exchange resources between partners encourage learning through alliances.[57]

BOX 14.2   THE ROYAL BANK OF SCOTLAND AND THE BANCO SANTANDER

An alliance between the Royal Bank of Scotland and the Banco Santander of Spain, was formally announced on 3 October 1988. It was an open-ended collaboration rather than a formal joint venture, though as a demonstration of commitment, the two companies exchanged a small percentage of their equity. At the time, the alliance was motivated primarily by the desire of both banks to find a European partner to help position themselves in the approaching European Community single market. Each bank was looking for a partner of similar size, with compatible cultures and activities and similar attitudes towards the single market.

Although these similarities were to prove beneficial for cooperation between the two banks, early difficulties in realizing potential synergies between them led to the establishment of *gateways* by appointing a special alliance director in each bank through whom alliance communication would pass. These gateways continued to play an essential role in promoting joint projects as vehicles for mutual learning.

The alliance evolved through an intensification of cooperation between the two banks, most notably in the development and launch of an Interbank Online System in 1994. Senior officials from both partners perceived the alliance as having promoted organizational learning of mutual benefit. Each partner was able to learn about and absorb improvements in banking operations as well as learn over time how to deepen the process of working together. Initially, the major areas of cooperation between the two banks included access to branches, shared ownership of German and Belgian banks, offshore banking in Gibraltar, merchant banking, technology development, and acquisitions.

Comments by senior managers in both banks illustrate the learning that was achieved with the alliance partner, again, not all of it anticipated. The chief executive of the Royal Bank commented:

> "We have been surprised by the intangible benefits from the alliance, as each side has got to know and observed the working practices of the other. Simple things like the differing ways in which we prepare and organize meetings; the nature and content of papers presented to internal audiences; and differences in structures and reporting relationships have all provided ample food for thought."

With reference to business lending, the Royal Bank's alliance director remarked:

> "Santander have put a huge amount of time and expertise into that area. And there is a huge amount of money that can be saved in terms, not just of cost, but also of time. So I think that is learning from what they have learned . . . it's the capability of the other organization, it's being prepared, both ways, to help out."

The director of the alliance for Banco Santander added other examples:

> "We have learnt how best to launch an interest bearing current account after seeing what RBS's experience has been. We admire how they develop business by phone, even selling loans that way. At top management level we are exchanging views on how best to handle credits, and geographical risks. On the Royal side, they look at our branch network with five people or less per branch, and compare it with their average of nine. Probably they will centralize the back office more. Also they are very good at serving customers, and we are very good at developing profitable customers . . . those are processes that are ongoing and enriching on both sides."

The same Banco Santander director noted that "Selling is one thing that very definitely, and from the top down, the Royal Bank has incorporated from our culture."

Sources: David Faulkner 1994. The Royal Bank of Scotland and Banco Santander of Spain. In Johan Roos (ed.) *European Casebook on Cooperative Strategies*. Hemel Hempstead: Prentice-Hall, pp. 157–173. John Child and Sally Heavens, personal interviews 1997.

◢ Implications for Practice

It has become apparent that there are plenty of obstacles in the way of achieving successful organizational learning. The most fundamental is lack of a top management intention to promote such learning, in which case it is unlikely that any of the other requirements will be put into place. A second major obstacle arises from lines of demarcation – both internal demarcations within organizations and the external boundaries between one organization and others. The problem arises partly because differentiation forms the basis for distinct social identities and perceptions of competing interests. Internally, individuals can regard themselves as competitors for advancement, and departments as competitors for a share of the overall budget. Externally, when two or more organizations form an alliance, such barriers are typically augmented by their different corporate cultures and, in the case of international alliances, by their different national cultures. If the organizations regard each other in a competitive light, the barriers to their mutual learning will be raised even further. Again, measures to integrate across lines of demarcation will not often arise spontaneously; they normally depend on managerial initiative.

The most important practical implication of what has been said in this chapter is therefore that *successful organizational learning has to be actively managed*. This applies equally to learning within firms and through inter-firm alliances. In line with this conclusion, Dodgson and his co-authors argue that three broad factors characterize an organization which is actively learning. These are a supportive learning environment in which members recognize the value of exploring new ideas and taking risks; formal arrangements to facilitate the learning process described in Figure 14.2; and leadership which encourages learning including a willingness to consider alternative viewpoints and to support experimentation.[58]

Within firms, top management, project coordinators and specialist experts each have important contributions to make. Senior management has to recognize the significance of organizational learning in order to legitimize the process and encourage it through the provision of suitable resources and incentives. More difficult, it should also be receptive to the possibility that it is standing in the way of organizational learning. Otherwise, as noted earlier, pressures to remove the top management team are liable to build up eventually.

Senior management also needs to recognize that the role of project coordinators or team leaders is a vital and difficult one, in view of the challenge of securing integration among the differentiated contributors to the learning process. It will need to lend considerable support to project and team leaders, and take care to choose people with the necessary abilities for these roles. Leading learning teams involves conflict management and requires a combination of considerable interpersonal skill and an ability to understand disparate bodies of knowledge. Because individuals and groups "own" different pieces of information and knowledge, sharing and reconciling these in an agreed manner can be a politically charged process. It requires active measures to promote a shared sense of purpose and identity among organizational members. The work of team leaders in achieving this can be assisted very importantly when senior management defines and explains the purpose of organizational learning. Chapter 13 showed how important a lead by senior management is for the achievement of organizational change and organizational learning inevitably implies change, not least in people's minds.

The focus of this chapter has been on an organization's learning capability and how to enhance it. The link between learning and change highlights the question of how much change an organization can cope with in any one period of time. This is a judgment that management has to apply to its policy on learning. If a firm pursues learning and change to the exclusion of all else, and this pursuit threatens its very culture and fabric, then it is soon likely to suffer the withdrawal of cooperation in that endeavor from the very groups on which the process relies. The reason is that these groups will have had no opportunity to redefine their role and identity within the organization in terms that they can accept. If, on the other hand, too much emphasis is placed on maintaining consensus and "not rocking the boat," rather little learning (and even less implementation) is likely to take place.

There are likely to be even more barriers to organizational learning in the hybrid forms that alliances take than in unitary firms. These barriers can be cognitive and emotional, as well as organizational. A lack of intent to learn can be an important cognitive barrier to realizing the learning potential of collaboration with other firms, and it may be due to ignorance of this potential. Emotional barriers can arise because of mistrust between alliance partners, and considerable efforts to develop personal relationships between the partners' senior managers may be required to overcome them.

Senior managers have a major role in reducing organizational barriers to learning through alliances. The actions they can take are, on the whole, comparable to those in unitary firms. Most important of all, they can signal the importance they attach to learning through collaboration in a way that influences the behavior of people throughout the partner firms. They are in a position to establish helpful organizational practices such as regular meetings and visits between partner staff, regular staff rotation between the alliance unit and partner companies, and sharing of information. Provisions for ensuring that communications are open, and that information technology is used appropriately in support, also help to reduce barriers to learning and to ensure that information is available to feed the learning process.

SUMMARY

1 Organizational learning stems from developments in the thinking and actions of individuals who belong to, or work with, organizations. It becomes "organizational" learning when individual learning becomes institutionalized into organizational properties. These properties take the form of new or revised routines, systems, structures, cultures and strategies.

2 Organizational learning can involve different levels of knowledge: technical systemic and strategic.

3 The ability to achieve organizational learning is an increasingly important strategic resource for firms, lending them a competitive edge.

4 It can take place through acquiring knowledge from external sources or through its creation within the firm.

5 Neither process is likely to take place very effectively, if at all, without certain supporting conditions being in place.

6 One condition is that management actively encourages learning throughout the firm and introduces organizational provisions to support learning. These organizational provisions include the necessary channels of communication, the appropriate balance between autonomy and control, the bridging of internal and external boundaries, and the use of teams.

7 Another condition is that the firm should have the capacity to learn. Among other things, this requires people who can absorb, evaluate and disseminate acquired knowledge.

8 The creation of new knowledge, both within firms and through inter-firm alliances, benefits from a pooling of complementary knowledge resources. This depends

critically on finding ways to promote cooperation and synergy between the groups of people involved.

9   There are many obstacles to organizational learning due to entrenched practice and thinking, and to the barriers in the way of communication and cooperation between different groups. Competition between the partners in an alliance can impose severe limits to the extent that they are prepared to pool their knowledge for the sake of achieving mutual learning.

10 A key requirement for successful organizational learning is that managers understand its strategic value and are aware of the conditions for achieving it. The process has to be actively managed.

QUESTIONS FOR DISCUSSION

14.1   What is organizational learning?

14.2   In what practical sense can organizations "learn"?

14.3   How can organizational learning contribute to superior performance?

14.4   Discuss the main processes by which individual learning and inventiveness can be transformed into an organizational property.

14.5   Describe and discuss the key requirements for organizational learning.

14.6   How can different forms of organization impact on the process of organizational learning?

14.7   Discuss the significance of team-working for organizational learning.

14.8   How can strategic alliances foster knowledge transfer and organizational learning?

14.9   What are the key features that affect an organization's capacity to learn?

NOTES

1   This chapter draws partly upon more detailed material originally presented in Meinolf Dierkes, Arianne Berthoin Antal, John Child, and Ikujiro Nonaka (eds.) (2001), *The Handbook of Organizational Learning and Knowledge*, Oxford, Oxford University Press, namely John Child and Sally J. Heavens, The social constitution of organizations and its implications for organizational learning, pp. 308–326; and John Child, Learning through strategic alliances, pp. 657–680. Readers seeking comprehensive sources on the subject of organizational learning are advised to consult this *Handbook* as well as Mark Easterby-Smith and Marjorie A. Lyles (eds.) (2011), *Handbook of Organizational Learning and Knowledge Management*, Chichester, Wiley, 2nd edition; and Linda Argote (2013), *Organizational Learning: Creating, Retaining and Transferring Knowledge*, New York, Springer, 2nd edition.

2   Max H. Boisot (1998), *Knowledge Assets: Securing Competitive Advantage in the Information Economy*, New York, Oxford University Press.

3   This description of organizational learning is similar to that suggested by Dusya Vera, Mary Crossan, and Marina Apaydin (2011), A framework for integrating organizational learning, knowledge,

capabilities, and absorptive capacity. In Mark Easterby-Smith and Marjorie A. Lyles (eds.) (2011) *Handbook of Organizational Learning and Knowledge Management*, Chichester, Wiley, Chapter 8.

4   Max H. Boisot (1998), op. cit.

5   On organizational change as learning see also Piers Myers, Sally Hulks and Liz Wiggins (2012), *Organizational Change: Perspectives on Theory and Practice*, Oxford, Oxford University Press, Chapter 8.

6   Lyndsay Rashman, Erin Withers, and Jean Hartley (2009), Organizational learning and knowledge in public service organizations: A systematic review of the literature, *International Journal of Management Reviews*, 11(4), 463–494.

7   Bertrand Moingeon and Amy Edmondson (eds.) (1996), *Organizational Learning and Competitive Advantage*, London, Sage.

8   David J. Teece (2007), Explicating dynamic capabilities: The nature and microfoundations of (sustainable) enterprise performance, *Strategic Management Journal*, 28(13), 1319–1350.

9   Calhoun W. Wick (1993), *The Learning Edge: How Smart Managers and Smart Companies Stay Ahead*, New York, McGraw-Hill. Quotation is from page 4.

10 Peter M. Senge (1990), *The Fifth Discipline: The Art and Practice of the Learning Organization*, New York, Doubleday.

11 James G. March (1991), Exploration and exploitation in organizational learning. *Organization Science*, 2(1), 71–87.

12 Gary Hamel and C.K. Prahalad (1994), *Competing for the Future*, Boston, MA, Harvard Business School Press.

13 Linda Argote and Ella Miron-Spektor (2011), Organizational learning: From experience to knowledge, *Organization Science*, 22(5), 1123–1137.

14 Jean Lave and Etienne Wenger (1991), *Situated Learning: Legitimate Peripheral Participation*, Cambridge, Cambridge University Press.

15 In particular, the sources listed in endnote #1.

16 Roland Villinger (1996), Post-acquisition managerial learning in Central East Europe, *Organization Studies*, 17, 181–206. The quotation is from page 185.

17 Chris Argyris and Donald A. Schön (1978), *Organizational Learning*, Reading, MA, Addison-Wesley. The quotation is from page 9.

18 Ikujiro Nonaka and H. Takeuchi (1995), *The Knowledge-Creating Company*, New York, Oxford University Press. The quotation is from page 59.

19 Michael Polanyi (1996), *The Tacit Dimension*, London, Routledge and Kegan Paul.

20 James G. March (1991), op. cit., *Organization Science*, 2(1), 71–87.

21 Manuel Becerra, Randi Lunnan, and Lars Huemer (2008), Trustworthiness, risk, and the transfer of tacit and explicit knowledge between alliance partners, *Journal of Management Studies*, 45(4), 691–713.

22 John Child and Suzana B. Rodrigues (1996), The role of social identity in the international transfer of knowledge through joint ventures. In Stewart Clegg and Gill Palmer (eds.), *The Politics of Management Knowledge*, London, Sage, pp. 46–68.

23 Chris Argyris and Donald A. Schön (1978), op. cit. See also Paul Tosey, Max Visser, and Mark N.K. Saunders (2011), The origins and conceptualizations of 'triple-loop' learning: A critical review, *Management Learning*, 43(3), 291–307.

24 James G. March (1991), op. cit.

25 Rafael Andreu and Claudio Ciborra (1996), Core capabilities and information technology: An organizational learning approach. In B. Moingeon and A. Edmondson (eds.), *Organizational Learning and Competitive Advantage*, London, Sage, Figure 6.2, p. 126. Reproduced with permission of Sage Publications.

26   Jan Schilling and Annette Kluge (2009), Barriers to organizational learning: An integration of theory and research, *International Journal of Management Reviews*, 11(3), 337–360.

27   Bo Hedberg (1981), How organizations learn and unlearn. In Paul C. Nystrom and William H. Starbuck (eds.), *Handbook of Organizational Design*, vol. 1, Oxford: Oxford University Press, pp. 3–27; Eric W.K. Tsang (2008), Tranferring knowledge to acquisition joint ventures: An organizational unlearning perspective, *Management Learning*, 39(1), 5–20.

28   Georg von Krogh, Ikujiro Nonaka, and Lise Rechsteiner (2012), Leadership in organizational knowledge creation: A review and framework, *Journal of Management Studies*, 49(1), 240–277. These authors spell out in some detail the contributions of leadership to learning at different levels.

29   Vijay Govindarajan and Srikanth Srinivas (2013), The innovation mindset in action: 3m corporation, *Harvard business review blog network*, august 6. Http://blogs.hbr.org/2013/08/the-innovation-mindset-in-acti-3/, accessed February 22, 2014.

30   Nicolai J. Foss, Kenneth Husted, and Snejina Michailova (2010), Governing knowledge sharing in organizations: Levels of analysis, governance mechanisms, and research directions, *Journal of Management Studies*, 47(3), 455–482. The quotation is from p. 456.

31   From Child and Heavens, (2001), op. cit., p. 314.

32   Communication among parties in other parts of the network to which an organization belongs, such as suppliers and research institutes, can also have important results for that organization's learning.

33   Nicole E. Coviello (2006), The network dynamics of international new ventures, *Journal of International Business Studies*, 37(5), 713–731.

34   Ikujiro Nonaka and H. Takeuchi (1995), op. cit. The quotation is from page 80.

35   Mark Dodgson, David M. Gann, and Nelson Phillips (2013), Organizational learning and the technology of foolishness: The case of virtual worlds at IBM, *Organization Science*, 24(5), 1358–1376.

36   Sally J. Heavens and John Child (2002), *Managing to Serve: Learning from Catering & Allied*, Cambridge, RH Business Books.

37   Robert Simons (1995), Control in an age of empowerment, *Harvard Business Review*, 73(2), 80–88.

38   Tom Burns and G.M. Stalker (1961), *The Management of Innovation*, London, Tavistock.

39   J. Stuart Bunderson and Ray E. Reagans (2011), Power, status, and learning in organizations, *Organization Science*, 22(5), 1182–1194.

40   Paul R. Lawrence and Jay W. Lorsch (1967), *Organization and Environment: Managing Differentiation and Integration*, Boston, MA, Harvard Business School Press. The quotation is from page 11.

41   John Child and Ray Loveridge (1990), *Information Technology in European Services*, Oxford, Blackwell.

42   Raymond van Wijk, Justin J.P. Jansen, and Marjorie A. Lyles (2008), Inter- and intra-organizational knowledge transfer: A meta-analytic review and assessment of its antecedents and consequences, *Journal of Management Studies*, 45(4), 830–853.

43   Alfred Kieser and Ulrich Koch (2008), Bounded rationality and organizational learning based on rule changes, *Management Learning*, 39(3), 329–347.

44   Michael A. West (2002), Sparkling Fountains or Stagnant Ponds: An Integrative Model of Creativity and Innovation Implementation in Work Groups, *Applied Psychology*, 51, 355–387.

45   Walter W. Powell, Kenneth W. Koput, and Laurel Smith-Doerr (1996), Interorganizational collaboration and the locus of innovation: Networks of learning in biotechnology, *Administrative Science Quarterly*, 41, 116–145.

46   Ikujiro Nonaka (1994), A dynamic theory of organizational knowledge creation, *Organization Science*, 5(1), 14–37.

47   Wesley M. Cohen and Daniel A. Levinthal (1990), Absorptive capacity: A new perspective on learning and innovation, *Administrative Science Quarterly*, 35, 128–152; Shaker A. Zahra and Gerard George (2002), Absorptive capacity: A review, reconceptualization, and extension, *Academy of Management Review*, 27(2), 185–203.

48 Peter Y.T. Sun and Marc H. Anderson (2010) An examination of the relationship between absorptive capacity and organizational learning, and a proposed integration, *International Journal of Management Reviews*, 12(2), 130–150.

49 Andrew C. Inkpen (2005), Learning through alliances: General Motors and NUMMI, *California Management Review*, 47(4), 114–136; Andrew C. Inkpen (2008), Knowledge transfer and international joint ventures: The case of NUMMI and General Motors, *Strategic Management Journal*, 29(4), 447–453.

50 Gary Hamel (1991), Competition for competence and inter-partner learning within international strategic alliances, *Strategic Management Journal*, 12 (Summer special issue), 83–103.

51 Neta Ron, Raanan Lipshitz, and Micha Popper (2006), How organizations learn: Post-flight reviews in an F-16 fighter squadron, *Organization Studies*, 27(8), 1069–1089.

52 Bernard L. Simonin (1997), The importance of collaborative know-how: An empirical test of the learning organization, *Academy of Management Journal*, 40, 1150–1174; Jacky Swann, Harry Scarbrough, and Sue Newell (2010), Why don't (or do) organizations learn from projects? *Management Learning*, 41(3), 325–344.

53 Ikujiro Nonaka and H. Takeuchi (1995), op. cit. Quotations are from pages 62, 64, 67, 69 and 70 respectively.

54 Niklas Lindholm (1997), Learning processes in international joint ventures in China, *Advances in Chinese Industrial Studies*, 5, 139–154.

55 Tarun Khanna, Ranjay Gulati, and Nitin Nohria (1998), The dynamics of learning alliances: Competition, cooperation, and relative scope, *Strategic Management Journal*, 19, 193–210.

56 Gary Hamel (1991), op. cit. p. 84.

57 For example, Senthil K. Muthusamy and Margaret A. White (2005), Learning and knowledge transfer in strategic alliances: A social exchange view, *Organization Studies*, 26(3), 415–441.

58 Mark Dodgson, David M. Gann, and Nelson Phillips (2013), op. cit.

CHAPTER 15

Generating and Utilizing Trust[1]

WHAT THIS CHAPTER COVERS

This chapter is concerned with the role that trust plays in the creation and maintenance of effective organizational relationships. After signaling the importance of trust in the modern business world, the chapter discusses the nature of this subtle and complex concept. It then identifies two major sources of trust. One is traditional and this is where trust arises from close personal relationships. Another basis for trust is institutional, where trust is underwritten by formal safeguards. These two foundations offer insights into the ways in which trust in business collaborations can develop through calculation, mutual understanding, and bonding.

The chapter reviews the benefits that accrue from trust in and between organizations, with reference to two areas of collaboration that are of particular importance in modern business. These are teamwork and partnerships between organizations. Its benefits make it imperative to generate, maintain, and even repair organizational trust, and the chapter closes with guidelines for so doing.

◢ Introduction

The modern global economy is characterized by a need for people with different skills and backgrounds to collaborate. Forms of collaboration range from cross-functional teams to alliances and other networks crossing organizational and national boundaries. As we have seen in previous chapters, the old organizational models of self-sufficiency within boundaries tightly drawn around specialties and nationalities are less and less applicable. Companies are using teams increasingly for a range of purposes that include reducing new product development lead times and promoting organizational learning. International collaboration has also grown markedly with global mergers, acquisitions, and strategic alliances, and the development of global networks. Getting collaboration to work successfully is therefore a prime requirement for success in the new business environment. The key to this is trust between the people who are involved.[2]

Managers are discovering the vital role that mutual trust plays in the success of partnerships and projects. Formal agreements and specifications, such as project briefs for teams and contracts between alliance partners, play a necessary part in establishing the conditions and performance milestones for collaboration. Indeed, they may provide the only basis on which people can begin to work together in the first instance. But formal provisions are rarely enough by themselves. Informal understanding, based on trust, often proves to be a more powerful factor in determining how the collaboration works out. Of course, trust is itself likely to be reinforced by a successful relationship and this virtuous circle is an ideal one, if it can be achieved.

Trust makes a particularly important contribution in situations where one person, group or organization depends heavily on another and when the context of that dependence is uncertain and risky. This is because trust stabilizes the expectations people have of one another. Such situations include ones where:

1   interdependence between the parties is high and long-term, as in a continuing supplier relationship, a strategic alliance, or a team of co-workers;
2   the likelihood of misunderstanding or error is high because what the parties expect of each other is complex or ambiguous;
3   where control is fragile, for example where it is difficult to draw up or enforce adequate contracts; or
4   when the price of failure in the relationship is high, for instance in terms of financial loss.[3]

It is not surprising therefore that people engaged throughout business and industry, and in every country, say they value trust and trustworthiness. At the same time, they recognize that it is not an easy thing to obtain. Here are two examples.

The first example concerns a UK industrial printing company, one of the technologically most advanced in the world, which undertook a joint development project with its US subsidiary, a large American customer and a specialist printing materials supplier. The project aimed to develop the effective application of rapid industrial printing using the laser technology possessed by the subsidiary, and which was the main reason why the subsidiary had been acquired. The collaboration was based entirely on trust and goodwill – no contract was signed. The UK company's technical director commented:

> We were able to achieve the benefits of collaboration as a consequence of the personal relationships that built up, that recognized we could be more exploratory, that we could understand each other's good and bad points . . . This is an informal relationship which has simply developed out of a mutual wish to move the business forward and from an adequate level of trust in each other's goodwill.

The second example is an extract from a conversation between two senior executives of a leading IT systems services company involved in a range of strategic alliances:

A: "No partnership will work without trust and it is one of the most difficult things to achieve."

B: "Yes. I think it has all sorts of dimensions to it. But essentially the way I think I gained the trust of [one of the company's partners] was that I could make our company do what it said it would do . . . I could deliver this and that's when they started to trust me."

The first example was one of building trust primarily on the basis of mutual *goodwill*. The second example was one in which trust was based at least partly on a belief in the other party's *competence* to deliver on what executive B promised. Whereas in purely personal relationships, trust may be based on a belief that the other person has goodwill towards oneself, in business and working relationships competence – the ability to deliver on what one promises or is contracted to do – is also an essential condition for trust to develop and be maintained.

Despite the value placed on it, trust remains a poorly understood phenomenon. What is trust? Can one speak of organizational trust as well as personal trust? Is it a universal or a culturally specific phenomenon? What benefits can it bring? What generates and sustains trust? Are there some guidelines for "growing" and "managing" trust? These questions provide the agenda for this chapter. It pays special attention to the creation and maintenance of effective relationships in two areas of collaboration that are of particular importance in modern business. These are teamwork and partnerships between organizations. When these collaborations involve people from different cultures, they are potentially very productive, but difficult to turn into a success.

What is Trust?

Because it is so central to human relationships, many definitions of trust have been offered. They tend to agree that it is a psychological state in which one person or group is willing to relate to another in the belief that the other's actions will be beneficial rather than detrimental, even though this cannot be guaranteed. A willingness to accept vulnerability vis-à-vis another person or party is frequently regarded as a feature of trust, as expressed in the often quoted definition offered by Denise Rousseau and her colleagues: "Trust is a psychological state comprising the intention to accept vulnerability based on positive expectations of the intentions or behaviors of another."[4] In the world of business, this can mean having sufficient confidence in others to commit valuable resources, such as finance and know-how, to collaborating with them despite the risk that they may take advantage of this commitment. Even collaboration between different groups and nationals within an organization can appear risky to them. They may fear that, if their unique knowledge or personal connections are shared with others, their employment value to the company and their career prospects could be reduced.

While it is obvious that people can trust other people and be trusted by them, the question arises whether the same can be said of organizations. The phrase "organizational trust" is often used but its meaning is not necessarily clear. Organizations cannot themselves trust, although the extent to which those in charge of organizations trust others like their members, suppliers or customers, is manifested in the organizational contracts, rules and practices that they devise. For instance, one can infer that a management which exercises restrictive behavioral control practices does not trust either the intentions or competences of its employees (see Chapter 6). On the other side of the coin, people do have variable degrees of trust in organizations whether this is dealing with them as employees, customers, suppliers, members of the local community or regulators. The sad truth is that a lot of people do not trust organizations, or more precisely, their leaders.[5] Many laws and regulations reflect this lack of public trust. In their marketing literature or websites, firms claim to be trustworthy because they hope this will attract and retain customers, but the reality often falls short of what they assert.

In so-called collaborative relationships between organizations or between people within an organization, the more that the specific assets and unique proprietary resources of a partner organization or team member are sunk into the collaboration, the greater the risk should the other party(ies) renege on the understanding between them. Trust between the parties is necessary to help offset this risk, yet the threat posed by the risk itself can inhibit the development of trust. It is therefore a major challenge to get a process of trust-building underway. Trust is also a fragile phenomenon. It is easily lost and may take a great deal of time and effort to re-establish – what has come to be called "trust repair."[6] The following chapter illustrates this point by indicating how corporate misdemeanors and problems of corporate governance created a serious breach of trust between senior management and employees. Later on in the present chapter I consider what can be done to repair trust that has been broken.

Trust is vital for any relationship, business or otherwise, when there is insufficient knowledge and understanding of the other person or group. We have to bear in mind that the trust involved in collaboration between departments or organizations reflects the quality of relationships between the people, often very few of them, who represent or symbolize those units. It is a way of dealing with ignorance and uncertainty, and involves something like a leap of faith over and above any basis that we have for certainty. Uncertainty can arise about future contingencies and about how one's collaborators will react to them. Under conditions of uncertainty, trust stabilizes the expectations that people have of one another and provides the reassurance necessary for them to continue working or transacting with each other. This is not, however, to recommend trust in others without having any basis for so doing. To trust blindly would be extremely naive and is not a prescription for survival in business.

Broadly speaking, two types of social institution can support trust. The first type is *traditional* in nature. Trust can be supported by sharing membership of the same social group and it is reinforced by the group norms that govern approved behavior. Traditional trust is based on personal relationships and is strengthened by a positive experience of those relationships. Family normally provides the strongest basis for mutual trust; others are belonging to the same local community, having a shared education, and having a long history of mutual dealing that may go back several generations. When both parties share a positive experience of working together, the trust between them will inevitably rise and, as we note later, this becomes an important factor in cultivating trust in international and other business dealings. Many traditional foundations for trust are, however, synonymous with belonging to the same culture, which is why relations between people from different cultures can present a considerable challenge in international business.

The other type of institutional support for trust is formal in nature. Legally enforceable contracts and guarantees of competence and quality provided by officially recognized certification, such as qualifications and standards maintained by the International Organization for Standardization (ISO), are prime examples. Contracts backed by an effective legal system, and certification that is given on the basis of rigorous testing and subsequently monitored, can reduce the risk of entering into new business and employment relations involving people about whom there is limited knowledge and experience.

When people share a common social membership or take the protection of institutions for granted, trust can usually be offered without too many qualms. The problem is that, in global business relations, both of these conditions may be rather weak. Entry into newly emerging economy markets is a significant instance.

If trust is a characteristic of interpersonal relationships, does this mean that the assumptions behind it are specific to different cultures? If they are, this could create particular difficulties for international collaboration. Some, like Francis Fukuyama, distinguish high trust societies from low trust ones. This boils down to whether or not a country has developed a strong institutional basis on which its citizens can rely when taking the risk of trusting others. In this respect, the United States is a high trust society because it has a highly developed system of law that protects the individual, assuming he or she can afford recourse to it. This encourages people to place a high value on honesty, openness, and treating individuals equally and fairly. By contrast, other countries such as many in sub-Saharan Africa could be regarded as low trust environments because their systems offer only limited effective protection and conditions for doing business remain somewhat arbitrary.

Although this kind of broad characterization does indicate the conditions under which companies operate in these respective countries, we still have to take the analysis down to the level of the individual in order to draw useful action guidelines. It is then that we come across a paradox. In societies where there is a high degree of uncertainty and a generally low level of trust, whom you can actually trust becomes a vital consideration. In other words, when institutional supports for trust are weak, people have to resort to supports of a traditional nature. In these circumstances, trust provides an extremely significant bond in personal relationships that assume much greater significance than in the so-called high trust societies. At the same time, because people then depend on trust so highly, they require assurances of a traditional kind before they are willing to trust in others. In a society like China, this means that successful business collaboration depends very much on establishing trust between people, but it requires more time and effort. This is also to some extent true of other East Asian societies, such as Japan. Once it has been established, people in this type of culture place an extremely high value on trust and will react with great bitterness should it be betrayed. Business people in East Asian countries are therefore reluctant to terminate business relationships, as when an alliance no longer meets their strategic objectives, whereas westerners are more likely to take a less personalized view of the matter. Honda managers, for example, were said to have felt a sense of betrayal when Rover backed away from their automotive alliance after being purchased by BMW.

Trust is a fundamental component of human relationships throughout the world. Because of their specific historical experiences and current institutional conditions, however, societies vary substantially in the meaning their members attach to trust, and the conditions for building it. While these differences may be reducing as emerging and transitional economies introduce "modern" institutions, they still present a challenge to trustbuilding in global collaboration.

◢ The Benefits of Trust

Trust is a particularly important factor in the success of alliances between companies.[7] As James R. Houghton, Chairman of Corning Glass Works has said, "the key ingredient in a successful alliance is trust." It is also proving to be a very significant condition for successful teamwork and joint knowledge creation among different units within a company, especially when these span cultural and national boundaries.[8]

Evidence for the way that trust can contribute to performance comes from a variety of sources.[9] One is the contrast between auto industry supplier relationships in Japan and the United States, at least as they were up until relatively recently. For instance, Toyota developed long-standing social and economic relations with a network of suppliers. These customer-supplier relations were characterized by higher levels of trust and less fear of opportunistic behavior than was normal in the United States. Toyota relied far less on formal contracts than a company like GM. The result was that Toyota and its suppliers felt able to undertake a large amount of joint development work, exchange potentially sensitive technical information, and operate a tight, just-in-time component delivery system that supported "lean production." By contrast, GM could not rely on this close, trust-based relationship, nurtured over a long period of time, to reduce the risks of opportunism. Instead, it tried to deal with such risks by reducing its commitment of specific investments to any one supplier, by drawing up elaborate inflexible contractual safeguards, and by internalizing supplies rather than outsourcing them. Japanese producers like Toyota have derived major performance advantages from operating on a high trust basis. They have been more efficient than US or European producers in terms of the total engineering hours needed to develop a new car and the number of months required to complete and deliver a new product. Their quality levels have also been generally superior, and trusting suppliers to keep close to zero defects has saved on inspection and guarantee costs.

To take another example, a study of 177 international strategic alliances between UK and foreign partners found that trust between the partners enabled them better to manage complexities due to strategic and organizational dissimilarities between partner firms. In this way trust contributed towards higher alliance performance. The investigators concluded that trust enables actors in complex situations to synchronize critical tasks better by supporting personal ties that facilitate coordination and the sharing of knowledge. They also concluded that the positive effect of trust diminishes as the size of the alliances increases. In line with the argument advanced in Chapter 4 of this book, they argue that this size effect is due to a concomitant increase in bureaucracy which opposes and eventually nullifies the beneficial effects of trust based largely on informal relationships.[10]

Other examples of the benefits that high levels of trust can bring come from the management of foreign-invested operations in mainland China. I noted that the business environment of China is like that of many emerging economies, in which personal trust is treasured because the institutional supports for guaranteeing business agreements, which people in the West take for granted, are limited. In these circumstances, trust becomes a particularly important business asset to cultivate.

A study colleagues and I conducted of 615 Hong Kong companies with units operating across the border in mainland China found that the trust their managers could place in their mainland managers and staff was the single strongest predictor of how successful those units were.[11] As might be expected, high levels of trust were closely linked to the development of skills among Chinese personnel and to technological improvements in their units. Trust strengthened the resolve to invest in the development of local staff. At the same time, evidence of the staff's enhancement increased the Hong Kong managers' confidence in them, including a willingness to delegate to them. As one manager put it, "mainland employees are hard working and loyal to the company, and so I trust them. I believe that it is fine to delegate to them. A reliable and efficient workforce makes my business prosper." This virtuous circle also contributed to better operational and financial performance among the mainland China units.

Previous research that colleagues and I carried out in Sino-British joint ventures also indicated that high levels of trust between senior executives from the partners are an important success factor. It was particularly important for avoiding a destructive breakdown in confidence between the partners, of which we came across several examples. When the foreign partner does not have a majority share of the joint venture's equity, the generation of mutual trust through inter-partner relationship building can create a basis for sharing influence in circumstances where contractual and other legal rights do not provide for formal control. It was especially important for smaller companies that their leading executives find personally compatible Chinese counterparts and then invest heavily in building trust with them. For while such firms can take advantage of niche market opportunities in areas such as specialized electronic control systems, they do not have the financial resources to risk going-it-alone or the human resources to undertake all the necessary activities themselves. They have to rely heavily on their local partner.

Sally Heavens and I examined the experience of six cross-cultural project teams created to achieve specific organizational learning objectives.[12] Each team was chosen for study because it had accomplished a clearly evident example of knowledge-creation. Despite their disparity, and the fact that intra-team processes varied according to whether time schedules and budgetary constraints were imposed, the strong common element in their success lay in each team's ability to generate mutual trust among its members. This was a particularly important consideration for those teams whose members did not know one another beforehand.

The teams faced problems caused by differences in national identity and perceived interest between the members of the teams. It was evident that the way the teams were managed could reduce their internal differences and facilitate their work. When care and time were taken to create a non-threatening atmosphere and to develop personal friendships between team members, trust grew between them. This personal trust was in turn a vital enabling factor for the teams to achieve the conditions necessary for learning and knowledge creation to be achieved, such as an open sharing of information and views. Trust helped the team members to transcend the factors defining their separate social identities and which otherwise threatened to jeopardize the collective learning process. As closer relationships developed between team members, they gradually became more comfortable in sharing their views and knowledge and they became more aware of a common learning goal. The team and its goal came to provide a common identity for them.

Our conclusions on the importance of trust coincided with the team members' own observations. They are consistent with the theme developed in Chapter 14 that mutual trust is a condition for promoting learning. They also lend support to an observation once made by Claudio Ciborra that "even institutional economists interested in the architectures of transactions between opportunist 'models of man' admit that productivity and efficiency of team arrangements are strongly influenced by . . . all the subtleties of the quality of human relationships that emerge in a team."[13] This observation is illustrated in Box 15.1 by one of the cases we studied, a water company.

Another indicative study in 88 Canadian retail stores examined the impact on performance of employees' collective perceptions of being trusted by management. It found that the more employees felt they were trusted by management the more they believed it important to

BOX 15.1 DEVELOPING KNOWLEDGE-CREATING TEAMWORK THROUGH TRUST

The scenario for cross-national teamwork in this case developed through a series of takeovers. These were prompted by a desire on the part of a British water and waste treatment company to expand in a certain business area, with the initial acquisition of a Swedish firm in possession of the required technology. Subsequently, this latter firm bought out a smaller, Norwegian company, whose patents therefore went to the British company as overall owner. It was the work with this smaller company on new waste-water processes that was studied, one of a number of collaborative projects with the Scandinavians.

Teamwork with the Swedes and Norwegians, based on technology developed by the latter, took a long time to evolve. The company's British head of technology innovation had the mission to establish the ground rules and an appropriate research program, but he was hindered by the fact that the Norwegian company was reluctant to tell him anything. There were two main reasons for this: first, the company, being small and therefore vulnerable, feared being "emptied out," with their patents being taken and sold on; second, and more generally, the Norwegians have a dislike of the English on account of contentious issues relating to their occupational identity as water engineers, such as acid rain and pollution from UK coastal outlets. It was only through withholding knowledge and distorting channels of information that the Norwegian subsidiary felt it could preserve its worth, and therefore its identity and security. A lack of trust held the Norwegians back from contributing to learning by the wider organization. It is significant that the initial, formal framework of procedures and programs, devised for mutual working and intended also to promote mutual confidence, was insufficient to facilitate the learning process.

Barriers to knowledge sharing were becoming apparent about one year into the project. The initial barriers, created by fear and mistrust on the part of the Norwegian subsidiary, were overcome primarily through the personal relationship developed by the new project manager with his counterpart in Scandinavia. This relationship opened up communication between the British and Norwegian groups and enabled them to recognize mutual benefits and objectives. A joint R&D program also served importantly to assuage the Norwegians' fears and to provide a bridge across the national divide based on a sharing of their common scientific identities. This illustrates the importance of perceived goal congruence, a reconciliation of social identities and a sense of psychological safety as conditions for team members to develop sufficient mutual trust to share knowledge and so generate organizational learning. The joint R&D program enabled findings from the project to be applied throughout the British and Scandinavian companies. Informants agreed that both operational processes, concerning the day to day running of waste-water treatment works, and process knowledge – the actual technological processes of waste water treatment – were considerably enhanced through the teamwork that was developed. The R&D program was also a symbolic indication of the new organizational identity that was being forged within the international corporate group.

accept responsibility for their organization's performance. In turn, their willingness to be accountable for their organization's performance led directly to better sales and improved customer service.[14]

To summarize, trust can bring a number of important benefits to collaboration, as evidenced by its association with superior organizational performance:

1   Trust generates a willingness to overcome cultural differences and to work through other difficulties that arise in collaboration.
2   Trust between people encourages them to work together to cope with unforeseen circumstances. This permits them to adjust more rapidly, and with less conflict, to new circumstances that contracts and other formal agreements have not foreseen.
3   Trust can provide an alternative to incurring the costs and potentially demotivating effects of close control and a heavy reliance on contracts.
4   Trust between collaborating organizations or between units within an organization encourages the openness in exchanging ideas and information that is a necessary condition for innovation and other forms of new knowledge creation.
5   For these reasons, trust is a particularly vital ingredient in the success of global teams and alliances.

Generating and Sustaining Trust

Trust plays a positive role in business relationships, but it is an asset that requires effort, sensitivity, and time to build up and maintain. The question then is how trust might be generated and sustained. I shall address this in two stages, taking the challenging case of international alliances between firms as a case in point. I first analyze the bases for generating trust in business and on which it can evolve over time. I then offer practical guidelines for cultivating trust, which follow from the analysis.

Alliances are business relationships that have a clear starting point and often a clear termination point. They pass through a number of stages of development – formation, implementation and evolution – which, if successful, are likely to run parallel to a corresponding development of trust between the cooperating partners. They therefore provide a useful basis for understanding how trust between organizations and their agents can be generated and sustained.[15]

Trust based on calculation – often the start

Trust based on calculation appears at first sight to be a contradiction in terms.[16] However, some calculation is likely to underpin a belief that another party's action will be beneficial and reliable rather than the opposite. The calculation that business partners have the ability, competence, and motivation to deliver on their promises and that there are sufficient deterrents, based on law and reputation, to their letting you down, is a vital condition for being prepared to cooperate with relative strangers. Some authorities therefore talk about this in terms of "calculative trust." This form of trust is a commitment to enter into a business relationship based on a calculation of the likely outcomes relative to the costs and risks of maintaining (or later severing) it. It is clear that legal and other formal safeguards will be important to the calculation.

Trust based primarily or solely on calculation is likely to be found in relationships that are new, and which are formed between partners or team members who do not have any other prior social connections. It may be the only type of trust that can apply to purely arms-length and hence impersonal economic transactions. It cannot rely on any of the more traditional foundations for trust and it therefore has to proceed on the basis of institutional protection and the reputation of the partner. Joint investment in the common venture can provide a "hostage" against cheating. A further requirement, which can also lessen the motivation to renege later on, is that the partners should only agree to a basis of collaboration that they regard as fair and equitable in its division of projected returns.

We can apply the concept of calculative trust to the formation of a new alliance between two companies. Early in the formation process, the future partners will have come to the conclusion that they favor an alliance out of a range of possible alternatives. For example, if one partner's purpose is to enter a new market, it has a range of possibilities for accomplishing this objective: these include exporting into the market using local agents, licensing technology or franchising a brand name to a local producer, forming an alliance with a local firm (in the form of a collaboration, equity joint venture, or merger), and setting up a wholly-owned subsidiary. The choice between these alternatives is likely to be informed by the partner's strategic intentions and previous experience of managing different forms of market entry. It will rest primarily on a *calculation* of the relative costs and benefits of each alternative. At this stage, the calculation has to rely primarily upon business intelligence.

If it is decided to explore the possibilities of forming an alliance, the selection of a partner is also likely to be based importantly upon calculation. In principle, the potential partners try to find out as much as they can about each other and then compare the information obtained against a range of selection criteria in order to assess the degree of strategic fit between them. In reality, however, information about prospective partners will be limited, especially that relating to their internal cultures, competences, and values. This means that judgments will have to be made on the basis of the partners' reputations, including those for trustworthiness. This has sometimes been called the "information stage," during which the prospective partners try to find out as much as possible about each other, and it will normally precede their entry into negotiations on a contract. In learning about the other, the partners are also embarking on the processes of "getting to know" each other.

In the case of a putative *international* strategic alliance, the nature of cultural differences between the prospective partners will also become evident. Cultural differences could inhibit the development of mutual understanding and trust, and jeopardize the process of moving towards a formal agreement. This is a quite realistic possibility when alliances are being discussed between partners from societies that are culturally and institutionally dissimilar. The exchange of information during this phase depends on an initial development of trust that, in turn, depends on how the relations between the partners are affected by their cultural distance.

When the process of information gathering moves into the negotiation phase, each party will be able to supplement its knowledge of legal and other institutional safeguards with the direct information they gather about each other through personal contact. This enables them to begin a relationship and starts to lay down the second foundation for trust, namely mutual knowledge. A successful negotiation is not just the achievement of a mutually agreed contract; it is also the beginning of a trust-based relationship. The two phases of trust building, calculation, and mutual understanding therefore overlap. It is in any case not possible to anticipate all the issues that will arise in alliance operation through the terms of a formal contract. Such issues will have to be resolved, and trust will make the difference in this resolution taking the form of constructive problem-solving rather than hostile confrontation.

Formalizing the contractual conditions and managerial arrangements for a new alliance establishes what Yves Doz has called "initial conditions" for the alliance's future development. If these initial conditions are appropriate, the chances that the alliance will evolve successfully are enhanced.[17]

Trust based on mutual understanding – building on working together

The second main foundation for trust is more traditional in nature. This builds mutual confidence on the basis of mutual knowledge and common experience among the partners. As a purchasing manager once said, "So long as I have been working here, company X has never let us down. When they promise a delivery, it always comes through. I think they are an honest company who would never deliberately do the dirty on me." When repeated exchanges live up to the parties' expectations, they can become confident that the partner does not cheat and that he or she is capable of delivering on their promises. This is significant, because in business trust depends on the capability to do what is agreed as well as the intention to do so. The perception of risk involved in the initial phase of calculative trust is reduced through a positive experience of working together. This explains the common finding that business people tend to attach less significance to the terms of formal contracts the longer they have been dealing with one another.

At this stage, the partners accumulate more knowledge about each other and they are likely to develop common ways of thinking through their sharing of experience and information. Let us again consider this in the case of a strategic alliance. Following its foundation, with the allocation of capital and other resources to it, there is a phase of implementation during which it is commissioned as a productive venture. During implementation, people are appointed, technology and systems installed, and operations commenced. Implementation is of crucial importance for the quality of co-operative relations within the alliance. The people appointed to work together may or may not possess the necessary technical competences for the alliance to succeed, and this is equally the case with their cultural competences. If these competences are lacking and as a result the alliance founders, the underlying calculus for the alliance can no longer remain valid.

It is therefore essential not to violate the basis of calculation that initially made the partners willing to enter into a cooperative relationship, with the investment and risk this involved. Once an alliance is being implemented, however, or a team is starting to work, the members have the opportunity of getting to know each other more intensively than before. The growing ability of each to understand and predict the thinking and actions of the other can provide a further basis for trust between them. This mutual understanding should reduce the sense of uncertainty that alliance partners and team members experience about each other.

The systems that are installed during the implementation phase, particularly those for control and information reporting, are for this reason very significant. The ways they are designed and operated can determine the quality of knowledge that is available to each partner. For example, if one partner's systems for accounting, marketing, operational, and technical information reporting are installed in a joint venture, this adds to the quality of the knowledge available to that partner, but not necessarily to the other. The one partner therefore enjoys a basis for growing confidence in the alliance that is being denied to the other. Similarly, if the personnel appointed to work together within the alliance do not bother to understand each other's cultures, the likelihood of their achieving a close cooperative relationship based on mutual knowledge and respect will be diminished.

Trust based on bonding – building on liking each other

A third basis for trust is associated with strong personal relationships such as those within a family or between close friends. This form of trust arises between people who share a common identity, meaning that they hold similar values, including a shared perception of mutual obligation. Psychologically, people in this situation will have "bonded" with each other.

Bonding is not so uncommon in business relations as one might think. If a business relationship is maintained for a long period of time and the parties meet each other regularly on a personal basis, they can come to identify with each other and establish a mutual psychological bond. This evolutionary process permits stable, ongoing relationships to develop. The openness that follows from a close relationship allows the people concerned to accumulate knowledge about each other, which tends in its turn to reinforce the relationship.

As relationships develop over time within the context of a successful collaboration, so there is a natural tendency for those concerned to identify increasingly with one another's interests as well as for emotional ties to grow. In this way, bonding can form between partners, which some commentators argue is a significant requirement for collaborative success. Thus a virtuous circle may be established, which reinforces both trust and the cooperation that it nurtures. This circle can, of course, be broken and reversed, as we note shortly. Although bonding usually emerges after some years of successful collaboration, it can under some circumstances provide the initial basis for establishing collaboration, as when close friends or family members decide to set up a business or when a team is formed of people who have already established strong friendships.

The successful collaboration between the Royal Bank of Scotland and the Banco Santander, referred to in Chapter 14, illustrates the possibilities of evolving trust to the level of bonding. These two banks held a small minority of each other's stock, but did not establish a legal framework for their collaboration. When I studied this case at the end of the 1990s, the collaboration had already prospered for over a decade. Two mid-level directors, one British and one Spanish, shared responsibility for facilitating the stated business objectives of the alliance; (i) developing profitable customer bases in Europe; (ii) providing services to corporate and personal customers of both groups; and (iii) marketing improved cross-border financial services. They reported jointly to a surveillance committee comprising the chief executive officers and executive directors of each bank and which met every six weeks to review progress and strategies for the alliance.

The relationship between the banks, mediated by the two alliance directors, has evolved along the trust curve. As the Spanish director said to me:

> "The first accomplishment is that we are still together, we have become closer friends than we were; at first, it took quite a bit of effort on both sides because I can vividly recall on presentations

you would call in a regional manager to explain what he did, and he would whisper, 'How far do I go, what do I tell them?' and the answer was 'Everything.' Talk about your accomplishments, your failures, your frustrations, your profit, your loss. The whole thing."

Through this open approach in sharing their experiences of branch networking and processes, "Little by little, we started to say, we can learn about this, that they are doing this better than we are. They would say the same thing about certain things we were doing." The only barrier to learning identified by both the British and Spanish alliance directors was language; the former referred to "our inability, corporately, to speak Spanish" while the latter observed that "language has turned out to be an almost insurmountable obstacle." Ultimately, however, it did not detract from the overall success of an alliance the importance of which, the British director notes, "on business, is probably less than average; but jumps over the average when you add the learning aspect, the sharing of ideas."

The work of the two alliance directors was to monitor opportunities for joint business development and, as the British director noted, "to encourage as many linkages for business purposes." This included the ongoing facilitation of personal relationships, to mirror that between himself and his Spanish colleague who said:

> "What we try and do is, we take the head of one unit (in our bank) and the head of that unit in (our partner) bank, put them together, and hope something happens. But it's difficult. One can never forget human personalities. With (the British director) and myself . . . I am sure we could exchange places and be just as effective in the other's bank because we've become so intimate in all areas of business and of thought. And that has helped enormously."

The collaboration led to marked improvements in the selling capabilities and organizational efficiency of the British bank, while the Spanish partner benefited in areas such as service quality and corporate banking.

Figure 15.1 summarizes the evolution of trust-based relationships that has been analyzed in this section.

It is important to make two further observations in connection with this analysis. First, as we saw with the two banks, there will often be only relatively few *individuals* relating with each other across the boundaries of cooperating organizations. The same is true of teams. The trust that can be said to exist between organizations and within teams therefore comes down to the quality of mutual trust that exists between those individuals. The organizational members upon whom successful collaboration depends could therefore justifiably be called their *"trust guardians."* In addition to the two banks, some other companies like Hewlett-Packard explicitly designate roles of this kind: in H-P's case they are called "relationship managers." The contribution that these trust guardians make to inter-organizational cooperation will depend on (a) the mutual trust they have developed; (b) the influence they enjoy within their respective organizations; and (c) how many there are of them in each organization.

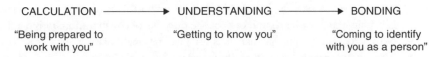

Figure 15.1 Phases in the evolution of trust.

It follows that, if there is a frequent turnover of the personnel allocated to an alliance or to a team, the opportunities for developing trust-based cooperation between them will be diminished. Overseas tours of duty for the personnel of a foreign alliance partner are often limited in duration, especially when the other partner is located in a developing country where "hardship" conditions apply. This can inhibit the development of trust in international alliances, especially when the culture of the local partner attaches high value to transactions based upon personal relationships.

Secondly, trust-based cooperation through alliances is vulnerable. As noted in Chapter 11, alliances are based on cooperation between partners whose interests do not usually wholly coincide and who, in the case of horizontal alliances, could become competitors at a future point in time. The multi-stage model of trust evolution indicates the danger of collapse in an alliance relationship at any stage of its development if the previous bases of trust are withdrawn. Bonding is unlikely to sustain a business relationship if one or both of the partners conclude that the calculative or predictive basis of their co-operation has disappeared. I suggested previously that this is particularly the response of Western managers.

Equally, if there is a problem in building the basis for a higher level of trust development, such as the emergence of a personal antipathy, it may prove necessary to return to the initial foundations for the relationship in order to rebuild it. For instance, if a personal dislike arises between two inter-organizational trust guardians, it may still be possible to rescue the relationship between the organizations themselves through their leaders recognizing that it continues to retain a basis in mutual economic benefit. A hierarchy of foundations for trust and cooperation is, in effect, being posited here with calculation at the base, prediction in the middle, and bonding at the apex.

◢ Guidelines for Cultivating Trust

The fact that trust in business relations develops through several stages, and rests upon a number of different foundations, helps us to identify the kind of policies and practical measures that can be taken to develop and promote it.

Create a clear and calculable basis for mutual benefit

It is vital, when entering into any collaboration, to maintain clarity and realism in the commitments that the participants promise to make to each other. There are five aspects to this:

1 Their commitments must be realistic and therefore subject to careful calculation and scrutiny. The participants must be seen to be able to honor those commitments.
2 The partners must also have good intentions to honor their commitments. For this reason, their reputation for reliability and trustworthiness needs to be investigated. This is usually much easier to find out for the purpose of collaboration within a firm, or even within the same country, than it is for international alliances between firms.
3 The commitments each participant offers must together be sufficient to meet the purpose of their collaboration.

4   At this early stage, before any significant trust has been established, it is important to research the formal safeguards that are available should one party to the collaboration renege on the other(s). Within a firm, this framework can be contained in management's directives or handled by the firm's customary practices. In collaborations between firms, it is relevant to check the legal and other institutional safeguards that are available in the event of the other partner reneging on its promised commitments.

5   Last, but particularly important for an inter-firm collaboration, the agreement between the partners should be committed to writing, in detail and with the minimum of ambiguity.

The rationale behind these guidelines stems from the likelihood that the first step in establishing collaboration, even within a firm, involves mutual calculation. If the calculation is wrong in the first place, the relationship immediately becomes hostage to blame and recrimination. "Bedding down" with other team members or alliance partners is essential, and it is a false economy to rush the process. This may anyway be accomplished quite quickly, perhaps in a matter of a few weeks in the case of a new team formed from members of the same firm who mostly know one another already.

The situation is likely to be different in the case of forming new international joint ventures. It may be difficult to identify a clear and calculable basis for mutual benefit if the prospective partner's ability to deliver market access or specific competences is not well known. In such cases, which are more common with partners from developing economies, it is imperative to attempt a thorough appraisal of the prospective partner and the context in which it operates, and not to rely on what the other party itself provides by way of estimates or assurances. It is tempting for a potential partner to promise more than it can realistically deliver when it is keen to achieve the cooperation of another company whose financial or technical assistance it considers to be a strategic priority. In addition to establishing a clear basis for mutual benefit, there is also the need to progress from a situation in which the parties remain conscious of their separate social identities to one in which they construct a new joint identity. This may in practice take several years to accomplish, and can sometimes never be achieved.[18] In view of these challenges along the road to establishing mutual trust and reducing the risks in collaboration, some companies like Corning Glass for this reason favor a "courtship" approach whereby collaboration starts on a limited basis and, if successful, moves forward toward full-blown joint ventures.

Improving mutual predictability: strive to resolve conflicts and keep communication open

Conflicts are bound to arise between team members and partners, even if there is very little inherent conflict between their underlying interests.[19] They arise frequently in teams within a single organization and are therefore all the more likely to occur in the cooperation between people from different organizations. There is often a mixture of disputes over "hard" financial or technological issues and frictions of a "softer" cultural and inter-personal nature. In each case, it is important to try and avoid unsettling surprises, as well as having mechanisms for resolving conflict in place from the very outset of the collaboration.

Studies into the dynamics of working groups have shown that two forms of leadership are typically required. One is "task leadership" and the other has been called "maintenance leadership." Task leadership basically keeps the team's eye on the ball, so that its efforts remain directed toward the goal that the team has been brought together to reach. Maintenance leadership is directed toward maintaining the team as a group through defusing conflicts, enhancing motivation, and so forth. Since teams are groups that do not work in isolation from other parts of an organization or, in the case of an alliance, do not work in isolation from their members' parent companies, another leadership function is managing the external boundary of the team.[20]

As we have seen, trust requires an initial foundation provided by sound task leadership that clarifies a team's objectives and ensures that the team receives adequate support to achieve them, so reducing the threat of failure. Thereafter, the maintenance aspect becomes more prominent for trust development, including the maintenance of supportive relations with external groups and organizations. "Trust guardians" in strategic alliances can perform both task and maintenance functions with respect to the quality of collaboration between the partner firms. They play an invaluable role in preparing the ground for new collaborative projects, avoiding surprises, and assisting conflict resolution.

The risk to trust posed by "hard" disputes can also be reduced by certain routines that provide information among team or alliance members. These should help develop trust based on knowledge and predictability. An example in alliances is the arrangement for regular and frequent meetings between the managers and staff seconded or appointed to the alliance by the partners. These meetings should establish the facts of any matters at issue, recording the discussion and any solutions proposed. The records of such meetings provide a basis on which problems can be addressed at a higher level between the partners if a resolution is not forthcoming within the alliance unit, or collaborative team, itself. An important aim of meetings and other formal conflict-resolution mechanisms is to ensure that relatively "hard" disputes do not get turned into, or mixed in with, inter-personal antipathies. The intention is to de-personalize the issues as far as possible.

Another important approach toward reducing the incidence of "hard" disputes is to invest in a formal specification of appropriate rules and guidelines. These clarify matters such as the performance expectations placed on teams and joint ventures. They can also indicate the recognition that team members will receive for disclosing their tacit knowledge and the recognition of proprietary rights over technology within an alliance. A potential leakage of proprietary technical knowledge has been found to reduce trust between business partners (customers and suppliers), so formal agreements to protect such knowledge may be particularly significant.[21] It will probably require an investment of time by senior managers to agree on the formalization of rules at a very early stage of the collaboration.

Formal provisions can, in addition, play a role in encouraging the sharing of information among the members of an alliance or team, within any bounds of confidentiality and intellectual property right protection that have been agreed in the terms of the cooperation. While they cannot guarantee the amount and quality of information-sharing, procedures such as password access to computer networks, the circulation of well-documented material before meetings, and the regular dissemination of data on the alliance's performance, or the team's progress, can be of considerable assistance. The sharing of information should, over time, contribute to a breaking down of barriers between people from different backgrounds and responsibilities who have been assigned to work together. In so doing, it will help to generate the mutual confidence that takes trust forward beyond a basis of calculation on to one of shared understanding and predictability.

Some degree of structuring appears to facilitate the development of trust, even when collaborating personnel come from culturally similar territories. The previously mentioned study of Hong Kong companies with operations in mainland China serves as an illustration. Reliance on traditional trust-building policies, aimed at building up personal relationships between Hong Kong and mainland personnel, was certainly helpful. However, the introduction of the companies' standard practices into their China units contributed rather more to trust development, largely because this helped to stabilize expectations. This approach amounts to a "micro" institutionalization of attitudes and behavior, which lies within a company's control and can be backed up by appropriate training provisions.

Approaches to reducing conflicts of a "softer" interpersonal nature within a cooperative relationship are less formal, but still need to be organized. The building of sensitivity about how people coming to work together from different departments, units, or firms perceive each other is central to this effort. There are well-known techniques western organizational development consultants have devised for achieving this and which generally work within a western cultural setting. Other approaches will, however, be necessary for collaboration in non-western cultures. These do not require the quick "confrontations" favored in the United States, but a more patient and less personally exposing process of mutual discussion and socializing.

The organizational "politics of envy" and problems arising from perceived discrimination in the treatment of staff from different backgrounds have to be tackled systematically as well. For example, serious interpersonal problems can arise within foreign joint ventures established in developing countries over the often quite substantial disparities in the pay offered to foreign and local managers. Local resentment over high expatriate compensation may be eased somewhat by charging this to the foreign partner directly rather than having it as a direct charge on the alliance. However, a more effective solution lies in making the basis for compensation quite clear to all concerned in terms of qualification, performance, market factors, and so forth. This helps to demonstrate the rationale for the compensation system, and also indicates potential channels for betterment that are open to local managers and staff.

It is evident that measures such as these, taken to eliminate the sources of interpersonal conflict, will, if successful, also help to remove barriers to establishing personal friendships between alliance and team members. Personal friendship is conducive to the third major basis for trust, namely mutual bonding.

Moving toward mutual bonding

The careful selection of people who are to work together in a team or an alliance assists the prospects of mutual bonding. They should be selected, not merely on the basis of technical competence, important though this is, but also on an assessment of their ability to form good relationships with people from other organizational, occupational, or national cultures. Track record can tell a lot in this respect. Some global companies have, for this reason, now created opportunities for successful alliance and expatriate managers to be able to remain in inter-organizational and international assignments without detriment to their long-term advancement within the home corporation. People with open-minded and prejudice-free personalities are likely to be more successful at personal bonding within alliances and teams. These characteristics can be assessed through careful observation and, if appropriate, systematic personality tests.

Bonding is promoted by socializing and it is important to encourage as much of this between the people directly involved in collaborations as possible. If people are brought together to work in a cross-cultural team or an international alliance, their participation in sports and social events can do a lot to break down barriers between them. In the case of expatriates seconded to alliances, joint activities like these, together with charitable and sponsorship activities in the local community, and avoidance of creating expatriate housing ghettos, can help to promote mutual bonding. Such initiatives help to create a common social identity.

In the case of alliances, one very important way of encouraging bonding between the people directly involved in the collaboration is for the leaders of the cooperating organizations to maintain regular, friendly contact with each other. This means planning for personal visits between partner chief executives at least once a year, and giving these full publicity. Apart from the intrinsic merit such visits have in ironing out any differences of view between the partners and laying down broad plans for the future, they set a very important example and establish a climate of cooperation for the people working further down within the alliance. Senior management support is equally vital for the success of collaboration through international teams. It must be visible to all those working under them.

The length of appointment or secondment of personnel to a collaborative activity is also an important consideration. The shorter this is, the less the chance of achieving mutual bonding. Project teams usually work to a short timescale, but bonding between their members should be helped if they have previously worked together in another team. The time it takes for the members of alliances and project teams to overcome a lack of personal familiarity will be extended if they need to learn a new language as well. Longer-term appointees to a collaborative activity are also more likely to invest in establishing relationships within it, for they see it as a more significant part of their overall career path. Western, and especially American, companies tend to attach people to alliances on contracts of four years' maximum, whereas Japanese companies tend to attach their people for up to twice as long. This reflects a cultural difference in the importance attached to establishing close relationships. Partners coming from countries where personal relationships are a requirement for business cooperation commonly complain that personnel assignments to their alliances are too short for any bonding to occur.

It is, of course, not possible to legislate for the development of personal friendship among those working together in a strategic alliance or a cross-national team. There is inevitably an element of unpredictability in interpersonal dynamics. Nevertheless, policies such as those just outlined can help a great deal, especially in circumstances where there are no fundamental conflicts of interest driving a wedge between the people concerned. And, once established, personal bonding and a sense of mutual identity between alliance and team partners can reinforce their determination to solve business problems, and provide a solid basis for their mutual confidence when so doing.

Repairing broken trust

As mentioned earlier, the top managements of many companies have suffered from a massive breakdown of trust in them due to financial misdemeanors and poor decision making. Adding to this loss of confidence has been the general disenchantment in their leaders among the citizens of many countries associated with a sense of unfairness about increasingly unequal distributions of income and wealth. These developments have damaged the expectations that people previously had concerning the good intentions and competence of their leaders.

Whether damaged or broken trust in organizations can be repaired, and if so how, has therefore come onto the agenda of management discussion. While trust can be broken very quickly, it can be a long and difficult process to restore it. In fact, if trust has been broken as a result of causing deep offence to the norms of conduct in a particular culture, it may never be possible to repair the damage fully. There is a greater chance of rectification if trust has been damaged but not broken. Even so, experts on the subject stress that quick fixes will not rectify low trust. Rather, underlying conditions have to be put in place that will enhance and maintain trust over the long term.[22] As Chapter 4 noted when discussing downsizing, it is unrealistic to lay people off one year and then expect this to be forgotten by employees the next year.

If trust is damaged, what can be done to repair it? In their review of the evidence, Kramer and Lewicki identify several possibilities. One is to apologize for the actions or conditions that caused trust to be damaged. The danger is that apologizing may be dismissed as "cheap talk" especially if it is not accompanied by any reparation. However, apologizing appears to be better than not doing so and is more effective in helping to repair trust when it comes quickly after the event, and when it is seen to be sincere with the offender taking the blame rather than trying to shift it on to someone else. Also apologies for a lack of competence appear to be more effective than apologies for a lack of good intention and also when the breach of trust was an isolated event rather than a systematic repeated failing. Apologies have to be credible and commit the offender to putting matters right for the future. Another possibility, which could accompany an apology, is to offer reparation. Research suggests that inviting the victim to discuss the terms of reparation is more effective in restoring cooperation than making a specific targeted offer, and that offering a small amount of reparation is generally as effective as offering a large amount. A further approach to repairing trust is through introducing appropriate structural measures such as rules, contracts and monitoring procedures designed to deter and/or punish future trust violation. There is quite a lot of evidence indicating that such structural measures can be effective.[23]

High-trust organization

As Kramer and Lewicki observe, it is better to lay the foundations for organizing in a high-trust manner than to spending time and energy trying to repair breaches of trust. This chapter has offered guidelines on generating and sustaining trust. These are consistent with the suggestions that Six and Sorge draw from their detailed comparison of two matched Dutch consulting organizations which differed in the levels of interpersonal trust their members reported.[24] The researchers identified four types of organizational policy that, in combination, appear to encourage the building of trust between people within the organizations. The first three of these policies aim to foster the goodwill aspect of interpersonal trust, while the fourth policy aims to develop competence as a basis for that trust. The four policies are:

1   To create an organizational culture in which relationships are important and showing care and concern for other people's needs is valued.

2   To facilitate what the authors call "unambiguous relational signaling" among colleagues both in vertical and horizontal communications; by this they mean fostering good communication skills so as to avoid misunderstandings and opportunities for colleagues to meet and discuss informally outside the normal run of work.

3   To take great care in the selection and initiation of new staff to make them aware of the values and principles of the organization – "how we do things around here."

4   To enhance the competence basis for interpersonal trust through means such as training, manuals, matching employees' competences and experience to the tasks they were expected to carry out and monitoring their performance and development needs.

SUMMARY

1   Trust concerns the readiness of one person or group to relate to another in the belief that the other's actions will be beneficial rather than detrimental, even though this cannot be guaranteed. A belief in another's goodwill and competence are important foundations for trust. For trust to exist in business and work contexts both goodwill and competence are necessary.

2   Trust is the key to successful collaboration in organizational relationships, especially those involving people from different backgrounds and cultures. Such collaboration ranges from teams to alliances and other networks crossing organizational and national boundaries. Research has demonstrated the performance benefits of trust.

3   Trust encourages a willingness to work together in coping with unforeseen circumstances and to make necessary adjustments not anticipated in formal agreements. It can provide an alternative to incurring the costs and potentially de-motivating effects of close control and a heavy reliance on contracts; and it encourages the openness in exchanging ideas and information that is a necessary condition for innovation and organizational learning.

4   Informal understanding, based on trust, often proves to be a more powerful factor in determining the success of collaboration than formal arrangements such as contracts.

5   Analysis of the conditions supporting trust are important for understanding how trust can be developed, maintained and, if necessary, repaired.

6   Considering goodwill and competence as bases for trust offers insights into the ways in which trust in business collaborations can develop through the three stages of calculation, mutual understanding, and bonding. The first of these stages amounts to a willingness to transact or work with the other person, group or organization. While little or no trust may be present at this stage, a belief in the other party's competence backed by formal contractual or institutional guarantees, should serve to get the relationship going. At the second stage, trust starts to develop on the basis of mutual predictability as the parties come to understand each other better. The third stage – bonding – strengthens their relationship on the basis of personal friendship.

7   These insights in turn lead to practical guidelines aimed at creating a clear and calculable basis for mutual benefit, improving mutual predictability, and moving toward mutual bonding.

QUESTIONS FOR DISCUSSION

15.1   How would you define "trust"?

15.2   Discuss the differences between traditional and institutional foundations of trust. What are their practical implications for management?

15.3   What is the role of calculation in creating and sustaining trust?

15.4   How does trust contribute to the success of team working and collaboration through strategic alliances?

15.5   What are the specific benefits one could expect from high-trust relationships in organizations?

15.6   Referring also to Chapter 14, discuss the connection between trust and organizational learning.

15.7   In the light of your reading of previous chapters, what is the significance of trust for new organizational forms?

NOTES

1   Some of this chapter is based on John Child (2001), Trust – the fundamental bond in global collaboration, *Organizational Dynamics*, 29, 274–288.

2   Reinhard Bachmann and Akbar Zaheer (eds.) (2008), *Handbook of Trust Research*, Cheltenham, Edward Elgar; Maria Sousa-Lima, John W. Michel, and António Caetano (2013), Clarifying the importance of trust in organization as a component of effective work relationships, *Journal of Applied Social Psychology*, 43(2), 418–427.

3   Peter Ping Li (2012), When trust matters the most: The imperatives for contextualizing trust research, *Journal of Trust Research*, 2(2), 101–106.

4   Denise M. Rousseau, Ronald S. Burt, Sim B. Sitkin, and Colin Camerer (1998), Not so different after all: A cross-discipline view of trust, *Academy of Management Review*, 23, 393–404. Quotation is from p. 395.

5   Edelman Trust Barometer (2013), http://www.edelman.com/news/2013-edelman-trust-barometer-finds-a-crisis-in-leadership, accessed 27 February, 2014. This barometer is based on a survey of over 30,000 people in 26 countries.

6   Roderick M. Kramer and Roy J. Lewicki (2010), Repairing and enhancing trust: Approaches to reducing organizational trust deficits, *Academy of Management Annals*, 4(1), 245–277.

7   Arvind Parkhe (1998a), Understanding trust in international alliances, *Journal of World Business*, 33(3), 219–240; Arvind Parkhe (1998b), Building trust in international alliances, *Journal of World Business*, 33(4), 417–437.

8   Amy Edmondson (1999), Psychological safety and learning behavior in work teams, *Administrative Science Quarterly*, 44(4), 350–383; Jane E. Salk and Oded Shenkar (2001), Social identities in an international joint venture: an exploratory case study, *Organization Science*, 12(2), 161–178.

9   Arvind Parkhe (1998a), Understanding trust in international alliances, op. cit.

10   Matthew J. Robson, Constantine S. Katsikeas, and Daniel C. Bello (2008), Drivers and performance outcomes of trust in international strategic alliances: The role of organizational complexity, *Organization Science*, 19(4), 647–665.

11   John Child and Guido Möllering (2003), Contextual confidence and active trust development in the Chinese business context, *Organization Science*, 14(1), 69–80.

12 Sally Heavens and John Child (1999), Mediating individual and organizational learning: the role of teams and trust, paper presented at the 3rd International Conference on Organizational Learning, Lancaster, June.

13 Claudio U. Ciborra (1993), *Teams, Markets and Systems,* Cambridge, Cambridge University Press. The quotation is from p. 56.

14 Sabrina Deutsch Salamon and Sandra L. Robinson (2008), Trust that binds: The impact of collective felt trust on organization performance, *Journal of Applied Psychology*, 93(3), 593–601.

15 Bo Bernhard Nielsen (2011), Trust in strategic alliances: Toward a co-evolutionary research model, *Journal of Trust Research*, 1(2), 159–176.

16 There is a continuing debate among academics about the relation of trust to calculation. Some economists like Oliver Williamson maintain that the notion of calculative trust is a contradiction in terms and that economic relationships, at least, can always be analyzed solely in terms of calculation. The idea of trust is therefore redundant. Other authorities disagree. They maintain that trust and calculation are distinct, but accept that calculation can contribute importantly to establishing conditions that favor trust. This latter position is the one I adopt. See Guido Möllering (2014), Trust, calculativeness, and relationships: A special issue 20 years after Williamson's warning, *Journal of Trust Research*, 4(1), 1–21.

17 Yves L. Doz (1996), The evolution of cooperation in strategic alliances: Initial conditions or learning processes? *Strategic Management Journal*, 17(S1), 55–83.

18 Jane E. Salk and Oded Shenkar (2001), op. cit.

19 Petru Lucian Curşeu and Sandra G. L. Schruijer (2010), Does conflict shatter trust or does trust obliterate conflict? Revisiting the relationships between team diversity, conflict, and trust, *Group Dynamics: Theory, Research, and Practice*, 14(1), 66–79.

20 Eugene McKenna (2012), *Business Psychology and Organizational Behaviour*, 5th edition, Hove, Psychology Press, Chapter 11.

21 Werner Bönte (2008), Inter-firm trust in buyer-supplier relations: Are knowledge spillovers and geographical proximity significant? *Journal of Economic Behavior & Organization*, 67, 855–870.

22 Roderick M. Kramer and Roy J. Lewicki (2010), op. cit.

23 Roderick M. Kramer and Roy J. Lewicki (2010), op. cit., pp. 252–256.

24 Frédérique Six and Arndt Sorge (2008), Creating a high-trust organization: An exploration into organizational policies that stimulate interpersonal trust building, *Journal of Management Studies*, 45(5), 857–884.

CHAPTER 16

Corporate Governance in New Organizational Forms[1]

WHAT THIS CHAPTER COVERS

This chapter begins by pointing out the surprising lack of communication between the study of corporate governance and that of new organizational forms. It describes the growing concern about corporate governance, which is normally regarded as the problem of how to hold managers to account as the agents for stockholders or stakeholders. The chapter examines the agency implications of two developments in organizational form, namely devolved initiative within firms and partnerships between firms. While new organizational forms present new agency challenges, they also offer opportunities for placing corporate governance on a more inclusive basis that may help to heal the serious breach of trust between senior management and employees.

Introduction

Corporate governance and new organizational forms are two of the most frequently visited themes in business and management. They are complementary in that corporate governance is concerned with ways in which managerial agents can be held to account for the attainment of the goals given to firms, while the impetus to develop new forms of organization comes from the need to achieve such goals more effectively in the changing conditions of the contemporary business world.

It is therefore surprising to find that there has been very little communication between the two fields of inquiry. Specialists in accounting, finance, and law have dominated discussions of corporate governance. Most take for granted a conventional model of organization in which accountability is guaranteed through hierarchical "command and control" relationships. Even this conventional model makes heroic assumptions about the control effectiveness of hierarchies. In practice, many corporations are moving beyond it. For their part, sociological studies of organizations have been concerned with governance from the perspective of the legitimacy and status of organizations in modern society. However, experts on organizational design tend to adopt a narrower view and rarely take governance into account.

The result has been that discussions of corporate governance generally do not venture below the CEO level, whereas the consideration of organizational design generally goes no higher than that level. There is little meeting of minds across the threshold. This mutual disconnect is untenable, particularly as new organizational forms present a significant challenge for the process of corporate governance just at a time when its reform has become an issue of considerable urgency.

This chapter begins by reviewing the growing calls to improve corporate governance. The most powerful of these argue for its strengthening along conventional lines, the adequacy of which is questioned by developments in organizational form. A comparison between the governance characteristics of conventional hierarchical organization and newer forms helps to clarify their implications for agency and control. The more fluid relationships implicit in new organizational forms make it more difficult to guarantee the behavior of agents through conventional mechanisms. New organizational forms, however, offer opportunities to place governance onto a different basis that engages organizational members more completely and may restore some of the trust in management that has been lost in recent years. The chapter concludes by exploring these possibilities.

◢ Growing Concern about Corporate Governance

Concern with the governance of firms goes back a long way. Following industrialization, some social theorists were alarmed at the power of business owners in society.[2] Others, on the contrary, have worried about the dilution of owners' control over professional managers in modern large corporations.[3] In recent years, concern over the accountability of managers has revived in line with a number of developments, especially in the Anglo-Saxon countries. Weaknesses in corporate governance were brought to light when the major recessions of the early 1980s, 1990s and post-2008 exposed poor or fraudulent management in a number of failing US and UK companies that had previously received reassuring audit reports. The catastrophic effects of the major corporate failures in the early 2000s on people's well-being as employees, pension fund holders, and investors represented what *Business Week* in a report on "How to Fix Corporate Governance" called "capitalism's biggest crisis since the trustbuster era."[4] The collapse of major financial institutions such as Lehman Brothers, AIG, RBS and Citigroup in 2007/8, not to mention General Motors and Chrysler, added further to the crisis of confidence in how large corporations were being run, especially when extremely highly paid "fat cats" were in control.

The globalization of capital markets has also exerted pressure on companies to adopt international standards and practices of corporate governance, with the markets offering access to larger sums of cheaper investment capital in return for greater accountability and transparency. The damage inflicted on investors and local economies by the Asian financial crisis of the late 1990s added fuel to demands for greater transparency and accountability for performance. With financial markets becoming more sensitive to corporate performance, mechanisms to remove under-performing managements, such as acquisitions and leveraged buy-outs, have been employed with increasing frequency. One consequence of using these mechanisms has been widespread job loss, which has in turn eroded the trust that employees, including managers, are willing to place in their employers.[5] The institutional ownership of most large corporations has become more concentrated and this, combined with increasing competition among financial service providers to offer better returns to their clients, has further encouraged such institutions to seek ways of improving the accountability of directors and top managers for corporate performance.

Further pressures for corporate accountability are also emerging from beyond the realm of stockowners and financial markets. Major environmental disasters at the hands of prominent corporations, such as the Bhopal, Exxon Valdez and Deepwater Horizon incidents, have accentuated the pressures for corporate managements also to be held more accountable to the communities in which they operate. Pressures for social responsibility are being enhanced by the growing expectation that rich multinational corporations should serve as agents for the development of emerging economies rather than exploiting them.[6] This has given rise to the concept of "ethical sourcing," and benchmark standards have been proposed for it.[7]

The issue of top management accountability has also been highlighted by evidence that levels of trust in companies and their corporate managers are declining worldwide. As the previous chapter noted, many surveys across a wide range of countries confirm this decline. They indicated that people placed their lowest levels of trust in large companies and national legislative bodies. An international survey conducted in 2013 found that only 20 percent of the general public questioned trusted business leaders to tell the truth.[8] Surveys in the UK confirm the general decline in trust, and also indicate that, on average, senior managers are not trusted even by a majority of their own employees.[9] At the time of writing, trust in business among citizens of the European Union was continuing to decline.[10]

A large-scale survey of employees conducted in the fifteen European Union countries (as of 2003) concluded that their trust in employers has been significantly damaged by a number of developments.[11] One of these is the widespread and large-scale downsizing of the 1990s that is still continuing today. The cutting of employers' pension contributions and, in particular, the closure of company final salary pension schemes is another. The revelations that followed the Enron, Worldcom, and other corporate scandals, of collusion between corrupt employers and the supposedly independent financial institutions that were advising investors, further eroded trust (BBC, 2003).[12] There can be no doubt that there is widespread mistrust of business today among people, both in their roles as employees and as members of the public. This mistrust has further eroded confidence in the effectiveness of corporate governance.

These problems, in particular corporate scandals and the failures of financial institutions, have placed governance high on the agendas of academics, government officials, international institutions, and consulting firms. The debate concerns both who should have rights and powers in allocating corporate resources and returns and how their use of such rights and powers can be made sufficiently transparent and accountable. Another contentious issue concerns the parties whose interests the corporation should satisfy, be these shareholders or various categories of stakeholder such as employees, suppliers, customers, and the community. The dominant view informing most discussion of the subject remains oriented to shareholders' interest, focusing on their relations with company boards and top management.

Supporting the shareholder value principle is the fact that many members of the general public now depend on the returns they receive from stocks and shares as members of pension funds, holders of managed funds, and individual stockowners. It is the threat to these interests, and to employment, that has prompted the greatest anger at corporate wrongdoing. Thus the codes on principles of good corporate governance, which bodies such as the OECD have developed, define the prime objective of the corporation to be the optimization over time of return to its shareholders.[13] In terms of practices to render this objective effective, the OECD gave by far the greatest attention to the rights of shareholders concerning voting, disclosure of information, and protection of minority shareholders, as well as the responsibilities of the board.[14]

Shareholders, especially financial institutions, have over time moved toward a more active role in monitoring the performance of boards and chief executives, although scandals such as the Enron collapse and the failure of large banks such as Royal Bank of Scotland show how difficult this can be to achieve. A number of prominent CEOs have been ousted for presiding over poor corporate performance or auditing, including Thorsten Heins at Blackberry, Jacques Nasser at Ford, Rick Wagoner at General Motors and Fred Goodwin at Royal Bank of Scotland. Institutional investors have also been expressing their impatience more forcefully at the lack of effective links between executive pay and corporate performance and this has become an issue of wider public concern.[15] The importance that institutional investors attach to "good" corporate governance is indicated by surveys showing that they would be prepared to pay premiums of between 18 and 27 percent more for the shares of a well-governed company than for a poorly governed one with a comparable financial performance. The level of premium investors would be willing to pay is higher in Asian and Latin American countries where the quality of financial reporting is lower.[16]

These developments reflect support for, and a strengthening of, the shareholder-value principle. They focus, however, on the relationship between two groups only. The first group consists of owner-shareholders, and the second of companies' boards and top managers. In what the OECD has characterized as the "outsider" system of corporate governance, owners have to rely on external levers and mechanisms in order to ensure that their managerial agents will act in accordance with their interests. This system does not take account of the "insider" issues of accountability and control within the company that are raised by organization theory.

◢ The Agency Problem

There is a concern that shareholders be provided with sufficient inducements and protection for them to be willing to bear the risk of being the recipients of residual returns from a company's activities once all other contractual claims have been met. This concern informs the "outsider" system of corporate governance. It is assumed that the bearing of residual risk encourages shareholders to allocate corporate resources to their best use in order to maximize the size of the residual. This is taken to mean that, when corporations are run to maximize shareholder value, both the interests of shareholders and the performance of the whole economic system should benefit.

Financial economists point to the benefits of a separation of residual risk bearing from corporate executive management. They are, however, worried about the agency problem that enters into the relationship between the two parties. As Mary O'Sullivan has noted, "The governance problem of the modern corporation, as financial economists conceptualise it, is that those who bear the residual risk – the shareholders or "principals" – have no assurance that the corporate managers or "agents" who make the decisions that affect shareholder wealth will act in shareholder interests."[17] Financial economists have therefore been preoccupied with the analysis of mechanisms to mitigate this "agency problem," including incentives such as stock options and constraints imposed by efficient markets, such as the threat of takeover if shareholders do not receive adequate returns.

Agency theory focuses on the ability of "principals" to ensure that their "agents" are fulfilling their objectives. It assumes that agents cannot necessarily be trusted, and that this creates a serious risk for principals when there is an asymmetry of information in favor of their agents. It is therefore concerned with the governance mechanisms that limit agents' self-serving behavior. Such behavior, ranging from excessive top management rewards to downright fraud, reduces the residual returns available to owners or indeed other claimants.

Agency theory has become firmly associated with the shareholder value principle. This is misleading and regrettable, because an agency problem can arise in *any* relationship whereby one person, or group of persons, is acting on behalf of another. The issues identified by agency theory remain when groups other than shareholders are the principals of business corporations. Agency is a general problem inherent in modern complex business and organizational relationships, which arises whenever there is a division of labor or function between people that makes them dependent on others. This is one of the reasons why there is so much concern today to improve the level of trust within and between organizations.

◢ The Double Agency Problem

A double agency relationship arises when a principal has to rely upon agents at more than one stage in the process between the expression of his or her interests and actions taken to realize those interests. This kind of relationship is to be found in the larger, more complex firms that dominate many sectors today. Here, the process of holding agents to account for the attainment of goals given to organizations involves two sets of control relationships, reflecting the presence of agents at two main levels. The first relationship is that between owners and other stakeholder groups on the one hand, and corporate management, on the other. The second relationship, which has been largely ignored in discussions of corporate governance, is that between corporate management and other managers and employees within the company.

Organization theorists refer to the first relationship in terms of "strategic control." Chapter 6 notes that the focus of control at the strategic level is on the means and methods on which the whole conduct of an organization depends. These include its capital, the form of assets in which capital is embodied, and also its strategic dispositions such as the markets or areas of need to be served, the communities and labor markets in which the organization is located, and its relations with competing organizations, suppliers, and government. Corporate management is the agent of ownership and/or other stakeholders at this strategic level.

A key assumption in the governance literature is that the board of directors has the capacity to ensure that the managers of capital do the right thing by the owners of capital. It is based on the premise that corporate managers can control the behavior of their own agents within the organizations they supervise. In other words, the conventional view of corporate governance assumes that strategic control is sufficient both to avoid misinformation and to ensure a level of operational effectiveness that will provide a good return to shareholders. It requires top management to have the authority and knowledge to ensure that a firm's operations are aligned with its strategic objectives. Strategic control is seen as underwriting operational control, which is control over the production or service provision process within an organization, in the sense of determining and monitoring how the people contributing to that process behave and perform. A strong hierarchy, with clearly defined reporting relationships, has been the traditional approach to achieving operational control on the part of top managers, who in turn are accountable to the board or other governing bodies.

In practice, this conventional approach and the assumption behind it are problematic. Even in organizations with clearly delineated hierarchies, there are risks attached to the implementation of corporate strategies through agents situated at lower levels. As three consultants with Booz Allen Hamilton remarked, "cooking the books isn't the only sure path to notoriety for companies these days. Far more endemic is corporate dysfunction. From the CEO down, the laments are familiar: 'We have the right strategy and a clear action plan, but we can't seem to execute'.[18]

One reason lies in a striving for autonomy among subordinates, leading to "control loss" and the failure to realize corporate intentions fully. Another reason stems from the fact that hierarchies are career and advancement ladders as well as control systems, and that subordinates therefore seek to present their actions in the best possible light. The hierarchical control process is thus weakened by the tendency for people in subordinate positions to reinterpret orders flowing downward and, at the same time, to pass upward information presented in such a way as to make it look good. There are even occasions when the authority of top management is openly challenged through industrial action. Employees at the point where strategy is applied through operations have always had the potential to challenge top management power through undertaking various forms of organized action. They may maintain informal practices over long periods of time in ways that also distort management intentions.[19]

Among the conventional approaches to organization, it has been thought that the multi-divisional form is better able than the traditional, functionally structured form to transmit top management goals throughout the firm and to keep top management informed about how far such goals have been achieved.[20] The multi-divisional form permits performance targets to be allocated to divisions that comprise focused and distinct areas of value creation. It therefore typically substitutes reliance on the reporting of results (output control) for the use of personal supervision and reporting (behavior control). This, it is argued, should reduce opportunistic behavior and empire building by lower-level managers and improve the focus of a firm's efforts on profit maximization to the benefit of its owners.

However, studies of decisions having major strategic significance, such as on capital investment, demonstrate the dependence of top management in multi-divisional firms upon the information and proposals passed to them by those lower down within the divisions.[21] In other words, both conventional forms of organization – divisional as well as functional – remain vulnerable to the double agency problem. As Demsetz has put it, "Which form of organization causes more serious distortions in the firm's policies will be a function of which can create the most biased information for top management to act upon."[22]

The double agency problem is therefore present in all forms of organization that are of a scale as to create a personal and often physical distance between top managers and the agents on whom they rely for policy implementation at lower levels. It is not a new problem, albeit one scarcely recognized in the mainstream corporate governance literature, which has assumed at least implicitly that well-designed hierarchies, control systems and incentives will do the job. Serious though the problem is, we shall see that moves from hierarchical to less or non-hierarchical forms of organization, and towards the opening of organizational boundaries through joint ventures and networks, may well make it even more challenging to deal with.

The Multiple Agency Problem

Multiple agency refers to a situation in which there is more than one party in agency relationships, either as principals, agents or both. An important instance of multiple agency arises when firms enter into partnerships with other firms through so-called strategic alliances. These partnerships may be formed for specific purposes such as assisting foreign market entry or accessing technology and other resources, or they may comprise the components of wider business networks. Chapter 11 noted that equity-based joint ventures are a common form of strategic alliance in which there is a pooling of ownership assets and usually a degree of joint management between two or more partner firms. They are in effect "hybrid organizations."[23]

The multiplicity of agency relationships in equity joint ventures and similar organizational forms arises from three of their salient characteristics. First, there are several, though normally few, owners. They have to be regarded as multiple principals because each has its own rationale for entering into the alliance and each is sufficiently salient to require its interests to be respected. Indeed, if just one partner decides to withdraw, the alliance usually breaks down. Second, because the owner partners usually contribute complementary tangible and intangible assets to the joint venture, they also in effect become agents for each other in ensuring its viability. Third, the managers of the joint venture act as agents for its owners. Their agency role is often complicated by the presence of multiple owners, when each places its own expectations upon venture managers. Further problems can arise if a joint venture is managed by a mixture of personnel supplied or appointed by the different partners, and if they come from different cultures and management traditions.

Implications for Corporate Governance

Previous chapters have described how new organizational forms reduce the emphasis on hierarchy in favor of horizontal team-based relationships, devolve initiative to self-organizing units, and tolerate a diversity of arrangements such as controls with a firm. Chapters 9, 10 and 11 indicated how firms are also making greater use than before of networked systems of production and partnerships.

There is no reason to think that new organizational forms will replace conventional bureaucracies in areas of work where the consistency and efficiency offered by hierarchy and routine are necessary, such as government internal revenue departments. At the same time, it is very unlikely that new organizational forms simply represent a passing fashion. We have seen that they are a response to a range of contextual developments of profound and lasting significance, including globalization, information and communications technologies, intensifying competition, and the growing significance of knowledge as a source of value creation and competitive advantage. As such, new organizational forms are a response to the step change in

Table 16.1   Organizational forms and implications for agency and control

Organizational form	Chief characteristics	Implications for agency and control
Traditional hierarchy	Centralized initiative and unified authority; top-down leadership through formal processes and hierarchical channels; mandatory compliance with rules. Stress on conformity and efficiency	Reliance on vertical "command and control" process; unified management structure (agency) accountable to principals' representatives, normally the board of directors
Devolved Initiative	Distributed initiative and authority; use of teams; recognition of positive role of intra- and inter-group contest in innovation; leadership through guidance and response to bottom-up initiatives; discretionary compliance with rules. Stress on innovation, intrapreneurship, and flexibility	Difficulty in applying traditional control mechanisms; greater reliance on arms-length "output control," complemented by attempts to generate shared understanding and corporate culture; intrapreneurship and innovation increase risk of control loss and need to revise principals' objectives in the light of new developments
Partnerships	Negotiated definition of objectives; complementarity of resource contributions; mode of management and joint working evolves through accommodation and learning	Problems of control loss by each principal arising through inherent managerial role conflict and likelihood of role ambiguity; risk of opportunism and breakdown of collaboration

the business environment that is taking place with increasing speed. They present a new landscape, for which students of corporate governance require new maps.

Two major implications arise for corporate governance from the adoption of new organizational forms. The first is the dilution of top-level control arising from the *devolving of initiative*. This adds to the problem of double agency. The second implication concerns the complications of multiple agency arising from the growing use of network *partnerships*, especially equity-based alliances. Table 16.1 summarizes the chief characteristics of these new organizational forms and their implications for the agency and control aspects of corporate governance. The Table starts with the *traditional hierarchy* for purposes of comparison.

Devolved initiative and the dilution of control

I have argued that corporate governance extends beyond external supervision, to include the process of control within the firm exercised through its form of organization. This two-stage supervision process creates the problem of double agency. I also indicated that the double agency problem exists even within firms organized along conventional hierarchical lines. This is despite the presence typically within such firms of clear lines of authority, reinforced by formalized practices such as job descriptions, procedure manuals, and the agreement of goals and targets with subordinates. A tenet of the theory of bureaucracy is that the senior executives of a firm make the most important decisions, control and influence the most significant resources, and have the power to execute the plans approved by the board. This assumes that corporate managers can control the behavior of their agents within the company.

This assumption is less likely to hold in an organization that has de-emphasized hierarchy. The decentralized initiative and flexibility it aims to foster implies a greater reliance on "output control": focusing upon performance targets and "responsibility accounting" systems rather than on hierarchical supervision or a specification of approved behavior. Chapter 6 noted that output controls become more appropriate when managers have only limited knowledge of the transformation processes involved in the work of an organization. The rapidly changing and uncertain conditions that have stimulated a search for new organizational forms, however, may even militate against the *a priori* specification of output targets. Moreover, the inability to specify appropriate behavior requires a heavy reliance on the rather uncertain efficacy of organizational cultural norms.

Top managers, and the boards of directors they report to, may therefore have only limited impact over the most critical locus of activity in the organization. This is because under the new organizational approach the role of senior executives is effectively confined to articulating a vision and shaping a collective culture rather than supervising behavior. In new-form organizations, initiative is widely dispersed, both within and outwith the firm, and in effect what has come about is a dilution of the agency relationship to scattered quasi-autonomous agents. The consequence can be that a board is helpless to have much impact on the activities of the organization, even if it has tremendous impact on its senior executives. Despite its ability to dismiss a CEO, a board can have relatively little influence on the organization as a whole. For example, many of Enron's new businesses, some of which moved beyond top management control and contributed to the company's collapse, were the results of entrepreneurial initiatives by middle managers rather than the top brass (see Box 16.1).[24] Fresh thinking is urgently required on how to preserve the benefits of devolved initiative without incurring the disastrous loss of control that ruined Enron.

The Enron case illustrates how innovation is one of the primary drivers behind new forms of organization. The innovation process is cumulative and collective, meaning that it involves people within organizations working together, often in teams, to generate organizational learning. It is also uncertain both in the sense that it may not realize superior returns and that it may lead a firm's strategy in directions not foreseen by its leaders. This presents a challenge for top management's accountability as well as to the conventional view of corporate governance.

Corporate governance debates generally focus on the allocation of corporate returns and neglect the relation between the allocation of resources and the innovation process.[25] They also neglect the dependence of innovation on the way people, especially knowledge workers, are organized. In so doing they fail to consider the extent to which new forms of organization, mostly intended to promote innovation and flexibility, challenge the fundamental assumption of conventional corporate governance that the CEO and top management team are in total control of, and therefore to be totally accountable for, the actions taken by lower-level individuals and groups in the course of innovation. There is a potential tension here between the need for innovation and the need for control.

The decomposition of large integrated firms into networked value chains also creates a new governance challenge to firms that are held to public account for the actions of other network members. They are held accountable because the value chain product is marketed to the public

BOX 16.1   ENRON – OUT OF CONTROL?

Enron was celebrated by a number of prominent writers on management for the ways that its devolved and loosely coupled organization encouraged innovation and intra-preneurship. Gary Hamel, for example, wrote that Enron is "an organization where thousands of people see themselves as potential revolutionaries." Kathy Eisenhardt praised Enron's ability to decentralize initiative so as to allow managers to develop new businesses where competitive advantage was to be gained from market confusion.

Enron's collapse has been attributed to shortcuts in financing new ventures, managerial arrogance, and sheer fraud. Part of the problem lay in a failure of control associated with the devolved initiative that the company's organization had encouraged. Many of Enron's new businesses, the failures of which were hidden through accounting manipulations, resulted from entrepreneurial initiatives made by middle managers rather than those at the top. Jeffrey Skilling, the company's former chief executive, claims not to have known of the irregular dealings that went on, or even about some of the private partnerships that hid debts from investors and at the same time enriched a number of the company's officers.

This claim does not absolve Skilling of ultimate responsibility, or of blame for condoning a morally lax atmosphere in the company. Nevertheless, the Enron case demonstrates how a loose, networked structure can lead to a situation in which the CEO is neither concerned nor informed about initiatives taken lower down.

Sources: Financial Times, December 4, 2001, p. 16; August 22, 2002, p. 26; August 23, 2002, p. 21.

under their brand name. Nevertheless, they claim that their power to control behavior within the network is severely circumscribed, and that they face a variant of the double agency problem. This is because the integration of a production network or value chain relies heavily upon standardized systems for sharing operational information,[26] and such systems do not easily handle behavioral issues of a non-standardized and ethical nature. The question therefore arises: when leading core firms become disassociated from their supporting organizational network, who takes responsibility for the behavior of firms within that network?

This issue has come into prominence in recent years. Multinational corporations can permit (wittingly or otherwise) their sub-contractors in developing countries to apply codes and practices that are different from their policies in their country of origin. Nike and Gap are examples of leading brand MNCs whose Asian subcontractors' exploited local labor. While one attraction for leading firms to adopt the new organizational philosophy may have been the prospect of sloughing off non-core employees and responsibility for their welfare, public opinion is no longer prepared to condone this. For however loosely-coupled and disaggregated a value chain, it remains a system that enables and supports the proprietary brand of the leading firm in that system.

Partnerships and multiple agency

Strategic partnerships present additional complications from the point of view of corporate governance. These are particularly acute in the case of equity joint ventures (EJVs). They arise as a result of the mutual dependencies and multiple agency relationships built into the shared ownership and management of such ventures. In international joint ventures, the legal and social contexts of the parent companies, which shape their experience and expectations of the corporate governance process, will also differ.

The legal aspects of corporate governance applied to EJVs is primarily concerned with the rights of partners in relation to their share of equity. They focus on voting power in JV boards as the lever to ensure participation in strategic control. Clearly if that power is divided, as in the case of a 50/50 equity split, there is a risk of serious deadlocks arising.

The divided ownership structure of equity JVs leads naturally to problems of agency. When EJVs are formed, the most evident principal–agent relationship is that between the partner owners and the venture managers. The situation becomes complicated if the partners disagree over objectives and/or have different risk or time preferences. Partners often decide to form an EJV because they perceive cooperation to provide the means to achieve their respective objectives, but the fact that those objectives are typically not identical can easily lead to conflicts over priorities. Cultural differences, and the misunderstanding these create, increase the liability to conflict. An example of how these multiple agency problems led to a breakdown in an Anglo-Chinese equity joint venture is given in Box 16.2.

The possibility of disagreement between partners recalls the fact that JVs are cooperative arrangements intended to enhance the partners' ability to achieve their objectives through joint contributions that exploit the presence of complementarities between them. So, in addition to employing agents to manage the JV itself, each partner is also an agent for the other. This heightens the importance of the control they can each exercise over the JV in relation to each other. At the same time, for one partner to exercise too much control over the other(s) will defeat the point of forming a partnership in the first place.

Many alliances are between multinational corporations (MNCs) and local companies, especially in developing countries. These alliances pose different problems of governance for each partner. For the MNC, greater control helps to protect it against technology leakage and to keep a hand on knowledge and information. Yet this increases managerial costs, especially if it means employing expensive expatriates in key positions. The local partner may have personal control of many of the venture's operational activities, but often does not have the final say in strategic issues. If such a potentially unstable relationship is to be long-lasting, learning and trust building are essential ingredients which should decrease the need to rely on personal control and also increase effective accountability.

The multiple agency problems arising with equity joint ventures can extend throughout an "equal-partner network."[27] In such cooperative networks there is no single partner that sets up and controls the networks' activities. Power relationships between the partners, while relatively equal, are liable to shift with the fortune of the members. While this kind of network has potentially great flexibility, and an ability to respond to often turbulent environments, it lacks a permanent "brain" and "central nervous system" of networks led by strong-brand firms. The multiple agency issue therefore becomes particularly diffuse and difficult to handle within equal-partner networks and is subject to almost constant negotiation.

BOX 16.2   BREAKDOWN DUE TO MULTIPLE AGENCY PROBLEMS

An Anglo-Chinese equity joint venture in the branded fast-moving consumer goods sector was experiencing increasing problems leading to a crisis in its performance. The venture's equity was divided 50/50 between the British and Chinese partners. The British partner had contracted to provide technology and systems support as well as one of its international brands, while the Chinese partner provided vital access to the domestic market. The achievement of the two partners' objectives for establishing the joint venture depended on their cooperation as agents for each other.

The Chinese partner holds a provincial monopoly over the market for its product. Potentially, this provides an assured market and a sound basis for profitability. However, the partners soon came into dispute over the pricing of the internationally branded product. The Chinese partner believed that the UK side sought a price that was too high for the local market. It lost its commitment to promoting the joint venture brand and eventually began production of a cheaper substitute competing directly with that product. The local partner's command of the market and domestic distribution turned from being a valuable asset to a stranglehold.

The UK partner's ability to exercise strategic influence was undermined further by a split within its organization. Most communication went through its Hong Kong and Singapore regional offices, and there was normally little direct contact with the UK head office. The split gave rise to inconsistencies in policy that were keenly noticed by the Chinese partner and led to further frustration on its part. Although receiving regular emails, the UK office was ill informed of the situation and thus tended to intervene sporadically in a manner that was regarded as highly destabilizing by the Chinese side. Strategic issues became a divisive factor between the joint venture partners rather than a foundation for their cooperation.

Operational management was specialized between the two partners. UK appointees headed marketing and production. The general manager was a Chinese appointee, as were the heads of the other functions. In the hostile atmosphere, rather than being integrated, this specialization led to a split in operational management with many decisions being blocked by the other partner's personnel. Not surprisingly, the joint venture experienced serious problems of internal communication and low trust. Language was a natural barrier, but the provision of assistance by interpreters turned into a source of continuing friction in the prevailing atmosphere of low trust. Eventually the Chinese partner withdrew its provision of interpreters. At the time of my visit, the joint venture had experienced a decline in both profit and sales over the previous three years and was running a loss.

Source: Author's field research.

In the case of networks, accountability is confused by the fact that the use of assets may not be conditional upon their ownership. The virtual organization provides an instance of this, where a company such as Dell Computers in effect utilizes the assets of its network partners to produce under the corporate brand name. It is not, however, accountable in law for the conduct of its network producers towards their shareholders, employees, communities and environments. There is a case for a company that benefits from its dominance of a network to assume a larger measure of accountability for the conduct of firms within its network, thereby recognizing how the organization of value-chain systems has become externalized beyond its own boundaries.

◢ Applying Organizational Insights to Corporate Governance Practice

Limitations of contract and hierarchy

None of the issues identified in this chapter is receiving much attention in current discussions on corporate governance, as perusal of a leading text such as that by Monks and Minow will confirm.[28] Yet they arise from major developments in the nature of the firm that render the conventional view and practice of corporate governance untenable. This conventional view draws on a model of organizations that assumes they are based on contracts and structured by hierarchical obligations, rules and controls. Chief executives positioned at the apex of these hierarchies are presumed to know, understand and control what is going on in their firms and partnerships. The limitations of hierarchy are ignored, as are problems of double and multiple agency.

Perhaps the most important insight provided by an organizational perspective is that effective corporate governance cannot be guaranteed through reliance on contracts. It has been suggested that contracts can become "farsighted" by anticipating hazards and future contingencies.[29] However, in conditions of rapid change and uncertainty, there are severe limits to what can be anticipated and farsighted contracts by themselves are clearly not enough. In any case, contracts will not necessarily motivate people to behave in ways that meet the interests of owners and other stakeholders. The ongoing processes of interpretation and adaptation within organizations are more significant to the actions people take than is the formal basis on which they are contractually bound.

Discussions of corporate governance also tend to view organizations as structured by hierarchical obligations, rules and controls. In practice, many companies are reducing their reliance on hierarchy and are instead devolving initiative further down their organizations because they wish to make better use of their employees' capabilities. They particularly want to engage their contribution toward innovation and adaptation to new requirements. They realize that they cannot rely on contracts or rules to achieve these benefits. However, this partnership with employees entails some risk. At best, they will sometimes make mistakes and embark on ill-advised initiatives. At worst as in the case of Enron, some of them will take advantage of the freedom that they are given. This risk can clearly undermine the process of corporate governance.

So we have two desirables that, on the face of it, do not seem to be easy to reconcile. One concerns the benefits that can be offered by new approaches to organization, while the other is the generally accepted need to strengthen corporate governance. Nevertheless, despite the challenge that new organizational forms create for corporate governance as a result of double and multiple agency problems, we have to recall that such governance was not necessarily in good shape even in conventionally organized firms. There are in fact some measures, which are quite consistent with newer approaches to organization that can actually help to improve corporate governance. These include mutual monitoring and questioning by employees, transparency aided by new information technologies, a broader approach to control, the fostering of trust, and the co-optation of employees and middle managers through stock ownership and gain-sharing schemes. Although the following discussion is centered on organization within a single company, the principles that inform some of these measures, especially shared control, trust and mutual benefit, can also provide a sound basis for managing a partnership between companies.

Mutual monitoring

If the advantages of new devolved organizational forms are to be retained, then additional steps have to be taken to ensure responsible behavior and good governance. One such step is to recognize that conflicts of interest are endemic to the organization of firms and have to be managed through a combination of negotiations and bargaining, disclosures and approvals, and mutual monitoring.[30]

In a devolved organization, let alone a partnership network, it is not sufficient to rely only on the monitoring of the chief executive by the board and its committees, and of the board by shareholders. Given that it is impossible in practical terms for a chief executive, or even senior managers, to know the details of what is going on, it becomes necessary for the parties involved in a company's ongoing activities to monitor each other and to make any concerns public. This means that stakeholders such as employees, creditors and network partners should be allowed due voice. In a joint venture it means listening to a minority partner rather than trying to dominate it. In particular, corporate leaders have to encourage what Michael Useem calls "leading up" – criticism and questioning from their employees and others. Practices such as whistle blowing should be encouraged rather than punished. If Enron had done this, disaster might have been avoided (see Box 16.3).

BOX 16.3   THE NEED TO "LEAD UP"

Kenneth Lay, Enron's (former) chief executive, apparently failed to listen when Sherron Watkins, vice-president, warned of the accounting problems . . . Two other executives told a board committee of the financial risks created by the special-purpose entities. An internal lawyer wrote to his superiors that it could appear that "the financial books at Enron are being 'cooked' in order to eliminate a drag on earnings that would otherwise occur under fair value accounting." Managers should resist the temptation to ignore warnings from below.

Source: Eric Orts 2002. Law is never enough to guarantee fair dealing. *Financial Times*, August 23, p. 9.

Evidence has accumulated to show how serious corporate misdemeanors, as well as failings in public service provision such as health care, could have been avoided if the warnings of whistle blowers had been heeded. There has also been mounting public pressure for organizations to recognize the value of responsible whistle blowing and to protect those who draw attention to failures in conduct. The US Sarbanes-Oxley Act of 2002 extended whistle-blower protection to publicly traded companies for the first time; it contains significant protections for corporate whistleblowers. The breadth of its provisions means that it may turn out to be one of the most important whistleblower protection laws. As a result of these developments, many organizations have announced policies on whistle-blowing, as a quick check of the Internet immediately shows. For example, the Anglo American mining group is one of the leaders among large companies in operating an official whistle-blowing policy. It is called Speakup and encourages employees to report in confidence any violations of Anglo American's rules of good business practice or any ethical and legal concerns they may have. At the time of writing just under 300 alerts were being received each year.[31]

Transparency

From the point of view of shareholder value, more effective governance requires greater transparency in corporate dealings and better mechanisms for sounding due warnings of malpractice or impending problems. Mutual monitoring is intended to promote transparency. Moves towards greater transparency are in tune with the aims of new organizational forms, especially the promotion of learning and innovation. For although these processes are often aimed at generating new proprietary knowledge that is then guarded in secrecy, the generation of such knowledge or other forms of organizational learning requires greater internal transparency. Unless relevant information is shared within an organization, the effectiveness of collective learning will be impaired. The same open organizational climate can facilitate both learning aimed at avoiding governance errors and learning aimed at making innovative improvements.

Transparency requires open communication and the sharing of information within organizations, as well as between them and their stakeholders. The availability of the Internet, and especially social media, are technological developments that can be used to share information widely and improve its transparency. Just as the almost instantaneous broadcasting and mobilization of collective opinions through Twitter are impacting on the voting intentions of elected political representatives,[32] so in principle a similar technology could be used to promote an active ongoing process of disseminating and sharing information, expressing opinions and, when appropriate, mutually monitoring behaviour within organizations. The provision of information electronically tends to encourage a more active level of participation, which is a necessary condition for good governance. For example, it is reported that in companies like DaimlerChrysler AG or Allianz AG up to 80 percent of shareholders who are informed electronically tend to respond either by ordering admission cards to shareholders' meetings or by granting power of attorney and instructions to the proxies. This level of participation is much higher than the response to paper information.[33]

The demand for transparency is in some degree the inevitable result of a more knowledge-based society, in which educated citizens demand the right to know and managements need to share information so that people's competencies can be applied to adding value most effectively. It is also a reaction to the accumulation of managerial power noted earlier, which leads to an uneven access to information unless it is otherwise checked. The outcome of this tension between power asymmetry and demands for transparency will have a direct bearing on the future of organizational forms. If the case for transparency wins, it is likely that more extensive mechanisms for consultation and participation will be introduced, and that practices such as 360-degree assessment will be extended to the upper reaches of organizations. Smaller organizational units operating more like organic teams and closer to local interests also enhance transparency. MNCs may well come under pressure to devolve more autonomy in recognition of local sensitivities, and the shift from conventional hierarchies towards networks of semi-autonomous units will be further encouraged.

Greater transparency in the form of more open monitoring and reporting of concerns should reduce the risk of opportunism in new forms of organization – indeed in any form of organization. It does not, of course, remove the double agency problem and the consequent necessity for control over what people do within an organization, or in its name. It does, however, speak for a more open and participative approach to control.

A broader approach to control

In order to reduce the double agency problem in present day organizations, a more sophisticated approach toward control is required that moves beyond the purely top-down focus on the chief executive that we find in most discussions of corporate governance. As Chapter 2 described, this top-down perspective characterized the analysis of control within traditional organization theory. There was concern for instance about how, as firms grew larger, the limitations of centralized personal supervision by higher-level executives could be compensated by a suitably designed system of rules, including those incorporated in procedures like "management-by-exception."[34]

Today, the discussion has progressed much further. Chapter 6 described the broader range of control strategies that have since been developed. In addition to personal supervision and "behavior control" through the enforcement of rules, there are other options such as output control based on agreed targets, control through cultural norms, and control through HRM processes such as selection and appraisal. Reward systems can also function as supports for control (see Chapter 7). Control through agreed targets, the appraisal process, and common cultural norms is conducive to participation in a process of joint commitment by managers and their staff. These different forms of control have been developed in response to the challenge of maintaining accountability under an increasingly varied set of organizational conditions and organizational forms. They can be employed to suit different types of staff, working under different circumstances. Less formal approaches such as personal contact and cultural norms can reinforce more formal control mechanisms, and vice versa.

Nowadays, effective managers recognize the competitive advantage of gaining the whole-hearted support of their staff, as well as that of their partners when they form alliances and networks. Any imposition of control in a one-sided manner either by design or default, that does not allow for staff and partners to discuss and agree both the criteria and methods to be applied, excludes their potentially valuable contribution and undermines their commitment to the goals that control is supposed to help achieve. In other words, a good control system must operate with participation, transparency and evident fairness. The "new organization" ethos of empowerment and transparency has to be applied to the way control systems operate if they are to support the aims of devolved initiative *and* provide an effective means of ensuring accountability. This is why thoughtful managers are keenly interested in the possibilities of increasing the extent of self-control within their firms, based on trust and shared objectives. Trust and the sharing of objectives also reduce the likelihood of opportunistic behavior, the primary concern of corporate governance.

Trust

The widespread unwillingness of organizational members and many stakeholders to trust corporate managers is one of the most serious failings of contemporary business. People who do not trust the management they work for are unlikely to give of their best. This goes against the intentions of newer organizational perspectives, which recognize the talents that organizational members possess and aim to enlist these. From a corporate governance perspective, employees who do not invest trust and commitment in their organizations are more likely to abuse their employment and behave opportunistically at the expense of their principals. Trust therefore is an essential requirement.

The previous chapter identified ways in which trust can be fostered. It is a two-way process. If people feel they can trust those they work for, they in turn will tend to exhibit trustworthy behavior. A necessary start to developing trustworthiness among employees is to avoid threats to their security, through assurances that they will not be forced out of employment, through having equitable policies for recognition and rewards, transparent procedures for dealing with grievances and matters of discipline, and the like. On this sound basis, trust can then be reinforced and deepened through open communication and the wide dissemination of information. This will make organizational members aware of relevant events and proposals, and should therefore generate greater mutual understanding. It will also reduce the likelihood of employees being taken by surprise and consequently feeling threatened and let down. Efforts to develop social interaction between employees and managers at all levels and across units, should further strengthen trust within the company on the basis of personal bonding and mutual identification.

These policies are all compatible with the spirit of new organizational forms. They help to promote flexibility and innovation, as well as to facilitate the processes complementary to these aims such as change, learning and renewal. The very same trust-building policies should also strengthen corporate governance by underwriting the provisions already mentioned: greater transparency, a broader approach to control and a positive attitude toward mutual monitoring.

Co-optation of agents into ownership

There is a further path toward reducing the risk of opportunism on the part of staff and of increasing their commitment to the goals of the firm. This is to co-opt them into ownership, or at least into the right to share the rewards due to ownership, so that they become principals as well as agents. Chapter 8 discussed Employee Stock Ownership Plans (ESOPs) and gain-sharing plans as components in a payment system.

Shoshana Zuboff, of the Harvard Business School, and James Maxim support the principle of employee ownership in their landmark book and indeed take it further. They note that capitalism is a robust economic system that has weathered crises before through appropriate adaptation. They believe that the next stage in its development will be what they call "distributed capitalism" in which ownership will be spread more widely and firms will be as responsive to their employees and communities as to their shareholders.[35] Even gain-sharing plans, which do not offer employees a share in ownership, do at least enable them to share in the rewards of improved organizational performance and to contribute ideas for such improvement through meaningful participation.

While the financial value of each employee's ownership stake will normally be a tiny proportion of the whole, its absolute value to individuals and their families is more significant. The symbolic value for such individuals of a share in ownership of the firm where they work is also of potential importance because it signifies an identity of interests with the company and a commitment to its common objective. The same principle has been widely applied to senior managers in the form of share allocations or stock options, and many writers on corporate governance have applauded it. When confined to a small elite group, however, the potential gains to be had have sometimes encouraged deceptive and opportunistic behavior at the expense of the rest of the company – in other words, the opposite of transparency. Having a large number of informed inside members of a firm, motivated as owners to monitor senior managerial behavior, would provide a significant check on this abuse of power.

It has been suggested that the managerial dishonesty and hubris that led to recent corporate crises reflect an arrogant culture of "smartness" on the part of managers and consultants who have been trained in business and law schools and who almost feel compelled to devise ever more complex and creative ways of exploiting the system.[36] Acceptance of the ideology of managerial expertise has come to justify the right to use executive power beyond effective control or redress from shareholders, customers, or members of the general public. The democratization of voice within corporations through the corporate governance reforms I have mentioned would provide an antidote to this dangerous trend. Senior managers in privileged positions have often claimed that this would open the door to irresponsibility. Apart from being a hollow claim in the light of recent scandals, previous chapters, especially 4 and 13, have shown how the weight of evidence disproves it.

Does effective corporate governance require the retention of some bureaucracy?

One of the virtues of traditional bureaucracy was that its officials and managers were given clearly-defined duties which made it easier to hold them accountable for their performance in carrying out those responsibilities. Although I have noted many times already how this approach has come to be criticized for its rigidity and over-constraint on qualified staff, there is the possibility that effective corporate governance requires some degree of bureaucracy to be retained not least in organic network-type organizations. Some of the worst corporate scandals have taken place in organizational regimes that were flexible to the point of licentiousness, and intrapreneurial to the point of allowing initiatives that served personal rather than collective interests.

The editors of a special journal issue on the governance of networks suggest that "a little bureaucracy might be a good thing."[37] They point out that although network organizational forms may appear to be non-hierarchical and democratic, they do nevertheless require a degree of coordination and control to ensure that the collective efforts of their members lead to a value-adding output. This means that hierarchy will inevitably be present within networked organizations although this may operate mainly on an informal basis.[38] Once such hierarchy emerges, there is a potential internal agency problem. This raises the need for adequate organizational governance, which, it is suggested, benefits from formalized obligations and accountability mechanisms.

In this respect some interesting insights are offered by a study of governance mechanisms in ten Italian local public utilities.[39] Many such utilities in Italy have become joint-stock companies in which both public and private entities can invest. They have boards of directors. These utilities experienced multiple agency problems including conflicts of interest between majority and minority principals. Nor were their boards of directors adequate to ensure accountability of their local government managers (acting as agents) to the general public (the main principal). One of the provisions that have been introduced into Italian public service organizations to make them more responsive to direct users is that of "service charters." These were pioneered in the UK following the privatization of many public services. Service charters hold administrators accountable for specified quality standards, and lay down consultative mechanisms, complaints procedures and the information to be provided to citizens. They represent an injection of bureaucratic formalization into the governance process. Although the authors of the study believe that the best solution to agency problems in the utilities would be the direct involvement of citizens in decision-making, they conclude that service charters are a good start.

◢ Conclusion

My conclusion therefore is that companies can make a virtue of the necessity to rely increasingly on devolving initiative to their members. By co-opting those members as partners into the system of governance, the adoption of the new organizational philosophy can be allied to good corporate governance and performance. This co-optation can be fostered through affording members a real stake in corporate ownership and the rewards from future success, and by nurturing their trust in management through openness and taking espoused values seriously. There are examples of successful companies that have benefited from following this approach, from the John Lewis Partnership to Southwest Airlines both of which are examined in Chapter 18. Box 16.4 gives the example of the Springfield ReManufacturing Corporation.

I would conclude in similar vein for partnerships between companies, where the risks arising from deceit and opportunism are equally serious. There have to be certain contractual safeguards in an alliance to protect each partner's interest, especially if proprietary resources are being supplied. The alliance also has to be based on a good strategic fit between each partner's strategic interests. A common strategic interest and stake in shared ownership will help to provide the alliance with a sound foundation. Once this foundation is established, however, it is the psychological commitment of each partner to the alliance, strengthened by transparency and mutual trust, that best guarantees both its good governance and future success (see Chapter 11).

BOX 16.4 OPEN ORGANIZATION AND SOUND GOVERNANCE

In the late 1980s, the Springfield ReManufacturing Company, led by Jack Stack, emerged as a model for how management and labor could work together successfully in a culture of transparency, mutual trust and ownership. Stack persisted with this approach even when it got out of tune with the heady, get rich quick, days of the late 1990s. During this time, the company maintained its "open-book management" culture. By sharing information on all of the company's financials with all its employees, and giving them an ownership stake in the company, it had built up an unusual level of mutual trust and respect. This highly successful approach saw the company's stock price of just 10 cents per share when it was founded in 1983 grow to over $199 per share.

As Stack commented in an interview: "It drives you crazy when you see the Arthur Andersons and the Enrons and everything that's happening in our society today, and you know that it's due to the lack of transparency. You know that if we were practicing open books those things wouldn't happen, because too many people know about it."

At Stack's company, there are weekly get-togethers between managers and workers, prominent scorecards on the factory wall charting the progress of work, and a continuing emphasis by managers on building a company rather than just a product. Workers undergo training so that they can understand balance sheets and income statements.

Sources: John A. Byrne. After Enron: The Ideal Corporation. *Business Week*, August 26, 2002: 32–35. Stephen Hicks interview with Jack Stack recorded 2011 and published by the Center for Ethics and Entrepreneurship, http://www.ethicsandentrepreneurship .org/20110411/interview-with-jack-stack/

SUMMARY

1 Corporate governance is concerned essentially with the conduct and performance of people who act as agents for shareholders and other stakeholders of companies.

2 Corporate scandals, such as those around 2001 and 2008, have strengthened the public demand for more comprehensive and effective systems of corporate accountability. Top executives are now placed on the line as never before for the standards of conduct and reporting throughout their companies. Governance remains high on the public agenda for corporate reform.

3 Corporate governance calls for corporate directors and chief executives to be held accountable for the performance and standards of conduct of their companies in their role as agents for shareholders or other groups possessing rights over companies.

4 In so doing, it assumes that these senior officers can effectively know and control what takes place within their businesses. This assumption is based on a traditional

hierarchical model of corporate organization, but it is questionable even for that conventional form.

5 The new organizational developments described in previous chapters make it much more difficult to satisfy this assumption. The devolution of initiative within more loosely coupled firms increases the problems associated with double agency. When partnerships and networks are formed, problems associated with multiple agency arise.

6 In these ways, there is a potential for moves toward new organizational forms to conflict with the accountability required by corporate governance. This conflict reflects a tension between the need for control and that for adaptability and innovation.

7 Nevertheless, newer approaches to organization envisage forms of control and reward that should assist good governance by facilitating participation and transparency of information. New communication and social media technologies have opened up new opportunities for this facilitation.

8 These developments, combined with other measures such as a wider spread of corporate ownership, offer the prospect of reconciling new organizational forms with improved corporate governance. An approach to corporate governance that is based on inclusion should also help to heal the breach of trust in between senior management and employees.

QUESTIONS FOR DISCUSSION

16.1 Drawing also on your reading of earlier chapters, describe and discuss the complementarity of corporate governance and organization.

16.2 What agency problems can arise in different forms of organization?

16.3 Do new organizational forms add to or reduce problems of corporate governance?

16.4 How does the analysis of corporate governance inform our understanding of strategic alliances?

16.5 What is the role of "mutual monitoring" and "transparency" in promoting better corporate governance?

16.6 Referring also to Chapter 15, discuss the relevance of corporate governance to people's trust in senior corporate management.

NOTES

1 This chapter draws in part from John Child and Suzana B. Rodrigues (2003), Corporate Governance and New Organization Forms, *Journal of Management and Governance*, 7, 337–360.

2 Among them Karl Marx and Thorsten Veblen. Marx, K. and Engels, F. 1948 *Manifesto of the Communist Party* (1959 translation), Moscow: Foreign Languages Publishing House; Veblen, T. (1904), *The Theory of Business Enterprise*, New York: Scribners.

3   A.A. Berle and G.C. Means (1932), *The Modern Corporation and Private Property*, New York, Macmillan.

4   *Business Week* (2002), How to fix corporate governance. Special Report. May 6, 43–50.

5   John Child and Suzana B. Rodrigues (2004), Repairing the Breach of Trust in Corporate Governance, *Corporate Governance*, 12, 143–151.

6   Russell Mokhiber and Robert Weissman (2001) September in Washington, DC http://www .corporatepredators.org62, September 7.

7   See reports issued by The Ethical Sourcing Forum. http://www.ethicalsourcingforum.com/esf-reports/.

8   Edelman Trust Barometer (2014), http://edelmaneditions.com/wp-content/uploads/2014/01/ FINAL-BROCHURE-2014.pdf, accessed May 4, 2014. This barometer is based on a survey of 33,000 people (27,000 General Public and 6,000 Informed Public respondents) in 27 countries.

9   Chartered Institute of Personnel and Development (CIPD) (2013), *Employee Outlook: Focus on Trust in Leaders*. London: CIPD. Based on a sample of 2,918 working adults. http://www.cipd.co.uk/ binaries/6348%20EO%20Focus%20Trust%20in%20leaders%20WEB.pdf. Accessed March 29, 2014.

10   Edelman Trust Barometer (2014), European Results. http://www.edelman.be/wp-content/ uploads/2014/01/2014-Trust-Barometer-Europe-FINAL.pdf. Accessed March 29, 2014.

11   M. Skapinker (2003), Building trust and profits by telling staff the truth, *Financial Times, Survey of 'Best Workplaces 2003'*, March 28, p. 2.

12   BBC (British Broadcasting Corporation) (2003), *The Banks that Robbed the World*. BBC Money Programme, January 9.

13   For an overview see Robert A.G. Monks and Nell Minow (2011), *Corporate Governance*, 5th edition, Chichester, Wiley.

14   OECD (1999), *Corporate Governance: Effects on Firm Performance and Growth*, Paris, OECD.

15   See for example, the weekly blog, *Too Much* issued by the Institute for Policy Studies Program on Inequality and the Common Good. toomuchonline.org.

16   P. Coombes and M. Watson (2000), Three surveys on corporate governance, *McKinsey Quarterly*, (4), Special edition, 74–77.

17   Mary O'Sullivan (2000), The innovative enterprise and corporate governance, *Cambridge Journal of Economics*, 24, 393–416. Quotation is from page 395.

18   G. Neilson, D. Kletter, and J. Jones (2003), Treating the troubled corporation, *Strategy+Business Enews*, March 28, http://www.strategy-business.com.

19   For example, David J. Hickson (1961), Motives of workpeople who restrict their output, *Occupational Psychology*, 35(3), 111–121; Melville Dalton (1959), *Men Who Manage*, New York, Wiley.

20   Oliver E. Williamson (1970), *Corporate Control and Business Behavior*, Englewood Cliffs, NJ, Prentice-Hall.

21   Joseph L. Bower (1970), *Managing the Resource Allocation Process*, Boston, Division of Research, Harvard Business School.

22   H. Demsetz (1992), *The Emerging Theory of the Firm*, Acta Universitatis Upsaliensis no. 33, University of Uppsala, Sweden. Quotation is from page 21.

23   John Child, David Faulkner, and Stephen Tallman (2005), *Cooperative Strategy: Managing Alliances, Networks and Joint Ventures*, 2nd edition, Oxford, Oxford University Press.

24   S. London (2001), Enron: revolution can fail the people, *Financial Times*, December 4, p. 16.

25   William Lazonick and Mary O'Sullivan (2000), *Perspectives on Corporate Governance, Innovation, and Economic Performance*, Report for EU research contract no. SOE1-CT98-1114, project no. 053, Fontainebleau: INSEAD.

26   R. Häcki and J. Lighton (2001), The future of the networked company, *McKinsey Quarterly*, 3, 26–39.

27   Child, Faulkner, and Tallman (2005), op. cit.

28   Robert A.G. Monks and Nell Minow (2011), op. cit.

29   Oliver E. Williamson (1996), *The Mechanisms of Governance*, New York, Oxford University Press.

30   Michael Carney, Eric Gedajlovic, and Sujit Sur (2011), Corporate governance and stakeholder conflict, *Journal of Management and Governance*, 15, 483–507.

31   See http://www.angloamerican.com/development/approach-and-policies/transparency-and-ethics/ethics.aspx

32   John Naughton (2013), Twitter and the transformation of democracy, *The Observer*, 14 September. http://www.theguardian.com/commentisfree/2013/sep/14/twitter-flotation-facebook-politics-social-network, accessed March 26, 2014.

33   Caspar Rose (2012), The new European shareholder rights directive: removing barriers and creating opportunities for more shareholder activism and democracy, *Journal of Management and Governance*, 16, 269–284.

34   See for example, John Child (1972), Organization structure and strategies of control, *Administrative Science Quarterly*, 17(2), 163–177.

35   Shoshana Zuboff and James Maxim (2002), *The Support Economy*, New York, Viking Books.

36   Tony G. LeTrent-Jones (2002), What lies beneath: A critical look at the role of management consulting and business education in the Enron-Andersen case, Unpublished paper. LeTrentJones@CS.COM.

37   Denita Cepiku, Riccardo Mussari, Sara Poggesi, and Christoph Reichard (2014), Special issue on governance of networks: challenges and future issues from a public management perspective: Editorial, *Journal of Management and Governance*, 18, 1–7.

38   Thomas Diefenbach (2013), *Hierarchy and Organisation: Toward a General Theory of Hierarchical Social System*, London, Routledge.

39   Andrea Calabro, Mariateresa Torchia, and Francesco Ranalli (2013), Ownership and control in local public utilities: the Italian case, *Journal of Management and Governance*, 17, 835–862.

PART V

Designing Organizations for the 21st Century

◢ Introduction to Part V – Designing Organizations for the 21st Century

Part V steps back from the detail of previous chapters to make sense of how organization can be designed to help meet the strategic business and social criteria of the present century. The twin chapters in this last part of the book reflect the two fundamental faces of organization. In one face we see organization as a set of arrangements for undertaking collective goal-directed activities in a cohesive and coherent manner. This is the side of organization that contributes to meeting strategic business needs.

Chapter 17 illustrates how each strategic business need, and different combinations of them, has a corresponding appropriate form of organization. It has become increasingly necessary to use a mix of organizational forms within the one company or system while at the same time preserving consistency and integration between them. The capability of doing this has become known as "ambidexterity." Returning to the theme of Chapter 3, a consideration of how these needs are changing helps us to make better sense of how organizational forms are evolving and tending to become increasingly complex.

Chapter 18 turns to the other face of organization, in which we see a set of arrangements that distributes power, rewards, and personal wellbeing. If this aspect of organization is seen to be failing, it will have deleterious performance effects as well as calling the legitimacy of business into question. Deficiencies in this aspect of organization are not only undermining trust within companies and public institutions; they are also threatening the social contract that underpins society at large. Some firms have taken organizational initiatives that address this problem.

CHAPTER 17

Meeting Strategic Business Needs

WHAT THIS CHAPTER COVERS

Previous chapters have identified an increasing variety of organizational forms. New forms are being developed, while at the same time conventional forms persist. The aim of this chapter is to make sense of this varied picture in the wider economic context, and to consider emerging developments. The conventional approach to organization developed historically in relatively stable and simple environments. Under such conditions, it can promote efficiency through its emphasis on clarity of responsibilities and conformity to rules. These attributes are conducive to accountability, predictable behavior and low managerial over-heads, but they can inhibit innovation and adaptability. However, Chapter 3 indicated that very few firms, or even public organizations, operate under stable and simple conditions any more.

The need for innovation and adaptability has therefore become significantly more important. At the same time, financial pressures from market competition or from tight budgets mean that efficiency and cost effectiveness continue to be a further requirement. Organization has to be designed in ways that reflect the balance between these various pressures. They can justly be called "strategic business needs" because the performance, even survival, of organizations depends on meeting them.

Understanding these three strategic needs – innovation, adaptability, and efficiency – can help us to make sense of organizational design choices. This chapter illustrates how each need and different combinations of them is reflected in an appropriate form of organization. Contemporary thinking recognizes the necessity of using a mix of organizational forms within the one company or system while at the same time preserving consistency and integration between them. The ability to do this is expressed by the idea of ambidexterity. The aim of achieving ambidexterity is to be able to manage complexity.

Strategic Needs

Chapter 3 described the general trends that are today impacting heavily on organizations. In the public sector, pressures to cut costs in view of high government budget deficits are being accompanied by the penetrating exposure by social and other media of service failures. Whereas in business, there are very few sectors in which the intensity of competition is not increasing. The internationalization of competition and the entry into markets of new competitors from countries like Brazil, China, India and South Korea are very evident. Particularly significant is the fact that these new cost-effective competitors are catching up fast on technology and product design. One of the consequences of the globalization of markets is that the distinction formerly drawn by Michael Porter between two types of competitive advantage that firms could aim at – lower cost and differentiation – is now breaking down.[1] Firms competing in open markets must increasingly seek to develop both cost and differentiation advantages. Their value proposition has to be based on both the price of their product or service and its intrinsic worth. Much the same combination of requirements applies to public organizations which are facing pressures to find costs savings while at the same time improving standards.

Cost advantages may derive from cheap inputs, especially labor; otherwise they have to be achieved through superior *efficiency*. Efficiency has a physical basis, as with economies of scale and high productivity. There is also an important organizational contribution to efficiency, such as when administrative overheads are kept low and jobs are highly focused on activities that add greatest value. Differentiation advantages can derive from the capability to provide distinctive and superior products through *innovation*. They can also come from the ability to respond to rapid changes in the market or to customized requirements – this is the ability to be *adaptable*. Very often a strong foundation for successful differentiation rests on a combination of innovation and adaptability. However, there are forms of adaptability that do not necessarily depend on innovation. These are more a question of being able to select quickly, and efficiently, from an existing portfolio of capabilities to meet a customer need than to have to develop something new. All three strategic needs are relevant to all organizations, though their relative significance will vary. Designing organizational arrangements to facilitate the satisfaction of multiple strategic needs presents a particularly difficult challenge.

This chapter examines the implications for organizational design of the fundamental strategic needs to which organization has to be attuned – *innovation*, *adaptability* and *efficiency*. I shall start by considering each need separately. This offers the opportunity for some clarification, especially in the case of innovation, and to summarize the aspects of organizational design that support the activities required to meet each need. I continue by considering combinations of strategic needs. After pursuing this perspective which is oriented toward the economic contribution of organizational design, the next chapter then turns to its social implications. Here the question concerns the impact that the form of organization has on the community, environment and wider society. The overriding issue then becomes how the design of organization can support social responsibility while remaining functionally effective as well.

Innovation

The stimulus to innovate arises from several sources. One is the growing sophistication of generally well-educated consumers who collectively account for the greatest purchasing power. These are purchasers located in developed countries and in the rapidly developing regions of emerging economies such as China's coastal cities. Such consumers are demanding more complex and elaborate products and services. They are attracted by the continuous development ("improvement") of existing products and the invention of new ones. Smart phones, tablet computers, and the software that drives them, are familiar examples. The increasing complexity of products leads to a growing heterogeneity of inputs to be supplied for their production, especially as firms take advantage of trade liberalization and improved global information in order to outsource activities to suppliers can offer the most competitive transactions.

Another stimulus to innovation has come from the other end of the income scale – the realization that new business opportunities lie in providing goods and services for poor communities located at "the bottom of the pyramid," especially in developing economies.[2] It is argued that companies can help eradicate poverty by providing goods and services for the four billion people who live on less than $2.50 a day and profit from this market, although its aggregate purchasing power remains a matter of debate. Much of the innovation to suit bottom of the pyramid consumers is operational, requiring new ways of distributing, sizing and paying for products, but some also requires new designs such as low power consumption products.

The pressure to offer steady improvements to most products except basic staples curtails their life cycles and adds to the pressures for innovation. Rita McGrath has argued that the 21st century challenges of fluctuating competition, short-lived opportunities and constant challenge means that a competitive advantage in Porter's terms is always under threat and temporary. This places an absolute premium on innovation. It means that companies have to adopt policies of constant early-stage innovation. Compared to their competitors, companies must generate more ideas, implement them more rapidly and be faster to abandon those that fail.[3]

Exploration and exploitation in the innovation process

The innovation process encompasses both the generation of new ideas and their application in the form of products or services that are attractive to the market. These two aspects correspond to James March's dichotomy between the generation or "exploration" of new knowledge, and its "exploitation."[4] Exploration is commonly associated with fundamental or radical innovations, while exploitation is associated with incremental innovations that build upon what is already known. So, while exploration is often described as "basic research," exploitation is frequently described as "applied research," "development" or "implementation." Exploitation can also take the form of upgrading and efficiency improvements, in both cases applying existing knowledge.

Fundamental questions arise over (1) the relationship between these two aspects of innovation and (2) whether they can be organized as distinct stages in the overall innovation process or whether the required speed to market is nowadays often so short that ways need to be found to carry out exploration and exploitation simultaneously, or at least with considerable overlap. The responses to these questions are highly consequential for the design of appropriate organizational support. The conventional approach has been to identify exploration and exploitation as separate activities that place conflicting demands on a company's resources or may even be conducted by different organizational units. I shall accept this assumption for a while, so as to indicate separately the organizational implications of exploration and then exploitation. I then qualify the assumption in order to discuss some more complex considerations.

Exploration, or new idea and knowledge generation, tends to be encouraged by an organizational context that stresses the significance of creativity but is non-directive over the exact form it takes. Exploration is also encouraged by the presence of active communication networks to enable the exchange of new ideas both within and between organizations. The kind of organizational approach supportive of creative exploration activity incorporates many of the attributes of new organizational forms identified in Chapter 3, in particular:

- A fuzzy definition of organizational roles and their boundaries.
- Distributed initiative and authority – high levels of autonomy in carrying out tasks.
- Open and intensive communications.
- Use of teams.
- Systems of accountability focused on the achievement of research targets.
- Rewards in terms of autonomy and recognition; also opportunities to participate in financial reward from innovations.

Organizational design features such as fuzzy roles, job autonomy, and open communications are easier to achieve within small units. In the attempt to boost their performance in basic drug research, some companies like Aventis and GlaxoSmithKline have decentralized their research activities into smaller teams of scientists from various disciplines who exchange information and knowledge intensively within their units. They are also encouraged to network closely with universities, biotech firms and other pharmaceutical companies. However, these units tend to be highly specialized, working in very strongly delineated niches. This can create a barrier to cross-fertilization between them as well as a barrier to integration with other functions in the company when the development stage is reached.[5] Chapter 3 noted how the Danish hearing aid company, Oticon, adopted an autonomous team approach in order to boost its creativity and achieve basic innovative breakthroughs. This led to a significantly improved stream of product innovations, but it also gave rise to problems of coordination among projects and to managerial control loss.

Successful exploration will lead to a demonstrable "proof of concept" or similar indication that new concepts or theories have the potential for real-world application. However, this does not necessarily mean that a marketable idea or prototype has emerged. It only indicates the likely operational and financial viability of new concepts. The fruits of exploration need to be exploited. Exploitation is broadly synonymous with the development of the output from exploratory research. The emphasis in exploitation is on refining new ideas or prototype products so that they match buyers' requirements or anticipated market demands, in terms of specification and price. Other categories of personnel now have a significant role to play in decision-making. Production engineers or other operational specialists can advise on the feasibility of putting new concepts into routine production. Cost accountants can advise on what the emerging outputs will cost. HR specialists can advise on the availability and training needs of the people who will staff production and, possibly, after-sales support. There may also be a requirement for legal advice concerning a range of issues ranging from safeguarding the intellectual property embodied in the new product to its health and safety aspects. Throughout the exploitation process, the contribution of marketing and staff in direct contact with potential customers is particularly crucial since commercialization is innovation's acid test.

Successful exploitation therefore depends on a mode of organization which will help provide sufficient integration of the wider range of required specialized contributions. Two organizational arrangements, discussed in Chapter 5, are candidates to achieve this. One is the cross-functional product development team which brings together different contributors and their perspectives. If the development process is long and complex, the membership of cross-functional teams can be varied to suit different stages and priorities within that process. The other arrangement is the project champion who steers and coordinates the development process as well as speaking on behalf of the innovation project with higher management. A project champion should be a person of sufficiently high standing within the organization as a whole both to enjoy the respect of the development team (which he or she might formally lead) and of higher management whose continued support for and understanding of the project is vital to its success. The combination of cross-functional team and project champions should provide valuable support to exploitation projects.

There is a caveat to what has just been said. I have focused on the type of exploration and exploitation that takes the form of specific projects and often requires a sizable investment. But just as Chapter 13 distinguished the contributions that planned change (usually periodic and often large-scale) and emergent continuous change can both make, so one cannot assume that all innovation is, or should be, planned. Exploration can result from chance discoveries even made by individuals. Chapter 14 noted that the 3M Corporation has organizational arrangements to encourage and allow space for bottom-up unplanned innovations, some of which, like the "Post-It Note" have contributed massively to the company's fortunes. Similarly, exploitation can arise from suggestions by individual organization members or from informal discussions that a company encourages. It may establish a formal framework for such discussions, as with "quality circles," as well as for their high-managerial support, but their contribution to exploitation does not necessarily follow a formal agenda.

At this point, I need to qualify the earlier assumption that a clear distinction can be made in practice between exploration and exploitation within the ambit of innovation. In fact, the relation of exploration to exploitation has been a matter of keen debate over several questions. What are their independent and interdependent effects? Is there a trade-off between them in terms of resource allocation? Does a focus on one run the risk of driving out the other, especially if they each compete for resources and if the optimum organizational forms to support them are contrasting? James March in his pioneering distinction between exploration and exploitation envisaged a trade-off between them implying that, if both have a necessary contribution to make, some kind of balance between them has to be achieved:

> It is clear that exploration of new alternatives reduces the speed with which skills at existing ones are improved. It is also clear that improvements in competence at existing procedures make experimentation with others less attractive . . . Finding an appropriate balance is made particularly

difficult by the fact that the same issues occur at levels of a nested system – at the individual level, the organizational level, and the social system level.[6]

A contrasting view is that there may be important synergies between exploration and exploitation at each of the system levels that March mentions. This means that it is misleading to view the relation between the two only in terms of a trade-off and competition for resources. These synergies arise for several reasons. It is exploration that provides the scientific and technological advances that open up possibilities of profitable exploitation. Exploitation depends on the outputs from exploration, whether these are produced in the same firm or from collaborating firms. An example of the latter occurs when biotech companies feed new research-based formulations into pharmaceutical companies for their exploitation in the form of field trials, securing regulatory approval, and commercialization. The other side of the coin is that the experience of exploitation and commercialization can provide valuable feedback information for identifying promising avenues for further fundamental research (exploration). Also, the profits from successful exploitation may help to fund exploration. So, in contrast to the view that there is tension between exploration and exploitation, a focus on their potential synergies highlights the resource complementarities between them.

Although exploration and exploitation are distinct activities, the importance of potential synergies between them point to the drawbacks of separating them organizationally. It is true that specialization between them reflects inherent differences in the nature of work and people involved, and their cultures, and in this respect it is beneficial. It may therefore be appropriate to have different units within the same company, or even different companies, specialize on exploration and exploitation respectively. As Lavie, Stettner, and Tushman point out, exploration and exploitation can be conducted separately in several ways – through being situated in different organizational units; through coexisting in the same organization but being carried out at different points in time; or through being carried out in separate units within the same organization.[7] Nevertheless, as we saw in Chapter 5, it is a fundamental organizational insight that specialization ("differentiation") has to be balanced by the degree of integration necessary to realize interdependencies and synergies between the specialized activities.

There are several dangers of separating fundamental research from its implementation, either within the same company or between companies. Exploration may be commercially misdirected or even not taken forward into development, while exploitation (development) may be starved of usable new concepts and prototypes. A classic case of this happening is the experience of Xerox, whose Palo Alto Research Centre (PARC) was located in Silicon Valley almost 3,000 miles away from the company's main center of operations. PARC produced a stream of breakthrough new technological inventions most of which were not adopted by the company but instead were successfully commercialized by competitors such as Apple.[8] The extract in Box 17.1 clarifies how this was due to a failure of organization.

Li and Liu argue that the relationship between exploration and exploitation is a paradoxical duality. On the one hand, there is an inherent trade-off between the two activities when it comes to focus and resourcing. On the other hand, they are fundamentally complementary and offer vital potential synergies. Li and Liu's empirical study of 508 Chinese firms supported this duality perspective, finding that exploration and exploitation had partially independent effects on both radical and incremental innovation as well as some interdependent effects.[9] They suggest that the challenge for management and organization is to achieve the minimum

BOX 17.1   XEROX – LACK OF ORGANIZATION TO LINK EXPLORATION AND EXPLOITATION

Through the 1960s and early 1970s, Xerox invested in a series of very innovative technology development research efforts. Xerox managed this research effort by creating a stand-alone research laboratory (Xerox PARC, in Palo Alto, California) and by assembling a large group of highly creative and innovative scientists and engineers to work there. Left to their own devices, these scientists and engineers developed an amazing array of technological innovations including the personal computer, the "mouse," windows-type software, the laser printer, the "paperless office," Ethernet, and so forth. In retrospect, the market potential of these technologies was enormous.

Unfortunately, Xerox did not have an organization in place to take advantage of these resources. For example, no structure existed whereby Xerox PARC's innovations could become known to managers at Xerox. Indeed, most Xerox managers – even many senior managers – were unaware of these technological developments through the mid-1970s. Once they finally became aware of them, very few of the innovations survived Xerox's highly bureaucratic product development process – a process where product development projects were divided into hundreds of minute tasks, and progress in each task was reviewed by dozens of large committees. Even those innovations that survived the product development process were not exploited by Xerox managers . . . Xerox's formal reporting structure, its explicit management control systems, and its compensation policies were all inconsistent with exploiting the valuable, rare and costly-to-imitate resources developed at Xerox PARC. Not surprisingly, Xerox failed to exploit any of these potential sources of sustained competitive advantage.

Source: Jay B. Barney. Looking inside for competitive advantage, *Academy of Management Executive*, 9(4), 1995, pp. 56–57.

trade-off and maximum synergy between exploration and exploitation. I shall return to the implications of the relation between exploration and exploitation for organizational design later on when considering the idea of "ambidexterity."

Examples such as the Xerox experience demonstrate that there is a need to encourage active communication and shared understanding between creative research staff and their colleagues who are closer to the operating and commercial end of a business. This is especially important when research (exploration) and development (exploitation) are intended to be sequential stages in the innovation process. A pioneering, and particularly insightful, investigation into the factors favoring the commercial success of innovation projects in two industries, chemicals and scientific instruments, highlighted the key importance of a strong user-orientation and attention to marketing throughout such projects. The successful innovators also performed their development work more efficiently, eliminating technical problems before products were launched. A further characteristic of successful innovating firms was that they had better contacts with the external scientific community and made better use of outside scientific and technical advice.[10] The results of this and subsequent studies indicate that a key organizational requirement is to link a firm's creative and technical experts with those in other functional areas who will then have to take the project forward. It is normally appropriate to arrange for some marketing input at the very beginning of the innovation process. Then during the development/exploitation phase, other specialists – from the production, quality, accounting and finance, HR, legal, distribution, and customer support areas – have essential contributions to make. While the successful commercialization of innovations clearly depends on new knowledge and research in the first place, it also requires a sound understanding of production costs and other practicalities and, above all, customer needs and wants.

At the development stage, the focus is on how new knowledge can best be exploited and adapted to the market. From the perspective of successful commercialization, it is necessary to find ways to bring different professional contributions to bear and to integrate these, while at the same time avoiding the danger of unduly delaying, even suffocating, the project. This returns us to the way exploration and exploitation are organized in relation to each other within the innovation stream. There has to be both an appropriate balance and degree of integration between exploration and exploitation activities in an attempt to avoid two pitfalls. One pitfall lies in inadequate attention to, or resourcing of, exploitation, so that research investment is wasted on new ideas that do not meet user needs, or a firm's reputation is damaged by launching products in the marketplace before technical problems have been ironed out. Another pitfall lies in an inappropriate organization of exploration so that creativity is stifled by too much behavior control over how the staff involved carry out their work.

Adaptability

The second fundamental strategic need to which organization has to be attuned is adaptability. Here it is important to distinguish between adaptability and adaptation. Adaptation is one way in which available knowledge or existing designs are exploited. They are modified to suit a particular need or purpose. This modification normally entails some incremental innovation. For example, the specifications of core software programs are often modified or elaborated through additional design work to suit different customer requirements. Adaptability, by contrast, is the capacity to adjust rapidly to new circumstances. It requires flexibility in the sense of being able to respond rapidly to customer requirements or other changing circumstances. Although this may entail some incremental innovation, this is not necessarily the case because an organization's flexibility may lie in a capacity to rapidly assemble or configure a set of existing tasks or technologies. An example of this is the "same-day" bespoke tailoring services available in many East Asian cities, in which new orders from customers walking into the shop are rapidly met using traditional methods but coordinated through an extremely efficient network of local subcontractors. General (community) medical practice is another example of an occupation in which high adaptability is essential. Every day, physicians face a wide range of client needs which are often not known in advance and which they have to diagnose and respond to rapidly. However, that response does not normally involve applying any new knowledge or technique. The distinction between adaptability and adaptation through incremental innovation is an important one because the two strategic needs do not carry the same implications for organizational design.

The most crucial requirement for competitive adaptability lies in the rapid communication of new information and the ability to respond quickly to it. Organizational arrangements therefore have to be put in place to ensure closeness to the customer or scene of action. There has to be provision for relevant decisions to be taken quickly and for any resources necessary to support those decisions to be marshalled rapidly and flexibly. However, unlike the case with innovation, the nature of appropriate action to meet new circumstances may be well known and understood. This can permit some aspects of conventional organization to be applied such as the standardization of action categories and procedures, the formalization of relevant technical specifications, and possibly a clear definition of the roles to be undertaken. The following organizational features support adaptability:

- The provision of specialized roles for maintaining close contact with customers or clients in the relevant external environment. The means of contact can vary. It may, for example, be achieved through personal meetings with customers, or through direct selling using the telephone or Internet. The key requirement is to become aware of any changes in customers' needs as early as possible.
- The delegation of authority to make decisions rapidly in response to new information from the market or other clients.
- Systems that specify the actions to be taken in response to new requirements or developments – if such responses fall into already known categories they can benefit from codification and preparatory training.
- Clear specification of who has the authority to call upon resources, allocate staff and ensure their coordination, so as to provide a rapid response to new situations. Who has this authority may depend on the significance of the situation (its urgency, its importance for the organization, etc.) and on who has direct knowledge of it (see Box 17.3 below).

Efficiency

Efficiency is the most pervasive of the strategic needs. Even a firm that is securing considerable differentiation advantages through rapid innovation or effective adaptability cannot neglect its efficiency without incurring some loss of profit. If intrinsically superior products and services have to be offered at an inflated price because of producer inefficiencies, this means that customers are being offered less than optimal value for money. It opens the door to competitors. When firms compete on the basis of differentiation but incur high costs, they face the threat that lower-cost imitators or "followers" will enter the market and undermine their position. An increasing number of emerging economy multinational companies are today exploiting a competitive advantage deriving from their insight into customer needs combined with low cost production and innovation.[11] In other words, whichever way a firm chooses to organize, it has to be done efficiently. Outside the field of competitive business, in the public sector where services are paid from taxation and where a consistent standard of delivery is expected, efficiency is often the overriding criterion by which the success of the agency is judged.

It is a strength of conventional forms of organization that their rule-based practices are intended to enhance efficiency under stable conditions. Being based on relatively simple single-dimension structures, they are also inherently economic in themselves. When they have failed to be economic, as when they build up an excess of administrative staff, this often points to a pathological condition such as an unwarranted accumulation of hierarchical levels, rather than to a fault that is necessarily inherent in the organizational approach itself.

The following organizational features are oriented toward efficiency needs:

- Clear definition of the specialized responsibilities attached to roles within the organization.
- Differentiation of roles to accord with levels and areas of responsibility (i.e. hierarchy and specialization of function respectively).
- Systems of control focused on accountability for the performance of responsibilities.
- Units controlled and coordinated by higher management.
- Simple structures in order to reduce administrative cost and to maximize the visibility of leaders.
- Clear and transparent provisions for rewarding organizational members according to how well they perform their roles.
- Use of rules and standard practices as repositories of accumulated experience and knowledge.
- A strong organizational identity and commitment to it among staff ("esprit de corps").

The widespread opinion that the conventional organization of the past is no longer suited to present-day needs runs the risk of ignoring its potential benefits, which are to administer collective activities efficiently, reliably and impartially. In cases where these remain important criteria – sometimes the most overriding ones – we therefore have to ask whether and to what extent we should discard the accumulated organizational wisdom of the past 4,500 years which achieved some very impressive results.[12] Should we be open to thinking in terms of refining conventional organization when this is appropriate rather than replacing it wholesale? Could this, on the other hand, lead to mixed, modular or hybrid forms of organization which are very challenging to manage? These are the kind of questions that arise when we now turn to consider the organizational implications of different strategic needs in the light of the desired balance and relationship between them. The concept of ambidexterity helps to identify the issues that are involved.

Combinations of strategic needs

AMBIDEXTERITY

Ambidexterity is a concept that draws attention to the need to balance and reconcile the requirements of different strategic needs.[13] It has been specifically applied to balancing the requirements of just two needs associated primarily with innovation – exploration and exploitation – which, as Turner and his colleagues note, "is both a theoretical and a practical challenge."[14] However, the concept can usefully be extended to having the capability of (1) balancing more than one strategic need, and to (2) finding ways of organizing and managing so as to accomplish this balance as well as to achieve a flexible coordination of the activities that address the multiple needs. Chapter 12 noted how this capability is essential for operating the "transnational" model of multinational organizations.

Some writers see ambidexterity as characterized by the ability to manage the separation of organizational tasks that meet different strategic needs – exploration and exploitation in particular. This separation could be temporal (focusing on exploration and exploitation at different times depending, for instance, on prevailing competitive conditions), or organizational (having separate units carry out exploration and exploitation). Other views on ambidexterity place greater emphasis on realizing the potential synergies between different activities through organizational arrangements that improve their ability to adapt to change in a coordinated manner. The idea of "contextual ambidexterity" has been proposed which refers to a managerial and behavioral capacity to achieve an appropriate alignment or coherence between separated activities while at the same time being able to adapt them to changing circumstances or priorities. It is suggested that contextual ambidexterity requires an organizational context which encourages individuals and teams to make their own judgments as to how to handle the conflicting demands that can arise in maintaining ambidexterity.[15]

For successful innovation, both structural differentiation and integration are normally required.[16] This takes us back to the paradox noted in Chapter 5 that a structural differentiation between intrinsically contrasting activities has to be balanced by methods to ensure adequate integration between them when their contributions to the overall goal of an organization are interdependent. This is particularly the case when exploration and exploitation are part of the same innovation stream. For example, Tushman and his colleagues concluded from a study of innovation streams that ambidextrous designs were relatively more effective than other designs such as functional, cross-functional and spin-out designs. Ambidextrous designs were defined as "those designs that coupled high structural differentiation with targeted linkage and senior team integration."[17] So, although some studies lend empirical support for the organizational partitioning of exploration and exploitation,[18] such partitioning benefits from adequate control and coordination. This conclusion also applies to situations where the two activities are conducted by different companies. The respective specialization of biotech and pharmaceutical companies in the exploration and exploitation of new drugs is a case in point.

Turner and his colleagues suggest from their review of available research that three methods can help to achieve ambidexterity, in terms of allowing some differentiation between different strategic activities while also integrating them to secure potential synergies and an appropriate balance between them. Organizational design (which Turner et al. call "organizational capital") is one of these methods. The others are to build "social capital" including knowledge-sharing relationships, and to foster "human capital" including the vision, quality and flexibility of managers. These "soft" integrating mechanisms have been recommended as approaches that are particularly suited to fostering collaboration and motivating the growing number of knowledge workers.[19] An important practical implication highlighted by the research into ambidexterity is that its achievement depends on capabilities and processes at levels below that of an organization as a whole. Interfaces between organizational sub-units and key individuals, and the skills to handle communications between them in the light of changing situations emerge as essential to make ambidexterity a reality, so as to combine the generation and development of ideas within small units with the effective sharing of such ideas with other units.[20] This is consistent with the notion of "contextual ambidexterity" mentioned above.

Although the term ambidexterity has been interpreted in a variety of ways, there is consensus that it arises from the recognition that an organization has to pursue more than one strategically key activity and that the challenge therefore arises of how to maintain a balance and/or combination of the several activities. Investigations have shown with reasonable consistency that ambidexterity is associated with firm performance, especially rate of growth. It appears that the achievement of ambidexterity at the level of the organization as a whole has a stronger performance effect than ambidexterity at lower levels. Also the benefits of ambidexterity for performance have emerged as more marked in service industries, possibly because many of these are knowledge-intensive firms operating in more dynamic environments where the need to explore new opportunities as well as to exploit existing resources is acute.[21]

Organizing for different combinations of strategic need

Ambidexterity is the underlying aim for organizational designs intended to support different but complementary strategic needs. I now discuss how the principle of ambidexterity can be applied to organizing for various combinations of strategic need. In order to analyze as simply as possible the strategic choice confronting firms, I start by focusing on the relative *weight* given to each of the two foundations of strategic differentiation – adaptability and innovation – and then later consider how to balance these with the need to maintain efficiency.[22]

Adaptability and innovation

Figure 17.1 provides examples of organizations that fall into the categories identified in terms of high and low needs to adapt and innovate respectively. The existence of several categories serves as a reminder that different firms, or the various units within a firm, do not necessarily operate within identical environments.

Two categories can be distinguished among organizations that are confronted with high needs to be adaptable. The first category (box A in Figure 17.1) includes those organizations

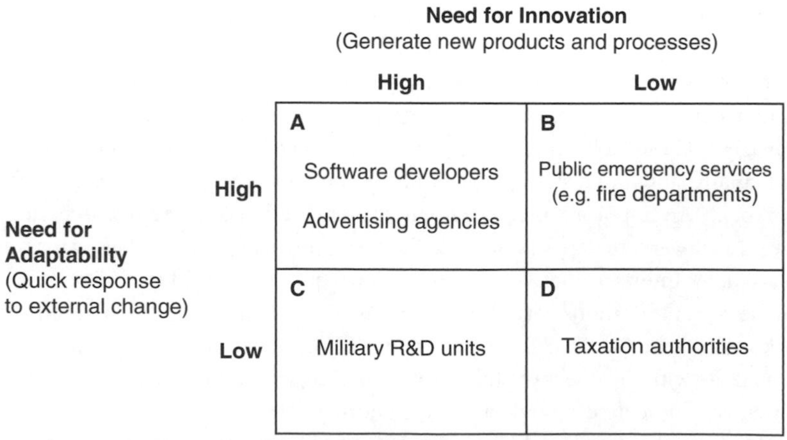

		Need for Innovation (Generate new products and processes)	
		High	**Low**
Need for Adaptability (Quick response to external change)	**High**	**A** Software developers Advertising agencies	**B** Public emergency services (e.g. fire departments)
	Low	**C** Military R&D units	**D** Taxation authorities

Figure 17.1 Examples of high and low needs for adaptability and innovation

that have to be both adaptable and innovative. Companies offering to develop new software for clients will have to adapt, often under time pressures, to the special circumstances that may accompany a new commission. Although much software can be written from existing modules, it may well be necessary to create new software as well, or at least to develop aspects of existing software. Advertising agencies find themselves in a similar situation. They have to adapt at frequent intervals to clients' requirements for new innovative campaigns and other services, or to the needs of new clients, within the context of a highly competitive industry.

When a firm needs to be both highly adaptable and highly innovative, this translates into two main organizational requirements. It has to employ an organizational arrangement that will allow for changing market requirements to be analyzed and inform the firm's innovative activities. This has to be combined with an organizational form that will also stimulate the learning and innovation that are needed to meet these requirements. In the case of an advertising agency, market requirements are normally expressed by a brand manager or account executive who is in direct contact with clients and can articulate their wants in terms of performance, delivery and price. In this highly competitive industry, clients often impose very tight timetable and budget demands on the agency. The preferred organizational mode for generating the creativity required for a new advertising campaign is the project team comprising various creative specialists in areas such as graphics, copy, and production. The link between innovation (exploration) and adaptability to client requirements (exploitation) is normally achieved by the participation of account executives in project meetings.

This solution combines a "vertical" leadership mode that has the legitimacy of market criteria behind it, with a predominantly "horizontal" team working mode. This combination presents a major organizational design challenge because of inherent conflicts in this situation between market and artistic criteria, which are heightened by budget and time pressures. The ADD agency in Box 17.2 provides an illustration.

Companies or other organizations in the second category (B) do not have to compete or justify their existence through innovation. They are faced with new demands on their activities, the *nature* (technology) of which can be known in advance, though *when* they will occur cannot. The public emergency services provide a typical example. They can devise standard procedures for handling different types of emergency, and on the whole the nature of these emergencies does not change appreciably in the short-to-medium term. All public services are expected to be efficient, so as not to waste taxpayers' money and to provide a fair and effective service. A conventional organizational form should suit this requirement. An emergency service nevertheless needs to be organized in a way that permits it to respond rapidly to a critical incident when it arises and to be sufficiently flexible in the deployment of resources to cope with the unique scale and scope of the incident. This means that a unit that has high adaptability needs but a relatively low need for innovation can be organized along conventional bureaucratic lines, so long as it includes among its portfolio of procedures ones that enable it to cope with sudden changes. In other words, it requires a capacity to "modulate" between different organizational forms. The case of the fire-fighting services in California, summarized in Box 17.3, illustrates this point.

Military R&D units and companies developing fundamentally new high-technology products and systems fall into category (C). Organizations in this category are required above all to achieve innovation. They may be facing keen competition from rival innovators, but they can program their projects over a time-period that is sufficient to avoid the need to

BOX 17.2 ACCOMPLISHING ADAPTABILITY AND INNOVATION THROUGH GUIDED TEAMS

The ADD agency faces the need to generate a new campaign for each of its client companies approximately every three months. Clients expect most campaigns to be new products, with new copy and new visuals, even when they wish to maintain certain themes or values through different campaigns. Some advertisements also have to be adapted to suit different cultures, markets and media. The agency's contact with its clients is channeled through "account executives." They provide the vital client interface for the agency and are highly sensitive to client requirements, which can change frequently even at a late stage of formulating a new campaign. Account executives represent the client's wishes to the creative teams that are formed for each new commission. Specialist scriptwriters, designers, and production people usually comprise the core of each team, but accountants, media planners and various advisors also come to meetings as required. Account executives attend key team meetings, especially at the formative stage of the campaign, when possibilities need to be checked with the client and when presentations are being prepared and given. There are frequent conflicts between account executives and creative personnel over how to apply the different criteria of adapting to the client's wishes and innovating in a manner that is profession-ally satisfying and perceived to be good for the agency's reputation. There can also be disputes between creative staff and the company's accountants or senior managers over campaign budget overruns.

Source: Author's personal research.

adapt to short-term external changes. NASA's program to land astronauts on the moon was a prime example.

An organization with high innovation needs has to establish arrangements that can both stimulate invention and later on apply that creativity to a useful outcome (innovation). The initial requirement is to identify people who can provide promising ideas, and to open up channels to new ideas and other relevant information that may come from outside the organization such as from the scientific activities of universities. Initial ideas are likely to be relatively uncoded and abstract, so a further step is to refine ideas into more specific, codified and hence usable new knowledge. As already indicated, the cross-functional team is a favored organizational arrangement to achieve this result. It can bring people together who represent different relevant specialties and perspectives, including scientific, engineering, accounting, and commercial.

If the process of innovation can be allocated a specific time period and is not subject to frequent changes initiated by customers, it should be possible to accomplish the work through relatively stable project teams with appropriate membership changes even planned in advance. These teams can be resourced and controlled through budgets and plans that incorporate progress milestones. Through the flexible self-organization of tasks, the teams themselves can

BOX 17.3   AN ADAPTIVE BUREAUCRATIC SYSTEM

Gregory Bigley and Karlene Roberts studied the way that fire departments in California cope with suddenly occurring and potentially massive fires, such as forest fires. The fire departments can classify the different types of fire that can occur singly or in combination, including forest fires, chemical fires, fires involving domestic dwellings, and so forth. However, they do not know in advance which kind of fire will break out next. When it does, they must respond quickly, and on the spot.

The fire departments in collaboration with the California Department of Forestry and state and federal governments, have devised the "incident command system" (ICS), which is today used widely throughout the United States and applied to a wide range of emergency situations. ICS denotes a particular approach to assembly and control of the highly reliable, temporary organizations employed by many firefighters, police, and other public safety professionals to manage diverse resources at a wide variety of emergency scenes. The ICS is a basically bureaucratic standardized system that produces remarkably flexible and reliable arrangements for handling complex, volatile, and risky task environments.

Bigley and Roberts identified three main features that enable the ICS to work effectively. The first of these involves various structural mechanisms to permit rapid on-the-spot adaptability. Such mechanisms include the ad hoc building of local resources and teams, activating roles according to the immediate needs of the situation, reallocating authority according to need and the expertise of staff who are available, and immediate changes to fire-fighting plans when necessary. The second feature is the allocation of considerable discretion to incident commanders and supervisors to improvise rules and routines within the broad terms established by the organization's objectives and performance criteria. The third feature is the building up over time of a shared understanding of operational conditions that is realized through intensive communications.

The research undertaken by Bigley and Roberts suggests the possibility of new organizational forms able to capitalize on the control and efficiency benefits of bureaucracy, while at the same time avoiding or overcoming the considerable tendencies toward rigidity that are thought to accompany bureaucratic systems.

Source: Gregory A. Bigley and Karlene H. Roberts, The incident command system: high reliability organizing for complex and volatile task environments, *Academy of Management Journal*, 44, 2001, pp. 1281–1299.

handle their internal needs for adaptability, for example in the light of unexpected technical problems.

A team, commissioned to develop a new mini computer, illustrates the flexible self-organization of tasks to achieve a major innovation within a specified time period (Box 17.4).

The fourth category (D) comprises organizations that do not have a high need for either adaptability or innovation. This means that they can adopt efficiency as their main operational

BOX 17.4   THE INNOVATIVE TEAM

A brilliant and aggressive team of young computer wizards working for the US company data general was given one year to design and make a new mini computer. In his graphic account of the team's progress over that year, Tracy Kidder describes how the members of the team worked for long hours, often under intense pressure, largely from a sense of commitment to the challenge of the task. The team, the "eclipse group" was largely self-organizing:

> "The entire eclipse group, especially its managers, seemed to be operating on instinct. Only the simplest visible arrangements existed amongst them. They kept no charts and graphs or organizational rules that meant anything. But those webs of voluntary, mutual responsibility, the product of many singings-up, held them together . . . of course, someone who favored rigid control might have felt ill at the spectacle . . . in fact the team designed the computer in something like six months and may have set a record for speed." (p. 111)

Source: Tracy Kidder, *The Soul of a New Machine,* Harmondsworth, Penguin 1982.

criterion, concentrating on performing routine activities in the most cost-effective and efficient way. There is a danger that all the attention that is being given to changes in the environment and to new organizational forms can obscure the fact that some organizations still exist in this category. I have argued that efficiency is in any case always a continuing strategic need. This is because it contributes to maintaining cost advantage, which is necessary within any firm's competitive strategy. It also helps to meet political expectations that public services will provide value for money. Some routine functions within firms, such as payroll administration, will also be charged with meeting efficiency needs first and foremost.

The activities of routine organizations continue to have a significant impact in society and to employ large numbers of people. There are fewer such organizations among business companies than before, but they remain relatively common among the governmental and other public institutions of society. The taxation and civil law enforcement authorities in most countries would be examples. For such organizations, the conventional form of bureaucracy remains the most appropriate form of organization, because efficiency, incorruptibility and reliability remain the primary attributes we expect of them. Box 17.5 provides an example of a government agency dedicated to law enforcement. The agency was required to enforce given legal regulations, using established practices and referring to formalized guidelines, rather than innovating or even adapting to circumstances in any major way.

Hybrid organizational forms

Every firm or public institution will have its own combination of innovation, adaptability and efficiency needs arising from the basis on which it chooses to compete in the marketplace or justify its role to the public. Priorities between these needs will also vary between different

BOX 17.5   A GOVERNMENT BUREAUCRACY

A US federal agency was responsible for the enforcement of practices designed to bring about the uniform application of the provision of federal laws by business companies. This required the inspection of business establishments to ensure faithful adherence to these laws, which were relatively new at the time. The main duties of the agents were therefore carried out in the field. Firms to be investigated were assigned to them individually by a supervisor. Agents had to evaluate the reliability of the information they obtained and then decide whether violations had taken place on the basis of a large and complex body of legal regulations. Every agent was in possession of a manual containing over 1,000 pages of regulations, to which he or she constantly referred. When as was often the case, the manual did not suffice, an agent would consult the volumes of administrative explications and court opinions, which occupied two library shelves [They would today, of course, be computer files – *author*].

Source: Peter Blau, *The Dynamics of Bureaucracy*. Chicago: University of Chicago Press, revised edition 1963, chapter VII.

activities within the same firm. For example, R&D will normally score high on innovation need, product promotion and production-to-order will score high on adaptability need, while quality control, the production of standard products, and routine support services, will all score high on efficiency need. Galbraith suggests that even under complex and fast-moving modern conditions, large companies consist of a stable as well as a variable part.[23] This accounts for the internal variation in modes of control, coordination and work organization that is evident within many firms, and which Chapter 12 noted was particularly characteristic of multinational corporations. It also helps to explain survey findings suggesting that new organizational forms are complementing rather than replacing conventional ones.[24] Organizational forms are often hybrid in nature and an identification of the contrasting needs they are called upon to support helps to make sense of this internal diversity.

Nicolai Foss has distinguished two classes of hybrid organizational form.[25] "Internal hybrids" are forms of organization that infuse hierarchy with elements of market control, such as devolving responsibility for attaining agreed goals to project teams that enjoy a high level of autonomy in deciding about how to conduct their work. Incentives might well be offered to such teams to focus and motivate their efforts toward goal attainment. The combination of a high level of self-direction with an incentive element amounts to the incorporation of control through quasi-market means alongside, and partially in replacement of, hierarchical control. The hierarchical element remains in that progress may continue to be monitored at intervals in respect of achievement, costs incurred, behavioral ethics, and so forth. External hybrid forms are market exchanges that are infused with elements of hierarchical control. These include outsourcing arrangements, virtual value-chains and alliances, examples of which were discussed in Chapters 9, 10 and 11. External hybrid forms incorporate aspects of hierarchy into their contractual relations in order to gain various benefits. Such benefits can include optimizing operational integration through the application of standardized protocols, controlling the use of proprietary knowledge, and introducing a personal element into external relationships that allows trust to develop.

The idea behind hybrid forms is to meet two or more of the strategic needs I have identified and to accommodate the different modes of working and managing that are appropriate to each. With the exception of firms in category D that do not have significant adaptability or innovation needs, such needs have to be balanced against the continuing need for efficiency. The experience of the Danish hearing-aid company, Oticon, provides an illustration of the need for this balance and also of how difficult it can be to achieve. Box 3.2 in Chapter 3 described the highly devolved, flat, and flexible form of organization that Oticon had introduced in 1990 in order to boost its flagging ability to innovate in a highly competitive market where new product development was essential for success. Although this radical organizational form proved to be highly effective in boosting the company's new product development performance, it decided in 1996 on a partial retreat to a more conventional matrix structure. This move can be explained largely in terms of the unanticipated costs (efficiency losses) that the highly devolved form had incurred.[26] These costs arose from problems of coordinating employees who were not restricted in the number of projects they could join, the failure to track the use of employee time on different projects, and the over-complexity of systems that had been developed to monitor employee behavior. Interventions by management to correct these problems had serious de-motivating consequences because employees saw this as arbitrary behavior that was inconsistent with the company's declared bottom-up philosophy.

As a result, the company focused its activities through the introduction of three business teams. This amounted to the addition of an extra layer of management. It also established a "Competence Center" to take charge of all projects and their financing and of an operational group to control administration, IT, logistics, sales and exports. The leaders of the business teams, together with the head of the Competence Center and the CEO comprise a "Development Group" that was now in charge of overall strategy formulation and also provided most of the initiatives for starting new projects. This introduction of additional hierarchy and formalization appears to have avoided some of the efficiency losses incurred by the previous organizational form without necessarily impeding the company's capacity to innovate. Although it broke with the bottom-up approach it had previously adopted, Oticon retained a considerable devolution of initiative. The changes the company introduced after 1996 were an attempt to improve its efficiency while retaining its capacity to innovate.

Oticon's experiment was an attempt to shift the balance within its organization from an emphasis on control through centralization and hierarchical relationships towards the encouragement of innovation through self-organization. It was not easy to get this balance right, especially as it requires the addressing of multiple strategic needs through hybrid organizational forms. As the case of Eli Lilly in Chapter 12 also illustrated, it can become horrendously complicated to manage with contrasting organizational forms within the scope of a single firm. Accusations of inequitable treatment could easily arise when different activities are subject to different forms of control and styles of management. Confidence could be lost in a management whose calculated inconsistency of organizational form could easily be mistaken for incompetence. This is one of the reasons why many firms have dis-aggregated the organization of their different activities and networked them in a loosely coupled manner, giving each activity its own identity and goals within a strongly defined overall corporate mission.

This process is taken one step further through the use of modular organizational forms for production or other value-adding systems. These involve external hybrid arrangements such as outsourcing and the construction of value chain networks of different firms that are bound together through contracts and partnerships. The use of modular forms appears to be encouraged by heterogeneity in inputs and outputs within the value chain, and hence likely variation in the organization of each module in the system. As Chapter 10 described, when such networks are coordinated on a virtual basis, tightly integrated information flows and the strict application of technical standards provide for the necessary control over the value chain.[27] A virtual network can readily cope with a variety of organizational forms among its members, so long as they all adhere to standard technical and operational protocols. This solution is being used increasingly both for manufacturing and for service provision. Continued advances in ICT are reducing its costs and increasing its technical feasibility. It has the considerable virtue of combining all three of the basic needs I have identified without the intolerable strains that could accompany the attempt to achieve this combination within the same organizational unit.

Miles and his colleagues predict that firms in rapidly developing and high innovation sectors such as ICT will adopt a network kind of organizational design which they call "a collaborative community." This will enable them to achieve a flexible and rapid assembly of multiple specialized capabilities which are constructively integrated and offer economies of scale and experience. They comment:

> "We believe that a viable new organizational type is presently available, as pioneering managers and firms have succeeded in bringing together the capabilities, structures, and processes to create *collaborative communities* of independent firms capable of producing virtually continuous product and market innovations."[28]

Miles et al. identify two types of situation in which this large-scale multi-party collaboration can help the successful pursuit of global opportunities or, particularly in the public sphere, resolve global problems. One situation is that typically found with large strategic alliances such as the Star Alliance among airlines where a large number of actors share a common goal which they can best attain if they agree to provide their complementary contributions to the larger system in a coordinated manner (see Chapter 11). Another situation is increasingly relevant to dealing with common problems such as climate change and resource shortages. This is where organizations and governments jointly hold and rely on a resource such as water which collaboration can help to preserve and even augment. They argue that:

> "The process of large-scale collaboration places heavy strains on existing forms of organizing, which typically are based on hierarchy as the primary means of coordination and control. Hierarchy, however, is not well suited to managing the collaborative process, particularly collaboration that extends beyond the boundaries of the firm. Therefore, pioneering firms in knowledge-intensive, rapidly evolving environments are experimenting with organizational designs that are less reliant on hierarchy."[29]

It is possible, then, to make a lot of sense of new organizational forms by reference to the increasing importance of meeting strategic needs for innovation and adaptability. In competitive markets, the increasing reliance on differentiation strategies is increasing the salience of both these needs. Yet at the same time, organizational arrangements still have to meet efficiency needs, which are especially important in some sectors and for some routine activities within organizations. The combinations of strategic need give rise to different mixes of organization in which conventional elements usually coexist with new forms. Attempts to create efficient yet creative and adaptable organizations are therefore giving rise to various forms of integrated differentiation. Differentiation can be achieved through:

- Using multiple organizational forms for different activities and processes within a company, as illustrated by the Eli Lilly case.
- Disaggregating value chains through outsourcing, alliances and networking, which results in smaller modular units each of which can be differently organized to suit the tasks it is performing.
- Building in practices and procedures that permit the organizational mode to switch between dealing with routine and new events, thus allowing rapid response to the latter. This approach has sometimes been called "modulation" between organizational forms, and an example was given in Box 17.3.

Increasing organizational differentiation in these ways implies the devolution of initiative and decision making as well. It becomes inappropriate, and indeed impossible, to provide the necessary integration between different units and activities primarily through hierarchical coordination. The sheer complexity of the system precludes this.[30] An attempt to impose hierarchical constraints would not only generate major delays but also vitiate the direct contributions to creativity and adaptability that are required from organizational members or partners. Accordingly, integration within these new organizational forms has to depend primarily upon a number of arrangements that have been examined in previous chapters:

- The common use of standardized protocols and specifications for transactions between differentiated units.
- The use of ICT to enable instant and precise communication of market-led requirements between members of the value chain.
- Direct personal relations based on trust between the members of teams and networks, especially to handle non-routine matters requiring negotiation, problem-solving and the like.

SUMMARY

1   The conventional approach to organization developed historically in relatively stable and simple environments. It emphasized control and was suited to promoting efficiency through its emphasis on clarity of responsibilities and conformity to rules.

2   These attributes are conducive to accountability, predictable behavior and low managerial overheads, but they can inhibit the meeting of two strategic needs that

tend to dominate under the more complex and dynamic competitive conditions of today. These needs are for innovation and adaptability.

3 Nevertheless, financial pressures from market competition or from tight budgets in the public sector mean that efficiency and cost effectiveness continue to be a strategic requirement.

4 Organization has to be designed in ways that reflect the balance between these various pressures. They can justly be called "strategic business needs" because the performance, even survival, of organizations depends on meeting them.

5 These three strategic needs – innovation, adaptability, and efficiency – speak for different approaches to organization. It is a major challenge to devise organizational forms for the increasingly common situation in which all three needs have to be catered for simultaneously.

6 Contemporary thinking recognizes the necessity of using a mix of organizational forms within the one company or system while at the same time preserving consistency and integration between them. The ability to do this is expressed by the idea of ambidexterity. The aim of achieving ambidexterity is to be able to manage complexity.

7 Newer approaches to combining the differentiation and integration of activities have been considered in this book. Examples include coordinated outsourcing, networked value chains using elements of virtual organization, strategic alliances. Guided or targeted team-working is frequently used to support innovation and adaptability within such arrangements.

QUESTIONS FOR DISCUSSION

17.1 Why do you think conventional forms of organization continue to be used in practice, despite the many criticisms leveled against them?

17.2 What are the different strategic business needs that organization is expected to support as a set of arrangements for achieving goals through collective activity?

17.3 Which forms of organizing are most likely to help promote successful innovation?

17.4 How might hybrid organizational arrangements help companies to meet different strategic business needs simultaneously?

17.5 What do you understand by the concept of "ambidexterity"? What are the different forms it can take as a way of conducting qualitatively different activities within the same organization?

17.6 What do you understand by "a collaborative community"? Provide some examples of this form of inter-organizational cooperation.

17.7 The present chapter, as well as others in this book, has talked about "new" forms of organization. Do you think they are really new and, if so, in which ways?

NOTES

1   Michael E. Porter (1985), *Competitive Advantage*, New York, Free Press.

2   Stuart L. Hart and Clayton M. Christensen (2002), The great leap: Driving innovation from the base of the pyramid, *Sloan Management Review*, 44, 51–56; Prahalad, C-K. (2005), *Fortune at the bottom of the pyramid: Eradicating poverty through profits*, Upper Saddle River, NJ, Wharton School Publishing.

3   Rita G. McGrath (2013), *The End of Competitive Advantage*, Boston, MA, Harvard Business Review Press.

4   James G. March (1991), Exploration and exploitation in organizational learning, *Organization Science*, 2(1), 71–87.

5   Paola Criscuolo and Rajneesh Narula (2007), Using multi-hub structures for international R&D: Organisational inertia and the challenges of implementation, *Management International Review*, 47(5), 639–660.

6   Reprinted by permission. James G. March (1991), Exploration and exploitation in organizational learning, *Organization Science*, 2(1), 1991, pp. 71–87. Copyright 1991, the Institute for Operations Research and the Management Sciences (INFORMS), 5521 Research Park Drive, Suite 200, Catonsville, MD 21228 USA.

7   Dovev Lavie, Uriel Stettner, and Michael Tushman (2010), Exploration and exploitation within and across organizations, *Academy of Management Annals*, 4(1), 109–155.

8   Jay B. Barney (1995), Looking inside for competitive advantage, *Academy of Management Executive*, 9(4), 49–61.

9   Peter P. Li and Heng Liu (2012), Exploration-exploitation balance as a duality of tradeoff and synergy, unpublished paper, Copenhagen Business School. On this duality, see also M. Farjoun (2010), Beyond dualism: stability and change as a duality, *Academy of Management Review*, 35, 202–225.

10 Science Policy Research Unit (SPRU) (1971), *Project SAPPHO: A Study of Success and Failure in Innovation*, University of Sussex, 2 vols. See also Christopher Freeman (1974), *The Economics of Industrial Innovation*, Harmondsworth, UK, Penguin, especially Chapter 5.

11 Ravi Ramamurti (2012), Competing with emerging market multinationals, *Business Horizons*, 55, 241–249.

12 Ancient Egypt provides one of the earliest examples of an administration which was highly organized along conventional lines and was capable of achieving considerable feats of collective effort such as the construction of the three pyramids at Giza around 2500 BC.

13 See Lavie et al. (2010), op. cit., pp. 129–135.

14 Neil Turner, Juani Swart, and Harvey Maylor (2013), Mechanisms for managing ambidexterity: A review and research agenda, *International Journal of Management Reviews*, 15(3), 317–332.

15 Cristina. B. Gibson and Julian Birkinshaw (2004), The antecedents, consequences, and mediating role of organizational ambidexterity, *Academy of Management Journal*, 47(2), 209–226.

16 Justin J.P. Jansen, Michiel P. Tempelaar, Frans A.J. van den Bosch, and Henk W. Volberda (2009), Structural differentiation and ambidexterity: The mediating role of integration mechanisms, *Organization Science*, 20(4), 797–811.

17 Michael Tushman, Wendy K.Smith, Robert Chapman Wood, George Westerman, and Charles A. O'Reilly III (2010), Organization designs and innovation streams, *Industrial and Corporate Change*, 19(5), 1331–1366. "Spin-out" designs had a distinct innovation unit without general manager control and/or senior team support, whereas ambidextrous designs had general manager control and senior team support.

18 See the studies mentioned by Turner et al. (2013), op. cit., p. 324.

19 Jetta Frost, Margit Osterloh, and Antoinette Weibel (2010), Governing knowledge work: Transactional and transformational solutions, *Organizational Dynamics*, 39(2), 126–136.

20 Neil Turner and Liz Lee-Kelley (2012), Unpacking the theory on ambidexterity: An illustrative case on the managerial architectures, mechanisms and dynamics, *Management Learning*, 44(2), 179–196; Christina Fang, Jeho Lee, and Melissa A. Schilling (2010), Balancing exploration and exploitation through structural design: The isolation of subgroups and organizational learning, *Organization Science*, 21(3), 625–642.

21 Paulina Junni, Rikka M. Sarala, Vas Taras, and Shlomo Y. Tarba (2013), Organizational ambidexterity and performance: A meta analysis, *Academy of Management Perspectives*, 27(4), 299–312; Charles A. O'Reilly III and Michael L. Tushman (2013), Organizational ambidexterity: Past, present, and future, *Academy of Management Perspectives*, 27(4), 324–338.

22 March (1991) in his seminal article regarded efficiency as an aspect of exploitation. He also included implementation and execution in exploitation, which could refer to what I am calling adaptability. The difference arises because March's point of reference was organizational learning, whereas our point of reference is market-oriented strategic need.

23 Jay R. Galbraith (2010), The multi-dimensional and reconfigurable organization, *Organizational Dynamics*, 39(2), 115–125.

24 Andrew M. Pettigrew and Evelyn M. Fenton (eds.) (2003), *The Innovating Organization*, London: Sage; Andrew M. Pettigrew et al. (eds.) (2003), *Innovative Forms of Organizing*, London, Sage.

25 Nicolai J. Foss (2003), Selective intervention and internal hybrids: Interpreting and learning from the rise and decline of the Oticon Spaghetti Organization, *Organizational Science*, 14(3), 331–349.

26 Nicolai J. Foss (2003), op. cit.

27 Melissa A. Schilling and H. Kevin Steensma (2001), The use of modular organizational forms: An industry-level analysis, *Academy of Management Journal*, 44, 1149–1168.

28 Raymond E. Miles, Charles C. Snow, Øystein D. Fjeldstad, Grant Miles, and Christopher Lettl (2010), Designing organizations to meet 21st-century opportunities and challenges, *Organization Dynamics*, 39(2), 93–103. The quotation is from p. 97.

29 Miles et al. (2010), op. cit., p. 100.

30 Shona L. Brown and Kathleen M. Eisenhardt (1998), *Competing on the Edge: Strategy as Structured Chaos*, Boston: Harvard Business School Press; Rita G. McGrath (2013), op. cit.

CHAPTER 18

Meeting Strategic Social Needs

WHAT THIS CHAPTER COVERS

There are growing pressures for companies and institutions to be socially responsible. The need to respond constructively to these social pressures is also a strategic one because the continued legitimacy of business and public bodies, and ultimately their survival, depends on doing so. This social perspective shines a light on the other face of organization, as a set of arrangements that distribute power, rewards and the conditions for well-being. If the organizational form in use fails to meet people's expectations in these respects, not only the legitimacy but also the performance of a business are likely to suffer. This chapter notes the presence of deep-seated failures in society that are, in part at least, attributable to the way in which business is organized. It also presents examples of how some companies are addressing the problem in a constructive manner. The overall purpose of the chapter is to consider how organizational design can help to reconcile social responsibility with other strategic needs.

As mentioned in Chapter 3, organization has two faces. One face is organization as a system for allocating and managing work so as to achieve certain strategic objectives. Here, organization makes an essential contribution to adding value that is primarily economic. The other face is organization as a means for differentiating and allocating power and reward. This applies particularly to the hierarchical aspect of organizational structure. In this respect, organization is a distributive mechanism that is socially very sensitive. Organization is therefore never just a technical issue. It also has a major impact on the level of economic and other benefits (such as personal fulfillment at work) that people receive. The value that organization adds, or takes away, in social terms can be judged by the extent to which it sustains personal well-being and avoids excessive inequalities and differences in peoples' life chances.

The analysis offered by Chapter 17 focused on the first face of organization, whereas this chapter is concerned with the second face. Ideally, organization should be designed so as to serve both economic (business) and social purposes together. In practice, this seems to happen rather rarely, which presents companies with a significant challenge at a time when they are expected to be socially responsible.

The previous chapter referred to strategic business needs to understand some key recent developments in thinking about organizational form. These included a de-emphasis on hierarchy in favor of enlisting the contributions of members on a more devolved and cooperative basis. Clearly, an organization's performance depends on its people: on their capabilities and their motivation to use them. Evidence is accumulating that "progressive HRM policies" can facilitate the achievement of strategic needs and in that way contribute to better company performance. These findings endorse the so-called "resource-based perspective of the firm" insofar as they indicate the special value that people can offer as "human resources." The policies in question entail moves away from many of the features of conventional organization. They include teamwork and decentralization, narrow status differentials and plentiful open communication. Other components in these policies involve the protection of employees' interests and an investment in people – policies such as employment security, careful recruitment, extensive training and personal development, and generous levels of pay with an incentive element tied to performance.

On the basis of his review of research into HRM and organizational performance, Paauwe makes a plea for progressive HRM to be regarded as an "enabler" for a whole range of strategic options. He writes:

> "Enabling" implies that the HR architecture's main goal is the development of a workforce with a sufficient degree of flexibility/adaptability to implement a range of strategic options. This places high demands upon employees, since they need to be eager to learn and display a ready willingness to change and to be adaptable and flexible. Of course, this is only possible once the organization has taken proper care of employees' needs and has ensured that they are treated fairly and with due consideration for their well-being. So the HRM system should be based not only upon added value, but also on moral values.[1]

The argument that an HRM system should be based on moral values implies that more is at issue than just people as resources. People also have their own concerns which center on providing a livelihood for themselves and their families and ultimately being able to enjoy respect and dignity as human beings. It is no coincidence that a condition for the success of HRM policies is that people are given some assurance of security based either on a guarantee of continuing employment or sufficient investment in developing their capabilities so that they can survive on their own account. There is a lesson here that carries over to forms of organization and the way they are used. If they impose significant personal costs on people and threaten them, they are very likely to demotivate and even alienate them from their work. Ultimately, socially dysfunctional forms of organization run the risk of undermining the legitimacy of corporate management and even the whole business system. As we shall see, there is evidence that conventional modes of organization are having negative effects, which result in alienation and a loss of managerial legitimacy. If anything, the gap between people's expectations of working in or for organizations and what they actually experience is increasing. This problem gives a further impetus to the search for alternative organizational forms, and in the long run may prove to be the most important single criterion to be applied to them.

The view I adopt in this chapter is that moral criteria should be applied to all aspects of organization and how these impact on people at work and in the community. This approach places the notion of Corporate Social Responsibility (CSR) at the core of management. It means, however, that CSR is not to be practiced merely as a superficial PR exercise or as compensation for deficiencies at work through, for instance donating conscience money to charity or the community. Rather, it means that CSR should involve an examination of the very structures and processes of organization and management so as to ensure that they have a positive impact on employees, consumers, the environment, communities and all other members of society who can be considered as stakeholders. This is further than many companies are prepared to go at present, though as we shall see, there are some notable (and generally very successful) exceptions. Critics have therefore suggested that many professions of CSR are merely window-dressing. Such window-dressing could be designed to ward off the potential restrictions that governments in their roles as watchdogs may place on powerful multinational corporations; or it may be part of a promotional policy intended to gain favor with consumers and enhance market share; or it may be an attempt to (re)gain corporate legitimacy in the wake of highly publicized scandals.

The aim of this closing chapter is to elaborate on the assertion that how we choose to organize has significant consequences not only for economic performance but also for the health of society and the people in it. My argument is that conventional forms of organization are helping to create a major social problem. The new forms of organization I have described in previous chapters reduce this problem to a certain extent, though they do not resolve it entirely. The next section outlines the social problem and the negative contributions of conventional organization to it, especially hierarchy. I then illustrate how alternative approaches can mitigate the problem and at the same time offer performance advantages.

The Social Problem

It is clear that all is not well with contemporary organizations, especially "big business." Their managers are experiencing a serious loss of trust on the part of employees. There is a rapid growth of income inequality between people located at the top and bottom of organizations. The psychological and health-related costs of working in organizations are rising every year. Increasing numbers of people are seeking to quit employment in large organizations in order to find fulfillment in self-employment or working in small communities. I now examine each of these problems before considering how they are exacerbated by inappropriate organization, especially hierarchy.

Loss of trust

Employee mistrust of their employers is not a new phenomenon. Its association with perceived conflicts of interest and alienation from work has been recognized for a long time. Social scientists have seen these phenomena as endemic within the capitalist system and enhanced by institutions that grant primacy to shareholder interests. Nevertheless, following the Second World War, many companies made strenuous efforts through training and development, job enrichment programs, and corporate culture building to enhance the attachment and trust their employees felt towards them. These efforts were encouraged by the shift in employment towards categories of people who would be relatively responsive to them, notably female, white-collar and knowledge workers, and they also coincided with a secular decline in trade union membership.

Although popular confidence in corporations did appear to grow for a while on both sides of the Atlantic, the picture has changed markedly in recent years. Chapters 15 and 16 reported evidence from surveys indicating that levels of trust in companies and business leaders are declining worldwide. There can be no doubt that there is widespread mistrust of business today among people, in their roles as employees and members of the public.

Growing inequality

There has been a dramatic widening of differentials in reward between people at the top and bottom of firms. The trend in the United States is shown in Box 18.1. More specifically, by 2013 the ratio of CEO-to-worker pay had increased 1000 percent since 1950 according to data from Bloomberg. In 2013, Fortune 500 CEOs made 204 times the pay of regular workers on average. This ratio of 204-to-1 had risen from 120-to-1 in 2000, 42-to-1 in 1980 and 20-to-1 in 1950.[2] Income inequality is greater in the United States than in Europe (particularly Northern Europe), but lower than in most Latin American countries.[3]

This situation has had several very harmful consequences. The prospect of such huge rewards, especially when bolstered by stock options, has led some top managers to act in ways that are detrimental to their firms. They have jacked up short-term profits instead of focusing on long run opportunities, and they have disregarded paying out dividends to their share-holders.[4] There have been many claims that firms cannot afford pay rises for their ordinary employees while at the same time awarding huge rises to under-performing top managers.

For instance, on the same day, December 16, 2002, the *Financial Times* carried two reports. One featured the fact that Tony Isaac, chief executive of the British Oxygen Company received a 47 percent pay increase despite a second consecutive year of falling profits. The other report mentioned that average pay settlements for manufacturing employees were running at 2.3 percent and those for service sector employees at 3.7 percent. It is not surprising that "fat-cat pay" has become a divisive social issue incurring the wrath both of employees and shareholders. What is more surprising is that the yawning income gap has continued to widen with many more cases of high CEO pay rises regardless of performance.

Even the prospect of receiving a steady level of pay has been eroded, at least in the UK, by the increase in the number of employees on so-called "zero-hours" contracts. These contracts provide payment only for hours worked and place people on call without specifying any hours or times of work. It is instructive to quote the conclusion of a report concerning the effects of this development:

> It is possible that zero-hours contracts may suit some groups of workers employed on them . . .
> [However] given the potential for work on a zero-hours contract to negatively impact on the
> management of household budgets, to impinge on family commitments, to undermine employment

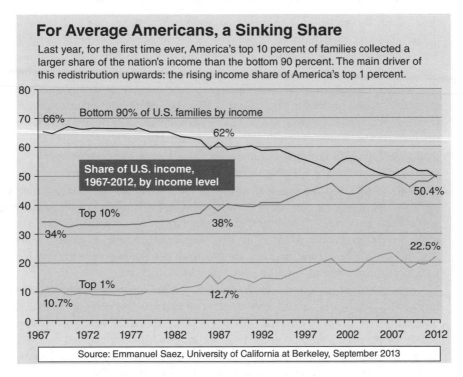

Figure 18.1 Share of US income 1967–2012, by income level.
Source: Too Much, December 2, 2013, Washington, DC: Institute for Policy Studies, editor@toomuchonline
.org.

rights and relations, and to complicate access to tax credits and other benefits, the continued rise in their use is of growing concern. Yet their impact also extends beyond those working under them, impacting on staff morale, team cohesion and turnover in a way that can damage the quality of the service being provided.[5]

Psychological and health-related costs

There is mounting evidence that working in organizations today is taking a rising toll of people's health. For example, a total of 27 million days were lost in 2011/12 in Britain due to occupational illness – primarily stress. This figure had risen from 18 million days lost in 1996.[6] The cost of absence for British business rose to £13.8 billion ($22 billion) in 2010/11. Surveys in the United States indicate that stress at work "has become a common and costly problem in the American workplace, leaving few workers untouched."[7] It was reported that people working in large organizations rely on spiritual therapies worth £670 million in order to cope with the demands of employment.[8] Stress is, of course, a complex issue and it is difficult to identify its precise causes, but it is likely that hierarchical and bureaucratic modes of organizing work contribute to the problem. The reasoning behind this statement is as follows.

The tendency for people who occupy higher positions in society (i.e. belong to a higher social class) to enjoy superior health and longevity is a statistically demonstrated phenomenon replicated across many societies.[9] Once a minimum economic threshold has been reached, the position people occupy relative to others in the same society is a more consistent predictor of their personal health than is their absolute standard of living. We have seen how income differentials have risen dramatically between people working at different organizational levels. Since organization impacts directly in this way upon income differentials, it must be assumed that the effect on the health of ordinary employees has become increasingly negative.

A further negative health impact of how people are being organized also arises from its non-economic effects on them. The reason is that the greater the hierarchical differentiation between people, the greater the differences between them in their status, self-esteem, and personal control of work, as well as in their income.[10] A study of a large cohort comprising over 18,000 male UK government employees found a strong association between the grade of employee and mortality rates. Men in the lowest grade (messengers, doorkeepers, etc.) had a mortality rate three times higher than that of men in the highest grade (administrators). A second cohort was set up in 1967 comprising approximately 10,300 male and female government employees. This suggested that the way work is organized and the work climate were two factors that contribute to the declining social gradient in health. The implication is that variations in health and longevity are due to the fact that as people rise up a hierarchy they gain increasing power to determine how they work and live.[11]

Large-scale organization adds to the problem. Larger organizations typically contain more hierarchical levels and exhibit greater personal distance between people at the top and bottom.[12] From this perspective, downsizing and delayering can have positive benefits for the quality of people's working lives if they are introduced on a planned basis that does not threaten personal security. Larger organizations also tend to be more bureaucratic, and this is another source of frustration for the people who work in them. The US National Institute for Occupational Safety and Health identifies negative features of bureaucracy, such as poor communications, a low sense of autonomy in carrying out tasks, and a lack of participation in decision-making, as among the organizational conditions that can lead to stress.[13] People with the most valuable competencies, based on a high level of professional training and experience, are the most likely to have this negative experience. They tend to regard attempts to control their activities through formal job definitions and the imposition of rules as unnecessarily constraining their ability to apply their informed judgment to specific cases.[14] The considerable increase in paperwork that has accompanied the bureaucratization of sectors such as the UK National Health Service further frustrates medical and other professionals by reducing the time they can devote to the work for which they were trained. Many physicians are choosing to retire early, with an accompanying loss of their valuable skills.[15]

Desire to escape from large organizations

Despite the rise in home working, many people still spend a large part of their adult lives working in organizations. Research suggests that such employment plays a central role in the formation of people's self esteem and identity in industrial societies, yet for reasons just outlined the experience of work and the workplace in large organizations is often found to be limiting and even damaging. It appears that, as a result, an increasing number of people are seeking to leave modern large organizations and choosing alternative forms of work.[16] These include self-employment and working in small communities of a cooperative nature. A common feature of these alternatives is that they free the people concerned from the managerial constraints and associated values imposed on them by conventional organizational forms.[17]

◢ Organization as a Culprit

No doubt part of the problem just outlined has to be attributed to human failings such as the misuse of their power by senior executives. Therefore any form of organization is liable to be used for personal advantage if it distributes information and authority differentially. Nevertheless, there are certain common organizational features that of themselves are liable to accentuate the problem. Hierarchy, the backbone of conventional organization, comes in for particular censure.

Hierarchical control and coordination has enabled outstanding collective achievements, such as the building of the Egyptian pyramids, the ancient empires of China and Rome, the medieval church in Europe, and the modern business corporation. Hierarchy, it seems, embodies a wisdom born of experience about how to organize complex activities that involve quite large numbers of people. But this means it is equally possible that hierarchy has over time simply become "conventional" – embedded in our expectations and very convenient for leaders to preserve.[18]

Hierarchy has certainly come in for a lot of criticism.[19] Nevertheless, most companies that have grown beyond the small start-up stage, and virtually all public organizations, seem to find it very difficult to do without hierarchy. Evidence from surveys in Europe, Japan and the United States indicate that innovations in organization have, on the whole, supplemented rather than replaced hierarchy and other features of "conventional organization."[20] The characteristics of new organizational forms discussed in Chapter 3, and summarized in Table 3.2, signal a less centralized and more consultative use of hierarchy rather than its actual abolition.

What lies behind this persistence of hierarchy? Some of the reasons are ostensibly rational, and linked to the need for efficiency discussed earlier in this chapter. From this perspective hierarchy:

- Gives a focus to leadership.
- Distinguishes between levels of authority and responsibility.
- Separates routine from non-routine decision-making.
- Allocates managers according to levels of responsibility and decision-making.
- Permits tasks and responsibilities to be defined and supervised by managers directly in charge of work at different levels.
- Provides for coordination and control.

Other reasons for the survival of hierarchy are, however, more political than rational in nature. This is the side of hierarchy that panders to some of the weaknesses in human nature and certainly the one that leads it to cause social problems. From this perspective, hierarchy:

- Offers some people better rewards than others, often on the basis of seniority rather than performance.
- Indulges people's needs to feel more important than others.
- Gives people a sense of personal progression through promotion up the ladder.
- Legitimizes the exercise of power by some people over others.
- May provide people with a sense of security that comes from feeling that they are "in good hands" – i.e. have good leaders.

More precisely, what is it about hierarchy that helps to engender the social problems mentioned earlier? The answer lies in the way that it is the source of the two-faced nature of organization mentioned in the preamble to this chapter. Hierarchy is a means for getting work done through allocating tasks and responsibilities, as well as coordinating and controlling that work. At the same time, hierarchy is a basis for distributing rewards, privileges, and powers differentially, and for creating different social identities. Fundamentally, this means that any organization based on hierarchy divides people at the same time as it endeavors to unite them. On the one hand, hierarchy provides a vertical division of labor for allocating the different decisions and tasks to be undertaken within a collective effort. On the other hand, it takes on the attributes of a status and authority ladder. It is indicative how the term "superior" is commonly used in descriptions of hierarchies, which implies that for every superior there must be an inferior!

It is this basic paradox in hierarchical organization that contributes to the social problem mentioned earlier. The so-called "breach of trust" between senior managers and other employees stems in large measure from a perceived inconsistency in the criteria that are applied to the well being of people at different hierarchical levels of an organization, often accompanied by a veil of secrecy. We have already seen how pay differentials between the top and bottom of large organizations have grown out of all proportion to the respective contributions that are made. The divorce of reward from contribution among executives has been notorious in the case of the "too big to fail" banks. The payment of generous bonuses to bank executives despite performance failures is a particularly stark example of apparent contempt for public opinion. For example, in February 2014, the 81 percent publicly-owned Royal Bank of Scotland sparked wide public outrage after what the Unite trade union called its "astonishing betrayal" to taxpayers in paying £576 million in bonuses despite going further into the red with annual losses of £8.2 billion.[21] The MG-Rover automobile firm provides another example. The company collapsed in 2005. It later came to light that the five directors had siphoned off £42 million in pay and pensions while the firm was failing and when its employees faced the loss of their jobs. The directors refused to discuss these payments publicly and details of their self-serving conduct only came to light four years later following a government investigation.[22]

The distance that hierarchy creates between members of the same organization encourages secrecy of this kind and this makes corporate abuses easier to hide. If it were not for these effects of hierarchy, it is unlikely that executive pay would have become an issue of such contention as to attract the label of "scandal." The reforms that Chapter 16 suggested to improve corporate governance within firms are all measures that aim to reduce hierarchical distance. They involve greater transparency of information, the rights of employees to share in ownership benefits, monitoring behavior upwards as well as just top-down, and greater participation in decision-making.

Organizational contributions to social responsibility[23]

The problems just outlined have led to the view that an alternative to hierarchy and other features of conventional organization is necessary on social grounds, over and above any dividend it may bring for performance. A performance dividend is indeed expected on the basis that committed and contented members of an organization will give more to it. This also brings in the other face of organization, given that contemporary conditions place a premium on innovation and adaptability. A capability to innovate and to adapt depends much more on the willingness of an organization's members to work together constructively and intelligently than it does on the ability of managers to command or apply established organizational rules.

As we have seen, there is plenty of evidence pointing to the negative effects of organizational hierarchy. At the same time, hierarchy is a persistent phenomenon. Although some of this persistence has to be attributed to the self-interested reproduction of differences in power and privilege, the regularity with which the number of hierarchical levels is associated with organizational size suggests that there may be inherent drivers towards hierarchy in today's mega-organizations. Realistically then, the question we have to ask is not what can be done to abolish hierarchy, but rather what can be done to (1) reduce it and/or (2) offset its socially negative effects.

Reducing hierarchy

Chapter 4 discussed how a direct reduction in hierarchical levels can come through "delayering." In recent years, this has been associated with the break-up of organizations into smaller units and the shedding of activities and employment through outsourcing.[24] In view of the close relationship between hierarchical levels and total employment, delayering normally requires downsizing. In principle, moves toward smaller organizational units should also be beneficial in reducing the alienation that stems from the impersonality of the large organization over and above its hierarchical character. A distinction was drawn in Chapter 4, however, between downsizing in a manner that clearly harmed employees' interests and could leave considerable psychological scars and "responsible restructuring" in a manner that built upon the suggestions of employees and was acceptable to them. Movement in a socially acceptable way towards a combination of smaller sized and less hierarchical workplaces would undoubtedly tend to mitigate some of the psychological costs of modern employment.

The substitution of horizontal for vertical coordination through teamworking may also facilitate some delayering. However, while a reduction in hierarchical layers and organizational size may improve the ability of employees to know what is going on, if only through informal communication, it does not necessarily alter the underlying asymmetry of power within organizations; nor does it necessarily reduce senior management's ability to manipulate parameters such as rewards and employment conditions in its own interests.

There are companies that have tried to minimize hierarchy and its negative effects, as well as adopting other new forms of organization. Not many of them have been reported and even fewer emulated, despite their often dramatic success. Two often-discussed examples are Southwest Airlines in the USA and Semco in Brazil. They illustrate very successful practical applications of new organizational thinking.

SOUTHWEST AIRLINES[25]

Southwest Airlines, founded in 1966, has become one of the most successful airlines in history. Southwest has topped the list of most admired airlines in the world each year since 1997. It was one of the first cut-price airlines flying initially on very limited routes. By 2013 it had become a

$19.34 billion business, serving 96 American cities and employing 45,000 people. As soon as the company was founded, competitors like Braniff Airlines and Texas International used every legal and political strategy to keep it grounded. They failed to do so. Since it first became profitable in 1973, the company has never recorded a loss and it rode the post 9/11 crises in the industry far better than any other major US airline.[26]

From its inception, Southwest encouraged its employees to identify with their colleagues in the company, to deliver customer service, and to have fun in their work. Its motto is "We are a company of people, not planes." Southwest has been recognized as a top-10 employer among *Fortune's* list of "America's Most Admired Companies" since the program began in 1993. People want to work for it. For instance, in December 2013, 10,000 people applied for 750 openings to work as flight attendants for Southwest Airlines in just two hours and five minutes.[27]

Southwest has also achieved a remarkable level of productivity, which sustains its low fares services. In 2010, it had an average of 63 employees per aircraft, whereas American, Continental, Delta and United each had over 100.[28] This high productivity is not, however, simply the product of a relaxed and employee friendly corporate culture. The company has also pushed its employees to the limit. They are paid about the industry average, but are expected to work harder through undertaking extra unpaid duties. The company has in fact had a number of labor disputes although only one full-blown strike. One dispute was with its flight attendants over their pay in relation to the effort and flexibility expected of them. Labor relations are said to have deteriorated since the retirement of co-founder Herb Kellerher.[29]

Competitors have tried to imitate the Southwest model, including its focused route planning. They include America West, Reno Air, Kiwi Air, United, Continental, US Airways, and Delta. The competition understands the technology, cost structures and route planning. They have the same equipment, locations and market knowledge. Yet they have been unable to replicate Southwest's success largely because they have not adopted its approach to organization and people.

What kind of approach does Southwest follow? Basically, it respects people whether they are employees or customers. Box 18.1 lists the salient features.

1   *Job security.* The company has never had any redundancies, even in the wake of September 11. However, it has in recent years experienced several disputes over

---

BOX 18.1 SOUTHWEST AIRLINES

- One of most successful airlines in history.
- A leader in productivity.
- Competitors have tried to imitate its strategy, but failed to replicate its success because they did not adopt its approach to organization and people.
- The Southwest Airlines policy is one of:
  # Job security
  # Minimal hierarchy and bureaucracy
  # Consistently applying its declared corporate culture

employment rationalization and plans for outsourcing some work. The airline faces the same pressures as its competitors from high labor costs and these threaten its labor relations. Some sources see trouble ahead on this front.[30]

2   *Minimum hierarchy and bureaucracy.* The company cuts across hierarchical and job distinctions. For example, flight attendants and pilots will if necessary help clean the aircraft, load bags, or check passengers in at the gate. The co-founder and CEO until 2001, Herb Kelleher, summed up his philosophy on this point by referring to what his Mother taught him. "She talked a lot about how you should treat people with respect. She said that positions and titles signify absolutely nothing . . . She taught me that every person and every job is worth as much as any other person and any other job."[31]

3   *A consistently applied corporate culture.* The company takes its mission statement seriously when it says "We are committed to provide our employees a stable work environment with equal opportunity for learning and personal development . . . above all, employees will be provided the same concern, respect, and caring attitude within the organization that they are expected to share externally with every Southwest customer." The company is also committed to making work fun. Serious attention is paid to parties, awards and celebrations. But providing job security is the most important witness to the importance the company vests in its declared philosophy.

SEMCO[32]

According to available reports and the writings of its CEO Richard Semler, the Semco Company in Brazil has adopted one of the most radical approaches seen today toward reducing, almost eliminating, the attributes of hierarchy. One should treat these sources with some caution, because most of what has been written about the company refers to the period up to 2000 and also does not appear to have been independently verified. Whenever I have asked local experts about Semco during recent visits to Brazil, they say that there is very little recent information about the company. Nevertheless, what Semler and Semco claim to have achieved is thought-provoking at the very least.

Semco is an industrial equipment manufacturer located in and around Sao Paulo, Brazil. Its owner and CEO, Ricardo Semler, has attracted attention because of the unorthodox yet highly successful ways in which he has broken away from conventional organization. When he took the company over from his father in 1980 at the age of 21, it was run on traditional lines but was almost bankrupt. Since Semler introduced his reforms, the company has been consistently successful and has weathered several stormy periods in the Brazilian economy. For example, sales volume adjusted for inflation increased fivefold between 1980 and 1992 and tripled between 1990 and 1996. Under Ricardo Semler, the company has never made a loss despite the background of an erratic economy during the 1980s and 1990s, with four currency devaluations, hyperinflation, record unemployment and a virtual cessation of all industrial production. It became a $100 million-a-year conglomerate.

Many Fortune 500 companies have visited Semco in an attempt to discover the secret of its success.

Box 18.2 summarizes its key features.

BOX 18.2 SEMCO

- Outstanding commercial success in a difficult economy
- A distinctive approach to organization based on:
  - \# Participation
  - \# Profit sharing
  - \# Minimum hierarchy and bureaucracy
  - \# Freedom of information

Following three interdependent core values – employee participation, profit sharing, and the free flow of information – Semco has overturned conventional organization. Among other things, it introduced:

1. *Participation*: Self-managed groups of six to ten manufacturing employees were placed in charge of all aspects of production. They decide on how to organize their work. They set their own budgets and production goals. Salaries are tied to monthly budget and production performance. It is claimed that managerial staff set their own salaries and bonuses and that the result has been highly responsible.

2. *Profit-sharing*: Employees receive roughly one-quarter of the net profits of their respective divisions. A democratically elected committee decides on these distributions, which can easily double or even triple a worker's salary.

3. *Reducing hierarchy and bureaucracy*: "Semco's distinguishing feature is the utter liberation of its employees from the control of hierarchies and the rigidity of uniform rules."[33] What was once twelve layers of management bureaucracy were reduced to three, and the corporate staff have been reduced by 75% since 1982. Outsourcing many administrative functions has assisted this. Hierarchical distinctions have been reduced to a minimum. Semco has no receptionist, secretaries or personal assistants. All employees, Semler included, receive their own guests, make their own copies and draft and send their own correspondence. There are no private offices, workers set their own hours and office attire is at the discretion of each employee. Job titles carry little significance. Top management consists of six Counsellors who determine general policy and strategy. Each of the Counsellors, including Semler, takes a six-month turn as CEO.

   Semco's standard policy is not to have one. Its policy manual is a twenty-page booklet filled with cartoons and a brief declaration outlining the culture of the organization. On "organization chart" it states: "Semco doesn't use a formal organization chart. Only the respect of the led creates a leader. When it is absolutely necessary to sketch the structure of some part of the company, we always do it in pencil, and dispense with it as soon as possible."[34] On "participation," it states: "Our philosophy is build on participation and involvement. Don't settle down. Give opinions, seek opportunities and advancement, always say what you think. Don't be just one more person in the company."[35]

4. *Freedom of information*: Semco has made all of its financial data available to all employees. In fact, it developed a course to train employees in the interpretation of balance sheets and cash flow statements. Everyone knows the salaries of senior managers, which are

capped at ten times the average entry-level salary. All meetings, including those of the Counsellors, are open to all employees who wish to attend and they are free to question managers on any aspect of the business.

The company survived a nationwide liquidity crisis in the early 1990s, which led to many bankruptcies, because rather than facing layoffs, the workers' committee was willing to take a pay cut and suggested more flexible work arrangements to raise productivity, including free movement between functions. The negotiations at this time marked a major cultural shift towards democratic worker management, including worker participation in planning, decision-making and the devolution of authority to work teams to hire and fire co-workers and managers by a democratic vote. This not only saved the company, but also produced a highly cross-trained and knowledgeable staff.

Offsetting the socially negative effects of hierarchy

A large organization can only go so far toward reducing hierarchy in direct ways. However, there are always possibilities for offsetting its negative effects, particularly the ways in which it distances employees from top management. The British retailer, the John Lewis Partnership, provides a good example of what can be done, with highly successful consequences for the bottom line.

THE JOHN LEWIS PARTNERSHIP[36]

The John Lewis Partnership comprises two leading UK retail businesses – the John Lewis department stores and Waitrose supermarkets. The company has achieved consistent profitability and growth in sales revenue. It is a highly successful and well-regarded company, which has also taken a lead in the area of corporate social responsibility.[37]

Its 91,000 employees, called "Partners," own the company through a trust which its then owner, John Spedan Lewis, established in 1929. In 1950 Spedan Lewis made a further deed of settlement, which transferred the entire ownership of the John Lewis Partnership to trustees to hold for the benefit of those who worked in the business. Every Partner receives an annual bonus, which is a share of the company's profits. In 2014 the bonus amounted to 15 percent of annual salary (approaching two months' additional salary) and since 2000 it has ranged from 9 to 20 percent of annual salaries. The Partners are also enrolled in a favorable pension scheme and have other benefits such as generous holidays. It is instructive to note that back in 1957 Spedan Lewis publicly reflected a concern about the widening gap in incomes when he expressed the desirability of setting limits to the rewards for financial risk-taking and stating that "differences in reward must be large enough to induce people to do their best, but the present differences are much too great."[38]

Of particular interest is the way that employee ownership of the John Lewis Partnership provides a basis for offsetting some of the negative effects of organizational hierarchy. It does this through an extensive system of participation and though attention to maintaining open communication of information. At departmental and store level, every Partner belongs to forums which discuss local issues in every store. At the next level up, there are elected councils for the John Lewis and Waitrose Divisions of the company. Above these is the Partnership Council, which has the right to discuss any issue. The Partnership Council is responsible for the non-commercial aspects of the business such as its social and charitable activities. The Partners elect at least 80 percent of the Council's 82 representatives, and the Chairman appoints the remainder. The Partnership Board is responsible for commercial activities. The Partnership Council elects five Board directors while the chairman appoints another five. There are also three non-executive directors. At the time of writing, all but one executive director had risen to the top within the company. Partners get time off to fill representative roles. An independent department, called the Registry, oversees these participative arrangements.

The company tries to maintain open communications through its policy that every non-management Partner has the right to express his or her views directly to senior management and the Chairman. The company also publishes a weekly in-house magazine, while each John Lewis store has its own weekly magazine. It is significant that Partners can write anonymous letters to either of these magazines, holding management to account.

The John Lewis Partnership is very conscious and deliberate in its approach towards CSR. It claims to adopt a long-term policy towards serving the interest of stakeholders, whom it defines as its community, customers, employees, suppliers, and the environment. Each year since 2001, it has publicly accounted for its CSR performance through "Sustainability Reports" that "set out our policies and principles and summarize how we are managing our environmental impacts, how we are working with suppliers and local communities, and how our employees or Partners contribute to and share in the rewards of our commercial success."[39]

There are more examples that could be cited from companies such as Lincoln Electric and the Springfield ReManufacturing Corporation.[40] Case examples are particularly useful in drawing attention to the specific actions that pioneering companies have taken to reform organization to make it more beneficial to people. They also indicate how such change has been accomplished, sometimes against considerable opposition from managers who fear losing some of their power and privilege.

Although they all differ, one can discern some common features among companies that have progressed along the road of acting with greater responsibility to their employees, and often other stakeholders as well. They have reduced hierarchical layers. Where large size makes this difficult, as with the John Lewis Partnership, they have introduced provisions to reduce the negative effects of hierarchy through sharing information, increasing participation, minimizing privileges, and devolving authority. They also have often sought to minimize the negative effects of bureaucracy through measures such as introducing teams with powers to act flexibly in pursuit of agreed objectives, reducing the status of formal structures and abolishing rigid job demarcations.

There is increasing evidence that non-conventional approaches to organization of this kind produce real benefits for people. In turn, these policies elicit remarkable commitment from employees of a kind that has often very significantly helped firms to resolve crises and gain a competitive edge. Some of this evidence has been discussed in this book, and other sources present it in detail.[41] This evidence is important because it indicates that examples such as those just mentioned should not be dismissed as simply quirky or oddball.

◢ A Concluding Comment

Organization is not just a means to achieving better economic performance. It also exerts a profound influence on the societies in which we live. For this reason, it is vital that we understand what organization is, what it does, and the grounds on which it can be justified. We always have to bear in mind that while the type of organization we have reflects our wider society, its structures of power and cultural assumptions, that same organization in turn helps to shape the kind of society in which we live. The form of organization we employ carries certain values back into society and communicates a message about how to treat other people. In being used day-to-day, organization legitimates workplace practices so that there is always the danger that these will come to be taken for granted. They become "conventional" and this is why we can speak of "conventional" organization. Given the social costs that the conventional can inflict, it is hugely important to break away from the limits it places on our thinking.

This book has argued that the conventional approach to organizing we have inherited over many centuries *can* be modified so as both to meet the strategic needs of firms better and so provide for fulfilling experiences at work. Nevertheless, only relatively few firms and public bodies have taken any really significant steps along this road, despite the impressive results that they have achieved. Most progress appears to have been made in the Nordic countries.[42] Organizational reform clearly faces considerable inertia. There is reluctance at the top to sacrifice the vested interests that conventional organization can support, and to some extent even conceal. It is more comfortable to maintain practices that preserve a distance between managers and workers, especially when this is accompanied by the huge differentials in reward and privilege that were noted earlier. Similarly, recent experience has demonstrated a reluctance to reform corporate governance in ways that meaningfully reduce the distance between top managers and stakeholders. The result is that often only lip service is paid to socially desirable policies. It does appear that many top executives will only introduce meaningful changes when forced to by the public reaction to their misdemeanors and to the harmful effects of the ways they organize their businesses or public services.

Should we be pessimistic in the light of this apparent reluctance? Not entirely. The general message of this book has been that even if social ethics do not oblige managers to change their approach to organization, economic realities eventually will. The context of business and work is changing dramatically in ways that will oblige firms and other institutions to value people more and adjust their forms of organizing accordingly. Heightened competition in which success requires a distinctive competence, the need to have learning organizations that can innovate and adapt to change, and the growing reliance on knowledge workers to provide this distinctive edge, are among the obvious developments. Employers who decide to organize in a more enlightened way will win out in the quality of people they can attract. Nevertheless, in order to speed up the process of reform it could be helpful to establish standards for new practices, perhaps along the lines of a further ISO (International Organization for Standardization) scheme.

Importantly, research indicates that what pays off is adopting the mutually supporting aspects of new organization *together* – fewer hierarchical layers, devolved initiative, teamwork, positive human resources policies, and IT support – rather than just bits and pieces.[43] This is a significant finding because it implies that a move toward adopting alternative arrangements has to be done with a clear philosophy and commitment that ensures consistency and comprehensiveness.[44] Just tinkering or following the fad of the moment is no good.

SUMMARY

1 Growing pressures for companies and institutions to be socially responsible are stimulating interest in alternative forms of organization.

2 As well as a set of arrangements for achieving goals through collective effort, organization is also a set of arrangements that distribute power, rewards and well-being.

3 This means that some of the intrinsic features of conventional organizational forms, especially hierarchy, add to contemporary problems such as inequality and lack of trust.

4 If the organizational form in use fails to meet stakeholders' expectations, not only the legitimacy but also the performance of a business are likely to suffer.

5 There is evidence that reductions in hierarchy, and measures to bridge the gap between organizational leaders and members, can have a positive impact on people's wellbeing and on their commitment to achieving high performance.

6 A few companies have made significant organizational reforms that enfranchise their members and pay respect to their needs. These companies have attained exceptional levels of performance and are therefore exemplars which others could consider following.

7 On the whole, the new forms of organizing adopted by such companies are consistent with meeting the strategic needs for adaptability and innovation that have become prominent in current competitive conditions.

8 The ability to adapt and innovate depends heavily on securing the commitment and initiative of employees, especially knowledge workers. This affirms the truth of the often quoted saying in business that "people are our most precious resource."

QUESTIONS FOR DISCUSSION

18.1 Are the commercial and social criteria that are being applied to business today mutually compatible or not?

18.2 Does the bigness of "big business" make it more difficult to meet the criteria of corporate social responsibility?

18.3 Which approaches to organizing are best suited to meeting social criteria?

18.4 How much do you think the high commitment of members to an organization's goals stems from a vision and culture laid down by inspired leadership rather than from a particular form of organization?

18.5 Why do you think that relatively few companies have developed radically new forms of organization despite their apparent success and the wide academic interest in them?

18.6 Are the new forms of organizing described in this chapter better suited to a western "liberal" culture than to other cultures?

NOTES

1 Jaap Paauwe (2009), HRM and performance: Achievements, methodological issues and prospects, *Journal of Management Studies*, 46(1), 129–142. The quotation is from p. 138.

2 http://www.bloomberg.com/news/2013-04-30/ceo-pay-1-795-to-1-multiple-of-workers-skirts-law-as-sec-delays.html. Although the growth in income inequality has accelerated in recent decades, long-term increases in inequality were evident in capitalist economies during the 18th and 19th centuries. See Thomas Piketty (2014), *Capital in the 21st Century*, Cambridge, MA, Belknap, Harvard University Press.

3 Max Fisher (2013), Map: How the world's countries compare on income inequality. *Washington Post* blog, September 27. http://www.washingtonpost.com/blogs/worldviews/wp/2013/09/27/map-how-the-worlds-countries-compare-on-income-inequality/ accessed May 5, 2014.

4 Margit Osterloh and Bruno S. Frey (2004), Corporate governance for crooks? The case for corporate virtue, in Anna Grandori (ed.), *Corporate Governance and Firm Organization*, Oxford, Oxford University Press, pp. 191–211.

5 Resolution Foundation (2013), *A Matter of Time: The Rise of Zero-hours Contracts*, London, June. The quotation is from p. 21. Reproduced with permission.

6 Health and Safety Executive (2013), *Annual Statistics Report for Great Britain 2012/13*. http://www.hse.gov.uk/statistics/overall/hssh1213.pdf, accessed April 2, 2014.

7 National Institute for Occupational Safety and Health [NIOSH] 1999. *Stress at Work*. www.cdc.gov/niosh/stresswk.html.

8 Jo Revill (2003), Life makes you sick, *The Observer*, October 12, p. 19.

9 Richard G. Williams (ed.) (1986), *Class and Health: Research and Longitudinal Data*, London, Tavistock; Michael Marmot (2004), *The Status Syndrome: How Social Standing Affects our Health and Longevity*, New York, Henry Holt; Richard Wilkinson and Kate Pickett (2011), *The Spirit Level: Why Equality is Better For Everyone*, London: Penguin.

10 Michael Prowse (2002), Is Inequality good for you? *Financial Times FT Weekend*, December 7, pp. I–II; Michael Marmot (2004), op. cit.

11 *Whitehall II Study* (2013), University College London, Research Department of Epidemiology and Public Health, http://www.ucl.ac.uk/whitehallii/history, accessed April 3, 2014. Other factors also doubtless contribute to the greater incidence of ill health and shorter lifespans among people with lower incomes – such as a relatively greater consumption of junk food leading to obesity and diabetes.

12 John Child (1984), *Organization: A Guide to Problems and Practice*, London, Harper & Row, Chapter 3.

13 National Institute for Occupational Safety and Health (NIOSH) 1999, op. cit.

14 John Child (1982), Professionals in the corporate world: Values, interests and control, in David Dunkerley and Graeham Salaman (eds.), *International Yearbook of Organization Studies 1981*, Routledge & Kegan Paul.

15 6 in 10 doctors considering early retirement. *The Guardian*, March 23, 2014, http://www.theguardian.com > News > Society > GPs. Accessed April 6, 2014.

16 However, some young people go to work in a large corporation for the experience and training it provides and have the intention of leaving later on to set up on their own.

17 Emma Bell and Scott M. Taylor (2015), *Spirituality and Organization*, London, Sage. See also Catherine J. Casey. *Critical Analysis of Organization: Theory, Practice, Revitalization*. London, Sage 2002.

18 Thomas Diefenbach (2013), *Hierarchy and Organisation: Toward a General Theory of Hierarchical Social System*, London, Routledge.

19 Thomas Diefenbach (2013), op. cit.; John Child (2009), Challenging Hierarchy, in Mats Alvesson, Hugh Willmott, and Todd Bridgman (eds.) *Oxford Handbook of Critical Management Studies*, Oxford, Oxford University Press: 501–514.

20   Andrew M. Pettigrew and Richard Whittington (2000), *The New Internal Network Organization: Process and Performance*. Final Report to the Economic and Social Research Council, Warwick Business School; Mats Alvesson and Paul Thompson (2005), Post-bureaucracy? In Stephen Ackroyd, Rosemary Batt, Paul Thompson, and Pamela S. Tolbert (eds.), *The Oxford Handbook of Work and Organization*, Oxford, Oxford University Press, 485–507. See also Thomas Diefenbach (2013), op. cit.

21   Maria Tadeo (2014), RBS bonus fury as bankers walk away with £576m in 'astonishing betrayal' to taxpayers, *The Independent*, February 27, http://www.independent.co.uk/news/business/news/rbs-bonus-fury-as-bankers-walk-away-with-576m-in-astonishing-betrayal-to-taxpayers-9156438.html, accessed April 5, 2014.

22   Department for Business Innovation and Skills (2009), *Report on the Affairs of Phoenix Venture Holdings Limited, MG Rover Group Limited and 33 Other Companies*, Vols I and II, London, http://www.bis.gov.uk/files/file52782.pdf and http://www.bis.gov.uk/files/file52783.pdf, accessed April 5, 2014.

23   Some of this section draws from John Child (2009), op. cit.

24   Andrew M. Pettigrew and Evelyn M. Fenton (eds.) (2000), *The Innovating Organization*, London, Sage.

25   Sources: Jody H. Gittell (2002), *The Southwest Airlines Way*, New York, Mcgraw-Hill; Wayne F. Cascio (2002), *Responsible Restructuring*, San Francisco, Berrett-Koehler, pp. 83–87; Kevin Freiberg and Jackie Freiberg (1998), *Nuts! Southwest Airlines' Crazy Recipe for Business and Personal Success*, New York, Broadway Books; www.fortune.com/fortune/mostadmired 2004, company literature and various Internet sites.

26   http://southwest.investorroom.com/2014-01-23-Southwest-Airlines-Reports-Record-Fourth-Quarter-And-Full-Year-Profit-41st-Consecutive-Year-Of-Profitability, accessed March 31, 2014.

27   http://www.businessinsider.com/flight-attendant-applications-flood-southwest-airlines-employment-2013-12#ixzz2xVe0cgYg, accessed March 31, 2014.

28   http://www.airlinefinancials.com/airline_data_comparisons.html, accessed March 31, 2014.

29   Jack Nicas and Susan Carey (2014), Southwest Airlines, once a brassy upstart, is showing its age. Carrier copes with labor strife, high costs; some pine for days of co-founder Herb Kelleher. Wall Street Journal, April 1, 2014, http://online.wsj.com/news/articles/SB10001424052702303949704579459643375588678, accessed April 5, 2014.

30   See: http://aviationblog.dallasnews.com/2013/03/southwest-airlines-ground-employees-picket-at-dallas-love-field.html/; http://centreforaviation.com/analysis/southwest-airlines-solid-financial-performance-for-fy2013-but-challenges-are-piling-up-149650; both accessed April 4, 2014.

31   Quoted in K. Brooker (2001), Herb Kelleher: The chairman of the board looks back, *Fortune*, May 28, pp. 62–76.

32   *Ricardo Semler and S.A. Semco* (2001), Thunderbird, The American Graduate School of International Management, case study A07-98-0024, 1998; Ricardo Semler, (2001), *Maverick!* New York, Random House.

33   Roberto Guimaraes and John Southerst (2003), Semco: Work + space = freedom, www.steelcase.com/en/pdf/knowledgepapers/Semco.pdf.

34   Ricardo Semler (2001), op. cit., p. 300.

35   Ibid., p. 309.

36   Keith Bradley and Simon Taylor (1992), *Business Performance in the Retail sector: The Experience of the John Lewis Partnership*, Oxford, Clarendon Press; John Lewis Partnership, *Wikipedia*, http://en.wikipedia.org/wiki/John_Lewis_Partnership, accessed March 31, 2014; Editorial: An eye for retail, editorial, *People Management*, July 16, 2009, http://www.cipd.co.uk/pm/peoplemanagement/b/weblog/archive/2009/07/88/an-eye-for-retail-2009-07.aspx, accessed March 31, 2014.

37   http://www.johnlewispartnership.co.uk/csr/our-progress-and-reports/csr-reports/latest-reports.html

38   Editorial, *People Management*, July 16, 2009, op. cit.

39 http://www.johnlewispartnership.co.uk/csr/our-progress-and-reports/csr-reports/latest-reports. html, accessed April 5, 2014.

40 On Lincoln Electric, see: Wayne F. Cascio (2002), op. cit., pp. 75–77; Frank Koller (2010), Spark: How Old-Fashioned Values Drive a Twenty-First Century Corporation. Lessons from Lincoln Electric's Unique Guaranteed Employment Program, New York, Public Affairs Books. Also The Lincoln Electric Company, Harvard Business School case 376-028, 1983 and Lincoln Electric Co., George Willis, video, Harvard Business School case 9-889-517. On Springfield see Chapter 16 (Box 16.4) and John A. Byrne (2002), After Enron: The ideal corporation, *Business Week*, August 26, pp. 32–35. Stephen Hicks interview with Jack Stack recorded 2011 and published by the Center for Ethics and Entrepreneurship, http://www.ethicsandentrepreneurship.org/20110411/interview-with-jack-stack/. Accessed April 5, 2014.

41 For example: Frank Heller, Eugen Pusic, George Strauss, and Bernhard Wilpert (1998), *Organizational Participation: Myth and Reality*, Oxford, Oxford University Press; Jeffrey Pfeffer (1998), op. cit.; Wayne F. Cascio (2002), op. cit.

42 Peer Hull Kristensen and Kari Lilja (eds.) (2011), *Nordic Capitalisms and Globalization: New Forms of Economic Organization and Welfare Institutions*, Oxford, Oxford University Press.

43 See Boston Consulting Group (2011), *High-Performance Organizations: The Secrets of their Success*, http://www.bcg.com/documents/file84953.pdf, accessed April 5, 2014. Also Andrew M. Pettigrew and Evelyn M. Fenton (eds.) (2000), op. cit.

44 I first pointed out the performance benefits of organizational consistency in John Child (1977), *Organization: A Guide to Problems and Practice*, London, Harper & Row, pp. 169–173.

Author Index

SUBJECT INDEX